Contemporary Selling

Building Relationships, Creating Value

Published in previous editions as *Relationship Selling*, the latest edition of Mark Johnston and Greg Marshall's *Contemporary Selling: Building Relationships, Creating Value* continues to set the standard for the most up-to-date and student-friendly selling textbook available anywhere today.

The latest edition incorporates a new chapter on social media and technology-enabled selling, as well as a new chapter on selling globally. To support student engagement, the book also features:

- "Expert Advice" chapter openers showing how each chapter's sales concepts are applied in the real world
- In-chapter "Ethical Dilemmas" that help students identify and handle effectively the numerous ethical issues that arise in selling
- Mini-cases to help students understand and apply the principles they have learned in the classroom
- Role plays at the end of each chapter enabling students to learn by doing
- Special appendices on selling math and developing a professional sales proposal
- Video material available on the Companion Website, featuring new content with sales experts discussing best sales practices from a recent PBS television special on selling produced by HR Chally.

The Companion Website can be accessed at www.routledge.com/cw/Johnston

Mark W. Johnston is the Alan and Sandra Gerry Professor of Marketing and Ethics at Rollins College, USA.

Greg W. Marshall is the Charles Harwood Professor of Marketing and Strategy at Rollins College, USA.

"A great text if you want to combine professional selling and sales management in one book."

—James S. Boles, Georgia State University, USA

"It is an excellent compilation of the principles of selling and sales management for undergraduate students."

—Subhra Chakrabarty, Mississippi State University, USA

"Johnston and Marshall successfully deliver a very readable text with everything you need to know about selling and the sales process. Its approach is very contemporary. Particularly insightful for post-graduate students with many valuable supporting learning material. This text will be recommended to all my students on 'selling and sales strategies' modules."

—Tony Douglas, Edinburgh Napier University Business School, Edinburgh

"This textbook facilitates an outstanding introduction to business-to-business selling. New sales students often approach selling with some skepticism and bring with them the stereotype of the salesperson as a mere product peddler willing to manipulate naive prospects. *Contemporary Selling* will open students' eyes to the concept of the mutually beneficial exchange—in the competitive marketplace, sellers can only satisfy customers by building relationships that center around the customer's needs and customers will only commit to sellers willing to do so. I have used previous editions of this book and have found it invaluable—the new edition's inclusion of sales technology is particularly exciting. With this textbook, Dr. Johnston and Dr. Marshall are providing an outstanding resource at a particularly critical time when students need to understand the true nature of selling and the vital role that salespeople play in fostering a functioning marketplace and a thriving economy."

—Ronald L. Jelinek, PhD., Providence College, USA

"If you are hunting for a book to teach young college students the art and science of modern selling, look no further than *Contemporary Selling* by Mark Johnston and Greg Marshall. The book must rank among the top few on the subject. What sets it apart are its honing the concept of value creation as the underpinning of today's selling, the expert advice from practitioners, and inclusion of ethics and global perspectives... just a few powerful ideas that make the book what it shouts aloud—contemporary."

—Bala Shankar, Adjunct Faculty, Singapore Management University; Consultant, Entrepreneur

"Johnston and Marshall's *Contemporary Selling* is a valuable asset for mastering the skills of selling in recent times. Discussions compiled through fourteen logical chapters are easy-to-follow but exhaustive in content. Some of the book's key strengths are its discussion of the relationship between technological change and selling, its new perspectives on territory and time management, and its treatment of globalized environment issues as they impact selling. All in all, this book offers great insights for any course on Selling."

—Kavita Sharma, University of Delhi, India

Contemporary Selling

Building Relationships, Creating Value

4th Edition

MARK W. JOHNSTON AND GREG W. MARSHALL

Routledge
Taylor & Francis Group

NEW YORK AND LONDON

Please visit the companion website for this title at www.routledge.com/cw/Johnston

This edition first published 2013
by Routledge
711 Third Avenue, New York, NY 10017

Simultaneously published in the UK
by Routledge
2 Park Square, Milton Park, Abingdon, Oxon OX14 4RN

Routledge is an imprint of the Taylor & Francis Group, an informa business

© 2013 Taylor & Francis

First edition published by McGraw-Hill, 2005
Second edition published by McGraw-Hill, 2008
Third edition published by McGraw-Hill, 2011

Library of Congress Cataloging in Publication Data
Johnston, Mark W.
    Contemporary selling : building relationships, creating value /
Mark W. Johnston and Greg W. Marshall.
        p. cm.
    Rev. ed. of: Relationship selling. 3rd ed. c2010.
    Includes bibliographical references and index.
    1. Selling. 2. Relationship marketing. 3. Customer relations. I. Marshall, Greg W.
II. Johnston, Mark W. Relationship selling. III. Title.
    HF5438.25.J655 2013
    658.85—dc23   2012030579

ISBN: 978-0-415-52349-3 (hbk)
ISBN: 978-0-415-52350-9 (pbk)
ISBN: 978-0-203-12096-5 (ebk)

Typeset in Berkeley by
Keystroke, Station Road, Codsall, Wolverhampton

Printed in the United States of America by Courier, Kendallville, IN

Brief Table of Contents

Preface		*xiii*
PART ONE	WHAT IS CONTEMPORARY SELLING?	**1**
CHAPTER 1	**INTRODUCTION TO CONTEMPORARY SELLING**	**3**
CHAPTER 2	**UNDERSTANDING SELLERS AND BUYERS**	**29**
CHAPTER 3	**VALUE CREATION IN BUYER–SELLER RELATIONSHIPS**	**55**
CHAPTER 4	**ETHICAL AND LEGAL ISSUES IN CONTEMPORARY SELLING**	**83**
CHAPTER 5	**CRM AND SALES TECHNOLOGIES**	**109**
PART TWO	ELEMENTS OF THE CONTEMPORARY SELLING PROCESS	**129**
CHAPTER 6	**PROSPECTING AND SALES CALL PLANNING**	**131**
CHAPTER 7	**COMMUNICATING THE SALES MESSAGE**	**157**
CHAPTER 8	**NEGOTIATING FOR WIN-WIN SOLUTIONS**	**191**
CHAPTER 9	**CLOSING THE SALE AND FOLLOW-UP**	**211**
CHAPTER 10	**SALESPERSON SELF-MANAGEMENT**	**235**
PART THREE	MANAGING THE CONTEMPORARY SELLING PROCESS	**259**
CHAPTER 11	**SALESPERSON PERFORMANCE: BEHAVIOR, MOTIVATION, AND ROLE PERCEPTIONS**	**261**

CHAPTER 12 **RECRUITING, SELECTING, AND TRAINING SALESPEOPLE** **283**

CHAPTER 13 **COMPENSATING AND EVALUATING SALESPEOPLE** **325**

CHAPTER 14 **GLOBAL PERSPECTIVES ON CONTEMPORARY SELLING** **357**

Glossary *375*
Endnotes *391*
Index *403*

Table of Contents

Preface   xiii

PART ONE
WHAT IS CONTEMPORARY SELLING?   1

CHAPTER 1
INTRODUCTION TO CONTEMPORARY SELLING   3

Learning Objectives   3
Expert Advice: David B. Edmonds   4
Introduction to Contemporary Selling   5
A Model for Contemporary Selling   5
Building Relationships, Creating Value 6
Understanding Sellers and Buyers 10
Ethics 10
Technology 11
Selling Process 12
Sales Management 13

Issues Outside the Circles: The Global Selling Environment   15
Internal Environment 15
External Environment 17

Expert Advice: Follow-up   20
Summary   21
Key Terms   21
Role Play   21
Discussion Questions   23
Mini-Case 1: Creekside Outdoor Gear   24
Appendix: Additional Information on Role Plays   25

CHAPTER 2
UNDERSTANDING SELLERS AND BUYERS   29

Learning Objectives   29
Expert Advice: Anjai ("A.J.") Gandi   30
Overview of Selling as a Career   31
Why Sales Jobs Are So Rewarding 32

Key Success Factors in Contemporary Selling   35
Listening Skills 36
Follow-up Skills 37
Ability to Adapt Sales Style from Situation to Situation 37
Tenacity—Sticking with a Task 37
Well Organized 37
Verbal Communication Skills 37
Proficiency in Interacting with People at All Levels of a Customer's Organization 37
Demonstrated Ability to Overcome Objections 38
Closing Skills 38
Personal Planning and Time Management Skills 38

Selling Activities   38
Types of Selling Jobs   40
Selling in B2C versus B2B Markets 41
Types of B2B Sales Jobs 41

Participants in the Organizational Buying Process   42
Selling Centers and Buying Centers 44

Organizational Buying Decision Stages   45
Stage One: Anticipation or Recognition of a Problem or Need 45

*Stage Two: Determination and Description of the
    Traits and Quantity of the Needed Item(s)* 46
*Stage Three: Search for and Qualification of
    Potential Suppliers* 47
*Stage Four: Acquisition and Analysis of Proposals
    or Bids* 47
*Stage Five: Evaluation of Proposals and Selection
    of Suppliers* 47
Stage Six: Selection of an Order Routine 48
*Stage Seven: Performance Evaluation and
    Feedback* 48

Types of Organizational Buying Situations   49
Expert Advice: Follow-up   49
Summary   50
Key Terms   50
Role Play   51
Discussion Questions   52
**Mini-Case 2: National Agri-Products
    Company**   52

CHAPTER 3
**VALUE CREATION IN BUYER–SELLER
RELATIONSHIPS**   55

Learning Objectives   55
Expert Advice: Howard Stevens   56
Adding Value Is "Marketing 101"   57
Role of Selling in Marketing 57
Role of Marketing in Selling 59

Clarifying the Concept of Value   59
Value Is Related to Customer Benefits 59
The Value Chain 60
The Lifetime Value of a Customer 61

Communicating Value in the Sales Message 62
Product Quality 63
Channel Deliverables (Supply Chain) 64
Integrated Marketing Communications (IMC) 64
Synergy between Sales and Marketing 64
Execution of Marketing Mix Programs 65
Quality of the Buyer–Seller Relationship (Trust) 65
Service Quality 65
Salesperson Professionalism 67
Brand Equity 67
Corporate Image/Reputation 67
Application of Technology 67
Price 67

Managing Customer Expectations   69
Expert Advice: Follow-up   69
Summary   69

Key Terms   69
Role Play   70
Discussion Questions   71
Mini-Case 3: BestValue Computers   71
Appendix: Selling Math   73

CHAPTER 4
**ETHICAL AND LEGAL ISSUES IN
CONTEMPORARY SELLING**   83

Learning Objectives   83
Expert Advice: David B. Edmonds   84
**The Importance of Ethics in the 21st
    Century**   85
Renewed Emphasis on Ethical Practices 85
Companies Take the Lead in Social Responsibility 86

Ethical Concerns for Salespeople   86
Issues with Customers 88
Issues with Employers 90

Ethical Concerns for Management   91
Issues with Salespeople 92
Issues with Company Policies 92

Legal Issues in Contemporary Selling   95
*Uniform Commercial Code: The Legal Framework
    for Selling* 95
Unlawful Business Activities 96

A Code of Sales Ethics   98
Corporate Code of Ethics 98
Individual Code of Sales Ethics 99

Expert Advice: Follow-up   102
Summary   102
Key Terms   103
Role Play   103
Discussion Questions   104
Mini-Case 4: Health Sense Pharmaceuticals 106

CHAPTER 5
CRM AND SALES TECHNOLOGIES   109

Learning Objectives   109
Expert Advice: Gerhard Gschwandtner   110
**What Is Customer Relationship
    Management (CRM)?**   111
From Mass Marketing to One-to-One Marketing 112
CRM Process Cycle 114
Toward a Relationship-Based Enterprise 115

The Technology of Selling   115
A Peek at Historical Sales Technology 118

Sales Technology in the Informational Decade 120
Gaining Technology Acceptance by Salespeople 125

Expert Advice: Follow-up 126
Summary 126
Key Terms 126
Discussion Questions 127
Mini-Case 5: Who "Owns" CRM 127

PART TWO
ELEMENTS OF THE CONTEMPORARY
SELLING PROCESS 129

CHAPTER 6
PROSPECTING AND SALES CALL
PLANNING 131

Learning Objectives 131
Expert Advice: Walter Friedman 132
Prospecting: Customers Don't Start Out as
   Customers 133
Qualifying the Prospect 133
Why Prospecting Is So Important 137

Sources of Prospects 137
Loyal Customers 138
Endless Chain Referrals 138
Networking 139
Directories 140
Internet 140
Telemarketing 141
Written Correspondence 142
Trade Shows 143
Conferences 143
Cold Calls and Warm Calls 143
Other Issues in Sourcing Prospects 144

Set a Systematic Prospecting Plan 144
Make the Best Use of CRM in Prospecting 145
Resist Call Reluctance 145

Planning the Sales Call: The Preapproach 145
Establish Goals for the Initial Sales Call 146
Learn All You Can about the Prospect 146
Plan to Portray the Right Image 147
Determine Your Approach 148
Prepare a Sales Proposal 148

The Sales Manager's Role in Prospecting
   and Sales Call Planning 148
Expert Advice: Follow-up 149
Summary 149
Key Terms 149

Role Play 150
Discussion Questions 150
Mini-Case 6: Strong Point Financial
   Services 151
Appendix: Sales Proposals 153

CHAPTER 7
COMMUNICATING THE SALES MESSAGE 157

Learning Objectives 157
Expert Advice: David B. Edmonds 158
Communicating the Sales Message 159
Getting Ready for a Sales Presentation 159
Characteristics of a Great Sales Presentation 159
Sales Presentation Strategies 161

Setting Objectives and Goals 163
Approach the Customer: Initiating the
   Relationship 164
Tips for Making a Good First Impression 164
Approach Strategies 166

The Sales Presentation: Building the
Relationship 168
Identify Customers' Needs 168
Listen 171
Apply Your Knowledge to Customer Needs 173
Satisfy Customer Needs 174

Keys to a Great Sales Presentation 175
Demonstrations 175
The Value Proposition 178
Nonverbal Communication 179
What to Do When Things Go Wrong 180

The Sales Manager's Role in the Sales
Presentation 181
Managers Are Essential to a Great Presentation 183
Providing the Tools for Success 183

Expert Advice: Follow-up 183
Summary 183
Key Terms 184
Role Play 184
Discussion Questions 186
Mini-Case 7: Bright Colors Paint 187

CHAPTER 8
NEGOTIATING FOR WIN-WIN
SOLUTIONS 191

Learning Objectives 191
Expert Advice: Tom Kadien 192

Negotiating Win-Win Solutions　193
**Negotiations: The Heart of the Win-Win
　　Solution**　193
Common Customer Concerns　193
Do I Need Your Product?　194
Do I Trust Your Company?　195
I Don't Really Know You　195
I Need More Time to Consider Your Product　197
Is This Your Best Price?　197

**Basic Points in Negotiating Win-Win
　　Solutions**　198
Plan and Prepare　199
Anticipation Enhances Negotiations　199
Say What You Mean and Mean What You Say　199
Negativity Destroys Negotiations　199
Listen and Validate Customer Concerns　200
Always Value the Value Proposition　200

Specific Negotiation Strategies　200
Question　201
Direct Denial　201
Indirect Denial　202
Compensating for Deficiencies　202
Feel—Felt—Found　202
Third-Party Endorsements　203
Bounce-Back　203
Defer　204
Trial Offer　204

**The Sales Manager's Role in Negotiating
　　Win-Win Solutions**　204
Expert Advice: Follow-up　205
Summary　205
Key Terms　206
Role Play　206
Discussion Questions　207
Mini-Case 8: Mid-Town Office Products　208

CHAPTER 9
CLOSING THE SALE AND FOLLOW-UP　211

Learning Objectives　211
Expert Advice: Gerhard Gschwandtner　212
What Is a Close?　213
Selling Is Not a Linear Process　213

Closing Methods　214
Assumptive Close　214
Minor Point Close　215
Alternative Choice Close　215
Direct Close　215
Summary-of-Benefits Close　215

Balance Sheet Close　216
Buy-Now Close　216
In Closing, Practice Makes Perfect　216

Dealing with Rejection　216
Attitude Is Important　217

Identifying Buying Signals　218
Verbal Buying Signals　218
Nonverbal Buying Signals　219
Trial Close　219

Common Closing Mistakes　219
**Follow-up Enhances Customer
　　Relationships**　220
Customer Expectations and Complaint Behavior　221
*Don't Wait for Complaints to Follow Up with
　　Customers*　223
Other Key Follow-up Activities　225
CRM and Follow-up　225

**The Sales Manager's Role in Closing the
　　Sale and Follow-up**　226
Expert Advice: Follow-up　226
Summary　226
Key Terms　227
Role Play　227
Discussion Questions　228
Mini-Case 9: St. Paul Copy Machines　229
**Appendix: Checklist for Using Effective
　　Closing Skills**　231

CHAPTER 10
SALESPERSON SELF-MANAGEMENT　235

Learning Objectives　235
Expert Advice: Tom Kadien　236
**The Importance of Salesperson
　　Self-Management**　237
Reasons for Salespeople　237
Reasons for Sales Managers　238

**Salespeople's Role in Salesperson
　　Self-Management**　240
Efficient Time Management　240
Effective Territory Management　242

**Sales Managers' Role in Time and Territory
　　Management**　243
Design the Most Effective Sales Territories　245
Measure Sales Territory Performance　250

Expert Advice: Follow-up　254
Summary　254

Key Terms   254
Role Play   255
Discussion Questions   256
Mini-Case 10: Diagnostic Services Inc.   256

PART THREE
MANAGING THE CONTEMPORARY
SELLING PROCESS   259

CHAPTER 11
SALESPERSON PERFORMANCE: BEHAVIOR,
MOTIVATION, AND ROLE PERCEPTIONS   261

Learning Objectives   261
Expert Advice: David B. Edmonds   262
Why Is It Important for Management to
    Understand Salesperson Performance?   263
Salesperson Performance   263
Role Perceptions 264
Sales Aptitude: Are Good Salespeople Born or
    Made? 265
Sales Skill Levels 265
Motivation 266
Organizational, Environmental, and Personal
    Factors 267
Rewards 268
Satisfaction 268

How Salespeople Influence Performance   269
The Salesperson's Role Perceptions 269
The Salesperson's Role Is Affected by Many Factors
    272

How Managers Influence Performance   273
Role Perceptions 273
Motivation 275
Incentive and Compensation Policies 276

Expert Advice: Follow-up   277
Summary   277
Key Terms   278
Role Play   278
Discussion Questions   279
Mini-Case 11: Ace Chemicals   280

CHAPTER 12
RECRUITING, SELECTING, AND
TRAINING SALESPEOPLE   283

Learning Objectives   283
Expert Advice: Bill Scannell 284
Recruitment and Selection Issues 285

Establish Responsibility 288
Analyze the Job and Determine Selection Criteria 288
Find and Attract Applicants 290
Develop and Apply Selection Procedures 294

Issues in Sales Training   299
Objectives of Sales Training 299
Improve Customer Relationships 300
Increase Productivity 300
Improve Morale 300
Lower Turnover 301
Improve Selling Skills 301

Developing Successful Sales Training
    Programs   302
Analyze Needs 302
Determine Objectives 302
Develop and Implement the Program 302
Evaluate and Review the Program 304

Training Needs Change with Time   304
New Recruits 304
Experienced Salespeople 305

Sales Training Topics   306
Product Knowledge 307
Market/Industry Orientation 307
Company Orientation 307
Time and Territory Management 308
Legal/Ethical Issues 308
Technology 309
Specialized Training Topics 309

Sales Training Methods   309
On-the-Job Training 310
Internet (Online) 310
Classroom Training 311
Role Playing 311

Measuring the Costs and Benefits of Sales
    Training   312
Measurement Criteria 313
Measuring Broad Benefits 313
Measuring Specific Benefits 314

Expert Advice: Follow-up   314
Summary   314
Key Terms   315
Role Play #1   315
Role Play #2   317
Discussion Questions   318
Mini-Case 12.1: Right Times Uniform   319
Mini-Case 12.2: House Handy Products   321

CHAPTER 13
COMPENSATING AND EVALUATING
SALESPEOPLE   325

Learning Objectives   325
Expert Advice: Anjai ("A.J.") Gandi   326
Overview of Salesperson Compensation
    and Incentives   327
Straight Salary, Straight Commission,
    and Combination Plans   330
Other Types of Compensation   332
Sales Contests 332
Expense Accounts 333
Nonfinancial Rewards 333

Deciding on the Mix and Level of
    Compensation   334
Dangers of Paying Salespeople Too Much 335
Dangers of Paying Salespeople Too Little 335

Evaluating Salesperson Performance   336
Performance versus Effectiveness 336

Objective Measures of Performance   338
Ratio Measures 339

Subjective Measures of Performance   339
Problems with Subjective Performance
    Measurement 341
Avoiding Errors in Performance Evaluation 342
BARS Systems 342

360-Degree Performance Feedback   344
Expert Advice: Follow-up   346
Summary   346
Key Terms   347
Role Play #1   347
Role Play #2   349
Discussion Questions   350

Mini-Case 13.1: MedTech Pharmaceuticals   351
Mini-Case 13.2: American Food Processors   352

CHAPTER 14
GLOBAL PERSPECTIVES ON
CONTEMPORARY SELLING   357

Learning Objectives   357
Expert Advice: Tom Kadien   358
Selling is Global   359
The Global Marketplace and Contemporary
    Selling 359

Global Challenges in the Sales Process   360
Culture 361
Business Practices 364
Technology 367

Global Challenges in Managing the Sales
    Process   368
Sales Organizational Structure 368
Hire the Right People in a Global Sales
    Environment 368
Training for Effective Global Selling 369
Motivation of the Global Salesperson 370
Compensation of the Global Salesperson 371
Evaluation of the Global Sales Force 372

Expert Advice: Follow-up   372
Summary   372
Key Terms   373
Discussion Questions   373
Mini-Case 14: Gen Tech Corporation   374

    Glossary   375
    Endnotes   391
    Index   403

Preface

Fundamental to the success of any organization is its relationship with customers. As we move into the second decade of the 21st Century the relationship between organizations and customers is in a period of profound change. Technology, globalization, ethical concerns, corporate strategic decisions, and a host of other issues have created a revolution in the selling process. Customers are no longer interested in working with companies that cannot add substantial value to their business. They seek better, more strategic partnerships with suppliers. And the changes in the buyer–seller relationship have also led to dramatic changes in the management of salespeople. Issues of home/virtual offices, new approaches to communication technology, and general demographic changes in the sales force and buyers (to name just a few) have created significant challenges for salespeople and their managers. The 21st Century selling model is a very different process from that of ten years ago. As a result, any book about selling and sales management must reflect the *contemporary* nature of this new business reality.

Published in three previous editions by McGraw-Hill as *Relationship Selling*, we're pleased to report that Routledge/Taylor & Francis Group is our publisher for this fourth edition of this market-leading book. We've been very impressed with Routledge's position as a truly global business publisher and the energy, support, and creativity they've added to this new edition. The editors and marketing people at Routledge have made a strong point that the book will continue to set the standard as the most up-to-date and student-friendly textbook in the sales area available anywhere in the world today. To reflect the many changes in the field and celebrate the next generation of the book, we've retitled it *Contemporary Selling: Building Relationships, Creating Value*. This new edition continues to present clearly and concisely the true nature of the selling process in the 21st Century and it remains the only book to integrate the critical tools of the contemporary selling process with the unique challenges managers face working with salespeople in a highly dynamic competitive environment. Mark Johnston and Greg Marshall, your authors, combine backgrounds in selling and sales management with long-established research records and consulting experience in the field.

WHY DID WE WRITE THIS BOOK?

The idea for writing the original edition of this book evolved over several years and many conversations with colleagues and sales professionals. There was no single moment of creation; rather a series of conversations that ended with "Gee, I wish there was a book that combines a relevant and current model of professional selling with the sales management skills needed for effective buyer–seller relationships."

Our own review of the books in the Personal Selling and Sales Management areas has found no single source for a complete, holistic approach to selling that incorporates not only state-of-the-art sales methodology but also the knowledge base and skill sets necessary to manage such a critical area in the organization. A gap exists between the many Professional Selling books that provide a "drill-down" approach covering everything from A to Z (and back again) and Sales Management books that discuss in detail the many challenging issues involved in managing a sales force. As co-authors of *Sales Force Management*, 11th edition (Routledge/Taylor & Francis Group), we were already keenly aware of the depth of coverage in available Sales Management books around the world.

Our colleagues presented us with an interesting challenge: was it possible to create a book that combines 21st-Century professional selling processes with 21st-Century sales management practices in a way that maximizes value and utility for both instructors and students? A key element in the challenge was to extend the knowledge of the selling process and incorporate new thinking on relationship building into the creation of a 21st-Century selling model. Most importantly, we did not want to simply patch together a book about "selling with a little sales management sprinkled in." Quite the contrary: our primary goal in writing *Contemporary Selling, 4e: Building Relationships, Creating Value,* as in the previous editions, was to create a single, comprehensive, and holistic source of information about the selling function in modern organizations focused on building relationships and creating value. As you read the book, note that our approach is to link the process of selling (what salespeople do) with the process of managing salespeople (what sales managers do). In order to provide a pictorial representation of this linkage and to create an easily referenced thematic thread throughout the book, we have developed a "Model of Contemporary Selling" that serves as a road map all the way through. The model is introduced in chapter 1.

Building strong, sustainable customer relationships is no longer optional—today it is *required* for long-term business success. As the importance of relationships has grown, the selling function has become assimilated into the rest of the organization. Selling now is truly a "boardroom topic," as companies realize that effective management of the contemporary selling process is a key to gaining overall competitive advantage. Thus, this book incorporates state-of-the-art sales practices and research to develop a comprehensive model of selling in the 21st Century.

WHO IS THE AUDIENCE FOR THE BOOK?

The overarching theme of this book is enabling salespeople to build relationships and create value with customers. As such, the book has broad appeal and high value-added in sales-related courses. In addition, the book offers new opportunities for two distinct groups. First, many schools have only a limited number of courses in the sales area—maybe only one. As a consequence they are often forced to choose between a Personal Selling course and a Sales Management course. In such cases, Personal Selling is the course chosen as it offers students the immediacy of developing skill sets necessary to be successful in selling. Unfortunately, students receive at best a limited understanding of how selling fits into the firm and (more importantly) of the unique challenges and issues managing the selling process. Other times, Sales Management is the chosen single course as it provides the managerial perspective business students are presumed to desire. But in that instance, students may get no direct experience in understanding buyer–seller relationships, leaving these topics to on-the-job training by their first employer. In our discussions with colleagues at many colleges and universities we consistently heard a call for a book that offers a comprehensive approach to contemporary selling and a concurrent, integrated discussion of managing this process (i.e., sales management). This book addresses that need.

Second, you may have noticed (as we have) a growing trend in sales-related courses. More and more students who are not majors in marketing (or even in business) are taking courses in selling and sales management. This trend recognizes the inherent value of such courses to the personal growth and success of any student. As such, we believe *Contemporary Selling, 4e: Building Relationships, Creating Value* serves this emerging market very well in that it allows non-sales majors wanting a single sales-related course to fully benefit from understanding the overall sales area instead of only one part of it (i.e., just Personal Selling or Sales Management).

In addition, the book is written to complement and enhance a variety of teaching approaches. Most importantly, *Contemporary Selling, 4e: Building Relationships, Creating Value* incorporates a comprehensive role-play series that integrates exercises on the selling process and sales management topics with most chapters. Role-playing is one of the most used sales training tools by the top companies. Our end-of-chapter role plays are tied together throughout the book within a common scenario that students will readily and enthusiastically identify with as they progress through the course. Beyond the role plays, a variety of other teaching enhancements are provided within the book. For those interested in a lecture/discussion format an abundance of material is presented in the chapters and reinforced in discussion questions at the end of each chapter. Learning objectives and key terms help focus students on the most important material. Mini-cases are included at the end of each chapter for instructors taking a more case-oriented approach. A variety of other features embedded within each chapter add value to the students' experience in the course, including the boxed features Ethical Dilemma and Global Connection. This fourth edition also expands the use of experts on a variety of topics throughout the book, as each chapter begins with an Expert Advice video giving firsthand opinions on the issues in that chapter.

STRUCTURE OF THE BOOK

As we have discussed, the contemporary selling model based on building relationships and creating value defines the connection between companies and customers in a new way. As a result, we have developed a framework that breaks down the selling process into three distinct yet interrelated components.

1. **Part One: What is Contemporary Selling? (Chapters 1–5).** The book begins with an introduction to contemporary selling and the environment in which this process takes place. The opening chapter introduces the Model for Contemporary Selling and demonstrates how it serves as a road map for the entire book and course. Next, in chapters 2 and 3, is a comprehensive discussion of two critical precursors to the selling process—understanding sellers and buyers and the concept of value creation, both of which are central to the buyer–seller relationship. In chapter 4 the important area of ethical and legal issues in selling is discussed. Finally, and this is new for the fourth edition, chapter 5 provides a comprehensive discussion of CRM and sales technologies that have become such a critical component of salesperson success.

2. **Part Two: Elements of the Contemporary Selling Process (Chapters 6–10).** In this part, each of the elements in the contemporary selling process is identified and examined in detail. These include prospecting and sales call planning (chapter 6), communicating the sales message (chapter 7), negotiating for win-win solutions (chapter 8), closing the sale and follow-up (chapter 9), and management of time and territory (chapter 10).

3. **Part Three: Managing the Contemporary Selling Process (Chapters 11–14).** Key to effectively implementing successful buyer–seller relationships is an understanding of the many issues involved in managing a sales force. The topics addressed include salesperson performance: behavior, motivation, and role perceptions; recruiting, selecting, and training salespeople; and compensating and evaluating salespeople. Part Three concludes with an in-depth discussion of the unique challenges and opportunities in a global selling environment.

Features of the Text

A. CRM and Sales Technologies Chapter—NEW

CRM is the foundation for many companies' overall marketing programs and is an integral tool for contemporary selling. At the same time there are a number of specific sales technology tools that are part of the selling process. The chapter presents a "state-of-the-art" discussion on the use of technology in contemporary selling.

B. **Global Selling Chapter—NEW**

In addition to the box feature—Global Connection—in each chapter, a new chapter (chapter 14) focusing on the unique challenges of a global selling environment brings together all the current information on global selling and sales management.

C. **Expert Advice—NEW**

In partnership with global sales consultancy Chally Group Worldwide, Expert Advice is a dialogue with an expert in the sales field with firsthand experience applying aspects of the principles and concepts discussed in the chapter. You can view a video clip from Chally's PBS television special of the expert talking about an issue, then read the chapter. At the end of the chapter you will find a follow-up that links together the expert's comments with chapter content. Designed to be a great chapter kick-off by providing real-world information, these openers satisfy the desire of both students and instructors to demonstrate how people actually use the chapter concepts to be successful in business practice.

D. **Learning Objectives—UPDATED**

Each chapter begins with a set of Learning Objectives for the students. The objectives guide students as they read and seek to identify the key takeaways from the chapter.

E. **Boxed Feature—Global Connection—NEW and UPDATED**

One of the keys to success in contemporary selling is the ability to take a global perspective. Each chapter contains a boxed feature that connects chapter content with a global focus and provides real-world examples and questions for consideration. Instructors will benefit from these boxes, as they are excellent discussion starters in class

F. **Boxed Feature—Ethical Dilemma—NEW and UPDATED**

Demonstrating ethical behavior in buyer–seller relationships has never been more important than it is today. Each chapter contains an Ethical Dilemma designed to place students in realistic scenarios that require one or more decisions, prompted by questions provided. These scenarios can be used as discussion starters in class or assigned to students to reflect on and report back individually or in groups.

G. **Key Terms—UPDATED**

At the end of each chapter Key Terms are listed. These terms are also bolded the first time they appear in the body of each chapter. As a result, students can use these terms to get a quick read on their understanding of the material. They will also find these terms defined in the Glossary at the end of the book.

H. **Role Plays—UPDATED**

It is accepted in the field and classroom that role-playing is a valuable tool for helping salespeople and students apply what they are learning. A comprehensive role-play scenario has been developed for *Contemporary Selling 4e: Building Relationships, Creating Value* that flows through most chapters for continuity of learning. It involves a sales district of the "Upland Company," and includes a cast of characters students come to know and empathize with as they move through each chapter's role play. Each part of the role play will enable students to employ aspects of selling and sales management they have learned within a particular chapter.

I. **Discussion Questions—UPDATED**

Each chapter contains a set of questions designed to generate classroom discussion of key concepts and ideas from the chapter material, Expert Advice videos, and boxed features. These questions can also be used by students to enhance their own understanding or by instructors as review questions.

J. **Mini-Cases—UPDATED**

Cases have consistently been shown to be an effective tool for students in learning and applying material. Each chapter incorporates a mini-case that supports chapter subject matter. All the cases are original—written especially for the book, incorporating the latest in contemporary selling issues.

K. **Sales Proposal Appendix—NEW and UPDATED**

Creating an effective sales proposal is an essential element of a successful sales presentation. The

Appendix to chapter 6 references additional detail for use in developing a sales proposal, which is posted on the book's website (www.routledge.com/cw/Johnston). This material guides you through the process, linking it back to specific chapters and other source material.

L. **Contemporary Selling Math Appendix—NEW and UPDATED**

The value proposition provides the basis for the customer's perception of your product. As part of the value proposition a good salesperson will develop a quantitative analysis that demonstrates and supports that product value. This Appendix to chapter 3 and the accompanying spreadsheet on the book's website (www.routledge.com/cw/Johnston) lead the student through interactive exercises detailing the process of putting together a financial analysis for a sales proposal and buyer presentation.

In addition, on the book's website (www.routledge.com/cw/Johnston) you will find the following items:

M. **Videos—UPDATED**

As mentioned earlier, in support of the chapter openers' Expert Advice, videos of the experts providing their opinions about aspects of each chapter's material are provided via the book's website.

N. **PowerPoint Slides—UPDATED**

A complete set of PowerPoint slides has been developed to enhance the in-class experience of both instructors and students. The package of slides is flexible enough for instructors to include their own material yet comprehensive enough to stand alone. Links to sales-related sites are imbedded in the PowerPoint presentation to enable the instructor to go directly to relevant websites if they are online.

O. **Instructor Manual—NEW and UPDATED**

A newly created instructor manual provides an overview of each chapter, answers to discussion questions, and a discussion guide to Role Plays, Ethical Dilemmas, Global Perspectives, and Mini-Cases. A comprehensive test bank is included.

P. **Flashcards and Other Ancillary Website Materials—NEW and UPDATED**

Students will find the Flash Cards for each chapter included on the website to be highly useful in preparing for exams. Instructors and students also benefit from a variety of extra materials on the book's website, many of which are periodically updated. There you will also find important information on the two Appendices mentioned above: Contemporary Selling Math (chapter 3 Appendix) and Sales Proposals (chapter 6 Appendix).

Acknowledgments

Writing a book is never the result of the authors alone. Many people contribute in a variety of ways to the process. We would like to begin by thanking the many colleagues and sales professionals who inspired us to take on the challenge of creating a text that encompasses the gamut of contemporary selling issues. Over many conversations we developed the ideas and concepts you will find in the book. More specifically, we offer a special thank you to the reviewers who provided valuable insights and guidance through the writing process. They are:

- Somjit Barat, *Pennsylvania State University, USA*
- James Boles, *Georgia State University, USA*
- Tony Douglas, *Edinburgh Napier University, UK*
- Shane Hunt, *Arkansas State University, USA*
- Dan Ladik, *Seton Hall University, USA*
- Amit Mukherjee, *Stockton State College, USA*
- Jay Mulki, *Northeastern University, USA*
- Mallery Nagle, *University of Central Oklahoma, USA*
- Bala Shankar, *Singapore Management University, Singapore*

- Kavita Sharma, *University of Delhi, India*
- Yiu-hing Wong, *Hong Kong Polytechnic University, Hong Kong*

We would also like to thank the great people at Routledge/Taylor & Francis Group, including Sharon Golan, Holly Davis, and James Driscoll for their exceptional work and support during the process. Working with professionals who are also fantastic people makes the task easier and more enjoyable—thanks again to everyone at Routledge/Taylor & Francis. In addition, we greatly appreciate the hard work of Danielle Cosco, Jessica Dunn, and Morgan Filteau here at Rollins College—your efforts greatly enhanced the quality of this new edition. And finally, we want to offer a very special thank you to our families and friends. Without their encouragement and support over many months you would not be reading this book. You are special and you are appreciated. Enjoy the book!

Mark W. Johnston, Rollins College
Greg W. Marshall, Rollins College
April 2013

A VISUAL TOUR OF *CONTEMPORARY SELLING:*
BUILDING RELATIONSHIPS, CREATING VALUE
4TH EDITION

PEDAGOGICAL FEATURES

Contemporary Selling offers numerous features to facilitate the instructor's task, and to engage students and help them understand the topics under discussion.

THE MODEL FOR CONTEMPORARY SELLING

Developed by the authors to portray visually the notion that everything builds outward from a customer focus, this model serves as a road map for the book and for selling courses. The Model is introduced in Chapter One.

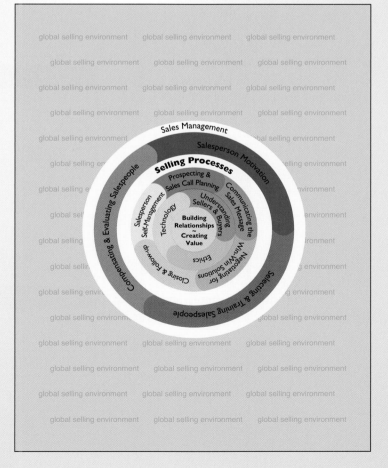

EXPERT ADVICE boxes at the beginning of each chapter are linked to video clips of sales experts discussing best sales practices hosted on the book's companion website. Students are then asked to consider questions relating to the video clip at the end of each chapter.

EXPERT ADVICE

Chally Group WORLDWIDE

EXPERT: David B. Edmonds
Senior Vice President, Worldwide Services, FedEx Corporation

TOPIC: The sales role and sales job characteristics.

SUMMARY: Mr. Edmonds talks broadly about the contemporary world of selling and sa management. He describes what makes for great global selling opportunities at Fee and strongly emphasizes that customers today expect a salesperson to be a trust business partner. They want you to help them win in the increasingly competit marketplace. Because the business-to-business (B2B) selling environment is incredi complex, he recommends that a salesperson bring to the table a business mindset fi

EXHIBITS are woven throughout the text, highlighting key points and incorporating visual materials to aid students' understanding.

EXHIBIT 1.1 TEST YOUR CUSTOMER MINDSET

External Customer Mindset	Internal Customer Mindset
I believe that . . .	I believe that . . .

External Customer Mindset:
- I must understand the needs of my company's customers.
- It is critical to provide value to my company's customers.
- I am primarily interested in satisfying my company's customers.
- I must understand who buys my company's products/services.
- I can perform my job better if I understand the needs of my company's customers.
- Understanding my company's customers will help me do my job better.

Internal Customer Mindset:
- Employees who receive my work are my customers.
- Meeting the needs of employees who receive my work is critical to doing a good job.
- It is important to receive feedback from employees who receive my work.
- I focus on the requirements of the person who receives my work.

GLOBAL CONNECTION boxes in each chapter draw out global issues and differences between cultures within the context of selling.

GLOBAL CONNECTION

SHIFT TO VALUE-ADDED SELLING IS BIGGEST CHALLENGE IN GLOBAL SALES

Making the transition from transactional (price- and product-oriented) selling to consultative (value-added) selling is now the most frequent challenge faced by sales professionals around the world, according to a survey of 134 sales managers by global consultancy Sales Performance International:

What difficulties do your salespeople have in the marketplace?

Moving to solution-type selling	69%
Selling value	67%
Inexperience	63%
Negotiating	58%
Prospecting	55%
Closing	55%
Unable to get to decision maker	51%

ETHICAL DILEMMAS are included each chapter, to help students identify and handle effectively the numerous ethical issues that arise in selling.

ETHICAL DILEMMA

WHOSE FAULT IS IT ANYWAY?

Ted Gaitlin has been an insurance agent with All Star Insurance for 13 years. He has enjoyed success with the company and won a number of sales awards. In addition, he has developed a reputation as an honest agent who works hard for his clients.

Over the last several years, however, the insurance market in his area became extremely competitive. Even though he was working harder than ever, he was not performing as well as he had during the 1990s. Management was beginning to wonder if Ted would be able to continue as an agent with the company.

Two months ago a sales contest was announced. Ted saw it as an opportunity to reestablish his position. The company wanted to drive new business in the last quarter of the fiscal year, and the contest was based on submitting new insurance policies for underwriting. Ted worked hard to write new business during the period and his efforts yielded good results. Now, as the contest entered its last month, he was concerned about winning. Biweekly results of all the agents across the country showed the contest was down to Ted and two other agents.

This morning Ted got a call from a friend, also an agent with All Star, who encouraged him to go all out to win the contest and suggested Ted submit proposals that would most likely be rejected by

ROLE PLAYS at the end of each chapter enable students to learn by doing.

ROLE PLAY

BEFORE YOU BEGIN

Each chapter in *Contemporary Selling* has a role-play exercise at the end. These role plays are designed to provide you the opportunity to work with one or more other students in your class to put into practice, or "act out," some of the important learning from that chapter.

All the role plays involve a cast of characters from a fictional firm, the Upland Company. You will need to know some basic information about Upland and its customers, as well as meet each of the characters you will be asked to role-play, before you begin. The Appendix to this chapter provides the company and character profiles you need to get started preparing your role play. It also provides valuable tips on how to get the most out of a role-play exercise and specific instructions on how to put your role play together.

Before attempting to go further with this first role play, please refer to this chapter's Appendix.

MINI CASES at the end of each chapter help students to understand and apply the principles they have learned in the classroom.

MINI-CASE 1 CREEKSIDE OUTDOOR GEAR

Creekside Outdoor Gear is a Philadelphia-based company that produces and markets clothing sold exclusively in retail stores specializing in apparel for outdoor enthusiasts. The product line includes shirts, pants, jackets, ski-suit bibs and jackets, hats, gloves, and underwear. The stores also sell equipment for mountain climbing, kayaking, skiing, snowboarding, canoeing, and hiking, items for which Creekside's products are a natural complement. Creekside is known throughout the Northeast for high quality. Joe Edwards, Creekside's founder and owner, often tells his employees, "If you provide a quality product, people will want to buy it from you." However, Joe is beginning to detect some changes in his business and is wondering how those changes will affect his company.

One change that Joe has noticed is that the customers visiting the retailers that carry his products look younger and younger. As a member of the baby boomer generation, Joe realizes that his peers are getting older. The group of customers that has spurred his company's growth since its founding in 1978 will likely be a smaller piece of his business in the future. Joe has also noticed the growth in extreme sports. Not only are the people who participate in these sports youngsters, but they also have unusual (to Joe) buying habits. They seem to want what Joe would describe as a sloppy look and attractive color schemes at the same time.

Such customer desires take advantage of new, high-tech materials that provide greater warmth

DISCUSSION QUESTIONS at the end of each chapter provide students with the opportunity to apply their knowledge to exam style questions.

DISCUSSION QUESTIONS

1. Think about the general concept of a relationship, not necessarily in a business setting, but just relationships in general between any two parties. What aspects of relationships are inherently favorable? What aspects tend to cause problems? List some specific ways one might work to minimize the problems and accentuate the favorable aspects.

2. What is *value*? In what ways does a relationship selling approach add value to your customers, to you the salesperson, and to your sales organization?

3. When a firm shifts from transactional selling to a value-added approach, a number of changes have to take place in the way a salesperson approaches customers as well as his or her own job. List as many of these changes as you can and explain why each is important to making value-added selling work.

4. Has transactional selling gone the way of the dinosaur? That is, are there ever any situations in which a transactional approach to selling would be an appropriate approach today? If so, what are those conditions and why would transactional selling be appropriate in those cases?

5. Why is it important to talk about selling *solutions* instead of products or services? How does selling solutions further the success of a relationship selling approach?

6. The chapter mentions negotiating for win-win solutions. Think of a time when you negotiated with

COMPANION WEBSITE

 www.routledge.com/cw/johnston

Visit the Companion Website for a whole host of instructor and student resources that support and enhance the textbook, including:

Instructor resources:

- An Instructor's Manual including chapter outlines, helpful hints for the instructor, teaching notes, and outline answers to questions in the text
- A comprehensive Test Bank of questions, including MCQs, true-false questions and open questions to assign to your students
- All of the exhibits from the book available to download for your own use
- PowerPoint Slides for classroom use.

Student resources:

- An interactive Flashcard Glossary to test your understanding of the key terms
- Multiple Choice Questions to test your knowledge of each chapter's key points
- Videos of sales experts discussing best sales practices produced by HR Chally (as featured in the "Expert Advice" sections in the book)
- Links to relevant YouTube Videos, organized by chapter.

WHAT IS CONTEMPORARY SELLING?

CHAPTER 1
Introduction to Contemporary Selling

CHAPTER 2
Understanding Sellers and Buyers

CHAPTER 3
Value Creation in Buyer–Seller Relationships

CHAPTER 4
Ethical and Legal Issues in Contemporary Selling

CHAPTER 5
CRM and Sales Technologies

PART ONE introduces the concept of the customer-centric firm. In selling today, the focus in customer-centric organizations is on securing, building, and maintaining long-term relationships with profitable customers. In chapter 1 we introduce many important concepts in contemporary selling and provide a pictorial model for Contemporary Selling that tracks the remaining chapters in this book. The discussion in chapter 1 follows along with our model, working from the inside out.

Success in selling requires a good understanding of sellers and buyers, the topic of chapter 2. On the selling side, this includes the key drivers of change in selling and sales management today, aspects of selling as a career, key success factors in contemporary selling, selling activities, and types of selling jobs. On the buying side, important questions include who participates in the organizational buying process, what are the stages in the buying decision process, and what are the different organizational buying situations.

Value creation is a central theme in most business models today. Chapter 3 takes a close look at the concept of value, how sales organizations and salespeople can create value for customers, and how salespeople can effectively communicate and deliver on that value proposition for their customers.

No business topic has received more attention recently than companies' ethical and legal behavior. Chapter 4 provides insight into the importance of ethics in selling and sales management, outlines a variety of key ethical concerns in the field, and gives guidance on legal issues that are particularly relevant for salespeople and their managers.

Finally, technology continues to transform the sales role and impact the customer relationship. Chapter 5 provides an important focus on technology and how key technology tools are best utilized in contemporary selling and sales management.

Sales Management

Salesperson Motivation

Compensating & Evaluating Salespeople

Selecting & Training Salespeople

Selling Processes

Prospecting & Sales Call Planning

Communicating the Sales Message

Salesperson Self-Management

Technology

Understanding Sellers & Buyers

Building Relationships ~ Creating Value

Closing & Follow-up

Ethics

Negotiating for Win-Win Solutions

Introduction to Contemporary Selling

LEARNING OBJECTIVES

Selling has changed. The focus of much selling today is on securing, building, and maintaining long-term relationships with profitable customers. To accomplish this, salespeople have to be able to communicate a value proposition that represents the bundle of benefits their customers derive from the product being sold. This value-driven approach to selling will result in customers who are loyal and who want to develop long-term relationships with a salesperson and his or her firm. This chapter provides an overview of the book by way of an integrative model for Contemporary Selling.

After reading the chapter, you should be able to:

- Appreciate key aspects of contemporary selling.
- Understand the importance of a firm being customer-centric.
- Explain why value is a central theme in contemporary selling.
- Identify the processes involved in selling.
- Recognize the key elements in sales management.
- Discuss and give examples of the components of the external and internal environment for contemporary selling.

EXPERT ADVICE

EXPERT: David B. Edmonds
Senior Vice President, Worldwide Services, FedEx Corporation

TOPIC: The sales role and sales job characteristics.

SUMMARY: Mr. Edmonds talks broadly about the contemporary world of selling and sales management. He describes what makes for great global selling opportunities at FedEx and strongly emphasizes that customers today expect a salesperson to be a trusted business partner. They want you to help them win in the increasingly competitive marketplace. Because the business-to-business (B2B) selling environment is incredibly complex, he recommends that a salesperson bring to the table a business mindset first and sales aptitude second. Overall, today's successful salesperson has to cultivate a new set of thinking from salespeople of the past.

NEXT STEPS: Go to the website for *Contemporary Selling* (www.routledge.com/cw/Johnston), watch the chapter 1 video, and then read the chapter. You will find an Expert Advice follow-up at the end of the chapter with questions that connect elements of your learning.

COMPANION @ WEBSITE

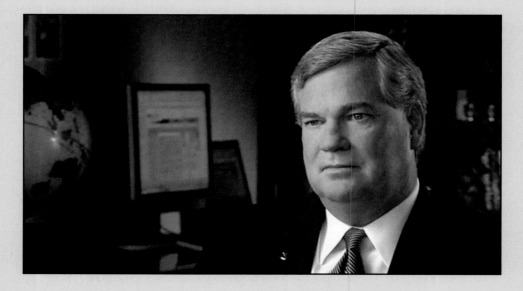

INTRODUCTION TO CONTEMPORARY SELLING

No matter what you sell, selling primarily based on having the best price is no way to build long-term clients. Low prices are very easy for competitors to match, and fickle buyers who are focused only on price will drop you as soon as a competitor beats your price. Second, the concept of creating value for your customers is an important way to get around the problems associated with price selling. **Value** represents the net bundle of benefits the customer derives from the product you are selling. Often this is referred to as your **value proposition**. Certainly low price may enhance value, but so do your expertise, your quality, and your service. Value creation in buyer-seller relationships is the subject of chapter 3. Finally, firms must focus on keeping customers coming back again and again. This idea of building **customer loyalty**, giving your customers many reasons not to switch to competitors, is central to successful selling today.

This book does not use the title "*Contemporary Selling*" lightly. That is because, in this day and age, the whole field of selling is much more sophisticated than in days past. Old-fashioned and traditional approaches to customers simply are insufficient in today's dynamic, global, technology-driven business environment. In the 21st Century world of business, it is critical to think in terms of **relationship selling**, whose central goal is securing, building, and maintaining long-term relationships with profitable customers. Relationship selling is oriented toward the *long term*. The salesperson seeks to keep his or her customers so satisfied with the product, the selling firm, and the salesperson's own level of client service that they will not switch to other sources for the same products. The book is also about **sales management**, meaning the way the various aspects of selling are managed by the salesperson's firm.

In modern organizations, the process of selling and sales management is quite integrated.[1] The managers in the sales organization have taken time to think through the most efficient and effective way to manage the overall customer side of the business. This might include using all sorts of technologies, gathering information to make decisions on customer strategies, employing different selling approaches for different kinds of customers, and having a system in place that connects all this together through information management. Such a system is often called **customer relationship management (CRM)**, which refers to an organizationwide customer focus that uses advanced technology to maximize the firm's ability to add value to customers and develop long-term relationships. The role of CRM, and technology in general, in contemporary selling will be discussed in chapter 5.

A MODEL FOR CONTEMPORARY SELLING

A firm that is **customer-centric** puts the customer at the center of everything that occurs, both inside and outside the firm. Customers are the lifeblood of any business! They are the center of your business universe. Without them you have no sales, no profits, ultimately no business. The starting point for learning about selling, and ultimately sales management, is the customer. The model for Contemporary Selling that you saw earlier serves as a road map for this book and for your course. Like customer-centric firms, the model places the customer firmly in the center of everything you will read about in this book.

Firms that are customer-centric have a high level of **customer orientation**. That is, they:

1. Instill an organizationwide focus on understanding customers' requirements.
2. Generate an understanding of the marketplace and disseminate that knowledge to everyone in the firm.
3. Align system capabilities internally so that the organization responds effectively with innovative, competitively differentiated, satisfaction-generating products and services.[2]

What does customer orientation mean to the individual salesperson? One way to exhibit a customer orientation is through a **customer mindset**, which may be defined as a salesperson's belief that understanding and satisfying customers, whether internal or external to the organization, is central to doing his or her job well. It is through this customer mindset that a customer orientation comes alive within a sales force. Exhibit

EXHIBIT 1.1 TEST YOUR CUSTOMER MINDSET

External Customer Mindset	Internal Customer Mindset
I believe that . . .	I believe that . . .
<ul><li>I must understand the needs of my company's customers.</li><li>It is critical to provide value to my company's customers.</li><li>I am primarily interested in satisfying my company's customers.</li><li>I must understand who buys my company's products/services.</li><li>I can perform my job better if I understand the needs of my company's customers.</li><li>Understanding my company's customers will help me do my job better.</li></ul>	<ul><li>Employees who receive my work are my customers.</li><li>Meeting the needs of employees who receive my work is critical to doing a good job.</li><li>It is important to receive feedback from employees who receive my work.</li><li>I focus on the requirements of the person who receives my work.</li></ul>

Score yourself from 1 to 6 on each item. 1 = strongly disagree and 6 = strongly agree. The higher your total score, the more of a customer mindset you've achieved.

Source: Karen Norman Kennedy, Felicia G. Lassk, and Jerry R. Goolsby, "Customer Mind-Set of Employees Throughout the Organization," *Journal of the Academy of Marketing Science* 30 (Spring 2002), pp. 159–71. Reprinted by permission.

1.1 provides example descriptors of a customer mindset both in the context of people you sell to (external customers) and people inside your own firm you need to deal with to get the job done (internal customers). Score yourself to see how much of a customer mindset you have.

Throughout this book, time and again we will come back to this notion of the customer at the center of the business universe. The concentric circular style of the model for Contemporary Selling was created to visually portray the notion that everything builds outward from a customer focus. The next sections describe the rest of the model from the inside out and lay the groundwork for future chapters, which focus in detail on each component of the model. The remainder chapters in the book follow the flow of the model. The most fundamental issues related to building relationships and creating value with customers are the focus of Part One of the book, comprised of chapters 1–5.

Building Relationships, Creating Value

As mentioned, building relationships and creating value with the customer is in the center of the model to connote a customer-centric organization, and the idea of a customer mindset is at the heart of this circle. Fundamentally, the onus is on the salesperson to ensure that each sales call results in a meaningful, relationship-building exchange that creates value. When problems occur—and they are bound to occur—in things like shipping, billing, out-of-stocks, after-sale service, or anything else, the salesperson must stand ready (and must be personally empowered) to work with the buyer to solve the problem. On the buyer's side, sales organizations must calculate how much time, money, and other resources should be invested in a particular customer versus the anticipated return on that investment. This ratio, often called the **return** on customer investment, is central to our discussion of value creation in chapter 3. More broadly, the customer's long-term value to the sales organization is referred to as the lifetime value of a customer.

Earlier we described value as the net bundle of benefits the customer derives from the product you are selling. A more direct way to explain value is as a "give–get" ratio. What does each party "get out of a sale" compared to what they invest? This investment might be money, time, labor, production, or any other resources used up in moving the sale forward. For many years, organizations gave little consideration to using value creation to build relationships with customers. Instead, they were content to simply conduct business as a series of discrete transactions. This approach to selling has come to be called transactional selling.

Exhibit 1.2 portrays a convenient way of distinguishing between transactional approaches to selling and those more focused on developing long-term relationships.[3] The relationship-oriented approaches are referred to as consultative selling and enterprise selling. The basis of the approach is segmenting the sales effort by the type and amount of value different customers seek to derive from the sales process.

EXHIBIT 1.2 TRANSACTIONAL SELLING VERSUS RELATIONSHIP SELLING

Transactional Selling

Transactional selling is the set of skills, strategies, and sales processes that meets the needs of buyers who treat suppliers as a commodity and who are mainly or exclusively interested in price and convenience. From the customer's point of view, in the transactional sale there are no additional benefits the seller can bring to the party beyond price.

Transactional selling *reduces* resources allocated to selling because customers don't value or want to pay for the sales effort. So transactional selling creates its value by stripping cost and making acquisition easy, with neither party making much investment in the process of buying or selling.

Relationship Selling

We earlier described relationship selling as an approach whose central goal is securing, building, and maintaining *long-term* relationships with profitable customers—the emphasis on long-term is a key. Rackham and DeVincentis distinguish between two forms of relationship selling: consultative selling and enterprise selling. The difference hinges largely on the importance of the customer and the willingness of both firms to invest in more of a strategic partnership.

Consultative Selling   Consultative selling is the set of skills, strategies, and processes that works most effectively with buyers who demand, and are willing to pay for, a sales effort that creates new value and provides additional benefits outside of the product itself. Consultative selling depends on having salespeople who become close to the customer and who have an intimate grasp of the customer's business issues. It involves a mutual investment of time and effort by both seller and customer. Listening and gaining business understanding are more important selling skills than persuasion; creativity is more important than product knowledge. In the consultative sale, the sales force creates value in three primary ways:

- It helps customers understand their problems, issues, and opportunities in new or different ways.
- It helps customers arrive at new or better solutions to their problems than they would have discovered on their own.
- It acts as the customer's advocate inside the sales organization, ensuring the timely allocation of resources to deliver customized or unique solutions that meet the customer's special needs.

Because these are demanding skills, good consultative salespeople are hard to find. Diagnostic tools, sales processes, and CRM and other information systems can help "ordinary mortals" perform well in the increasingly sophisticated consultative selling role.

Enterprise Selling   Enterprise selling is the set of skills, strategies, and processes that work most effectively with strategically important customers who demand an extraordinary level of value creation from a key supplier. Both the product and the sales force are secondary. The primary function of the enterprise sale is to leverage any and all corporate assets of the sales organization to contribute to the customer's strategic success. No single salesperson, or even a sales team, can set up or maintain an enterprise relationship. These sales are initiated at a very high level in each organization. They are deeply tied to the customer's strategic direction, and they are usually implemented by cross-functional teams on both sides.

Enterprise selling requires continuous redesign and improvement of the boundary between supplier and customer. Frequently, hundreds of people from each side are involved in the relationship and it's impossible to tell where selling begins and ends. Because enterprise selling is a very expensive process, firms must be selective in implementing this approach to relationship selling.

Source: Neil Rackham and John DeVincentis, *Rethinking the Sales Force: Redefining Selling to Create and Capture Customer Value* (New York: McGraw-Hill, 1999), pp. 25–27. Reprinted by permission of the McGraw-Hill Companies.

Basically, transactional selling works to strip costs and get to the lowest possible sales price. In contrast, relationship selling works to add value through all possible means. **Value-added selling** changes much of the sales process. Exhibit 1.3 illustrates the major differences in how a salesperson's time is best invested in the two types of selling. Relationship selling requires the salesperson to spend more time developing an understanding of the buyer's needs, which results in a more "front-loaded" selling process. Information, analysis, and communication become much more important to success with the customer. In contrast, in transactional selling focused on price, much more time and energy must be put into closing the sale.[4]

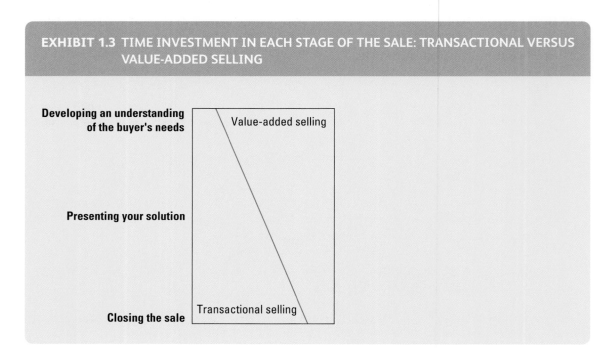

EXHIBIT 1.3 TIME INVESTMENT IN EACH STAGE OF THE SALE: TRANSACTIONAL VERSUS VALUE-ADDED SELLING

GLOBAL CONNECTION

SHIFT TO VALUE-ADDED SELLING IS BIGGEST CHALLENGE IN GLOBAL SALES

Making the transition from transactional (price- and product-oriented) selling to consultative (value-added) selling is now the most frequent challenge faced by sales professionals around the world, according to a survey of 134 sales managers by global consultancy Sales Performance International:

What difficulties do your salespeople have in the marketplace?

Moving to solution-type selling	69 %
Selling value	67 %
Inexperience	63 %
Negotiating	58 %
Prospecting	55 %
Closing	55 %
Unable to get to decision maker	51 %

"The findings suggest today's sales organization has a more sophisticated focus than a few years ago," said Sales Performance International CEO Keith Eades. "While more than half of respondents still cite frustration with basic sales techniques, like prospecting and closing, more encounter trouble at the higher end of the sales process, specifically consultative and value-added selling. This reflects a shift in emphasis as much as the complexity of the tasks involved."

For more than a decade, managers in the global arena have tried to move their sales force toward consultative selling, observed Eades. "As the survey implies, solution selling is where leading companies want to be. Not only does a consultative approach afford a competitive advantage, but it also makes for a more honorable seller. The salesperson becomes a problem solver and builds a better relationship with the customer."

But organizations in all regions of the globe find consultative selling a major challenge, Eades explained. "The accepted dogma is don't push product on customers—address their business problem and show value. Frequently, however, sellers have to deal with customers who need to be in control, want to define what they need, and seek the best price. And when all else fails, the seller falls into old habits and ends up shaving the price to win the deal."

A mistake made by management is to see consultative selling as merely a technique, said Eades. "Effective solution selling requires a culture change, top-to-bottom engagement, and an organizationwide commitment. Otherwise, the organization doesn't speak a common language and gives out different messages."

Questions to Consider

1. Do you know of any unique cultures around the world that might create particular challenges to implementing a value-added selling approach? Discuss the cultural nuances and how it might impact the ability of a salesperson to utilize value-added selling.
2. What does it mean when Mr. Eades says that solution selling requires an organizational culture change? What organizational culture changes would be necessary to make sure solution selling is successful outside the firm's home country?

Adapted from "Consultative Selling Now Seen as Biggest Challenge," *American Salesman* (September 2006), p. 29.

Shifting to value-added selling is not easy. In fact, a survey by global consulting firm Sales Performance International indicates it is the challenge most often faced by sales professionals around the world. 'Global Connection' presents the results of this survey and insights on how to foster value-added selling.

Understanding Sellers and Buyers

In the model for Contemporary Selling, the first of three elements in a band that rings the center circle focuses on fundamentals of sellers and buyers. Before we can go much farther in our learning about selling, it's essential to know something about sales jobs—what activities do salespeople perform, what factors make great salespeople so successful, what types of sales jobs exist, and why a career in selling can be highly satisfying and rewarding. At the same time, you need to know something about the person that sits on the other side of the proverbial desk—your buyer. This is a book about professional selling in a business environment, and organizational buying centers and the roles of the various participants in the buying process can be complex. Firms buy for many different reasons and they go through a series of decision-making stages before placing an order. The more complex the buying situation, the more likely the selling firm will utilize a team selling approach with the client.

In chapter 2 you will learn a great deal about professional sellers and buyers and why and how things must line up between them in order to build a strong relationship that creates value for both parties over the long run.

Ethics

The second element in the band that rings the center circle in the model for Contemporary Selling is ethics. **Ethics** are moral principles and standards that guide behavior. According to a *Sales & Marketing Management* magazine/Equation Research survey, 83 percent of 220 respondents said they train their salespeople to sell their companies' ethics and integrity along with their products and services. Nearly 70 percent said they believe their clients consider a company's ethical reputation when deciding whether to make a purchase. And, while 48 percent said their companies haven't changed their emphasis on ethics and values recently, another 48 percent said they recently have placed somewhat more or much more emphasis on ethics.[5]

The values of a society affect contemporary selling and sales management in a variety of ways. They set the standards for ethical behavior. Ethics is more than simply a matter of complying with laws and regulations. A particular action may be legal but not ethical. For instance, when a salesperson makes extreme, unsubstantiated statements such as "Our product runs rings around Brand X," he or she may be engaging in legal puffery to make a sale, but many salespeople (and their customers) view such little white lies as unethical.

Two sets of ethical issues are of particular concern in contemporary selling and sales management. The first set arises from the interactions between salespeople and their customers. These issues involve the sales manager only indirectly because the manager cannot always directly observe or control the actions of every salesperson. But sales managers have a responsibility to establish standards of ethical behavior, communicate them clearly, and enforce them vigorously. Managers must be diligent in smoking out unethical practices by their salespeople when dealing with customers.

The second set of ethical issues relates to the sales manager's dealings with the salespeople. Issues include fairness and equal treatment of all social groups in hiring and promotion, respect for the individual in supervisory practices and training programs, and fairness and integrity in the design of sales territories, assignment of quotas, determination of compensation and incentive rewards, and evaluation of performance.

Chapter 4 provides insight into a wide variety of ethics topics related to the salesperson–buyer and salesperson–sales manager relationships. In addition, within each chapter you will be challenged by an Ethical Dilemma related to topics in that chapter, along with questions to consider. In fact, here's the first one now!

ETHICAL DILEMMA

WHOSE FAULT IS IT ANYWAY?

Ted Gaitlin has been an insurance agent with All Star Insurance for 13 years. He has enjoyed success with the company and won a number of sales awards. In addition, he has developed a reputation as an honest agent who works hard for his clients.

Over the last several years, however, the insurance market in his area became extremely competitive. Even though he was working harder than ever, he was not performing as well as he had during the 1990s. Management was beginning to wonder if Ted would be able to continue as an agent with the company.

Two months ago a sales contest was announced. Ted saw it as an opportunity to reestablish his position. The company wanted to drive new business in the last quarter of the fiscal year, and the contest was based on submitting new insurance policies for underwriting. Ted worked hard to write new business during the period and his efforts yielded good results. Now, as the contest entered its last month, he was concerned about winning. Biweekly results of all the agents across the country showed the contest was down to Ted and two other agents.

This morning Ted got a call from a friend, also an agent with All Star, who encouraged him to go all out to win the contest and suggested Ted submit proposals that would most likely be rejected by underwriters but count during the contest period. Ted dismissed the strategy during the phone call. Although many agents engaged in this practice, Ted had never booked insurance business unless he was confident the underwriter would accept it.

After the phone call, however, Ted began to think about the contest and his future with All Star. Technically, he would not be violating the rules of the contest, since it was based solely on generating new policies for underwriting. He had been working hard the last few years, and he felt it was not his fault that business was down all across his area. Finally, he was sure that winning the contest would improve his standing with management. On the other hand, he knew that writing policies that will be rejected is not in the best interest of the customer or the company. The booked customers would be upset because they could not get the insurance they counted on, and having underwriters review policies that could not be approved wastes the company's money.

Questions to Consider

1. What should Ted do? Why?
2. What conflicts do salespeople run into when they try to balance the needs of the company and their customers?
3. Is it OK for Ted to violate the spirit of the contest so long as he does not violate the letter of the contest rules?
4. Who bears more of the ethical responsibility: management (for creating a contest with poorly written rules) or Ted?

Technology

The third and final element in the band that rings the center circle of the model for Contemporary Selling is technology. Think of information as the engine that drives a salesperson's success in building relationships and creating value for customers. Technology plays a major role in using information to manage customer relationships. The term "customer relationship management" has come to signify a technology-driven organizationwide strategic focus on the customer. CRM began primarily as a software package designed to collect and mine data and has evolved into an overarching organizational philosophy of doing business. Chapter 5 provides insights on the use on CRM, and also on various sales technologies—including the use of social media—that must be mastered by salespeople today in order to be successful.

Selling Process

In the model for Contemporary Selling, the second circle outside the core represents the various *process elements* of contemporary selling: prospecting and sales call planning, communicating the sales message, negotiating for win-win solutions, closing and follow-up, and time and territory management. These five selling processes are represented by chapters 6–10, which comprise Part Two of the book. The following sections provide an overview of these important topics.

Prospecting and Sales Call Planning. In any business, today's customers weren't always customers. Chances are they started out as **prospects**—a set of potential customers you or your firm identified as *very likely* future customers. Building a business involves being on the lookout for great prospects, for it is a pipeline of prospects that ensures a growing, thriving customer base. Salespeople sometimes look at identifying and developing prospects as a "necessary evil" in selling—that's an unfortunate (and unproductive) attitude to take. Nowadays, CRM systems, social media, the Internet, and other technology-driven tools have the capability to provide a wealth of information to salespeople about potential customers if the systems are properly implemented and utilized.

Chapter 6 provides insights on how to systematically and successfully go about identifying and developing prospects, and then details how to prepare in advance for the first sales call once you have qualified a prospect as a high potential future customer.

Communicating the Sales Message. Selling involves **persuasive communication**. When you persuade, you hope to convince someone to do something. In transactional selling, the focus tends to be on communicating a hard sell message. This is because by definition in transactional selling there is no real relationship. With a hard sell approach, buyers and sellers are likely to be adversarial, little trust exists between them, and they are not working for long-term or win-win solutions.

The hard sell has been replaced by a communication approach of mutual problem solving. In contemporary selling, communication is handled by multiple means—from traditional email and phone to texting and social media. The salesperson acts as a consultant or problem solver for buyers and sells value-added solutions, popularized by the term **solution selling**, in which the salesperson's primary role is to move the buyer toward visualization of a solution to his or her problem (need).[6] Today, almost all of us seem to be selling "solutions," as opposed to "products," whether our wares are cell phones, financial services, computer software, or just about any other product or service (even college courses in selling) that solves a problem or fulfills some buyer's need. Chapter 7 explores the issue of communicating effectively when selling solutions, solving buyer problems, and managing long-term relationships.

Negotiating for Win-Win Solutions. Even when buyers have been doing business with you for a very long time, they will develop **objections** to various aspects of your proposed solution. An objection is simply a concern that some part of your product offering (solution) does not fully meet the buyer's need. The objection may be over price, delivery, terms of agreement, timing, or myriad other potential elements of a deal. Even though typical buyer–seller interactions in a relationship selling environment are far from adversarial, negotiation still must take place. Chapter 8 includes details on planning for, recognizing, and handling common objections from buyers and strategies for negotiating win-win solutions.

Closing and Follow-Up. The rapport, trust, and mutual respect inherent in a long-term buyer–seller relationship can take some of the pressure off the "close" portion of the sales process. In theory, this is because the seller and buyer have been openly communicating throughout the process about mutual goals they would like to see fulfilled within the context of their relationship. Because the key value added is not price but rather other aspects of the product or service, the negotiation should not get hung up on price as an objection. Thus closing becomes a natural part of the communication process. (Note that in many transaction selling models, the closing step is feared by many salespeople—as well as buyers—because of its awkwardness and win-lose connotation.)

A big part of this process of maintaining loyal customers over the long run is follow-up, which includes service after the sale. Effective follow-up is one way that salespeople and their firms can improve customer perceptions of service quality, customer satisfaction, and customer retention and loyalty. These issues are central to successful selling, and they will be discussed in detail at various points throughout the book. Many salespeople try to "underpromise and overdeliver," a catchphrase that reminds salespeople to try to deliver more than they promised in order to pleasantly surprise the buyer. Managing customer expectations is an important part of developing successful long-term relationships. Customer delight, or exceeding customer expectations to a surprising degree, is a powerful way to gain customer loyalty. Overpromising can get the initial sale and thus may work once in a transactional selling environment, but a dissatisfied customer not only will not buy again but also will tell many others to avoid that salesperson and his or her company and products.[7]

Chapter 9 provides a variety of ideas on how to move customers toward closure in contemporary selling and presents key issues in effective follow-up after the sale.

Self-Management. In chapter 2 you will read about various characteristics of sales jobs that make them unique, challenging, and rewarding. One thing that makes selling an attractive career choice for many people is the autonomy, which means the degree of independence the salesperson can exercise in making his or her decisions in the day-to-day operation of the job. Salespeople today have tremendous autonomy to develop and execute their selling strategies. Chapter 10 presents a host of important salesperson self-management issues, including organizing the job, designing and routing the sales territory, classifying and prioritizing customer potential, using technology to improve efficiency, and exercising good time management skills.

Sales Management

In the model for Contemporary Selling, the third circle outside the core is about managing salespeople: salesperson motivation; selecting and training salespeople; and compensating and evaluating salespeople. And, of course, the whole scope of these activities takes place in the context of the global stage. These managerial areas of focus comprise the first three chapters of Part Three of the book, chapters 11–13. The final chapter in Part Three, chapter 14, deals with the global selling environment and will be highlighted later in this chapter.

Motivating Salespeople. Psychologists classically view motivation as a general label referring to an individual's choice to (a) initiate action on a certain task, (b) expend a certain amount of effort on that task, and (c) persist in expending the effort over a period of time.[8] Thus, for clarity let's consider motivation as simply the amount of effort a salesperson chooses to expend on each activity or task associated with the job. This general view of motivation is based on expectancy theory, which holds that a salesperson's estimate of the probability that expending effort on a task will lead to improved performance and rewards. The expectancy theory of motivation provides the framework for our discussion of motivating salespeople in chapter 11.

Selecting and Training Salespeople. With the shift in focus from transactional to relationship approaches, the various skills and knowledge components required to successfully perform the sales role have shifted accordingly. Identifying these **key success factors** in contemporary selling is the first step selecting new salespeople (chapter 2 discusses sales success factors in more detail). Whereas in the past these success factors tended to be related to fairly traditional selling activities (prospecting, overcoming objections, closing, etc.), nowadays they have broadened substantially. A survey of 215 sales managers across a wide variety of industries identified the following seven success factors as the most important to sales managers interviewing prospective salespeople. Notice in particular how each supports a relationship selling approach:[9]

1. Listening skills
2. Follow-up skills
3. Ability to adapt sales style from situation to situation
4. Tenacity (sticking with a task)
5. Organizational skills
6. Oral communication skills
7. Ability to interact with people at all levels of customer's organization

Chapter 12 considers the overall process of selecting salespeople based on the skills and knowledge needed to succeed in today's business selling environment. Although a salesperson's ability to manage customer relationships generally improves with practice and experience, it is inefficient to expect a rep to gain skills solely through on-the-job experience. Good customers might be lost due to the mistakes of an unskilled salesperson. Consequently, many firms have a formal training and development program to give new recruits some knowledge and skills before they are expected to pull their own weight in calling on customers.

Training generally focuses on building specific skill and knowledge sets needed to succeed in the job. **Development** is more about providing a long-term road map or career track for a salesperson so he or she can realize professional goals. The rapid changes in technology, global competition, and customer needs in many industries have accelerated the need for effective training in sales organizations. Chapter 12 also discusses training and development of salespeople in detail. It explains that salespeople go through a variety of career stages (exploration, establishment, maintenance, and disengagement) and each stage brings a unique set of training and development needs.[10]

Compensating and Evaluating Salespeople. Professional salespeople are very results-oriented. They crave recognition and rewards for a job well done. Their motivation to expend effort on the various aspects of their job is largely a function of the rewards they expect for a given job performance. **Compensation** involves monetary rewards. **Incentives** include a variety of financial and nonfinancial rewards. Nonfinancial incentives include recognition programs, promotions to better territories or to management positions, or opportunities for personal development. Chapter 13 provides insight on these important issues, including ways to put together an effective sales force reward system.

One trend in contemporary selling is that today's salespeople often work as part of a team assigned to manage a specific client relationship. Team-based selling requires that rewards must be created both for individual and team aspects of the sales job.[11] For example, the entire selling process at Bristol-Myers Squibb (BMS) is team-driven. A Fortune 100 firm, BMS is one of the world's leading makers of medicines and related healthcare products. BMS, based in New York City, had 2012 sales of over $20 billion and employed over 30,000 people. A key account manager serves as a team leader for a major retail account (Walgreens Drug Stores, for example). A category management specialist tracks sales and competitive trends and provides information to the team and the client for decision making about the product line. Also on the team are BMS merchandisers, who work with the various Walgreens regions and stores to ensure the BMS–Walgreens merchandising program is carried out; local BMS salespeople, who make presentations to pharmacists and front-end managers at Walgreens stores in their area; and members of the BMS product management group in New York, who work with the team and client on new-product development and promotion planning for their respective brands. As you might expect, compensation and incentives reward team performance, as well as individual performance.

Another aspect of the sales management process is evaluating the performance of salespeople. Team-based approaches to selling and managing customer relationships make it harder for sales managers to evaluate the impact of individual salesperson performance and determine appropriate rewards. Chapter 13 also provides insights into linking rewards to the new sales roles defined by relationship approaches to selling. It also discusses the best practices in evaluating today's salespeople.

ISSUES OUTSIDE THE CIRCLES: THE GLOBAL SELLING ENVIRONMENT

In the model for Contemporary Selling, the concentric circles exist inside a broader field labeled "Global Selling Environment." This implies that the process of selling, as well as the process of managing salespeople, takes place not in a vacuum but rather within a dynamic environment that includes issues relevant to and controllable by your own firm (the **internal environment**, or organizational environment) and issues outside the control of your organization (the **external environment**, or macroenvironment). Throughout this book, all the ideas and examples we will discuss about how to be successful in selling must be considered in the context of the internal and external environments facing you and your customers on the global stage. You saw the Global Connection feature earlier in this chapter—within each chapter you will be challenged by a Global Connection related to topics in that chapter, along with questions to consider. And chapter 14 provides a detailed discussion of global aspects of contemporary selling. We want to be sure that when you finish this book and your course, you are fully up to speed on the major issues and idiosyncrasies of doing business outside one's home country.

Internal Environment

The policies, resources, and talents of the sales organization make up a very important part of the internal environment. Salespeople and their managers may have some influence over organizational factors in the long run due to their participation in making policy and planning decisions. However, in the short run a firm's selling initiatives must be designed to fit within organizational limitations. Components of the internal environment can be divided into six broad categories: (1) goals, objectives, and culture, (2) human resources, (3) financial resources, (4) production and supply-chain capabilities, (5) service capabilities, and (6) research and development (R&D) and technological capabilities. These are depicted in Exhibit 1.4.

Goals, Objectives, Culture. Successful management of customer relationships begins with top management's specification of a company mission and objectives that create a customer-centric organization. As the mission and objectives change, customer relationship initiatives must be adjusted accordingly. A well-defined mission, driven by top management's values and beliefs, leads to the development of a strong **corporate culture**. Such cultures shape employees' attitudes and actions and help determine the plans, policies, and procedures salespeople and their managers implement.

Periodically, *Sales & Marketing Management* magazine, a major trade publication covering the selling industry, publishes a special report on the 25 best sales forces. Global firms that appear regularly on the list include Baxter International (healthcare), Cisco Systems (information technology), Charles Schwab (financial services), and General Mills (consumer products), among others. A common thread among these and other top-performing sales organizations is a culture, embraced from top management all the way throughout the firm, that focuses on getting and staying close to customers. Their customer-centric culture is manifest in their missions, goals, and objectives.

EXHIBIT 1.4 COMPONENTS OF THE INTERNAL ENVIRONMENT

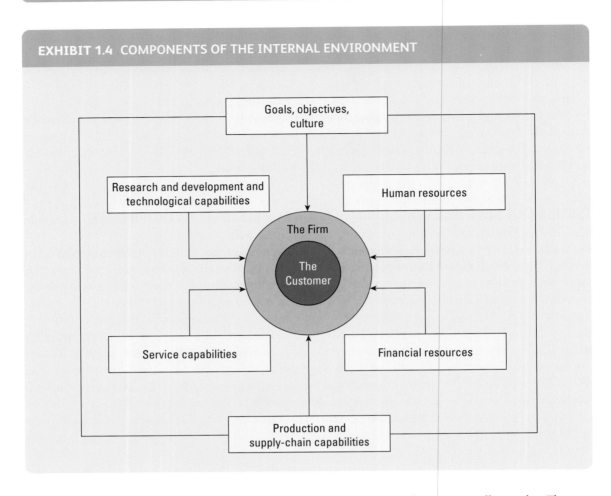

We have already mentioned the central role of ethics and legal considerations in selling today. The tone and expectations set by upper management and the overall culture of the firm drive ethical behavior in sales organizations.

Human Resources. Modern sales organizations are highly complex and dynamic enterprises, as are their customers' firms. The sheer number of people in many sales organizations and their broad scope of global coverage, together with the complexity and diversity of key success factors needed in selling, create challenges. Because it takes time to recruit highly qualified people for sales positions and then to train them, it is often difficult to expand a sales force rapidly to take advantage of new products or growing global markets. Sometimes, however, a firm can compensate for a lack of knowledgeable employees by hiring outside agencies or specialists on a fee-for-service or commission basis. For example, many companies use independent distributors when entering new markets, particularly markets outside their home country, because using such preexisting sales forces speeds up the process of market entry.

Financial Resources. An organization's financial strength influences many aspects of its customer relationship initiatives. A tight budget can constrain the firm's ability to develop new value-adding products as well as the size of its promotional budget and sales force. Companies sometimes must take drastic measures, such as merging with a larger firm or one outside their home country, to obtain the financial resources necessary to realize their full potential in the global marketplace. For example, Procter & Gamble's acquisition of Gillette in the highly competitive consumer health products field several years ago gave P&G quick entry into the lucrative razor blade market, while benefiting Gillette through P&G's strong supply chain expertise outside the U.S.

Production and Supply-Chain Capabilities. An organization's production capacity, the technology and equipment available in its plants, and even the location of its production facilities can influence the selling initiative. A company may be prevented from expanding its product line or moving into new areas of the globe because it does not have the capacity to serve increased demand or because transportation costs make the product's price uncompetitive.

Walmart, though U.S.-based, is achieving most of its growth through outside-U.S. expansion. Vendors doing business with Walmart are expected to fulfill orders within 24 hours and to deliver the goods to the Walmart warehouses within a two-hour assigned appointment window. Suppliers who don't meet this requirement pay Walmart for every dollar of lost margin. It is no wonder Walmart's vendors are willing to invest the capital to tie their information and supply-chain systems directly to Walmart's system so the whole ordering and fullfillment process can be handled at maximum efficiency and speed. Because of Walmart's massive size, being a preferred vendor for the firm can often push the supplying organization to a whole new level of global scope, benefiting it with other customers as well.

As an example of supply-chain efficiency on the e-commerce side, founder Jeff Bezos at Amazon developed a network of global distribution centers long before Amazon's sales volume could financially support the warehouse capacity, principally because he wanted to ensure seamless distribution and service after the sale and avoid inventory stockouts.

Service Capabilities. We have already mentioned the importance of delivering high service quality in the follow-up stage after the sale. Actually, a sales organization's ability to provide a consistently high level of service is an important source of value-added throughout the whole process of contemporary selling. This will be discussed further in chapter 3. For now, be assured that firms committed to providing great service typically enjoy a strong competitive advantage in the global marketplace and make it difficult both for (a) other firms to compete for the same customers and (b) customers to switch to competitors even if they offer price advantages.[12]

R&D and Technological Capabilities. An organization's technological and engineering expertise is a major factor in determining whether it will be an industry leader or follower in developing value-adding products and delivering high-quality service. Excellence in engineering and design can also be a major promotional appeal in a firm's marketing and sales programs, as customers are attracted to innovators and industry leaders. When companies are investing heavily in technology, salespeople can communicate the R&D and technological sophistication to customers as important value-adding aspects of the company and its products. This capability helps avoid the trap of overrelying on price to get the sale.

External Environment

By definition, factors in the external global environment are beyond the direct control of salespeople and managers. Companies do try to influence external conditions through political lobbying, public relations campaigns, and the like. But for the most part, the salesperson and sales manager must adapt customer relationship initiatives to fit the existing environment in the countries in which they operate. Exhibit 1.5 groups the components of the external environment in five broad categories: (1) economic, (2) legal-political, (3) technological, (4) social-cultural, and (5) natural.

Economic Environment. People and organizations cannot buy goods and services unless they have the money. The total potential demand for a product within a given country depends on that country's economic conditions—the amount of growth, the unemployment rate, the level of inflation, and the gross domestic product (GDP). Sales managers must consider these factors when analyzing market opportunities and developing sales forecasts. Keep in mind that global economic conditions also influence many firms' ability to earn a profit. Companies of all kinds were impacted by the credit crunch created by the general financial

EXHIBIT 1.5 COMPONENTS OF THE EXTERNAL ENVIRONMENT

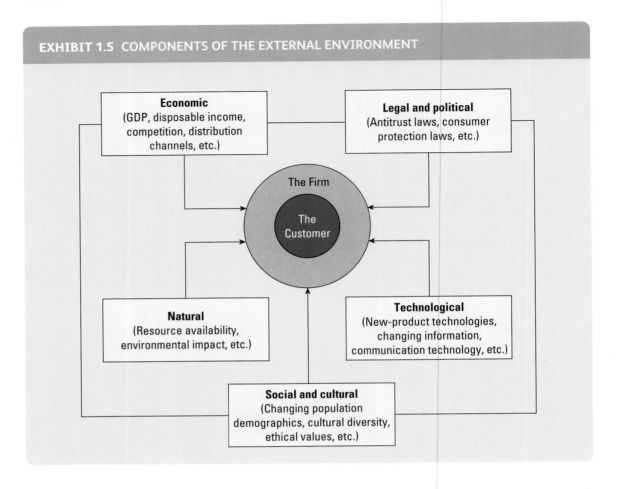

and economic crisis that began in the late 2000s, making it difficult to secure capital for investment in growth of products and markets. Then too, currency exchange rates can make trade more or less favorable for a sales organization depending on the direction of the flow of products and money.

A second aspect of the economic environment is the existing distribution structure in an industry within areas of a firm's global reach. This includes the number, types, and availability of wholesalers, retailers, and other intermediaries a firm might use to distribute its product. Much of a firm's selling effort may be directed to persuading such intermediaries to stock and provide sales and marketing support for the company's products.

A third economic factor is the amount of competition in the firm's industry, both the number of competing firms and the relative strength of each in the marketplace. Ideally, a company's customer relationship initiative should be designed to gain a differential advantage over competitors. For example, rather than trying to compete with the lower prices of non-U.S.-based competitors (such as Komatsu) Caterpillar has succeeded in the heavy construction equipment business by providing superior product quality and excellent service, while charging prices as much as 10 to 20 percent higher than its competitors. A great way to thwart competitive threats is to focus the sales message on value-adding aspects of the product or service rather than price, the topic of chapter 3.

Salespeople go head to head with competitors on a daily basis, so they are often the first to observe changes in competitive strategy and activity in the various markets around the world in which the salespeople are based. One critical issue is getting information from the sales force back to the company so that the firm can act on those observations. CRM systems, discussed in chapter 5, provide an infrastructure for managing such competitive information (and many other types of customer information).

Legal and Political Environment. Laws and political action affect all organizations, and for those doing business globally this aspect of the environment can be daunting due to idiosyncrasies from country to country. In selling, common legal issues include antitrust, truth in advertising, restriction of telemarketing and spam, product liability, issuance of credit, transportation of materials, and product claims, among many others. In addition, differing political administrations at all levels of governments can bring changes to the marketplace and sales arena. Sales organizations must always be mindful of laws relevant to doing business in each country and must take laws and political action into account when developing plans and strategies there. Also, it is very important that salespeople be trained on the impact of the law on their role.

As discussed earlier in this chapter, ethics is different from the law. Something unethical may not be technically illegal, but it should still be avoided. Perceptions and norms for what is and isn't ethical can vary by country and culture. Many reasons exist for practicing highly ethical behavior in contemporary selling and sales management. The ethical environment is the focus of chapter 4.

Technological Environment. An earlier section under "Internal Environment" discussed the impact of a sales organization's own technological capabilities. Here, we focus on the overall impact of macrolevel technology trends on selling. One obvious impact is the opportunity for new-product development. Technological advances occur faster all the time, and new products account for an increasing percentage of total sales in many industries. For example, historically at 3M, more than half of the current sales volume is generated by products that did not exist five years ago. And, of course, at Apple, a few short years back all of their sales came from computers and related items. Today, the bulk of Apple's customers are buying iPods, iPads, and iPhones (not to mention downloading iTunes).

Most analysts believe new products and services will become even more important to the success of many firms. Rapid development of new products affects many selling activities. New selling plans and messages must be developed to appeal to customers in various regions of the world, salespeople must be retrained to update technical knowledge, in some cases new salespeople must be hired to augment the sales effort, and new reward and performance evaluation systems must be established that match the new sales roles.

Improvements in transportation, communications, and information management across global markets are changing the way customers are targeted, sales territories are defined, salespeople are deployed, and salesperson performance is evaluated in many companies. New communication technologies, together with the escalating cost of a traditional field sales call, are changing how the selling function is carried out. Much selling today on the global stage is accomplished by a combination of face-to-face communication and various electronic forms of communication. Consequently, the nature of many sales jobs and the concurrent role of the sales manager in supervising the salespeople have changed dramatically in recent years.

Social and Cultural Environment. The values of a society affect contemporary selling and sales management in a variety of ways. Firms develop new products in response to trends in customer tastes and preferences. For example, in the United States, the well-documented demographic trends of aging society, greater influx of minorities as a percentage of total population, two-income households, greater mobility, and ever-increasing desire for more leisure time and more convenience-oriented products all have greatly affected selling. Likewise, in China and India many sales organizations are finding an increasing openness to doing business with global partners, and to a large degree the level of success outside sales organizations will achieve in those markets hinges on their ability to adapt their business models to the needs of those cultures.

The attacks of 9/11 in New York City provide a vivid example of social-cultural impact on a global stage. Societal values shifted quickly and sharply toward family, home, safety, and comfort after the attacks. People became more cautious of travel and security measures were greatly increased all over the world and have not diminished since. Direct sellers especially saw a resultant change in shopping pattern and intensity. Direct sellers (like Avon, Amway, and Mary Kay) typically do business in customers' own homes, where relationships among buyers and sellers are warm, friendly, and high in trust. Most direct sellers, as well as the direct selling industry as a whole, experienced a significant increase in global business after the 9/11 attacks as customers gravitated closer to home for many of their purchases.

Natural Environment. Nature influences demand for many products. Of course, natural disasters such as tsunamis, typhoons, and floods increase demand for building products and the like. The winter 2012 season brought historic warmth and nearly no snow to parts of Europe and record cold to other European regions, creating all sorts of challenges for any firms selling and distributing typical winter products across the affected areas. But unseasonable weather can either damage or enhance sales, depending on the type of product you are selling. Hurricanes and typhoons are massive and violent storms that wreak havoc wherever they hit, yet firms selling batteries and building materials see unprecedented sales spikes as a result. And when the massive volcanic eruption in Iceland took place a few years ago, sellers of travel saw transatlantic flying impacted for weeks. The devastating Japanese tsunami of 2011 severely impacted the selling and distribution process for several global automobile and consumer electronics manufacturers, resulting in shortages of products fromJapan-based firms and a shift of market share to brands that are manufactured elsewhere.

The natural environment is an important consideration in the development of selling approaches. It is the source of all the raw materials and energy resources needed to make, package, promote, and distribute a product. Since the 1970s, firms in many industries—among them cement, steel, aluminum, wood, plastics, and synthetic fibers—have periodically encountered resource or energy shortages that have forced them to limit sales. You might think salespeople could simply take things pretty easy under such circumstances, letting customers come to them for badly needed goods. But the sales force often has to work harder during product shortages, and at such times well-developed customer relationships become even more crucial for the firm's success.

During periods of shortage, a company may engage in **demarketing** part or all of its product line. In such cases, the sales force often helps administer rationing programs, which allocate scarce supplies according to each customer's purchase history. Shortages are usually temporary, though. So sellers must be sensitive to their customers' problems in order to retain them when the shortage is over. Salespeople must treat all customers fairly, minimize conflict, and work hard to maintain the customer relationship as well as the firm's competitive position for the future.

Over recent years, oil prices have skyrocketed globally. Most outside salespeople depend on automobiles or commercial airlines to travel from customer to customer. Gasoline and jet fuel prices have upped the costs of travel substantially. As the trend toward higher energy costs continues, look for sales organizations to find more creative ways to build relationships and create value while simultaneously reducing physical travel by salespeople.

Growing social concern about the impact of products and production processes on the natural environment also has important implications for selling. For instance, countries in the European Union have passed legislation requiring manufacturers to take back—and either reuse or recycle—materials used in packaging and shipping their products. And in general, the movement toward **sustainability**—succinctly defined as firms doing well by doing good, across the multifaceted aspects of their operations—significantly impacts relationships with client firms as well as with the public at large. Some firms have made their sustainability initiative a central theme in their sales and marketing strategies. Unilever, for example, is well regarded by its customers as a leading proponent of sustainability on a global scale.

EXPERT ADVICE: FOLLOW-UP   Chally Group
                                      WORLDWIDE

After watching the video of Mr. Edmonds and reading the chapter, consider the following questions:

1. How does what you learned in the chapter corroborate Mr. Edmonds' advice about how to best succeed in the contemporary selling environment?

2. How do you stack up in terms of meeting his expectations for success in global B2B sales today? How can you best cultivate the development of requirements you may presently be lacking?

SUMMARY

In the contemporary world of global business, it is important to think in terms of relationship selling, which is focused on securing, building, and maintaining long-term relationships with profitable customers. Firms that practice relationship selling are customer-centric. They place the customer at the center of everything that happens both inside and outside the organization. This focus on long-term customer relationships requires value-added selling, in which a salesperson communicates a broad range of benefits the customer can achieve by doing business with his or her firm. Value-added selling changes much of the sales process. It especially aids in moving purchase decisions away from simply price.

The model for Contemporary Selling is a road map for this book and for your course. This first chapter provided a brief introduction to each element of the model, which will be developed in much greater detail in later chapters. This chapter also provides an overview of the global environment of contemporary selling, highlighting key internal and external elements.

KEY TERMS

value	return on customer investment	persuasive communication	training
value proposition		solution selling	development
customer loyalty	lifetime value of a customer	objections	compensation
relationship selling		follow-up	incentives
sales management	transactional selling	customer delight	internal environment
customer relationship management (CRM)	consultative selling	autonomy	external environment
	enterprise selling	motivation	corporate culture
customer-centric	value-added selling	effort	demarketing
customer orientation	ethics	expectancy theory	sustainability
customer mindset	prospects	key success factors	

ROLE PLAY

BEFORE YOU BEGIN

Each chapter in *Contemporary Selling* has a role-play exercise at the end. These role plays are designed to provide you the opportunity to work with one or more other students in your class to put into practice, or "act out," some of the important learning from that chapter.

All the role plays involve a cast of characters from a fictional firm, the Upland Company. You will need to know some basic information about Upland and its customers, as well as meet each of the characters you will be asked to role-play, before you begin. The Appendix to this chapter provides the company and character profiles you need to get started preparing your role play. It also provides valuable tips on how to get the most out of a role-play exercise and specific instructions on how to put your role play together.

Before attempting to go further with this first role play, please refer to this chapter's Appendix.

Characters Involved

Bonnie Cairns

Chloe Herndon

Alex Lewis

Rhonda Reed

Abe Rollins

Justin Taylor

Setting the Stage

Rhonda Reed, sales manager for District 100 of the Upland Company, has called an early-morning meeting of all five salespeople in her district. Within a few weeks, Rhonda must work with each salesperson to set goals for the upcoming year. The purpose of this meeting is to discuss any external environmental factors that are likely to affect sales next year. Upland sells a variety of health and beauty aid products through supermarkets, drugstores, mass-merchandise stores such as Target and Walmart, and other similar retail environments. Example products include shampoo, hairspray, deodorant, and skin lotion.

Rhonda Reed's Role

Rhonda's objective is to stimulate discussion about the full spectrum of external environmental factors that are likely to impair Upland's industry/business during the next year. Of course, this also implies she wants to discuss the factors that will affect Upland's customers' business. She will systematically solicit her salespeople's views on the potential impact of changes/issues in each of these elements of the external environment: economic (including the competition), legal-political, technological, social-cultural, and natural. She must be sure that each person has the opportunity to contribute to the discussion and that the impact on Upland's customers is discussed.

Others' Roles

The five members of District 100 will soon be working with Rhonda to develop their sales goals for next year. This meeting is important to everybody, since if there are any external factors that are likely to affect Upland's sales and the sales of Upland's customers, those factors must be taken into account when the annual goals are developed. Much of the income earned by Upland's salespeople comes from the percentage accomplishment against annual goals. Therefore, each of the five salespeople is eager to share his or her best ideas about the potential impact of these external factors on next year's business.

Assignment

First, each student in the class should develop a list of the key issues within each external environmental factor that are likely to affect Upland and its customers.

Once the individual lists are developed, break into groups of six to act out the role play as described above. Allow about 15 minutes for the meeting. One student from each group (other than the student playing Rhonda) will take notes. After all role plays are complete, these students will share their findings with the full class.

DISCUSSION QUESTIONS

1. Think about the general concept of a relationship, not necessarily in a business setting, but just relationships in general between any two parties. What aspects of relationships are inherently favorable? What aspects tend to cause problems? List some specific ways one might work to minimize the problems and accentuate the favorable aspects.

2. What is *value*? In what ways does a relationship selling approach add value to your customers, to you the salesperson, and to your sales organization?

3. When a firm shifts from transactional selling to a value-added approach, a number of changes have to take place in the way a salesperson approaches customers as well as his or her own job. List as many of these changes as you can and explain why each is important to making value-added selling work.

4. Has transactional selling gone the way of the dinosaur? That is, are there ever any situations in which a transactional approach to selling would be an appropriate approach today? If so, what are those conditions and why would transactional selling be appropriate in those cases?

5. Why is it important to talk about selling *solutions* instead of products or services? How does selling solutions further the success of a relationship selling approach?

6. The chapter mentions negotiating for win-win solutions. Think of a time when you negotiated with someone over something and one of you "lost" and the other "won." How did that happen? Why didn't you work toward a win-win solution? If you could do it over again, what might you do to promote a win-win approach?

7. Another salesperson in your company says to you: "Closing techniques today are moot. We know all our customers and their needs too well to have to employ 'closing' techniques on them. Doing so would ruin our relationships." How do you respond to this? Is the person correct, incorrect, or both? Why?

8. Think about the various courses you have taken during your college career. What *motivates* you to work harder and perform better in some courses than others? Why? What rewards are you seeking from your college experience?

9. Sales managers ranked success factors for sales recruits as "listening skills" first, "follow-up skills" second, and "ability to adapt sales style from situation to situation" third in importance. Why do you think managers find these particular success factors so important? How does each contribute to a relationship selling approach?

10. A wise and weathered sales sage tells you: "Today, all selling is global." Is the sage right? Why or why not?

11. Like all firms, Apple operates within an external environment of factors beyond its immediate control. Consider the various aspects of the external environment portrayed in the chapter. What specific external factors have the most impact on Apple's ability to practice successful relationship selling? Why is each important?

MINI-CASE 1 CREEKSIDE OUTDOOR GEAR

Creekside Outdoor Gear is a Philadelphia-based company that produces and markets clothing sold exclusively in retail stores specializing in apparel for outdoor enthusiasts. The product line includes shirts, pants, jackets, ski-suit bibs and jackets, hats, gloves, and underwear. The stores also sell equipment for mountain climbing, kayaking, skiing, snowboarding, canoeing, and hiking, items for which Creekside's products are a natural complement. Creekside is known throughout the Northeast for high quality. Joe Edwards, Creekside's founder and owner, often tells his employees, "If you provide a quality product, people will want to buy it from you." However, Joe is beginning to detect some changes in his business and is wondering how those changes will affect his company.

One change that Joe has noticed is that the customers visiting the retailers that carry his products look younger and younger. As a member of the baby boomer generation, Joe realizes that his peers are getting older. The group of customers that has spurred his company's growth since its founding in 1978 will likely be a smaller piece of his business in the future. Joe has also noticed the growth in extreme sports. Not only are the people who participate in these sports youngsters, but they also have unusual (to Joe) buying habits. They seem to want what Joe would describe as a sloppy look and attractive color schemes at the same time.

Such customer desires take advantage of new, high-tech materials that provide greater warmth with lighter materials, which support the increased mobility needed to participate in extreme sports. Joe has never used these new materials and he wonders how they would work in his production process. Finally, Joe is concerned about the buying power of this new group of potential customers. Do people in their late teens and early twenties have enough income to purchase Joe's products, which typically command premium prices?

Another concern is geographic expansion. To help offset the impact of some of the trends described above, Joe would like to sell his products in stores in Colorado, Utah, Wyoming, Oregon, and Washington. However, Joe has always been a regional producer (Northeast U.S.), and such an expansion will require a significant investment. Establishing distribution channels and developing relationships with buyers is both expensive and time consuming. Furthermore, Joe doesn't employ a sales force. His operating philosophy has always been that a good product will sell itself. Consequently, he's wondering how best to represent his product to outdoor store buyers in those Western states.

One factor that keeps weighing on Joe's mind as he thinks about these issues is that he believes in developing relationships with his retail partners. Joe has read some information about transactional selling and relationship selling, but he's not at all sure how either one of these methods is actually implemented. Nor does he know how to decide which method of selling will better meet his objectives for sales in the Western states. Needless to say, Joe has much to consider as he decides whether or not to pursue expansion. If he does decide to expand, he needs to determine how best to set up his sales force.

Questions

1. Identify and explain aspects of the internal environment that are affecting Creekside Outdoor Gear's business. What external environmental factors are especially important to Creekside Outdoor Gear and the decisions that Joe faces? Why?

2. If Joe interviewed two different candidates for a sales position, one who has been using a transactional approach to selling and the other who has been using a relationship selling approach, how would he recognize the difference between the two?

3. Should Joe hire a sales manager and allow him or her to hire a sales force, or do other options exist? Why?

Appendix: Additional Information on Role Plays

The following information pertains to the role-play exercises at the end of the chapters. Each chapter except for chapters 5 and 14 has a role-play exercise; chapters 12 and 13 have two role-play exercises each. It is important to read and study this information before doing the role play in chapter 1 and also to refer back to this information as needed before conducting the role plays in subsequent chapters.

UPLAND COMPANY

The role plays involve a fictional consumer products company called the Upland Company. Upland sells a variety of health and beauty aids through supermarkets, drugstores, mass-merchandise stores like Target and Walmart, and similar retail environments. Example products include shampoo, hairspray, deodorant, and skin lotion. The sales force follows a relationship approach to selling and calls on headquarter buying offices for retail chains as well as some larger independent stores. Competition in this industry is fierce, and salespeople must find ways to add value beyond just low price.

Upland is organized into 45 sales districts in the United States and Canada. Sales outside North America are handled by various international subsidiaries. Each district has a district manager and four to seven account managers (salespeople) who have geographically defined territories. Each district manager reports to one of four regional managers; regional managers report directly to the VP of sales.

Each district manager also has direct selling responsibility for a few large or particularly complex accounts. Districts have two-digit numbers with a third number representing the territory number tacked onto the end. The district of interest in our role plays is District 10, managed by veteran Upland sales manager Rhonda Reed. The next section provides a profile of each person currently working in District 10.

Profiles of District 10 Personnel

District 10: Rhonda Reed, District Manager. Age 38. Married with three children. Five years' experience as district manager with Upland, always in District 10. Previously had seven years' experience as account manager with Upland in another district out of state; three years' experience with another consumer health product firm. Has a BS degree in business administration, marketing major. Is working on an MBA with tuition support from Upland. Would like to move up to a regional manager position with Upland someday.

Territory 101: Bonnie Cairns, Account Manager. Age 23. Single. Upland is first professional job; she was hired right out of college. Has BS in Psychology with a minor in Business. Has been on the job two weeks. Completed first week-long Upland initial sales training program at the home office. Previous account manager in this territory, Gloria Long, was recently promoted to district manager out of state.

Territory 102: Alex Lewis, Account Manager. Age 41. Married with two children. Has been in current position for 18 years. Previously spent two years as a customer representative with a major bank. Has a BA in Communications. Spouse holds a professional position locally and neither wants to move.

Territory 103: Justin Taylor, Account Manager. Age 28. Married with one child (infant). Has been in current position four years. Previously spent two years with Upland's leading competitor. Worked in a supermarket to put himself through college. Graduated with honors with a BS in Business Administration, dual major of Marketing and MIS. His goal (and Upland's) is for him eventually to move into management.

Territory 104: Chloe Herndon, Account Manager. Age 31. Single. Has been in current position for three years. Previously was in the buying office of one of Upland's customers (Doug's Drug Stores Inc.) for five years. Has BS in General Business.

Territory 105: Abe Rollins, Senior Account Manager. Age 55. Married with four grown children (one still lives at home and is in college locally). The "senior" designation in his title is reserved for account managers who have chosen not to pursue management positions but who are long-term contributors to Upland's sales success and who manage particularly high-volume territories. Served in the army right out of high school, then completed BA in Economics in college while working full-time as an assistant manager at a motel to support his family. Has been with Upland 27 years, but has moved twice with the company for better sales territories.

Territory 106: Currently vacant. Rhonda needs to recruit for this position. Previous Territory 106 account manager Rocky Lane lasted 15 months before deciding he wanted to pursue a different career track from sales. He left two weeks ago.

Additional Information

On each role play, you will need additional information to fill in some gaps and to prepare and act out the role play. This may involve various customers of Upland, recruits for the open position, compensation background, or many other possibilities. This information will be provided with each role play as needed. Think of the process as building the story or plot as we go along from chapter to chapter.

TIPS ON PREPARING ROLE PLAYS

Role-play exercises are fun and provide a great learning opportunity. The following tips will prove useful as you get the hang of doing them. Most importantly, it is unlikely that anyone in your class is a professional actor, so don't worry about how well you come across as a thespian. Simply follow the instructions for the role play, prepare the script, rehearse as needed, and then enjoy acting out your part and receiving feedback.

Tip #1: Take the Role Plays Seriously but Have Fun

These role plays expose you to various aspects of successful contemporary selling and put you into the action by giving you a part to play. Role plays are an excellent surrogate for real on-the-job experience. Topics come off the page from your book and into a real exchange of dialogue among the role players. You will want to do good preparation and take the task you are assigned seriously, but remember that the role play itself should be fun!

Tip #2: Follow These Steps

Each role play is inherently different. However, following some important general steps will enhance your experience with each.

1. **Team up.** Under the direction of your instructor, you will need to team up with one or more students to complete each role play. Although the characters in the role plays are gender-identified, if your role-play partner or group does not have sufficient gender distribution to fill each male part with a male, and each female part with a female, you can certainly have one gender play another.
2. **Prepare a script.** The role-play partners or groups should collaborate to prepare a proper script that fulfills the goals of the role play. *Important: There is no one right way to portray any given role play!* Follow instructions, be open and creative, and incorporate the input of everyone who will be part of your script.
3. **Rehearse the role play.** Except for chapter 1, all the role plays require rehearsal prior to presentation. Carefully stay within the suggested time parameters for each.
4. **Present the role play.** Your instructor may have you present your role play live in front of the class. Or he or she may ask you to videotape your role play as an outside assignment and bring it to class to turn in or play for the full class. Either way, you want your preparation to result in a professional-looking and -sounding presentation.
5. **Receive and provide feedback.** The role-play experience is not over when you complete your presentation. One of the best learning opportunities with role play is the chance to receive feedback from your instructor and the other students and for you to provide the same for others. The important thing to remember here is that your feedback should always be *constructive* (not critical) and focused on the relevant issues in the role play.

Tip #3: Broaden Your Learning

As you work on your own role-play exercises, and especially as you witness other presentations, you have a golden opportunity to broaden your learning about contemporary selling. Take good notes, be open to ideas and suggestions from others, and integrate what you learn from the role plays with the remainder of the material in this book. This process will teach you valuable skills and knowledge that will help you succeed at securing, building, and maintaining long-term relationships with profitable customers.

Sales Management

Salesperson Motivation

Selling Processes

Compensating & Evaluating Salespeople

Selecting & Training Salespeople

Prospecting & Sales Call Planning

Communicating the Sales Message

Salesperson Self-Management

Understanding Sellers & Buyers

Building Relationships ~ Creating Value

Technology

Ethics

Closing & Follow-up

Negotiating for Win-Win Solutions

global selling environment

Understanding
Sellers and Buyers

2

LEARNING OBJECTIVES

This chapter focuses on gaining a better understanding of the roles of sellers and buyers in today's organizational marketplace. The many factors discussed in chapter 1 are transforming the nature of the field and creating a challenging yet invigorating and rewarding environment in which to pursue a career in selling. First, aspects of sales careers are introduced. Then perspectives are provided from both a seller's and organizational buyer's points of view.

After reading this chapter, you should be able to:

- Explain the historical basis for stereotyped views of selling in society.
- Point out a variety of reasons why sales jobs can be highly satisfying.
- Identify and explain key success factors for salesperson performance.
- Discuss and give examples of different types of selling jobs.
- List and explain the roles of various participants in an organizational buying center.
- Describe the relationship between buying centers and selling centers and the nature of team selling.
- Outline the stages in organizational buyer decision making.
- Distinguish among different organizational buying situations.

EXPERT ADVICE

EXPERT: Anjai ("A.J.") Gandi
               Managing Director of the Sales Practice of the Corporate Executive Board

TOPIC: The sales role and sales job characteristics.

SUMMARY: Mr. Gandi provides a number of important insights about the changing dynamics and complexities of selling in the 21st Century. He relates the ideas to selling in China in particular, highlighting the ways that cultural differences impact the sales role and selling activities. He gives sage advice for students that may be considering (or discounting) professional selling as a possible career track, encouraging them to get past the stereotypes and overly simplistic notion of what selling is. He inspires us to consider contemporary selling as a vibrant, challenging, and rewarding enterprise and a great way to enter into a business career.

NEXT STEPS: Go to the website for *Contemporary Selling* (www.routledge.com/cw/Johnston), watch the chapter 2 video, and then read the chapter. You will find an Expert Advice follow-up at the end of the chapter with questions that connect elements of your learning.

OVERVIEW OF SELLING AS A CAREER

This chapter provides you with important insights to better understand the world of contemporary selling. First, you will have the opportunity to take a look at selling as a potential career path, including the many attractive aspects that explain why selling is such a popular and rewarding job. Sales jobs in the 21st Century contribute significantly to the world economy and of course to the success of individual firms in the marketplace. But like any other position, misunderstandings exist among people that have never been in selling about what the jobs are really like—and many of these misperceptions are based on stereotypes about selling that are best put out in the open and discussed right now. Then, you will learn about factors that can make one salesperson more successful than another, as well as what activities salespeople perform and different types of sales positions. Finally, we turn the tables and you get to see what organizational buying is all about.

Let's begin by dispelling some myths and mistaken impressions about selling in general. This is a true fact: well-run selling initiatives can produce enthusiasm and job satisfaction for salespeople, yet, despite this, recruiting and keeping excellent salespeople can be very difficult. One reason is that, unfortunately, some college students hold certain negative attitudes toward selling as a career because they think of the field based on old styles of selling where salespeople used hard-sell techniques to get buyers to do things they didn't really want to do and buy products they didn't really need.

Where do these notions come from? For one thing, the old style of selling is embodied in icons of media through the decades including plays, movies, and television shows.[1] Probably the most famous play by an American author is Arthur Miller's Pulitzer Prize-winning *Death of a Salesman,* which most students encounter sometime during their high school or college English courses. Miller immortalized old-style selling through the play's principal character, Willy Loman (as in "low man" on the totem pole of life). Poor Willy left for long sales trips on the road at the beginning of every week, returned a tired and disheartened peddler at the end of every week, and worked his customers based "on a smile and a shoeshine." His family was collapsing in his absence, his self-esteem was at rock bottom, his customers were defecting to other vendors at an alarming rate, and there seemed to be no hope of improvement for Willy on any front. This awful image, while certainly dramatic, has emblazoned on every schoolkid who ever read or acted in the play a sad, demoralizing image of selling.

A classic movie that also dramatically reinforces negative stereotypes about salespeople is the 1992 movie *Glengarry Glen Ross,* adapted from David Mamet's Pulitzer Prize-winning play of the same name. It features a stellar cast, including Al Pacino and Jack Lemmon, and has become an incredible cult favorite as a pay-per-view. In the movie, times are tough at Premier Properties, a boiler-room real estate sales company. Shelley "The Machine" Levene and Dave Moss are veteran salesmen, but only Ricky Roma is on a hot sales streak. Sales leads for the new Glengarry property development could turn everything around, but the front office is holding the leads back until the "losers" prove themselves on the street. Then someone decides to steal the Glengarry leads and leave everyone else wondering who did it. The verbal exchanges among these men desperate to make sales are riveting and very scary to someone interested in sales as a possible career.

Then in the 2000s came the TV show *The Office,* which started in Britain and was exported to the U.S. The "office" that is subject of the U.S. show is a branch of a fictional old-school office supply sales firm Dunder Mifflin. The salespeople use all forms of gimmicks and hard-sell tactics in a desperate struggle to try to stay ahead of the big box retailers like Staples, Office Max, and Office Depot as well as the general trend toward a paperless office. If you're into retro TV, you can catch reruns of the classic *WKRP in Cincinnati,* about a lovable cast of characters employed at a third-rate rock-and-roll radio station. One character who was arguably not so lovable was station sales manager Herb Tarlek. Herb was played as a back-slapping, white-shoe-and-polyester-suit-wearing buffoon who exhibited questionable ethics and made sales only through pure dumb luck. Google "Herb Tarlek WKRP" for fun and you'll see what we're talking about! And there's plenty of imagery of Herb on YouTube as well.

These images of salespeople have become embedded in the global culture. It is true that some unprofessional and unethical salespeople always have existed and always will exist (just as unprofessional people exist in any profession—witness the crisis in accounting, banking, and housing during the recent global recession). In selling, we seem to have to prove our value to society just a little more than in other professions. But the effort is worth it to those who love the profession, because there's no doubt about it— sales jobs are important to society, they're challenging and invigorating to those who occupy them, and they are also potentially one of the most rewarding career tracks available.

Why Sales Jobs Are So Rewarding

For most professional salespeople, it is precisely the complexity and challenge of their jobs that motivate them to perform at a high level and give them a sense of satisfaction. A number of surveys over the years have found generally high levels of job satisfaction among professional salespeople across a broad cross-section of firms and industries. Even when these surveys do find areas of dissatisfaction, the unhappiness tends to focus on the policies and actions of the salesperson's firm or sales manager, not on the nature of the sales job itself.[2]

Why are so many professional salespeople so satisfied with their jobs? Attractive aspects of selling careers include the following:

1. *Autonomy.* Freedom of action and opportunities for personal initiative.
2. Multifaceted and challenging activities (these *sales activities* will be addressed later in this chapter).
3. Financial rewards. Salespeople hired right out of college tend to start at higher salaries than most other professions and tend to keep up well during their careers with the compensation of their peers outside of sales (due to sales compensation being linked directly to performance).
4. Favorable working conditions—often via telecommuting with a virtual office, and with less minute-to-minute direct supervision than most other careers.
5. Excellent opportunities for career development and advancement.

Each of these advantages of selling jobs will now be discussed in more detail.

Job Autonomy. A common complaint among workers in many professions is that they are too closely supervised. They chafe under the micromanagement of bosses and about rules and standard operating procedures that constrain their freedom to do their jobs as they see fit. Salespeople, on the other hand, spend most of their time working directly with customers, with no one around to supervise their every move. They are relatively free to organize their own time and to get the job done in their own way as long as they show good results.

The freedom of a selling career appeals to people who value their independence, who are confident they can cope with most situations they will encounter, and who like to show personal initiative in deciding how to get the job done. However, with this freedom come potential pressures. Salespeople are responsible for managing their existing customer relationships and developing new ones. Although no one closely supervises their behavior, management usually keeps close tabs on the *results* of that behavior: sales volume, quota attainment, expenses, and the like.

To be successful, then, salespeople must be able to manage themselves, organize time wisely, and make the right decisions about how to do the job. Ethical Dilemma examines how the nature of this high degree of freedom—job autonomy—can sometimes create opportunities that also can cause challenges.

Job Variety. If variety is the spice of life, sales jobs are hot peppers. Most people soon become bored doing routine tasks. Fortunately, boredom is seldom a problem among professional salespeople, whose work tends to be high in *job variety*. Each customer has different needs and problems for which the salesperson can develop unique solutions. Those problems are often anything but trivial, and a salesperson must display insight, creativity, and analytical skill to close a sale. Many sales consultants expect creative problem solving to become even more important to sales success in the future.

ETHICAL DILEMMA

TOO MUCH JOB AUTONOMY?

Jennifer Lancaster found herself in an uncomfortable situation. Two years ago she graduated from college at the top of her class and took a sales job with Gracie Electronics. Although she had several offers and different career options, Jennifer felt a career in selling offered the best chance to apply her skills while doing something she enjoyed. After an extensive training period, she was given her own territory in Arizona with several large, established clients and great potential for new business.

Jennifer also began volunteering in an after-school program for high-risk teenagers. As part of Gracie Electronics' commitment to employees and local communities, the company supports employees' involvement with local charities and gives them time off to volunteer. Her involvement with the after-school program had made her much more visible in the community and she felt that she was really making a difference. The CEO of Gracie Electronics, Grace Jordan, had personally thanked Jennifer for her work in the community. Jennifer found her sales work very rewarding but was faced with a significant challenge: balancing the time commitment to her job with her volunteer work in this important nonprofit organization.

At first it was small changes to her schedule. She would choose to call customers from her smartphone on the way home in early afternoon instead of going to their office in person. Soon, however, her volunteer commitments represented a growing part of each day. She would occasionally take off entire afternoons and not report it to the company. She justified it to herself by the fact that she was helping needy teenagers and the company did support charity volunteer work. Moreover, she was still on target to hit her performance goals for the year—so what's the worry?

Yesterday Jennifer was faced with a difficult choice. One of her customers, Dynamic Manufacturing Systems, asked her to visit its site in Flagstaff to review their contract that could mean new business. Jennifer told the client she would have to check her schedule before committing to the meeting. However, she had recently been named Board Chairman at the nonprofit, and that day had been set aside for a strategic planning seminar to chart the direction of the organization for the next five years. She had already planned to take the day off. She knew the meeting with Dynamic Manufacturing was important but was seriously considering not going because of her other commitment.

Questions to Consider

1. What should Jennifer do?
2. As a salesperson, how would you balance the demands of a sales career with a personal life?
3. Can you identify some other challenges a person might face in balancing a sales career and personal life?

To make the sales job even more interesting, the internal and external environments are constantly changing (as we learned in chapter 1). Salespeople must frequently adjust their sales presentations and other activities to shifts in economic and competitive conditions.

Opportunities for Rewards. For many people in the selling profession, variety and challenge are the most rewarding aspects of their jobs. These aspects help develop a sense of accomplishment and personal growth. As we will see in chapter 11, they are important sources of **intrinsic rewards** (rewards inherent to satisfaction derived from elements of the job or role itself), as opposed to **extrinsic rewards** (rewards bestowed on the salesperson by the company).

Make no mistake, though—selling can be a very lucrative profession in terms of extrinsic rewards as well! More importantly, a salesperson's earnings (particularly one who receives a large proportion of incentive pay) are determined largely by performance, and often no arbitrary limits are placed on them. Consequently, a salesperson's compensation can grow faster and reach higher levels than that of employees at a comparable level in other departments.

Favorable Working Conditions. If the stereotypes of sales jobs addressed earlier were true, salespeople would be expected to travel extensively, spend much of their time entertaining potential clients, and have little time for home and family life. Such a situation represents a lack of balance between work life and family life such that work is encroaching on family—**work/family conflict**. But it is not an accurate description of the working conditions of most salespeople. Some selling jobs require extensive travel, but most salespeople can be home nearly every night. Indeed, with the increasing use of computer networks, email, and video conferencing, the trend for over a decade has been toward **telecommuting**. More and more salespeople work from a remote or **virtual office**, often at home, and seldom even travel to their companies' offices.[3] Telecommuting offers many advantages for salespeople and efficiency and cost savings to the sales organization, but virtual offices do create a challenge for sales managers. They must keep the sales force fully socialized to the culture of the organization.

Ability to Move Up in the Organization. Given the wealth of knowledge about a firm's customers, competitors, and products—and the experience at building effective relationships—that a sales job can provide, it is not surprising that iconic leaders like Sam Palmisano, former CEO at IBM and A. G. Lafley, former CEO at Procter & Gamble, often come up through the sales ranks into the executive suite. Jeff Immelt

---

EXHIBIT 2.1 FROM SALESPERSON TO CEO

As companies focus on customer satisfaction and building long-term relationships with customers, they are increasingly tapping the sales and marketing ranks to fill CEO positions. Here are five steps you can take to place yourself in that swanky corner office.

- *Understand the whole business.* Sales and marketing people can become quite focused on just sales and marketing. Customer relationships are vital, but make sure to learn how the rest of your company works. No executive can be CEO without being able to talk the talk about every aspect of the company.
- *Take on extra responsibilities.* To understand other parts of your business, spend time with other departments. Learn what it's like to be a factory worker or a researcher. Not only will this give you overall insight, but it will undoubtedly get you respect throughout the organization.
- *Show you want it.* Knowledge and experience are important for attaining the top spot, but proving your desire is vital. Let the people above you know your aspirations and constantly prove to them why you're qualified.
- *Gain self-awareness.* No CEO can lead without fully understanding his or her strengths and weaknesses. Ask for honest assessments from your employees, your bosses, and your customers. Process that knowledge and improve with it.
- *Network, network, network.* You have to know the top people to become one of them. It may feel like a game sometimes, but no executive can get the head job unless he or she continuously has meaningful conversations with top brass.

Adapted from Eilene Zimmerman, "So You Wanna Be a CEO," *Sales & Marketing Management* (January 2000), p. 33.

EXHIBIT 2.2 FROM SALESPERSON TO CEO

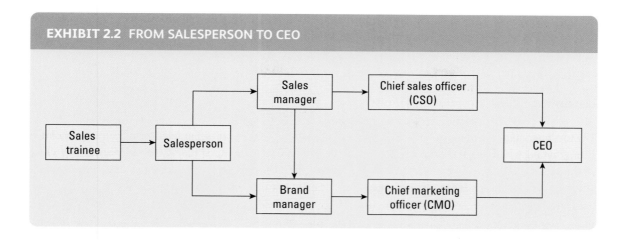

spent more than 20 years in various sales and marketing positions at General Electric before being named the successor to Jack Welch as CEO. Anne Mulcahy, former Chairwoman and CEO of Xerox, spent most of her 30 years at the company in sales. She advises that those who climb the corporate ladder from the sales rung need to be willing to take on nonsales-oriented assignments along the way to broaden their experience. Exhibit 2.1 advises aspiring salespeople on how to improve their odds of one day becoming CEO.

Although salespeople are sometimes reluctant to give up their high-paying jobs to move into managerial positions, most firms recognize the importance of good managerial talent and reward it appropriately, particularly as a person reaches the top executive levels of the sales organization. Total compensation of over $250,000 a year is not unheard of for national sales managers or vice presidents of sales in large firms.

Of course, many managerial opportunities are available to successful salespeople at lower levels of the corporate hierarchy as well, most obviously in sales management, product or brand management, and general marketing management. A survey of human resource managers found that sales professionals are among the most sought-after employees.[4] Exhibit 2.2 shows several possible career tracks for salespeople.

Despite the obvious upside, promoting top salespeople into management can sometimes cause problems. Successful selling often requires personal skills and abilities that are different from those required for successful management. There is no guarantee that a good salesperson will be a good sales manager. Also, successful salespeople have been known to refuse promotion to managerial positions because they enjoy selling, or they can make more money in sales than in management, or both. Finally, recent trends toward corporate downsizing, flatter organizational structures, outsourcing, and cross-functional selling teams have changed the number and nature of managerial opportunities available for successful salespeople. The sales manager of the future is more likely to be a coach or team leader than an authority figure isolated in the upper reaches of a corporate hierarchy. We will explore these ongoing changes in the nature of the sales manager's job in more detail in Part Three of the book.

KEY SUCCESS FACTORS IN CONTEMPORARY SELLING

Although many career advancement opportunities are available to successful salespeople, not all sales recruits turn out to be successful. Some are fired, others quit and seek different careers, and some simply languish on the lower rungs of the sales hierarchy for years. Not everyone possesses the key success factors needed to make it in selling. What personal traits and abilities are related to successful sales performance? This question is somewhat difficult to answer because different types of sales jobs require different key success factors. The factors sales managers consider critical to success in managing customer relationships are different from those required in the transactional approach to selling. Knowing what sales managers look for when hiring a salesperson is very useful for anyone thinking of selling as a career.

One study asked 215 sales managers from a variety of industries to rate the importance of 60 key success factors developed from interviews with salespeople and sales managers.[5] The top 20 factors are presented in Exhibit 2.3. Let's examine the top 10 in more detail.

Listening Skills

The top-rated item is listening skills. Other research has found that buyer–seller relationships are significantly strengthened when salespeople consistently employ effective listening skills.[6,7] Good listeners pay close attention to the buyer, carefully assessing his or her needs. Ironically, selling courses and sales training seminars almost always focus more on teaching salespeople to speak and write than to listen.

EXHIBIT 2.3 SUCCESS FACTORS FOR SALESPEOPLE

Success Factors	Mean	S.D.
Highest level of importance		
Listening skills	6.502	0.683
Follow-up skills	6.358	0.772
Ability to adapt sales style from situation to situation	6.321	0.687
Tenacity—sticking with a task	6.107	0.924
Well organized	6.084	0.889
Verbal communication skills	6.047	0.808
Proficiency in interacting with people at all levels of a customer's organization	6.000	0.991
Demonstrated ability to overcome objections	5.981	1.085
Closing skills	5.944	1.109
Personal planning and time management skills	5.944	0.946
Proficiency in interacting with people at all levels of an organization	5.912	0.994
Negotiation skills	5.827	0.975
Dresses in appropriate attire	5.791	1.063
Empathy with the customer	5.723	1.074
Planning skills	5.685	0.966
Prospecting skills	5.673	1.209
Creativity	5.670	0.936
Ability to empathize with others	5.549	1.105
Skills in preparing for a sales call	5.526	1.219
Decision-making ability	5.502	1.023

Note: All items were scaled as follows: 1 = of no importance at all in hiring decisions, 7 = of the utmost importance in hiring decisions. S.D. = Standard Deviation.

Source: Reprinted from Greg W. Marshall, Daniel J. Goebel, and William C. Moncrief, "Hiring for Success at the Buyer-Seller Interface," *Journal of Business Research* 56 (April 2003), pp. 247–55, Copyright 2003, with permission from Elsevier.

Follow-up Skills

As we learned in chapter 1, a key difference between transactional and relationship selling is the effort devoted to the ongoing maintenance of the relationship, especially in between face-to-face encounters with the customer. EMC Corporation, a computer storage company, has a reputation for being obsessed with follow-up. Its sales and service teams work hard to anticipate and fix trouble before the client even recognizes a problem. Anything from a toppled storage system to a change in the storage room's temperature causes the boxes to beam home warning messages and activate a response from EMC reps, often before the client is aware of the situation. Locations in 24 countries position their more than 250 individuals and teams to quickly follow up in person if necessary. In fact, the CEO of EMC has been known to respond in person within eight hours in the case of a severe service failure.

Ability to Adapt Sales Style from Situation to Situation

Adaptive selling is the altering of sales behaviors during a customer interaction or from one situation to another based on information the sales rep gathers about the nature of the selling situation.[8] Adaptive salespeople are more successful since understanding customers' needs and problems lets them provide solutions that add value.

Tenacity—Sticking with a Task

Nurturing customer relationships is a long-term proposition. The objective is not to simply close a sale with one client and then move on to the next. The process of managing relationships requires patience and the willingness to work with a client, often over very long periods, before the potential benefits of the relationship to both parties are realized. Along the way setbacks often occur that must be overcome. Great salespeople always keep the big picture in mind while working on the details. This perspective facilitates tenacity and yields results that are worth the wait.

Well Organized

As the content and responsibilities of sales jobs have increased in complexity and buying organizations have become more complicated for salespeople to navigate, the ability to skillfully prioritize and arrange the work has become a more important success factor. Good organization is a component of effective time and territory management. These and other aspects of self-management are covered in detail in chapter 10.

Verbal Communication Skills

Salespeople must be great communicators, especially of their value proposition. Communicating the sales message is the topic of chapter 6. Note that talking skills, while obviously critical to sales success, *are* rated lower in importance than listening skills.

Proficiency in Interacting with People at All Levels of a Customer's Organization

Selling often involves communication and interaction with many people within the client's firm besides the purchasing agent. Later in this chapter we will identify individuals in other roles within customers' firms that may be just as important to the sales rep as the actual buyer.

Demonstrated Ability to Overcome Objections

As mentioned in chapter 1, customers often have a number of concerns about any given purchase that the salesperson must work to overcome. Objections are a natural and expected part of any sales process. The sales rep can minimize them by developing a trusting relationship with the client over the long run and by working to negotiate win-win solutions. Chapter 8 takes up the topic of customer objections in more detail.

Closing Skills

Closing is of paramount importance, but a win-win approach to negotiating makes closing a much less arduous process for a salesperson. In chapter 9 you will learn about a variety of different approaches to closing a sale.

Personal Planning and Time Management Skills

Like being well organized, being good at personal planning and managing your time will serve you well in a sales career. Nowadays, both these success factors are aided substantially by technology, including smartphones, laptop computers, and email. Chapter 10 addresses a variety of self-management topics.

SELLING ACTIVITIES

Given what you have learned so far about the complexities of contemporary selling, as well as the key success factors sales managers believe are important, you will not be too surprised to learn that salespeople who develop solutions for client firms spend much of their time *collecting information* about potential customers and then using that information to plan and coordinate the activities of other functional departments, service existing customers, and make sales calls. It is difficult to specify the full range of activities in which salespeople engage because they vary greatly across companies and types of sales jobs.

However, in one extensive study, 1,393 salespeople from 51 firms rated 121 possible activities on a seven-point scale according to how frequently they performed each activity during a typical month. These responses were examined statistically to identify the underlying categories of various activities. Ten different job factors were identified.[9] These factors are shown in Exhibit 2.4, along with examples of the specific activities each involves.

One obvious conclusion from Exhibit 2.4 is that a salesperson's job involves a wide variety of activities beyond simply calling on customers, making sales presentations, and taking orders. Although the first two factors in Exhibit 2.4 are directly related to selling and order taking, factors 3 and 5 focus on activities involved in servicing customers after a sale is made (follow-up). Similarly, factors 4, 6, and 7 incorporate a variety of administrative duties, including collecting information about customers and communicating it to sales and marketing executives, attending periodic training sessions, and helping to recruit and develop new salespeople. Factors 8 and 9 focus on physically getting to customers and on entertaining them with meals, sports events, and other social interactions. Finally, some salespeople also expend a good deal of effort helping to build distribution channels and maintain reseller support (factor 10).

Several follow-up studies have been conducted over the years to update this list of selling activities based on changes in selling as described in chapter 1. The vast majority of new activities involve the deployment of various types of technology in the sales role and more than ever before technology is an important part of many sales activities. Ten years ago a sales presentation using overhead slides was considered high-tech and five years ago the same thing could be said of bringing a laptop into a sales call. But times have changed and technology has literally transformed almost every facet of the sales job. From smartphones to social

EXHIBIT 2.4 SALES JOB FACTORS AND SELECTED ASSOCIATED ACTIVITIES

1. **Selling function**
   Plan selling activities
   Search out leads
   Call on potential accounts
   Identify decision makers
   Prepare sales presentation
   Make sales presentation
   Overcome objections
   Introduce new products
   Call on new accounts

2. **Working with others**
   Write up orders
   Expedite orders
   Handle back orders
   Handle shipping problems
   Find lost orders

3. **Servicing the product**
   Learn about the product
   Test equipment
   Supervise installation
   Train customers
   Supervise repairs
   Perform maintenance

4. **Managing information**
   Provide technical information
   Receive feedback
   Provide feedback
   Check with superiors

5. **Servicing the account**
   Stock shelves
   Set up displays
   Take inventory for client
   Handle local advertising

6. **Attending conferences and meetings**
   Attend sales conferences
   Attend regional sales meetings
   Work at client conferences
   Set up product exhibitions
   Attend periodic training sessions

7. **Training and recruiting**
   Recruit new sales reps
   Train new salespeople
   Travel with trainees

8. **Entertaining**
   Entertain clients with golf, etc.
   Take clients to dinner
   Take clients out for drink
   Take clients out to lunch
   Throw parties for clients

9. **Traveling**
   Travel out of town
   Spend nights on the road
   Travel in town

10. **Distribution**
    Establish good relations with distributors
    Sell to distributors
    Handle credit
    Collect past-due accounts

Source: Adapted from William C. Moncrief III, "Selling Activity and Sales Position Taxonomies for Industrial Sales Forces," *Journal of Marketing Research* 23 (August 1986), pp. 261–70.

networking, tremendously powerful technologies are available for a salesperson's everyday use across a gamut of job activities. And huge database-driven CRM systems provide salespeople with heretofore undreamed of resources in their jobs. CRM and the gamut of technology in sales will be discussed in detail in chapter 5.[10]

Several important conclusions can be drawn from the evolving and expanding selling activities. First, salespeople have experienced rather substantial job enlargement over the past decade. That is, the sales role today is broader and contains substantially more activities. Let's hope the efficiencies gained from the technological advances help offset the sheer number of additional activities salespeople perform. Second, sales

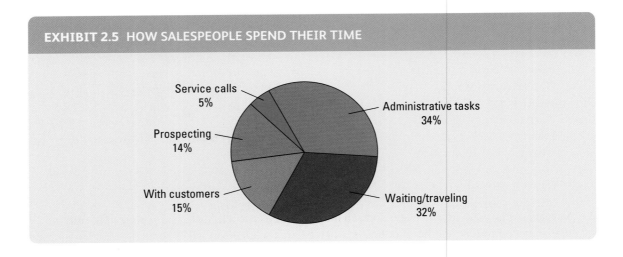

EXHIBIT 2.5 HOW SALESPEOPLE SPEND THEIR TIME

Service calls 5%

Prospecting 14%

With customers 15%

Administrative tasks 34%

Waiting/traveling 32%

organizations need to ensure that all salespeople receive proper training and support so they can accept and use the available technology. Finally, performance management systems (appraisals, rewards) must be updated to reflect the dimensions and activities of sales positions today so that salespeople are not evaluated and rewarded based on an out-of-date model of their jobs.

An increasing number of nonselling and administrative activities means that many salespeople spend only a small portion of their time actually selling. Exhibit 2.5 shows the results of a survey of salespeople in a variety of industries. The survey found that, on average, sales reps devote less than half their time to direct contact with customers, either selling or servicing.[11] In firms that sell complicated or customized products or service systems to large customers, the proportion of selling time may be even lower.

The increasing involvement of salespeople in nonselling activities is one major reason why the **average cost of a sales call** has risen consistently in recent years. A rep must perform many nonselling activities over a long period of time in order to successfully build relationships and create value. The average cost of a single sales call is estimated to be over $450, depending on the industry, and this cost is increasing by about 5 percent per year.[12] To make matters even more costly, another survey found that it took an average of three calls to close a sale with an existing account and seven calls were required to win a sale from a new customer. This means selling expenses might average as much as $3,000 per sale to new accounts.[13]

This rapid escalation of selling costs helps explain the urgent search for new ways to improve sales force efficiency. Using new technologies, reallocating sales effort to customer retention, and purifying the sales job by eliminating nonessential tasks are some of the strategies companies have used to reduce selling costs and increase sales force efficiency.

TYPES OF SELLING JOBS

Not every salesperson engages in all of the activities discussed above, nor does every salesperson devote the same amount of time and effort to the same kinds of activities. Neither do they all employ the various available technologies equally. The many different types of selling jobs involve widely different tasks and responsibilities, require different types of training and skills, and offer varying compensation and opportunities for personal satisfaction and advancement. Perhaps most importantly, different kinds of selling jobs bring different levels and types of opportunities for managing customer relationships. Two broad categories of selling are business-to-consumer markets and business-to-business markets.

Selling in B2C versus B2B Markets

In terms of sheer numbers, most salespeople are employed in various kinds of **retail selling**. These jobs involve selling goods and services to *end-user consumers* for their own personal use. These salespeople are selling in the **business-to-consumer (B2C) market**. Examples are direct sellers (Avon, Tupperware, etc.), residential real estate brokers, and retail store salespeople. However, much more contemporary selling is accounted for by the **business-to-business (B2B) market** (which used to be commonly called **industrial selling**)—the sale of goods and services to buyers who are not the end users. Business-to-business markets involve three types of customers:

1. *Sales to resellers,* as when a salesperson for Hanes sells underwear to a retail store, which in turn resells the goods to its customers.
2. *Sales to business users,* as when a salesperson for General Electric sells materials or parts to Boeing, which uses them to produce another product; or when a Xerox salesperson sells a copier to a law firm for use in conducting the firm's business.
3. *Sales to institutions,* as when a salesperson for Lenovo sells 20 laptops to a nonprofit hospital or a government agency.

Sometimes the key success factors and sales activities relevant to B2C and B2B markets and to managing the two types of sales forces are very similar. Success in both types of selling requires interpersonal and communications skills, solid knowledge of the products being sold, an ability to discover customers' needs and solve their problems, and the creativity to show customers how a particular product or service can help satisfy those needs and solve these problems. Similarly, managers must recruit and train appropriate people for both types of sales jobs, provide them with objectives consistent with the firm's overall marketing or merchandising program, supervise them, motivate them, and evaluate their performance.

But B2C and B2B selling also differ in some important ways. Many of the goods and services sold by B2B salespeople are more expensive and technically complex than those in B2C. B2B customers tend to be larger and to engage in extensive decision-making processes involving many people. Therefore, the key success factors and activities involved in selling to business buyers are often quite different from those in retail selling. Furthermore, the decisions made to manage a B2B sales force are broader than those required for a B2C sales force. Although some topics in this book apply reasonably well to both types of selling situations, others apply more directly to the B2B. Overall this book focuses more on the B2B side of contemporary selling.

Note that many sellers work in both the B2C and B2B markets. An insurance agent, for example, sells automobile policies to both individual drivers and company fleet managers.

Types of B2B Sales Jobs

Even within B2B selling, many different types of jobs exist that require different skills. One of the most useful classification systems for sales jobs identifies four types of B2B selling found across a variety of industries.[14]

1. *Trade servicer.* The sales force's primary responsibility is to increase business from current and potential customers by providing them with merchandising and promotional assistance. The "trade" referred to in the label is the group of resellers, such as retailers or distributors, with whom this sales force does business. A Procter & Gamble rep selling soap and laundry products to chain-store personnel is an example of trade selling.
2. *Missionary seller.* The sales force's primary job is to increase business from current and potential customers by providing product information and other personal selling assistance. Missionary salespeople often do not take orders from customers directly but persuade customers to buy their firm's product from distributors or other wholesale suppliers. Anheuser-Busch does missionary selling when its salespeople

call on bar owners and encourage them to order a particular brand of beer from the local Budweiser distributor. Similarly, pharmaceutical company reps, or *detailers,* call on doctors. When Pfizer first introduced Celebrex, an arthritis drug, its salespeople alerted the physicians in their areas to the efficacy of the product, explained its advantages over traditional pain relievers, and influenced them to prescribe it to their patients. Note that Pfizer sales reps normally don't "sell" any product directly to physicians.

3. *Technical seller.* The sales force's primary responsibility is to increase business from current and potential customers by providing technical and engineering information and assistance. An example is a sales engineer from the General Electric jet engine company calling on Boeing. Most technical selling nowadays is accomplished through cross-functional selling teams because many of the products and associated services are so complex that it is difficult for any one salesperson to master all aspects of the sale.

4. *New-business seller.* The sales force's primary responsibility is to identify and obtain business from new customers—that is, securing and building the customer relationship. Salespeople performing this role are sometimes referred to as Business Development Managers.

Each type of sales job involves somewhat different activities and thus different key success factors.

Like many firm activities in the 21st Century, the selling function in a firm is sometimes outsourced. An **outsourced sales force** entails hiring sales agents—who usually work for a broker organization—that specialize in selling particular types of product lines within the hiring firm's channel of distribution. These brokers usually represent numerous product lines that are not in direct competition in order to avoid conflict of interest. They are most often paid a straight percentage of sales revenue, thus shifting the sales function for the hiring firm to a purely variable cost model. For the broker salesperson him/herself, the characteristics and activities involved in the job are not much different from those of company-specific salespeople.[15]

In order to truly understand the selling process, why successful salespeople do what they do, and how they manage their efforts effectively, you must understand how customers make purchase decisions. The next sections shift the focus of our discussion from the selling side to the buying side. We will examine the participants in the B2B buying process, the stages of this buying process, and finally the nature of organizational buying situations.

PARTICIPANTS IN THE ORGANIZATIONAL BUYING PROCESS

To make a decision on a technologically sophisticated IT solution from a firm like IBM or Microsoft, a wide variety of individuals in a client firm may participate in the decision process, including computer analysts, customer service reps, procurement personnel, end users, and others. The various participants in a buying process may be grouped into seven categories: initiators, users, influencers, gatekeepers, buyers, deciders, and controllers.[16] Together, the individuals in these roles form the **buying center**, which represents all the people who participate in purchasing or influencing the purchase of a particular product.

American Airlines operates the largest commercial aviation maintenance and equipment base in the world in Tulsa, Oklahoma. Mechanics there use a wide variety of products purchased by American from hundreds of vendors. A variety of people at American participate in the purchase of these products in one way or another. Participants in that buying process include the following.

- *Initiators* are the people who perceive a problem or opportunity that may require the purchase of a new product or service. They start the buying process. The initiator can be almost anyone at any level in the firm. Complaints from maintenance workers at American Airlines about outmoded and inefficient equipment, for instance, might trigger the purchase of new machinery. Or the decision to replace the equipment might come from top management's strategic planning on how to make the airline more cost efficient and effective.

- *Users,* the people in the organization who must use or work with the product or service, often influence the purchase decision. For example, drill-press operators at American Airlines might request that the purchasing agent buy drill bits from a particular supplier because they stay sharp longer and reduce downtime in the plant. Users also often initiate a purchase, so the same people may play more than one role.

- *Influencers* provide information for evaluating alternative products and suppliers and often play a major role in determining the specifications and criteria to use in making the purchase decision. Influencers are usually technical experts from various departments. They may include users. At American Airlines, for example, flight engineers and pilots often influence purchase decisions based on their experience with various vendor options.

- *Gatekeepers* control the type and amount of information provided to other people involved in the purchasing process. A gatekeeper may control information going to the organization's purchasing agents, the suppliers' salespeople, and others on the selling and buying teams. IT people are often gatekeepers because they frequently hold the information that is key to decision making. There are two types of gatekeepers: *screens* (like receptionists and administrative assistants at American Airlines, who decide whose phone call is put through to the executive or purchasing agent) and *filters* (like the American Airlines purchasing agent who gathers proposals from three companies and decides what to tell others in the buying center about each company). The purchasing agent filters information, choosing to pass along some but not all of it to influence the decision.

- The *buyer* is the person who actually contacts the selling organization and places the order. In most organizations, buyers have the authority to negotiate purchases. In some cases, they are given wide discretion. In others, they are constrained by technical specifications and other contract requirements determined by technical experts and top administrators. At American Airlines, the level of authority to buy is determined by the size and type of purchase involved. In many organizations, the decision may be referred to a buying committee, which may either vote or reach a consensus on which vendor to buy from or which product to buy.

- The *decider* is the person with the final authority to make a purchase decision. Sometimes buyers have this authority, but often it is retained by higher-level executives. When American Airlines buys a complete, systemwide computer installation and upgrade, for instance, the final decision is likely to be made by the Chief Information Officer or a top management committee.

- The *controller* is the person who determines the budget for the purchase. Sometimes the budget is set independently of the purchase. For example, the administrative office at American Airlines' Tulsa facility may receive a budget for office equipment set by corporate headquarters in Fort Worth at the start of the fiscal year. If a copier needs to be replaced or some other unexpected high-dollar expense looms, the cost somehow has to fit into that budget. Alternatively, sometimes the controller may be an engineer or a line manager who is trying to keep the cost of the new maintenance procedure within a certain budget.

Three to 12 people are likely to be in the buying center for a typical purchase. Different members of the buying center may participate—and exert different amounts of influence—at different stages in the decision process.[17] At American Airlines, people from engineering, quality control, and R&D often exert the greatest influence on the development of specifications and criteria that a new maintenance product must meet, while the purchasing manager often has more influence when it comes time to choose among alternative suppliers.

The makeup and size of the buying center vary with the amount of risk the firm perceives when buying a particular product. The buying center tends to be smaller—and the relative influence of the purchasing manager greater—when reordering products the firm has purchased in the past than when buying something for the first time or buying something that is seen as risky.[18] **Perceived risk** is based on the complexity of the product and situation, the relative importance of the purchase, time pressure to make a decision, and the degree of uncertainty about the product's efficacy. The buying center is likely to involve more participants when it is considering the purchase of a technically complex or expensive product, such as a computer system, than a simpler or less costly product.[19]

Selling Centers and Buying Centers

Since major customers' buying centers often consist of people from different functional areas with different viewpoints and concerns, those concerns often can be addressed most effectively by a team of experts from equivalent functional departments in the selling firm, or even from different divisions within the company. Recently, companies have begun to use a **selling center** approach that brings together individuals from around the organization (marketing, customer service, sales, engineering, and others) as a team to join the salesperson who has primary responsibility for a customer. In this way, just as customers have buying centers, the selling organization works together to present a unified, well-coordinated effort to the customer.[20]

The key is establishing a **team selling** structure within the sales organization to meet customer needs. One common structure makes the salesperson (account manager) responsible for working with the entire selling team to manage the customer relationship. Often such customer relationship teams include representatives from functional departments like R&D, operations, and finance. Increasingly, customer relationship teams maintain offices in or very near the customer's facilities.

Since different members of the buying center may be active at different stages of the purchase process, an important part of sales planning involves determining whom the sales organization should contact, when each contact should be made, who within the selling team should make each contact, and what kinds of information and communication each buying center member is likely to find most useful and persuasive.

At Siebel Systems, a part of Oracle and the world's largest producer of CRM software, the team for a major account like Marriott is led by a Siebel account executive who has a global team of salespeople as direct reports but can also draw from the full functional resources of Siebel to provide solutions for GM at any location in the world. This approach creates a **matrix organization** of direct reports and supporting internal consultants at Siebel who bring their collective expertise to bear for this major client.

GLOBAL CONNECTION

GLOBAL VIRTUAL SALES TEAMS

International sales opportunities, consolidation of global accounts, and advancements in communication technologies have led to the prevalence of global virtual sales teams. These teams span the globe in terms of geographic location of the team members and bring their capabilities to bear on clients that are equally dispersed geographically. Thus, much of the engagement with the client—as well as among selling team members themselves—is through technology enabled processes. Time zone differences create challenges in these environments as expertise required by a client may be half a world away and scheduling virtual meetings is not as easy as simply setting a time during "normal business hours." In fact, the norm for doing business has rapidly become a 24/7 proposition in which selling team members are expected to be available for consult based on the client's schedule. Although this arrangement clearly saves on the hassles of travel and speeds up response time to clients, the "always on call" mindset can lead to stress on the part of salespeople. Welcome to the 21st Century!

Questions to Consider

1. How does the global virtual sales team approach impact the sales role and selling activities?
2. Would you like to be part of a global virtual sales team? Why or why not?

Adapted from Vishag Badrinarayanan, Sreedhar Madhavaram, and Elad Granot, "Global Virtual Sales Teams (GVSTs): A Conceptual Framework of the Influence of Intellectual and Social Capital on Effectiveness," *Journal of Personal Selling & Sales Management* 31 (Summer 2011), pp. 311–24.

Team selling can present some coordination, motivation, and compensation problems. Lou Gerstner, former Chairman and CEO of IBM, has frequently spoken out publicly on the difficulties of performance management in team selling environments. In fact, it is a key theme in the book *Who Says the Elephant Can't Dance? Inside IBM's Historic Turnaround* that Gerstner released after retiring, about rebuilding IBM toward a truly global I.T. consultancy.[21, 22] Given that today's sales environment is by nature global, new opportunities exist for utilizing technology to make the team experience more seamless on a global basis. Global Connection provides ideas on using global virtual sales teams.

Team selling is expensive and involves a substantial commitment of human resources, including management. Thus, team-based approaches tend to be most appropriate for the very largest customers (especially those with buying centers) whose potential business over time represents enough revenue and entails enough cross-functional interaction among various areas of both firms to justify the high costs. Such customers are often referred to as **key accounts**. They generally have a senior salesperson as the key account manager (KAM).[23,24,25]

ORGANIZATIONAL BUYING DECISION STAGES

You have seen that different members of a buying center may exert influence at different stages in the decision process. What stages are involved? One widely recognized framework identifies seven steps that organizational buyers take in making purchase decisions: (1) anticipation or recognition of a problem or need, (2) determination and description of the traits and the quantity of the needed item(s), (3) search for and qualification of potential suppliers, (4) acquisition and analysis of proposals or bids, (5) evaluation of proposals and selection of suppliers, (6) selection of an order routine, and (7) performance evaluation and feedback.[26] These organizational buying decision stages are portrayed in Exhibit 2.6 and described in detail on the next few pages.

Stage One: Anticipation or Recognition of a Problem or Need

Many organizational purchases are motivated by the requirements of the firm's production processes, merchandise inventory, or day-to-day operations. Such demand for goods and services is **derived demand**. That is, needs are derived from the firm's customers' demand for the goods or services it produces or markets. For example, the demand for luggage is derived in part from the demand for air travel. The luggage department at Macy's Department Store loses customers, and Samsonite (a leading luggage manufacturer) loses customers, when people don't travel. This characteristic of derived demand can make organizational markets quite volatile, because a small change in the market can result in a large (relatively speaking) change in the organization's sales.

Many different situations can lead someone to recognize a need for a particular product or service. Need recognition may be almost automatic, as when the computerized inventory control system at Walmart reports that the stock of an item has fallen below the reorder level. Or a need may arise when someone identifies a better way of operating, as at the American Airlines Maintenance and Equipment Base when an engineer or mechanic suggests a better procedure than the current practice.

New needs might also evolve when the focus of the firm's operations changes, as when top management decides to make a new product line. Procter & Gamble introduced Crest Whitestrips, which sell for considerably more on the grocer's shelf than most other Crest products such as toothpaste and mouthwash, because P&G wanted to get into the business of more professional products that will raise its average sale and profit per item. In all these situations, needs may be recognized—and the purchasing process initiated—by a variety of people in the organization, including users, technical personnel, top management, and purchasing managers.

EXHIBIT 2.6 ORGANIZATIONAL BUYING DECISION STAGES

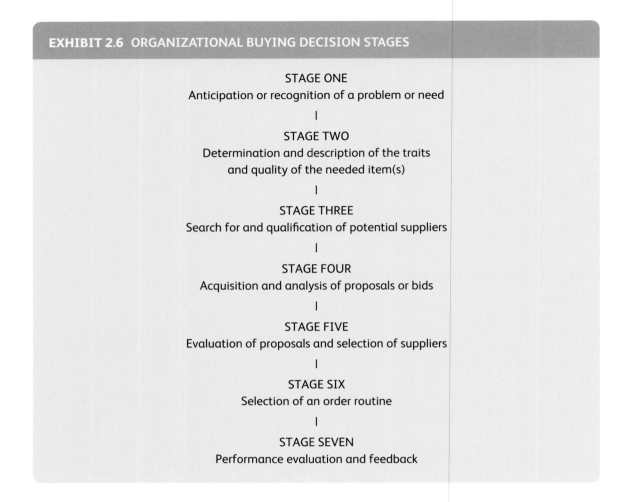

STAGE ONE
Anticipation or recognition of a problem or need

|

STAGE TWO
Determination and description of the traits
and quality of the needed item(s)

|

STAGE THREE
Search for and qualification of potential suppliers

|

STAGE FOUR
Acquisition and analysis of proposals or bids

|

STAGE FIVE
Evaluation of proposals and selection of suppliers

|

STAGE SIX
Selection of an order routine

|

STAGE SEVEN
Performance evaluation and feedback

Stage Two: Determination and Description of the Traits and Quantity of the Needed Item(s)

In organizational buying settings, the types and quantities of goods and services to be purchased are usually dictated by the demand for the firm's outputs and by the requirements of its production process and operations. The criteria used in specifying the needed materials and equipment must usually be technically precise. Similarly, the quantities needed must be carefully considered to avoid excessive inventories or downtime caused by lack of needed materials. For these reasons, a variety of technical experts, as well as the people who will use the materials or equipment, are commonly involved in this stage of the decision process.

It is not enough for the using department and the technical experts to develop a detailed set of specs for the needed item, however. They must also communicate to other members of the buying center and to potential suppliers a clear and precise description of *what* is needed, *how much* is needed, and *when* it is needed. When the design and marketing groups of Nissan or Hyundai decide to change the specifications of a car's interior and electronic systems, the changes must be communicated effectively to purchasing so that the vendor (often Lear Corporation) can begin changing the parts these important customers rely on to satisfy picky consumers in this market.

Stage Three: Search for and Qualification of Potential Suppliers

Once the organization has clearly defined the type of item needed, a search for potential suppliers begins. If the item has been purchased before, this search may be limited to one or a few suppliers that have performed satisfactorily in the past. (See the section later in this chapter on types of organizational buying situations.) From the seller's perspective, one distinct advantage to cultivating strong long-term buyer relationships is that under such circumstances this step is often skipped. The buyer has enough familiarity and trust that it gives the favored seller the first opportunity to bid on supplying the new products. Historically, many automobile manufacturers have gone with single-source suppliers wherever possible to minimize the variation in quality of production inputs. This approach bodes well for Lear whenever a manufacturer announces spec changes on aspects of car models for which Lear supplies parts. If the purchase involves a new item, or if the item is complex and expensive (again, if the product represents a *risky* decision), organizational buyers often search for several potential suppliers and select the one with the best product and most favorable terms.

Stage Four: Acquisition and Analysis of Proposals or Bids

After potential suppliers are identified, the buyer may request proposals or bids from each. When the item is a frequently purchased, standardized, or technically simple product (for example, nails or copier paper), this process may not be very extensive. The buyer may simply consult several suppliers' catalogs or make a few phone calls. For more complicated and expensive goods and services, the buyer may request lengthy, detailed sales presentations and written proposals from each potential vendor. Governmental and other institutional buyers almost always are required to formally solicit bids.

Stage Five: Evaluation of Proposals and Selection of Suppliers

During this stage of the purchasing process, members of the buying center examine the acceptability of the various proposals and potential suppliers. Also, the buying organization and one or more potential vendors may engage in negotiation about various aspects of the deal. Ultimately, one or more suppliers are selected and purchase agreements are signed.

The people in the buying organization's purchasing department (the buyers) usually evaluate offerings and select the supplier. Others in the buying center, such as technical and administrative personnel, may also play a role in supplier selection, especially when the purchase is complex and costly.

What criteria do members of the buying center use in selecting a supplier? Organizational buying is largely a rational decision-making process, so rational criteria are usually most important—the value-added aspects of the product, the service offered, and the like. However, social and emotional factors can also influence this decision. Organizational buyers and other buying center members are, after all, human, just like buyers in the B2C marketplace. Some differences between consumer and organizational buyer behavior are summarized in Exhibit 2.7.

The relative importance of different supplier selection criteria varies across organizations and the types of products or services being purchased. For example, product quality tends to be more important in the purchase of technically complex products, whereas price and customer service are relatively more important for more standardized, nontechnical items or commodity products. Fortunately, a strong relationship between buyer and seller greatly increases the likelihood that buying firms will not use price as the sole determinant of vendor selection. Instead, because buyers will have much more complete knowledge about you and your products, they will better understand the overall value to their organization of buying from you versus one of your competitors with whom they do not have a long-standing relationship. Chapter 3 considers the issue of value creation in buyer–seller relationships in detail.

EXHIBIT 2.7 CONSUMER VERSUS ORGANIZATIONAL BUYER BEHAVIOR

Aspect of the Purchase	Consumer Buyer	Organizational Buyer
Use	Personal, family, or household	Production, operations, or resale
Buyer motivation	Personal	Organizational and personal
Buyer knowledge of product or service	Lower	Higher
Likelihood of group decision making	Lower	Higher
Dollar amount of purchases	Lower	Higher
Quantity of purchase or order size	Smaller	Larger
Frequency of purchase	More	Less
Number of cyclical purchases	Lower	Higher
Amount of negotiation and competitive bidding	Little	Much

Stage Six: Selection of an Order Routine

Until the purchased item is delivered, it is of no use to the organization. Consequently, after an order is placed with a supplier, the purchasing department often tries to match delivery of the goods with the company's need for the product. Other internal activities also must occur when the order is delivered. The goods must be received, inspected, paid for, and entered in the firm's inventory records. These activities represent additional costs that may not be readily apparent to the buying firm. Retailers have become very aggressive in asking vendors to cover these costs by charging sales organizations slotting allowances, fees for the privilege of having the retailer set up a new item in its IT system, program it into inventory, and ultimately distribute the item to the stores. Slotting allowances can cost manufacturers thousands of dollars per new item stocked.

Stage Seven: Performance Evaluation and Feedback

When the goods have been delivered, evaluation by the customer begins. This evaluation focuses on both the product and the supplier's service performance. This is a stage where follow-up by the salesperson is critically important. The goods are inspected to make sure they meet the specifications described in the purchase agreement. Later, users judge whether the purchased item performs according to expectations. The supplier's performance can also be evaluated on such criteria as promptness of delivery, quality of the product, and service after the sale.

In many organizations, this evaluation is a formal process, involving written reports from the user department and other persons involved in the purchase. The purchasing department keeps the information for use in evaluating proposals and selecting suppliers the next time a similar purchase is made. Chapter 9 provides tips for sellers on successful ways to follow up after a sale.

TYPES OF ORGANIZATIONAL BUYING SITUATIONS

The steps just described apply largely to (1) a **new-task purchase**, where a customer is buying a relatively complex and expensive product or service for the first time (e.g., a new piece of production equipment or a new computer system), or (2) **modified rebuy** purchase decisions, where a customer wants to modify the product specs, prices, or other terms it has been receiving from existing suppliers and will consider dealing with new suppliers to make these changes if necessary.

At the other extreme is the **straight rebuy**, where a customer is reordering an item he or she has purchased many times (e.g., office supplies, bulk chemicals). Such a **repeat purchase** tends to be much more routine than the new-task purchase or the modified rebuy. Straight rebuys are often carried out by members of the purchasing department (buyers) with little influence from other members of the buying center, and many of the steps involved in searching for and evaluating alternative suppliers are dropped. Instead, the buyer may choose from among the suppliers on a preapproved list, giving weight to the company's past satisfaction with those suppliers and their products.

Purchasing departments are often organized hierarchically based on these different buying situations. For example, at Walmart's buying office, new buyers begin as analysts and assistants, primarily monitoring straight rebuys. New-task purchases and modified rebuys that require more direct vendor contact are handled by more seasoned veterans.

Being an "in" (approved) supplier is a source of significant competitive advantage for a seller. For potential suppliers not on a buyer's approved vendor list, the selling problem can be difficult. The objective of such an **outsupplier** is to move the customer away from the automatic reordering procedures of a straight rebuy toward the more extensive evaluation processes of a modified rebuy.

Since, as we've seen, any member of a firm's buying center can identify and communicate the need to consider a change in suppliers, an outsupplier might urge its salespeople to bypass the customer's purchasing department and call directly on users or technical personnel. The salesperson's goal is to convince users, influencers, and others in the buying center that his or her products offer advantages on some important dimension—such as technical design, quality, performance, or cost—over the products the client is currently purchasing. Finding someone to play the role of initiator can be difficult, but it is possible if latent dissatisfaction exists.

Kamen Wiping Materials Co., Inc., in Wichita, Kansas, sells high-quality recycled cloth wiping rags to manufacturers. The business essentially consists of banks of huge industrial-size washing machines. Kamen buys soiled wiping cloths, cleans them, and then resells them to manufacturers in a variety of industries at prices much lower than paper or new cloth rags. Founder Leonard Goldstein became famous for getting Cessna, Beechcraft, and other heavy users of wiping materials to change wiping-cloth vendors (and even change from paper to cloth, which is a big switch) by scouting out who in the company can benefit the most from the change. This person then becomes the initiator. As with most organizational buying decisions, what benefits the company ultimately benefits the members of the buying center (especially the purchasing agent). If buying from Kamen makes certain members of the buying center look like heroes for saving money or being environmentally friendly, Kamen knows they have a great chance of getting the sale—and keeping the customer.

EXPERT ADVICE: FOLLOW-UP ⟨Chally Group⟩ WORLDWIDE

After watching the video of Mr. Gandi and reading the chapter, consider the following questions:

1. What are some of the most important tips he provides for selling in China?
2. When he urges "people graduating from college and considering a new career to actually take a much deeper look at the sales profession," what characteristics cause him to make this recommendation?

SUMMARY

Selling is a great career path that can also lead to significant upward mobility. Contemporary selling bears no resemblance to the stereotyped view of old-style selling. Sales jobs today offer autonomy, variety, excellent rewards, favorable working conditions, and the opportunity for promotion.

The key success factors needed in contemporary selling all point to professionalism, strong skills, and broad and deep content knowledge that allow the salesperson to maximize his or her performance (and thus rewards). Quite a few new sales activities have been added in recent years, driven largely by technology and the move from transactional to relationship selling. Understanding the types of selling jobs available will help you decide whether and where to enter the selling profession.

Because customers are the primary focus of relationship sellers, gaining knowledge about the world of organizational buying greatly enhances the effectiveness of a salesperson in his or her role as a customer relationship manager. Many people in a client firm may influence the buyer–seller relationship and the decision of what to buy, and salespeople must study their customers carefully to learn what dynamics are at play within each buying center situation. Selling firms often form selling centers and initiate team selling to better serve buying centers, especially with large and complex customers (key accounts). Of course, salespeople need to fully understand and appreciate the stages of the buying decision process that their customers go through so they can work to add value throughout the purchasing process. Different organizational buying decision situations require different communication between buyer and seller, and the seller must know enough about the nature of each purchase to manage the process properly.

Overall, the more expertise a salesperson has about how his or her own organization operates and how the customer's firm operates, the more likely the salesperson will be able to sell solutions for the customer and add value to both organizations.

KEY TERMS

intrinsic rewards	retail selling	perceived risk	new-task purchase
extrinsic rewards	business-to-consumer (B2C) market	selling center	modified rebuy
work/family conflict		team selling	straight rebuy
telecommuting	business-to-business (B2B) market	matrix organization	repeat purchase
virtual office		key account	outsupplier
adaptive selling	industrial selling	derived demand	
job enlargement	outsourced sales force	single-source suppliers	
average cost of a sales call	buying center	slotting allowances	

ROLE PLAY

BEFORE YOU BEGIN

Before getting started, please go to the Appendix of chapter 1 to review the profiles of the characters involved in this role play, as well as the tips on preparing a role play.

Characters Involved

Bonnie Cairns
Rhonda Reed

Setting the Stage

Bonnie Cairns has now been on the job for four weeks, two of which have been in the field beginning to call on her buyers (mostly with the help of Rhonda Reed, her sales manager). The past week or so, she has begun to feel a lot more comfortable in her new position. Rhonda told her yesterday that in about a week she plans to begin doing some campus recruiting at Stellar College, from which Bonnie graduated last year, to look for potential candidates to interview for the open Territory 106. She mentioned that she would like Bonnie, as the newest member of the District 100 sales team, to join her to help tell graduates why selling careers can be great. The goal is to attract good students to interview for the vacant Upland Company sales territory. Bonnie and Rhonda are meeting for breakfast in a few minutes to discuss this.

Bonnie Cairns's Role

Bonnie has never done any recruiting before, and at age 23 she is only a year older than most of the students she will talk to during the campus visit. She needs to find out what to tell them to convince them that the old stereotypes of selling are not true in contemporary professional selling situations. She wants to use this meeting to get Rhonda to give her ideas on how to "sell" top students on considering a career with Upland.

Rhonda Reed's Role

Rhonda comes to the breakfast meeting to give Bonnie some ideas on how to present selling careers with Upland Company to students at the Stellar College campus recruiting day in a way that will lead top candidates to consider interviewing with Upland. Rhonda needs to explain the various reasons why sales jobs are rewarding compared to other career options. She also needs to prepare Bonnie for hearing resistance to selling careers from top candidates due to incorrect stereotypes about the profession.

Assignment

Work with another student to develop a 5–7 minute dialogue on these issues. Be certain to cover both the stereotypical "bad" and the actual good aspects of contemporary professional selling careers. Be sure Bonnie is prepared to both convey the many rewarding aspects of selling and to deal with questions about the stereotypes.

DISCUSSION QUESTIONS

1. It is often said that successful salespeople today must be "nimble." What does it mean to be nimble as a salesperson and as a sales organization?

2. Take a piece of paper and draw a line down the middle. Write "Pros" on the top left and "Cons" on the top right. Now, from your own perspective, come up with as many issues as you can on both sides regarding selling as a career choice for you. Be sure to note *why* you list each item as you do.

3. Creativity is important to sales success. What is creativity? Give specific examples of several things you have done that you think are especially creative. How might creativity be taught to salespeople?

4. Telecommuting and using a virtual office are major aspects of many professional sales positions. How do you feel about telecommuting and virtual offices? What aspects of them are you most and least attracted to?

5. What aspects of sales jobs do you believe provide a strong foundation for moving up in an organization?

6. Review the top 20 key success factors for salespeople as listed in Exhibit 2.3. Which of these factors are currently *your* strongest points? Which need the most work? How do you plan to capitalize on your strengths and improve on your weaknesses?

7. Pick the three selling activities presented in Exhibit 2.4 that you would *most* like to perform. Then pick the three you would *least* like to perform. Explain the rationale for your choices.

8. This chapter outlines the roles different members of a buying center play within an organizational buying context. Think of a purchase process you were involved in as an end-user consumer (not an organizational buyer). Can you list people who played these buying center roles in your purchase? Try to connect as many specific people to specific buying center roles as you can.

9. Explain the differences among a new-task purchase, modified rebuy, and straight rebuy. How will each situation alter the way a salesperson approaches a client?

MINI-CASE 2 NATIONAL AGRI-PRODUCTS COMPANY

Sue Wilson, purchasing manager for the Humboldt, Tennessee, plant of National Agri-Products Company, is back in her office reviewing her notes from a meeting she just finished with Tom Roberts, Vicki Sievers, and Greg Runyon. Tom is the plant manager of the Humboldt plant, Vicki is the plant engineer, and Greg the production manager. The four met for the last hour to discuss the equipment National needs to buy to complete expansion of the Humboldt plant.

National Agri-Products Company produces various agricultural products at its four manufacturing locations throughout the Midwest. The Humboldt plant was built seven years ago to produce cornstarch and dextrose for use as food ingredients. Five and a half years after the plant was completed, upper management decided to expand it to produce corn syrup, which is an ingredient in soft drinks, candy, and various baked goods. Humboldt will be the second National Agri-Products Company plant with the capability to produce corn syrup.

As Sue reviews her notes, she notices that Tom, Vicki, and Greg have various requirements for the equipment that would be needed to produce the corn syrup. During the meeting, Tom said it was very important to "get everything right" in completing this project. The company already had invested a lot of money in the expansion, and Tom didn't want to risk that investment by installing equipment that would produce syrup inferior to National's standards. Tom said that, although he expected to be consulted when needed, he thought Vicki and Greg could handle this assignment without his daily input.

Vicki knew that quality equipment would be needed to produce high-quality corn syrup. She wondered if the plant could meet the deadline National's home office had given of producing corn syrup in six months. Vicki said she was already working on equipment specifications and she would get them to Sue as soon as possible. Greg's main concern was producing the corn syrup efficiently and making sure his maintenance people could "keep the stuff running." Both Vicki and Greg asked Sue to let them know when she had more information about potential suppliers.

After reviewing these notes, Sue knew this was going to be a big job. She has no direct experience buying equipment to produce this type of product line. She decided to call Vijay Sethi, National's VP of purchasing, to discuss a few options. Vijay reminded Sue that National's policy is to get three bids on purchases of this amount and suggested that she start with the storage tanks and tubing since they are the most time-consuming items to fabricate. Vijay also gave Sue the number of Larry McDermott, a salesperson for New Products Steel Company, as a potential supplier. Finally, Vijay asked Sue to keep him up to date on progress, as this was the most expensive expansion project the company was undertaking this year.

After talking with Vijay, Sue decided to call Larry McDermott.

LARRY: Larry McDermott, New Products Steel. May I help you?
SUE: Larry, this is Sue Wilson at the Humboldt, Tennessee, plant of National Agri-Products Company. Vijay Sethi gave me your name as a potential bidder on the stainless-steel tanks and tubing we are installing for our new corn syrup product line.
LARRY: I'll certainly be glad to help you out with that, Sue. As you may know, we provided similar equipment for your Hawarden, Iowa, plant when they added the corn syrup line there. We worked with Jim Fisher in Hawarden.
SUE: I didn't know that, but I'll certainly give Jim a call. Anyway, our plant engineer will have specs on the equipment available early next week. When can you come in to go over them?
LARRY: Next Wednesday around 2:00 looks good to me. How does that sound?
SUE: Great. I'll get our team assembled here and we'll look forward to meeting you next Wednesday.

Questions

1. Who are the various members of the buying center that Larry should take time to get to know? What role or roles within the buying center is each person filling?

2. What are the primary *needs* of each member of the buying center? How much influence do you expect each member of the buying center will have on the final decision?

3. Discuss the buying process being followed by National Agri-Products Company. How does this buying process differ from that discussed in the chapter? At what stage of the buying process is it most beneficial for Larry to get involved?

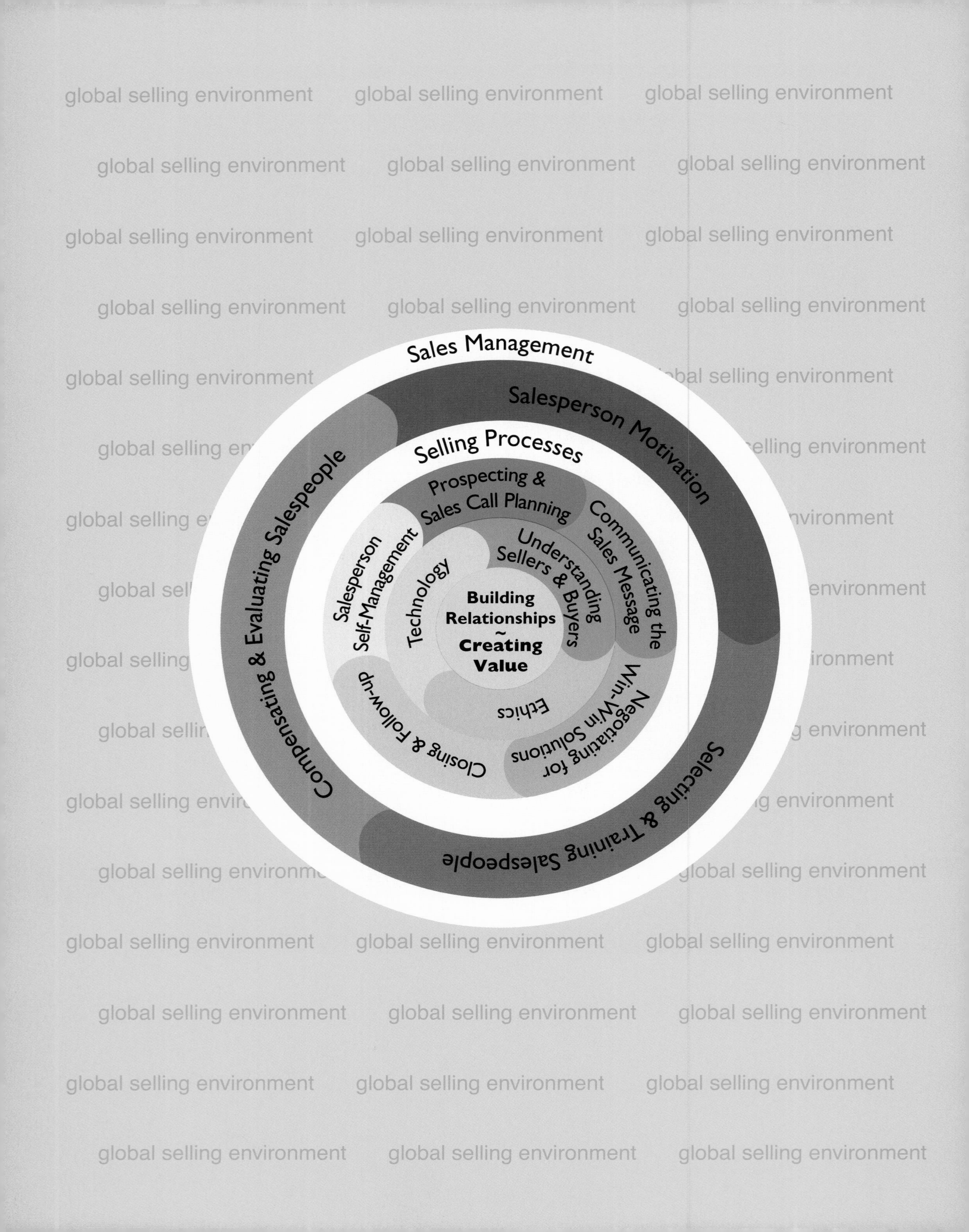

Value Creation in Buyer–Seller Relationships

3

LEARNING OBJECTIVES

This chapter focuses on one of the most important concepts in contemporary selling: value. Value-added selling sums up much of what securing, building, and maintaining customer relationships is all about. Taking advantage of the opportunity to really understand value and value creation will help you immensely as you move into the selling process chapters in Part Two of the book.

After reading this chapter, you should be able to:

- Understand the concept of perceived value and its importance in selling.
- Explain the relationship between the roles of selling and marketing within a firm.
- Explain why customer loyalty is so critical to business success.
- Recognize and discuss the value chain.
- Identify and give examples for each category for communicating value in the sales message.
- Understand how to manage customer expectations.

EXPERT ADVICE

EXPERT: Howard Stevens
                Chairman, HR Chally Group

TOPIC: Service as a value-added in sales.

SUMMARY: Mr. Stevens builds a strong case that salespeople must turn to factors beyond the features of the product itself in order to build relationships and add value. In particular, he mentions that in some regions of the globe there is a disconnect between what is considered fundamental service versus other regions. For example, he argues that in the U.S., service has been devalued and in fact many of the service functions previously attached to the sales value proposition have now actually been shifted offshore to developing economies such as India. Ultimately, he suggests that the distinction/separation between sales and service needs to be rectified in order to truly compete globally.

NEXT STEPS: Go to the website for *Contemporary Selling* (www.routledge.com/cw/Johnston), watch the chapter 3 video, and then read the chapter. You will find an Expert Advice follow-up at the end of the chapter with questions that connect elements of your learning.

ADDING VALUE IS "MARKETING 101"

In chapter 1 we defined *value* as the net bundle of benefits the customer derives from the product you are selling and said that the communication of same is often referred to as a firm's *value proposition*. It is up to the salesperson and the firm's other forms of marketing communications to ensure the customer perceives these benefits as its value proposition. In transactional selling, the goal is to strip costs and get to the lowest possible sales price—in essence, the value proposition to the customer is low price. But relationship selling works to add value through all possible means, which is why we titled your book *Contemporary Selling: Building Relationships, Creating Value* and why we placed the elements of building relationships and creating value at the core (center circle) of the model for Contemporary Selling.

Value-added selling changes much of the sales process. As you will see in this chapter, the sources of value (or, more properly, **perceived value**, meaning that whether or not something has value is in the eyes of the beholder—the *customer*) are varied. Moving to more value-added approaches to selling is not easy, and selling value is the single biggest challenge faced by sales professionals.[1]

Why a chapter focused solely on value? Two simple reasons: (1) The evidence is clear that success in selling depends greatly on the degree to which customers perceive that they achieve high value from a vendor relationship, and (2) many salespeople have trouble making a shift from selling price to selling value.

Role of Selling in Marketing

A good place to start understanding the role of value is with a brief review of marketing and the role of selling within marketing. For years, introductory marketing textbooks have talked about the **marketing concept** as an overarching business philosophy. Companies practicing the marketing concept turn to customers themselves for input in making strategic decisions about what products to market, where to market them and how to get them to market, at what price, and how to communicate with customers about the products. These **4 Ps of marketing** (product, place or distribution, price, and promotion) are also known as the **marketing mix**. They are the toolkit marketers use to develop marketing strategy.

Personal selling fits into the marketing mix as part of a firm's **promotion mix**, or **marketing communications mix**, along with *advertising* and other elements of the promotional message the firm uses to communicate the value proposition to customers. Other available promotional vehicles are *sales promotion,* including coupons, contests, premiums, and other means of supporting the personal selling and advertising initiatives; *public relations and publicity,* in which messages about your company and products appear in news stories, television interviews, and the like; and *direct marketing,* which might include direct mail, telemarketing, electronic marketing (via website or email or social media), and other direct means.[2]

These elements of marketing communications are referred to as a "mix" to emphasize that, when developing a strategy and budget for marketing communications, companies must decide how to allocate funds among the various promotional elements.

Several factors may affect the marketing communications mix, as shown in Exhibit 3.1. The size and importance of the purchase, complexity of the product, how much information buyers need, degree of price negotiation, number and dispersion of buyers, and whether postpurchase contact is required all drive decisions about the marketing communications mix.

To ensure that the message about a company and its products is consistent, the firm must practice **integrated marketing communications (IMC)**, as opposed to fragmented (uncoordinated) advertising, publicity, and sales programs. IMC is very important to selling, as it keeps the message about the value proposition consistent, which in turn supports the overall brand and marketing strategy. Key characteristics of effective IMC programs are:

1. IMC programs are *comprehensive*. All elements of the marketing communications mix are considered.
2. IMC programs are *unified*. The messages delivered by all media, including important communications

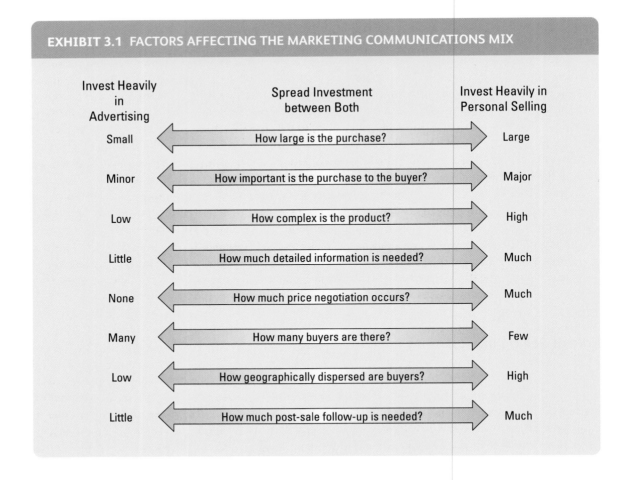

EXHIBIT 3.1 FACTORS AFFECTING THE MARKETING COMMUNICATIONS MIX

Invest Heavily in Advertising	Spread Investment between Both	Invest Heavily in Personal Selling
Small	How large is the purchase?	Large
Minor	How important is the purchase to the buyer?	Major
Low	How complex is the product?	High
Little	How much detailed information is needed?	Much
None	How much price negotiation occurs?	Much
Many	How many buyers are there?	Few
Low	How geographically dispersed are buyers?	High
Little	How much post-sale follow-up is needed?	Much

among **internal customers** (people within your firm who may not have external customer contact but who nonetheless add value that will ultimately benefit external customers) are the same or support a unified theme.

3. IMC programs are *targeted*. The various elements of the marketing communications mix employed all have the same or related targets for the message.
4. IMC programs have *coordinated execution* of all the communications components of the organization.
5. IMC programs emphasize *productivity* in reaching the designated targets when selecting communication channels and allocating resources to marketing media.[3]

FedEx has been very successful at IMC, in both B2B and B2C markets. This is important, since the core of FedEx's business is adding value through high-priced but fast and dependable service. To achieve this, internally all employees are trained to behave as though they have customers whether they actually interface with external users or not. That is, various departments within FedEx practice relationship-building among each other. Good **internal marketing** provides a consistency of message among employees and shows that management is unified in supporting FedEx's key strategic theme of adding value through reliability. Externally, FedEx uses all the elements of the marketing communications mix—advertising, personal selling, sales promotion, public relations/publicity, and various methods of direct marketing, including a strong web and social media presence. FedEx is careful to communicate its value proposition consistently via each element of the mix.

Role of Marketing in Selling

You just saw that selling plays a crucial role in the success of marketing strategy. But how do things work in the other direction—that is, how does marketing affect selling? As we discussed, the marketing communications mix (or promotion mix) is one element of the overall marketing mix that a firm uses to develop programs to market its products successfully. Products may be physical goods or services. Some firms market primarily services (such as insurance companies), while others market both goods and accompanying services (such as restaurants).

We know that the marketing mix consists of the famous 4 Ps of marketing: product, place (for distribution, or getting the product into the hands of the customer), price, and promotion (marketing communications). Like the elements of the marketing communications mix, each element of the marketing mix plays a large part in forming and communicating the overall bundle of benefits that a customer ultimately will perceive as the value proposition. This is why salespeople benefit from a well-executed marketing mix strategy.

Marketing also has an important role in gaining input and ultimate buy-in from the sales force on marketing strategies. The best way to do this is to involve salespeople and their managers in the marketing planning process from the ground up. Also, good communication lines must always be open between sales and marketing so that salespeople can contribute their considerable insight gained "on the firing line" to marketers engaged in strategic market planning, product development, and all aspects of IMC strategy development and execution.[4]

Recently, there has been considerable talk of something of a "war" between sales and marketing in many organizations. That is, salespeople are from Mars; marketers are from Venus—the idea being that a variety of differences in the goals and roles of sales and marketing people create tension within a firm that can be a challenge to avoid and, if unchecked, can sub-optimize the customer's experience. Strong executive leadership on the sales and marketing teams, coupled with an organizational culture of mutual respect for each role, can go a long way toward gaining crucial cooperation and collaboration between sales and marketing. Also, regular joint exercises in goal-setting and planning between sales and marketing are a key toward maximizing the customer's experience with the firm and its offerings. Finally, identifying some performance metrics that both sales and marketing will be evaluated against greatly helps to promote a spirit of mutual focus on the customer's experience.[5]

At the end of the day, in order for an organization to do the best possible job of building relationships and creating value, sales needs marketing and marketing needs sales. Both groups must work together to make the customer's experience with the firm and its offerings the very best experience possible.

CLARIFYING THE CONCEPT OF VALUE

Later in the chapter we will discuss ways value can be created by a firm and communicated by its salespeople. First, however, let's clarify a few issues related to value.

Value Is Related to Customer Benefits

Value may be thought of as a ratio of benefits to costs. That is, customers "invest" a variety of costs into doing business with you, including financial (the product's price), time, and human resources (the members of the buying center and supporting groups). The customers achieve a certain bundle of benefits in return for these investments.

One way to think about customer benefits is in terms of the utilities they provide the customer. Utility is the want-satisfying power of a good or service. There are four major kinds of utility: form, place, time, and ownership. *Form utility* is created when the firm converts raw materials into finished products that are desired by the market. *Place, time,* and *ownership utilities* are created by marketing. They are created when products are available to customers at a convenient location, when they want to purchase them, and facilities of exchange allow for transfer of the product ownership from seller to buyer. The seller can increase the value of the customer offering in several ways:

- Raise benefits.
- Reduce costs.
- Raise benefits and reduce costs.
- Raise benefits by more than the increase in costs.
- Lower benefits by less than the reduction in costs.[6]

Suppose you are shopping for a car and trying to choose between two models. Your decision to purchase will be greatly influenced by the ratio of costs (not just monetary) versus benefits for each model. It is not just pure price that drives your decision. It is price compared with all the various benefits (or utilities) that Car #1 brings to you versus Car #2.

Similarly, the value proposition a salesperson communicates to customers includes the whole bundle of benefits the company promises to deliver, not just the benefits of the product itself. For example, Dell Computer certainly communicates the customization and bundling capabilities of its PCs to buyers. However, Dell is also careful to always communicate its service after the sale, quick and easy access to their website, and myriad other benefits the company offers buyers. Clearly, perceived value is directly related to those benefits derived from the purchase that satisfy specific customer needs and wants.

For years, firms have been obsessed with measuring **customer satisfaction**, which at its most fundamental level means how much the customer likes the product, service, and relationship. However, satisfying your customers is not enough to ensure the relationship is going to last. In relationship-driven selling, your value proposition must be strong enough to move customers past mere satisfaction and into a commitment to you and your products for the long run—that is, a high level of **customer loyalty**. Loyal customers have lots of reasons why they don't want to switch from you to another vendor. Those reasons almost always are directly related to the various sources of value the customer derives from doing business with you.

Loyal customers, by definition, experience a high level of satisfaction. But not all satisfied customers are loyal. If your competitor comes along with a better value proposition than yours, or if your value proposition begins to slip or is not communicated effectively, customers who are satisfied now quickly become good candidates for switching to another vendor. The reason building relationships with customers is so crucial to building loyalty is that its win-win nature bonds customer and supplier together and minimizes compelling reasons to split apart.

The Value Chain

A famous approach to understanding the delivery of value and satisfaction is the **value chain**, envisioned by Michael Porter of Harvard to identify ways to create more customer value within a selling firm.[7] Exhibit 3.2 portrays the generic value chain. Basically, the concept holds that every organization represents a synthesis of activities involved in designing, producing, marketing, delivering, and supporting its products. The value chain identifies nine strategic activities (five primary and four support activities) the organization can engage in that create both value and cost.

The *primary activities* in the value chain are:

- Inbound logistics—how the firm goes about sourcing raw materials for production.
- Operations—how the firm converts the raw materials into final products.
- Outbound logistics—how the firm transports and distributes the final products to the marketplace.
- Marketing and sales—how the firm communicates the value proposition to the marketplace.
- Service—how the firm supports customers during and after the sale.

EXHIBIT 3.2 THE GENERIC VALUE CHAIN

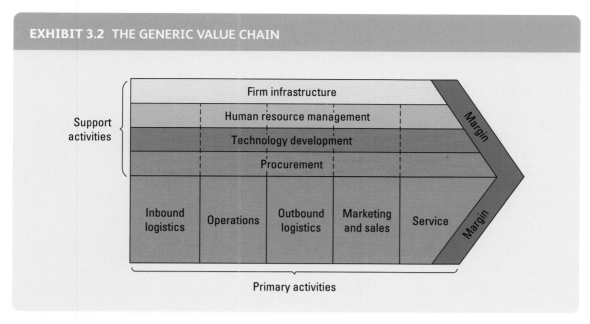

Source: Reprinted with permission of The Free Press, a Division of Simon & Schuster Adult Publishing Group, from *Competitive Advantage: Creating and Sustaining Superior Performance*, by Michael E. Porter. Copyright © 1985, 1998 by Michael E. Porter. All rights reserved.

The *support activities* in the value chain are:

- Firm infrastructure—how the firm is set up for doing business. (Are the internal processes aligned and efficient?)
- Human resource management—how the firm ensures it has the right people in place, trains them, and keeps them.
- Technology development—how the firm embraces technology use to benefit customers.
- Procurement—how the firm deals with vendors and quality issues.

The value-chain concept is very useful for understanding the major activities that can create value at the organizational level. CEOs in recent years have been working hard to *align* the various elements of the value chain, meaning that all facets of the company work together to eliminate snags that may impair the firm's ability to secure, build, and maintain long-term relationships with profitable customers.

When the supplier's value chain is working well, all the customer tends to see are the *results:* quality products, on-time delivery, good people, and so on. If the value chain develops just one weak link, the whole buyer–seller relationship can be thrown off. For example, a glitch in the value chain of one of Walmart's vendors can delay delivery, resulting in stockouts in Walmart stores. If this happens repeatedly, it can damage the firms' overall relationship. To reduce the potential for this happening, Walmart (which is known as a leader in implementing the value chain) requires all vendors to link with its IT system so that the whole process of order fulfillment is as seamless as possible.

Lifetime Value of a Customer

One element depicted in Exhibit 3.2 is margin, which of course refers to profit made by the firm. Back in chapter 1 we were careful to say that the goal of *relationship selling* is to secure, build, and maintain long-term relationships with *profitable* customers. If this seems intuitively obvious to you, that's good. It should.

EXHIBIT 3.3 CALCULATING THE LIFETIME VALUE OF A CUSTOMER

Estimated annual revenue from the customer	$15,000
Average number of loyal years for our customers	×5
Total customer revenue	75,000
Company profit margin	×10%
Lifetime customer profit	$7,500
Cost of securing a new customer	$3,500
Cost of developing and maintaining the customer (est. 6 calls per year @ $500 each)	3,000
Average number of loyal years for our customers	×5
Total selling cost	15,000
Estimated costs of advertising and promotion per customer (from marketing department)	500
Lifetime customer cost	$15,500
Lifetime value of the customer (lifetime profit − lifetime cost)	− $8,000

In the past, many firms focused so much on customer satisfaction that they failed to realize that not every satisfied customer is actually a profitable one! Today, firms take great care to estimate the lifetime value of a customer, which is the present value of the stream of future profits expected over a customer's lifetime of purchases. They subtract from the expected revenues the expected costs of securing, building, and maintaining the customer relationship. Exhibit 3.3 provides a simple example of calculating the lifetime value of a customer.

Selling to this customer is a money-losing proposition in the long run. Firms should not attempt to retain such customers. The analysis raises the prospects of firing a customer, which is a rather harsh way to express the idea that the customer needs to find alternative sources or channels from which to secure the products he or she needs. Of course, this assumes that other, more attractive customers exist to replace the fired one.[8] Firms engaged in value-chain strategies who don't pay attention to margin usually don't stay in business long.

On the other hand, for profitable customers, increasing the retention rate—meaning keeping customers longer—by increasing loyalty can yield large increases in profits. This is because, as you can see from the calculations in Exhibit 3.3, it is much less costly to retain existing customers than it is to acquire new ones. Exhibit 3.4 shows the potential impact of customer retention on total lifetime profits in different industries. These issues are closely related to CRM, which will be discussed in chapter 5.

Quantifying the value proposition is an important element of successful selling. The Appendix (Relationship Selling Math) at the end of this chapter provides an approach, in spreadsheet format, to quantitative analysis of a product and its value to a customer.

So far, we have looked at important issues of value creation from the perspective of the selling firm via the value-chain concept. In the next section, we identify specific value-creating factors the salesperson can communicate to the customer.

COMMUNICATING VALUE IN THE SALES MESSAGE

In the chapters in Part Two of the book we will discuss the *process* a salesperson follows to successfully communicate the sales message. But now we turn our attention to one of the most important *content* issues in selling: value proposition. In chapter 7 you will learn how to translate the idea of value into specific benefits

EXHIBIT 3.4 IMPACT OF 5 PERCENT INCREASE IN RETENTION RATE ON TOTAL LIFETIME PROFITS FROM A TYPICAL CUSTOMER

Industry	Percentage Increase in Profits
Advertising agency	95 %
Life insurance company	90 %
Branch bank deposits	85 %
Publishing	85 %
Auto service	81 %
Auto/home insurance	80 %
Credit card	75 %
Industrial brokerage	50 %
Industrial distribution	45 %
Industrial laundry	45 %
Office building management	40 %

Source: Reprinted by permission of Harvard Business School Press. From *The Loyalty Effect,* by Frederick Reichheld and Thomas Teal. Boston, MA. Copyright 2001 by the Harvard Business School Publishing Corporation, all rights reserved.

to the buyer. To help you organize your thinking about value, now we focus on 12 broad categories from which you can draw these benefits in order to practice value-added selling. Keep in mind that it is customers' *perceptions* of these factors that are relevant. For example, Toyota might have excellent product quality, but if this is not communicated to customers, they may not perceive it as excellent. The 12 categories for communicating value are:

1. Product quality.
2. Channel deliverables (supply chain).
3. Integrated marketing communications (IMC).
4. Synergy between sales and marketing.
5. Execution of marketing mix programs.
6. Quality of the buyer–seller relationship (trust).
7. Service quality.
8. Salesperson professionalism.
9. Brand equity.
10. Corporate image/reputation.
11. Application of technology.
12. Price.

Product Quality

David Garvin has identified eight critical dimensions of product quality that can add value.[9]

- *Performance.* A product's primary operating characteristics. For a car, these would be traits such as comfort, acceleration, safety, and handling.
- *Features.* Characteristics that supplement the basic performance or functional attributes of a product. For a washing machine, they might include four separate wash cycles.

- *Reliability.* The probability of a product malfunctioning or failing within a specified time period.
- *Conformance.* The degree to which a product's design and operating characteristics meet established standards of quality control (for example, how many pieces on an assembly line have to be reworked due to some problem with the output). Conformance is related to reliability.
- *Durability.* Basically, how long the product lasts and how much use the customer gets out of the product before it breaks down.
- *Serviceability.* Speed, courtesy, competence, and ease of repair for the product.
- *Aesthetics.* How the product looks, feels, sounds, tastes, or smells.
- *Perceived quality.* How accurately the customer's perceptions of the product's quality match its actual quality. In marketing, perception is reality.

For manufacturers of physical goods, product quality is the most fundamental of all sources of value. In the consumer health products space, the name Johnson & Johnson (J&J) has for years been synonymous with product quality. On every dimension listed above, J&J products have excelled. But over the past few years J&J experienced a raft of bad press about contamination in some of its most famous brands of over-the-counter medications. Bottles of tablets and capsules were reported by consumers as containing foreign elements that turned out to be residual materials from a lax production line. For J&J, like any manufacturer, news like this is devastating to its customer relationships—not just end users of the products like us, but also the many retailers that sell J&J products in stores around the globe. The sales force at J&J has been racked by multiple recalls that have left some shelves bare and retail customers scrambling to make up for lost sales and profits by promoting other manufacturers' items in substitute. The lesson is that, in today's competitive marketplace, one can never allow product quality to be compromised. At this stage, it remains to be seen if J&J will ever recoup the lost market share based on its highly publicized recent problems in this area.

Channel Deliverables (Supply Chain)

Firms that have excellent **supply-chain management** systems add a great deal of value for customers. A supply chain encompasses every element in the channel of distribution. FedEx is an organization that brings to its clients excellent supply-chain management as a key value proposition. FedEx salespeople, as well as FedEx's overall IMC, constantly communicate this attribute to the marketplace.

Integrated Marketing Communications (IMC)

We have already seen how important integration of the marketing message is in managing customer relationships. When Lou Gerstner, former CEO of IBM, took the job, one of the first things he noticed as he visited various IBM field operations was that the image, message, and even the logo of IBM varied greatly from market to market. Such variance is almost always due to poor IMC. IMC starts with a firm's people understanding and accepting its mission, vision, goals, and values. Then the message about the value proposition gets communicated to employees through internal marketing. Finally, it gets communicated to customers and other external stakeholders through all the elements of the promotion mix. Clients expect and deserve consistency in the way your value proposition is put forth. With great IMC, salespeople can refer to a well-known message about their firm that is all around to solidify the client relationship. IBM's Gerstner put a great deal of emphasis on cleaning up the firm's global IMC, which resulted in a clear and consistent message about what IBM stands for and how it delivers value to customers.

Synergy between Sales and Marketing

An easy definition of *synergy* is that the whole is greater than the sum of its parts. Sales and marketing exhibit synergy when they are both working together for the greater benefit of customers. The whole concept of our model for Contemporary Selling centers on synergy—seamless organizational processes focused on managing customer relationships. When sales and marketing are out of sync, customers are marginalized and the value proposition is weakened. One way to ensure synergy is with cross-functional selling teams that include members of marketing in key roles.

Procter & Gamble is a firm that has put a great deal of energy into this issue. A vivid example of creating value through synergy is the way P&G develops its regular promotion schedule for its brands. Brand management works directly with field sales management to create a schedule and product mix for the promotions that best serve P&G's clients. Thus, when a salesperson presents a new promotion to a customer, he or she can sell the value of the thoughtful planning that took into account the customer's needs and wants in making P&G's promotional decisions.

Execution of Marketing Mix Programs

Firms that do a great job of integrating the marketing mix provide opportunities for value-added selling. Salespeople enjoy communicating with clients about their firm's plans for product changes, new-product development, and product line extensions. And a history of a strong marketing mix program gives salespeople and the firm credibility that helps turn prospects into new customers. Thus, customers have confidence that your firm will support its products through effective marketing mix programs.

Quality of the Buyer–Seller Relationship (Trust)

A key issue in relationship quality is trust. Trust is a belief by one party that the other party will fulfill its obligations in a relationship.[10] Obviously, building trust is an essential element of selling. It represents confidence that a salesperson's word (and that of everyone at his or her company) can be believed. It signifies that the salesperson has the customer's long-term interests at the core of his or her approach to doing business. An atmosphere of trust in a relationship adds powerful value to the process.

Service Quality

Services are different from products. In particular, services exhibit these unique properties:

- *Intangibility.* Services cannot be seen, tasted, felt, heard, or smelled before they are bought.
- *Inseparability.* Unlike goods, services are typically produced and consumed simultaneously.
- *Variability.* The quality of services depends largely on who provides them and when and where they are provided.
- *Perishability.* Services cannot be stored for later use.

These unique properties of services create opportunities for firms to use them to add value to the firm's overall product offerings and for salespeople to communicate this value to customers. Ethical Dilemma provides you with an interesting situation in which the future viability of service quality as a value-adding aspect of a customer relationship is called into question.

Because of the unique properties of services, it should not be too surprising that the dimensions of service quality are different from those for goods:

ETHICAL DILEMMA

HANDLING A DECLINING ACCOUNT

Ben Lopez has been with Bear Chemicals for seven years and has earned a reputation as one of the best salespeople in the company. Starting as a detail salesperson calling on small specialty companies, he worked his way up to key account manager, calling on some of Bear's largest customers.

Today, Ben was faced with a difficult decision. Midwest Coatings, Ben's smallest account, called again this morning, wanting him to come out and talk about problems with its new manufacturing operations.

When Ben first started with the company, Midwest was Bear's largest customer. However, over the last few years Midwest has become less competitive and has seen significant declines in its market share, with a corresponding reduction in the purchase of chemicals. Of even greater concern was the trend for foreign competitors to deliver higher-quality products at lower prices than Midwest.

Unfortunately, Midwest still views itself as Bear's best customer. It demands the lowest prices and highest level of service. Its people call frequently and want immediate attention from Ben, even though Bear has customer support people (customer service engineers) to help with customer problems and service. For Ben, a growing concern is his personal relationship with several senior managers at Midwest. The chief marketing officer and several top people at Midwest are Ben's friends and their children play with Ben's kids.

After the phone call this morning, Ben called his boss, Jennifer Anderson, to get direction before committing to a meeting. He explained that the problems at Midwest were not Bear's fault and a customer support person should deal with them by phone. Ben was worried that going out there would take an entire afternoon. He did not want to waste his time when a customer service engineer could handle the situation. Jennifer, who knew about the problems at Midwest, suggested it was time for a full review of the account. She also told Ben that it might be time to classify the company as a second-tier account, meaning Ben would no longer be responsible for calling on Midwest. While acknowledging the problems with Midwest, Ben is hesitant to lose the account because it might create personal problems for him at home.

Questions to Consider

1. Should Ben drop Midwest as his account and let it become a second-tier customer?
2. What obligation does a company have to customers who no longer warrant special service or attention?

- *Reliability.* Providing service in a consistent, accurate, and dependable way.
- *Responsiveness.* Readiness and willingness to help customers and provide service.
- *Assurance.* Conveyance of trust and confidence that the company will back up the service with a guarantee.
- *Empathy.* Caring, individualized attention to customers.
- *Tangibles.* The physical appearance of the service provider's business, website, IMC materials, and the like.[11]

Nowadays, even when selling physical goods, these dimensions of service quality often trump other sources of value for customers (assuming no product quality problems, of course!).

Salesperson Professionalism

Your own level of professionalism in the way you handle yourself with customers is a great potential source of value to them. What is professionalism? It includes little things such as clear and concise correspondence, proper dress, good manners, and a positive attitude and can-do demeanor. Part Two of this book covers many aspects of how to exhibit professionalism as you go about relationship selling.

Brand Equity

Brand equity is the value inherent in a brand name in and of itself.[12] Brand equity is a bit like the concept of goodwill on the balance sheet, since if a company liquidated all its tangible assets, a great brand would still add terrific value to the firm. Examples of brands with high equity are Coke, IBM, McDonald's, and Apple. In selling, when all else is equal, your job is generally easier if you can sell the value of your brand. Global Connection builds an interesting case for salespeople developing their own personal global brand.

Corporate Image/Reputation

Closely related to brand equity is the concept of how corporate image or reputation adds value. Some firms that have financial difficulties continue to gain new clients and build business simply based on their reputation. On the other hand, the perils of losing and then trying to regain company reputation are well documented. Many firms in the financial services sector saw their brands tarnished as they were blamed (rightly or wrongly) for contributing to the economic downturn that began in the late 2000s. It is demoralizing for a salesperson to have to represent a firm to customers when its name is in the press as a "bad guy." Selling for an organization with a strong, positive image provides a leg up on competition, and the confidence that image brings to clients can overcome many other issues in making a sale.

Application of Technology

Some firms add substantial value to customer relationships through technology. Fortunately for the salesperson, communicating this value-adding dimension is usually quite straightforward. Pharmaceutical companies like Pfizer and Merck have developed sophisticated software for medical professionals that help them organize their daily jobs. Such activity is one example of strategic partnerships, which are more formalized relationships where companies share assets for mutual advantage. We'll look more closely at value-adding technology in chapter 5.

Price

Now we are back to where we started in this chapter: price. As we said before, many salespeople have difficulty transitioning from selling price to selling value. You may be surprised to see price mentioned as a value-adding factor in selling. However, remember the discussion on value as a ratio of benefits to costs. For customers, value is the amount by which benefits exceed their investment in various costs of doing business with you (including the product's price). And one of the ways we pointed out that you can increase value is by reducing costs (in this case, lowering price).

For some firms, low price is a key marketing strategy. Usually, such firms manage to compete on price by having consistently lower costs than competitors. The lower cost structure may have a number of sources, among them greater production efficiencies, lower labor costs, or a better supply-chain management system.

GLOBAL CONNECTION

BE YOUR OWN GLOBAL BRAND

What comes to mind when people see you? Or hear your name? That's your personal brand. It's the sum total of what people know about you—what they think of you after you've had a conversation, given a speech, or they've seen you in the public eye in some way. The idea is no different from what comes to mind when you see a product brand like Nike, Apple, or any global brand.

Every time you speak, you are branding yourself, and it's important to think strategically about what and how you are delivering that message. Your conversations, presentations, emails, phone calls, and conversations in the hallway all send signals. Are you talking about big ideas? Are you clear, concise, and interesting? Do people appear to sit up and pay attention when you speak?

People have a feeling about others, almost as soon as they meet and work with them. They continue to shape that feeling with the more interactions they have. Pretty soon, they see them walking down the hall, and something registers, positive or negative. It's within your power to make that feeling positive. What constitutes a strong personal brand? There are seven aspects of a powerful personal brand. A personal brand:

- Is instantly recognizable.
- Stands for something of value.
- Builds trust.
- Generates positive word of mouth.
- Gives a competitive advantage.
- Creates career opportunities.
- Results in professional and financial success.

Wherever you are today in your professional life, you can start sending strong, positive signals that will cut through the clutter of day-to-day business and create buzz about you. Everyone has the power to create their own positive personal brand. In fact, you could argue, they must if they want to succeed in a competitive global economy. It's up to you to create the strategy and messages needed to create a buzz and a powerful brand.

Questions to Consider

1. Identify two or three great global brands. What do they do that makes them a great brand globally?
2. Consider yourself as a brand in the context described above. What activities and steps can you take now to ensure that you will have a solid personal brand that will add value to your own career on a global basis?

Adapted from Suzanne Bates, "Is There Buzz about You? The Power of Building a Personal Brand," *American Salesman* (October 2006), p. 27.

Famously, Southwest Airlines has competed successfully for years using a low-cost strategy. Its operating efficiencies translate into not only lower prices but also better profit margins.

Sometimes firms feel relegated to competing on price because they see themselves as being in a commodity market. That is, their offering has no real differentiation from that of competitors and therefore a purely transactional selling approach is deployed (we discussed transactional selling in chapter 1). Put another way, the salesperson has none of the other value-adding sources above to bring to the customer. An interesting question that is more for a marketing strategy course than a selling course is how or if a firm can escape commoditization and find ways to strategically differentiate itself through some of the means above. For now, suffice it to say that transactional selling is unlikely to provide you with the kind of stimulating career opportunity we laid out in chapter 2 and it is not the approach that is the focus of this book.

MANAGING CUSTOMER EXPECTATIONS

We have seen that salespeople can draw on a wide array of factors in communicating their firm's value proposition. Each factor provides a rich context for communicating benefits to customers, a key topic in chapter 7. A final caveat deserves mention as we close our discussion of value. For any potential source of value or benefit, it is essential that the salesperson (and their firm) not *overpromise and underdeliver*. Instead, in relationship selling it makes sense to engage in *customer expectations management* and thus *underpromise and overdeliver*, which creates customer delight.

As we discussed in Chapter 1, customer delight—exceeding customer expectations to a surprising degree—is a powerful way to gain customer loyalty and solidify long-term relationships. Overpromising can get you the initial sale, but a dissatisfied customer will likely not buy from you again—and will tell many other potential customers to avoid you and your company. In executing the various selling process steps in Part Two of this book, remember the power of managing customer expectations.

EXPERT ADVICE: FOLLOW-UP   Chally Group WORLDWIDE

After watching the video of Mr. Stevens and reading the chapter, consider the following questions:

- Why does he focus on service as a value-adding element in selling?
- From a customer's perspective, what are some problems associated with a disconnect between sales and service?

SUMMARY

Salespeople who really know how to communicate the value proposition to customers are well on their way to success. In selling, it is a customer's *perceptions* of the value added that are key. Sales and marketing play major roles in communicating the value proposition. This message must be consistent in all forms in which it is communicated—hence the importance of integrated marketing communications (IMC).

Michael Porter's value-chain concept provides a very useful model for understanding value creation at the firm level. At the salesperson level, we present a variety of categories from which a salesperson can draw to communicate various aspects of value as benefits to customers.

KEY TERMS

perceived value	integrated marketing communications (IMC)	customer loyalty	retention rate
marketing concept		value chain	supply-chain management
4 Ps of marketing	internal customers	margin	trust
marketing mix	internal marketing	lifetime value of a customer	brand equity
promotion mix (marketing communications mix)	utility		strategic partnerships
	customer satisfaction	firing a customer	

ROLE PLAY

BEFORE YOU BEGIN

Before getting started, please go to the Appendix of chapter 1 to review the profiles of the characters involved in this role play, as well as the tips on preparing a role play.

Characters Involved

Alex Lewis
Abe Rollins

Setting the Stage

As part of a realignment of territories in District 10, Alex Lewis has just acquired a few customers from Abe Rollins. The realignment took place to better equalize the number of accounts and overall workload between the two territories, and both Alex and Abe welcome the change.

Unfortunately, one of Alex's new accounts, Starland Food Stores, is giving him some problems. On his first call on buyer Wanda Green, she took the opportunity to hammer hard on Alex that (to quote) "The only thing that matters to me is price, price, price. Get me a low price and I will give you my business." Alex knows that over the three years Abe called on Wanda, the two of them developed a strong professional relationship. Therefore, Alex gave Abe a call to see if they could get together over lunch to discuss how Alex might shift Wanda's focus away from just price to other value-adding aspects of the relationship with Upland.

In truth, Upland is pretty competitively priced item-to-item versus competitors. However, it is definitely not the lowest-priced supplier, nor would Alex have the discretion to make special prices for Wanda.

Alex Lewis's Role

Alex should begin by expressing his concern about Wanda's overfocus on price as the only added value from Upland. He should be open to any insights Abe can provide from his experience on how to sell Wanda on other value-adding aspects of the relationship.

Abe Rollins's Role

Abe should come into the meeting prepared to give a number of examples of how Alex (and Upland Company) can add value beyond simply low price. (Note: be sure the sources of added value you choose to put forth make sense in this situation.) Abe uses the time in the meeting to coach Alex on how he might be able to show Wanda that, while Upland's products are priced competitively, they offer superior value to the competition in many other ways.

Assignment

Work with another student to develop a 7–10 minute exchange of ideas on creating and communicating value. Be sure Abe tells Alex some specific ways he can go back to Wanda with a strong value proposition on the next sales call.

DISCUSSION QUESTIONS

1. Select any firm that interests you. Which aspects of the 12 categories for communicating value you learned in the chapter do you believe are most relevant for the firm you selected, and why is each particularly important to that firm?

2. What do you think are the most important ways sales can contribute to a firm's marketing, and vice versa?

3. Why is it so critical that marketing communications be integrated?

4. What is customer satisfaction? What is customer loyalty? Is one more important in the long run than the other? Why or why not?

5. Take a look at Exhibit 3.2 on the value chain. Pick a company in which you are interested, research it, and develop an assessment of how it is doing in delivering value at each link in the chain.

6. Consider service quality as a source of value. Give an example of a firm of which you have been a customer that exhibited a high degree of service quality. Also, give an example of poor service quality you have experienced at a firm.

MINI-CASE 3 BESTVALUE COMPUTERS

BestValue Computers is a Jackson, Mississippi, company providing computer technology, desktops, laptops, printers, and other peripheral devices to local businesses and school districts in the southern half of Mississippi. Leroy Wells founded BestValue shortly after graduating from college with an Information Technology degree. Leroy began small, but soon collected accounts looking for great value at reasonable prices with local service. When Leroy started his business in Jackson, he believed that anyone could build a computer. In fact, other than the processor and the software that runs computers, many of the components used are sold as commodities.

Leroy initially viewed his company as a value-added assembler and reseller of technology products. This business model was so successful that Leroy decided to expand from Jackson throughout southern Mississippi. To facilitate this expansion, Leroy hired Charisse Taylor in Hattiesburg to sell his products to all of south Mississippi, including the Gulf Coast, where a number of casinos were locating.

Before hiring Charisse, Leroy made sure that she had a reputation for developing long-term relationships with her customers and that she was a professional with integrity. Charisse did not disappoint Leroy. She has grown the business significantly in the two years that she has been with BestValue. Charisse credits her success to being honest with customers, which includes explaining exactly what BestValue can provide in terms of software and hardware. That way, no one is surprised with the result. In fact, many times customers have remarked to both Charisse and Leroy that they received more than they expected.

Now Leroy has set his sights on the New Orleans and Memphis markets. In addition, many of his initial customers have grown beyond a couple of desktop computers. They are starting to ask Leroy if he can provide and service local area networks (LANs), which allow many computers to share a central server so that workers can share files and communicate much more quickly. Leroy has decided to pursue the LAN business because selling, installing, and servicing LANs seems to be a natural extension of his current business.

However, adding the LAN products and accompanying services to his existing line of business represents a big addition to his current method of operation, which is to provide high-quality, high-value computers and peripheral devices. This new venture into providing more of a service than a product seems somewhat risky to Leroy, but he recognizes that LANs are the wave of the future and that to remain viable he will have to start viewing his company as more of a service provider than a product provider.

To facilitate Leroy's expansion into Memphis and New Orleans, he has hired two new salespeople. They are similar to Charisse in that they are relationship builders who believe providing clients with more than they promised is the key to successful selling today. This attitude is important because the competition in these two markets will be tough. Much larger competitors like Dell, IBM, and Hewlett-Packard have been selling equipment in these areas for a long time, so it will be very important for the sales reps to communicate BestValue's message of great value, including reasonable prices and local service. In fact, Leroy realizes that the only way to compete with the big boys is to be better than they are, by providing value over and above what they offer. That philosophy has made BestValue a success so far, and Leroy thinks it will work in these new markets too.

Questions

1. Identify and describe the categories of value creation on which BestValue currently relies most.

2. How can BestValue utilize the service quality dimensions to make sure it is communicating a consistent message of high-quality service and value every time someone from the company interacts with a customer?

3. Even though BestValue provides basically a commodity product, what role can the concept of brand equity play for BestValue's sales reps as they begin contacting customers in the New Orleans and Memphis areas?

4. What is the role of the BestValue sales reps in managing customer expectations? How can they ensure that new customers in the New Orleans and Memphis areas are delighted with their purchases? Be specific and explain.

5. What are some dangers that BestValue must take into account as it moves into the new markets and begins to provide LAN products and services? How will value creation change for it with the addition of LANs?

Appendix: Selling Math

An important element in relationship selling is developing an effective and persuasive value proposition. In the vast majority of sales presentations a critical component of the value proposition involves a quantitative analysis of your product and its value to the customer. This Appendix, which we call Selling Math, provides the tools to develop the quantifiable justification for a value proposition. All of the spreadsheets discussed in this Appendix can be found at the website for *Contemporary Selling* (along with other important information). Please go to www.routledge.com/cw/Johnston and download the spreadsheets before you continue. Working through the spreadsheets as you read the Appendix is the best approach for understanding and applying Selling Math. In addition, the spreadsheets are interactive, so you can create your own scenarios and see how a change in one component of the analysis alters other elements.

Most quantitative analysis involves a spreadsheet and is usually in one of two formats:

- If you are selling a product that is sold to a reseller (for example a retailer), use the *profit margin spreadsheet*.
- If you are selling a product or service that is used in the production of the business, use the *return on investment (ROI) spreadsheet*.

In customer relationship management (CRM) the customer value proposition is ascribed to one of three scenarios: (1) acquisition of new customers, (2) retention of existing customers, or (3) additional profitability (see Chapter 5). When creating a value proposition it is a good idea to identify which of these three is the most important objective in the presentation and create your spreadsheet around that goal. For example, if you were going to sell a new brand of clothing to a department store, you might argue that it would bring in new customers who are loyal current customers of the brand that had not shopped at the store previously. You might also argue it will increase retention by offering existing customers a larger selection which results in their greater satisfaction. Finally, you could argue the addition of the new brand would increase profitability because of the demand for the new product from existing and new customers, which would result in increased sales and profits. Analyzing the customer's needs and then matching the company's products to those needs is essential in choosing the most appropriate objective and spreadsheet model. This is not to say the other advantages should be ignored, just not quantified in the spreadsheet. Let's consider each scenario more closely and give some examples.

ACQUISITION OF NEW CUSTOMERS

In a retail purchase situation a customer may have many concerns and questions. Often a critical question in taking on a new product or service is, would the addition of your product or service actually bring new customers to the store? Keep in mind that consumers today are overloaded with product choices and a vast array of convenient purchasing options. When was the last time you went out of your way to find a particular product? Most likely this would occur when the product is a specialty good with high brand recognition. In this selling scenario, you would want to prepare a *ROI spreadsheet.*

RETENTION OR RETAINING NEW CUSTOMERS

Does the addition of your product or service allow the buyer to have better customer satisfaction? As we have discussed in relationship selling, exceeding customers' expectations results in keeping customers. It is much less expensive to keep existing customers than to attract new ones. How much is this actually worth to the company? It is possible to see the value of retaining particular customers through different kinds of analysis.

- If the goal is to determine the worth of a customer you would use the *lifetime value formula* (see Chapter 3).
- If the objective is customer retention, you would choose an *ROI spreadsheet* using the lifetime value of the customer offset by the inventory costs of your product.

PROFITABILITY

Profit is generated by a reduction in costs or an increase in sales. Questions that are frequently addressed in this selling scenario include: Does the addition of your product or service reduce labor or operational costs? Will the purchase of the product by the reseller increase sales? The information to address these questions can be measured and dealt with in a quantitative analysis.

If the profitability objective is based primarily on reducing costs, you should choose the *return on investment spreadsheet.* The cost savings would be compared to the cost of purchase to see if the ROI is positive. The bottom line of the ROI spreadsheet is the *net savings or return to the company.* If the purchase produces a positive ROI—in other words, if the savings are greater than the costs—it is a good match between the buyer's needs and the seller's product/service. If the purchase would produce a negative ROI—the cost is greater than the savings—it may mean the prospect is not a qualified buyer or the value proposition is not well developed (for example, there are too many product features relative to the cost targets for the customer).

If the value proposition is profitability based on increasing sales, you should choose the profit margin spreadsheet. The revenue from additional sales would be compared to the cost of purchase to project profit margin. The reseller spreadsheet is a simple calculation of costs less discounts, offset by retail price. An actual seller would supply costs and discounts. It is always important to be as accurate as possible in assigning costs and discounts; a thorough analysis of the customer's business and your company's own pricing flexibility is crucial to developing an accurate forecast. All research including interviews with store personnel should be documented and/or presented as evidence in your sales presentation. Let's examine each of these spreadsheet models.

UNDERSTANDING THE PROFIT MARGIN SPREADSHEET

Units	Unit Cost	Total Cost	Quantity Discounts	Co-op Allowance	Net Cost	MSRP	Revenue	Net Profit	Profit Margin/ Unit	Markup Up/Retail

- The *Units* column indicates the size of the purchase in the multiples in which they are sold. For example, some products are sold only by the case and therefore units would be number of cases. If products were sold individually then it would be the number of individual units.
- *Unit cost* is the wholesale price of the unit. If your unit were a case, it would be the price of the case. As stated above, this information would be readily available to you in your industry. It is not easily ascertained outside the company. You might have to find an industry average, ask for a range from an employee, or work backwards from retail price. To work backwards, you could take the retail price less the markup and discover the cost. For example, if you see a product advertised for $100 and you research the industry and discover there is usually 100 percent average industry markup, you can deduce that the cost would be $50. Another option would be to check prices at online discounters or cost clubs. They sell closer to wholesale and you could use their numbers as your wholesale cost.
- *Total cost* is number of units multiplied by the unit cost. Be sure you are using concurrent numbers. For example, if you discover the wholesale cost of a bottle of water is .29, but it is sold in cases of 12, you will first need to translate the unit cost to the cost for a case (12 × .29), or break down the number of units from number of cases to number of actual bottles.

Example

Cases	Units per Case	Total Units	Unit Cost ($)	Total Cost ($)
10	6	60	50	3,000
20	6	120	50	6,000
50	6	300	50	15,000

- In B2B *quantity discounts* are often used to encourage larger purchases. The amount of the discount varies by industry and research can determine an industry standard. Quantity discounts are normally expressed as a percentage of the total cost.
- Another common discount in B2B, especially in heavily advertised brands, is *co-op allowances*. This is money allocated for promotion of the seller's product by the reseller. Co-op discounts are often a percentage of the total cost. These discounts would be offered only if the reseller engaged in advertising that would significantly promote the seller's product. Co-op discounts are not usual for small orders or commodity items.
- *Net cost* would be the result of subtracting all discounts from total cost.

Example

Cases	Units per Case	Total Units	Unit Cost ($)	Total Cost ($)	Quantity Discounts ($)	Co-op Allowance ($)	Net Cost ($)
10	6	60	50	3,000	0	0	3,000
20	6	120	50	6,000	180	0	5,820
50	6	300	50	15,000	450	750	13,800

- *Manufacturer's suggested retail price (MSRP)* is the price of the product to the end user. It is the price without promotional allowances (markdowns, on sale, clearance, etc.). To find the best MSRP you should go to an actual brick-and-mortar retail location, not a discounter, and research the price at which your product is selling. Online resellers may discount the price and therefore you will not get an accurate MSRP. Manufacturers suggest a retail price to maintain brand equity. If you shop at a reseller location that also maintains strong brand equity you will get a more accurate MSRP.
- *Revenue* is the amount of sales generated by the order. The MSRP would be multiplied by the number of units. Be especially careful that you convert units into individual units because the MSRP will be for one unit. If your total cost was figured by the case, you will need revenue projections that include all the units.

Example

MSRP ($)	Revenue ($)
100	6,000
100	12,000
100	30,000

- *Net profit,* the bottom line, is revenue minus net cost. The buyer is most focused on this number. You should create a graph showing the increasing levels of profit with increased order size.
- *Profit margin per unit* could be a persuasive indicator. The revenue from the sale of the product or service is reduced by the cost of goods sold to determine profit margin. If the profit margin generated by the unit were significantly higher than the average margin experienced by the buyer, this would be of value. For example, in a grocery store markup on staple items is generally low, often below 30 percent. If your product could generate a pm/unit of more than 50 percent, especially if shelf space needs were low, the purchase would be highly valued.

Example

Net profit ($)	Profit Margin/Unit ($)
3,000	50
6,180	52
16,200	54

- Markup is the percentage added to the cost of the product to determine the selling price. *Markup based on retail* price should be included if you worked backwards to find the wholesale cost. The formula for markup is Cost / (100% − GM%) = Selling price. You can replace GM in the formula with the average markup to determine cost. Markup could be an industry average if specific numbers are unavailable. Markup is often used to determine if the return on the space your product occupies is worth the investment. For example, retail stores calculate their return on shelf space based on the sales generated from the square footage of selling space available. If your product requires more selling space than the revenue it will generate, it would be a bad purchase decision for the customer.

Understanding the ROI Spreadsheet

	Plan 1	Plan 2	Plan 3
Expenses			
Daily			
Average number of staff			
Average amount of time			
Labor minutes used			
Labor hours			
Monthly			
Labor hours			
Average hourly wage			
Total monthly cost			
Yearly			
Investment			
Product/service cost			
Additional costs			
Total yearly cost			
Net savings			
Over time . . .			
ROI/month			

The ROI spreadsheet requires a deeper understanding of your buyer's business than the profit margin spreadsheet. It also requires access to sensitive information about the company's operations. If you are selling a product or service that will decrease costs to the customer's business and consequently increase profitability, you need to show your buyer the value of buying/investing in your product. Profitability from the purchase is called the return on investment (ROI). In many cases the main expense is labor costs, as in the example. You can use the same format, substituting rows as needed to adapt to the other expenses.

In this example we have chosen to present three options to the buyer with each providing a greater return. It is not always necessary to have numerous options, but it does help illustrate the financial advantage of building the relationship with a long-term contract.

The purpose of the ROI spreadsheet is to persuade the buyer to invest in your product or service. The payoff of their investment, or the return, is the difference between their current expenses and the new purchase.

- The spreadsheet begins by addressing the *expenses*. The buyer will be more comfortable discussing the current situation from this point of view. It is also a good idea to show the need for your product before introducing the price.
- If your product/service is going to reduce labor costs, you first need to know the current labor costs. Begin by determining the current cost of labor associated with the task the sale will impact. If you are selling accounting software, this could be the number of people who will use the software. If you are selling Internet access, this would be the number of employees who will benefit from faster connections. In this example we have started with *daily usage* and built into the larger picture. Many buyers will find it easier to think in smaller time blocks. "How many minutes would you estimate you spend waiting on the phone per day?" is much easier to answer than asking the same question for minutes per year.
- *Average amount of time* is the current use of time by the employees included in the staff calculation above. For example, if they use about 30 minutes a day on a task that will now be eliminated or streamlined, that would be put in the cell. Time wasted while waiting on connections or slow computers could also be included.
- *Labor minutes used* are the number of staff members multiplied by the average amount of time worked. This tells us the total usage for the company on a daily basis.
- Since most wages are calculated per hour we need to convert minutes into hours. Thus, *labor hours* are the labor minutes divided by 60.

Example

	Plan 1	Plan 2	Plan 3
Expenses			
Daily			
Average number of staff	10	10	10
Average amount of time	12	12	12
Labor minutes used	120	120	120
Labor hours	2	2	2

- *Labor hours/month* is calculated to build the bigger picture. Since investments are not made on a daily or even monthly basis, we need to build up to the yearly usage. Labor hours multiplied by 30 gives us the labor hours per month.
- To determine the actual cost of the labor hours we need an *average hourly wage*. Be sure to note that this is an average. In some cases all employees impacted by the investment will be comparable in earnings, in other cases there may be great disparity between management and staff. This is your best attempt at parity and can be quite easily researched.
- *Total monthly cost* is calculated by multiplying average wage by labor hours/month. This amount is the cost to the buyer of not buying your product or service.

Example

Monthly

Labor hours	54	60	66
Average hourly wage	$9.00	$9.00	$9.25
Total monthly cost	$486	$540	$611

Most investments in B2B are long term, not merely for 30 days. To calculate the yearly cost of not buying, we would multiply total monthly cost by the number of months in the year.

Example

Yearly	$5,832	$6,480	$7,326

The next section of the ROI spreadsheet is the introduction of the investment or cost to buy your product/service. These costs are usually easy to find, as they are the retail price of the good or service.

- *Product/service cost* is the actual amount the business needs to "invest" in the solution. It should be expressed in the total cost for the year to keep our analysis logical.
- *Additional costs* might be installation, training, maintenance, support, compatibility upgrades, etc. In building strong relationships, all costs should be discussed. Hidden costs are unethical and do not contribute to long-term relationships.
- The *total yearly* costs are the sum total of the investment for that year. Services are often repeating investments. Many times a discounted price is offered for multiple year contracts. In some buying situations, a large purchase could be amortized over an extended period. All costs should appear when presenting the ROI.

Example

Investment

Product/service cost	$5,000	$6,000	$5,500
Additional costs	1,200	0	0
Total yearly cost	$6,200	$6,000	$5,500

The bottom line of the ROI spreadsheet is the *net savings*. If the purchase produces a positive ROI—in other words if the savings are greater than the costs—it is a good match between the buyer's needs and your (the seller's) product/service. If the purchase would produce a negative ROI—the cost greater than the savings—it may mean the prospect is not a qualified buyer or that price negotiation is needed.

As stated previously, there are often advantages to making a commitment to purchase for more than one year. It is an advantage to the seller to know they will have the repeat business, and an advantage to the buyer to know they have created a relationship with the seller that can provide them with benefits from customer service and reduced ordering costs. In the case of some B2B purchases, the one-time purchase price is spread out over the life of the product. In both these instances it is important to show the ROI over the life of the contract or product. In the example, we chose to look at the investment over a three-year period. The yearly return for each year is added together to determine the actual return over the three-year life of the investment.

Since many businesses use monthly cash-based accounting methods, it is a persuasive tool to break down the large investment dollars into monthly returns. If you take the three-year ROI and divide by the number of months in the same time period (36) you find the *ROI per month*. As consumers we find $99 per month easier to accept than $1,200. In B2B, the same psychology applies.

Example

Investment

Total yearly cost	$6,200	$6,000	$5,500
Net savings	280	480	1,826
Over time . . .	840	1,440	5,478
ROI/month	$23	$40	$152

If you are using the ROI spreadsheet to quantify the *acquisition of new customers*, a few modifications would be made. You would need to forecast the number of new customers that would be attracted. You would also need a lifetime value for the customer (see Exhibit 3.3). This would determine the revenue stream.

Example

	Minimum	Average	Exceptional
Acquisition			
Number of new customers	3	4	5
Lifetime value	$5,000	$5,000	$5,000
Revenues	$15,000	$20,000	$25,000
Investment			
Product/service cost	$13,000	$17,000	$20,000
Additional costs	1,500	1,500	1,500
Total yearly cost	$14,500	$18,500	$21,500
ROI	$500	$1,500	$3,500

The revenues generated would be offset by the cost of the product/service and any related costs. Be sure to include all costs that will be associated with the decision. In this example we are selling advertising space. The additional cost of artwork for the ad design is shown as an additional cost. If you were selling a product that would provide value through *customer retention*, your product cost would be the investment.

The ROI in the acquisition example shows that a $20,000 yearly investment in advertising could return $25,000 in sales revenue and thereby not only recover the expense but actually return $3,500. The spreadsheet also shows that in the worst-case scenario the return on the investment would be $500.

As you work through the spreadsheets it is important to note the challenge of these analyses is not the calculations but, rather, verifying the accuracy of the data. Without valid data the analyses are not very valuable to you as the salesperson, or the customer. Indeed, a poor analysis with invalid data could do more harm than good to the relationship. Mastering the relationship selling process means, in part, becoming comfortable with understanding, creating, and then explaining these kinds of analyses to customers.

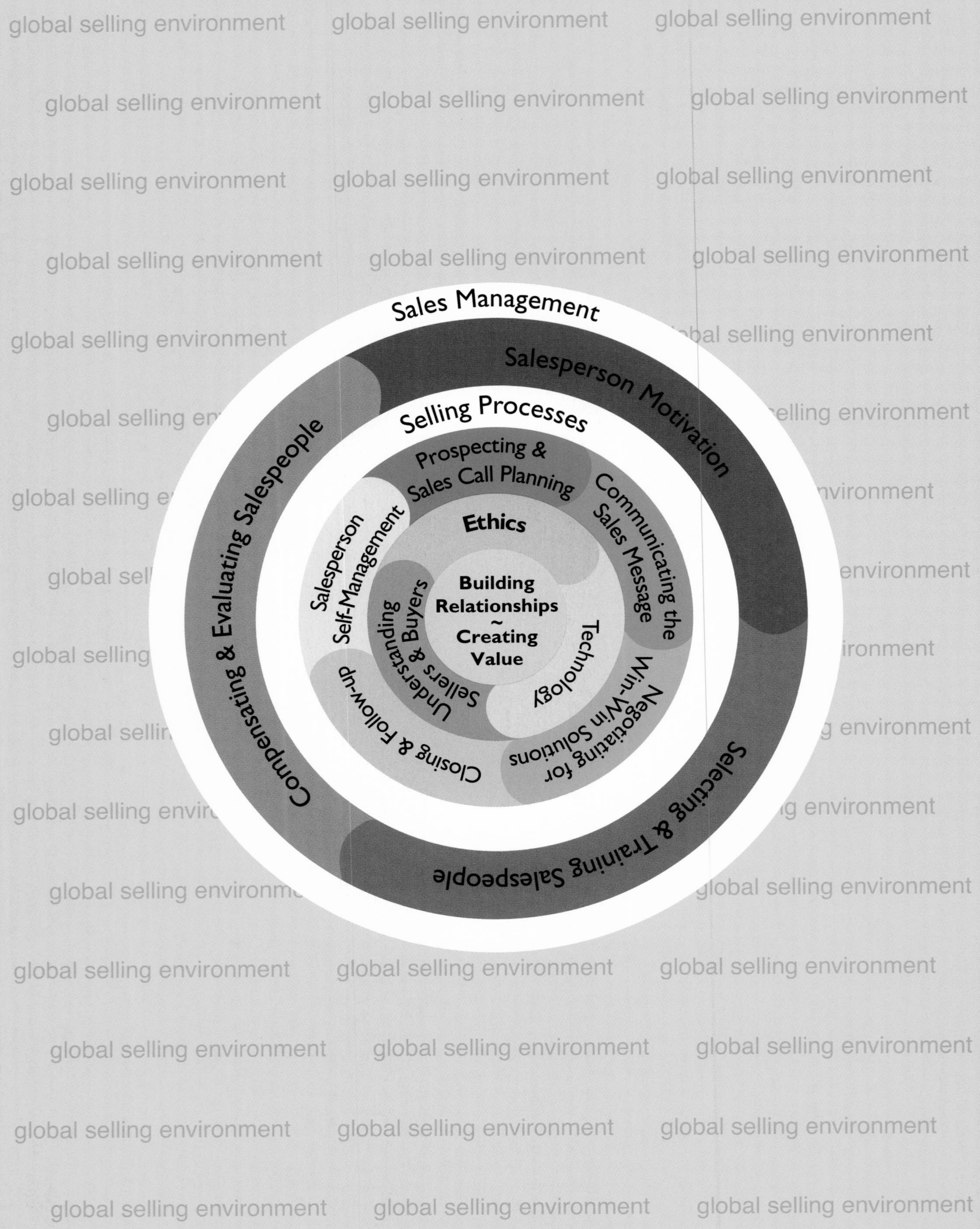

Ethical and Legal Issues in Contemporary Selling

4

LEARNING OBJECTIVES

As we have said, ethical relationships are the foundation of contemporary selling. Every day salespeople are asked to make ethical judgments. Likewise their managers must make ethical decisions that affect company policies as well as individual salespeople. The events of the last several years have made it clear that ethical behavior cannot be assumed. It needs to be taught and become a fundamental element of the corporate culture. This chapter will explore the many ethical concerns facing salespeople and managers and discuss legal issues that affect sales behavior. The chapter ends with tips on creating a personal code of sales ethics.

After reading this chapter, you should be able to:

- Understand the importance of ethical behavior in contemporary selling and sales management.
- Identify the ethical concerns facing salespeople as they relate to customers and employers.
- Identify the ethical concerns facing sales managers as they relate to salespeople, company policies, and international sales issues.
- Discuss the legal issues in contemporary selling.
- Create a personal code of sales ethics.

EXPERT ADVICE

EXPERT: David B. Edmonds
Senior Vice President, Worldwide Services, FedEx Corporation

TOPIC: The role of trust in building a successful customer relationship.

SUMMARY: Mr. Edmonds discusses the characteristics of a successful salesperson in today's competitive environment. In his discussion he speaks to a number of important characteristics that are part of contemporary selling. He also talks about how that role has changed over the last decade. He notes that a critical success factor is becoming a "trusted" business partner with the customer. Trust is based on honesty and ethics, the topic of this chapter. Learn how sales people (and managers) deal with critical issues to become a trusted business partner.

NEXT STEPS: Go to the website for *Contemporary Selling* (www.routledge.com/cw/Johnston), watch the chapter 4 video and then read the chapter. You will find an Expert Advice Follow-Up at the end of the chapter with questions that connect elements of your learning.

COMPANION @ WEBSITE

THE IMPORTANCE OF ETHICS IN THE 21ST CENTURY

All of us are faced with decisions that test our ethical principles every day. For example, what do you do when the clerk at the grocery store gives you too much change? When your classmate asks you for an answer during a test? What principles guide you as you make decisions about ethical dilemmas?

Given the unique nature of their jobs, it is not surprising that salespeople face ethical issues all the time. As shown in the model for Contemporary Selling and Sales Management at the beginning of the chapter, ethics is a core principle of the buyer–seller relationship. Without a commitment to ethical behavior, it is impossible to have a successful long-term relationship with buyers. However, salespeople encounter pressure from a variety of sources, including their managers, customers, and other outside parties (family, friends), and research suggests that this pressure, particularly the conflict between work and family, can lead to more unethical, even illegal behavior.[1] Making the right decision for one can mean disappointing another, which complicates the decision even more. For example, refusing to sell a long-term service contract to a customer who doesn't really need it may be in the customer's best interests but is not the most profitable decision for the company.

Also, ethical norms change over time. This can lead to anxiety as salespeople get caught in the middle of changing corporate policies and customer demands. For example, the nature of contemporary selling today often means buyers and sellers share sensitive information about manufacturing and pricing. However, many companies are still wary of sharing too much information about sensitive topics with customers.

Unfortunately, defining ethical behavior is difficult. Our focus is on **business ethics**, which comprises moral principles and standards that define right and wrong and guide behavior in the world of business.[2]

Renewed Emphasis on Ethical Practices

In recent years, business ethics has become front-page news as companies like Enron have engaged in unethical, and in some cases illegal, activities. Whether or not salespeople in these companies were directly involved in illegal activities, they suffered as a result of management's ethical lapses.

One outcome of these scandals has been a renewed interest in ethics at every level in the organization. From the board of directors to the lowest level, employees have become more aware of their company's ethical practices. Many large companies have published their code of conduct or values (there are many phrases), which defines the way they do business. Exhibit 4.1 is a summary of Dell Computer's Code of Conduct.

Not surprisingly, one of the areas most affected by the focus on ethics is selling. The relationship between buyer and seller is based on mutual trust. Any ethical lapse by the seller can severely damage the customer's trust. A recent survey of sales managers reported that 70 percent of their clients consider a company's ethical reputation when making purchase decisions. In addition, companies are starting to realize the importance of ethics training in improving salesperson and sales manager satisfaction.[3] Ethics will play an increasingly important role in the sales decision process for both buyer and seller.

The focus on ethics is not limited to the United States. Around the world, companies are reacting to and in many cases proactively dealing with ethical problems by establishing worldwide ethical policies. This is difficult because ethical practices vary by region and even from country to country. What is acceptable behavior in Latin America may be against the law in the United States or Europe. For example, offering bribes or payments to enhance the probability of success is often seen as part of doing business in parts of Latin America and the Middle East but is illegal in the United States. As we explore in chapter 14, internationalizing ethical practices and policies is not easy for any company, no matter where it is from originally.

EXHIBIT 4.1 CODE OF CONDUCT DELL COMPUTER

"How We Win," Dell's Code of Conduct, provides general guidance to all team members on how to behave legally and ethically, and in compliance with the letter and spirit of applicable legal requirements, Dell policies and our ethical principles. It serves as a guidebook for living our value of winning with integrity.

Our Code of Conduct, a fundamental component of our culture of integrity here at Dell, has been extensively revised and updated to bring it into alignment with our purpose and values, as well as with our business, brand and people strategies.

Our reputation as an ethical company and trustworthy business partner is one of our most valuable assets and critical to our success. To safeguard our reputation and our brand, we hold ourselves to standards of ethical behavior that go well beyond legal minimums.

Our ethical principles are:

- **We are honest.** What we say is true and forthcoming—not just technically correct. We are open and transparent in our communications with each other and about our business performance.
- **We are trustworthy.** Our word is good. We keep our commitments to each other and to our stakeholders. We do the right thing without compromise. We avoid even the appearance of impropriety.
- **We treat others with respect.** We value their contributions and listen to their point of view. We maintain fairness in all relationships.
- **We are courageous.** We speak up for what is right. We report wrongdoing when we see it.
- **We use good judgment.** We think before we act. We use our purpose, values and ethical principles as decision filters to guide our behavior.
- **We are responsible.** We accept the consequences of our actions. We admit our mistakes and quickly correct them. We don't retaliate against those who try to do the right thing by asking questions or raising concerns.

Companies Take the Lead in Social Responsibility

Beyond the question of ethical behavior is a larger question that companies face on a daily basis. What are my social responsibilities as a corporate citizen? As Enron demonstrated, lost shareholder wealth and thousands of layoffs are only two of the consequences of poor ethical judgments. Those decisions, which hurt thousands of people in many ways, are prime examples of bad corporate citizenship. Companies have a responsibility to many groups. Certainly they have a responsibility to their customers. They also have employees (who count on continued employment), shareholders (who invest their money for a financial return), and a host of other entities (among them suppliers, government, and creditors) who expect the company to act in an ethical manner. Exhibit 4.2 details the best corporate citizens, as identified by *Corporate Responsibilty* magazine.

ETHICAL CONCERNS FOR SALESPEOPLE

This section discusses the ethical issues salespeople deal with as they interact with customers and their own companies. As you will see, these issues can be complex, and much of the time there is a great deal riding on the salesperson's decision.

Exhibit 4.3 summarizes the ethical concerns for salespeople.

EXHIBIT 4.2 THE BEST CORPORATE CITIZENS

For the last 12 years, *Corporate Responsibility* magazine has published an annual list of the 100 best corporate citizens. The study highlights companies that balance social responsibility and other business ethical issues with traditional financial returns. The purpose of the list, as stated by the magazine is:

> In a perfect world investors, regulators, customers, suppliers, employees, and neighbors would know everything instantly about companies they invest in, do business with, and work for. We do not live in a perfect world. And in the past few years we've paid the price of now knowing … Corporate Responsibility Magazine and the Corporate Responsibility Officers Association (CROA) share a common purpose in advancing corporate accountability and responsibility. The 100 Best Corporate Citizens Methodology fulfills that purpose by transparently assessing the degree to which companies hold themselves accountable and let others … hold them accountable as well.

In putting together the list of 100 best corporate citizens, *Corporate Responsibility* magazine examines information in the following areas (the number in parentheses denotes it weighting):

Environment (19.5%)
Employee Relations (19.5%)
Climate Change (16.5%)
Human Rights (16.0%)
Financial (12.5)
Philanthropy (9.0%)
Governance (7.0%).

Ranked in order, the top 15 corporate citizens in 2012 were as follows:

1. Bristol-Myers Squibb Co.
2. International Business Machines Corp.
3. Intel Corp.
4. Microsoft
5. Johnson Controls Inc.
6. Accenture plc.
7. Spectra Energy Corp.
8. Campbell Soup Company
9. Nike, Inc.
10. Freeport-McMoran Copper & Gold Inc.
11. Sara Lee Corp.
12. Mattel, Inc.
13. Gap, Inc.
14. Coca-Cola Company
15. Altria Group Inc.

For a more complete discussion of the 2012 100 Best Corporate Citizens, go to www.thecro.com and click on "100 Best Corporate Citizens."

Adapted from *Corporate Responsibility* magazine, June 2012, www.thecro.com

EXHIBIT 4.3 ETHICAL CONCERNS FOR SALESPEOPLE

Customers	Employers
Dishonesty	Cheating
Gifts, entertainment, bribes	Misuse of company resources
Unfair treatment	Inappropriate relationships with employees and customers
Breaking confidentiality	

Issues with Customers

There are four primary ethical concerns for salespeople in their relationships with customers. They are dishonesty, gifts (entertainment, bribes), unfair treatment, and confidentiality leaks. We will explore each in detail.

Dishonesty. Salespeople sell. That is their job, and as part of that job they are expected to present their products to customers in the best possible light. It is perfectly acceptable for a salesperson to be passionate about products and services; however, there is a line between enthusiasm and illegal, dishonest behavior. Under no circumstances is it acceptable to be **dishonest** and provide false or deliberately inaccurate information to customers. However, what happens when the customer asks if the company can meet certain shipping deadlines for a product and the salesperson is *not sure* if recent delays in manufacturing could severely push back the requested shipping dates? The question here is not legal but ethical. How does a salesperson ensure that enthusiasm does not become poor ethical judgment? This is a question salespeople face almost every day.

The adage that defined the 20th Century sales model was **caveat emptor** ("let the buyer beware"). It was generally considered the buyer's responsibility to uncover any untruths in the seller's statements. Even in 21st-Century-contemporary selling, the salesperson must decide how much information to give the customer. Successful contemporary selling is based on mutual trust and ethical behavior, which means the salesperson should not hold back information or tell half-truths.[4] When customers become aware of such half-truths (as they always do), the long-term damage to the relationship can be far worse than any short-term pain caused by being honest.[5] Dishonesty not only harms the customer relationship but can lead to legal action (which we will discuss later in this chapter) and huge financial judgments against the company.

The salesperson who chooses to provide complete information even when it presents the company in a less than favorable light can create a high degree of credibility with the customer. Cisco, for example, instructs its salesforce to be totally open and honest with customers, to present the most accurate information available even if the information is not positive. Interestingly, the mere fact that the company states this policy has had a positive effect with customers.

Gifts, Entertainment, Bribes. A **gift** is a nonfinancial present. A **bribe** is a financial present given to a buyer to manipulate the purchase decision.

Meeting a customer for lunch is an accepted business custom. Historically, it has been a way for the buyer and seller to build a more personal relationship while getting work done. The vast majority of salespeople take their customers to lunch at least occasionally. But what about taking them to dinner or a nightclub? Does it make a difference if the lunch cost $15 per person or $75? These are the kinds of questions salespeople must answer on a regular basis.

Why do some salespeople offer bribes or illegal gifts to customers? Unfortunately, the answer is, it works. Research suggests that gifts can affect whether or not the order is given and the size of the order.[6] Customers often place salespeople in an almost impossible situation. Even if the salesperson desires to be ethical, a customer may ask for "special consideration" in getting the order.

To deal with these difficult ethical questions, many companies on both sides of the buyer–seller relationship have established policies for handling gifts and entertainment. On one hand, companies like Hewlett-Packard tell their salespeople explicitly that under no circumstances should they offer gifts of any kind to secure an order. On the customer side, companies like Target and Home Depot significantly limit the scope of gifts (pencils, coffee mugs) and type of interaction (they must meet at corporate offices) between their purchasing agents and salespeople. It is important to note that ethical issues are not just a domestic concern; in many countries the same ethical challenges occur. Check out the Ethical Dilemma to experience a very real ethical challenge.

ETHICAL DILEMMA

IS IT A BRIBE OR A RETIREMENT FUND?

Your company gets a call from a large company that is based in Latin America and has operations around the world. It is the industry leader in this region of the world. The vice president of sales for your company has been trying to enter the Latin American market for several years with no luck and considers this a tremendous opportunity.

The VP calls you into her office to tell you that you have been chosen to explore the potential for a relationship with this company. After several visits over the next six months, you realize the customer is impressed with your company's reputation for quality and is seriously considering giving you a substantial contract. This contract will open up all of Latin America for your company.

At the final meeting with the potential new customer, you expect to sign the contract. However, the company's CEO, who is running for national public office in the country, suggests it would be very helpful if you (and your company) make a substantial contribution to a prominent charity in the country. The CEO is not specific about the reasons for the contribution, but strongly suggests that the contribution is necessary to get the contract.

Questions to Consider

1. What do you do?
2. If you were the vice president of sales, what would you tell your salesperson when he contacts you for advice?

Unfair Treatment. By their very nature, each customer is different. Some customers buy more or have greater potential for new business. It is quite appropriate to offer special pricing or better terms to them. However, salespeople need to be aware of ethical concerns when customers ask for more than is reasonably expected in the course of business.

There are several problems associated with unfair treatment. First, providing special treatment to customers is costly and may not be a good use of the salesperson's time. Consider, for example, the established customer who expects a busy salesperson to drop off orders. Diverting the salesperson away from his or her primary focus could lead to lower productivity. Second, providing special services to some customers will almost surely lead other customers to feel as though they are not important enough to warrant special treatment, which will lead to a weaker relationship with those customers.

Confidentiality Leaks. A key element of the trust between buyer and seller is **confidentiality**, which is the sharing of sensitive information. Salespeople learn critical facts about their customers all the time. At a minimum they know how much, at what price, and when shipments of their own products will be purchased by their customer. Today their knowledge often goes much deeper. For example, in working with customers they may learn about the development and introduction of new products. They can also learn a great deal about the pricing structure and strategy of existing products. This information would be useful to the customer's competitors, some of whom could be the salesperson's customers already.

It is essential for the credibility of a salesperson and his or her company that any information shared by the customer be held in the strictest confidence. Divulging sensitive information to others, even to non-essential employees in the salesperson's company, is one of the surest ways to lose a customer. Customers have long memories in these situations and do not easily forget or forgive any salesperson who shares confidential information with individuals or organizations not authorized by the customer.

Issues with Employers

Not all of a salesperson's ethical concerns deal with the customer relationship. Three ethical concerns related to the salesperson's employer are (1) cheating, (2) misuse of company resources, and (3) inappropriate relationships with other employees. Let's look at each issue more closely.

Cheating. Salespeople work, for the most part, away from their employer, so the company relies on their honesty and integrity. More importantly, the salesperson is the primary (if not the only) source of direct communication with the customer, and companies must have confidence in that information in order to make sound business decisions. Salespeople report on things like the number of sales calls, expenses, and even how sales are recorded to the company and this information is assumed to be true and accurate.

Unfortunately, when salespeople do not make enough sales calls, want to win a sales contest by booking orders within a certain period of time, or any of hundreds of other situations they can be tempted to cheat. For example, if a salesperson is evaluated on the number of sales calls he or she makes each week but has not made that number, is it ethical to list a sales call with a customer *this* week that he or she intends to contact by phone *next* week? What would you do in a similar situation?

Misuse of Company Resources. Salespeople need a number of resources to do their jobs effectively, so it is expensive to equip and maintain a sales force in the field. Among the resources are technology (smartphones, computers) and transportation (cars, air travel). Legitimate business expenses include taking a customer to lunch, for which the salesperson is entitled to be reimbursed. Salespeople are often given direct control of some resources, such as cell phones and computers. For other expenses, such as travel, they submit expense reports and are reimbursed by the company. In still other situations, salespeople are given a budget for items like a car and submit a report at the end of the year detailing how they used the money.

If salespeople misrepresent their business expenses to generate additional income, they cross the ethical line. Often this happens when the salesperson believes the compensation is not adequate or company policies are not sufficient to cover legitimate business expenses. Sadly, this practice is not uncommon. A study by the Department of Commerce estimated employee theft in the United States at $60 billion. Another study reported that 30 percent of all business failures are caused by employee theft. More specifically, 60 percent of sales managers said they had caught one of their salespeople cheating on an expense report.[7]

It may be true that the company compensation plan is inadequate and policies regarding reimbursement of expenses are not fair, but this does not justify illegal or even unethical behavior. We'll discuss in the section on ethical concerns for management the wisdom of having plans and policies in place that are fair to salespeople.

A good rule of thumb is to adopt your own standard of living when you are incurring business-related expenses. Companies should not ask their salespeople to have a lower standard of living on business than at home, but salespeople should not use the opportunity of business travel to live a more lavish lifestyle than they do at home either.

It is not always clear whether the use of business resources for personal use is unethical. Some companies permit the personal use of business assets. Consider the company cell phone. After business hours, is it unethical for a salesperson to use the cell phone for personal use when it does not interfere with business activities? Companies almost always have a stated policy on the personal use of business resources, and the salesperson needs to become familiar with that policy. Violating it can have serious implications for a salesperson's continued employment with the company.

Inappropriate Relationships with Other Employees and Customers. In today's workplace, men and women work closely together in a variety of situations, as members of the same organization (peers and co-workers), or as buyer and seller. For the most part, men and women work in an environment of mutual respect and professional business behavior. However, occasionally these relationships become more personal and intimate, which can be dangerous for everyone involved. In a survey, 57 percent of respondents had personally witnessed romantic relationships between salespeople in their companies, but only 15 percent of the companies had a stated policy on personal relationships between employees.[8] This creates a gap between what individuals in the organization are doing and company policy on such behavior.

The biggest ethical issues for individuals are the potentially negative implications of the relationship on them, their loved ones, and the company. What happens when the relationship ends? Might the company be charged with sexual harassment? If the relationship is with a customer, how will it affect the business relationship between the two companies? These are tough questions that involve not only business but also personal decisions.

While a number of companies do not expressly prohibit personal relationships among co-workers, it is important to realize there are serious implications crossing the line into a personal, nonprofessional relationship. Simple common sense can help you avoid such compromising situations. For example, always keep the conversation professional and on business topics. Even joking about sexual matters or personal business can give someone the wrong impression. Also, don't put yourself in a situation that could be misinterpreted. Taking a co-worker to dinner alone after business hours could give that person the wrong idea.

ETHICAL CONCERNS FOR MANAGEMENT

Salespeople are not the only members of the sales force who face ethical concerns. Management must address significant ethical issues with salespeople and company policies. Let us explore each of these issues in greater detail.

Exhibit 4.4 summarizes the ethical concerns for management.

EXHIBIT 4.4 ETHICAL CONCERNS FOR MANAGEMENT

Salespeople	Company Policies	International Ethics
Sales pressure	Unethical climate	Cultural differences
Deception	Unfair corporate policies	Differences in corporate selling policies
Abusing salesperson rights		

Issues with Salespeople

Sales managers face a number of ethical questions with their employees. If companies expect their salespeople to behave ethically, they must behave ethically as well. Management has a significant role in setting the overall culture of ethical behavior for the sales force.[9] In their relationship with salespeople, managers most often deal with three ethical issues: (1) sales pressure, (2) deception, and (3) abuse of salespeople's rights.

Sales Pressure. Pressure is part of the selling profession. Salespeople are evaluated all the time on how much they have sold, how profitable the order is, and the configuration of the sales order, among other issues. However, when sales pressure is applied unfairly or too forcefully, management may be crossing the line into unethical behavior. Professional salespeople expect management to define clear sales goals without threatening undue pressure.

Unfortunately, some managers do exert unfair pressure for sales results and set goals they know their salespeople cannot attain. Setting unrealistic goals can, over time, demotivate people, especially if they feel that there is nothing they can do to reach sales targets. It can also cause salespeople to consider unethical practices. Setting sales targets and holding salespeople accountable for hitting those targets are part of the manager's job, but it is important to set realistic goals that motivate salespeople.

Deception. Deception, the practice of misleading or misrepresenting something, has no place in the manager–salesperson relationship. However, managers are often in situations when being totally honest has negative consequences. Consider, for example, what happens when a salesperson is forced to leave the company. What does the manager tell a prospective employer asking for a reference? Should the manager be honest and say the employee was a consistent poor performer and has no future in sales? In today's legal environment, being totally honest can lead to expensive lawsuits. In general, though, honesty is still the best policy.

In dealing directly with salespeople, managers must be honest and clear in their discussions. For example, when a salesperson is performing poorly and the future is not bright, it serves no purpose to put him or her in an impossible situation (for example, assigning a poor-performing territory or customers with little business potential) to force the salesperson out of the company. While confrontation is not easy, misleading the person is more harmful in the long run.

Abuse of Salespeople's Rights. All employees have certain rights, which managers must be aware of to avoid legal and ethical problems. These rights cover a variety of employment matters, including (1) following the policies and procedures related to termination, (2) maintaining the confidentiality and security of personal information, (3) creating a work environment free of any form of discrimination or bias (for example, race or gender bias), and (4) following established policies and rules regarding performance appraisals, compensation, and benefits. Essentially, they involve doing the right thing when you say you are going to do it.

Many problems arise when managers do not follow established company policies and procedures. For example, not reporting instances of bias or discrimination is not only unethical but also illegal (as we shall discuss later in this chapter). Terminating salespeople without proper notification and not following established procedures is also unethical and potentially illegal. Frequently, managers' mistakes result from omission (not knowing the appropriate procedures) rather than commission (deliberately abusing the rights of the salesperson). It is critical that managers aggressively protect and defend the rights of their salespeople.

Issues with Company Policies

A primary role for any sales manager is to delineate, implement, monitor, and enforce the procedures and policies of the organization as they relate to the sales force. In the vast majority of instances, these policies are fair and ethical. Unfortunately, some company policies create significant ethical challenges for managers and salespeople. We will examine two such examples: unethical climate and unfair corporate policies.

Unethical Corporate Culture. Every organization has a corporate culture, a set of unwritten norms and rules that influence the behavior of its employees. On one hand, companies like CNL Investments follow a strong code of personal and corporate ethics. The climate at CNL encourages people to behave in an ethical manner. It is based on the personal beliefs of senior management, conveyed in the Core Values statement and other documents and demonstrated as a matter of management practice. One of the challenges in today's global business environment is the impact of a country's culture on a company. While there are certainly differences among cultures around the world the basic concepts of ethical business practices are remarkably similar. Global Connection lists the companies outside the United States ranked among the World's Most Ethical Organizations by Ethisphere, a leading research-based think tank on issues related to business ethics, corporate social responsibility, anti-corruption, and sustainability.

GLOBAL CONNECTION

COMPANIES OUTSIDE THE UNITED STATES LISTED AMONG THE WORLD'S MOST ETHICAL COMPANIES

Comme Il Faut
Apparel
Israel

Standard Chartered Bank
Banking
UK

William E. Connor &
   Associated Ltd.
Business Services
Hong Kong

Electrolux
Consumer Electronics
Sweden

Kao Corporation
Consumer Products
Japan

EDP Energias de Portugal
Energy and Utilities: Electric
Portugal

Northumbrian Water Group
Energy and Utilities: Water
UK

Stora Enso
Forestry, Paper, and Packaging
Finland

Shiseido Co.
Health and Beauty
Japan

National Bank of Australia
Banking
Australia

Westpac Group
Banking
Australia

Wipro Ltd.
Computer Software
India

Ricoh
Consumer Electronics
Japan

Premier Farnell plc.
Electronics
UK

ENMAX Corporation
Energy and Utilities: Electric
Canada

Statoil
Energy: Oil
Norway

Natura Cosmeticos
Health and Beauty
Brazil

Schneider Electric
Industrial Manufacturing
France

Rabobank
Banking
Netherlands

Accenture
Business services
Ireland

CRH plc.
Construction
Ireland

Henkel AG and Co. KGaA
Consumer Products
Germany

Encana Corporation
Energy and Utilities: Natural Gas
Canada

Vestas Wind
Energy and Utilities: Wind
Denmark

SCA
Forestry, Paper, and Packaging
Sweden

L'Oréal
Health and Beauty
France

Sompo Japan Insurance Inc.
Insurance: Property and Casualty
Japan

Tokio Marine Holdings, Inc. Insurance: Property and Casualty Japan	Swiss RE Insurance: Reinsurance Switzerland	The Rezidor Hotel Group Leisure and Hospitality Belgium
Coloplast Medical Devices Denmark	Royal Philips Medical Devices Netherlands	Tata Steel Ltd. Metals and Mining India
Umicore Metals and Mining Belgium	British Land plc. Real Estate UK	Kesko Retail: Food Stores Finland
SONAE Retail: Food Stores Portugal	The Co-operative Group Retail: Food Stores UK	Marks and Spencer Retail General UK
Portugal Telecom Telecommunications Services Portugal	Singtel Telecommunications Services Singapore	Nippon Yusen Kabushi Kaisah Transportation and Logistics Japan
Panama Canal Authority Transportation and Logistics Panama		

Adapted from Ethisphere.com, March 2013, http://www.ethisphere.com/wme/

On the other hand are companies like Enron, which in the late 1990s exhibited a consistent and profound lack of moral and ethical judgment beginning with senior management. The problem for many frontline sales managers is that the corporate culture is the result of many things beyond their control. Specifically, senior management style (do their actions match their words?), the established culture of the organization, and external pressures (like customer dissatisfaction) can create a climate where unethical or illegal behavior is tolerated, even encouraged. At Enron, salespeople perceived that unethical behavior was acceptable because they could see that was the company culture.

Managers need to create a climate in which ethical behavior is considered the norm, not the exception. Encourage open communication so that salespeople can be honest with management without fear of negative consequences. Generate an atmosphere of mutual respect that will not tolerate discrimination of any kind. Research suggests that an ethical climate can improve salespeople's job satisfaction, organizational commitment, and willingness to stay with the company.[10]

Unfair Corporate Policies. Often managers do not make corporate policies and procedures, but they must enforce them. Company policies are developed from a variety of areas inside the organization. In matters of hiring, termination, work rules, expense reimbursement, grievance procedures, and performance appraisals, the human resources department almost always approves company policies. Its focus is not necessarily on the sales force. Sometimes policies and procedures that work fine for the rest of the organization create a problem in the sales area. For example, a company might require that employees submit business expenses once a month, but a salesperson who travels a high percentage of the time can face an unfair financial burden while waiting for reimbursement.

Managers must be flexible enough to consider the unique situation of salespeople when they enforce company policies and procedures. Most of the time salespeople operate outside the company, spending their time with customers, which makes it difficult to follow all the company rules. Good managers understand the importance of applying corporate policies in a fair manner to their sales force.

LEGAL ISSUES IN CONTEMPORARY SELLING

So far we have focused on ethical sales standards and behavior. Society also sets legal standards that define and direct the behavior of sellers and buyers. While almost every country has its own laws, our focus is on United States laws and their effect on selling.

Over the years a number of laws have been enacted at the federal, state, and local levels that either directly or indirectly influence the buyer–seller relationship. Salespeople (or managers) who violate these laws put their companies and their personal reputations at great risk.[11] As a result of recent scandals, new laws have been enacted and existing laws strengthened to mandate large financial penalties as well as jail time for people who break them.

Uniform Commercial Code: The Legal Framework for Selling

We have talked a lot already about buyers, sellers, and a host of other important concepts in a successful sales relationship. But if someone asked you the legal definition of a sale, would you be able to tell them? What are the legal obligations of the salesperson and the buyer? What is the difference between an express and an implied warranty? These are all important terms, and salespeople must understand the legal implications of what they say and do with customers.

The **Uniform Commercial Code**, the most significant set of laws affecting selling, defines these terms (as well as many more). The UCC consists of nine articles and is modified by each state. It sets out the rules and procedures for almost all business practices in the United States. The most relevant section of the UCC for selling is Article 2, titled simply "Sales." It defines terms related to selling and spells out legal obligations for buyers and sellers. Exhibit 4.5 summarizes some of the key terms in selling.

The UCC is the most fundamental legal framework for selling and influences almost all transactions, so salespeople and managers need to become familiar with it. A mistake can cost the company a lot of money and the salesperson his or her job. The salesperson has significant legal responsibilities, which can be summarized as follows:

EXHIBIT 4.5 SUMMARY OF DEFINITIONS RELEVANT TO SELLING IN THE UNIFORM COMMERCIAL CODE

As you read the definitions, some will seem amazingly simple (salesperson, buyer), while others are more complex (express and implied warranties). Each term has legal meaning, and the UCC defines literally hundreds of terms. Some of the most significant terms for selling are defined here using the language of the UCC. The section where the definition is located is also identified.

1. **Salesperson**—a person who sells or *contracts* to sell *goods* (Section 2-103).
2. **Buyer**—a person who buys or *contracts* to buy *goods* (Section 2-103).
3. **Sale**—consists in the passing of title from the seller to the *buyer* for a price (Section 2-401).
4. **Contract for sale**—includes both a present sale of goods and a *contract* to sell goods at a future time.
5. **Goods**—all things (including specially manufactured goods) that are movable at the time of identification to the *contract for sale* other than the money in which the price is to be paid, investment

securities (Article 8), and things in action. "Goods" also includes the unborn young of animals and growing crops and other identified things attached to realty, as described in the section on goods to be severed from realty (Section 2-107).

6. **Person in the position of a seller** includes as against a principal an agent who has paid or become responsible for the price of *goods* on behalf of his or her principal or anyone who otherwise holds a security interest or other right in goods similar to that of a *seller* (Section 2-707).

7. **Express warranties** by the seller are created as follows (Section 2-316):

   (1)
   - a. Any affirmation of fact or promise made by the *seller* to the *buyer* that relates to the *goods* and becomes part of the basis of the bargain creates an express warranty that the goods shall conform to the affirmation or promise.
   - b. Any description of the *goods* that is made part of the basis of the bargain creates an express warranty that the goods shall conform to the description.
   - c. Any sample or model that is made part of the basis of the bargain creates an express warranty that the whole of the *goods* shall conform to the sample or model.

   (2) It is not necessary to the creation of an express warranty that the *seller* use formal words such as "warrant" or "guarantee" or that he or she have a specific intention to make a warranty, but an affirmation merely of the value of the *goods* or a statement purporting to be merely the seller's opinion or commendation of the goods does not create a warranty.

8. **Implied Warranty**

   (1) Unless excluded or modified (Section 2-316), a warranty that the *goods* shall be merchantable is implied in a *contract* for their sale if the *seller* is a *merchant* with respect to goods of that kind. Under this section the serving for value of food or drink to be consumed either on the premises or elsewhere is a sale.

   (2) *Goods*, to be merchantable, must be at least such as

   - a. pass without objection in the trade under the *contract* description; and
   - b. in the case of fungible *goods*, are of fair average quality within the description; and
   - c. are fit for the ordinary purposes for which such goods are used; and
   - d. run, within the variations permitted by the *agreement*, of even kind, quality, and quantity within each unit and among all units involved; and
   - e. are adequately contained, packaged, and labeled as the *agreement* may require; and
   - f. conform to the promise or affirmations of fact made on the container or label, if any.

   (3) Unless excluded or modified (Section 2-316), other implied warranties may arise from course of dealing or usage of trade.

Unlawful Business Activities

In addition to the Uniform Commercial Code, a number of federal laws have been passed over the years that affect selling. The laws include, but are not limited to, the Sherman Antitrust Act, Clayton Act, and Robinson-Patman Act. State and local municipalities have also adopted similar statutes and in many cases passed new laws that directly affect selling. For example, every state has its own set of real estate laws, which influence the sale of real estate in that state.

While there are a number of unlawful activities, this section summarizes the most significant: collusion, restraint of trade, reciprocity, competitor obstruction, defamation, and price discrimination. Exhibit 4.6 provides recommendations to help management create company policies that encourage legal behavior.

EXHIBIT 4.6 SALES MANAGEMENT POLICIES TO ENCOURAGE LEGAL BEHAVIOR

1. **Training**—Give salespeople relevant, specific information on laws and company policies. Role playing is an excellent technique to help the salesperson internalize and practice how to deal with legal issues.
2. **Mentor**—As laws, regulatory guidelines, and companies polices change be sure to update salespeople.
3. **Manage**—Design reward systems that encourage legal and ethical behavior and, conversely, punish illegal or unethical behavior.
4. **Evaluate**—Conduct regular salesperson performance reviews to identify illegal or unethical behavior quickly.
5. **Role Model**—A company and sales manager that wants legal and ethical behavior from its salespeople must demonstrate that behavior.

Collusion. When competing companies get together and fix prices, divide up customers or territories, or act in a way to harm a third party (often another competitor or customer), they are engaged in collusion. One example of this kind of activity occurs when two companies fix prices to force a third competitor into an unprofitable or uncompetitive position. Any activity between two competitors that serves to lessen competition is illegal.

Restraint of Trade. It is not uncommon with today's complex distribution systems to find companies that exert powerful influence over their channel of distribution. However, it is illegal for any company to engage in restraint of trade, which is forcing a dealer or other channel member to stop carrying its competitors' products as part of its arrangement with the dealer.

Reciprocity. The practice of suppliers buying from one another is called reciprocity and is not illegal per se. A company buys from a supplier and then turns around and sells it another product or service. However, if the arrangement effectively shuts out other competitors, it is illegal and must be stopped.

Competitor Obstruction. It is illegal for salespeople or their companies to actively participate in competitor obstruction, which is the practice of impeding competitor access to a customer. For example, altering a competitor's products or marketing communications clearly interferes with the competitor's right to do business and is illegal. A good rule is: steer clear of your competitors' products when you encounter them with a customer.

Competitor Defamation. While direct competitor obstruction happens occasionally, a much more common problem for salespeople is competitor defamation. It is illegal to harm a competitor by making unfair or untrue statements about the company, its products, or the people who work for it. Unfair statements are statements that are difficult to prove (or disprove) and put the competitor at a disadvantage in the marketplace while untrue statements are deliberate falsehoods. Among the remedies open to the injured party are cease-and-desist orders, which effectively force the guilty company to stop or face several penalties. It can also take the offending party to court and pursue other remedies (financial compensation).

There are two basic types of defamation:

Slander is unfair or untrue *oral* statements (for example, a salesperson making false statements during a presentation) that materially harm the reputation of the competitor or the personal reputation of anyone working for the company.

Libel is unfair or untrue *written* statements (for example, a salesperson writing unfair statements in a letter or sales proposal) that materially harm the reputation of the competitor or the personal reputation of anyone working for the company.

Examples of statements that defame a competitor:

- "That company has not met any target delivery dates for new products in the last five years" (untrue statement about the competitor's ability to meet contractual obligations).
- "I heard they were going to lay off a lot of people due to poor sales over the last four quarters" (untrue statement about the company's financial condition).
- "You know, the salesperson for that company is not very knowledgeable about their products and services" (unfair statement about the personal qualifications of a legal representative of the company).

Not only is defamation illegal, it is also a bad idea. Disparaging the competition is bad selling and will not help build a strong customer relationship. While factual comparisons between your products and competitors' are accepted sales practice, it is always best to focus on your product rather than belittle your competition.

Price Discrimination. Put simply, it is illegal to discriminate based on price. While the original law, Robinson-Patman, focused on interstate commerce, most states have passed legislation that provides the same protection to intrastate business transactions. **Price discrimination** is the practice of giving different prices or discounts to different customers who purchase the same quality and quantity of products and services. Of course, companies are legally allowed to charge different prices if (1) they reflect differences in the cost of operations (manufacturing, sale, or delivery), (2) they meet, in good faith, competitor pricing to the same customer, or (3) they reflect differences in the quality or quantity of the product purchase. It is perfectly legal, for example, to charge a lower price to a customer who buys more (quantity discount) or has received a better price from a competitor. At the end of the day the issue is the fair treatment of customers.

A CODE OF SALES ETHICS

What are the rules that govern your life? How do you make ethical decisions? We all grow up learning a sense of right and wrong that, over time, becomes our **code of ethics**. We use our personal code to guide us in life; regrettably, situations and people that force us to either reaffirm or compromise our code of ethics often test it. As we examined the many ethical concerns and issues salespeople and managers face, you saw how difficult it can be to make the right ethical decision. Let's examine how a code of ethics can be helpful for salespeople as they face ethical issues every day.

Corporate Code of Ethics

Salespeople (indeed, all employees) make ethical decisions using two ethical frameworks: their own personal code of ethics and the company's ethical code. Not all companies have a written code of ethics, but all companies have a culture that defines acceptable and unacceptable ethical behavior.

Corporate codes of ethics are important for three reasons. First, they are—or at least should be—the framework for the company's approach to doing business. Second, by defining the company's values, corporate ethical codes can serve as a point of reference for individual employee behavior. Third, a strong corporate code of ethics can have a positive effect on customers and other organizations that interact with the company.

As we saw earlier in the chapter, companies like Dell have a code of conduct that defines what they believe and how they expect employees to conduct the company's business. A corporate code of ethics, like a personal code of ethics, does not define what to do in every possible ethical situation. Rather, it identifies certain key traits to help direct the salesperson's decision making. "We avoid even the appearance of impropriety" (see Exhibit 4.1) tells customers clearly that Dell salespeople will do the right thing in every situation. This is a powerful tool for salespeople who know the company will support them as long as they act with integrity.

Of course, it is essential that the values and behaviors spelled out in the code of ethics (or whatever it is called) are actually part of the company's corporate culture. Companies like Adelphia embraced ethics in their codes, but *key senior managers* behaved in an unethical and illegal manner anyway. Senior management, in particular, must not only "talk the talk" but "walk the walk" and actually support an ethical business climate.

Individual Code of Sales Ethics

Everyone has his or her own code of ethics, which influences the decisions that a person makes in certain situations. Unfortunately, in some cases salespeople make unethical choices. The vast majority of salespeople and managers, however, are ethical and seek direction in making the difficult decisions we have examined in this chapter.

A personal code of sales ethics can be a valuable tool for everyone in selling. It provides a framework for evaluating situations and helps individuals coordinate their own personal values system with their corporate ethics code and established guidelines for ethical sales behavior. The process begins with your own definition of what is right and wrong. Very early in life we develop a value system that is learned from our parents and reinforced by religious or moral beliefs. We also learn from our company's code of ethics and accepted business practices. Research suggests salespeople are generally more successful when their personal code of ethics is consistent with those of the company and management.[12]

It can be helpful to evaluate the current circumstances and possible decisions against a code of sales ethics. One example is from the Sales and Marketing Executives Institute (a leading professional organization for salespeople and managers). Exhibit 4.7 is the SMEI Sales and Marketing Creed. Many salespeople subscribe to this and other codes that delineate ethical conduct in selling.

It also helps to use a checklist to walk through the ethical issues. One such checklist (and there are many) is Exhibit 4.8, which allows you to quantify your ethical analysis and determine how well you have assessed the situation.

The goal of these analyses is to help each salesperson make the best ethical decision. The time to think about ethics is not in the middle of a difficult ethical situation but before you get caught up in the circumstances. This is one reason corporate and personal codes of ethics are important—they give salespeople greater confidence in their final ethical decisions.

EXHIBIT 4.7 SMEI SALES AND MARKETING CREED

Your pledge of high standards in serving your company, its customers, and free enterprise

1. I hereby acknowledge my accountability to the organization for which I work and to society as a whole to improve sales knowledge and practice and to adhere to the highest professional standards in my work and personal relationships.
2. My concept of selling includes as its basic principle the sovereignty of all consumers in the marketplace and the necessity for mutual benefit to both buyer and seller in all transactions.
3. I shall personally maintain the highest standards of ethical and professional conduct in all my business relationships with customers, suppliers, colleagues, competitors, governmental agencies, and the public.
4. I pledge to protect, support, and promote the principles of consumer choice, competition, and innovation enterprise, consistent with relevant legislative public policy standards.
5. I shall not knowingly participate in actions, agreements, or marketing policies or practices which may be detrimental to customers, competitors, or established community social or economic policies or standards.
6. I shall strive to ensure that products and services are distributed through such channels and by such methods as will tend to optimize the distributive process by offering maximum customer value and service at minimum cost while providing fair and equitable compensation for all parties.
7. I shall support efforts to increase productivity or reduce costs of production or marketing through standardization or other methods, provided these methods do not stifle innovation or creativity.
8. I believe prices should reflect true value in use of the product or service to the customer, including the pricing of goods and services transferred among operating organizations worldwide.
9. I acknowledge that providing the best economic and social product value consistent with cost also includes:

   - recognizing the customer's right to expect safe products with clear instructions for their proper use and maintenance.
   - providing easily accessible channels for customer complaints.
   - investigating any customer dissatisfaction objectively and taking prompt and appropriate remedial action.
   - recognizing and supporting proven public policy objectives such as conserving energy and protecting the environment.

10. I pledge my efforts to assure that all marketing research, advertising, and presentations of products, services, or concepts are done clearly, truthfully, and in good taste so as not to mislead or offend customers. I further pledge to assure that all these activities are conducted in accordance with the highest standards of each profession and generally accepted principles of fair competition.
11. I pledge to cooperate fully in furthering the efforts of all institutions, media, professional associations, and other organizations to publicize this creed as widely as possible throughout the world.

Source: Sales and Marketing Executives Institute website (www.smei.org), March 2013.

EXHIBIT 4.8 ETHICAL CHECKLIST

Circle the appropriate answer on the scale; 1 = not at all; 5 = totally yes

1. **Relevant Information Test.** Have I/we obtained as much information as possible to make an informed decision and action plan for this situation?	1	2	3	4	5
2. **Involvement Test.** Have I/we involved all who have a right to have input and/or to be involved in making this decision and action plan?	1	2	3	4	5
3. **Consequential Test.** Have I/we anticipated and attempted to accommodate the consequences of this decision and action plan on any who are significantly affected by it?	1	2	3	4	5
4. **Fairness Test.** If I/we were assigned to take the place of any one of the stakeholders in this situation, would I/we perceive this decision and action plan to be essentially fair, given all of the circumstances?	1	2	3	4	5
5. **Enduring Values Test.** Does this decision and action plan uphold my/our priority enduring values that are relevant to this situation?	1	2	3	4	5
6. **Universality Test.** Would I/we want this decision and action plan to become a universal law applicable to all similar situations, even to myself/ourselves?	1	2	3	4	5
7. **Light-of-Day Test.** How would I/we feel and be regarded by others (working associates, family, etc.) if the details of this decision and action plan were disclosed for all to know?	1	2	3	4	5
8. **Total Ethical Analysis Confidence Score.** Place the total of all circled numbers here.					
How confident can you be that you have done a good job of ethical analysis?					
7–14			Not very confident		
15–21			Somewhat confident		
22–28			Quite confident		
29–35			Very confident		

EXPERT ADVICE: FOLLOW-UP

After watching the video of Mr. Edmonds and reading the chapter, consider the following questions.

1. What does it mean when Mr. Edmonds says, "Customers today expect salespeople to be trusted business partners."
2. What role do you think trust does (or should) play in contemporary selling?

SUMMARY

Ethics is a core principle of successful contemporary selling. This chapter examined the ethical and legal issues of salespeople and managers. Salespeople are placed in difficult ethical situations every day, and the decisions they make affect not only themselves but their companies. Management also faces a number of ethical challenges.

The last few years have brought a new focus on the importance of ethical behavior and decision making. As a result of recent scandals, salespeople and, by extension, their managers confront customers who demand integrity and honesty and evaluate their suppliers on their business practices. There is also a growing emphasis on demonstrating social responsibility in the community (whether it is the local, national, or even global community). Companies understand that being ethical also means being a good corporate citizen.

Salespeople face two fundamental ethical arenas. First, they encounter a number of ethical challenges with their customers: dishonesty; gifts, entertainment, and bribes; unfair treatment; and confidentiality leaks. Dishonesty should never be an accepted business practice, and salespeople will find it impossible to have a strong relationship with any customer after engaging in dishonest behavior. It is appropriate to offer small tokens of appreciation and take customers to business lunches; however, at some point gifts and entertainment cross a line and become unethical and even illegal. Not all customers are equal, but it is unethical to provide unfair or unwarranted treatment to customers. Some customers demand unfair service as part of the terms of business. In these situations, their companies must support salespeople. Finally, in light of today's complex selling relationships, salespeople need to maintain the confidentiality of their customers. There is no better way to destroy a good customer relationship than to betray a confidence.

A second area of ethical issues for salespeople involves their employer. There are three basic issues a salesperson needs to be aware of: cheating, misuse of company resources, and inappropriate relationships with other employees. Cheating (as in giving false information) as it relates to employers is grounds for dismissal and never tolerated in any company. Likewise, misusing company resources (as in misrepresenting expenses) is unethical. In effect, it's stealing from the company—no matter how unfair company policies may be. Finally, the highly interactive nature of selling puts salespeople in contact with many co-workers and customers. Developing inappropriate relationships is dangerous and not in the salesperson's or the company's best interests.

Management must also deal with three areas of ethical concern: salespeople, company policies, and international ethics. Management should avoid putting too much pressure on salespeople to hit sales targets, which can create a climate that encourages or at least condones unethical behavior. Just as companies expect their salespeople to be honest, it is unethical for management to practice deception on salespeople. Finally, salespeople deserve certain rights in working with management. The company should follow established policies for termination and performance appraisals and create an environment free from discrimination. Managers who violate company policies in working with salespeople are behaving unethically.

All companies have a **business climate** or culture, which is a set of unwritten rules and policies that influence salespeople's behavior. Management should create a climate that encourages salespeople to make ethical decisions. It should also create (when possible) and enforce fairly company policies and procedures that directly affect the sales force. It is wrong to punish salespeople with company policies that do not consider the unique aspects of their job (such as having to wait for expense reimbursement).

In addition to ethics, laws at the local, state, and federal level define and place limits on sales activities. The most fundamental set of laws affecting sales is the Uniform Commercial Code which legally defines business practices in the United States and, more specifically, the responsibilities of a salesperson. Illegal business activities include collusion, restraint of trade, reciprocity, competitor obstruction, competitor defamation, and price discrimination.

A code of ethics can be a useful tool in helping salespeople work through difficult ethical situations. Most salespeople use two codes in making ethical decisions. A personal code of ethics is their own definition of right and wrong. The company's code of ethics defines conduct for all employees in the organization.

KEY TERMS

business ethics	bribe	collusion	slander
social responsibility	confidentiality	restraint of trade	libel
dishonesty	sales pressure	reciprocity	price discrimination
caveat emptor	deception	competitor obstruction	code of ethics
gift	Uniform Commercial Code	competitor defamation	business climate

ROLE PLAY

BEFORE YOU BEGIN

Before getting started, please go to the Appendix of chapter 1 to review the profiles of the characters involved in this role play, as well as the tips on preparing a role play.

Characters Involved

Chloe Herndon
Lenny Twiggle

Lenny is the new head buyer at Buster's Supermarkets, a chain of 20 stores that is one of Chloe's top five accounts. Before Lenny started at Buster's, Chloe had called on former head buyer Edith Greer there for about eight years (three representing Upland Company and five representing a competitor of Upland's) and had an outstanding professional relationship with Edith and Buster's. Edith left to take a position with another supermarket chain out of state.

Setting the Stage

While meeting with another account this morning, Chloe received a voice mail from Lenny Twiggle, the head buyer at Buster's Supermarkets, asking her to stop by there to see him at 4:30 p.m. today. Lenny has been on the job for about three months. Chloe has made four calls on him during that time and has been generally pleased with the business she has received from the account. It is a little unusual for his office to summon her in between regular appointments and very unusual for Lenny to call personally instead of his assistant. When she calls back to confirm that she can make it, she attempts to find out the agenda for the meeting. But Lenny just says, "We'll talk when you get here." Puzzled but not concerned, Chloe heads for Lenny's office.

Lenny closes the door and says, "Chloe, I have been pleased with your service and with Upland so far. I want to give you a chance to really perform. What I need are some special concessions from you. If you can get me what I want, I will increase your orders next quarter 20 percent over last year."

Chloe Herndon's Role

Chloe has been in her job for three years. Before that she worked for a competitor for five years. She has had buyers ask for all sorts of inappropriate things during her career. Tempting as Lenny's offer might be, she knows she cannot succumb to the temptation, as his expectations of special favors will only escalate over time and eventually she (and Upland Company) will be the big loser. She must formulate a response right now that lets him know where she stands on this sort of thing but also lets him know she wants to do business with him legitimately.

Lenny Twiggle's Role

Lenny is looking for a variety of what he calls "special concessions": gifts, entertainment, extra merchandise for free, unauthorized lower prices—even a dinner date with Chloe if he can get it (he's single). Basically, he is trying to see how far he can push her to give him things that enhance his professional position with Buster's as well as his personal situation. He is quite insistent and proposes several ideas for how she might meet his request. He will back down only when he understands that losing Upland Company as a vendor would severely impair his performance as perceived by management.

Assignment

Work with another student to develop a 7–10 minute dialogue on the issues that might occur in Lenny's office. Chloe must be firm in her unwillingness to behave unethically but at the same time keep her reasons for not doing what he asks on a professional (not personal) level. Lenny should start out nearly contemptuous in attitude, but if Chloe does a good job fending off his various requests he should end up agreeing to the value of continuing to do a healthy legitimate business with Upland.

DISCUSSION QUESTIONS

1. Much has been made of the scandals at Enron and other large companies. What effect do you think these scandals have had on the salespeople who work for these companies? Do you think it makes their jobs easier or harder? Why?

2. Companies talk a lot about being socially responsible. What do you think that means for a company like General Electric or IBM? As a salesperson, would you incorporate your company's social responsibility into your presentation. If so, how?

3. The chapter talks about the business practice of "caveat emptor," or "let the buyer beware." Do you think this philosophy is consistent with contemporary selling? Why or why not?

4. As a sales manager, how would you handle this situation? One of your salespeople (not a top performer but one who consistently comes close to hitting sales objectives) has turned in a receipt for a very expensive dinner with a client that is above the company's stated guidelines for customer entertainment expenses. When questioned, the sales rep says the customer is thinking of giving the company a large order and the salesperson was looking to close the deal. However, it's been three weeks and there's no

contract. Other salespeople have heard about the dinner and are questioning why this employee was allowed to spend that much entertaining the customer. What do you do?

5. A large customer has just told you it expects to introduce a new product over the next 45 to 60 days. This product will definitely enhance this customer's position in the market. Your company also sells to this customer's major competitors. While you have none of these companies as customers, this information would be helpful for salespeople working with these other companies. Should you share with them?

6. As part of a mid-year cost reduction effort, your company has reduced your bonus for achieving annual sales targets. This is widely perceived as unfair; even your manager declares the company should not have instituted this policy. At the same time, the company has a very flexible expense reimbursement policy that allows salespeople to claim mileage. Historically, you have been very conservative in submitting mileage for reimbursement. However, talking with a group of sales colleagues the other night, you heard that several of them are going to start inflating the mileage to their expense reports, since the company has unfairly cut their bonuses. What will you do?

7. You are a district sales manager for a high-tech company selling IT services in the Southeast. Sales have been down in the last year and senior management is putting significant pressure on you to hit the sales targets for the rest of the year. Your superior, the Eastern Regional Manager, implied that if the Southeast does not achieve sales numbers, your job may be in jeopardy. How will you deal with this pressure from management? What kind of pressure will you apply to your sales force?

8. You are head of sales for a large company with operations around the country. The top-performing saleswoman in your western region has come to you with a sexual harassment complaint. She says her immediate boss, a 20-year veteran with the company who is well liked and in line for a promotion to regional vice president, has made improper comments and touched her inappropriately. He denies everything and says she is upset because her performance has been slipping over the last two years. What do you do?

9. How would you create an ethical business climate?

10. You travel a lot for your company and fly at least twice a month, accumulating thousands of frequent flyer miles with your airline of choice. Is it ethical to keep the miles even though you earned them traveling on business for your company?

11. As a sales manager, how would you educate your sales force about the Uniform Commercial Code? Go to www.law.cornell.edu/ucc and review the UCC. What topics do you think are most relevant for salespeople?

12. A salesperson is giving a sales presentation to a customer purchase committee. At the end, the Head of Purchasing looks at her and asks, "You know our specific requirements. Can your product do the job?" The salesperson responds, "Yes." Has she just offered an implied warranty?

13. What policies and procedures can a company use to discourage salespeople from discriminating on price with certain customers? As a manager, how would you deal with the problem of price discrimination?

14. Develop a personal code of sales ethics using the ethical checklist in Exhibit 4.8 as a guide.

MINI-CASE 4 HEALTH SENSE PHARMACEUTICALS

Karen Simmons awoke early one cold winter morning because she had almost 70 miles to drive to begin her day as a pharmaceutical sales representative with Health Sense Pharmaceuticals. Karen knew the trip might take a little longer that day because the forecast called for about three inches of snow and a high temperature of 35 degrees, the ideal conditions for a very sloppy day. Even though most of the trip was on the interstate highway, Karen didn't want the snow to make her late for any of her 10 appointments scheduled that day. Karen has worked for Health Sense for almost three years and enjoyed much success during that time—often outselling more senior representatives in nearby territories. She attributes her success to dedication and the desire to "give the company a full day's work for a full day's pay." As Karen looked out her bedroom window, she realized that, for once, the weatherman had gotten it right.

After making all of her sales calls for the day, Karen attended a social gathering sponsored by the local chapter of Sales Representatives International (a worldwide trade association dedicated to the advancement of the sales profession). There she ran into Mike Johnson and Lisa Wright, two Health Sense Pharmaceuticals reps with territories that border Karen's.

MIKE: Hi, Karen. How's it going?

KAREN: Pretty good. Today's weather was kind of bad, wasn't it? I had to go all the way up to the northern end of my territory, and you know how people drive in the snow.

MIKE: I wouldn't know. I downloaded this really cool golf game for my iPad over the weekend, so when I saw today's weather I decided to play golf! I did a little paperwork this afternoon but the golf game works really well. I guess I'll have to make up a few calls on doctors just to fill my day.

LISA: Why does it always have to snow or rain on Mondays? When I saw that snow I decided to go to the mall—at least it's indoors. I did make it to my 2:00 appointment though, because I had been trying to get in to see that doctor for quite a while.

KAREN: Well, you two had interesting days. Hey, there's Dave. I think I'll go say hi. You both take care and I'll see you at the next meeting.

Dave is a sales rep for Midtown Copiers. Karen met him in a doctor's office two weeks ago while they were both waiting to see the same doctor—Karen to discuss pharmaceuticals and Dave to sell the doctor a new copy machine for his practice.

DAVE: Hi, Karen. How's business?

KAREN: Pretty good. I had a good day today. You know, customers seem to really appreciate you making the effort to keep your appointments in bad weather. Did you ever get that doctor to buy a new copy machine? I've been hearing the office workers complaining about the copier.

DAVE: Well, the office workers may be complaining, but that doctor didn't think he needed a new copier. In fact, he still thought his copier was under warranty and that the manufacturer could fix any problems.

KAREN: So, was the copier still under warranty?

DAVE: Yeah, I think so. That manufacturer offers five-year warranties and the machine in that office is only four years old. However, the nice thing is that he doesn't have the invoice any longer and the dealer for that machine is out of business now. I was able to convince him that, without a local dealer, he wouldn't be able to get service—even though the manufacturer maintains a service center 50 miles away in Springfield.

KAREN: I guess you sold him a new copier, then?

DAVE: I sure did, but the nice thing is that I got him to hold off on placing the order until this week. That way the order will count toward a sales contest our firm is holding over the next two months. Waiting until March to place the order will put me on the path to winning a trip to Cancun, Mexico.

KAREN: Well, good luck with that, Dave.

DAVE: Hasta la vista, Karen.

Questions

1. Discuss the ethical situation faced by Mike and Lisa. What did they do that was unethical? Pretend that you are the manager of Mike, Lisa, and Karen. How could you find out if Mike and Lisa acted unethically? What would you do about it?

2. What do you think of Dave's behavior in selling the doctor a new copier? Did Dave act unethically at all? If you believe that Dave acted unethically, how did he do so and what should his manager do about it? Finally, how will Dave's actions affect his relationship with this doctor?

Sales Management

Salesperson Motivation

Selling Processes

Compensating & Evaluating Salespeople

Prospecting & Sales Call Planning

Communicating the Sales Message

Salesperson Self-Management

Technology

Building Relationships ~ Creating Value

Understanding Sellers & Buyers

Ethics

Closing & Follow-up

Negotiating for Win-Win Solutions

Selecting & Training Salespeople

CRM and Sales Technologies

LEARNING OBJECTIVES

This chapter begins by providing a discussion of important issues related to Customer Relationship Management (CRM). CRM is much more than merely a technology application, as you will learn. In fact, in many ways CRM is a key enabler of sales organizations to build relationships and create value with customers. You will also learn about a wide variety of sales technologies and how they can enhance contemporary selling. Gaining a grounding in these technology issues now will be very useful for you as we cover the various elements of the sales process and its management in Parts Two and Three of the book.

After reading this chapter, you should be able to:

- Understand and identify the key components and goals of CRM.
- Explain the CRM process cycle.
- Outline the history and progression of modern sales technology and its impact on selling and the sales role.
- Become familiar with the various types of contemporary sales technology and their application.

EXPERT ADVICE

EXPERT: Mr. Gerhard Gschwandtner
Founder and Publisher, *Selling Power* magazine

TOPIC: Technology as a change driver.

SUMMARY: Mr. Gschwandtner makes the case that when you look at the global business environment there are two key change factors: number one is technology and number two is entrepreneurism. Together, these drivers have changed the face of business generally and the salesperson/customer relationship specifically. The business creation cycle has been accelerated tremendously. To be competitive today, it's not a matter of *whether* a sales organization embraces and utilizes technology to improve productivity and effectiveness; rather, the issue is *how well* they use the technology versus competition.

NEXT STEPS: Go to the website for *Contemporary Selling* (www.routledge.com/cw/Johnston), watch the chapter 5 video, and then read the chapter. You will find an Expert Advice follow-up at the end of the chapter with questions that connect elements of your learning.

WHAT IS CUSTOMER RELATIONSHIP MANAGEMENT (CRM)?

For many years, introductory marketing textbooks have talked about the marketing concept as an over-arching business philosophy. At its essence, companies practicing the marketing concept turn to consumers themselves for input in making strategic decisions about what products to market, where to market the products and how to get them to market, at what price, and how to communicate with consumers about the products. These four elements (product, distribution, price, and promotion) are referred to as the marketing mix. The elements of the marketing mix represent the "toolkit" marketers use to develop marketing strategy. Personal selling fits into the marketing mix as part of a firm's marketing communication mix, or promotion mix, along with the other elements of the promotional approach used by a firm to communicate with customers: advertising, sales promotion, direct marketing, and public relations and publicity.

The operationalization or implementation of the marketing concept is known as a **market orientation**. That is, the actions taken by a firm that is market-oriented would be focused on aligning all the various organizational processes and functions toward maximizing the firm's success in the competitive marketplace.[1] Not surprisingly, a successful market orientation requires that the firm place the customer in the center of all strategic decisions and firm activities. Thus, a key component of market orientation is exhibiting a customer orientation in all levels and units of an organization, which we discussed in chapter 1. Considerable research indicates that firms with a higher level of customer orientation are usually more successful than less customer-oriented firms. Firms high in customer orientation are often referred to as customer-centric, because they have the customer at the center of their business model. Expanding this dialogue a bit, from a selling function perspective a customer-centric culture includes, but is not limited to, the following major components:[2]

1. Adopting a relationship or partnership business model, with mutually shared rewards and risk management.
2. Defining the selling role in terms of the provision of customer business consultation and solutions.
3. Increasing formalization of customer analysis processes and agreements.
4. Taking a proactive leadership role in educating customers about value chain and cost reduction opportunities.
5. Focusing on continuous improvement principles stressing customer satisfaction and loyalty.

The efforts a firm makes toward cultivating a culture that is market-oriented and customer-centric require a high degree of **formalization** within the firm. Formalization means that structure, processes and tools, and managerial knowledge and commitment are formally established in support of the culture. With these things in place, strategies and programs may be successfully developed and executed toward the goals related to customer centricity. In general, these goals center on establishing and maintaining long-term customer relationships. Today, the most prevalent formalization of a customer-centric culture is customer relationship management (CRM). CRM is a comprehensive business model for increasing revenues and profits by focusing on customers. More specifically, CRM refers to "any application or initiative designed to help your company optimize interactions with customers, suppliers, or prospects via one or more touchpoints—such as a call center, salesperson, distributor, store, branch office, Web, or e-mail—for the purpose of acquiring, retaining, or cross-selling customers."[3]

PricewaterhouseCoopers Consulting has defined CRM as "a journey of strategic, process, organizational, and technical change whereby a company seeks to better manage its enterprise around customer behaviors. This entails acquiring knowledge about customers and deploying this information at each touchpoint to attain increased revenue and operational efficiencies."[4] Touchpoints are viewed as the intersection of a business event that takes place via a channel using a medium (e.g., online inquiry from a prospect, telephone follow-up with a purchaser on a service issue, face-to-face encounter with a salesperson, etc.). At their essence, touchpoints are where the selling firm touches the customer in some way, thus allowing for information about customers to be collected.

Our discussion of CRM so far leads one to conclude that it is both an overarching philosophy of business that puts the customer at the center of strategic decision making (i.e., a customer-centric enterprise) and a programmatic, integrated implementation system (i.e., software-driven) involving a variety of channels and providers, all of which interact to contribute to the delivery of customer value. Most companies are now adopting CRM as a mission-critical business strategy and are redesigning internal and external business processes and associated information systems to make it easier for customers to do business with them. Because the focus of CRM is aligning the organization's internal and external systems to be customer-centric, marketing as a discipline becomes a core contributor to the success of CRM by virtue of its expertise on customers. Specifically, the sales force is a group within most firms that can add substantial value to the success of this process.

Many of the concepts underlying CRM are not at all new. One might open a principles of marketing textbook from 20 years ago and find a discussion of many of the tenets of what we now refer to as CRM, albeit not particularly integrated or cross-functional in scope. What has changed in the environment to allow for the more integrated approach to customers represented by modern CRM is *technology*. More sophisticated approaches to data management are a key enabler of CRM. Yet, it is a serious mistake to consider CRM as mere software. In fact, some firms have struggled with their CRM initiatives precisely because they have bought the sophisticated software but do not have the culture, structure, leadership, or internal technical expertise to make the initiative successful.

The next section provides a foundation for better understanding the concept of CRM. Then, in the remainder of the chapter we expand our discussion of sales technologies in general.

From Mass Marketing to One-to-One Marketing

CRM has its evolutionary roots in the progression of marketing, as enabled by advancing technology. Exhibit 5.1 illustrates this evolution from mass marketing, through target marketing, to customer marketing, to one-to-one marketing.

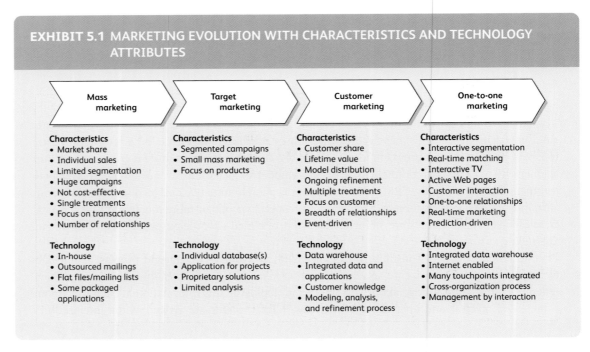

EXHIBIT 5.1 MARKETING EVOLUTION WITH CHARACTERISTICS AND TECHNOLOGY ATTRIBUTES

Mass marketing	Target marketing	Customer marketing	One-to-one marketing
Characteristics • Market share • Individual sales • Limited segmentation • Huge campaigns • Not cost-effective • Single treatments • Focus on transactions • Number of relationships	**Characteristics** • Segmented campaigns • Small mass marketing • Focus on products	**Characteristics** • Customer share • Lifetime value • Model distribution • Ongoing refinement • Multiple treatments • Focus on customer • Breadth of relationships • Event-driven	**Characteristics** • Interactive segmentation • Real-time matching • Interactive TV • Active Web pages • Customer interaction • One-to-one relationships • Real-time marketing • Prediction-driven
Technology • In-house • Outsourced mailings • Flat files/mailing lists • Some packaged applications	**Technology** • Individual database(s) • Application for projects • Proprietary solutions • Limited analysis	**Technology** • Data warehouse • Integrated data and applications • Customer knowledge • Modeling, analysis, and refinement process	**Technology** • Integrated data warehouse • Internet enabled • Many touchpoints integrated • Cross-organization process • Management by interaction

Source: Swift, Ronald S., *Accelerating Customer Relationships: Using CRM and Relationship Technologies,* 1st Edition, © 2001. Printed and Electronically reproduced by permission of Pearson Education, Inc., Upper Saddle River, New Jersey.

Mass marketing evolved in the early 1900s and dominated marketing management and strategy for decades. In the 1960s, many firms began to apply principles of segmentation, *target marketing*, and positioning to create different strategies and marketing programs for different consumer groups. A major change in mindset precipitates a shift from targeted consumer marketing (i.e., marketing to big groups of like-minded buyers) to *customer marketing*, or a focus on developing relationships with individuals customers. This approach first gained widespread attention in the 1980s. Many of the issues on relationship selling and strategic partnering discussed earlier in the book relate to customer marketing. Ultimately, the sophistication and multiplicity of available technology today enable true *one-to-one marketing*, as some firms are now able to truly customize offerings for individual users. This concept has been introduced and expanded on in several books by Don Peppers and Martha Rogers.[5]

As mentioned earlier, CRM enters the picture as a process that provides internal formalization for enabling successful customer marketing and one-to-one marketing. CRM has three major objectives:

1. *Customer retention.* The ability to retain loyal and profitable customers and channels to grow the business profitably.
2. *Customer acquisition.* Acquisition of the right customers, based on known or learned characteristics, which drive growth and increased margins.
3. *Customer profitability.* Increased individual customer margins, while offering the right products at the right time.[6]

Thus, a key realization is that CRM involves the process of acquiring, retaining, and growing profitable customers—consistent with a relationship selling approach. And consistent with our discussion of value in chapter 3, CRM requires a clear focus on the service attributes that represent value to the customer and that create loyalty. Simply put, **customer value** means that when the customer weighs the costs (monetary and otherwise) of a relationship with a seller, the benefits realized from that relationship outweigh the costs. Building customer loyalty is an important goal of CRM processes because loyal customers are typically highly satisfied with the relationship and the product offering and are very unlikely to switch to another company and its products or brands.

CRM has several advantages over traditional mass media marketing, as has been typically used in support of mass marketing and target marketing. The advantages are that CRM:

- Reduces advertising costs.
- Makes it easier to target specific customers by focusing on their needs.
- Makes it easier to track the effectiveness of a given promotional (marketing communications) campaign.
- Allows organizations to compete for customers based on service, not prices.
- Prevents overspending on low-value clients or underspending on high-value ones.
- Speeds the time it takes to develop and market a product (the marketing cycle).
- Improves use of the customer channel, thus making the most of each contact with a customer.[7]

One of the most important concepts in CRM is that of the lifetime value of a customer. In his books on customer loyalty, Fredrick Reichheld has demonstrated time and again that investment in CRM yields more successful long-term relationships with customers and that these relationships pay off handsomely in terms of cost savings, revenue growth, profits, referrals, and other important business success factors. It is possible to actually calculate an estimate of the projected financial returns from a customer, providing a very useful strategic tool for deciding which customers deserve what levels of investment of various resources (money, people, time, information, etc.). Such analysis has raised the prospects of firing a customer who exhibits a low predicted lifetime value and investing resources elsewhere. Of course, such action assumes other, more attractive customers exist for one's investment.[8]

CRM Process Cycle

The process cycle for CRM may be broken down into the following four elements: (1) knowledge discovery, (2) market planning, (3) customer interaction, and (4) analysis and refinement[9] (see Exhibit 5.2).

EXHIBIT 5.2 CRM PROCESS CYCLE

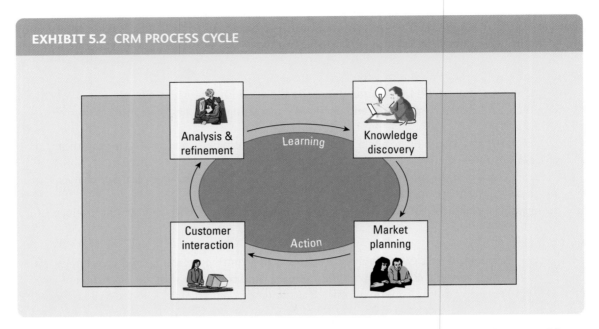

Source: Swift, Ronald S., *Accelerating Customer Relationships: Using CRM and Relationship Technologies,*, 1st Edition, © 2001. Printed and Electronically reproduced by permission of Pearson Education, Inc., Upper Saddle River, New Jersey.

Knowledge Discovery. This is the process of analyzing the customer information acquired through the touchpoints mentioned earlier. These might include point-of-sale systems, call center files, Internet accesses, records from direct sales, and any other customer contact experiences. A customer-centric **data warehouse** environment is the optimal approach to handling the data and transforming them into useful information for customer strategy development. A data warehouse environment affords the opportunity to combine large amounts of information and then use **data mining** techniques to learn more about current and potential customers. A variety of software products are available to help manage the knowledge discovery phase.

Market Planning. This is a key use of the output of the knowledge and discovery phase, in that marketing and customer strategies and programs are now developed. These involve the use of the marketing mix and especially the promotion mix in integrated ways. This process will be discussed in detail later in the chapter.

Customer Interaction. This phase represents the actual implementation of the strategies and programs, including the personal selling effort as well as all other customer-directed interactions. These must be aimed at all the customer touchpoints, or channels of customer contact, both in person and electronically.

Analysis and Refinement. Finally, the analysis and refinement phase of the CRM process is where learning takes place based on customer response to the implemented strategies and programs. This is a continuous dialogue with customers that is facilitated by all of the inputs for customer feedback. Over time, adjustments made to the firm's overall customer initiatives should yield more and more efficient investment of resources in the endeavor such that return on customer investment is maximized.

Toward a Relationship-Based Enterprise

As stated earlier, CRM represents both an overarching business philosophy and a process or tool to facilitate a truly customer-driven enterprise. Facilitating long-term, win-win relationships between buyer and seller firms is a central tenet of CRM. In order to move toward being a relationship-based enterprise, and to improve the effectiveness of CRM initiatives, ten critical questions must be answered.[10] These questions may be grouped into the following categories: customers, the relationship, and managerial decision making.

Customers

1. Who are our customers?
2. What do our customers want and expect?
3. What is the value potential of our customers?

The Relationship

4. What kind of relationship do we want to build with our customers?
5. How do we foster exchange?
6. How do we work together and share control?

Managerial Decision Making

7. Who are we?
8. How do we organize to move value closer to our customers?
9. How do we measure and manage our performance?
10. How do we increase our capacity for change?

Gaining satisfactory answers to these questions is fundamental to the success of CRM and to becoming a relationship-based firm. The answers guide (1) the evolution of the firm's relationships with customers, (2) the creation of a companywide relationship management game plan, and (3) the selection of solutions with the most appropriate combination and application of supporting technology.[11]

Given the promise of CRM, it is unfortunate that we must report a high failure and abandonment rate for CRM initiatives. Ethical Dilemma poses insights and challenges reasons why CRM fails.

THE TECHNOLOGY OF SELLING

One reason why this is a great time to be in a professional selling job is that salespeople today have an incredible number of choices and options when it comes to technology tools. Just like with everyday consumers, sometimes the array of possibilities can become overwhelming. Our strategic partner on this book, Chally Group Worldwide, has studied the use of technology in sales organizations extensively over the past 20 years, involving over 80,000 B2B customers and 7,300 sales forces. Their definitive conclusion based on this data is that the right technology, effectively executed, can add substantial value to customers and strengthen the salesperson–customer relationship. They are convinced—as are we—that sales force technology can and should be an outstanding source of competitive advantage in the business world today.[12]

An important clarification at this point requires addressing the basic question "What is technology?" Technology is the making, usage, and knowledge of tools, techniques, crafts, systems, or methods of organization in order to solve a problem or serve some purpose. Technologies significantly affect humans' ability to *control and adapt to their environments* and may include simple tools, such as a crowbar or wooden spoon, or more complex machines, such as a space station or particle accelerator. Tools and machines need not be

ETHICAL DILEMMA

IT'S THE MANAGEMENT, STUPID!

Here's a mantra worth repeating: *CRM software isn't stupid.* Nor is it inherently evil. People are stupid (or they can be)—especially the "sales management" kind of people. Problems leading to CRM misapplications and failures often are traced to organizational, not software, issues. The main reason that CRM is not successful is low user acceptance and utilization—in our case, the key user of interest is the sales force. This low acceptance level by those utilizing the system is mainly not a result of technical issues but rather the following organizational issues:

1. Disruption of established customer routines.
2. The perception that the software is intended as a micromanagement tool by sales management.
3. Differences in the expectations between salespeople and sales management as to what the system can do.
4. Perceived lack of management support for the system.
5. Disconnects between the salesperson's reward structure and any motivation for them to support the CRM system.

Managing these factors correctly provides a much higher chance of success. Salespeople must be involved in the CRM implementation process so that their own interests (and this means maximizing both success with customers and salesperson compensation) can be fully integrated with the new software.

From an ethical perspective, throwing a salesperson into the CRM creek and hoping he or she will swim is beyond unprofessional—it's simply unethical. Sales management must realize that salespeople require thorough training and clear communication regarding the expected benefits and pitfalls of the system. Turning a salesperson loose with CRM and no training or supervision is tantamount to a license to ruin customer relationships—especially in the touchy areas of data collection from clients and privacy violations in outbound communication to those clients. Only when sales managers and their salespeople work *together* to deploy CRM can a firm be assured that important professional and ethical lines between sales organization and customer are not crossed.

Questions to Consider

1. What aspects of the CRM Process Cycle are most relevant to salespeople, and where is the most potential to cross over ethical lines with customers?
2. From a customer's perspective, what would be the greatest concerns from a privacy/security perspective about involvement in a sales firm's CRM system?
3. Inside the sales organization, what are the most important steps a sales manager can take to ensure that salespeople never misuse or abuse a customer's relationship and trust through aspects of CRM?

material—virtual technology, such as computer software and business methods, also fall under this definition of technology. When combined with another term, such as "medical technology," "space technology," or "sales force technology," it refers to the state of the respective field's knowledge and tools.[13] As you see in Exhibit 5.3, the key outcome of technology implementation is control and adaptation to the relevant environment—be it in medicine, space, or (in the case of our focus) sales.

EXHIBIT 5.3 SUMMARY OF SALESPERSON ROLE DEVELOPMENT IN RESPONSE TO TECHNOLOGY

Salesperson role	Primary period of growth	What the role changed	New skills required	Key technologies
Mobile market developer	1850s–1920s	Expanded customer base by broadening geographic reach	Travel, territorial and route planning	• Railroad • Automobile
Long distance communicator	1850s–1910s	Allowed for customer communication that did not restrict buyer and seller to being in the same physical location.	Long distance communication	• Telegraph • Addressing machines • Telephone
Dynamic presenter	1850s–1970s	Enhanced buyer–seller interaction through use of audiovisual aids in sales presentations	Dynamic sales presentations and demonstrations	• Photography • Slide projection • 3D visual aids • Motion pictures • Audio/visual machines
Market intelligence gatherer	1910s–1950s	Provided timely feedback from salespeople to headquarters management about market changes	Customer and competitor analyses	• Telephone • Dictation machines • Tape recorders • Photocopiers
Prompt service provider	1950s–1980s	Strengthened customer service and satisfaction by reducing service response time and increasing communication between salespeople and customers	Prompt customer service and continual follow-up for fuller customer satisfaction	• Telephone recorders • Pagers and beepers • Mobile communication • Facsimiles • Computers

Source: Paul Christ and Rolph Anderson, "The Impact of Technology on Evolving Roles of Salespeople," *Journal of Historical Research in Marketing* 3 (February 2011), pp. 173–93.

Technology impacts most all areas of the salesperson and sales manager role, and the topics represented by all the chapters that follow in Parts Two and Three of the book have strong linkages to technology. Thus, it is important to set the stage now by providing an overview of sales force technology. We begin by providing a historical perspective, ultimately building a case that sales organizations and the sales role are literally being revolutionized by the capabilities that technologies such as social media, tablets, and smartphones (to name just a few) offer. Fortunately, based on the book's partnership with Chally Group Worldwide, we are able to share with you some of their key research findings on selling in the Internet era in a special feature box later in the chapter.

A Peek at Historical Sales Technology

Contemporary selling firms and their managers have always employed a wide array of devices and tools to carry out their jobs. While today we take quite advanced technologies for granted, the truth is that the sales role and especially a firm's relationship with its customers have evolved right along with technology. There are five historical salesperson roles that have been impacted and changed through the technology evolution, identified in Exhibit 5.3 as mobile market developer, long distance communicator, dynamic presenter, market intelligence gatherer, and prompt service provider.[14] Exhibit 5.3 shows how each role changed and what new skills were required, and provides examples of technologies that facilitated salesperson success in each of the role categories over time. Notice that many of even the older technologies have not completely disappeared—advancing technology sometimes displaces old ways but sometimes it simply adds additional choices to the toolkit.

The historical portrayal in Exhibit 5.3 stops with the 1980s, corresponding to the proliferation of personal computers—a technological development that was a game changer for sales organizations.

Global Connection points out an interesting and somewhat anti-cyclical recent development in personal computing driven largely by needs in emerging markets.

GLOBAL CONNECTION

PRICE OR POWER IN SALESPERSON COMPUTERS?

In the past, the main focus of the portable computer industry has been constant product upgrades to maximize performance (and drive new revenue, as customers feel they have to have the latest and fastest). Apple epitomizes this quest, with its rapid and seemingly endless stream of newer, faster, cooler, must-have devices. Sales organizations and their salespeople are no different from the general public and they typically want the latest, most powerful computing device in the smallest package.

But recently a very interesting reversal in this trend has begun to develop that is recasting "bang for the buck" as a winner over "smaller/faster" for firm-issued computers for salespeople. No doubt, the recent economic downturn contributed to this change, but it is perhaps even more attributable to the proliferation of salespeople in the global emerging marketplace, which, not surprisingly, tends to count its costs carefully. The net is that more firms around the world are definitely taking price into the equation and opting for low-cost, small, and lightweight netbooks over more trendy devices. Yes, netbooks—not exactly a new version of a portable, and certainly not as sexy as an iPad!

The cost of a fairly standard netbook, compared to the latest iPad with all the bells and whistles, can be many hundreds of dollars different. These devices use cheaper components, do not give the level of performance of full laptops, and do not match the light weight and elegance of an iPad or other tablet, but their excellent balance of portability and cost-effectiveness are winning over financially frugal sales organizations around the world at an increasing rate.

This also is a reversal of the often-commented-on "Moore's Law," which states that every 18 months double the computing power can be produced at the same price. This effect led to the ever-increasing power of computers—and the concurrent ever-increasing prices. Now, however, perhaps because the incremental value of power and elegance has reached a threshold of diminishing returns, more sales organizations are less concerned about power and want the price to be the variable that is reduced in the Moore's Law equation.

Most of the major portable computer manufacturers hopped on this "anti-cyclical" band wagon and are aggressively marketing these stripped down models to this emerging new target market. Acer, Dell, HP, Lenovo, Samsung, and Toshiba, among others, have all ramped up production and marketing of their network product line. In fact, Apple appears to be just about the only player in portable computing that has chosen to stay with a purely high-priced strategy. Apple may be concerned that coming out with a cheap netbook computer might sully its brand. But the downside of Apple's lack of a streamlined entry is that—especially on the global stage and more particularly in emerging markets—its market share in B2B sales organizations is basically nil.

Questions to Consider

1. Go online to any retailer that sells portable computers and review their current line and prices for the various brands of netbooks. Considering the entire bundle of functionality you get for the money, do you agree they are a good choice for salespeople? Why or why not? Are there any features missing that you believe are essential and, if so, what are they?
2. If you were issued one of the low-priced netbooks as your official company computer, would you be satisfied? Do you agree that the extra elegance and style of the iPad would be worth your firm's investment instead? Why or why not?
3. Do you agree with Apple's strategy of staying out of the low-priced netbook market? Why or why not?

Naturally we are much more interested in the role of sales technology today and going forward as opposed to technology of the past. The young generation of organizational sellers and buyers that comprise an ever-increasing portion of B2B relationships today can scarcely imagine what life must have been like doing business with such basic sales technology tools. Can you envision that, prior to basic cell phones, traveling salespeople had to stop at gas stations to use pay phones between sales calls? But remember that there are plenty of folks from that generation of salespeople (and their buyers) still in the field—a salesperson starting out in the late 1970s would be in his or her mid-fifties today and quite likely is in sales management by now!

Post-1980, Exhibit 5.4 identifies three evolutionary decades of more advanced sales technology: Origin, Formative, and Relationship. Several exemplar technologies are shown that became particularly relevant during each decade, and almost all of these technologies continue to be used to one degree or another by sales organizations. We believe the present decade (2010s—Informational) decade represents a true *revolution* in selling (rather than an evolutionary process, as before) because many of the current technology tools have resulted in extreme changes in how business is carried out. That is, the potential seems high that driving new opportunities through social media and related technology will permanently redefine certain aspects of selling and what a customer relationship actually means. If nothing else, these technologies have forever opened the flood gates for instantaneous, real-time, and fully participative communication between sellers and buyers as well as between both parties and anybody else that wants to be either party's Facebook friend or would like to follow them on Twitter.

EXHIBIT 5.4 PROGRESSION OF MODERN TECHNOLOGY IN SALES POST-1980

Evolutionary Process			Revolutionary
1980s **Origin Decade**	**1990s** **Formative Decade**	**2000s** **Relationship Decade**	**2010s** **Informational Decade**
Exemplar Technologies	Exemplar Technologies	Exemplar Technologies	Exemplar Technologies
Answering machine	Email	Database marketing	Social media and related technology
Phone land-locked	Internet	CRM	Smartphones
Paper reports	Laptops	Skype	Tablets
Traditional typewriter's last stand—IBM "Selectric"	Cellular phone	WebEx	Mapping software
PCs phase-in, such as Tandy TRS-80	Voice mail	USB drives	Apps
Dictaphone	Sales Force Automation Software	Original GPS devices	
Pager	Windows/Microsoft Office Suite	Virtual worlds and gaming approaches	
Telemarketing	Web pages		
Mobile phone	Early teleconferencing		
VCR	CD-ROM		
Fax			
WordStar, WordPerfect, Lotus 123—all DOS based			
Floppy disks			

Note: Several exemplar technologies are shown that were particularly relevant during three earlier decades. Some of these drop out in use over time; others continued to be used across the decades moving forward. Our intent here is to demonstrate the flow of technology development over those years, not to imply that some of the older technologies aren't still in use.

Sales Technology in the Informational Decade

Bringing us forward to today, the technology tools that we use as part of our daily lives—especially elements like social media, smartphones, and tablets—are revolutionizing the sales role and salesperson/buyer relationships beyond anything we might have imagined just a few years ago. The crux of why this can be called a revolution in selling can be summarized in the following two concepts: information access and portability. The capability for nearly instantaneous and real-time 24/7 access anywhere in the world to information required by buyers can alter the traditional role of a relationship salesperson of creating client through information. That is, if information is just as available to clients as to sales organizations, essentially information becomes a commodity and no longer a source of value-added. This does not mean that there aren't myriad other ways that salespeople can add value (review chapter 3 for some excellent approaches); what it does mean is that the old days of salespeople relying on simply providing customers with information they can't get elsewhere as the key to getting the sale are likely over.

Let's take a closer look at several categories of technology tools, some of the specific options in each, and how these tools can be best applied for B2B selling. This is not an exhaustive set but it does reflect some of the most applicable options for salespeople.

Communication Tools. In the past, most professional selling was done in person or by phone. Although often there are certainly great advantages to face-to-face communication, travel costs can be incredibly high, especially when selling on the global stage. Multiple tools are available now that mitigate the need to communicate in person. Examples:

* WebEx—The market leading web-based presentation tool, WebEx is widely used in B2B settings.
* Skype—Online and relatively inexpensive calling. Skype is replacing/enhancing a lot of traditional teleconferences and also allows sales team members from around the world to participate in a blended technology sales call—that is, a sales call on a buyer that includes some in-person salespeople and some via electronic means.

Presentation Tools. Laptops and standard PowerPoint have been the bellwether for in-office sales presentations for many years. Today there are numerous enhancements available for the creative-minded presenter. Examples:

* Plug-in Packages—Add-on PowerPoint plug-ins come in dozens of forms. One is Snap by Lectors, which provides great tools to create voiceover PowerPoint slides and also easily adds video and other enhancements so that the presentation feels "21st Century."
* Distribution and Feedback Options—Numerous cloud-based sites exist for editing, presenting, and commenting on information that has been shared (including shared PowerPoint presentations). Voice Thread is typical in that it allows users to leave feedback, questions, edits, etc. Salespeople can use it to create and sustain an ongoing two-way dialogue with a buying team about key aspects of a presentation, providing the sense that an interactive community has been developed throughout the sales process. Inside the sales firm, Voice Thread lends itself well to salesperson training when the manager and salesperson are not able to work together in person during part or all of the training process.

Mapping Software. Many outside salespeople travel extensively. Especially if they are regularly cultivating new customers in new geographic areas, modern-day spinoffs from the global positioning software all around the world (GPS) technology developed in the 2000s can be very useful in increasing productivity on the road (globally). Examples:

* Google Maps—Quite sufficient for most salesperson call routing needs.
* Map Quest—A representative example of the many different mapping applications that salespeople have at their fingertips. These programs offer a variety of features and most are (selectively) global in reach.

Social Media. Social media are Internet-based platforms that allow users to create their own content and share it with others that access the site. These platforms all aim to build community and communication-sharing among users. Recall that in chapter 2 we made a distinction between B2B and B2C? Don't make the mistake of thinking that social media are mostly applicable only in B2C situations. People that use these technologies in their daily lives for personal purposes tend to bring that usage straight over to the workplace setting. Younger generation organizational buyers not only are willing to do business with salespeople over social media, they expect it! Examples:

- LinkedIn—The gold standard of professional social media sites, LinkedIn is used heavily by salespeople for researching new and current customers and preparing for sales calls, and creating and maintaining social networks with buyers. Sales managers use it for recruiting new sales reps. In general, LinkedIn can be thought of as the "new business card" for salespeople.
- Facebook—Wildly popular globally for personal networking, Facebook is useful to salespeople and sales managers in much the same way as LinkedIn. Because it is not specifically business-focused, it can be more challenging to cull through the personal aspects to find information germane to the client. But many salespeople do heavily utilize Facebook as a primary means of communication and community building.
- Twitter—Twitter and the short Tweets it enables makes for a convenient and quick way for users to "follow" each other. The message size limit is perfectly adapted to smartphone usage, and the real-time nature of the process is appealing in terms of quickly identifying and reacting to trends. Twitter data can be mined for themes that can play into marketing and public relations campaigns.
- YouTube—A handy video-sharing website, YouTube is great for salespeople and their companies to post to for use with buyers in presentations and otherwise. Companies can make their offerings available through a YouTube channel dedicated to a particular company or product line. The audience is highly dispersed globally. Salespeople can also search for use other posted videos for general instructional or informational purposes with their clients. There is quite a lot of clutter on YouTube, so salespeople need to be savvy in culling through the postings to find ones that are useful and relevant.
- Blogs—**Blogs** are online journals and forums that are generally publically accessible. Tumblr and Flickr are two well-known blogs. Blogs preceded the current wave of social media sites and usership has gone down recently, particularly by younger people. But many very useful blogs still exist that salespeople can turn to for real-time information on an industry, competitive market, general trends, or just interesting thinking on timely topics. Many companies keep up their own blogs, so if a potential customer has one the salesperson can gain insight there that could be useful prior to making a sales call. In addition, some salespeople keep up their own blog and invite their customers to post regularly.
- Other Social Media Options—The social media space is rapidly expanding and relatively newer entries such as Four Square and Pinterest are available as communication tools for today's salespeople. Although it should be clear from the discussion above that social media affords some great opportunities for improving buyer–seller relationships, one caution is that salespeople should not become overconsumed in the social media world to an extent that other forms of communication with clients are underutilized.

Time Management Tools. Salespeople need to be very mindful of their use of time. In chapter 10 you will learn more about the importance of various aspects of self-management to salesperson success. Many technology options are available. Examples:

- MS Outlook—A simple solution to a variety of calendar, time management, and related needs. Most people think of Outlook as just an email program, but it is also a very powerful tool for schedule sharing and event scheduling.
- Smartphone Apps—As a device, the smartphone is rapidly becoming the primary hardware of choice for sales organizations. Not that companies are ready to totally replace tablets and laptops quite yet, but the portability and multitasking capabilities smartphones bring afford a high level of efficiency to a salesperson's daily routine. The range of apps available is staggering. One category that is particularly useful focuses on helping ensure that salespeople don't forget important tasks. Apple has a "Reminder" app, and there's another one called "To do," both of which do a great job of making sure that busy people stay on task!

Recruiting Sites. In chapter 12 you will find out about strategies to recruit the best possible people into professional selling jobs. Technology solutions for recruiting across multiple fields abound, and professional selling is no different. Examples:

- Monster.com and CareerBuilders.com—Selling and sales management categories on websites such as these are heavily utilized and never fail to contain numerous opportunities around the globe.
- Company Online Applications—Many sales organizations want potential recruits to start the process with them online. Before starting to make applications online, candidates need to seek some advice on how to put the best foot forward using this type of recruiting system. Numerous resources are available about how to rise above the pack in online applications.

Opportunities on the Frontier. Two particular technology areas seem to have a good deal of potential for future application in selling and sales management.

- Virtual Worlds—Most people think only of Second Life when they think of virtual worlds, and Second Life is certainly a pioneer. In virtual worlds, users participate through avatars and engage in activities that may or may not parallel the sort of things they do in their "real" world. Quite a few firms built sites within Second Life, usually for promotional purposes. But over the long haul, the usefulness of virtual world technology for selling is not likely to be through a public application such as Second Life, but rather through customized applications that are sponsored by individual sales organizations. Consider, for example, how a virtual world for Pfizer Pharmaceuticals could help train new salespeople in how to break through screeners (receptionists, nurses, etc.) to actually meet with physicians, or educate physicians directly on Pfizer's product specifications and usage protocols. For other types of products, buyers can view and experience product features and benefits, observe usage, and provide feedback to a firm on aspects of product development.
- Gaming—Video games are enormously popular with a large portion of the population throughout the world. **Gamification**, approaching other tasks and turning them into a videogame-like platform, is becoming popular all across the fields of education and training. An opportunity exists for sales organizations to invest in gamification as a way to make training of salespeople more fun and engaging. Chapter 12 covers training in detail, and a variety of traditional sales training tasks—from learning how to make a presentation to detailed product knowledge—could be translated into a gaming platform. Gamification can also enhance presentation of information to buyers. Imagine how a clever video game-style demonstration of a product might stimulate interest and separate the message from the regular routine of traditional sales presentation approaches.

Special Feature: Insights on Sales Force Technology, from Chally Group Worldwide, provides additional insights based on their research on specific technologies that are among the most important and cutting-edge in contemporary selling.

the areas where firms that develop and market technologies to sales organizations have been particularly active in recent years, including examples of the products available.

Lead Generation

Today, many tools exist to help sales teams create a more robust pipeline of potential new customers. The challenge here is to have some way to differentiate between leads that have high potential and leads that don't. Lead generation tools like InsideView, Hoovers, and Dow Jones provide in-depth background and current news about prospects' financial status and corporate strategies. Armed with that knowledge, a sales team can better qualify prospects, thereby building a pipeline that's full of high-quality opportunities.

Sales Cycle Acceleration

A great deal of technology now exists to help sales teams develop the deals in their pipeline so that they are quicker and easier to close. For example, sales research tools like Jigsaw, SalesGenie, and LinkedIn provide in-depth information on hundreds of thousands of decision makers. Having that "inside information" helps the sales team build additional contacts in the prospect's firm and create stronger relationships with those contacts. Similarly, sales analytics tools such as Cloud9 and Birst allow you to compare past opportunities with current ones, so that sales managers can better assign resources to opportunities likely to ultimately result in a client relationship.

Compensation Management

In the past, compensation and commissions were often handled haphazardly, which limited the ability of sales managers to drive strategic and tactical sales behavior. Today, sales compensation tools like Xactly and Makana allow sales managers to fine-tune commissions and quickly inform the team of the changes. As a result, sales professionals are now better informed and presumably better targeted toward pursuing the deals that sales management would like them to pursue.

Sales and Marketing Integration

Sales and marketing groups are traditionally at loggerheads, arguing over spending, lead quality, and sales execution among other issues. The resulting turf wars consume human energy that could otherwise be channeled into tactical execution of a sales and marketing strategy. Sometimes top executives have become so frustrated with these distractions, they create a new position that both sales and marketing must report to, such as Chief Revenue Officer or Chief Customer Experience Officer, in order to gain peace.

In addition, companies are using sales-oriented technology to measure the effectiveness of both sales and marketing. As a result, verifiable facts and figures begin to replace the opinions and subjective perceptions that lie at the core of these interdepartmental squabbles. One key to ending the strife between sales and marketing is finding and agreeing on some common metrics—measures that are relevant to both and that both can impact. Inherent in this approach, however, is the need to include these common metrics in the actual formal performance evaluations of organization members in both sales and marketing, holding both accountable for achievement of the metrics.

Sales Management

Many of the tools discussed above ultimately also provide sales management with deeper insight into both the sales process and individual salesperson performance within that process. This helps sales managers identify the areas (and people) that need improvement, and that can prove invaluable when a company is positioning itself for future growth while trying to hold expenses down.

However, even with this massive influx in new technology, many companies are struggling to keep up. The research firm CSO Insights recently conducted a survey of more than 2,000 sales and marketing professionals, and revealed that 85 percent of marketers believed they were doing a good job generating quality sales leads. By contrast, only 50 percent of the sales professionals—in those same organizations—were satisfied with those leads. Another CSO Insights survey, this one of 600 sales and marketing groups, revealed that marketers think they produce 38 percent of the leads that convert, while the sales thinks that number is only 23 percent.

Regardless whose numbers are more correct, the simple truth is that, despite a vast influx of new technology, many sales organizations continue to flounder in terms of performance achievements. According to CSO Insight's 2010 survey of 2,800 companies worldwide, "the percentage of reps making individual quotas dropped significantly, and the percentage of the overall company revenue target achieved dropped, as well." Ironically, 85 percent of the firms surveyed reported that they raised quotas for the subsequent year!

Source: Howard P. Stevens and Geoffrey James, *Selling in the Internet Age: How the Web is Transforming the Buyer/Seller Relationship* (Dayton, OH: Chally Group Worldwide, 2012).

Gaining Technology Acceptance by Salespeople

The Informational Decade we are now in when it comes to sales technology highlights the importance of information management and integration within an organization, focused on enhancing the customer experience and building strong customer loyalty over the long run. Much research has gone into understanding sales force technology adoption, including CRM. A famous model called the **technology acceptance model (TAM)** has been heavily tested and consistently predicts that salesperson attitude and behavioral intentions to use a technology are positively impacted by the perceived usefulness and perceived ease of use of the technology by the salesperson. As such, it is incumbent on sales managers to ensure that the available technology is presented to the sales force in such a way that maximizes those positive perceptions. Effective technology training, consistent technological support by the firm, and compensation systems that reward salespeople who deploy the technology ensure that a sales organization will go a long way in gaining technology acceptance. This investment in time and resources is definitely worth it—once technology acceptance is high, the research indicates that successful selling increases and overall salesperson performance improves. Thus, technology acceptance and usage is a very powerful element in sales organizational success.[15]

One important final caveat related to sales technology deserves mention. There is considerable evidence of a strong negative correlation between salesperson age and likelihood of embracing technological innovation. Simply put, it is much more likely that younger generation salespeople who essentially grew up in the midst of the lead-up to the Informational Decade will seek out and take on new technologies on the job simply as a matter of course. In contrast, older generation salespeople may tend to be slower to proactively seek job-enhancing technologies and may even resist using those required by the firm. The problem is exacerbated when it comes to sales managers, who are more likely to be older generation rather than younger and who are expected to not only lead by example in using new technology, but also to be able to train incoming salespeople on the applications.

This generational gap in technology is a sensitive situation for senior management in sales organizations. Experienced (translation: older) salespeople are the most likely group to call on the largest customers and to enjoy the deepest customer relationships. They may respond to pushes toward technology usage by saying that they're successful doing things the way they always have, and may even threaten to walk away and take important customers with them. And in the case of non-tech-savvy sales managers, they can experience a good deal of stress when it becomes clear that their newest recruits come onto the team much more technology proficient than they'll likely ever be themselves! There are no easy approaches to addressing this issue. In Part Three of the book you will become familiar with many issues of salesperson motivation, training, and rewards—at that time we will bring up the issue of career life cycles and some ideas for keeping and nurturing senior salespeople.[16]

EXPERT ADVICE: FOLLOW-UP   Chally Group WORLDWIDE©

After watching the video of Mr. Gschwandtner and reading the chapter, consider the following questions:

1. Consider his central point about using technology, combined with entrepreneurism, to create competitive advantage. What are some key ways that a salesperson's use of technology can add value to their customers and to the customer relationship?
2. Can you come up with any situations in which the use of technology by a salesperson could *detract* from a customer relationship? Describe the situations and explain your thinking.

SUMMARY

This chapter provides an overview of CRM and sales force technology. A strong understanding of CRM is essential for any successful salesperson today. CRM provides the firm with necessary formalization for maximizing available information. That is, a well-implemented CRM business model offers structure, processes and tools, and managerial knowledge and commitment in support of the customer-centric culture desired by the organization. CRM, through its process cycle of knowledge discovery, market planning, customer interaction, and analysis and refinement, is a critical enabler of one-to-one marketing.

After reviewing a brief history of technology usage by salespeople, a variety of currently available sales technologies are discussed and connected to how each might be best utilized. Regardless of the potential benefits of technology, it can only be effective if salespeople actually use it and use it as intended. Sales managers and the sales organization need to consistently provide the necessary salesperson support elements to ensure that the investment in technology is consistently and successfully deployed.

KEY TERMS

market orientation	data mining	gamification
formalization	technology	technology acceptance model (TAM)
touchpoints	blended technology	
customer value	social media	
data warehouse	blogs	

DISCUSSION QUESTIONS

1. One of the great debates in CRM is who should have ownership of the process. In many firms, IT people seem to be the guardians of CRM's secrets. This is because, as we have learned, a key facet of CRM is its information management capabilities. Who do you think should have ownership of CRM in a firm? Is it really necessary that CRM have an owner? What does ownership of the process imply in terms of actions and behaviors? What is the role of upper management in all this?

2. How does CRM offer advantages to salespeople in terms of information management? What are some of the problems you could predict for salespeople in firms that do not use CRM?

3. Why would a salesperson be reluctant to adopt CRM? What can management do to help gain salesperson adoption and usage?

4. Is it possible for a firm to be successful without a market orientation? Can you come up with examples of firms that are not very market-oriented but still are leaders in their competitive marketplace?

5. Consider any three of the newer types of sales technology presented in the chapter. For each, provide as many specific applications as you can think of that could enhance the buyer–seller relationship and the salesperson's performance.

6. Why do some salespeople not immediately embrace the use of the newest technologies? What are some ways in which a salesperson who is reluctant to adopt new technologies might be influenced to do so?

7. Are there actually situations in which the use of one or more of the older sales technologies might be superior to something new? When and why would older approaches perhaps be a better choice in this day and age?

MINI-CASE 5 WHO "OWNS" CRM

Alice Klein wondered what she should do next as she hung up the phone. As Vice President of Sales for New World Manufacturing, she was responsible for more than 200 salespeople around the country. New World is a manufacturer of precision components for bicycles (gearshift mechanisms). Among the company's clients are Cannondale and Giant Bicycles, as well as other leading bicycle companies around the world. In addition to the original equipment manufacturer (OEM) market, New World does a great deal of business selling after-market accessories to bicycle retailers.

Alice had pushed hard for a CRM system to be implemented at New World. Finally, as part of an overall upgrade of the IT system at the company, senior management purchased a CRM package that includes state-of-the-art software and hardware to help New World do a better job of managing its customer relationships. It was expensive to get the package that Alice and other executives knew was the best solution. The final cost ran into several million dollars, plus additional training time.

It is now six months since the purchase of the system. Elliot Whitney, Vice President of Information Technology, has just called Alice to say he still has not received a detailed summary of the information needed by the sales force. He told Alice that senior management was asking about the status of the CRM system. Management wanted the entire company to benefit from the system and were looking forward to its implementation.

The company had a lot of information about its customers as well as other data that could be incorporated into its CRM system (internal billing, price, and production schedules). Alice is well aware of the system's potential and has spent a great deal of time thinking about how the sales force can use it most effectively. After hanging up with Elliot, she knew it was time to decide how the new CRM system will be implemented with the sales force.

Questions

1. You are Alice Klein. What critical information do you think would be most helpful for the sales force to be able to access about the relationship between New World and its customers?

2. What device would you use to deliver this information from the CRM system to the salesperson (smartphone, laptop, tablet or something else), and why would you choose that device?

3. What kinds of issues do you think might come up for New World as it implements the CRM system with the sales force—for example, possible salesperson resistance to collecting information for the CRM system?

ELEMENTS OF THE CONTEMPORARY SELLING PROCESS

CHAPTER 6
Prospecting and Sales Call Planning

CHAPTER 7
Communicating the Sales Message

CHAPTER 8
Negotiating for Win-Win Solutions

CHAPTER 9
Closing the Sale and Follow-up

CHAPTER 10
Salesperson Self-Management

PART TWO describes the process of buyer–seller interchange that is the heart and soul of contemporary selling. Chapter 6 discusses two important tasks that must be done before meeting with a customer—prospecting and sales call planning, including a preapproach.

Once you have an appointment scheduled with your customer, preparing and delivering a great sales presentation becomes key. In chapter 7 you will learn about ways to make a good first impression, strategies for approaching the customer for the first time, and characteristics of different types of sales presentations. Then you will learn how to use the sales presentation to build the relationship and convey the value proposition to your customers. Chapter 8 gives you tips on keeping the buyer–seller dialogue focused on win-win solutions, and provides specific negotiation strategies to get there.

Closing is about achieving the goals set for a specific sales call. Chapter 9 provides several approaches to closing, as well as ideas for dealing with rejection and maintaining a professional attitude. Also in chapter 9 you will learn how to recognize buying signals and avoid several classic mistakes in closing, as well as how to do great follow-up after the sale.

Finishing out Part Two, chapter 10, provides a bridge from selling to sales management. It covers the importance of good time and territory management to salespeople and their managers, including a number of tips on efficient and effective self-management.

In order to directly connect the sales process to sales management, each chapter in Part Two concludes with a section on the sales manager's role in the element of the sales process covered in that chapter.

Sales Management

Salesperson Motivation

Compensating & Evaluating Salespeople

Selling Processes

Prospecting & Sales Call Planning

Communicating the Sales Message

Salesperson Self-Management

Technology

Understanding Sellers & Buyers

Building Relationships ~ Creating Value

Closing & Follow-up

Ethics

Negotiating for Win-Win Solutions

Selecting & Training Salespeople

global selling environment

Prospecting and Sales Call Planning

LEARNING OBJECTIVES

This chapter explores important issues in how salespeople successfully prospect and plan for a sales call (the preapproach). These important advance activities set the stage for success with the customer.

After reading this chapter, you should be able to:

- Describe how to qualify a lead as a prospect.
- Explain why prospecting is important to long-term success in selling.
- List various sources of prospects.
- Prepare a prospecting plan.
- Explain call reluctance and point out ways to overcome it.
- Describe elements of the preapproach and why planning activities are important to sales call success.
- Understand the sales manager's role in prospecting and sales call planning.

EXPERT ADVICE

EXPERT: Expert: Walter Friedman
Historian, Harvard Business School

TOPIC: Peddlers and drummers.

SUMMARY: Walter Friedman provides a rare glimpse of what selling was like just after the industrial revolution. Salespeople came in two primary forms—peddlers and drummers. Peddlers are colorful sales figures in early U.S. history that sold almost exclusively via cold calls on new clients. They might be on commission for a manufacturer, or they might purchase products from manufacturers, mark them up, and sell them directly to users. Peddlers are the legendary snake oil (patent medicine) salesmen—complete with requisite theatrics and production values. Drummers, on the other hand, worked for wholesalers (middle men) that were the most important channel for many manufacturers of the day. Drummers' jobs were more "respectable." They are analogous to today's relationship salespeople, in that they focused on selling the same customers over and over and in developing the business over time. Prospecting by drummers was methodical, as they traveled extensively on a route in order to keep their clientele supplied. The familiar phrase in sales "drum up business" comes from the historical drummers.

NEXT STEPS: Go to the website for *Contemporary Selling* (www.routledge.com/cw/Johnston), watch the chapter 6 video, and then read the chapter. You will find an Expert Advice follow-up at the end of the chapter with questions that connect elements of your learning.

PROSPECTING: CUSTOMERS DON'T START OUT AS CUSTOMERS

In Part One of the book we have talked a lot about customers and also had the chance to survey CRM and a variety of technologies that salespeople can utilize in their jobs. It is now time to fully realize an important aspect of selling that has not yet come up in our discussion: today's customers didn't start out as your customers at all. Somehow, your company, through its various selling and marketing efforts, brought them to you, you to them, or both by some means. This issue is the focus of this chapter. It's an exciting part of selling, especially in today's social media world!

By the time someone becomes your customer he or she has probably gone through a series of stages with you. The process may start out with a lead, which is the name of someone who *might* have the potential to buy from your company. Leads come from many places, and later in the chapter we will review those sources. Many (if not most) leads never make it past that stage to become prospects. Unlike mere leads, prospects have to meet certain criteria to be considered potential customers. Prospects are considered a *very likely* set of potential customers. The process of analyzing a lead to see if it meets the criteria to be a prospect is called qualifying the prospect.

Qualifying the Prospect

There are a variety of popular proprietary approaches to prospect qualifying—in fact, if you Google "qualifying prospects," you will discover that an incredible number of marketing and sales consulting firms would love to take your money to show you their miracle solution! There are also a variety of acronyms that can be handy for salespeople to use in remembering prospect qualifying elements. For example, the "MADDEN" test determines:

- Does the prospect have **M**oney?
- Is the prospect **A**pproachable?
- Is there a **D**esire to purchase?
- Is he or she the actual **D**ecision maker?
- Is the prospect **E**ligible to purchase—for example, has he or she already committed to someone else?
- Does the prospect have a demonstrated **N**eed?

In truth, any and all effective prospect qualifying approaches have several elements in common, which we've summarized for you below in the form of five basic qualifying questions along with an explanation of the scope of each element.

1. *Does the potential prospect appear to have a need for your product or service?* This criterion is fundamental. You have already learned that relationship-building approaches to selling don't involve arm-twisting, hard-sell techniques. You want to do business over the long run and eventually gain referrals (leads) from current happy customers about potential new customers. Thus, success in selling depends on understanding that what you sell can satisfy a potential buyer's needs.

2. *Can the potential prospect derive added value from your product in ways that you can deliver?* This criterion is closely related to #1. In chapter 3 you saw a number of ways beyond price and the product itself that a seller can add value for customers. To answer this question accurately, you must analyze the different ways you might do this with a potential customer. The more ways you can add value, the more likely you have a good prospect. Unless you are in a purely commodity business and everything hinges on just price, getting a fruitful answer to this question can be make or break.

3. *Can you effectively contact and carry on communication/correspondence with the potential prospect?* Contact and communication with potential customers might seem easy, but this is actually a very important point. Some customers look good on paper but are not really accessible. The potential customer's geographic location and your ability to get an appointment with him or her fall within this criterion. Opposite, some

customers loathe face-to-face contact with sellers and want to do business primarily electronically. For them, skillful use of smartphones and social media options can be the key. Consider what type of contact is needed to develop the relationship.

Here's a caution if you're a younger generation salesperson. Older generation customers are much more likely to want to talk to you by phone or even see you in person before they decide to do business with you. While your preference may be all things virtual, you have to adapt to them and you can't expect them to suddenly become Twitter-savvy to suit you! Bottom line: if access and communication lines are significant barriers, then it may be wise to move to another prospect.

4. *Does the potential prospect have the means and authority to make the purchase?* Quite often, as you learned in chapter 2 in the discussion of buying centers, a wide variety of people contribute to the ultimate purchase decision in B2B. The salesperson must determine (a) if the person being considered as a potential prospect can and will make a purchase and (b) how much effort and investment might be needed to see the purchase through to completion.

Xerox pioneered a sales training package Xerox PSS (for "Professional Selling Skills"). One of its classic training role plays partners a salesperson with a buyer to try to make a sale. The script (each player reads only the script for his or her role) gives the person playing the salesperson the task of making initial entry into the buyer's firm to present a new product. Unfortunately, the person role-playing the buyer is told in the script that he or she has no authority to buy and cannot do anything to further the relationship until the salesperson starts to ask questions relevant to means and authority to make the purchase. Most salespeople participating in the role play never solve the dilemma. Sadly, this is a common problem in qualifying prospects.

5. *Does the potential prospect have the financial capability to make the purchase?* This issue is directly related to #4. Obviously, little is to be gained by pursuing a potential customer who does not have access to the money needed to buy what you sell. Thus, an important criterion is determining the prospect's financial status. The credit department of your firm may perform this role, or you may have to personally investigate the prospect's financial strength. It is far better to determine in advance that a prospect cannot afford to buy than to waste time pursuing someone who ultimately will not become your customer for this very straightforward reason.

Qualifying prospects effectively is fundamental to success in selling. It often involves ranking leads according to their attractiveness. *A-level prospects* might be most attractive and most worthy of pursuit by the sales force, *B-level prospects* next, and *C-level prospects* last. Global Connection provides insights on four categories of prospects and how a salesperson might best prepare for each.

GLOBAL CONNECTION

FOUR CLASSIC CATEGORIES OF PROSPECTS

It happens over and over again. The sales representative delivers an outstanding presentation to the prospect. She not only knew all the facts about her product, but also about all of her competitors. Her vocal skills were impeccable, and she portrayed professionalism and confidence. Her close was strong and affirmative.

But her prospect—a very prominent physician—said he would "consider" using her product if it became "appropriate." He may as well have said, "No." What went wrong?

Although it is true that everyone is different and unique, it's also true that people tend to fall into four basic behavioral types when it comes to buying a service or product. The success (or failure) of the sales call is dependent on the sales representative being able to distinguish the correct behavioral type of the prospect, the quality of the sales message, and also the use of the appropriate communication style. For example, a sales representative cannot sell the same way to Donald Trump as he can to Richard Simmons, and vice versa. The product is the same in both sales calls, but in order to close the sale effectively, the approach and the message would (or should) be different to each of the four categories.

1.   **The Direct Type.** This buyer is usually a Type A personality—they are usually in a hurry and tend to be very direct in their conversation. Direct Type buyers are often blunt and even interrupt the sales representative constantly. They state their opinions as fact. They are impatient and demanding, wanting to get to "the bottom line" quickly.

     While you want to be direct and specific, provide alternatives so that the Direct Type buyer can make the decision to buy. Let this buyer speak and you listen. Do not go into all the details or try to control the situation. Ensure he/she "wins." You must act quickly, because this buyer type decides fast. Whatever happens, don't take issues personally.

2.   **The Interpersonal Buyer.** This buyer is very friendly and excitable, often animated. They cannot focus on details and jump from subject to subject. Because they don't always have the ability to listen for long periods, they may ask the same question several times. Interpersonal buyers are more interested in forming a relationship than they are in buying.

     Schedule time for chatting and let this buyer speak, giving recognition as appropriate. Talk about people and feelings. As you converse with this buyer type, move closer and maintain a positive atmosphere. You want to show how your product will help to achieve popularity and recognition for the buyer. Focus on the people aspects. Do not fail to socialize. Also, do not set hard restrictions, unless absolutely necessary.

3.   **The Safety or Status Quo Type.** These buyers usually appear calm and do not get easily excited. They listen carefully and ask specific questions. Completely new ideas/things make these buyers uncomfortable.

     It is critical to slow down your presentation and build trust. Provide the necessary information that this buyer needs logically, and secure commitment piece by piece. Ask specific questions to find out true needs, and then provide support. It is also advantageous to provide precedents or examples of previous success to reduce uncertainty. Be sincere and do not dominate.

4.   **The Contemplative Buyer.** These buyers are usually very quiet. They focus on details and ask questions. These characters study specifications and other information carefully. In fact, they may have even done some research on your product or service prior to your sales call.

     When selling to this type, patiently provide facts and plenty of detailed information. Go slowly and do not invade his or her private space. Avoid talking about personal issues or small talk. Listen carefully, and then answer questions calmly and carefully. Be thorough; remember to include all relevant information, utilizing written supporting documentation. Find out what the key issues are and focus on them. Don't move too fast, move too close, or lose patience in providing all the requested information. Also, don't expect decisions right away.

In order to be successful, salespeople must tailor their approaches and messages very differently to each buyer behavioral type. Let's examine the differences. First, as the numbers suggest, sales representatives who try to use the same "canned" message will be effective only 25 percent of the time, because the approach and message will be effective only for the buyer behavior type it was designed for. The ability to recognize the various behavior types and adapt the sales call appropriately takes training and practice.

Also, just as buyers fall into one of each of these buying types, so do sellers. More times than not, sales representatives will have to learn (and train) themselves on how to adapt their own behavioral type to the specific prospect they're calling on. Success in the sales arena will increase exponentially by training sales representatives on how to properly identify the behavioral type of their prospect, and how to adapt the sales approach and message appropriately.

Questions to Consider

1. Why is it useful for salespeople to categorize prospects? How does it help them do a better job of selling? Are there any downsides to categorization?
2. Think of people you know that you believe might fall under the various categories of buyer behavioral types. Provide evidence as to why you categorize each person as you do.

Adapted from Alan G. Bayham, "Do You Know Who You're Selling to?" *American Salesman* (April 2008), p. 7.

The overall process of moving from leads to prospects to customers is often portrayed as an upside-down triangle (see Exhibit 6.1). There are many, many leads, fewer leads that can be successfully qualified as prospects, and ultimately many fewer committed customers.

A CRM system as described in chapter 5 can be of great help in tracking, prioritizing, and qualifying leads. The database aspect of CRM provides bountiful information on potential customers that is readily available to anyone with a tablet, laptop, or (more and more) a smartphone. Today's successful salesperson is "plugged in" all the time by multiple synchronized devices, and with the power of a CRM system such as Salesforce (formerly referred to as Salesforce.com) can have at his or her fingertips the very information necessary for making these decisions. Obviously, and as we cautioned in chapter 5 on technology, the quality of the decisions will only be as good as the quality of the information used to make them.

Before we explore various specific sources of leads in detail, first let's ensure we understand *why* effective prospecting is so important to success in selling.

EXHIBIT 6.1 FROM LEADS TO CUSTOMERS

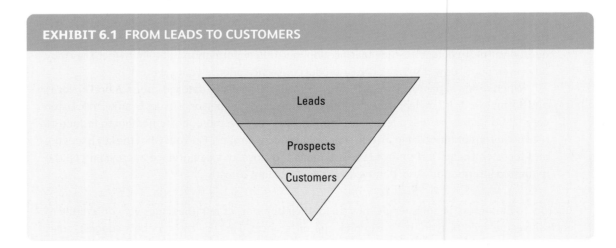

Why Prospecting is So Important

Think of prospecting, pursuing leads that you hope will develop into customers, as a way to fill your pipeline of future business. Today's business generated by current customers is well and good, but a salesperson always has to be thinking ahead to where business will come from next week, next month, and even next year. Prospecting is not a haphazard or part-time process in selling. Truly great salespeople are always engaged in prospecting in one form or another. They always have their sights set on where tomorrow's business is coming from.

Now you may be thinking: if we truly are engaged in *relationship* selling as we described it in Chapter 1, shouldn't we be able to relax some on prospecting? After all, doesn't the act of developing long-term relationships with our customers ensure they will stay loyal and provide business to us over and over for years? Why do we need to worry about getting new customers all the time? These are good questions with important answers. Yes, of course developing long-term relationships with your customers goes a long way toward sustaining your business. And keeping your current profitable customers is usually much more cost-effective than finding new ones. But all sales organizations are continually working to find new clients, take customers away from competitors, and build their market share. The lifeblood of business success is *growth*, from both existing customers and new ones.

Beyond this general growth perspective, below are a few other circumstances that may make prospecting for new customers an even higher priority.

- A *customer gets into financial difficulty or goes out of business entirely*. This can be quite unpredictable, as with a number of financial institutions during the credit crunch and mortgage bust that began in the late 2000s. If you have developed a long-term vendor relationship with a firm that is in financial trouble and have not also been engaged in prospecting for new customers, you may find yourself in as much trouble as your client.
- *Your main contacts in the client firm leave or change positions*. This may result in a change in the relationship. If the result is not favorable for you, ongoing prospecting can buffer any business losses from that client.
- *Your firm needs to increase revenues to pay for expansion or other items*. In such cases, the compensation and rewards system of your firm may be altered so that salespeople are paid more for prospecting and securing new customers than for developing and maintaining existing ones. Chapter 13 discusses linking sales force rewards with desired outcomes.
- A *customer moves to a new location outside your area of sales responsibility*. In this case, the business may simply move to another salesperson in your company, but you will need to find replacement business for yourself. Prospecting ensures a ready pool of potential new customers.

In sum, prospecting is a key activity of successful selling. How leads are developed (from which prospects and ultimately customers are derived) is the topic of the next section.

SOURCES OF PROSPECTS

Leads for potential prospects come from a wide variety of sources. Some sources involve activities initiated by the salesperson; others involve activities initiated at the sales organization level—such as leads provided by marketing—for which the salesperson can follow up. Some are generated the "old-fashioned way"—in person or by phone. Others are generated by using newer media tools like social media. The most successful sales firms train their salespeople how to best use the entire gamut of approaches to prospecting. Exhibit 6.2 summarizes various sources of prospects. Let's consider each of these now.

EXHIBIT 6.2 SOURCES OF PROSPECTS

Loyal customers
Endless chain referrals
Networking
- Friends and relatives
- Centers of influence
- Bird dogs
- Civic and professional groups

Directories
Trade shows
Conferences

Internet
- Social media
- Email

Telemarketing
Cold calls
Warm calls
Prospecting by others in your firm
Marketing and promotion

Loyal Customers

What better source of leads than existing customers, those who are loyal to you and your company and who are satisfied with your products and the service they have been receiving from you? Sometimes a loyal customer may give you a lead without being asked. More often, however, you will need to ask. This is a normal process of communication with your customers and you should not feel uncomfortable asking. This process is called getting a referral because the customer is referring more business your way. One study found that about 80 percent of customers are willing to provide a referral, but only about 20 percent of salespeople ask for one.[1]

An idea currently receiving much attention in selling is how to turn loyal customers into "advocates" for you and your business. Customer advocacy means that a customer is satisfied, loyal, and willing to spread the word that he or she is pleased with you. Satisfied customers are an important source of word-of-mouth advertising—a powerful source of leads that have a strong chance of resulting in qualified prospects.

Much of this advocacy through word-of-mouth occurs today through social media websites. Hopefully you and your current customers are on LinkedIn, follow each other on Twitter, and use such means to regularly share hot news flashes, best industry practices, and other value-adding information. A simple Tweet, well placed, can result in a referral! Customer referrals and advocacy are among the best sources of leads. These prospects are likely to meet your qualification criteria.[2]

Endless Chain Referrals

In an endless chain referral, the salesperson asks an open-end question during each customer contact, such as "Ms. Buyer, who else do you know that would benefit from our products?" When the question is phrased this way, the buyer is free to recommend as many potential prospects as possible. This can be done in person or via most any type of media. Later, when contacting these leads, the salesperson should use the buyer's name.

> "Mr. Prospect, I was talking with one of my clients recently, Ms. Buyer, and she mentioned to me that you might have a need for our products."

Although this method is probably best used when the person giving the referral is in a long-term customer relationship with you, it can and should be used even when the referrer is a prospect who doesn't buy from you. One way to turn a "no" from a prospective buyer into a win for you that doesn't cost the customer a thing is to ask for a referral. So always remember to ask for suggestions of potential new customers.

Networking

All salespeople have a variety of contacts. Using these contacts to develop leads is referred to as networking. Network relationships between salespeople and those with whom they interact can take several forms. Also, the communication channels can be by a variety of means, including electronic and non-electronic forms of communication—you the salesperson have to determine what form of communication to best use with each person in your network. Clearly, at this writing, LinkedIn is the social media platform of choice for much professional networking. It provides a straightforward, user-friendly, and widely accepted forum for prospecting. However, just because you favor LinkedIn and similar social media approaches, do not assume that all or even a majority of potential prospects will come from social media. The popular image of today's salesperson doing all their prospecting online while sipping a drink at their backyard pool is dramatically overstated—you've also got to be willing to network in more personal ways when the situation calls for it.[3]

Friends and Relatives. A primary network involves your friends and relatives. Northwestern Mutual Life Insurance Company encourages new agents to start their networking with this group. The idea is to think of friends and relatives as a core circle of potential leads for prospects and use an endless chain approach to work concentrically out from the core. Northwestern Mutual has shown that, after a few years, successful agents have developed an entirely new set of customers and prospects that are not even directly connected to the core of friends and relatives. But starting with that core group is fundamental to success.

Centers of Influence. People are centers of influence if they are in a position to persuade a salesperson's potential customers. For example, a salesperson selling sporting equipment to a school system might visit with coaches, trainers, and sports medicine experts to try to win influence over a purchasing agent. These people are analogous to the group we called influencers in the buying center (discussed in chapter 2).

Bird Dogs. No, not the canine kind! In selling, bird dogs (also often called "spotters") are people who come into contact with an unusually large number of people in the course of their daily routine. Salespeople can use bird dogs as their eyes and ears in the marketplace. For example, a tour operator might ask a bellman at a resort hotel for referrals of promising clients or even compensate the bellman for mentioning the tour guide's services to guests as they settle into their rooms. Some bird dogs work in client firms. Receptionists tend to hear much of what goes on in an organization. A long-standing rule of selling is to cultivate a rapport with anyone in a firm who is in a position to provide information about the potential for gaining business.

Civic and Professional Groups. One highly useful way of forming networks is to join groups. New agents with State Farm Insurance are encouraged to join Rotary International, Kiwanis, and the like, especially when they enter a new community. The friendships developed there are a terrific source of leads for the agents, and the agents' membership provides a source of strong goodwill for State Farm in the community. Likewise, if you are engaged in B2B selling, you can seek out primary prospects in industry and professional groups such as trade associations that represent the field you are targeting. And many of these memberships include access to great discussion boards, chat rooms, and even password-protected industry information. Below we mention directories as a particular possibility.

However, a note of caution is in order. Salespeople have been known to overdo it when joining organizations. Some become so tied up in leadership roles with groups that they lose too much valuable time from their core job of selling. Be careful to network selectively, targeting civic and professional groups that you believe will return the most leads for your time and effort invested.

Directories

A variety of directories are available that can serve as lead generators. These directories are most likely accessible as an online download for a fee and are available for most any target customer group imaginable. The usefulness of directories depends heavily on the type of business you are in and the types of clients you are targeting as customers. Many industry groups have their own directories, often published by trade associations and made available to salespeople for a fee. Also available are many general directories, such as *Moody's Industrial Manual*, the *Dun & Bradstreet Reference Book*, *Standard & Poor's Corporation Record Service*, and the *Thomas Registry of American Manufacturers*, to name only a few.

Many listings formerly available only in hard copy are now available online. Go to any search engine and type in the word "directory," you will be overwhelmed with sources of information on businesses and individuals. Whether online or in hard copy, a variety of specialty directories and listings are for sale. For example, a local medical society might sell a mailing list or database of all the physicians practicing in a particular geographic area for use by pharmaceutical reps.

Internet

In the age of Google, the Internet is obviously one of the richest (and most convenient) sources of leads for B2B selling. The Internet is used for lead generation in two primary ways. First, salespeople use it to research potential business clients and their industries, with a focus on gathering as much information as possible to try to answer the five qualifying questions for prospects presented earlier.

A second main way salespeople use the Internet for prospecting is by using their company's own website to generate inquiries from prospects. They either solicit information on a prospect's needs or make special offers to individuals who respond (probably by email) to a pop-up, banner ad, or other promotional offer or mechanism on the website.

One potential problem with this approach is that, believe it or not, even in the 2010s not every prospect either has access to the Internet on a regular basis or is inclined to use it. This necessitates providing alternate means of contact (such as phone or even fax) for prospects that do not regularly use the Internet. An even more nagging problem is that customer inquiries or requests must be responded to rapidly by the salesperson or another member of his or her firm. If the firm does not have a well-designed way to contact these prospects quickly, it can do more harm than good, since prospects are expecting a prompt response and are not receiving one.

Yet another problem is the growing consumer backlash against aggressive and invasive pop-ups, which are often viewed as detracting from the usefulness of the Internet. Finally, security concerns still linger in electronic commerce, although hopefully this issue will decline in importance as more and more sophisticated security protection continues to be developed. But today, firms must be aware that some percentage of prospects may want to provide contact and other information online (credit, for example) but ultimately fail to do so because of privacy and security concerns.

Email. Email prospecting can be thought of as a subset of using the Internet, expressly for communication purposes. It has been around for almost 20 years and typically involves outward communication from the sales organization to the prospect. Usually the firm creates or obtains an email list and sends an unsolicited communication to members of the list, with a means for the prospect to reply (by return email, going to a designated website, etc.) The proliferation of email prospecting over the years has led to considerable concern about spam, or junk email messages. Many email users (especially business users) filter the spam out of their email inboxes before they even have a chance to view the messages. Legislation against email spam has been discussed in many countries off and on during the past decade, so far without resolution.

Social Media. We've already mentioned several forms of social media above in the context of usage with some of the other prospecting sources. Building on what you learned about social media applications in selling in chapter 5, let's highlight a few particularly effective applications related to prospecting. Remember what prospecting is: pursuing leads that you hope ultimately will develop into customers, as a way to fill your pipeline of future business. And also remember: the key is not to just generate endless lists of people but instead to ensure truly *qualified* prospects. With this in mind, the activity of finding leads and cultivating them is perfectly matched to the functionality of social media, which aims to develop and nurture communities of various types. LinkedIn is clearly the leader in facilitating the networking and information sharing required in B2B prospecting. Anyone in B2B sales that is not on LinkedIn needs some career counseling! LinkedIn has an easy interface, is well organized, and members' pages generally contain a wealth of information that can be used to (a) make contact with and (b) begin the process of qualifying prospects.

Younger generation salespeople in particular are highly likely to come into the job already an old pro at Facebook, and certainly Facebook offers some of the same information potential as LinkedIn. The big difference, of course, is that Facebook pages also tend to include an enormous amount of more personal information and communication and is thus less focused on and less suited specifically for B2B prospecting. However, don't discount the power of Facebook in this regard; many firms regularly scan its postings for topical and other qualifiers that can lead to an effective first contact in prospecting. Twitter has different aims from Facebook and LinkedIn, and the ability to "follow" anyone in the community can provide some great insights for sales organizations savvy enough to mine the vast data in Twitter for prospecting purposes. For the individual salesperson, newer applications like Four Square, Pinterest, and others have yet different aims and sales organizations are beginning to mine the information in them as well in search of leads.

Although blogs and discussion boards may seem a little "yesterday" compared to the media above, the truth is that they also can be a rich source of information for B2B leads.

Telemarketing

Many firms support their salespeople through telemarketing. Telemarketers are frequently referred to as inside salespeople to denote that they do not call on clients face to face. In this context, salespeople that do call on clients in person are commonly called outside salespeople.

Outbound telemarketing involves unsolicited phone calls to leads in an attempt to qualify them as prospects. Because of past abuse by some unscrupulous firms, in the U.S. strict federal guidelines and regulations have been adopted about when telemarketers can call. Opt-out lists (also referred to as do-not-call lists) are available to ensure prospects do not receive such calls at all. Firms that ignore opt-out preferences of customers risk heavy penalities. The Federal Trade Commission (FTC) is the key agency regulating tele-marketing. The FTC website provides up-to-date information on telemarketing regulations. Other countries have rapidly adopted their own versions of anti-telemarketing laws. The declining reputation of outbound telemarketing, the resultant regulation and litigation, and especially the opt-out lists have drastically reduced the effectiveness of outbound telemarketing as a prospecting tool over the past decades. In particular, in some countries regulations have increasingly cracked down on unsolicited calls and (and texts) to smartphones. Ethical Dilemma explores the challenge of do-not-call lists and their limitations on the usefulness of telemarketing as a prospecting tool.

Outside salespeople, especially in B2B markets, often prospect by phone themselves rather than relying on mass telemarketing. This approach has the distinct advantage of allowing the salesperson to hear potential prospects' responses, favorable and unfavorable, firsthand. It also helps minimize the time and information gap between prospect identification and initial sales call.

Inbound telemarketing refers to responses from inside salespeople to inquiries from prospects that were generated by any means (advertising, social media, etc.). Inbound telemarketing holds promise for

ETHICAL DILEMMA

TO CALL OR NOT TO CALL

You read that telemarketing can be useful in generating prospective customers. But several years ago the U.S. Congress passed, and the President signed, the "Do Not Call" law. After several court challenges, the register is now in place. Similar actions have been taken by other countries and the trend is growing globally to block rampant telemarketing.

The national Do Not Call Registry (www.donotcall.gov) offers individuals the opportunity to register their phone number with the federal government. (Many state governments have similar registries.) Telemarketers must check the list and are prohibited from calling any phone number on it. Fines are high at over $10,000 per infraction, so telemarketers have a real motivation to follow the law.

There are exceptions to the prohibition. Companies that have had a business relationship with the individual in the last 18 months, telephone surveyors conducting a phone survey, and political organizations can still call numbers on the list. However, everyone agrees this should cut down on the ability of telemarketers to make unsolicited phone calls.

Telemarketers argue, and modern selling practices suggest, that although abuses occur telemarketing is a valid method for making prospective customers aware of new products and services. In addition, the telephone is one of the best methods for reaching certain target markets, such as senior citizens. Finally, fundamental questions about free speech and the ability to make a living are called into question if people are prohibited from engaging in a legal form of communication.

Questions to Consider

1. Should marketers be prohibited from using the telephone to solicit prospective customers? Why or why not?
2. Is there a cultural aspect to this issue? That is, is telemarketing more acceptable in some cultures than others?
3. If you worked for a company that has been using telemarketing to help generate new prospects, how would you feel about losing this source of customers? What would you do to replace this approach?

prospecting because, like websites, inbound telemarketing gives prospects a way to receive more information directly from a sales organization. As with other approaches, the key to success with this method is to ensure timely response by the inbound telemarketer to customer inquiries. If the prospect appears promising, depending on how the sales force is organized, the inside salesperson may go ahead and pursue the sale or may turn the prospect over to an outside salesperson to pursue the client further.

Written Correspondence

Can you believe that, in the second decade of the 21st Century, salespeople may choose to prospect via actual written correspondence with potential customers? Before you completely discount written correspondence as a dinosaur, consider that often a salesperson can differentiate his or her communication with clients from competition by occasionally employing a personal written letter or note. This approach is especially appreciated with older generation buyers and can be received as a pleasant surprise in this age of all things electronic.

One form of written correspondence that often is not so well received nowadays is an unsolicited mass direct-mail campaign by the firm. This type of prospecting, often called junk mail, can appear to be personalized but most receivers easily see through it as a mass mailing. This type of prospecting simply plays the odds and has the advantage of volume. It takes extremely large numbers of bulk mailings to generate reasonable numbers of leads.

Trade Shows

Most people are familiar with trade shows, major industry events in which companies doing business in a particular industry gather together to display their new products and services. Such events are usually held annually or semiannually. Examples include the annual housewares show in Chicago and the annual consumer electronics show in Las Vegas.

Trade shows provide leads in several ways. First, the listing of participants can be quite rich in terms of developing potential prospects. Generally, the leads developed at a trade show are later forwarded to the various salespeople responsible for making the next contact. Second, general networks can be developed and enhanced through contacts made at trade shows. And finally, there are opportunities to actually sell, as customers come by your booth to view and learn about your new products.

Conferences

Some sales organizations create their own conferences or other events to provide a forum for prospecting. Typically such conferences combine information sessions with social outings, and they are usually held in attractive locations. The global pharmaceutical industry historically has been a leader in sponsoring medical conferences in which physicians learn about new research findings and oncoming new medications. Because of concern about the ethics of having medical professionals potentially beholden to a particular pharmaceutical firm, many countries have clamped down on such events by limiting the ability to claim expenses from such conferences against their annual tax bill.

Cold Calls and Warm Calls

Classic cold calls, also referred to as canvassing, usually means the salesperson telephones or goes to see potential prospects in person, without invitation. Historically, many salespeople dislike cold calling. In many industries it is discouraged nowadays because it is very expensive to call on individuals whose likelihood of purchase is unknown. This is not to say that if you find yourself in a remote city with some extra time, a personal visit cold call on an interesting prospect company might not be worthwhile as a fact-finding mission. Such junkets often provide invaluable information (and sometimes surprises) that can lead to the development of a business relationship.

On the other hand, warm calls are a prospecting approach in which the salesperson makes a personal visit or phone call based on some pre-work in leads qualifying via one of the other sources of prospects discussed in this section. So much more information is available from these sources that, in many firms in the B2B space, cold calling is virtually obsolete.

Other Issues in Sourcing Prospects

Chapter 2 highlighted the trend toward the use of cross-functional teams in selling and chapter 3 discussed the intertwined roles of selling and marketing in modern organizations. These trends bring to light an important issue—prospecting by people in your firm *other than salespeople.* To the extent various support personnel, engineers, design people, and especially marketers and executives are out in the marketplace interacting with customers, they can employ the same approaches to lead generation and prospecting as salespeople. For this approach to provide any benefits, the firm must have a formal mechanism in place by which prospecting information collected by nonsales personnel can be recorded and disseminated to the sales force. Typical CRM systems allow for easy entry of such information into a database.

Then, too, mass-market advertising, public relations and publicity campaigns, and sales promotion methods also generate leads. A salesperson may get a text, Tweet, email, or call from a potential prospect responding to such promotion yet never know what generated the call. CRM systems typically require that, when such an unsolicited call is received, the salesperson ask the source of the referral and enter it into the system. Truly integrated CRM systems accumulate this information and distribute it back to the marketing department to show the effectiveness of various promotional initiatives (more leads generated means a more successful promotion).

SET A SYSTEMATIC PROSPECTING PLAN

You have seen that effective prospecting contributes to salesperson success by allowing for better qualification of leads as potential prospects. It is important to use a prospecting plan, which includes the following steps.

1. *Set goals for your prospecting activities before you begin.* Answer the question: What would you like to achieve by prospecting? Make sure your goals are:
   a. *Specific.* Goals should be clear, concise, understandable, and without ambiguity of purpose.
   b. *Measurable.* Put some numbers to your goals; include a time frame for accomplishment.
   c. *Attainable.* Be sure your goals are realistic, not "pie-in-the-sky" goals that you can't actually accomplish.

   Here is a goal that is specific, measurable, and attainable: "I will write a personalized follow-up letter to each potential prospect within one day after each prospecting appointment or phone call."
2. *Study and practice the various methods of prospecting.* Make it a point to use multiple prospecting approaches over time. Choose the approach for each situation that is most likely to pay off.
3. *Keep good records.* If your company has a database-driven system like CRM, always record prospecting information there. If not, keep your own records in an Excel file or other spreadsheet application.
4. *Be prompt in follow-up.* If a prospect contacts you for more information, respond to him or her right away. The term "hot" prospect means just what it sounds like. The prospect is stimulated to receive information about your product *now,* not later. Prompt follow-up shows prospects you are an efficient and caring salesperson.
5. *Pay attention to the results of your prospecting efforts.* Don't get into the grind of using a particular prospecting technique just because someone tells you to. It's not the prospecting itself that's important—it's the *results.* In your records, make notes about what worked and what didn't. Talk to your sales manager if you are having trouble using any of the prospecting methods.

Make the Best Use of CRM in Prospecting

By now you can see how useful CRM systems are in supporting your prospecting activities. Here are two keys to success.

- *Know your system.* Learn all you can about it. Understand its capabilities to help you as a salesperson.
- *Use your system.* Consider yourself very fortunate to have available a comprehensive tracking system for customers—a couple of decades ago salespeople tracked most everything by making written entries! Today, the recipe for successful selling likely is three parts great selling skills and two parts information technology and personal management skills.

Resist Call Reluctance

Chapter 2 examined buyer and seller roles. Although exceptions do exist, *sellers* are the ones usually expected to *initiate* customer relationships. Yet sometimes salespeople resist prospecting because (of all the activities required in successful selling) it is the one that may involve making cold calls. Salespeople must overcome this call reluctance if they are going to succeed.

There are many reasons for call reluctance. Most of them involve a lack of confidence in one's ability to perform the task.[4] The key is what to do about it. Much of the solution to call reluctance comes from effective training and support by management. Sales managers can help tremendously by employing the following approaches.

- Use role plays and exemplar videos to show various aspects of prospecting and potential prospect responses, as well as effective salesperson handling of questions and objections.
- Prospect together—salesperson and manager—until the salesperson is fully comfortable with the prospecting role.
- Set realistic goals. When we said that effective goals should be *attainable,* the point was not trivial. When sales managers set ridiculously high goals for converting prospects to clients, salespeople are bound to get discouraged and may even leave the company.
- Train salespeople to view prospecting as a numbers game. They must understand that to have a continuous pipeline of customers, a salesperson must continuously seek out new prospects.
- Keep as your target finding prospects who can become valued *long-term* clients. You already know the benefits of simultaneously cultivating current good customers and prospecting for new ones.

PLANNING THE SALES CALL: THE PREAPPROACH

At this point let us assume you have qualified a prospect as a potentially good future customer. You believe this person has the potential to develop a long-term relationship with you and your firm that will reap excellent returns for both parties. You clearly see that you and your product or service can add value for your prospect's firm. You are now ready to do some additional preparation for making a sales call on this prospect. Planning the sales call is called the preapproach because you are preparing some things before actually making the initial approach to set the appointment. (Note: The approach step will be discussed in chapter 7.)

In truth, many salespeople accomplish some of the preapproach activities in the process of prospecting. At least, they lay the groundwork for the preapproach based on the research they have done in identifying the target prospect. Think of preapproach activities as the things you focus on between qualifying a lead as a definite prospect and picking up the phone to make the appointment. The preapproach is a planning step. You are doing research, thinking about the potential client and how to approach him or her with your value proposition, and examining the best way to contact the client to make the appointment. A terrific amount of groundwork is laid during the preapproach that pays off during the actual sales call and beyond. The work you do here ensures that you make a good first impression on the prospect on the phone and/or face to face.

The preapproach includes the following elements:

1. Establish goals for the initial sales call.
2. Learn all you can about the prospect.
3. Plan to portray the right image.
4. Determine your approach.
5. Prepare a sales proposal.

These tasks do not need to be accomplished in order. In practice, you will likely be working on them simultaneously.

Establish Goals for the Initial Sales Call

It is amazing how many salespeople call on clients without setting specific goals for what they want to accomplish in the call. This is not professional, nor does it make good use of your client's valuable time (or your time). Like goals for prospecting, goals for the sales call must be specific, measurable, and attainable. They must take into account your firm's goals, your own goals as a salesperson, and the client's goals.[5] Use your judgment as to how much you can accomplish in one sales call—especially the first one, where you and the customer are just getting to know each other. Salespeople tend to map out in advance goals across several planned sales calls with a client. The nature and scope of your goals will vary depending on your business and the client. Some sample goals for a first sales call might be:

- To have the prospect agree to a demonstration of your product.
- To have the prospect agree to contact several of your references.
- To have the prospect initiate the process in his or her firm to allow your company to be set up as a vendor.
- To set up another appointment to address specific issues brought out in the initial sales call.

Note that none of these goals involves actually making a sale. If getting an order on the first sales call is realistic, then by all means set that goal. As time goes by and your relationship with a customer blossoms, you and the client can work together on mutual goal setting to build each other's business.

Learn All You Can about the Prospect

If you are engaged in B2B selling, you must pay attention to both professional and personal aspects of the potential customer. Some of the sources used in your prospecting research can serve you well here. You can turn to the Internet for more information on the professional (company) side. Other sources of information on the prospect and his or her company are noncompeting salespeople in your network who have been calling on the firm and members of the firm's buying center whom you can contact comfortably before the sales call. Exhibit 6.3 lists sample items you can research before making an initial sales call.

The idea is to obtain enough information to match yourself and your company to your prospect's situation and needs right from the very first sales call. It is also important to avoid mistakes such as mispronouncing a buyer's name or not knowing the client firm is going through a merger. Missing such major personal or professional aspects gives a very poor first impression.

EXHIBIT 6.3 SAMPLE ITEMS TO RESEARCH BEFORE THE SALES CALL

Information on the Person	Information on the Company
Name	Size of firm
Personal interests	Types of products offered
Personal goals	Other vendors currently used
Attitude toward salespeople in general	Corporate culture
Impression of your company and its products	How decisions are made (buying center or otherwise)
Any history of dealings with your company	Purchasing history of competing products
How rewarded/compensated by the firm	General policies on buying and vendor relations
Receptivity to socializing with salespeople	Any unusual or especially relevant current circumstances

Plan to Portray the Right Image

Image is important in forming a good first impression. In most cases, the first real impression you make on a prospect occurs when you meet him or her in your first face-to-face sales call. You can lay the groundwork for an excellent impression by sending written materials in advance along with a professional cover letter or email, or by being very professional when you set up the sales call appointment by phone. Planning the right image includes two key aspects: deciding what type of presentation to prepare and deciding what to wear for the sales call. Chapter 7 provides more on first impressions and image in the discussion about the approach.

Type of Presentation. Chapters 7 and 8 provide considerable detail about how to get ready for a great presentation as well as various sales presentation strategies. For now, you need to know that you actually decide what type of presentation you want to make at the preapproach stage. Here are some key issues to consider.

- How much technology should I employ in the sales call, and what types (PowerPoint, laptop, etc.)?
- How formal should the presentation be?
- How long should I allow for the presentation? How long for Q&A?
- What materials should I send the prospect in advance, how should I send them, and what should I bring with me?

To answer these questions, you must learn as much as you can, in advance, about the prospect's preferences. If you have trouble determining critical answers from your research, it is perfectly acceptable to directly query the prospect or his or her gatekeeper about preferences, either by phone (perhaps when you make the appointment), by follow-up letter, or by email.

Your goal at the preapproach stage should be to ensure you can show up at the prospect's office with the confidence of knowing that what you have prepared will be comfortable for the prospect, be a good fit to his or her style, and have the highest possible likelihood of gaining a favorable reaction. Bottom line: a great first impression!

Grooming and Attire. Grooming, or general personal cleanliness and professional appearance, is a given in professional selling. You *must* look the part of a competent, trusted business partner to succeed. Unclean fingernails, unkempt hair, and the like tell the prospect you are not playing in the professional leagues. People with poor grooming habits will *not* be successful in sales. In addition, visible tattoos and body piercings are still not generally accepted in most areas of professional B2B selling.

Attire is less dogmatic than grooming for several reasons. Of course you don't want your clothing to appear sloppy and unkempt, and you don't want unusual jewelry or accessories to distract from your sales message. However, many firms have shifted to business casual all the time, so you can choose whether to match that attire or dress up to a more professional image. Here are a few tips:

- If the client suggests dressing in business casual, do so.
- When in doubt, dress up to business attire.
- When you do the preapproach, ask the prospect or gatekeeper about the dress code.
- *Never* dress down below the client's level of attire.

Following these simple rules will ensure your first impression is enhanced, not hurt, by the way you are dressed.

Determine Your Approach

The approach means how you are going to contact the prospect initially to set up an appointment and begin the dialogue. Part of the preapproach is assessing options for the approach itself. Often the telephone is used, although other viable options include email, letter, or even an initial in-person interview. Your preapproach research should help you determine which of these is most appropriate for use with your particular prospect. Chapter 7 provides more information on making the approach.

Prepare a Sales Proposal

An excellent way to plan out the sales process in advance is through the use of written sales proposals. A sales proposal formalizes much of what we have learned in this chapter and focuses on the value proposition. It provides an effective means to approach the prospect. The Appendix at the end of this chapter guides you through the development of a sales proposal. The research, time, and energy you put into this preparation at the preapproach stage will pay off in multiple ways during the sales call.

THE SALES MANAGER'S ROLE IN PROSPECTING AND SALES CALL PLANNING

Given the critical importance of the tasks to be performed by a salesperson prior to the first meeting with a customer, sales managers often find themselves serving as a key resource to salespeople engaged in prospecting and sales call planning. As we have learned, prospecting sometimes can be a bit intimidating, and the best sales managers carefully monitor the progress their salespeople are making on their prospecting plan.

It is important for the manager to be especially sensitive to the potential for sales call reluctance. One highly effective way to coach and mentor salespeople on prospecting activities is through ongoing "workwiths" by the sales manager, in which he or she spends a day or so periodically traveling with the salesperson on visits to customers. The sales manager can occasionally reverse roles and actually do the selling while the salesperson observes, in order to provide an example. Besides the opportunity to observe a salesperson in action, work-withs often also provide ample time while traveling in between sales calls for general discussion between salespeople and their managers about prospecting, as well as two-way constructive debriefing of calls after they have taken place.

The sales manager can be a terrific source of ideas and information for the preapproach. Often, he or she will have direct access to more or different information that would help the salesperson better prepare for making the sales call. The salesperson can share a draft of a sales proposal or presentation materials with the manager beforehand to solicit input and ideas. And, importantly, sales managers are in the very best position of any manager in a company to ensure that the company's standards of professionalism, image, and branding are upheld consistently by the sales force through their interaction with the company's customers.

EXPERT ADVICE: FOLLOW-UP   Chally Group WORLDWIDE

After watching the video of Professor Friedman and reading the chapter, consider the following questions.

1. How do you imagine "peddlers" went about prospecting?
2. He says that drummers were an early day version of relationship salespeople. What similarities do you find between them and professional salespeople today?

SUMMARY

Prospecting is important to building new and future business. Leads must be qualified as prospects based on criteria established by the salesperson and his or her firm. Numerous approaches to prospecting exist. One of the most effective is referrals from loyal customers. In addition, various forms of social media can be a great boost to salespeople in lead generation. A prospecting plan can ensure that salespeople do a thorough and systematic job of prospecting. If a salesperson suffers from call reluctance, the sales manager should provide training support to help the rep overcome it.

The preapproach (the planning stage just before the sales rep approaches the prospect) is one of the most important aspects of the selling process. The preapproach is the salesperson's opportunity to prepare a presentation that will make a strong first impression. Good preparation during the preapproach also builds confidence that comes across in the sales call.

KEY TERMS

lead	endless chain referral	telemarketing	trade shows
qualifying the prospect	networking	inside salespeople	conferences
prospecting	centers of influence	outside salespeople	cold calls
referral	bird dogs	outbound telemarketing	warm calls
customer advocacy	directories	inbound telemarketing	call reluctance
word-of-mouth	spam	junk mail	preapproach

ROLE PLAY

BEFORE YOU BEGIN

Before getting started, please go to the Appendix of chapter 1 to review the profiles of the characters involved in this role play, as well as the tips on preparing a role play.

Characters Involved

Bonnie Cairns
Abe Rollins

Setting the Stage

Abe Rollins has just received a referral from a fellow Rotarian that Budget Beauty Biz (BBB) is going to open a new store in District 10, its first store in the area. BBB is a major chain that sells discount hair products, and several of Upland Company's products in the hair care category (shampoo, conditioner, creme rinse, hairspray, mousse, gel, and hair color) sell very well in BBB's stores. On further inquiry, Abe finds out the new store will be in Bonnie Cairns's sales territory. This will be the first new account Bonnie has opened, and Rhonda Reed (the district manager) asks Abe to help Bonnie develop her preapproach.

Bonnie Cairns's Role

Bonnie schedules a meeting with Abe to discuss preparing for making contact with the new customer. At this point, nothing is known about the new BBB store except that it will open in about six months and the buyer, José Reynaldo, will be in town in about a month to begin meeting with vendors for initial inventory orders. Bonnie needs to discuss with Abe the entire set of issues regarding the preapproach. She prepares a list of questions for Abe about what she should accomplish during the preapproach.

Abe Rollins's Role

Abe has a wealth of experience over the years in calling on new customers. He also enjoys helping Rhonda by coaching new salespeople. He is delighted to meet with Bonnie and prepares in advance an outline of the things she needs to accomplish during the preapproach on BBB.

Assignment

Work with another student to develop a 7–10 minute exchange about what Bonnie needs to accomplish during the preapproach stage with BBB. Both parties should come to the table prepared with extensive lists of preapproach issues, and the role play should be used to make decisions on specifically what Bonnie should do before calling José for that first appointment.

DISCUSSION QUESTIONS

1. Someone says: "Our firm focuses on maintaining long-term relationships with our customers. We don't have to do any prospecting." Evaluate this statement.

2. List three or four criteria you could use to qualify a lead as a likely prospect. How would you find out if the lead meets these criteria?

3. What are some reasons a potential prospect might not be readily accessible? How far should you go to try to overcome such an accessibility problem before you move to the next lead?

4. Pick any three of the sources of prospects discussed in the chapter and pick a product or service you like. Develop several ideas for how you would use each source to locate leads for the product or service you are interested in selling.

5. Who is currently in your own network that you could use for prospecting? How might you add to your network?

6. Why do you think a salesperson might experience call reluctance? How can it be overcome?

7. The chapter provides sample goals for an initial sales call on a prospect. (a) What other goals can you come up with that might be appropriate for an initial sales call? (Try for three or four more.) (b) Develop three or four goals that would be appropriate for a sales call on an *established* customer.

8. Why are grooming and attire so important in selling? How do you know if you are dressed appropriately for a customer?

MINI-CASE 6 STRONG POINT FINANCIAL SERVICES

Rafael Sanchez is about to begin his career as a financial investment representative with Strong Point Financial Services, a national company specializing in investment opportunities for individuals. Strong Point provides its customers with the ability to trade and own individual stocks and bonds. It also helps them manage Individual Retirement Accounts (IRAs) and 401(k) accounts.

Strong Point emphasizes a conservative investment philosophy of "buy and hold" and seeks clients who have the same philosophy. It differs from investment firms that encourage account holders to execute stock or bond trades often, thus creating commissions for the investment representative. The target market for Strong Point includes small business owners, empty nesters (people whose children have grown up and left home), two-income households with no children, and retired people. Strong Point's investment reps have had much success targeting this group of customers, and Rafael is eager to get started.

Rafael has just finished a seven-week training program for Strong Point's new investment representatives. He learned about the products and services Strong Point provides, who is included in the company's target market, how to identify potential customers, and how to represent and sell financial services. Now that Rafael is back in his company-assigned territory of southeast San Diego, he has been assigned a company mentor to help him through his first two years of employment with the company. Rafael's mentor, John Green, has been with the company for 11 years and has been extremely successful. In their first meeting, Rafael and John discuss how Rafael can begin to develop a list of prospects that will generate some clients for his new investment practice.

JOHN: Rafael, what do you plan to do to begin generating clients for your business?

RAFAEL: Well, at training, they said there is no substitute for knocking on doors and introducing myself to people. I'll start doing that tomorrow. I already have a couple of neighborhoods picked out—places where a lot of retired people live.

JOHN: That sounds like a good idea, and it looks as though you've picked the right neighborhoods. How many prospects do you plan to see in a day?

RAFAEL: I want to make at least 20 contacts, which as you know means getting their name, address, and phone number so I can follow up with them later. If I can get other information, such as whether they are already invested in the stock market or what their investment philosophy is, that will be great. But right now, I'll settle for an OK to contact them later with information about a potential investment in which they may be interested. If I reach my goal of 20 contacts per day, by the end of four weeks I'll have 400 names and addresses in my database. It'll require a lot of work and shoe leather, but I got into this business to be successful and that's what I plan to be.

JOHN: That sounds great. What else do you have planned?

RAFAEL: Well, I've contacted the local chamber of commerce. They keep a listing of all businesses owned by individuals and a separate list of businesses employing fewer than 50 people. I figure this will be a good source of information to begin targeting small business owners. They're sending me the lists and I should have them by the end of the week. Another thing I'm considering is having a booth at the local home show—you know, the one where home builders and building products suppliers display their home plans and products. I hear they get a big attendance at the show and I should be able to make some contacts there. What do you think?

JOHN: Those both sound like great ideas, especially the chamber of commerce lists. I'm not sure what your success will be at the home show, but it's worth a shot. In a couple of months you should consider putting on a seminar on one of the topics the company has provided, such as the difference between stock and bond investing. The last person I mentored, Maria Santiago, found that many of her current clients were people who had attended one of her seminars.

RAFAEL: Thanks for the tip. I'll keep the seminar idea in mind and start thinking about an appropriate topic. As you can tell, I'm eager to get started.

JOHN: That's great. I'll touch base with you later in the week to see how things are going. Good luck.

Questions

1. Which methods of prospecting discussed in the chapter has Rafael decided to use? Are they the most appropriate for his situation?

2. As Rafael continues to develop his client base, what other sources of prospects do you recommend he try? Why do you think these methods may be successful for him?

3. Assume you are Rafael's mentor, John Green. What recommendations would you make to help Rafael get the most out of his prospecting efforts?

Appendix: Sales Proposals

As mentioned in the introduction to Part Two, Chapters 6–10 are designed to systematically guide you through the entire sales process—prospecting and sales call planning; communicating the sales message; negotiating for win-win solutions; closing the sale and follow-up; and self-management. In practice, salespeople often plan out this process in advance through the use of written sales proposals that are provided to clients prior to making a sales call. Preparing a sales proposal accomplishes two important functions: (1) It forces the salesperson to formalize much of the advanced planning discussed in this chapter—the things that need to be done *before* going face to face with a buyer; and (2) it focuses the dialogue between buyer and seller on the *value proposition* from the very beginning, thus laying the groundwork for an effective long-term buyer–seller relationship. Sales proposals are an exceptionally professional way to approach the job of relationship selling.

In the course, your instructor may have you prepare a sales proposal and also role-play a complete presentation with a buyer (perhaps played by one of your classmates, by the instructor, or by someone else). On the website for this book (www.routledge.com/cw/Johnston) you will find a Sales Proposal Handbook, which includes a complete set of instructions and accompanying templates for a sales proposal assignment. In the handbook, the required content of the sales proposal is cross-referenced to the chapters in your book that contain information you will need to prepare each of the parts of the proposal. For now, let's briefly take a look at the four key components of a professional sales proposal.

- *Seller Profile.* Includes introductory information on you as the salesperson, your firm, and the products you foresee ultimately discussing with the buyer.
- *Critical Questions to Be Addressed.* You will learn in chapter 7 that a great way to establish initial communication with your buyer is through the use of well-reasoned, insightful questions. Asking the right questions will show the buyer that you have done your homework and are prepared for the sales call. One approach to using effective questions is a technique called SPIN selling, which will be described further in chapter 7.
- *Outline the Features, Advantages, and Benefits (FAB) of the Product.* Buyers today are very busy and pressed for time. They appreciate succinct, to-the-point information about sellers' offerings. One convenient way to provide what they need is through the FAB approach, which is also described in chapter 7.
- *Provide a Value Analysis in Financial Terms.* In chapter 3 and its Appendix you learned about the importance of conveying a strong value proposition in relationship selling. A key part of a sales proposal is quantifying for the buyer the value of doing business with you.

In this chapter, we built a strong case for the importance of taking time to do good prospecting and a thoughtful preapproach. The groundwork laid during these activities ensures a strongly favorable first impression with a buyer and pays off by getting the overall relationship off to a great start. Think of a sales proposal as a natural bridge between the prospecting/preapproach and the actual approach to the buyer. A sales proposal formalizes what you have learned during the analysis stage and presents an initial inquiry to a buyer in a way that will hopefully lead to the opportunity to meet with him or her in person. The next chapter prepares you for that in-person sales call.

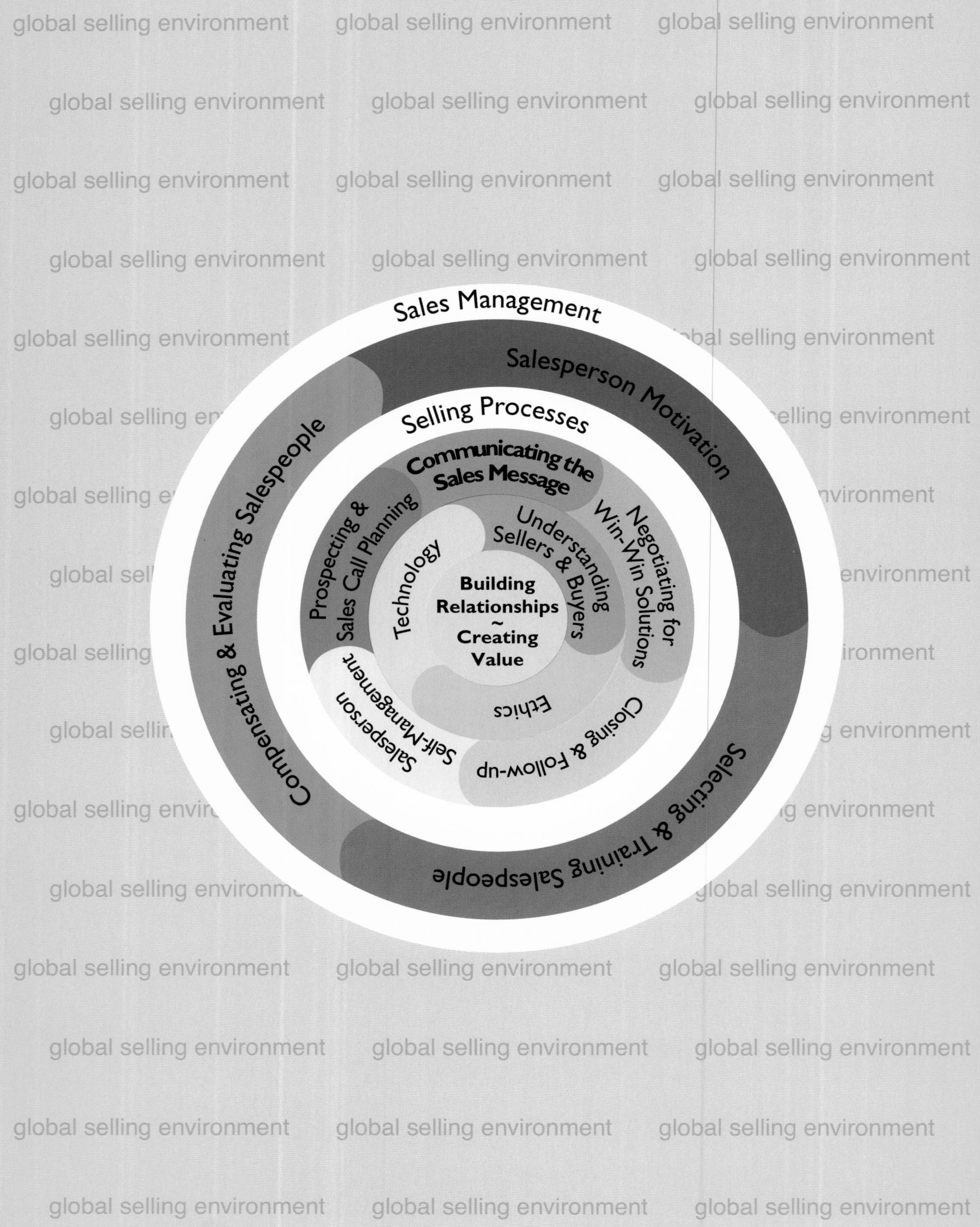
global selling environment
Sales Management
Salesperson Motivation
Selecting & Training Salespeople
Compensating & Evaluating Salespeople
Selling Processes
Communicating the Sales Message
Negotiating for Win-Win Solutions
Closing & Follow-up
Salesperson Self-Management
Prospecting & Sales Call Planning
Understanding Sellers & Buyers
Technology
Ethics
Building Relationships ~ Creating Value

Communicating the Sales Message

7

LEARNING OBJECTIVES

Watch the Expert Advice for chapter 7 and you will see how difficult and important it is to deliver a great sales presentation. Sales presentations are complex and require different skill sets for almost every situation. Successful salespeople know that building strong customer relationships depends in large part on their ability to do a good job presenting their products and services to customers.

In this chapter, you will learn about the building blocks of a sales presentation. The chapter will discuss how to prepare for the sales presentation and what specific information you need to get ready. It will also talk about the initial contact with the customer (the approach). Finally, the sales manager's role in the sales presentation will be discussed. While the salesperson is ultimately responsible for the presentation, the manager helps prepare the salesperson and does everything possible to ensure his or her success.

After reading this chapter, you should be able to:

- Understand the characteristics of a sales presentation.
- Identify sales presentation strategies.
- Discuss the steps in preparing for the sales presentation.
- Discuss the steps involved in approaching the customer.
- Understand how to apply your sales knowledge to the customer's needs.
- Understand how important product demonstrations are in the presentation.
- Define the keys to a great sales presentation.
- Understand the role sales managers play in sales presentations.

EXPERT ADVICE

EXPERT: David B. Edmonds
                Senior Vice President, Worldwide Services, FedEx Corporation

TOPIC: The importance of strong interpersonal communication in the sales presentation.

SUMMARY: Mr. Edmonds discusses the kinds of skills students need to be successful in a sales career. He highlights the need for good communication skills, the focus of this chapter. In addition, with the variety of products offered by FedEx and the complexity of their customer's businesses, it is important for the salesperson to have the strategic business insight to communicate the value proposition to the customer.

NEXT STEPS: Go the website for *Contemporary Selling* (www.routledge.com/cw/Johnston), watch the chapter 7 video, and then read the chapter. You will find the Expert Advice follow-up at the end of the chapter with questions that connect elements of your learning.

COMMUNICATING THE SALES MESSAGE

As you have seen, building winning relationships with customers is a long process. So far we have focused on the importance of understanding your own products and value proposition, gaining knowledge of the customer, prospecting for good potential customers, and developing a preapproach that puts your best foot forward when you first contact the prospect to gain an appointment. This chapter builds much of the *content* needed after the preapproach stage to prepare for the actual sales call. It then offers a road map for giving a great presentation when you are in the sales call.

With this chapter, you are ready to enter a critical stage in which you communicate the sales message to the customer in the sales presentation. (Refer to the model for Contemporary Selling and Sales Management at the beginning of the chapter to see where we are in the process.) So far you have focused on learning about your company (products, services, and capabilities), your customers, and the relationship selling process. In this chapter, you establish contact with the customer and begin a process that will culminate in a sale and strong relationship.

How important is the sales presentation? The sales presentation is the delivery of information relevant to solving the customer's needs. It often involves a product demonstration. Much of the time it also includes any data or other facts to support the case that the company's products and services are the best choice for the customer. It is in this critical stage that the salesperson begins to establish the link between the company's products and services and solutions to the customer's problem(s) in an open and honest way consistent with the company and salesperson's long-term goals.[1] As you have seen, customers move through a process that ultimately leads to the selection of a product. During the sales presentation, salespeople want to transition customers from mere interest to desire, conviction, and finally to purchase the product.

The stereotype of a sales presentation is a salesperson standing in front of a customer (or group of customers) talking and demonstrating the product. In reality, sales presentations are carefully choreographed interactions in which the salesperson tries to discern the customer's real needs and concerns while at the same time providing critical information in a persuasive way to help the customer appreciate the benefits and advantages of the product. Remember, the goal is not simply to "make the sale" but to create a strong value proposition that will lead to a mutually beneficial long-term relationship.

GETTING READY FOR A SALES PRESENTATION

Great sales presentations don't just happen. They are the result of careful planning and preparation. As you saw in chapter 5, getting ready for the presentation is just as important as actually meeting with the customer.

There are many elements to this part of the process. It is critical to know the characteristics of a great sales presentation, understand the various sales presentation strategies, and incorporate technology effectively. Salespeople must also establish the goals and objectives for the meeting and make sure that everything is set for a good first impression. They need to be able to answer two fundamental questions before a sales presentation: (1) What do I want to accomplish in this meeting? (2) Am I ready to make the sales call?

Characteristics of a Great Sales Presentation

If someone asked you, "What makes a great sales presentation?" would you be able to answer? Many of us could give examples of a bad presentation, such as not listening to the customer, but what are the characteristics of a great sales presentation? Exhibit 7.1 shows them. A great sales presentation explains the value proposition; asserts the advantages and benefits of the product; enhances the customer's knowledge of the company, product, and services; and creates a memorable experience.

EXHIBIT 7.1 CHARACTERISTICS OF A GREAT SALES PRESENTATION

1. Explains the value proposition. Answers the customer question: What is the value added of the product?

2. Asserts the advantages and benefits of the product. Answers the customer question: What are the advantages and benefits of this product?

3. Enhances the customer's knowledge of the company, product, and services. Answers the customer question: What are the key points I should know about this company, product, and services?

4. Creates a memorable experience. Answers the customer question: What should I remember about this presentation?

Explain the Value Proposition. First and foremost, a sales presentation must clearly explain the value proposition for the customer. As we discussed in chapter 3, identifying customer needs and creating solutions using your company's products and services is at the heart of the value proposition. However, a salesperson must have the skill and flexibility to adapt the value proposition based on customer feedback during and after the presentation. In addition, there is a huge difference between the salesperson knowing the value proposition and the customer understanding it clearly. Often the salesperson must use several tools to communicate how the company is creating value for the customer. In addition to an oral presentation, salespeople often use nonverbal communication, PowerPoint presentations, written proposals, and other support information to further explain the value proposition. By explaining the value proposition the salesperson plays a critical role in building the company's brand through the social interaction of the sales relationship and with today's technology the "salesperson" can even be an avatar.[2]

Assert the Advantages and Benefits of the Product. Customers want to know the specifics of how your product is better than the competition. As you shall see later in this chapter, identifying a product's features, advantages, and benefits is essential to a great sales presentation. They form the basis of a product's value to the customer.

At the same time it is important to understand any weaknesses associated with your product. It is essential that the customer believe you are answering the question "What's in it for me?"—in other words, how the product addresses the specific concerns of the customer—and that requires a good understanding of not only the strengths of the product but also the weaknesses.

Enhance the Customer's Knowledge of the Company, Product, and Services. Many products require detailed explanations for the customer to fully understand what is going on. Take, for example, an Oracle salesperson trying to explain a new feature in the Oracle Enterprise Manager Suite of software products. The salesperson could talk about the product's development and productivity, but it might be more effective to educate the customer about cost savings. Another option might be to demonstrate the product, an important presentation tool we will talk about later in this chapter. In any case, your presentation should enhance the customer's knowledge about the product.

In addition to specifics about the company's product, customers may want to know a variety of things about the company, other products and services, and even the people they will be working with. An effective sales presentation will educate customers about all these things.

Create a Memorable Experience for the Customer. Ultimately, for any sales presentation to be effective the customer must be interested in it. It needs to be an event the customer will remember after the salesperson is gone. There is no rule that says sales presentations should be boring. On the other hand, the presentation must always be professional and the salesperson should never substitute glitz for a skilled delivery of relevant information.

Sales Presentation Strategies

There are four basic types of presentation strategies, shown in Exhibit 7.2. The most appropriate one in a given situation depends on the salesperson's individual selling skills, feedback from the customer, and the company's preferences. Think of the four strategies on a continuum, with the memorized presentation at one end and the problem-solving presentation at the other.

EXHIBIT 7.2 SALES PRESENTATION STRATEGIES

Presentation Strategy	Focal Point of Presentation	Talk/Listen Ratio
Memorized	Product	90/10
Formula	Product	70/30
Need satisfaction	Customer	40/60
Problem solving	Customer	30/70

As you move along the continuum, you will find two fundamental differences. The first is the focus of the presentation strategy. In the memorized presentation the focal point is the product/company. At the other end of the continuum, the problem-solving strategy focuses on identifying customers' needs and solving their problem(s). The second difference is in the talk/listen ratio. In the memorized presentation, the salesperson does most of the talking and very little listening. As you move through the presentation strategies, that ratio begins to reverse. The customer talks more and the salesperson listens more. In a problem-solving presentation, the salesperson does very little talking (at least initially) as the customer explains his or her needs and problems. Let's look at each of these four presentation strategies in greater detail.

Memorized Presentation. At first glance the very structured memorized presentation strategy may seem inappropriate in most situations. The focus is on the product and the presentation is based on the memorization of specific canned statements and questions. The salesperson is not really interested in determining the needs of the customer. Companies, and salespeople, who adopt a memorized presentation strategy believe they can make a compelling argument for the product without spending time learning more about the customer's problems and needs.

There are a number of flaws in this presentation strategy. A primary disadvantage is that the salesperson may discuss aspects of the product that are not important to the customer while leaving out critical information. By not determining the customer's real needs, the salesperson risks wasting everyone's time. What is more, the very nature of memorized presentations limits customer participation. As much as 90 percent of the total presentation time may be taken up by the salesperson's dialogue. This is a big negative for many prospects, who wonder, "How can the product be the best choice for me if the salesperson does not listen or even ask me about my needs?" Finally, this type of presentation tends to seem high pressure, as it usually solicits the purchase decision several times. For all these reasons, the memorized presentation may not seem the best choice for building a customer relationship—and it's probably not. However, there are several advantages.

First, and most significantly, memorized sales presentations ensure consistent delivery. They are frequently the result of careful company analysis and development, and offer companies the assurance that critical information will be given to the customer in a uniform and reliable manner. The more you encourage customers to be involved, the less control you have in the presentation. Some companies believe that controlling the flow and order of the presentation increases the probability of success.

A second advantage is the ability to deliver more information in the same amount of time. By focusing on the product and not the customer's needs, the salesperson can convey more facts (making this a viable presentation style when time is very short). Next time you take a sales telemarketing phone call, notice that the caller is most likely working from a memorized presentation script.

This presentation strategy can also be reassuring for inexperienced salespeople. Since they can learn the presentation and have very little opportunity to change it, new salespeople may worry less about forgetting something or losing their place.

While set questions are included in a memorized presentation, they are most often designed to solicit a simple response that will move the customer through the purchase process. The salesperson may ask a question for which the answer is already known. "If I could save you 50 percent off your current copying charges, would you be interested?" The salesperson is not concerned about the customer's true copying charges (how they break down, what services the customer uses most often). Rather, the question is asked to get customer acceptance of the product. Most customers respond yes, and the salesperson has created buy-in for the product.

Formula Presentation. The formula presentation is also highly structured but increases customer interaction by soliciting more information. It follows a prepared outline that directs the overall structure of the presentation but enables the salesperson to gain some customer feedback. This type of presentation begins to shift the focus more to the customer. It still focuses on the product but encourages the customer—through questions, trial closes, and objections—to become more involved in the presentation. The talk/listen ratio changes to more listening (30–40 percent) and less talking (60–70 percent).

Formula presentations are based on the simple acronym "AIDA," which sums up the buying process. The salesperson must get the customer's *attention,* create *interest* in the product, develop a strong *desire* for the product, and move the customer to *action* (buying the product). Moving through the process requires buy-in and agreement, which means customer involvement.

The formula presentation strategy affords some definite advantages. Both company and salesperson can feel confident that critical information will be conveyed to the customer in a carefully constructed format. Moreover, the more ordered approach means salespeople will be better prepared to handle objections and questions. Finally, incorporating greater customer feedback into the presentation increases the likelihood of product acceptance and purchase.

On the other hand, if the salesperson does not do a good job of asking questions and anticipating objections, this strategy is not flexible enough to handle more complex selling situations and customer interaction. It is best used when a relationship has been established and the customer will be rebuying. The salesperson is already familiar with the customer's specific needs and is trying to gain acceptance of a new order, which could be a reorder of existing products or the sale of a new product into the customer's product mix.

Many companies, including Procter & Gamble, use some type of formula presentation with their frontline sales force around the world. Consumer products salespeople tend to know their customers well and the object is often for them to carry more of an existing product (more sizes of Crest toothpaste, greater inventories of Bounty paper towels). A highly structured presentation that lets them hit specific selling points in a predetermined formula while still soliciting customer feedback can be very effective. The key to the success of the formula strategy is customer knowledge, since the presentation itself is relatively inflexible. More sophisticated selling situations require different sales presentation strategies.

Need Satisfaction Presentation. Unlike the memorized and formula presentations, the need satisfaction presentation shifts the focus to the customer and to satisfying the customer's needs. The talk/listen ratio shifts in favor of listening, especially early in the presentation. As much as 60 percent of the first half of a need satisfaction presentation is spent asking questions, listening, and determining the customer's real needs. Even later in the presentation, the salesperson should be willing to ask additional questions to clarify problems and concerns.

The key to success with this strategy is the right combination of questions, listening, analysis, and presentation. Too many questions and the customer may doubt the salesperson's ability and knowledge. Too few questions and the customer will feel the salesperson is not really interested in his or her problems and needs.

Need satisfaction presentations can be broken down into three parts. The first stage, need identification, involves questioning the customer to discover his or her needs. This often begins with an open-ended question: "Ms. Grace, what exactly are you looking for in a new office network system?" Based on the customer response, the salesperson begins to ask more focused questions and zero in on a specific need. The questioning is not always linear. More circular questions uncover other needs, perhaps even problems or concerns the customer was unaware of. After identifying the customer's need(s), the salesperson moves from need identification to need analysis. Combining knowledge of the company's products and services with the recognition of customer needs, the salesperson must quickly (often during the presentation itself) analyze the customer's needs to determine how best to meet them. Finally, during need satisfaction, the salesperson presents the company's solution (products and services) to the customer's needs.

Creating a more interactive presentation can intimidate inexperienced salespeople. The salesperson gives up a degree of presentation control for a greater understanding of the customer's problems and concerns. If done well, need satisfaction presentations can establish profitable buyer–seller relationships. If done poorly, they can limit the company's access to that customer in the future. Salespeople generally need a great deal of training and confidence to use the need satisfaction presentation strategy successfully.

Problem-Solving Presentation. Considered the most complex and difficult presentation strategy, problem solving is based on a simple premise: The customer has problems and the salesperson is there to solve them by creating win-win solutions. We explore negotiating win-win solutions in chapter 8, but it is important to understand that problem solving is the preferred presentation strategy for building long-term customer relationships, and creating win-win solutions is a critical aspect of this strategy. The focus is on the customer, which means the salesperson spends much more time listening than talking. The salesperson does more analysis before the presentation. This strategy generally puts greater pressure on the salesperson, who must have the skills to identify and analyze the customer's needs and present the company's solution.

SETTING OBJECTIVES AND GOALS

The sales presentation is a critical time in the relationship-building process. You need to have a clear idea of what you want to accomplish. Ultimately, of course, the goal of the presentation is to secure a purchase commitment from the customer. However, you don't just walk in asking for the purchase order. Successful salespeople understand that the purchase order does not come until the customer believes the company's products and services offer the best solution to his or her needs. Often this will not happen in the initial meeting.

The goal of the presentation will dictate much of what happens during the meeting with the customer. In defining the goal, salespeople need to consider where the customer is in the buying process. They also need to have a clear understanding of the customer relationship. If the company has a long-established relationship, the salesperson can focus on other objectives than with a new customer. Finally, salespeople should know the specifics of the current situation. Is the company introducing a new product? Offering a new pricing program? Is the customer unhappy with something?

The presentation is affected by many factors. Based on their analysis of these factors, salespeople will identify at least one of five principal goals:

- Educate the customer by providing enough knowledge about the company's products and services.
- Get the customer's attention.
- Build interest in the company's products and services.
- Nurture the customer's desire and conviction.
- Obtain a customer commitment to action (purchase).

Every presentation should strive to meet at least one of these goals and often more than one. For example, it should be possible to move a customer from attention to interest in one presentation. Early in the relationship-building process, the salesperson may want to focus on educating the customer about the features, advantages, and benefits of the company's products and services. At some point, however, the goal of the presentation will be to obtain customer action.

You may think that once a relationship is established, the goals will change. But it will always be important to educate, maintain interest, nurture desire and conviction for your products, and, of course, keep the customer action oriented (buying). While it is important to have a goal for the presentation, the salesperson needs the skills and flexibility to deal with sudden opportunities (or threats) that may come up during the presentation.

APPROACH THE CUSTOMER: INITIATING THE RELATIONSHIP

Approaching the customer really means launching the buyer–seller relationship. You have spent a lot of time preparing the presentation. Now the approach is your first contact with the customer. It is a very important time as you move from introduction to transition into the sales presentation. Global Connection highlights the importance of creating a good first impression. Let's examine the customer approach more closely.

Tips for Making a Good First Impression

First impressions are important in setting the tone for the presentation.[3] Does a good first impression guarantee the sale? Absolutely not. Can a bad first impression lose a sale? Yes. Ultimately, a good customer relationship begins with the content and delivery of your presentation, but the first few minutes set the tone for everything else. Let's break down the first impression into three parts: before you meet the prospective customer, when you greet the customer, and the first three minutes of the presentation.

Before the Meeting. It is important to use your time before meeting the customer to put yourself in the right place at the right time. There is a simple rule in selling: Never make the customer wait. It is the salesperson's responsibility to be at the site before the presentation is scheduled to begin. Given the technology available today, there really is no excuse for being late. If you've never been there before, go online and get directions using MapQuest, Google Maps, or a similar site. If for some unexpected reason you are running late, use your cell phone to call the customer. Few things create a worse first impression than showing up late for a presentation.

Most salespeople make it a practice to arrive early. The "just-in-time" approach to making a sales meeting is not a good idea. A good rule of thumb is to get there at least 15 minutes before the scheduled start time. However, your time is also valuable, and all the time spent waiting for sales meetings would total many hours each year.

So it's helpful to have a checklist. First, be sure your customer knows you have arrived. Introduce yourself to the appropriate person (secretary, receptionist, assistant) and tell him or her you are there for the sales meeting. Second, as you wait, use the time to run over any last-minute notes or even the presentation itself. PowerPoint allows you to print a copy of the presentation; review it one last time so everything is fresh in

GLOBAL CONNECTION

THE POWER OF THE FIRST IMPRESSION AROUND THE WORLD

Here are five tips for creating a good first impression around the world.

1. *Be Confident*—Lack of confidence suggests the individual does not have command of the situation or the facts. There is always a risk of "stepping over the line" and appearing arrogant; this can be a problem in cultures where the sales process moves slower, such as China and Japan.

2. *Dress Appropriately*—As a professional it is important to present a positive image and dress appropriately. In a cross-cultural environment dress and personal habits play an important role; consider the customer's culture in selecting the appropriate attire.

3. *Make a personal connection*—Connect with the customer by developing a personal connection such as using his or her first name. However, keep in mind that in some cultures (many Asian countries, for example) it is important to acknowledge formal titles when meeting people early in the sales process.

4. *Be Punctual*—Nothing says more about the salesperson's commitment to the customer than being on time or, better yet, early. Even in many Latin cultures, which take a different view of time, it is always a good idea to be punctual—no matter the culture it is always better to wait on the customer than for the customer to wait on you.

5. *Do Homework*—Be ready and prepared to move confidently into the sales presentation. Customers all over the world appreciate a salesperson that is well prepared.

Adapted from Bill Brooks, "The Power of First Impressions," *American Salesman* (April 2006), pp. 3–6.

Questions to Consider

1. Do you believe first impressions really make a difference is a business-to-business setting? After all, aren't purchase decisions in a B2B setting based on rational decision-making criteria?

2. What does "do your homework" mean in the context of preparing for a first meeting with a client? What information is helpful to know before the meeting?

3. What additional information would you need to know if the meeting was with an international customer?

your mind. If it is an existing customer and you haven't checked with the office to learn the customer's latest activity, do so now. Update yourself on the status of the most recent order or find out what your company has done to address a current problem or issue. If you are confident that you are completely ready for the customer meeting, use the time to check voice mail or email.

Greeting the Customer. As we said earlier, the first few minutes of a presentation are critical to success.[4] Keep a few basic rules in mind as you create that first impression. First, make sure your overall look is appropriate. You may want to take a moment and freshen up. Second, make sure all wireless communication devices are turned off or put in silent mode. Having your cell phone go off just as you reach to shake hands will not start the meeting off on a good note. Third, be organized. Cause a minimum of disruption as you enter the customer's office. Walking in with stacks of paper or your laptop open sends a negative impression of your overall organizational skills.

If the customer extends his or her hand, shake it firmly. It is important to remember that the customer should extend their hand first; in some cultures shaking hands is less prevalent and you don't want to start the presentation off with a negative perception. If you are unfamiliar with the surroundings, look for a place to sit. In a conference room, if the customer sits at the head of the table, sit to one side close to the head. If the customer sits at a long side of the table, look for a chair across from him or her.

Most of the time, however, you meet customers in their office. The customer will give you verbal or nonverbal cues about where to sit. If there is a desk with chairs on the other side, move there immediately after greeting the customer. In large offices the customer may have a separate seating area (sofa and chairs with a coffee table) and you should follow his or her lead. If no cues are forthcoming, you may want to ask, "Where would you like me to sit?"

The First Three Minutes. The period just before the approach varies depending on your personal style, the customer's personal style, and the environmental situation at the time of the presentation. It's often helpful to spend some time developing a personal rapport with the customer.[5] Noncontroversial topics like the weather or sports (of course, depending on how the local team is doing, this may or may not be controversial) are the best subject choices. The key is to know when to make the transition from customer greeting to customer approach. Spend too long in small talk, and the customer will perceive you are wasting time. Be too abrupt, and you'll create an awkward moment. Initially, you may find these transitions difficult. However, in time you will develop a sense of the right moment to make the transition. Always remember the customer knows why you are there and it will not come as a surprise when you launch into the presentation.

Approach Strategies

The approach is what sales professionals call the first part of the sales presentation. It is a transition point from the greeting to the main body of your presentation where you will deliver the primary sales message to the customer. While you may have spoken by phone or email, most customers clearly prefer a face-to-face presentation. A well-executed approach can set up the rest of the presentation so you can move the buying process much more efficiently and effectively. The customer approach has two objectives: (1) get the customer's attention and (2) create enough interest in you, your company, and its products and services that you can continue the presentation.

The five common approach strategies are shown in Exhibit 7.3.

Referrals. One of the best ways to approach the customer is to be referred by a third party (often a satisfied customer). The referral is effective because of the third party's external endorsement of the company and by extension the salesperson as well. Research suggests the referral increases the credibility of the salesperson's points during the presentation and reduces customer anxiety about their validity.

A number of customers, however, do not wish to be used as referrals. There are many reasons for this reluctance. The relationship between the company and customer may deteriorate while the customer is being used as a referral with other prospective customers. Or the salesperson may also be calling on the customer's competitors.

Customer Benefit. Customers want to know how your products will benefit them, so telling them is a good way to begin a sales presentation. By starting the presentation with a solution to at least one of the customer's problems, you create an instant win-win situation. One caveat: It is essential that you be well prepared and have a thorough understanding of your customer's current situation, problems, and needs. Otherwise, the customer benefit approach could actually do more harm than good. The customer might be annoyed by your misperceptions.

EXHIBIT 7.3 APPROACHES TO THE SALES PRESENTATION

- **Referral**

  Mr. Render, my name is Charlie Smith. I am with Xentury Business Machines and you will remember we spoke by phone several times. Our networked copiers and printers offer great value and performance for businesses like yours. Indeed, you know Ms. Ferrino with Avalon Products and she suggested I give you a call. Ms. Ferrino has been a customer for five years and is very satisfied with our products and service.

- **Customer benefit**

  Ms. Santorum, your company needs reliable and cost-effective trucks to deliver your flowers every day. This new Ford van has the lowest costs per mile of any full-size van in the market, and our quality ratings [show appropriate studies] are among the highest in the industry. The new Ford van will not only get your flowers to their customers every day but will do so for the lowest cost of any full-size van.

- **Question**

  Our company can offer you a bundle of services that is the best in the industry. Are you interested in hearing more about them?

- **Assessment**

  Ms. Yeaple, as a successful businesswoman you want to be sure you are maximizing your current assets. I would like to evaluate your investment portfolio. There is no cost to you for this evaluation. If you would take a few moments to complete this short financial questionnaire, I will prepare an analysis of your current portfolio. Thank you.

- **Product demonstration**

Question. There are two advantages to the question method. First, getting the customer involved in the presentation is always a positive, and asking questions in the approach involves the customer right from the start. This goes a long way toward establishing customer buy-in to your sales message. Second, by getting customer feedback you are positioning yourself for success in the presentation. Ask questions that can focus the customer on the problem and help you gain greater acceptance; then structure the questions so they will lead into the presentation.

The risk of the question approach is that you may get an answer that will effectively end the presentation. If the customer answers yes, you are in an excellent position to transition into your presentation. But if the customer answers no, you will have to reestablish a point of contact or end the presentation.

Assessment. One technique that salespeople in certain industries (IT, insurance, financial services) have found effective is the assessment approach. You ask the customer to complete a set of questions. Then you collect the data, analyze the information, and make a presentation to the client based on your analysis.[6] The assessment approach is really a part of a larger problem-solving presentation strategy in which you put together a solution for the customer based on his or her feedback.

This approach can be effective for several reasons. First, it is relatively nonthreatening. You are not actually asking the customer to buy anything but simply requesting information that you will use to provide additional feedback. Second, the end result is generally an assessment that you can go over with the customer. Financial planners, for example, often ask prospective clients for a summary of their financial history. Based on the responses, the planner/salesperson prepares a financial plan for the customer. At the end of the presentation, the financial planner offers suggestions on how his or her company can help meet the customer's needs.

Product Demonstration. We will discuss the product demonstration in greater detail later in the chapter. Some salespeople find it an effective approach strategy. With certain products, such as automobiles, demonstrating the product is crucial to the presentation. Laptop computers and sophisticated graphics software let salespeople demonstrate products that are difficult to exhibit in a customer's office (security systems, for example).

Once you start the product demonstration, it is important to move quickly into the rest of the presentation, including the buying process. Salespeople often use the product demonstration in conjunction with another approach, such as the question, to get customer involvement while demonstrating the product.

THE SALES PRESENTATION: BUILDING THE RELATIONSHIP

Once the approach has established a relationship with the customer, it is time to move into the sales presentation. You did much of this work as you prepared for the sales meeting—but every salesperson will tell you there are always surprises. The customer might convey a new, critical piece of information, pose a new problem, disagree with your value proposition, or any one of hundreds of other challenges that a salesperson faces during a sales presentation. However, at the heart of the presentation is a simple process of identifying the customer's needs and applying your knowledge in a way that will solve the problem, add value to the customer's business (and your company), and build a successful relationship (Exhibit 7.4). Let's begin with identifying the customer's needs.

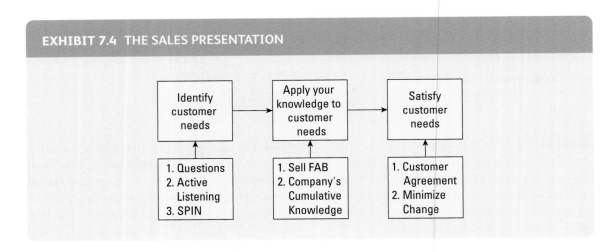

EXHIBIT 7.4 THE SALES PRESENTATION

Identify Customers' Needs

How important is identifying the customer's needs? Very. Research suggests that being able to focus on customers and correctly identify their needs is one of the key characteristics that distinguishes high-performing salespeople. Indeed, of all the elements in a sales presentation (approach, handling objections, and closing), the single factor shown to differentiate successful salespeople from the rest of the pack was their ability to discover the customer's need(s). Contemporary selling is based, in large part, on the salesperson's ability to identify those needs and develop win-win solutions that benefit both the customer and the company.

The need identification process really begins before the first customer meeting as you study the customer's business and get ready for the sales presentation. By learning about the customer, you will develop an initial assessment of needs. This will change as you talk with the customer and go through the need identification process. Even after the presentation, as you move forward in the relationship, you should continue to assess and update your understanding of the customer's needs.

Questioning Drives a Great Presentation. Identifying the customer's needs is not a complicated process, but it does require salespeople to perform several tasks very well. The first skill is asking the right questions at the right time. This may seem easy but, as we saw earlier, high-performing salespeople are significantly better at it than low performers. Asking questions and listening (which we will discuss shortly) are not easy for many people, especially in stressful situations like a sales presentation. Many inexperienced salespeople believe (incorrectly) that they should be talking and in control of the presentation.

A second, and sometimes more difficult, problem is the potential struggle within the customer. In the course of the presentation, he or she may become threatened by your questions. The customer may perceive that your proposed solutions could place him or her in jeopardy (if the presentation uncovers inefficiencies that are the customer's responsibility). In addition, remember that salespeople are change agents. By definition they are asking the customer to change by buying their product. Change creates conflict for the customer. What if you are wrong and the customer is blamed for buying your product? What if you are right and the customer fails to buy your product? As you can see, asking tough questions is threatening to both salesperson and customer. The basic categories of questions salespeople can ask during the presentation are summarized in Exhibit 7.5. Let's examine each type more closely.

EXHIBIT 7.5 CATEGORIES OF QUESTIONS

Question Type	Advantage	Disadvantage
Unrestricted	Encourages customer to speak	Is time consuming
Restricted	Gets specific information	Discourages dialogue
Data collection	Uncovers relevant data	Wastes customer time
Investigation	Helps uncover customer needs	Difficult to manage responses
Validation	Provides customer buy-in	Can derail presentation

UNRESTRICTED/RESTRICTED QUESTIONS. Encouraging the customer to open up and share information, unrestricted questions impose few limitations. Often referred to as open-ended or non-directed questions, they draw out information by allowing the customer to frame the answer. Restricted questions, on the other hand, require yes/no or very short answers. They direct the customer to a specific, very short response.

Most of the time salespeople will use both types of questions. Unrestricted questions encourage the customer to speak more freely and allow the salesperson to develop a richer, more complete understanding of the customer's issues. Restricted questions provide specific information the salesperson can use to shape the presentation. Indeed, it is common to move from one question type to the other. It is a good idea to get the customer more involved by asking unrestricted questions, but asking too many of them will almost certainly create time pressure on other parts of the presentation. There are particular pieces of information the salesperson may need during the presentation, and restricted questions are the most efficient way to get the information.

DATA COLLECTION QUESTIONS. These questions gather basic data about issues related to the customer's current business or historical perspective. While the information can be helpful, salespeople should limit data collection questions in a presentation for several reasons. First, customers may provide information that interferes with elements of the presentation. Given the access to information today, it is the salesperson's responsibility to be familiar with as much of the customer's business as possible. A general rule is to ask data collection questions that verify existing knowledge. Second, if a salesperson asks too many data collection questions, the customer may perceive a lack of preparation, and wonder, "Why doesn't this person already know this about my business?"

Inexperienced salespeople may incorrectly assume that asking customers questions about their business is the same as identifying their needs. This is not true; customers expect salespeople to know about their business before the presentation even begins. Data collection questions can be useful, but use them sparingly and do the customer homework before the presentation so that you don't waste time asking unnecessary questions.

INVESTIGATION QUESTIONS. These questions probe for information about problems, opportunities, or challenges in the business. The answers are often critical in correctly identifying the customer's needs. By encouraging the customer to talk about current issues and concerns in the business, salespeople gain valuable insight. Successful salespeople use these questions to assess the customer's current state of mind.[7]

VALIDATION QUESTIONS. At various critical points in the presentation, you may want to validate something with the customer. You might reaffirm the customer's needs or some key fact that came out of the investigation questions asked earlier in the presentation. Validation questions are important for two reasons. First, they help get agreement from the customer and move him or her through the buying process. Validating the customer's needs eliminates a point of disagreement later in the presentation. Second, they keep the customer involved in the presentation. Even if the response is simply yes or no, the customer is mentally engaged.

Keep in mind a few basic rules as you ask questions. First, go over them before the presentation. Poorly worded or inappropriate questions will do more harm than good. Second, always anticipate the answers. This is not to say you script the answers, but asking questions for which you have no general idea of the response can lead to real problems if you are surprised by a customer's response. Face-to-face time with the customer is limited, and fumbling for a response to an unexpected statement will not instill confidence in your abilities. Third (and most importantly), once you ask the question, listen to the customer's answer.

SPIN to Customers' Needs. Based on research conducted by Huthwaite, Inc. (and company founder Neil Rackham), the SPIN strategy is a comprehensive selling approach based on a series of questions about: **s**ituation, **p**roblem, **i**mplication, and **n**eed payoff.[8] This approach works very well with large, important sales. A number of multinational companies have adopted the SPIN selling approach, including UPS and Bank of America. Exhibit 7.6 summarizes the SPIN selling approach.

SITUATION QUESTIONS. These questions provide basic information about the customer's circumstances. Often they are broad questions designed to substantiate information the salesperson already knows. You don't want to overuse these questions, since customers may tire of answering them. Situation questions suffer from the same problems as the data collection questions we discussed earlier, but they do offer a format for establishing rapport with the customer.

PROBLEM QUESTIONS. Based on his or her own research, and responses to the situation questions, the salesperson moves on to more specific problems. Asking directed questions gets the customer concentrating on particular problems and issues. An effective tool when used by experienced salespeople, problem questions are much more useful in identifying the customer's needs than situation questions.

There are two goals for problem questions. First, the customer's responses offer critical information the salesperson will use in discovering the customer's needs. Second, in answering a carefully planned set of questions, customers will (if all goes well) admit they have a problem. While problem questions are valuable, the salesperson must continue to ask questions that will help the customer see the full effect of the problem.

IMPLICATION QUESTIONS. Once a problem has been defined, the salesperson must help the customer recognize its implications for his or her business. Implication questions help customers realize the seriousness of the problem and begin to search for solutions. You *must* get agreement on the problem before asking

EXHIBIT 7.6 THE SPIN SELLING APPROACH

Situation Questions—Finding facts about the customer's existing situations:

- Are overused by inexperienced salespeople.

Problem Questions—Learning about the customer's problems, difficulties, or dissatisfaction:

- Are used more in calls that succeed (especially for smaller sales)
- Are asked more by experienced salespeople.

Implication Questions—Learning about the effects, consequences, and implications, of the customer's problems:

- Are strongly linked to success in larger sales.
- Build up the customer's perception of value.
- Are harder to ask than situation or problem questions.

Need Payoff Questions—Learning about the value or usefulness of a proposed customer solution:

- Are strongly linked to success in larger sales. Increase the acceptability of your solution.
- Are particularly effective with influencers who will present your case to decision makers.

Adapted from Neil Rackham, *SPIN Selling* (New York: McGraw-Hill, 1988).

implication questions. These questions are instrumental in moving the customer closer to the value proposition you will offer in the presentation. As the customer comes to recognize the full implications of the problem, he or she becomes less concerned with the cost of the solution (your products and services) and more interested in solving the problem.

NEED PAYOFF QUESTIONS. The transition from problem identification and clarification to problem solution begins with need payoff questions. It is not enough to make the customer aware of a problem, nor to define its scope and potential ramifications. At some point the salesperson must move the customer to the solutions offered by the company. While problem and implications questions focus on establishing the customer's problem, need payoff questions directly connect the problem with the value proposition. If the customer agrees to the need payoff questions, the salesperson is in a strong position to successfully complete the sale. Conversely, if the customer disagrees, the salesperson has not yet established a significant problem for the customer to act on.

Listen

Should salespeople be better talkers or listeners? Many people unfamiliar with selling would probably say talking is more important, but the idea that salespeople are fast-talking individuals not really interested in customer's opinions is far from accurate. Listening, really listening, to customers is a vital trait of successful salespeople.

Despite its importance, most people (even those in selling) listen actively only 25 percent of the time. That means people don't really hear what is being said three-quarters of the time. Not surprisingly, the likelihood of correctly identifying a customer's needs if you are listening to only one quarter of what he or she says is pretty small. Interestingly, people can listen more effectively than they speak. Research suggests that most people can hear up to 800 words per minute but speak around 140 words per minute. The slowness of speech leads too many listeners to become distracted.

Active listening involves a commitment by the listener to focus on the speaker, concentrate on what is being said without thinking about other things, and take in nonverbal as well as verbal messages.[9] People speak with their voices, but they also speak nonverbally. Facial expression, arm and hand movements, body positioning, and eye contact all communicate just as much as the spoken word. Active listeners focus not just on what is being said but *how* it is being communicated. (We will talk more about nonverbal communication later in the chapter.)

Exhibit 7.7 summarizes recent research on how to enhance your active listening. When salespeople take the time to change from passive to active listening, they notice changes in the way customers react to them. Little things like providing nonverbal cues to a customer who is speaking (nodding your head, making

EXHIBIT 7.7 GUIDELINES FOR ACTIVE LISTENING

1. *Listen patiently to what the other person has to say, even though you may believe it is wrong or irrelevant.* Indicate simple acceptance, not necessarily agreement, by nodding or perhaps injecting an occasional "I understand."

2. *Try to understand the feeling the person is expressing, not just the intellectual content.* Most of us have difficulty talking clearly about our feelings, so it is important to pay careful attention.

3. *Restate the person's feeling briefly but accurately.* At this stage you simply serve as a mirror. Encourage the other person to continue talking. Occasionally make summary responses such as "You believe our product does not meet your needs" or "You feel our service is not meeting your expectations." Keep your tone neutral and try not to lead the person to your pet conclusions.

4. *Allow time for the discussion to continue without interruption and try to separate the conversation from more official communication of company plans.* Focus on sales presentation and not smaller, less vital company issues.

5. *Avoid direct questions and arguments about facts.* Refrain from saying, "You are wrong," or "You can't provide that." You may want to review evidence later, but a review is irrelevant to how a person feels now.

6. *When the other person touches on a point you want to know more about, simply repeat his or her statement as a question.* For instance, if he remarks, "Your company is much more expensive that your competitors," you can probe by saying, "So, you believe my company is expensive." With this encouragement, he will probably expand on his previous statement.

7. *Listen for what is not said, evasions of pertinent points or perhaps too-ready agreement with common clichés.* Such an omission may indicate something the person wishes was not true.

8. *If the other person genuinely appears to want your viewpoint, be honest in your reply.* In the listening stage, try to limit the expression of your views, since they may influence or inhibit what the other person says.

9. *Do not get emotionally involved yourself.* Try simply to understand first and defer evaluation until later.

10. *BE QUIET.* Let the other person talk. Actively listen to what he or she has to say.

Adapted from Dan Sharp, "Guildelines for Active Listening and Reflection," October 2008, www.salesconcepts.com

direct eye contact) and clarifying or rephrasing information can make the customer much more responsive. In turn, that customer is more likely to pay attention when you are speaking.

Apply Your Knowledge to Customer Needs

While identifying the customer's needs is essential in communicating the sales message, that's just the beginning of the salesperson's task. It is now time to take your knowledge of your company's products and services and apply it to the customer's needs. Providing solutions that solve customer problems is the essence of a salesperson's role in the relationship-selling process. You are the critical link between what the company has to offer the customer and the customer's needs.

Sell FAB. Good salespeople are very knowledgeable about their company's products and services. They know product performance characteristics, service turnaround times, and a host of other important features. These facts are important, but customers do not buy features. They buy solutions to their problems. So you need to link your knowledge of company products and services facts to solutions that meet customers' needs. This process is often referred to as FAB (**f**eatures, **a**dvantages, and **b**enefits).

By applying the FAB approach, salespeople can make the company's products and services relevant for the customer. A feature is any material characteristic or specification of the company's products and services (say, antilock brakes on a car). An advantage is a particular product/service characteristic that helps meet the customer's needs (antilock brakes stop the car faster and in a more controlled fashion). A benefit is the beneficial outcome to the buyer from the advantage found in the product feature (the car will provide greater safety for the driver and passengers).

Let's examine the FAB approach in greater detail.

FEATURES. All products and services are the sum total of physical characteristics and specifications. Consider the purchase of a new laptop computer. The buyer will learn the processor speed, hard disk drive size, screen size, and a host of other features. Go to the Lenovo computers website (www.lenovo.com) and click on products. Then go to the "Laptops" and click on "ThinkPad." Several models are listed and their product features are described.

By themselves, however, product features are not very persuasive. Indeed, most customers will never even see the processor or hard drive in a new computer. No matter what the buying situation, customers do not buy product features. They buy product benefits that meet their needs.

ADVANTAGES. Customers want benefits, but they also want to know how your product is better. What makes it better? Why should I buy your product/service over one of your competitors? In short, they want to see the advantages of your product.

If you return to the Lenovo web page, look at how the products are described as "lightning fast" and "torture-tested." Notice that these descriptions don't speak to the features of the product but, rather, the advantages. Lenovo ThinkPad laptops are fast and tough, two important features for heavy business users. This is a transition from talking about what the product does (features) to how it is better for the customer (advantages).

Unfortunately, most salespeople get a lot of training on the features of products and services but little training on the advantages and benefits. Remember, the task here is to apply your knowledge of the company's products and services to the customer needs you identified earlier in the sales presentation. Simply knowing the product's physical characteristics and specifications is not enough; understanding the product's advantages for your customer is good but still probably not enough to get a commitment. Ultimately, the customer must see how those advantages benefit him or her directly.

BENEFITS. Extending the application from product features to product advantages, and ultimately to product benefits, answers one of the most fundamental questions customers have in the relationship-building process:

"What's in it for me?" Ultimately, there will be no relationship if you cannot answer that question. Customers need to understand specifically how your product benefits them, solves their problem, or meets their needs.

Often, your customer will be comparing your product with at least one competitor. In the highly competitive, information-rich world of today, customers expect salespeople to have a thorough knowledge of their competitors' products and their benefits.

If you go back to the Lenovo web page one more time, notice it does not describe the benefits of a long-life battery. Why not? Because the company wants salespeople to do that. By phone call or visit, a Lenovo rep (direct salesperson or distributor's agent) will identify the particular customer's needs and then define the most relevant product advantages as benefits.

For example, engineers for a manufacturing company would find the high-speed Intel or AMD processor's ability to process the latest graphic-intensive software an advantage because it allows them to work sophisticated engineering programs while they are traveling. It is the salesperson's job to recognize the key customer issue (ability to work while traveling) and translate the product features into advantages (long battery life) and benefits (no more downtime while traveling).

This is an example of the synergy companies seek between their marketing communication (such as the Lenovo site) and the salesperson calling on the customer. While the website is outstanding at presenting product features and even identifying basic product advantages, direct contact with a salesperson (either inside or outside sales) is needed to connect the advantages to benefits for a given customer.

Collect the Company's Cumulative Knowledge. Salespeople are on the front line meeting customers and giving presentations. However, everyone in the organization supports them in one way or another. The support of areas like product development, customer service and support, and manufacturing is indispensable as salespeople apply the organization's cumulative knowledge to meeting the customer's needs. It is always helpful and often mandatory to tap into the knowledge base of the sales firm.

If a customer needs modifications to a product or has special service requirements, the salesperson calls in people from product development and manufacturing to get a true understanding of the issues and costs involved in making changes to existing products. When the customer has tight delivery and scheduling deadlines, it is important to contact the right people in the company to get the best, most up-to-date answers quickly.

Team selling is based in part on the premise that no one individual can successfully develop and manage large customer relationships. Applying your knowledge to the customer's needs really means applying the company's cumulative knowledge to those needs.

Satisfy Customer Needs

The ultimate goal of the presentation is to satisfy the customer's needs by identifying them, applying your knowledge to them, and creating a plan of action for the customer that incorporates your products and services to address them. Although the relationship-selling process certainly is not finished after the sales message is communicated (as you'll see over the next two chapters), every sales presentation should focus on customer satisfaction. No matter how much negotiating remains, no matter how tough it is to close the sale or build that long-term relationship, the customer should receive some satisfaction as a result of the sales presentation.

Get Customer Agreement. As you have undoubtedly noticed, a sales presentation is based on interaction with the customer. Through a prescribed process of preparation and customer communication, the salesperson comes to learn the customer's needs and develops a plan of action for solving the customer's problems. At every step in the presentation, it is important to get customer agreement.

This agreement can take many forms. Sometimes you ask a question: "Do you agree that my product provides the best value for your business?" Sometimes you make a statement. "We agree you need a product that offers great value and specific performance characteristics, and I have demonstrated how our product offers the best combination of performance and lowest cost of any product in the market." Often agreement can be a simple yes.

Customer satisfaction in the presentation is not a single event. It builds as a series of agreements during the presentation. When you secure agreement at many steps in the presentation, the customer will be much more compelled to agree to the purchase at the appropriate time. As you will see in chapter 9, closing the sale is a process that begins at the start of the presentation.

Minimize Change Conflict. As we discussed earlier, the sales presentation can create more stress for the customer than for the salesperson. The presentation is based on the assumption that you have a better solution than the customer is currently using, and customers can react negatively to your presentation even if (sometimes because) they find your product superior to their current choice.

One key to leaving a customer satisfied at the end of the presentation is to minimize change conflict. To help customers feel less conflict about the purchase, you can manage their expectations. Clearly explain the specifics of your value proposition and then deliver exactly what you promise. Overpromising and underdelivering is one of the surest ways to destroy a buyer–seller relationship. Also, make sure that details of the purchase agreement are known to everyone in the sales organization and all relevant individuals in the customer's company. Misunderstandings between other people often lead to disappointment later in the relationship.

Establish the Relationship. It is critical to build the buyer–seller relationship with every presentation, indeed every customer interaction. Building the relationship means creating trust and establishing a sense of loyalty.[10] Sales presentations are big events. Salespeople need to be sure that, no matter what happens to the potential sale on the table, the relationship is not damaged. Phone calls and emails are everyday occurrences, but getting face-to-face with the customer raises the stakes for you and your company.

Most of the time a sales presentation is the best opportunity for a company to forge a new relationship. Keep in mind the basic elements of relationship selling: Focus on creating value for the customer and always conduct business with the highest ethical standards.

KEYS TO A GREAT SALES PRESENTATION

Successful sales presentations don't just happen. They require preparation and a lot of hard work. This section examines ways to turn a good presentation into a great one.

Demonstrations

Have you ever heard the phrase "talk is cheap"? This cliché highlights a basic concept behind product demonstrations: At some point the salesperson must prove the claims and statements in the sales presentation. There are few selling tools more effective at proving the worth of a product than a product demonstration.[11] The product demonstration is not without risk (which we will discuss shortly), but when properly planned and executed, it offers three distinct benefits to the salesperson.

First, a successful buyer–seller relationship is based on trust and credibility. Fundamental to that trust is the customer's belief that your product will perform as promised in the sales presentation. Product demonstrations are an excellent tool that can *build credibility with customers*. When you prove the sales presentation with a product demonstration, the customer is more likely to accept you.

Second, seeing the product in action *creates a greater connection between the customer and the product.* Consider the last time you went shopping for clothes. By trying them on, you were demonstrating the product to yourself. If you liked the outfit, the demonstration worked and your probability of buying it increased dramatically. If you went into a clothing store and were told you could not try on that suit or dress, you would probably not purchase the product or even shop at the store. The same is true in all buying situations. Allowing the customer to interact with the product and see it in action can generate a strong affiliation between the customer and product. The product becomes more than words on a page or facts in a brochure.

Third, product demonstrations can *enhance the effectiveness of your communication.* People can process nonverbal information much faster than spoken words. By demonstrating the product, you are presenting information in a format that is probably more interesting and memorable for the customer.

Think about your own experiences. Would you rather have someone describe the horsepower, torque, and six-speed transmission of a new Porsche or experience it for yourself by test-driving one? If you are choosing a new printer for the office, what do you think will be more effective: (1) a brochure detailing the pages per minute, 256 color combinations, and networking capabilities, or (2) a file sent to your printer that is printed automatically in full color? Demonstrating the product makes all other communication during the presentation more effective. Once the customer sees the printer in action, the brochure the salesperson leaves takes on more meaning.

Exhibit 7.8 talks about the importance of good communication. Keep those points in mind as we examine product demonstrations more closely.

EXHIBIT 7.8 HOW TO BE A BETTER COMMUNICATOR

Good communication skills have to be learned. Most people are poor communicators. It's not that they don't try, but without proper training and practice it is difficult to listen or communicate effectively.

1. *It all starts with good listening skills.* This lets the other person know you are paying attention to his or her thoughts and expertise.
2. *Be sure your interpretation is correct.* Making sure you've heard the person correctly goes a long way toward keeping communication clear. Asking for clarification gives the person you are speaking with a chance to confirm exactly what he said or refine what she wants to convey.
3. *Be succinct.* Deliver your sales message in as few words as possible. The less you say, the more likely you are to be heard.
4. *Don't deliver the same message over and over.* Even if you don't get an acknowledgment that the customer agrees, don't try to drive your point home by saying it again a different way. Say it once and move on.
5. *Get confirmation.* Asking for feedback as you are speaking lets others know you are more interested in their reaction and creative input than in being right.
6. *Use open body language and non-verbal cues.* When customers feel that you are approachable, they are more likely to keep the lines of communication flowing.
7. *Be willing to laugh at yourself.* Research shows that the ability to laugh at oneself is a key indicator of emotional intelligence (the ability to connect well with other people). Connecting and listening are two key skills of good communicators.

As you can see, good communicators need many skills.

Adapted from Craig Harrison, "Tip Sheet: A Failure to Communicate Should Not be an Option When Doing Business," *PR News* (August 21, 2006), and "How to Be a Better Communicator," *Sales & Marketing Management* (February 2003).

Prepare for a Successful Demonstration. Clearly, the demonstration is an effective tool in the sales presentation—when it works. But when it fails or does not meet the customer's expectations the negative effect is significant. This is why it is so important to prepare for the presentation.

Exhibit 7.9 is a checklist of things to consider as your prepare for a product demonstration. Not all items are appropriate in every situation, but in general, when you have completed the checklist, you should be ready to give a successful demonstration. There are three key points to keep in mind as you prepare for a demonstration: develop objectives, get customers involved, and practice.

EXHIBIT 7.9 DEMONSTRATION CHECKLIST

- Justify the need for a product demonstration.

  "Does this sales presentation need a product demonstration?"

- State the objective of the demonstration.

  "What do I want to accomplish with the product demonstration?"

- Design the demonstration.

  "What will the demonstration look like?"

- Rehearse the demonstration.

  "Can I deliver the product demonstration effectively and efficiently?"

- Plan for unforeseen circumstances.

  "Have I identified key times or events when unforeseen events could disrupt the demonstration (power failure, lack of proper display facilities in the room, disruptions for the customer)?"

First, *develop objectives for the demonstration.* We spoke earlier about the importance of setting presentation objectives, and the same is true for product demonstrations. Most products have many characteristics that could be incorporated into a demonstration. Consider the specific customer's needs and develop a demonstration that shows how the product will address those needs. If the customer for a copier is interested in speed, the demonstration could focus on pages printed per minute. The objective could be, "The customer will know how fast and dependable the copier is as a result of the product demonstration."

Second, *get customers involved in the demonstration.* Imagine looking at a new car and not being allowed to test-drive it. It's the same principle in any product demonstration. The more involved the customer is in the demonstration, the more he or she will connect to the product and your presentation. Be sure the customer knows how to use the product. There are few things more dangerous in a product demonstration than a customer who does not know how to use the product correctly.

Third, *practice, practice, and practice the demonstration.* You generally have only one chance to be successful in a product demonstration. You must be absolutely comfortable with the product and the specific characteristics you are demonstrating and know how to do deal with unforeseen problems (which will almost surely appear at some point in time). Practice not only the demonstration itself but also your words and actions during the demonstration. Since you will be talking and showing the product at the same time, you need to know both very well. One benefit of practice is that it builds confidence. When you have mastered a demonstration, indeed an entire presentation, you are more confident in front of the customer.

The Demonstration: More than Just the Product. Is the product itself the best demonstration tool? Yes. Is it the only tool available to demonstrate the product's features, advantages, and benefit? No. Sometimes it is not possible to demonstrate the actual product in front of the customer, and you'll need to find other tools to help in the product demonstration. Evaluate the best possible format to demonstrate the product.

Many other tools can enhance the demonstration or even substitute for a live product display. In some cases, the product has not even been produced. Consider architects bidding on a big construction project. They have no product to show, so they must rely on models and drawings to demonstrate their vision of the final product (the building itself).

Another situation, often found in technology, is the demonstration of something that cannot be seen. How can a salesperson for Lenovo demonstrate how the ThinkPad actually processes information faster than the competition? One way is to compare a set of prescribed functions using a competitor or older model with a new ThinkPad. The demonstration should show the same functions being performed faster on the new machine. You don't really see the product working, but you see the results of the faster processor. Another tool might be charts that highlight the relative speed differences between the competitors and the ThinkPad.

A powerful tool commonly used in education and business is Microsoft's Office Suite of business software. Incorporating Excel, Word, and PowerPoint software into a presentation can enable the salesperson to convey a great deal of information. PowerPoint and programs like it can graphically display many elements of a product demonstration. Through the use of graphics software, embedded video, and other tools, the salesperson can develop a successful demonstration without actually having the product in front of the customer. Almost every computer manufacturer sells portable projectors. Among the more popular are Dell and Mitsubishi. With them, salespeople can take very sophisticated demonstrations right into the customer's office.

The Value Proposition

You remember the discussion on value creation in Chapter 3. We talked about the importance of value in the relationship-selling process. Creating value for their customers is really why companies are in business. However, customers must see the value of the company's products and services. The sales presentation is where that value is conveyed to the customer.

Chapter 3 highlighted many ways a company can create value for its customers. The job of salespeople is to identify their customers' needs and apply their knowledge of their company and its products to satisfy customers. Critical to that process is the value proposition, which is the summary of the value the customer receives based on the expected benefits and costs.

A realistic assessment of benefits and costs can be a persuasive tool to support the claims of the company's products and services. Customers today are often looking for a strong business case to justify the purchase decision. They ask a valid question, "How is your company adding value to my business?" Refer to the Appendix to chapter 3 ("Selling Math") for an in-depth discussion of building a financial business case in relationship selling.

A value proposition should be part of every presentation. Assessing the value proposition for your customer should be part of your preparation. Of course you will learn more about the customer's needs during the presentation, but by assessing the customer value of your company's products before the presentation, you can anticipate objections. As we shall examine in chapter 8, many customer objections deal with the value added by your company's products. If the price is too high (a common objection), the customer is really saying he or she has not been convinced the value of your product exceeds the cost. The customer does not believe your value proposition. Defining the customer value of your company's products and services and communicating it are essential to success in relationship selling.

Nonverbal Communication

Nonverbal communication is the single most important element in the communication process. Research suggests that over half of all communication is a result of things we see or feel. These include but are not limited to facial expressions, posture, eye contact, gestures, and even dress. Surprisingly, less than 10 percent of communication is based on the actual words we speak in a conversation. The remainder (about 40 percent) of what we take in is the result of *how* we hear the communication (vocal clarity, pitch, tone of voice).

Given the importance of nonverbal communication to the total communication process, salespeople need to know how to interpret their customers' nonverbal communication. They also need to know how to use nonverbal signals to communicate. How you sit, what you wear, even the amount of space between you and the customer sends a message. Let's examine nonverbal communication more closely.

Customer Nonverbal Communication. We spoke earlier about active listening and how important it is to focus intently on the customer. Customers, indeed all of us, speak volumes in the way we move. We communicate with almost every part of our body. Our hands, legs, facial expressions, even the way we hold our body (slumped over, sitting straight up) all convey a message. A person who has arms open and palms extended is sending a very different message than a person with folded arms and legs.

FACE. The face is the single most important feature of nonverbal communication. Without saying a word, a customer can convey acceptance or rejection, anger or amusement, understanding or confusion, with a facial expression. We all know the meaning of a smile or a scowl, but the face can convey many subtle messages as well.

"The eyes are the window to the soul" is a famous saying. Watching a customer's eye contact can tell you a lot about what he or she thinks of your sales presentation. A customer who stares blankly at the presentation is not really interested. Yet the more intently the customer stares, the greater the likelihood he or she is reacting negatively. When people are really focused on oral communication, they usually look down or up to enhance their concentration. Turning away indicates the customer believes the presentation is over—or wishes it were.

ARMS AND HANDS. Arms open, palms extended is one of the clearest signals the customer is open to the communication. Conversely, folded arms with closed hands indicate he or she is not receptive to what is being said.

Many gestures have different meaning around the world. Gestures and hand movements that are accepted in one culture can have very different meanings somewhere else. It is always helpful to know the customer's culture before interpreting these kinds of signals—or attempting to send them.

BODY LANGUAGE. When a customer leans forward in the chair, he or she is showing interest, while leaning back indicates a lack of concentration in the presentation. Quick movements indicate something has changed in the customer's mind. He or she may have a question, want you to conclude the presentation, or even feel bored.

No single customer movement or action should be taken out of context. People lean back in their chair for many reasons besides boredom. Without thorough knowledge of the customer's behavior patterns, it would be dangerous to infer too much from a specific gesture or even a single meeting.

Salespeople need to balance what they are seeing (nonverbal communication) with what the customer is saying (oral communication). When the presentation is going well and the customer accepts the information, verbal and nonverbal communication will likely be consistent. When the two forms of communication are inconsistent, the customer's comments may not express his or her true feelings about the presentation.

Salesperson Nonverbal Communication. Just as customers convey a great deal through nonverbal communication, so do salespeople. Literally hundreds of nonverbal signals are conveyed in every sales presentation, and salespeople need to be aware of their own nonverbal communication. Customers watch salespeople for nonverbal messages. Slight movements (looking away from the customer, glancing at the clock) can convey a message that was not intended. Here are some critical nonverbal cues.

THE SPACE BETWEEN YOU AND THE CUSTOMER. We all operate with concentric circles of space around us. The concept of territorial space is based on research that suggests that people have varying levels of space around themselves that they do not want people to enter without permission. Have you ever met someone and felt crowded? When their space is violated, people become uncomfortable. A salesperson should never violate a customer's space.

There are four levels of space around a customer. The most accessible is public space, which is at least 12 feet away. Almost anyone is welcome in this space, and this is often the distance between a salesperson and the group in a public presentation. Social space is from 4 to 12 feet and is often the space between customer and salesperson in a personal sales presentation. Think of it as the desk between the customer and salesperson in the customer's office. In this space, keep in mind your position relative to the customer. Standing while the customer is seated can be uncomfortable for the customer when you are this close. Personal space is 2 to 3 feet and should not be violated except for a handshake. Even then, the salesperson should be careful not to suffocate the customer. Finally there is intimate space (up to 2 feet). This space is reserved for family and close friends. Violating it is rude and even offensive.

BODY MOVEMENTS. When you look down or appear ill at ease, it suggests to the customer that you are not confident in the presentation. If the customer senses a lack of confidence or preparation, the presentation will probably not be successful, no matter what you say. You need to communicate confidence through your facial expressions and body movements. An open, accepting demeanor conveys a positive message to the customer before you have even said a word.

It is helpful to study your customers and match their style. Some people have a more conservative style than others, and being too gregarious or entering the customer's personal space can send negative nonverbal messages.

One caveat in nonverbal communication: Do what comes naturally. Don't try to be something you aren't. You'll just confuse and alienate customers. The key is to blend basic rules of nonverbal communication with your own communication style. Practice your nonverbal communication in front of a mirror or have a friend watch as you run through your presentation. Too often practicing a presentation consists of going over the words and PowerPoint slides without taking the time to practice the nonverbal messages you are sending the customer.

What to Do When Things Go Wrong

No matter how much planning and hard work you put into it, you can't control every aspect of the sales presentation. Indeed, most presentations offer at least one obstacle. Successful salespeople realize that, even when they have created the right setting for the presentation, things still come up to distract the customer. It is wise to consider what to do in difficult situations *before* they happen. While every situation introduces unique challenges, we will focus on three: interruptions during the presentation, inappropriate sales presentation environment, and a failure of technology.

Interruptions during the Presentation. Most of the time you are presenting at the customer's business, which means you do not control the environment. Of course it helps when the customer tells the staff to hold all calls, but that is no guarantee there will be no interruptions. Cell phones, pagers, and superiors can still find the customer when necessary.

What do you do when the customer is disturbed during the presentation? First, assess the nature of the call. If it's confidential, withdraw to give the customer space to deal with the issue in private. Second, consider any interruption an opportunity to assess the progress of the presentation and plan where you want to go from here.

Third, be patient and allow the customer to refocus attention on you before proceeding. Perhaps the customer needs to make some notes after the interruption or simply take a few moments to collect his or her thoughts. Don't proceed without first getting some indication that the customer is now focused again on you and the presentation. Fourth, briefly restate the key points you have covered in the presentation. You might validate where you left off with the customer by asking a question: "I believe we were talking about the benefits of our extensive product inventory to your manufacturing needs, is that correct?" Wait until you have the customer fully engaged before proceeding with the rest of the presentation.

Inappropriate Environment. Another issue for a salesperson meeting at the customer's place of business is the location of the presentation. A personal office or conference room with all the necessary equipment and privacy is ideal, but it's not always available. In pharmaceutical sales, for example, salespeople often meet with the doctor between patient visits and have only 5 to 10 minutes.

The key for dealing with less than ideal conditions for a presentation is preparation. Be knowledgeable and confident enough in your presentation that you can improvise in a difficult environment. If you have a 30-minute presentation and the customer says he or she has to leave in 15 minutes, make the necessary adjustments and go for it. Customers often appreciate salespeople who can accommodate unforeseen challenges in their presentation.

Technology Failure. In the high-tech world of today's selling environment, it is essential that salespeople know how to effectively incorporate technology into the sales presentation.[12] However, because technology is part of the sales process, salespeople need to be prepared when (not if) technology fails. What do you do when the computer crashes, the projector bulb burns out, or the customer wants the presentation in a room with no technology capabilities? As we have discussed already, technology can certainly enhance a presentation; however, it is not the basis for the presentation.

The solution is simple. Always have a backup plan when technology fails. If your presentation is in PowerPoint, bring a set of overhead transparencies and a hard copy of the presentation just in case. Even when the computers are down, you can usually get access to an overhead projector. The customer can follow your hard copy even if you cannot project it on screen. You should always bring a copy of the presentation anyway, to leave with the customer.

Many companies now are equipping their sales force with portable projectors to use when the customer does not have the proper equipment. This gives salespeople a great deal more flexibility in location. They are no longer dependent on the customer to set up for a computer-generated presentation. The key in these situations is to develop a plan of action to deal with any possible technology glitch. A good rule of thumb is to expect the unexpected. One of the most difficult ethical challenges in today's technology-oriented sales environment is the use of technology for personal use. Read the Ethical Dilemma to further explore these issues.

THE SALES MANAGER'S ROLE IN THE SALES PRESENTATION

Ultimately, the salesperson is responsible for the presentation. Yet salespeople do not operate alone. As part of their company's sales force, they are supported by hundreds (even thousands) of other employees. The sales manager plays a significant role in the overall success of a sales presentation. As the salespeople's immediate supervisor, he or she is responsible for providing all the tools they need. Let's examine the sales manager's role in more detail.

ETHICAL DILEMMA

WHOSE COMPUTER IS IT ANYWAY?

Jerry Gutel has been with Step Ahead Publishing for 11 years and witnessed firsthand its technology transformation. When he came to the company, Step Ahead salespeople carried large binders with all relevant information for hundreds of books (sometimes as much as 10 pages on each book). Often he would have to carry two or three of these heavy binders into a bookstore. Meeting with store managers in the Midlands (England) meant that Jerry was frequently on the road, and carrying the books was always cumbersome.

Five years ago Step Ahead management began to integrate technology into the sales force. Jerry began using the laptop as his only sales tool and was happy there were no more heavy binders. There was a great deal of sensitive information on the computer, such as individual book sales, wholesale prices, and new-product delivery dates. As a result, the company had a strict rule against the use of company laptops for personal use. It didn't want any outsiders gaining access to the data. It also wanted salespeople to view the laptop as strictly for company use and not as personal property. Recently the company updated their technology and now Jerry and the entire sales team has iPads loaded with up-to-date sales manuals and all the current data they need for operating in the field.

Jerry was becoming increasingly dependent on computers in his personal life and the iPad proved to be a great device for personal as well as business use. Two years ago he bought a new computer for his family. With two teenagers, however, Jerry had little access to the computer at home. Compounding the problem was the time Jerry had to work on personal matters while traveling and spending many nights in a hotel. He thought the company's policy was wrong, and other salespeople told him they used the company's laptops and tablet computers for personal business all the time. They even told him about software that would protect company files using secure passwords and encoding key data.

One day Jerry stopped by his bank and found out how he could use his iPad to do all his banking online. All he needed was an App on his iPad and Wi-Fi or wireless mobile service. While thinking about this, Jerry began to consider how he could use other apps to track his business expenses. The current system was still paper driven and Jerry spent an afternoon every two weeks going through his expenses and completing the paperwork. Jerry was seriously considering getting these apps and moving his banking onto the computer. In addition, he wanted to use apps to help monitor and complete expense forms. Before going to management, however, he wanted to try it for three months to be sure it would work. The question was, which computer: his home computer or the company's iPad?

Questions to Consider

1. If you were Jerry, on which computer would you install the new software? Why?
2. Does the company have a valid point in asking employees not to use the computer for personal business?
3. Should the company care if Jerry uses the iPad for personal use as long as he protects the sensitive information?

Managers Are Essential to a Great Presentation

Salespeople operate in the customer's environment, and they rely on the sales manager to support their efforts back at the office. Without that support they would be unable to sustain an effective presence with customers in the field. The two basic roles for the sales manager are mentor and salesperson.

Many managers come out of the sales ranks, and every manager is expected to work with salespeople to enhance their effectiveness during the presentation. Most organizations consider the role of mentor very important. Helping salespeople improve their skills is part of the job description.

The second role is that of salesperson. Yes, even sales managers have sales responsibilities. Customers, especially large customers, expect to see the manager as part of the sales presentation. The manager's presence makes customers feel important. Also, customers, at certain levels in their organization expect to negotiate with a sales manager.

We will discuss these roles in much greater detail in Part Three.

Providing the Tools for Success

The manager needs to equip salespeople for success. First, the salesperson needs the proper training to get the job done. Sending a salesperson in front of a customer without sufficient training will ensure failure. Second, the manager needs to provide the equipment for success. Today that means computers (laptop or desktop), mobile communications (cell phones), and other technologies the salesperson needs to deliver a persuasive message to customers. Third, the manager needs to develop and manage effective reward and compensation systems to ensure a highly motivated and satisfied sales force.

While we will explore the manager's tasks and responsibilities to the salesperson later in the book, it is important to recognize now that managers do play an important role in the salesperson's success during presentations.

EXPERT ADVICE: FOLLOW-UP

After watching the video of Mr. Edmonds and reading the chapter, consider the following questions:

1. Interview a local sales executive and ask them to define the key characteristics of a "good sales presentation." How do those characteristics compare with Mr. Edmonds' discussion?
2. After reading the chapter and seeing Mr. Edmonds, define the three most important elements of a successful professional sales presentation. Do you think they are same today as 10 years ago? If not, what has changed?

SUMMARY

Communicating the sales message is critical to the relationship-building process, and the most effective tool for communicating that message is the sales presentation. The sales presentation is direct, face-to-face communication with the customer that begins to establish the link between the company's products/services and the solution to the customer's needs.

There are three fundamental steps in communicating the sales message. First, it is important to spend the time getting ready for the sales presentation. A great sales presentation (1) explains the value proposition, (2) asserts the advantages and benefits of the product, (3) enhances the customer's knowledge of the company, products, and service, and (4) creates a memorable experience for the customer. The four basic sales presentation strategies vary by their focal point (product or customer) and talk/listen ratio. The salesperson must be able to work with technologies. Portable computing systems and wireless communication devices can greatly enhance the overall effectiveness of the presentation. Finally, every sales presentation needs a specific goal to answer the fundamental question: "What am I trying to accomplish in this presentation?"

The second step in a great sales presentation is approaching the customer. The approach begins with a good first impression, which has three distinct parts: (1) before the presentation, (2) greeting the customer, and (3) the first three minutes of the presentation. There are five approaches to starting the presentation: (1) referral, (2) customer benefit, (3) question, (4) assessment, and (5) product demonstration.

The third step in communicating the sales message is the actual presentation. Within the sales presentation, there are three elements. First, the salesperson needs to identify the customer's needs by asking questions and actively listening to the customer. The SPIN approach for identifying the customer's needs consists of four types of questions: (1) situation, (2) problem, (3) implication, and (4) need payoff. Second, the salesperson needs to apply his or her knowledge to the customer's needs. In this phase it is helpful to think in terms of features, advantages, and benefits (FAB). Customers do not buy features; rather, they buy the product benefits. Finally, the salesperson must satisfy the customer's needs in the presentation. Selling represents change, and change (even for the better) can be difficult for the customer. By minimizing conflict and getting customer agreement on major points, the salesperson can enhance the probability of success.

There are four keys to a great sales presentation. First, the product demonstration is one of the most valuable tools available. Second, every salesperson should have a clear idea of the value proposition for the customer. Third, realize that nonverbal communication is the single most influential component of the communication process. Finally, every sales presentation offers challenges. Very few presentations are totally trouble-free. The salesperson needs to understand what can go wrong and how to deal with it.

Salespeople are ultimately responsible for the sales presentation; yet sales managers play a critical role in supporting them. They should provide the tools for success (training, equipment, compensation/reward systems) that sustain the salespeople's efforts. Managers are mentors and also have a sales role. They are often responsible for major clients or for supporting salespeople in the field when they call on important customers.

KEY TERMS

sales presentation	need satisfaction	product demonstration	nonverbal communication
memorized presentation	problem-solving	SPIN strategy	public space
formula presentation	presentation approach	active listening	social space
need satisfaction	approach	FAB	personal space
presentation	customer benefit	feature	intimate space
need identification	question method	advantage	mentor
need analysis	assessment approach	benefit	

ROLE PLAY

BEFORE YOU BEGIN

Before getting started, please go to the Appendix of chapter 1 to review the profiles of the characters involved in this role play, as well as the tips on preparing a role play.

Characters Involved

Tracy Brown
Alex Lewis
Rhonda Reed

Tracy Brown (can be male or female depending on the composition of your student group) is buyer for Max's Pharmacy, a small (eight-store) chain in the area. Max's concentrates on its prescription business but also stocks typical "front-end" health and beauty aids. The front end of a Max's Pharmacy is not very big (average about 3,000 square feet of floor space), so Tracy has to be careful to only stock good sellers, items that are likely to appeal to customers who are in the store to pick up prescriptions, and items a pharmacist or physician might suggest customers purchase. Tracy runs a half-page ad in the local newspaper twice monthly to promote new and "hot" products merchandised in the front-end area of Max's stores.

Setting the Stage

Upland has just introduced "Happy Teeth," a teeth-whitening product to compete with the very successful Procter & Gamble product Crest Whitestrips. (Note: To familiarize yourself with this type of product and get information to use in your role play, visit the P&G website at www.p&g.com and click through to the Crest Whitestrips page. Also, drop by your local food or drugstore and take a look at a box of Crest Whitestrips.)

Upland sales rep Alex Lewis is about to call on Tracy to present Happy Teeth to Max's Pharmacies to gain distribution as a new product in Max's stores. Rhonda will be working with Alex on the day of the sales call. Because Alex has other business to discuss with Tracy during the call, he will have only 10 minutes to present Happy Teeth to her.

To develop this role play, Alex will need to identify and present to Tracy some features, advantages, and benefits (FABs) of Happy Teeth related to both (a) end users of the product (shoppers in Max's Pharmacies) and (b) Tracy's (Max's) business (what's in it for them). Benchmark what you learn about Crest Whitestrips to come up with these FABs. Assume that Upland will be introducing Happy Teeth at a 10 percent price advantage over Crest Whitestrips, that Happy Teeth has been shown through clinical testing to get teeth whiter faster than Crest Whitestrips, and that the whiteness provided by Happy Teeth lasts longer than that provided by Crest Whitestrips. Beyond that, make up any other reasonable FABs you like for use in the presentation.

Tracy Brown's Role

Tracy has been a customer of Alex's for 12 years, and a high level of trust exists in the business relationship. Although Tracy will have some questions and minor concerns/objections about the new product (you can make these up in advance as well as come up with some during the actual presentation), ultimately Tracy will agree to the purchase without giving Alex too much trouble.

Alex Lewis's Role

Alex must prepare and present a maximum 10-minute presentation to Tracy about Happy Teeth. He wants her to stock the product in the front end of each Max's Pharmacy and to feature Happy Teeth in an upcoming newspaper ad at a special price of $5 off, for which Upland will compensate Tracy in promotional "push" monies. Alex would like to sell three dozen per store for a total order of 24 dozen.

He needs to use the elements of a good "need satisfaction" presentation and incorporate all other relevant presentation tips provided in the chapter.

Rhonda Reed's Role

In the call itself, Rhonda should only briefly greet and engage in pleasant conversation with Tracy before and after Alex's presentation. Her key role is to observe Alex's presentation carefully during the sales call. Afterward, Alex and Rhonda will leave Tracy's office and Rhonda will give Alex at least 5 minutes of constructive feedback/coaching about his performance. The feedback should cover both verbal and nonverbal aspects of his presentation.

Assignment

Work together to orchestrate the sales presentation, buyer responses, and manager feedback/coaching encounter. Limit the sales call to 10 minutes and the manager feedback/coaching discussion to 5 minutes.

DISCUSSION QUESTIONS

1. As a customer, think back to a recent sales presentation that you felt went well. What made it good? What did the salesperson do (or not do) that most impressed you? Did you buy the product or service? What did the salesperson do that convinced you to buy from him or her?

2. Imagine you are working for a company that sells teleconferencing equipment. Draft a value proposition for selling your equipment to a sales manager who has 10 salespeople traveling two weeks a month to visit customers all over the country.

3. Identify three selling situations where a memorized sales presentation may be appropriate. Explain why they would be appropriate.

4. You are the sales manager for a company selling components to companies in the auto industry and are considering upgrading computer equipment for the sales force. Draft a document detailing the specifications for the new computer system. Your reps need access to a great deal of product information and need to run a simulation detailing the functions of the product. They need a computer that can handle a sophisticated simulation program.

5. Identify the five objectives of a sales presentation and develop an example of how a sales presentation would accomplish each one.

6. Pair off in class and practice a salesperson's approach to a customer. Develop an approach that lasts 3 minutes and includes a greeting.

7. Select two of the approach strategies and develop each one into a one-page dialogue between you and a customer.

8. You are a salesperson working for American Airlines calling on the vice president of a large manufacturing company. Many of the company's people travel all over the world, and you would like them to sign an agreement to use American Airlines exclusively. Develop a SPIN approach for this customer.

9. Choose a product and sell it using the FAB methodology.

10. You are a salesperson for the local cell phone company presenting to the sales manager of a company considering adopting a companywide cell phone provider. Develop a 5-minute product demonstration of any cell phone provider in your area.

MINI-CASE 7 BRIGHT COLORS PAINTS

Michael Lee is sitting in the lobby of Columbia Area Painting waiting to meet with the owner, Paul Ferguson. Michael is a salesperson for Bright Colors Paints. He's here to speak with Paul because Columbia was just awarded the contract to repaint all of the city's public recreation facilities. The facilities that Paul's company will be painting include five city pools, two water slides, pool snack bars, and locker rooms, as well as the snack bars and storage buildings at five city-owned baseball diamonds.

The business potential for this meeting is large, and Michael wants to make sure he understands Paul's job requirements thoroughly before making a proposal. Michael is a little nervous about the meeting because, in his 14 months with Bright Colors, he has never made a sale this large. He has never been able to sell anything to Columbia because Paul prefers a competitor of Bright Colors as his principal supplier. After a few moments, Paul's assistant tells Michael he is ready to see him.

MICHAEL: (sounding nervous and noticing his hands feel clammy) Mr. Ferguson, I'm Michael Lee with Bright Colors Paints. I'm very glad to meet you.

PAUL: (looking and sounding gruff) Nice to meet you. Call me Paul. I suppose you know why I agreed to meet with you. Although we usually deal with a competitor of yours, I'm not sure my usual supplier can provide me with everything I need to complete this new contract with the city. They're supposed to contact me later today, but I'm not convinced they can provide me with what I need when I need it to complete this job.

MICHAEL: (still feeling nervous about how this sales call will go) I appreciate the time you're giving me today, Paul. I found out about your contract to do work for the city Parks and Recreation Department when I was talking with Barb Montgomery, the purchasing director at Crestline Homes. I'm sure you are aware that Barb is on the city council. She told me that you might be interested in talking to me.

PAUL: (his tone starting to soften a little while he sits straight up in his chair with his arms on the arm rests) You know Barb at Crestline? I did some work for Crestline when their own painters got behind on some jobs. Crestline builds a nice house. I didn't know your company provided their paint.

MICHAEL: (beginning to relax some, given Paul's change in demeanor) Crestline was one of the first accounts I opened. We've been providing Crestline for over a year now. If you don't mind, I'd like to ask a few questions about your current needs with respect to the new contract before going on to suggest any particular paints.

PAUL: (still sounding very businesslike while maintaining intense eye contact with Michael) Go ahead, but you can be sure that I'll be giving Barb a call to find out how you are to work with.

MICHAEL: (finally realizing that Paul is not the most cooperative buyer he has ever met) I encourage you to call Barb. She'll give us a great recommendation. Tell me, how big is the contract that you were awarded from the city?

PAUL: (sounding defensive) You know what, I wasn't awarded anything. I worked hard to win that contract. It took a long time to calculate my bid. I'm still not sure I'm going to make any money off it. To answer your question, I'm going to need approximately 3,250 gallons of paint.

MICHAEL: (starting to settle into the interview) Do you anticipate any problems with respect to completing this job?

PAUL: (rolling his eyes) Yes.

MICHAEL: What kind of problems?

PAUL: (looking out the window of his office while crossing his legs) Well, weather is a potential problem. I don't want to apply a coat of paint to a pool or building and have rain wash it off before it dries. Also, I have never painted a pool before. I suppose there are special paints for pools, but I don't know if they'll work with my equipment.

MICHAEL: Would any of these problems harm your company if they were to happen on this job?

PAUL: (sounding exasperated) What do you think? Of course they would.

MICHAEL: If I can show you a paint that not only dries quickly but is also specially formulated for use on pools, would you be interested?

PAUL: (uncrossing his legs and leaning forward) I suppose. Tell me what you've got.

MICHAEL: Well, Paul, our new paint, QD21P, is just what you need for this job. The "QD" stands for "quick drying," while the "P" indicates that it is specially formulated for pools. The "21" means that the paint was developed in the 21st Century, so it's a brand-new product for us. What do you think?

PAUL: (sitting up straight with his elbows and hands resting on his desk) You haven't told me much about the paint other than its name. What does all of that stuff mean?

MICHAEL: The paint is quick drying, which you indicated as important. The paint is also suitable for use in pools. The paint is relatively new, so I'm not completely familiar with it, but it does meet some of your needs, doesn't it?

PAUL: (folding his arms and leaning back in his chair) I suppose. What else do you want to know?

The interview lasted about another 5 minutes and proceeded along the same path, only the discussion centered on the buildings that need to be painted.

Questions

1. Identify the type of approach Michael used in his sales call. What other options exist for approaching a customer and how can Michael change his approach to make it more effective?

2. What do you think of Michael's use of the SPIN technique for determining Paul's needs? Develop additional SPIN questions that Michael can use to determine Paul's needs, to illustrate the problems that could result from not fulfilling those needs, and to get Paul to agree to hear a proposal on how Bright Colors can satisfy his needs.

3. What nonverbal signals is Paul sending to Michael at each stage of the conversation?

Sales Management

Salesperson Motivation

Selling Processes

Compensating & Evaluating Salespeople

Selecting & Training Salespeople

Communicating the Sales Message

Negotiating for Win-Win Solutions

Understanding Sellers & Buyers

Closing & Follow-up

Technology

Building Relationships ~ Creating Value

Prospecting & Sales Call Planning

Salesperson Self-Management

Ethics

global selling environment

Negotiating for Win-Win Solutions

LEARNING OBJECTIVES

No matter how well you prepare, no matter how well you present your material to the customer—indeed, despite everything you do—the customer will seldom, if ever, buy the product based solely on your presentation. Does this mean you should not prepare the best sales presentation possible? Of course not. The presentation is the starting point for a successful buyer—seller relationship. But negotiating and working with customers to develop a win-win solution to their problems are at the heart of the contemporary selling process. There are many occasions when the customer will have legitimate, specific questions or objections about the nature of your material. Negotiations are the process whereby customer objections and questions are resolved.

This chapter explores the process of negotiating with customers. We will identify customer objections and how you can learn to respond successfully when customers raise objections about your product. It describes specific negotiating strategies designed to help you work through customer concerns. Finally, it discusses the sales manager's role in negotiating win-win solutions.

After reading this chapter, you should be able to:

- Understand the process of negotiating win-win solutions.
- Know the common objections most salespeople encounter working with customers.
- Know the basic points to consider in negotiating with customers.
- Understand the specific negotiating strategies.
- Understand the sales manager's role in negotiating win-win solutions.

EXPERT ADVICE

EXPERT: Tom Kadien
President, XpedX (distribution arm of International Paper)

TOPIC: The role of pricing in the sales process and negotiating the final sale.

SUMMARY: Mr. Kadien speaks about his early sales career and how it was dominated by a focus on pricing and the challenges that created for the customer and the salesperson. He then goes on to speak about the expanded responsibilities of salespeople today—helping the customer increase the value of their business.

NEXT STEPS: Go to the website for *Contemporary Selling* (www.routledge.com/cw/Johnston), watch the chapter 8 video and then read the chapter. You will find an Expert Advice follow-up at the end of the chapter with questions that connect elements of your learning experience.

NEGOTIATING WIN-WIN SOLUTIONS

"Obstacles are those frightful things you see when you take your eyes off your goal," Henry Ford observed. Dealing with customer objections is an element of the relationship-building process that many salespeople do not enjoy. However, as Ford pointed out, it is critical to keep your eyes on your goal: building the buyer—seller relationship. When a customer shares objections, it gives the salesperson an opportunity to strengthen the relationship.

The objections customers raise during the sales presentation are one reason salespeople are so important to the relationship-building process. If customers readily accepted the presentation, the company could just mail them a brochure or send them to the company's website to view a PowerPoint presentation. It is salespeople and their unique ability to answer customer objections that enables the company to sell products to customers.

This chapter examines the delicate process of negotiating win-win solutions. It is not particularly difficult to understand the basics of negotiation, but doing it well requires training, practice, and experience. By the end of the chapter you will have the tools to negotiate successfully with customers. The chapter also examines the role managers play in supporting the salesperson during the negotiating process.

NEGOTIATIONS: THE HEART OF THE WIN-WIN SOLUTION

Many books on personal selling speak to the issue of "customer objections" and how salespeople should deal with them. They seem to think that objections are a problem that salespeople need to manage. The contemporary selling process considers customer objections an opportunity for the salesperson to create a win-win solution, and that is the goal to focus on during the presentation. Refer to the model of Contemporary Selling at the beginning of the chapter to see where we are in the process.

Too often salespeople believe that when the customer wins, they lose. Or the customer believes he or she has lost and the salesperson has won. They think there can be only one winner. Presenting customer concerns as problems suggests that if salespeople can somehow develop a scheme to win, they are successful. This is simply not the case in contemporary selling.[1] If either the buyer *or* the seller loses, both have lost. An unhappy buyer is likely to seek out other suppliers, and the relationship will suffer. If, on the other hand, the seller is forced into an unprofitable contract, the customer will ultimately bear the cost through less service, poorer-quality products, or some other problem. In either case, there is no winner.[2] Successful buyer–seller relationships are based on both parties being satisfied with the customer's purchase.

Webster's dictionary defines negotiation as the act of "conferring with another so as to arrive at the settlement of some matter" and "arranging for or bringing about through conference, discussion, and compromise."[3] Notice the definition speaks about discussion and compromise with the customer. It does not include words like "exploitation" and "manipulation." We have spoken about the importance of building relationships based on mutual respect and customer value. Negotiating through customer objections is a critical element in that process.

COMMON CUSTOMER CONCERNS

Casual observation may suggest there are many different customer concerns; however, when you look closely, it is clear the anxieties fall into five areas. Note that customers may mask their true concern with general anxieties. Successful salespeople know that when they hear a customer objection, they need to clarify and determine its true nature. Exhibit 8.1 is a summary of the five main customer concerns.[4] Let's examine them.

> **EXHIBIT 8.1 SUMMARY OF CUSTOMER CONCERNS**
>
> - Do I need *your* product?
>
>   —Product need
>   —*Your* product need
>
> - Do I trust *your* company?
>
>   —Unease about your company
>   —Loyalty to existing supplier
>
> - I don't really know you.
> - I need more time to consider your product.
> - Is this your best price?

Do I Need *Your* Product?

Customer objections regarding the product fall into two broad areas that require different approaches to deal with the customer's concern.

Product Need. First, the customer may not be convinced that there is a need for the product. This is especially true if the customer has never used a product like it. He or she may simply not see the value in buying the product or the need that it satisfies. This view can be summarized as, "We've always done it one way. Why should we start something new now?"

Consider the Apple Newton. When it was introduced in 1993, the Newton was one of the original personal digital assistants (PDAs) and ahead of its time. Unfortunately, many corporate customers could not see the need for a personal organizer and thought of it as an expensive calendar and meeting organizer. Corporate buyers asked why they should spend $500 for a calendar. Where Apple failed, companies like Palm succeeded by demonstrating these were really little computers capable of many things besides being a calendar. Today, PDA functions are built into cell phones or other mobile wireless devices like the iPod Touch. The Newton lives, but only with a group of enthusiasts, as Apple discontinued the product in 1998.[5]

Ultimately, customers must see a clear and convincing reason to buy the product. If they don't, you shouldn't be surprised if they choose not to buy. Keep in mind that customers are not usually risk takers. With new products they are likely to wonder if the technology is too new or unproven. They may also question if it is significantly better than their current solution. The fundamental question is "Do I really need your product?" Key to the answer is a well-conceived value proposition that explains clearly how the product will benefit the customer and how it will be better than the existing solution.

Your Product Need. A much more common concern regarding product is whether the customer needs *your* product. Perhaps the configuration of your product is different or your competition's product has features that aren't on yours (or vice versa). Almost anything about your product may be of concern to the customer. Careful preparation is critical in dealing with questions about your product's superiority. This is why you must have a thorough knowledge of your competitor's products and services.

Since the customer has been using your competitor's products, he or she knows their configuration, terminology, and product benefits very well. You must clearly define your product's features, advantages, and benefits (FABs) so the customer will understand the value proposition of your company's products over your competition. Again, change is not easy, and buying your product means the customer will have to learn a new product, so your value proposition must consider the cost of change. Put simply, your product cannot be just as good as the competition because that will not be sufficient reason for the customer to change. Your product must be demonstrably better.

Do I Trust *Your* Company?

If a customer asked, "Why should I trust your company?" would you be able to answer? As we have discussed, contemporary selling is based in part on mutual respect and trust between buyer and seller, including trust between the buyer's company and your company. In most cases customers already have a supplier. They may not be totally satisfied with that supplier, but they're familiar with them. They know whom to call to get a problem resolved. They are also familiar with that company's policies and procedures. You must overcome the customer's reluctance to change suppliers.

There are two types of customer objections regarding the salesperson's company. Often these two issues work together to create a formidable concern for the customer.

Unease about Your Company. If customers are not aware of your company, they may simply be concerned about your ability to deliver when, where, and what they need. This is a legitimate concern, as they are putting their company at some risk by choosing you as a supplier. They need to know that you will do what you promise in the presentation.

Customers can be concerned about your company for many reasons. If you are small, they may be apprehensive about whether you can deliver what they need or whether you are even going to be in business in two years. If you are big, they may fear they will not be a valued customer. These objections can be difficult to overcome. How can you prove to the customer that your company will be around in two years? How can you demonstrate you will deliver what the customer needs when and where it's wanted, every time? Perhaps the customer has read or heard something negative about your company.

Loyalty to the Existing Supplier. A customer who has objections about your company may be showing loyalty to or satisfaction with the current supplier. The customer may say, "I have been buying from Mr. McAllaster at Steadfast for years and they have been excellent. I never had a problem they didn't fix." In those situations it is not that your company has done anything wrong; rather, your competitor has done things right. This problem must be handled carefully, or you will anger the customer and lose the opportunity to build the relationship. Long-term relationships with suppliers can create some challenges for the salesperson. Read the Ethical Dilemma to see how strategy partnerships sometimes present difficult problems.

Directly confronting the customer with negative comments about the supplier will almost surely fail. Remember, customers don't like change, and speaking critically about someone they have had a relationship with for a time will not endear you to them. The best approach is to stay focused on your product and company.

I Don't Really Know You

Customers may be concerned about the ability of a new, inexperienced salesperson to learn their business or their commitment to the company. (Is the salesperson going to be there for a while?) The salesperson has to earn the customer's respect. When salespeople are new, customers may ask to see their supervisor or want someone more experienced to handle their business. In these situations, it is important to be very prepared and demonstrate knowledge of the customer's value proposition. The salespeople shouldn't become defensive about their education or qualifications. Rather they should use the concerns as an opportunity to build the relationship and ask those customers to put them to the test. The salesperson is asking for a chance at their business.

Selling is a people business, and occasionally your personality will not be compatible with the customer's. Keep in mind Henry Ford's quote: "Stay focused on the goal." While you and the customer may not be friends or even get along, what matters is the relationship between your companies. Of course, you should notify

ETHICAL DILEMMA

HELPING A CUSTOMER OR SOMETHING ELSE?

Emily Hatch knows that this is an important moment in her company's relationship with World Manufacturing. For the past three years she has been the account manager for World, and business has grown steadily. Her company, Accurate Instruments, supplies a key component for World's leading product. World has bought this component from Accurate since the product was introduced over six years ago.

During that time, the relationship between World and Accurate has developed into a close strategic alliance. Emily's assignment three years ago signaled to everyone in the company that senior management thought Emily had a great future. She has not only managed the account well but actually increased business.

As she sits talking with Ben Griffin, senior vice president of manufacturing for World, there is a conflict. Recently the CEO of World told him to get a 10 percent cost reduction from all suppliers. The CEO said this is due to a recent sales slump. However, Ben believes it is a short-term tactic designed to enhance cost-cutting measures proposed by the CEO for the upcoming annual shareholders' meeting.

Ben points out that, as a major supplier to World, Accurate Instruments is expected to reduce its prices. However, he also proposes a solution. If Accurate will send an invoice showing a 10 percent reduction in prices, he will hold it. He's sure that once the shareholders' meeting is over in three weeks, Emily can send a new invoice with the original pricing.

The last thing Emily wants to do is create any friction between World Manufacturing and Accurate Instruments. She knows Ben Griffin and believes he must be under tremendous pressure to propose such a plan.

Questions to Consider

1. Should Emily submit the false invoice to World Manufacturing? Why or why not?
2. How much negotiating should a salesperson do when confronted with a customer making unfair or unethical demands?
3. What role should Emily's manager play in dealing with this situation?

your manager of the problems and seek his or her help on how to address personal compatibility issues. (We will talk about this later in this chapter when we examine the manager's role in negotiations.)

Even experienced salespeople run across personality conflicts when they take on a new account. Customers often develop a relationship with a salesperson as well as the selling company. When a salesperson is replaced, the new person and customer will naturally go through a period of getting to know one another. During this period, the salesperson should be supported by management so the customer understands the company has complete confidence in the new person. Some companies rotate the sales force to prevent this situation from developing with customers. The focus should always be on the relationship between the *company* and the customer, not the salesperson and the customer.

I Need More Time to Consider Your Product

Every day salespeople hear: "I need more time to think about your proposal." Customers have a legitimate concern about making a purchase decision too quickly. If the purchase involves several parts of the company (for example, the decision to build a new plant or develop a new product), there will most likely be a committee involved in the purchase process. In some industries (defense, airlines), the decision to purchase may take a year or more. Boeing, a world leader in manufacturing large commercial aircraft, is typical. Its Boeing 787 Dreamliner took years to develop, test, and market to commercial airlines around the world. When a customer says he or she needs more time to think about the purchase, it may be true.

However, customers frequently ask for more time because they wish to delay or stall the final decision for several reasons. First, customers may be reluctant to make a decision because of the uncertainty of something new. You are asking them to trust you, your company, and your solution to their problem. While you may know it to be the best solution to their problem, they may be anxious.

GLOBAL CONNECTION

NEGOTIATING PRICE IN A GLOBAL MARKETING PLACE

1. **Define value for the customer.** Customers all over the world are focused on getting value for their purchase. It is important for the professional salesperson to help the customer understand the true value of the sale. Often this involves prices but not always. For example, customers may be willing to trade a higher price for better reliablity or purchasing flexibility.
2. **Help the customer feel better about the purchase.** Every purchase requires the customer to make decisions and successful salespeople understand that a critical part of the sales process is helping the customer understand the wisdom of their purchase. It is important to minimize concerns that feed the buyers' fear of change.
3. **Probe the customer for unspoken concerns.** In some cultures, for example Japan, buyers are reluctant to state all their concerns and defer the decision until later. Salespeople must probe the customer to be sure all concerns have been addressed.

Questions to Consider

1. Do you think customers reference price in the same way around the world?
2. What are the primary challenges for negotiating price around the world?

The second (and more likely) scenario is that you have failed to prove the value proposition. The customers do not see the benefits of your product over their existing situation. It is important to realize, however, they are not saying no. They are indirectly asking you to build a stronger case for your product. Again, this is an opportunity to build the relationship. Go back into your presentation and ask questions to ascertain the source of the customers' anxiety. Summarize the value proposition to reinforce the positive results from a purchase decision.

Is This Your Best Price?

Salespeople will consistently tell you price is the concern they hear most often. This concern is voiced in many ways: "Your price is too high," "I don't have the budget right now," "I'd like to purchase your product but not at that price," "I can't justify that price for your product." In many cases, the customer has legitimate objections about the price of your product. Many customers, especially professional buyers, are directed to buy the lowest-cost product. Often they are evaluated and rewarded on their ability to drive down the price of the products they purchase. Professional buyers at Walmart are trained to negotiate the lowest price possible.

However, while price is a legitimate customer concern, a more likely explanation is that the customer has not accepted the value proposition. Remember that value is a function of price and perceived benefits. A customer who does not perceive that the product benefits exceed the price will not be inclined to purchase the product. You are left with two options to make the sale: lower the price until it is below the product's perceived benefits, or raise the perceived benefits until they exceed the price. A customer who says your price is too high is really saying, "The benefits I perceive for buying your product are not greater than the price you are currently charging." Here are some guidelines to follow in dealing with the price concern.

Add Value to the Total Package. Customers buy a bundle of benefits that includes the product, financial terms, customer support, the company's reputation, warranties—and not least, *you.* Getting customers to see the entire package of benefits will transform their perspective on the value of your presentation.

Price Should Never Be the Main Issue. When salespeople make price the center of the presentation, they are risking the long-term buyer–seller relationship. Price is an important part of the presentation, but the salesperson should never bring it up until after he or she has clearly defined the product's features, advantages, and benefits. Then they should mention price in the context of the value proposition equating it to outstanding service and quality products.

Price Is Your Friend, Not Your Enemy. Many salespeople treat price as the enemy and run away from it at the first sign of customer concern. When a salesperson offers price concessions, he or she is saying they believe the price is too high. This position will not enhance the value of the salesperson's product with the customer. Indeed, it will harm the customer perception of the product and create doubt as to the true product value. Embrace the price as an opportunity to highlight the value of the product benefits and customer service.

BASIC POINTS IN NEGOTIATING WIN-WIN SOLUTIONS

As you have seen, a number of customer objections can affect buyer–seller negotiations. Dealing with these objections may seem like a daunting challenge, but successful negotiations are about understanding the nature of buyer–seller relationships and recognizing some general guidelines for managing buyer concerns effectively. Exhibit 8.2 gives guidelines for negotiating win-win solutions.

EXHIBIT 8.2 GUIDELINES FOR NEGOTIATING WIN-WIN SOLUTIONS

1. Plan and prepare.
2. Anticipation enhances negotiations.
3. Say what you mean and mean what you say.
4. Negativity destroys negotiations.
5. Listen and validate customer concerns.
6. Always value the value proposition.

Plan and Prepare

Just as preparation is important to a successful presentation, it is crucial to managing customer concerns. Knowledge of your customer, anticipation of your customer's objections, and a carefully developed sales presentation can do more to resolve customer objections than almost anything else. Keep in mind that the customer knows why you are there and has agreed to see you, which shows a willingness to consider your product and company. The more you have thought about and dealt with possible objections before the presentation, the more likely the customer will be to accept your proposal. At a minimum, you have shown you are committed to his or her satisfaction and positioned yourself for success in the future.

Anticipation Enhances Negotiations

Basic customer objections run across all buyers and do not change over time. With training and experience, salespeople can learn to anticipate objections while preparing for the presentation.[6] We spoke in detail in chapter 7 about getting ready for a great sales presentation. A critical part of that preparation is to preempt customer objections. When you address a concern in your presentation, will the customer raise it anyway? Possibly, but by anticipating the customer's apprehension you will have a response already developed and can reinforce it if he or she brings the objection up again.

One benefit of anticipating customer objections is that you can solve a problem before the customer has a chance to mention it. Taking the time to work out solutions to customer objections in advance lets the salesperson offer choices so the customer doesn't feel compelled to say no. For example, if you foresee price as a customer concern, develop different combinations of benefit bundles (service levels, product quality, and financial terms) to demonstrate your willingness to work with the customer.

Say What You Mean and Mean What You Say

Plain-speaking, honest answers go a long way toward building trust and reducing customer anxiety. When customers come to realize that you have their best interests in mind and deliver on statements during the presentation, their overall concern about the company and about you is diminished. When you say you are going to follow up on a question and get back to the customer later that day, you must do it. Admitting you don't know the answer to a question is always a better strategy than trying to bluff. Customers don't expect you to have all the answers, but they do expect you to find out.

When customers trust you and your company, they are less likely to be concerned about price, ability to deliver products on time, product quality, and customer service. Of course, this means a great deal of communication inside your own company. When a salesperson says, "Yes, we can deliver the products by next Friday," he or she must have the knowledge to support that delivery date. Because you are the point of contact with the customer, your ability to represent the company honestly and accurately is essential in reducing customer objections about you and your company.

Negativity Destroys Negotiations

There is often a lot at stake in negotiations with the customer (purchase order, commissions, and reputation, just to name a few), and negotiations can become very tough. Both parties seek to do the best job for their respective companies, and conflict on a variety of issues (price, delivery, credit terms, product configuration) is a natural part of the process. There's always a risk of becoming emotionally involved in the proceedings. Frustration, even anger, at the customer, the circumstances, or the way the process is going is always possible and difficult to control. It is natural to defend yourself when you perceive an attack. But controlling your anger is critical to successful negotiations. Allowing negativity to enter the negotiations will lead to a similar reaction in the customer. Once this happens it is very difficult, sometimes impossible, to get the negotiations back on track.

When the situation is getting frustrating and you feel anger, step back from the process. Ask questions to keep the customer involved and allow him or her to voice concerns. Staying connected to the customer while managing your frustration is essential. It can help to remember the customer is likely frustrated as well. Maintaining control of one's anger demonstrates a willingness to work with the customer that will often be appreciated.

Listen and Validate Customer Concerns

Customers simply want the salesperson to listen and respond to their concerns. As we have discussed, the selling process asks customers to take a risk. New customers are risking a great deal, but even if they have been customers for a long time the selling process, by definition, is about change. Even though a salesperson has addressed their objections, customers may still feel the need to voice specific worries during the negotiations.

The concern may seem trivial to the salesperson, but it is important to the customer. Listening and validating the customer's concern acknowledges that it has value.[7] It is important to listen actively to customer concerns (as discussed in chapter 7). Focus on the customer, make sure you understand what he or she is saying, and then respond to the concern.

Always Value the Value Proposition

The most effective tool for negotiating with customers is a well-developed value proposition. Carefully explaining the benefits of your company, products, services, and yourself goes a long way toward alleviating customer objections during the presentation. When you link benefits to overall value, customers will tend to worry less about price (a major customer concern), as well as other issues, and focus more on how you have addressed their needs.

Value is more than price. While customers often direct their discussion toward price, it is the salesperson's responsibility to seek out and identify the real value of the company's product to the customer. The value added by your company could take many forms, including better customer service, enhanced product quality, or improved buyer–seller communication. After identifying the value added by your company and communicating that to the customer in the sales presentation, you may need to go back and reinforce it during negotiations.

SPECIFIC NEGOTIATION STRATEGIES

There are nine basic strategies for dealing with customer concerns. Each one can be effective in the right situation. However, learning how and when to use them requires training and experience. Unfortunately, using the wrong strategy or employing a particular strategy incorrectly can derail the negotiations.

There are going to be circumstances where the customer will not be satisfied with the negotiations no matter what you say or do. In those situations, it may be necessary to pull back from the negotiations to maintain the customer relationship. It is paramount to maintain the relationship. Never allow your personal feelings to affect negotiations.

Exhibit 8.3 details the various negotiation strategies.

EXHIBIT 8.3 NEGOTIATION STRATEGIES

1. Question
2. Direct denial
3. Indirect denial
4. Compensating for deficiencies
5. Feel—felt—found
5. Third-party endorsements
7. Bounce-back
8. Defer
9. Trial offer

Question

In the question strategy you take the customer's concern, turn it into a question, and refocus on one or more strengths of your value proposition. The goal is to get the customer thinking about your presentation in a new way and contrast his or her concern against an advantage. Notice in our example that the customer is concerned about the price of the product relative to the competition. The salesperson asks the customer to consider that, while the product has a slightly higher price, it is of better quality.

Think about possible customer objections before the presentation and formulate questions to address those concerns. Questions are a relatively nonthreatening method of handling customer objections, but you must listen to the customer's comments to develop a question that addresses the concern. Here's an example of this technique.

Buyer: Your product is 10 percent more than your competitor's. That's too much.
Seller: Yes, it is slightly more expensive, but do you agree that the higher quality of our product means fewer returns and lower service costs for your company in the long run?

Direct Denial

Perhaps the most confrontational strategy for dealing with customer objections is the direct denial method, which involves an immediate and unequivocal rejection of the customer's statement. Customers may find this kind of direct disagreement threatening and have a very negative reaction.

You are probably wondering if you should ever use this strategy to address a customer concern. When a customer states a clearly false and damaging statement about you, your company, or your product, it is important to respond to the statement immediately. Allowing such ideas to continue is usually more damaging than provoking the customer. If it is a simple case of misinformation, stating the facts directly will probably clear things up for the customer.

Critical to the success of this strategy is the manner in which you address the customer misstatement. If you are offensive and insulting, the customer will likely react negatively to the statements. The focus should be to create a win-win negotiation, but being condescending or demeaning eliminates that outcome.

Buyer: I was told recently that you had to recall all of your production for the last two months because of a faulty relay in your switch mechanism.
Seller: I'm not sure where you could have heard that. We have not had a recall on any of our products for over 10 years. If you like, I can provide the data for you. Your source was mistaken.

Indirect Denial

Indirect denial takes a less threatening approach. The salesperson begins by agreeing with the customer, validating the objection before explaining why it is untrue or misdirected. For this strategy, the customer's concern should have at least some validity. Perhaps you are priced slightly higher than the competition, or your product features do not match up exactly with the current supplier's. Address the concern by first acknowledging that part of what the customer is saying is true.

If the customer has raised a totally valid point, reconsider this strategy. You don't want to deny a legitimate customer point that makes the presentation weaker. If it is not possible to deny the customer concern with the information at your disposal, do not use this strategy.

Buyer: Demand for your products is strong. I'm not convinced you will be able to meet my order on time.
Seller: You are correct. My company has enjoyed tremendous success and we are thankful our customers have adopted our product. However, we pride ourselves on not missing order deadlines, and our customers will verify that. I will be working with my manufacturing and logistics departments to ensure on-time delivery of your order. One last note: you can check the status of your order any time by logging on to our website. If you are not satisfied, call me.

Compensating for Deficiencies

No product is perfect. Every product is a combination of advantages and disadvantages. Companies design, develop, and build products based on a bundle of features (product characteristics) they believe will be accepted in the marketplace. Customers must balance what they want with what they are willing to pay (the value proposition). They realize that the perfect product doesn't exist and they must decide which features, advantages, and benefits are most important to them.

Customers frequently object to some element of the product's FAB mix. The salesperson's task is to move the customer from focusing on a feature his or her product performs poorly to one in which it excels—to compensate for deficiencies in the product. The new feature must be important to the customer. Talking about a feature the customer is not interested in will only make the situation worse.

First, acknowledge the validity of the customer's concern about the feature in question. Second, move the customer to the new product feature by pointing out the trade-off between the two. If the customer insists the product must have this one feature, it is time to consider offering products that are closer to meeting that demand, even if you do not enjoy an advantage with these products. Ultimately, the customer is right and you must adjust your product offerings to meet his or her demands. Note that the example shifts the focus from response rate (one product feature) to price and quality.

Buyer: The response time on your product is too slow. Your competitor's response time is nine-tenths of a second, which is two-tenths of a second faster.
Seller: I agree with you. My product is two-tenths of a second slower. However, please note that it also costs 25 percent less per unit than the product you are currently using. You indicated price was an issue in your decision. I would also add that my product has 10 percent fewer returns than your current supplier's. I have the numbers right here if you care to take a look.

Feel—Felt—Found

There are times when customer objections are more connected to their attitudes, opinions, or feelings than to facts. "In my opinion" and "I believe" are indicators that the customer is moving from a fact-based to a feeling-based concern. In these situations, the feel—felt—found technique can be helpful.

First, acknowledge the customer's feeling ("I can see how you *feel*"). Second, extend the same feelings to a larger audience ("Other customers have *felt* the same way"). Third, counter with a legitimate argument ("However, I have *found* that our products . . ."). The sequence is important and should be followed exactly.

At first glance, this may seem like a good strategy for dealing with customer objections, as you are relating very specifically to the customer. However, it is an old technique and one most professional buyers know. Using it on the wrong person can create the impression you are being disingenuous and the presentation is prepackaged.

Buyer: In my opinion, your products are overpriced and not worth the extra cost.
Seller: Our products are slightly more than the competition's and I can certainly see why you *feel* that way. Other customers have *felt* that way at first. However, when they take the time to examine my company's higher product quality and improved customer service (which result in lower service costs) they have *found* the overall value of the product to be worth the investment. Let me show you those numbers again.

Third-Party Endorsements

This strategy is based on the use of outside parties to bolster your arguments in the presentation. It can be used in combination with other strategies, such as feel—felt—found and indirect denial. The use of third parties to endorse you, your company, or your product does add credibility. However, it is essential to get their permission before using them for an endorsement. Many customers do not wish to have their names used in this way. We spoke earlier of potential conflicts of interest if the customer you are calling on is a competitor of the endorsing party. In addition, you always run the risk the customer will have a negative reaction to the third party. Use this technique only when you know the relationship between your customer and the third party.

Buyer: Your customer service has been questionable, and it is important I have tech support 24/7.
Seller: I agree with you that our customer service was not what it should be several years ago. However, we made the investment to improve customer service, and it is now among the best in the industry. Gracie Electronics felt as you did but was willing to try us and is now one of our most satisfied customers.

Bounce-Back

An experienced salesperson knows when to turn a customer concern into a reason for action. The bounce-back is effective in many different situations (appointment setting, negotiating, and closing). It is more aggressive than some of the other strategies, so be careful not to seem pushy.

This technique can be particularly effective when you hear objections about needing more time or a lower price. Indeed, when you understand the value proposition of your product you will note that often it is designed to save the customer time and/or money. So when the customer raises a concern about time or cost, you have an opening to reinforce the cost savings and time efficiencies of your product.

Buyer: I've listened to your presentation but need more time to consider your proposal.
Seller: I can appreciate that this is a big decision for your company. However, delaying this commitment only costs your company money. As we agreed earlier, my products will save nearly 40 percent in manufacturing costs over your existing supplier. Delaying this decision simply means higher costs for your company.

Defer

Customers seldom let a salesperson complete an entire presentation without interrupting to ask a question. If the concern they raise is one you will address later in the presentation, you may want to defer it until you have had the chance to explain other material. Most of the time the customer will understand and let you continue with the presentation. Occasionally, the customer will demand an immediate answer. If pressed, you should respond immediately. However, suggest that the customer listen to the entire presentation in order to fully appreciate all the features, advantages, and benefits of the product.

The defer strategy is most common when the customer raises a concern about price early in the presentation before the salesperson has a chance to fully define the value proposition. Simply stating the price of the product without fully explaining the benefits bundle may lead the customer to the wrong conclusion— that the price is too high. You need to evaluate the customer and determine if he or she needs the information at that point to assess the product's value. (Some people process information differently than others.)

Buyer: (before the full value of the product has been explained): What is the cost of your product?
Seller: I can appreciate your interest in knowing the price of the product, but I would ask you to hold off just a minute until I know a little more about your product requirements and determine which of our products best suits your needs. Then I will be happy to show you what kind of investment you need to make.

Trial Offer

One of the best strategies to calm customer objections is the trial offer, which allows the customer to use the product without a commitment to purchase. It is especially effective with new products, because the customer can try the product, become familiar with it, and see the product benefits without risk.[8]

Here are some guidelines to keep in mind. First, the trial offer does not take the place of a good sales presentation. Second, clearly define the terms of the offer so there will be no confusion. A customer who does not know the offer is for three days may keep using it even after your company has sent a bill. These misunderstandings can do much more harm than good. Third, make sure the customer is fully checked out on the product. Don't leave a client with a product he or she does not know how to use correctly.

Buyer: I'm not willing to make a commitment to your copier today. It seems complicated and hard to use.
Seller: I can appreciate your concerns. How about I have our service department install one for you and let you try it for one week. I will come by and demonstrate it for you. You are welcome to use it for one week without any obligation. If at the end of the week you do not believe this copier solves all your copying needs, call me and I will come pick it up.

THE SALES MANAGER'S ROLE IN NEGOTIATING WIN-WIN SOLUTIONS

As mentioned earlier, the sales manager plays an important supporting role during negotiations between salespeople and customers. Salespeople need to know they have the authority to negotiate with customers and resolve their concerns. This may mean negotiating aspects of delivery, product configuration, even price. Salespeople need to have the confidence that they can negotiate whatever is necessary and (unless it violates company policy) the sales manager will endorse the negotiations. This means company policy must authorize salespeople to negotiate with customers. It is also important that managers work hard to provide the resources to help the salesperson satisfy the customer's needs; when resources are limited (such as in recessions) cutting back on sales force can lead to lower customer satisfaction.[9]

Company personnel must also know the salesperson speaks for the company. It can be very damaging if people inside the company question the salesperson's negotiations once the customer has committed to buy.

In situations where the customer objections exceed the salesperson's authority, the manager is there to step in and continue the negotiations. It is important for the manager to be fully briefed on the negotiations to that point. As the negotiations continue, the manager should keep the salesperson involved, since he or she will be responsible for taking care of the customer once the negotiations come to a successful conclusion. The manager's support is critical to the salesperson's success in negotiating win-win solutions.

EXPERT ADVICE: FOLLOW-UP

After watching the video of Mr. Kadien and reading the chapter, consider the following:

1. Interview a local sales executive and ask them what role price objections play in their customer relationships?
2. Do you agree with Mr. Kadien that selling paper can add value to the customer, or is it just a commodity?

SUMMARY

No matter how well a salesperson prepares or presents the material to the customer—indeed, despite everything the salesperson does—the customer will seldom (if ever) buy a product based only on the presentation. Customer objections are part of the relationship-building process, and negotiating win-win solutions separates successful salespeople from the rest of the pack. Negotiations are the process of arranging with customers (through conference, discussion, and compromise) a successful resolution to their concerns.

While there may appear to be many different customer concerns, in reality there are only five. The first is "Do I need *your* product?" There are two types of product concerns. First, the customer needs to be convinced he or she needs the product at all. Second, the customer may already use the product but buy it from a competitor. You need to convince the customer that your product is demonstrably better than the competition.

The second fundamental customer concern is "Do I trust *your* company?" Customers may not know your company and doubt your ability to deliver what, when, and where they require. Or they may have a good relationship with their current supplier and see no reason to change companies. In both cases, you need to work hard to show customers that your company is fundamentally capable of handling their orders and is better than the competition.

A third customer objection has to do with the salesperson—"Do I trust you?" Customers may need to be persuaded that trusting you is not risky. A fourth concern is "I need more time to consider your product." While there can be legitimate reasons why the customer needs more time, this is often an attempt to stall the purchase decision. The customer may be saying, "You have not yet made a strong value proposition and I don't fully understand the value of your product relative to the competition."

The final customer concern is "Is this your best price?" Customers often focus on price to the exclusion of other, more critical factors. The salesperson's job is to help the customers understand the value of the total benefits package and focus on issues other than price.

There are six basic points to consider in preparing to negotiate win-win solutions: (1) plan and prepare, (2) anticipation enhances negotiations, (3) say what you mean and mean what you say, (4) negativity destroys negotiations, (5) listen and validate customer concerns, and (6) always value the value proposition. Following these guiding principles greatly improves the probability of success in negotiations.

The nine basic negotiating strategies are (1) question, (2) direct denial, (3) indirect denial, (4) compensating for deficiencies, (5) feel—felt—found, (6) third-party endorsement, (7) bounce-back, (8) deferring, and (9) trial offer. Knowing when and where to use each strategy is critical. Using the wrong one at the wrong time (such as the direct denial) can create very negative feelings in a customer.

Finally, the sales manager plays a significant supporting role. First, he or she empowers salespeople to negotiate with customers. If customers don't believe salespeople have the authority, they will not negotiate. Second, the sales manager may on occasion have to get directly involved in the negotiations. In those cases, it is important to keep the salesperson involved.

KEY TERMS

negotiation	indirect denial	bounce-back
stall	compensate for	defer
direct denial	deficiencies	trial offer

ROLE PLAY

BEFORE YOU BEGIN

Before getting started, please go to the Appendix of chapter 1 to review the profiles of the characters involved in this role play as well as the tips on preparing a role play. This particular role play requires that you be familiar with the chapter 7 role play.

Characters Involved

Alex Lewis
Rhonda Reed

Setting the Stage

Assume all the information given in the chapter 7 role play, but flash back to *before* the sales call on Tracy Brown (Alex's longtime buyer at Max's Pharmacies). Alex and Rhonda have scheduled a meeting a few days prior to the Max's sales call so the two of them can brainstorm to develop a list of potential concerns/objections that Tracy may have regarding stocking the new Upland product "Happy Teeth" in the front-end space in her eight stores. Rhonda wants to role-play a buyer–seller dialogue about these potential concerns before Alex makes the actual sales call, so he will have a chance to practice handling Tracy's various potential objections. Tracy's concerns will relate both to end users of the product (customers who shop at Max's Pharmacies) and to her own business (why Max's should or should not stock and promote Happy Teeth in its very limited front-end space).

Alex's Role

Work with Rhonda to develop a thorough list of likely concerns/objections Tracy may have about Happy Teeth. Be sure all nine negotiation strategies in this chapter are represented at least once in your list. (You can have some represented more than once.) Refer to the sample buyer/seller dialogues in the section on specific negotiation strategies for ideas on developing the list and the role play dialogue.

Rhonda's Role

Work with Alex on the above.

Assignment

Present a maximum 10-minute role play in which Alex plays himself in a mock sales call on Tracy. (Rhonda gets to role-play Tracy.) Execute the nine specific negotiation strategies presented in the chapter. Be sure Rhonda asks tough questions and brings up concerns/objections in a way that is firm yet fair. Be sure Alex uses proper negotiation techniques to overcome each objection. At the end of the mock sales call, Rhonda should take no more than 5 minutes to provide constructive feedback/ coaching to Alex on how well he used the negotiating strategies.

DISCUSSION QUESTIONS

1. Have you ever bought a new (or used car)? What were the negotiations like? Did you enjoy the negotiations? Why or why not?

2. Do you think it is really possible to have win-win negotiations? Why or why not?

3. You have made an appointment with a new potential customer. As you prepare for the presentation you realize this person has never purchased this kind of product before. What do you do?

4. You have been meeting with a potential new customer regularly for three months. She likes the product but finally admits a loyalty to the existing supplier. The buyer says, "I have known Judith Gunther for 10 years and she has been a very good supplier." What do you do?

5. "I don't know you, and I very much liked working with Oscar Jones. Why was he transferred to Chicago?" The customer you have just met for the first time is unhappy because of his relationship with the old salesperson. As a new salesperson, how would you win over this important customer?

6. Your company has just announced a 7 percent price increase on your entire product line and you are meeting with your most important customer. She announces that your competitor has already been to see her and will not raise prices for at least 24 months. What do you do to keep the customer?

7. Think of a time you were talking with someone and felt yourself getting angry. How did you handle it? What steps would you take to keep from getting angry with a customer who was being unreasonable?

8. Your product is clearly not as good as the competition. The customer has been loyal to your company for years, but you will not come out with a replacement of your existing equipment for at least a year. What do you tell the customer?

9. Which negotiation strategy has the highest risk (possibility of making the customer angry)? Which strategy do you think has the lowest risk (is most effective with customers)?

10. You are calling on a very large company that has the potential to become your largest customer. How could your sales manager help you be successful in negotiations with this potential customer?

MINI-CASE 8 MID-TOWN OFFICE PRODUCTS

Ron Chambers arrives at work early on Friday morning. His anxiety has been growing throughout his final week of training with Mid-Town Office Products. Today Ron is going to work with his sales manager, Christine Wright, on negotiating customer concerns. He wants to make sure he has plenty of time to prepare and rehearse for the types of objections he is likely to encounter while calling on clients in his new territory (downtown Los Angeles). He will start working this territory next Monday. While Ron waits for Christine to arrive, he sits down and reviews his list of the concerns he is likely to hear from his potential customers.

Mid-Town is a regional distributor of office supply products ranging from pens and paper to small office machines like shredders and fax machines. The product line boasts over 11,000 catalog items. Mid-Town has been in existence for 12 years and operates a warehouse in Cucamonga, on the eastern outskirts of Los Angeles. Mid-Town has grown into a company with a reputation for providing customers with excellent value. It competes with other office supply firms by offering next-day delivery of all orders along with a price that, while not as low as some mail-order firms', is quite competitive from a total value perspective. In addition to volume discounts, the company maintains a database to help customers track how they use their office supplies. A final feature is a dedicated website so customers can place orders over the Internet. Orders placed via Internet by 4:00 p.m. are delivered the next day.

Mid-Town's extensive product line, reasonable pricing with volume discounts, next-day delivery, usage history, and Internet ordering have allowed the company to enjoy much success serving small businesses and companies in the eastern Los Angeles suburbs. This success has led the company to expand beyond its traditional customer base of suburban Los Angeles into the heart of the downtown area. Such an expansion is risky for Mid-Town because of the very different customer base and location. However, Mid-Town has decided it can afford to place one representative in downtown Los Angeles for up to two years to try and build the business. Knowing that the success of this venture hinges on his ability to win new business with the larger downtown prospects makes Ron even more anxious about his new assignment.

Ron accepted this position after a successful eight-year career selling copy machines to downtown businesses for a local distributor of a well-known brand. A competitor recently purchased his previous employer. Ron knows that selling office products for Mid-Town will be quite different from selling office machines, and a key part of that difference will be customer concerns. That's why Ron is eager to hone his skills so he can respond effectively to each objection. Ron also knows that, even though he'll be calling on some of the same accounts that used to buy his copy machines, the office supplies buyer has a lower job level and less responsibility than the copy machine buyer. As Ron refines the list of objections he expects to get from these buyers, Christine walks in and begins discussing how he can respond to them.

Questions

1. Identify the potential sources of concern that Ron is likely to encounter when he begins to make calls on his customers in downtown Los Angeles.

2. Write out two responses for Ron using two separate negotiation strategies to the following customer concern from an office supply buyer for a large downtown bank: "We don't want you delivering during banking hours. Bringing in big boxes of supplies will upset our operations and our customers who are here trying to conduct business. Our current supplier makes deliveries before 6:30 in the morning and I don't see any need to change."

3. How can Ron effectively respond to any concerns about the prices of Mid-Town's office supplies being higher than those of mail-order competitors?

global selling environment

Sales Management

Salesperson Motivation

Selling Processes

Compensating & Evaluating Salespeople

Closing & Follow-up

Negotiating for Win-Win Solutions

Technology

Understanding Sellers & Buyers

Salesperson Self-Management

Building Relationships ~ Creating Value

Ethics

Communicating the Sales Message

Prospecting & Sales Call Planning

Selecting & Training Salespeople

Closing the Sale and Follow-up

LEARNING OBJECTIVES

This chapter completes our journey through the selling process by examining closing the sale and following up to enhance customer relationships. Closing is a natural progression of the process. Because we are building toward win-win solutions with customers, closing simply connotes that both parties recognize the value-added of doing business with one another. Postsale follow-up presents a marvelous opportunity to add even more value to clients through problem solving and service.

After reading this chapter, you should be able to:

- Define closing and explain how closing fits into the model for Contemporary Selling.
- Understand different closing methods and provide examples of each.
- Discuss the concept of rejection and ways to deal with it.
- Identify various verbal and nonverbal buying signals.
- Know when to trial close.
- Recognize and avoid common closing mistakes.
- Explain aspects of follow-up that enhance customer relationships.
- Understand the sales manager's role in closing the sale and follow-up.

EXPERT ADVICE

EXPERT: Mr. Gerhard Gschwandtner
Founder and Publisher, *Selling Power* magazine

TOPIC: Closing.

SUMMARY: Mr. Gschwandtner discusses how technology and ubiquitous information has changed the sales role to one of trusted advisor. Customers depend on salespeople for expertise and value their professional input when making critical business decisions. He builds a case that trust and effective customer engagement lead to the type of seller–buyer relationship that makes the need for hard-sell closing techniques moot. Mr. Gschwandtner goes on to mention National Cash Register (now NCR) founder John Henry Patterson as a pioneer in developing a process approach to selling.

NEXT STEPS: Go to the website for *Contemporary Selling* (www.routledge.com/cw/Johnston), watch the chapter 9 video, and then read the chapter. You will find an Expert Advice follow-up at the end of the chapter with questions that connect elements of your learning.

COMPANION @ WEBSITE

WHAT IS A CLOSE?

Closing the sale means obtaining a commitment from the prospect or customer to make a purchase. Even long-time customers still need to be closed on specific orders or transactions. Also, as you learned in chapter 7, a salesperson should always enter a call with specific goals for that call. Closing denotes the achievement of those sales call goals.

Closing the sale should not be viewed as a discrete event that takes place at the end of a sales call. Such a perspective leads to much anxiety on the part of perfectly capable salespeople by focusing on a single element in developing the client relationship. Chapter 1 introduced the concept of closing the sale in the context of our overall model for Contemporary Selling:

> The rapport, trust, and mutual respect inherent in a long-term buyer–seller relationship can take some of the pressure off the "close" portion of the sales process. In theory, this is because the seller and buyer have been openly communicating throughout the process about mutual goals they would like to see fulfilled within the context of their relationship. Because the key value added is not price but rather other aspects of the product or service, the negotiation should not get hung up on price as an objection. Thus closing becomes a natural part of the communication process. (Note that in many transaction selling models, the closing step is feared by many salespeople—as well as buyers—because of its awkwardness and win-lose connotation.)

This chapter is designed to allay any fear you may have about closing the sale. Salespeople must be able to "pull the trigger" and close the deal, else they will never do any business. So relax, read on, and by the end of the chapter we believe you will agree that successfully closing sales in an environment where the goal is to build relationships and create value both for your firm and your customers is quite achievable.

Selling Is Not a Linear Process

The components of successful selling you have learned so far throughout this book liberate you from the need to use clever, tricky, and manipulative closing approaches with your prospects and customers. Note that our guiding model for Contemporary Selling is not linear. That is, it doesn't show "steps" of selling progressing one after another in order. This is because selling usually is decidedly nonlinear and the various components of the selling process take place simultaneously, always focused on building relationships and creating value. The circular layout of our model symbolically represents this approach.

Nowhere in the selling process does understanding the nature of the model for Contemporary Selling become more relevant than in closing the sale. Closing as a selling function is actually appropriate at *any point* in the selling process—not just at the end of a lengthy sales presentation. In this chapter, we advocate learning different approaches to closing, because knowing different ways to communicate to buyers the need to gain commitment to the goals of the sales call is a fundamental skill in seller–buyer communication. However, we also strongly advocate that these closing skills be used at the appropriate point in the dialogue with the customer—*not just at the end*. The salesperson must watch for buying signals, verbal and nonverbal cues that the customer is ready to make a commitment to purchase.

If a salesperson has done the job well on the tasks described so far in this book—understanding the buyer, creating and communicating value, behaving ethically, using information for prospecting and sales call planning, communicating the sales message effectively, and negotiating for win-win solutions—why should the close be anything other than a natural progression of the dialogue with the customer? That's the most healthy and constructive way to look at the task of closing the sale—and it focuses on doing a great job of the *whole* selling process, not just the "dreaded close" at the end.

What you learned in chapter 8 about always working to find win-win solutions has particular relevance in closing the sale. In their popular book *Getting to Yes*, Roger Fisher, William Ury, and Bruce Patton frame it this way. The core of selling is negotiation. The salesperson has goals and a perspective; the customer has goals and a perspective of his or her own. The art of selling is finding the common ground where both parties can win by developing a mutually beneficial business relationship. To do so, sellers must have a high level of empathy in dealing with their prospects and customers. An empathetic salesperson identifies with and understands the buyer's situation, feelings, and motives. Also, they must set goals for the sales call that are consistent with the customers' needs.[1] If both parties win from doing business together, surely this has been communicated *throughout* the dialogue between seller and buyer. Points of agreement have already been established. The idea that a win-win solution would somehow come as a revelation only at the end of the dialogue does not match the spirit or the process of relationship selling.

To summarize:

- Closing is a natural part of the selling process.
- The process is rarely linear. The close need not happen at the *end* of a lengthy sales presentation.
- Salespeople must watch for buying signals *any time* during the seller–buyer dialogue and act on those signals by closing then.
- It is important to take the *buyer's perspective* in closing, working toward win-win solutions for both parties by communicating and delivering value to the customer and to your own company.
- Based on the above, salespeople must understand and be able to use different approaches to closing.

CLOSING METHODS

There are many ways to close the sale. No salesperson can rely on just one or a few of them. Successful salespeople learn how and when to use many different approaches to closing so they can apply each appropriately in different situations. Just as you learned in chapter 7 that memorized or "canned" sales presentations have major limitations, canned approaches to closing do not give you the ability to adapt to a particular sales situation. It is critically important that any closing technique be customized to the particular buyer and situation. Like many aspects of selling, doing this successfully takes practice and improves over time.

A common theme of sales success that was discussed in chapter 7 is the need for salespeople to develop and practice *active listening* skills. In the context of closing the sale, active listening refers to carefully monitoring the dialogue with the customer, watching for buying signals, and then picking just the right time to close. Only when you listen actively will the buyer have the chance to register verbal and nonverbal buying signals that tell you it's time to close.

Another closing tool is silence. When you close, you have just put the ball into the prospect's court. It is now time to sit back, be quiet, and let the customer talk. Research indicates that effective use of silence in closing separates high-performing salespeople from the other kind.[2] Make no mistake, silence can be challenging to use in a sales call. If you bounce the ball to the prospect through a close and the prospect doesn't pick it up and run with it by either providing objections or making a commitment to buy, seconds of silence can seem like minutes (or hours!). However, try to resist jumping in. Give the prospect the maximum leeway to respond to your close.

The seven closing methods here are a sampling of some of the most used approaches. Examples are provided for each. However, remember that good salespeople adapt closing techniques to particular buyers and particular selling situations.

Assumptive Close

In a way, salespeople always assume they are going to close. Otherwise, they would be hard pressed to justify time spent on a prospect. The assumptive close allows the salesperson to verbalize this assumption to see if it is correct. Examples:

- "I can ship it to you on Monday. I'll go ahead and schedule that."
- "Let's get this paperwork filled out so we can get the order into the system."
- "You need Model 455 to meet your specifications. I'll call and reserve one for you."

Obviously, you are looking for the buyer to just naturally move along with your assumption. If he or she doesn't, as with any close you will likely uncover some additional objections you need to deal with.

Several of the other closing methods are assumptive in nature. In fact, it is generally favorable to handle all communication with the prospect with the attitude that he or she will ultimately buy. This creates an atmosphere in the sales call that supports the concept of moving to win-win solutions.

Minor Point Close

In the minor point close, the salesperson focuses the buyer on a small element of the decision. The idea is that agreeing on something small reflects commitment to the purchase, and the salesperson can move forward with the deal. Examples:

- "What color do you prefer?"
- "Do you want to use our special credit terms?"
- "When would you like our technical crew to do the installation?"

Alternative Choice Close

Usually the alternative choice close also focuses the buyer on deciding relatively minor points. This approach simply adds the twist of giving the prospect options (neither of which is *not* to buy at all). Focus on making the choice between *viable* options—options the prospect is most likely to accept. Examples:

- "Which works best for your application, Model 22 or Model 35?"
- "Would you like this delivered tomorrow, or would Monday be better?"
- "Do you want it with or without the service agreement?"

Direct Close

This approach is most straightforward. With the direct close, you simply ask for the order. Although simple, this close can be highly effective when you get strong buying signals and your buyer seems to be a straight shooter. Such buyers often appreciate the direct approach. Examples:

- "It sounds to me as though you are ready to make the buy. Let's get the order into the system."
- "If there are no more questions I can answer, I would sure like us to do business today. What do you say?"

Summary-of-Benefits Close

Throughout the sales process, you and the buyer have (we hope) found common ground for agreement on a variety of points. The summary-of-benefits close is a relatively formal way to close by going back over some or all of the benefits accepted, reminding the buyer why those benefits are important, and then asking a direct closing question (or perhaps ending with a choice or some other method). Example:

- "Ms. Buyer, we've agreed that our product will substantially upgrade your technical capabilities, allow you to attract new business, and all the while save you money over your current system, isn't that right? (Buyer agrees.) Given your timetable for implementation, let's go ahead and place the order for one of our systems today. We can have it delivered in two weeks and I will have my service technicians out then to begin training your staff on using the system. (Silence. Wait for response.)"

Balance Sheet Close

The balance sheet close, also sometimes called the t-account close, gets the salesperson directly involved in helping the prospect see the pros and cons of placing the order. In front of the customer, take a piece of paper and write the headings "Reasons for Buying" on the top left and "Remaining Questions" on the top right. (Don't put the word "Objections" on the top right; it sounds too negative.) Your job is to summarize the benefits accepted in the left column and use the right column to find out what is holding the prospect back from buying. You might set up the exercise like this:

- "Mr. Buyer, let's take a few minutes to list out and summarize the reasons this purchase makes sense for you, and also list any remaining questions you may have. This will help us make the right decision. (Pull out paper. Have a dialogue with the buyer to develop the points. When finished, use an appropriate closing method.)"

Buy-Now Close

The buy-now close, also sometimes referred to as the impending-event close or standing-room-only close, creates a sense of urgency with the buyer that, if he or she doesn't act today, something valuable will very likely be lost. In professional selling, manipulative closing techniques are strictly taboo, so you have to be *honest* here. That is, the reasons you set forth why the buyer will benefit if he or she doesn't hesitate must be *real*. Examples:

- "We have a price increase on this product effective in two weeks. Orders placed today can be guaranteed to ship at the current price."
- "My company is running a special this week. This product is currently 20 percent off the regular price."
- "Orders placed by Thursday receive an extra 30 days before the invoice is due."
- "I'm almost out of stock on this product in our warehouse."

In Closing, Practice Makes Perfect

There are many other forms of closing. In his book *The Art of Closing Any Deal*, James W. Pickens lists no fewer than 24 techniques he calls "the 24 greatest closes on earth."[3] However, not every closing technique you may read about is really appropriate. The above seven approaches are tried and true ways to move your buyer to commitment without resorting to unnecessarily tricky or questionable tactics. As a salesperson you will become more and more comfortable with using the different closing methods as you have the opportunity to practice them.

DEALING WITH REJECTION

In chapter 6 you learned that an important aspect of prospecting is qualifying the prospect and the better job a salesperson does of qualifying prospects, the more likely those prospects will eventually turn into customers. Prospecting is in many ways a numbers game. The more leads you can qualify as prospects, the more customers you develop, and ultimately the more sales you close.

Many times a salesperson can do everything right and still not get a customer to close a deal. It is important for anyone in the sales profession to reflect on this fact and to understand at a deep human level that failing to get an order or close a deal is not personal rejection. A salesperson's measure of accomplishment and self-worth should not be controlled by what someone else does or fails to do. Nobody can make you feel inferior without your permission!

It is one thing to be disappointed by not getting an order or closing a particular sale, and it is perfectly reasonable (and wise) to step back and analyze what might have caused this outcome and what you might do differently next time. This is simply learning and growing professionally. But successful salespeople never construe such business decisions by customers as personal rejection. They maintain their positive attitude about their job, their company, and their products and move on to the next customer.

Tom Reilly, a well-known authority on professional selling, developed five tactics for dealing with rejection, which he has used in successfully training salespeople for many years:

1. *Remind yourself of the difference between self-worth and performance.* Never equate your worth as a human being with your success or failure as a salesperson.
2. *Engage in positive self-talk.* Separate your ego from the sale. The prospect is not attacking you personally. Say to yourself, "This prospect doesn't really even know me as a person. The refusal to buy cannot have anything to do with me as a person."
3. *Don't automatically assume that you are the problem.* The prospect may be an intimidating, self-serving individual with some deep personal problems that cause the behavior you see. The prospect may be just having a bad day or may be like that all the time. You are not to blame for any of these possibilities.
4. *Positively anticipate the possibility of rejection and it will not overwhelm you.* Expect it, but don't create it. That is, think in advance what your response to rejection will be if it occurs. (Note: This does not conflict with an assumptive close approach.)
5. *Consider the possibility that not buying is a rational decision because of underlying reasons.* Possible reasons are bad timing, shared decision making, or budget constraints that truly do prevent purchase. The prospect may not feel comfortable revealing these reasons to you.[4]

The preparation you learned in chapter 8 for anticipating and handling buyers' objections will help buffer you against taking rejection personally. If you do a great job during the preapproach of researching reasons a customer might not buy and then planning appropriate responses for dealing with the objections, at the end of the day if the customer does not buy you can look at yourself in the mirror and say, "I did everything I could." This is a sign of professionalism in selling.

Excellence in call preparation yields a confidence and professionalism that cannot be equaled. This is why sales executives often call the preapproach the single most important stage in the selling process. (Interesting, isn't it, how this runs counter to the stereotype that the most important step is the close?) If, despite your preparation and presentation, the customer still doesn't buy, know when to pack up graciously and leave the door open to sell to this client another day.

Attitude Is Important

Books on successful closing agree that a critical determinant of whether or not a salesperson closes customers is attitude.[5] Attitude represents the salesperson's state of mind or feeling with regard to a person or thing. Everything else being equal, salespeople who believe in themselves and their product or service, show confidence, exhibit honest enthusiasm, and display tenacity (sticking with a task even through difficulty and adversity) will close more business than those who don't. Attitude is infectious. Customers pick up on a salesperson's attitude and outlook on life right away.

In a survey 215 sales managers across a wide range of industries were asked which success factors were the most important in their salespeople. Tenacity (sticking with a task/not giving up) ranked fourth out of over 50 key success factors.[6] Successful salespeople are successful in large measure because they don't give up easily. They stick with the process of developing customer relationships and moving customers to closing the sale. They aren't distracted from this core mission of selling, and they don't feel rejected when they don't make a sale.

One important way to approach closing involves envisioning a successful outcome with the buyer. Sit back and mentally rehearse how a positive outcome might unfold. Think about all the steps needed to close the sale. This exercise helps solidify the road map toward closing and also feeds your positive attitude and confidence before you actually engage in the close.

IDENTIFYING BUYING SIGNALS

As we mentioned, a close does not necessarily happen at the very end of a presentation. It can happen any time. The timing is driven by the buyer's readiness to commit—not the salesperson's need to cover a certain amount of material, present all the available features and benefits, or make it to the end of the presentation. Many salespeople, especially new ones, experience problems in closing because they ignore or are insensitive to buying signals, those verbal and nonverbal cues that the customer is ready to make a commitment to purchase.

Verbal Buying Signals

A buyer may not come right out and say "I'm ready to buy," at least not in those words. However, salespeople should look out for the following verbal signals, which essentially communicate the same message.

- *Giving positive feedback.* The most overt buying signal is a positive comment or comments from the buyer about some aspect of your product. Or the buyer may reinforce something you have said. Examples:

  - "I like the new features you described."
  - "Those extended credit terms really help me out."
  - "You certainly are right that our current vendor can't do that."

- *Asking questions.* When buyers become more engaged, they tend to ask more questions. Buyer questions come in many types, and not all signal a readiness to buy. But watch for questions that seem to open the door to close. Examples:

  - "When will it be available to ship?"
  - "What colors does it come in?"
  - "How much is it?" (Note: A price question may be a signal to close, or it may represent the beginning of an objection.)
  - "Can you explain your service agreement?"

- *Seeking other opinions.* Buyers usually don't ask for opinions about your product or company unless they are seriously considering purchase. This may involve someone else in their company, or it may involve asking you for references or even your own opinion about you versus the competition. Examples:

  - "Let me get Bob from our engineering department in to look at your specs."
  - "Who are some other firms that have bought your product recently?"
  - "Give me your honest opinion about how your product stacks up against your competitors."

- *Providing purchase requirements.* Watch for the point where a buyer begins to become very specific about his or her needs. Often these relate to relatively minor points, not the key attributes of your product or company. This signals acceptance of the major points. Examples:

  - "My orders must be split among four warehouses."
  - "The only way I can change vendors is if you are willing to train my people to use your equipment."

Nonverbal Buying Signals

As you learned in chapter 7 on communicating the sales message, often nonverbal communication tells as much or more about the buyer's readiness to buy as words. Watch closely for nonverbal signals that indicate it's time to close.

- *The buyer is relaxed, friendly, and open.* If the buyer moves to this mode during the call, it likely signals he or she is comfortable with what you are selling.
- *The buyer brings out paperwork to consummate the purchase.* A purchase order, sales contract, or other form is a sure signal to close.
- *The buyer exhibits positive gestures or expressions.* Head nodding, leaning forward in a chair, coming around the desk to get a better look at a sample, significant eye contact, and similar nonverbal signals denote interest and potential commitment to the purchase.
- *The buyer picks up your sample and tests it or picks up and examines your literature.* The more involved your customer is in your presentation, the more likely he or she is ready for a close.

Trial Close

When you detect one or more buying signals, it's time to engage in a trial close. "Trial" suggests that the buyer may or may not actually be ready to commit. A trial close can involve any of the closing methods discussed earlier. It may simply entail asking the buyer's opinion about something. Often a trial close elicits a negative response from the buyer because he or she still has some objections you must overcome. By nature, a trial close can be used at any time during the sales process. In fact, if you walk into a sales call and get a strong buying signal immediately, go ahead and do a trial close. If the customer commits, that's great. Never feel compelled to deliver a presentation to a buyer who is already sold! A trial close that works becomes *the* close.

COMMON CLOSING MISTAKES

You have already learned that closing the sale should not be viewed as an end in and of itself but rather as a natural part of the communication process. Over the long run, there will always be some orders you don't get and some deals you don't close. Avoiding a number of potential problems in closing will improve your success. The following are some classic closing errors.

- *Harboring a bad attitude.* We established earlier that salespeople who believe in themselves and the product, show confidence, exhibit honest enthusiasm, and display tenacity will close more business than those with a different attitude. A positive approach to life is infectious and carries over to your relationships with customers.
- *Failure to conduct an effective preapproach.* The preapproach stage is where you do the advanced research and planning needed to arm yourself with the knowledge to give the sales presentation, handle objections,

and ultimately provide win-win solutions to customers. This "behind the scenes" part of selling is very important, and failure to properly plan for the sales call usually leads to poor results in closing. Well-prepared salespeople exude confidence; ill-prepared salespeople come across as, well, ill prepared.

- *Talking instead of listening.* Listening is a key to understanding your buyer, getting to know his or her needs, uncovering objections, catching buying signals, and knowing when to trial close.
- *Using a "one size fits all" approach to closing.* Closing methods must be carefully selected and customized to fit a particular buyer and buying situation. You certainly do not want to come across as a "closing robot" that uses the same techniques every time. Practice and experience will raise your comfort level in applying multiple closing methods to different situations.
- *Fear of closing/failure to close altogether.* As mentioned earlier in the chapter, our hope is that by now you understand that asking for the sale is a natural part of the sales process when the focus is on building relationships and creating value. Any lingering fears about "pulling the trigger" to close the sale must be overcome in order to be a successful salesperson.
- *Uncertainty about what to do after the close.* Sometimes salespeople will hang around and keep talking about the sale after the buyer has already committed. Would you believe that this behavior can talk a buyer out of a sale? It's true! Once commitment is received, it's fine to firm up details (delivery, timing, support staff, etc.). But *never* linger and postmortem the sale with the buyer.

At the end of this chapter is an Appendix, "Checklist for Using Effective Closing Skills." Its extensive set of questions will help you identify what aspects of your closing skills are going well and what areas need more work. Especially for new salespeople, this checklist provides considerable insight into the complexity of issues in closing sales and is a source of ideas for use in closing.

Ethical Dilemma provides an interesting closing situation for your consideration.

FOLLOW-UP ENHANCES CUSTOMER RELATIONSHIPS

In chapter 3 on value creation in buyer–seller relationships, many foundation issues were developed that lead to long-term relationships with customers. Central to nurturing these relationships are how the sales organization creates value for customers and how salespeople communicate that value proposition through actions and words. One of the most important ways to add value is through excellent service after closing the sale, often referred to as follow-up.

During this follow-up, the various dimensions of service quality described in chapter 3 really come into play. Recapping, those are:

- *Reliability.* Providing service in a consistent, accurate, and dependable way.
- *Responsiveness.* Readiness and willingness to help customers and provide service.
- *Assurance.* Conveyance of trust and confidence the company will back up the service with a guarantee.
- *Empathy.* Caring, individualized attention to customers.
- *Tangibles.* The physical appearance of the service provider's business, website, marketing communication materials, and the like.[7]

The above descriptors of good service refer not only to salespeople but also to their whole organization. Often salespeople rely heavily on support people to aid in postsale service. Customer care groups, call centers, technicians, and many others frequently represent a firm during the follow-up process. Sometimes these after-sale service functions are even outsourced and offshored.[8] But no matter who else has contact with your customer, ultimately *you*—the client's primary salesperson—are the person your customer views as the main representative of your firm. So you must understand and involve yourself directly in follow-up activities with customers.[9]

ETHICAL DILEMMA

WHO WILL PLACE THE ORDER?

Jeff Hill of Southeast Distributors has a decision to make and not much time to make it. As Senior Account Manager for the Ronbev Technologies account, Jeff has a very good relationship with Ron Yokum, CEO and founder of Ronbev. In the four years since Jeff began managing the account, sales have increased 50 percent.

Ronbev has been a customer of Southeast for more than six years and the two companies have a close working relationship. Several years ago (after much hard work on Jeff's part), Ron signed an agreement to make Southeast his exclusive supplier, thereby ensuring price stability and enhanced service. Neither Southeast nor Ronbev has been disappointed in the relationship.

Despite the strong relationship between the two companies, Ron (CEO) and Hugh Jacoby (Head of Purchasing) insist that they personally initiate every order. While overall sales are worked out in strategic planning meetings every year, the configuration of each order and specific characteristics of product size, quantity, and delivery dates vary a great deal. As a result, Ron feels it is important for either Hugh or himself to sign off on every order to be sure it meets Ronbev's needs. Jeff often sits in on the strategic planning meetings and knows Ronbev's purchasing patterns quite well.

Today he sits in his office considering a difficult decision. It's the last day of the month and he is reviewing the Ronbev account. He knows that a big order is overdue, but Ron and Hugh are both out of town on vacation and aren't due back for another week. Jeff is also quite aware that today is the last day for sales to be counted in a sales contest that offers salespeople and their customer support teams the opportunity for a big bonus. Jeff's team of three support staff and two salespeople have worked hard on the Ronbev account all year, and the results have been very positive. He feels they deserve to win the award and the bonus.

Unfortunately, he is well aware of Ron's standing request to personally initiate orders. He has spoken to Ronbev often about creating a CRM system that would allow him to make assumptions about the order based on past history and feedback. Jeff knows that such a system would save Ronbev time and money. However, as he sits in his office today contemplating the situation, it is not in place.

Questions to Consider

1. Should Jeff go ahead and place the order he knows is coming and win the contest, while risking the anger of Ron Yokum?
2. How much latitude should a salesperson assume in closing the sale when he or she has an established relationship with a customer?

Customer Expectations and Complaint Behavior

During the sales process, you and your firm set certain expectations that customers have a right to believe you will meet. These expectations relate to all phases of your product and service. When customer expectations are not met, customers perceive a performance gap between what you promised and what you delivered. Performance gaps result in customer complaints.

Customer complaints are not something to be dodged or avoided. In fact, customers should be encouraged to share their postsale concerns. Otherwise, how will the sales organization ever know that a problem exists that needs to be corrected? The following performance gaps are among the most common sources of postsale complaints:

- *Product delivery.* Classically, when problems occur with product delivery, it is due to a service failure outside the direct control of the salesperson. However, you must not give excuses, blame someone else, or act as though delivery is not your problem. Your customer expects *you* to research and solve delivery problems.
- *Credit and billing.* Again, this problem is usually not due to some direct action or lack of action by the salesperson. Regardless, you are the customer's main contact person. If problems occur on the invoice, you should shepherd your credit department toward solving the problem and keep your customer in the communication loop during the process.
- *Installation of equipment.* If a delay occurs on a promised installation, or if something goes wrong with the installation, a customer can quickly become frustrated. Sometimes you must travel in person to the installation site to display empathy and responsiveness to the customer—even if you don't have the technical expertise to contribute to the installation itself.
- *Customer training.* Promising that your firm will train a client's users of your product is very common. If a breakdown occurs somewhere in this process, you must become involved in straightening out the mess.
- *Product performance.* A gap between a customer's expectations of your product's performance and its actual performance may evoke the most severe of complaints. While other complaint issues are relatively transient, problems with the product itself get at the core value the customer expected from the purchase. Guarantees and warranties can go a long way toward appeasing customers with product performance problems, but any customer would prefer to have a product that works right in the first place. Hence, the salesperson should work hard to communicate with the customer during a period of malfunction, and also help the customer find alternative solutions during a period of repair.

Communicating with Customers about Complaints. Salespeople are not absolved from communicating with customers just because they've closed the sale. In fact, properly handled complaints are strong opportunities for salespeople to show customers that they have the customers' long-term best interests at heart. Well-handled follow-up to customer problems—service recovery—can be a powerful solidifier of long-term customer relationships.[10]

Here are a few guidelines for salespeople to follow in communicating with customers about problems after the sale:

1. *Listen carefully to what the customer has to say.* Especially if he or she is upset, let the customer vent. Use active listening skills and good body language (eye contact, nodding in agreement, etc.). If the correspondence is by phone, interject verbally occasionally to let the customer know you are listening and you understand.
2. *Never argue.* Never get emotionally charged about the problem. Simply evaluate the complaint and work with the customer to formulate viable solutions.
3. *Always show empathy.* Understand the customer's point of view about the problem.
4. *Don't make excuses.* Don't say, "Your order was late because our truck broke down." Focus on *fixing* the problem. And never, ever, make negative remarks about or blame other people inside your company.
5. *Be systematic.* Work with the customer and your company to develop specific goals for solving the problem, including a timetable, action steps, and who will do what. Don't set unrealistic expectations for solving the problem. That will only widen the gap between your performance and the customer's expectations.
6. *Make notes about everything related to the complaint.* Keep the notes updated as things progress.
7. *Express appreciation.* Sincerely thank the customer for communicating the complaint and show by your words and actions that you value his or her business.

Don't Wait for Complaints to Follow Up with Customers

Although handling postsale problems and complaints is an important aspect of follow-up, successful salespeople are *proactive* in their follow-up. The idea is that the seller and buyer will communicate regularly to build each other's business. Many salespeople develop a communication plan with customers between sales calls that include touching base by phone, email, and mail. A particularly effective approach is to check with the customer right after delivery of an order just to ensure everything is as expected. Usually the customer will simply say everything is fine. But when a problem has occurred, the correspondence ensures the salesperson can deal with it quickly.

The predominant use of email for customer follow-up creates a need to educate salespeople about its effective use (and potential abuse). Global Connection explains important elements of email etiquette, especially in communicating across geographic borders and cultures. Following these rules will ensure that this outstanding communication tool enhances your relationship with customer around the world rather than detracting from it.

GLOBAL CONNECTION

PROPER EMAIL ETIQUETTE AVOIDS CROSS-BORDER FAUX PAS

Email correspondence continues to grow as a communication medium around the world and has usurped other more personal means of contact in most cases. The average businessperson sends and receives about 90 email messages daily.

Although email is certainly powerful and popular, it's *not always* the most effective way to get your ideas across to clients. This is particularly true when communicating across language and culture, as email cannot capture nuances and intent the way voice or face-to-face communication can. Between the limitations of ASCII text, odd line breaks inserted by mail servers, clients who use bizarre terms, spamming, never-get-to-the-point authors, tedious email lists, and hard-to-decipher unsubscribe routines, it's amazing anything at all gets properly communicated across borders.

To use email effectively in customer follow-up and make sure customers read and understand your messages, follow the six simple guidelines here:

1. *Always include a detailed subject line.* Because email messages don't go through a screening process or gatekeeper, many people use the subject line to determine which messages get read and which get instantly deleted. Even if your message is important for the recipient, if you make the subject line vague or leave it blank, there's a good chance the message will never get read. Be sure your subject line reflects the message's content. Trying to trick recipients with "sensational" subject lines will only make them wary of future correspondences from you. Keep your subject line brief—the more concise and truthful your subject line is, the greater the chance your recipient will read your message (and future messages from you).

2. *Allow ample time for a response.* Nearly everyone regards email as "instant communication" and expects an immediate response to every message. But immediate responses are not always feasible. Depending on your recipient's workload, log-on habits, level of smartphone usage, and time constraints, responding to your message may take several days. The general rule is to allow at least *three days* for a response. If you don't receive a reply, resend the original message and insert "2" into the subject line. So if your original message subject lines reads, "product information you requested," the resent subject line will read, "product information you requested—2." If your

second attempt doesn't get a response, consider calling your recipient and alerting him or her to your message.

3. *Know when and when not to reply to a sender.* One challenge with email is that everyone wants to have the last word. As a result, an email trail can continue for days without the new messages adding anything. Consider this typical email exchange:

Person 1: "Let's meet at 3 p.m. in the conference room."
Person 2: *That works for my schedule, too. See you then.*
Person 1: *Great. Looking forward to it.*
Person 2: *Me, too. Talk with you later.*
Person 1: *Okay. See you at 3:00.*

On and on the exchange continues, simply because neither person can resist the temptation to reply. Such correspondences not only waste time but take up bandwidth space on the server and add to people's frustration as their email boxes fill. If your intended reply does not add anything to the original message's objective, don't send it.

On the other hand, know when you definitely should send a response. If someone emails you a document to review, a simple acknowledgment that you received it and are reviewing it is sufficient. Don't force people to wait in limbo, unsure of the status of their request. Give a brief confirmation when you receive important messages, similar to the order acknowledgments you receive from online retailers.

4. *Use your reply button properly.* All email programs have a "reply" and a "reply to all" option. Using the wrong one could cause you undue embarrassment. Unless you want everybody on the original message to read your message, it's wise to simply use the "reply" button.

5. *Set up your reply features appropriately.* When you set up your email program's reply preferences, you have many options to choose from. To make replies easy for you and your recipient, set your new message to appear as the first block of text, above the original message. Placing your reply message below the original can confuse your recipient, who may not scroll all the way down and may think you did not add any new information. If you are replying to a series of questions, either restate the question before each answer or type "See answer below" at the top of your reply, then go back into the original message and type your answers there. Use this second approach only if you can easily distinguish your answers via different colored or styled text.

6. *Ask permission to add clients to your message list.* Because of the sheer number of emails your customers receive daily, always ask permission before you automatically put someone on any sort of listserves. And while you may enjoy receiving jokes, photos, and silly cartoons throughout the day, others may not appreciate such items taking up space on their server. Finally, be cautious how you convey very large file attachments. Often recipients become frustrated when you send really big files that are over their servers limit, resulting in emails without their planned attachments.

Strict adherence to these approaches will eliminate much of the ambiguity, confusion, and miscommunication by email that is common when doing business across borders.

Questions to Consider

1. Have you ever committed a major email faux pas? What was it and what did you do to fix it?
2. Why are the email etiquette tips above especially important to observe when communicating across borders?

Other Key Follow-up Activities

After the sale, companies have the opportunity to focus on several other important customer-building activities.

- *Customer satisfaction.* Sales organizations need an ongoing program to measure and analyze customer satisfaction—to what degree customers like the product, service, and relationship. Although the marketing department usually leads this initiative, the sales force often participates in the process. It certainly benefits from the information by altering sales approaches to better serve customer needs.
- *Customer retention and customer loyalty.* After the sale is a good time to work on building customer loyalty and retention rate. One reason periodic measurement of customer satisfaction is important is because a dissatisfied customer is unlikely to remain loyal to you, your company, and its products over time.

  Importantly, however, the corollary is not always true: Customers who describe themselves as satisfied are not necessarily loyal. Indeed, one author estimates that 60 to 80 percent of customer defectors in most businesses said they were "satisfied" or "very satisfied" on the last customer survey before their defection.[11] In the interim, perhaps competitors improved their offerings, the customer's requirements changed, or other environmental factors shifted. The point is that businesses that measure customer satisfaction should be commended—but urged not to stop there. Satisfaction measures need to be supplemented with examinations of customer behavior, such as measures of the annual retention rate, frequency of purchases, and the percentage of a customer's total purchases captured by the selling firm.
- *Reexamine the value added.* Customers should be analyzed regularly to ensure that your value proposition remains sufficient to retain their loyalty. Review the various sources of value discussed in chapter 3 to determine if you are maximizing the added value for your customers. Gaining feedback from customers after the sale has been institutionalized in many sales organizations. IBM, for example, includes such feedback as a formal part of its performance evaluation process for everyone who interacts directly with a client. This is part of a concept called "360-degree feedback," and it will be discussed further in chapter 13.
- *Reset customer expectations as needed.* This topic was discussed in chapter 3 but is well worth visiting again. Many salespeople try "to underpromise and overdeliver." This catchphrase encourages salespeople not to raise unrealistic expectations from their customers and reminds them to try to deliver more than they promised in order to pleasantly surprise the buyer. Overpromising can get the initial sale and may work *once* in a transactional selling environment, but a dissatisfied customer will likely not buy again—and will tell many others to avoid that salesperson.

  Managing customer expectations is an important part of developing successful long-term relationships. Customer delight, or exceeding customer expectations to a surprising degree, is a powerful way to gain customer loyalty. The follow-up stage is a great time to overdeliver and delight customers, as well as to close any lingering gaps between customer expectations and the performance of your company and its products.

CRM and Follow-up

All CRM systems allow for managing your business with any customer through all aspects of the relationship. As described in chapter 5, CRM systems use underlying data warehouses into which information about customers is entered at all touchpoints, or places where your firm interacts with the customer.

The follow-up activities in selling should all be documented in a CRM system. Among the analyses such documentation makes possible are:

- Tracking common customer postsale problems, sharing these problems with others in your firm, and creating viable solutions.

- Sharing postsale strategies among all members of the sales organization.
- Documenting and comparing levels of satisfaction, retention, and loyalty across customers.
- Developing product and service modifications, driven by customer input.
- Tracking performance of individual salespeople and selling teams against customer follow-up goals.

THE SALES MANAGER'S ROLE IN CLOSING THE SALE AND FOLLOW-UP

Very early in a salesperson's career an opportunity should be provided for him or her to learn and practice good listening skills. Then, these skills should be modeled and practiced periodically through role play—hopefully during sales manager work-withs—including sensitizing the salesperson to both verbal and nonverbal buying signals.

The onus is on sales managers to create a healthy environment for closing—an environment that recognizes the desired win-win nature of contemporary selling, not one that allows a high-potential customer relationship to be thrown offtrack by inappropriate, pushy closing techniques. Such a culture is created by training and reinforcement, and by everyone in the company (especially managers) practicing what they preach on a day-to-day basis.

You know from reading this chapter that salespeople should not translate the failure to get an order or close a deal into a personal rejection. The sales manager is in the best position of anyone in the firm to promote a healthy "can-do" attitude among his or her salespeople. When a sale is missed, the manager must work with the salesperson to debrief the sales process so that together they can come up with approaches that are likely to be successful with the next customer—or in future contacts with the customer who failed to close.

Finally, sales managers need to fully realize the power of follow-up after a sale to strengthen customer relationships, and then actively encourage their salespeople to invest in follow-up activities. Ideally, an assessment of how well salespeople engage in follow-up with customers should be a part of their performance review process and they should be rewarded accordingly. Evaluating salesperson performance is the topic of chapter 13.

EXPERT ADVICE: FOLLOW-UP

After watching the video of Mr. Gschwandtner and reading the chapter, consider the following questions:

1. According to Mr. Gschwandtner, how has technology and nearly limitless access to information by buyers necessitated changes in the sales role?
2. What did you learn from the video about John Henry Patterson's sales process and closing approaches?

SUMMARY

In contemporary selling, closing the sale should not be a traumatic experience for either the salesperson or the customer. Because the goal all along has been to work toward value-adding win-win solutions that benefit both parties and lead to a long-term relationship, closing is a natural outcome of the seller–buyer dialogue.

It is important for salespeople to become familiar with many closing methods so they can apply the best methods to different situations. Successful salespeople know that not getting an order is not a personal rejection. They understand the importance of learning from such experiences but not basing their self-worth on them. Attitude is very important to successful closing. Salespeople who believe in themselves and the product and show confidence, honest enthusiasm, and tenacity will close more business than those who don't. Empathy with customers and their needs is central to successful closing.

Good salespeople recognize a variety of verbal and nonverbal buying signals and respond appropriately with a trial close. It behooves salespeople, especially those new to the field, to become familiar with common closing mistakes in order to avoid them when dealing with their customers.

Postsale follow-up with customers provides an excellent opportunity to add considerable value to the client and the relationship. Excellent salespeople provide follow-up not just to handle customer problems and complaints but proactively to ensure customer satisfaction and loyalty.

KEY TERMS

closing the sale	minor point close	buy-now close	performance gap
buying signals	alternative choice close	rejection	customer complaints
empathy	direct close	attitude	service recovery
silence	summary-of-benefits close	tenacity	
assumptive close	balance sheet close	trial close	

ROLE PLAY

BEFORE YOU BEGIN

Before getting started, please go to the Appendix of chapter 1 to review the profiles of the characters involved in this role play, as well as the tips on preparing a role play. This particular role play requires that you be familiar with the chapter 7 and 8 role plays.

Characters Involved

Alex Lewis
Rhonda Reed

Setting the Stage

Assume all the information given in the chapters 7 and 8 role plays about Alex's sales call on Tracy Brown (Alex's longtime buyer at Max's Pharmacies). Again assume you are at the meeting between Alex and Rhonda a few days prior to Max's sales call and that the goal now is to brainstorm several potential closing approaches that Alex might use in the upcoming sales call on Tracy to present Happy Teeth. Again, Rhonda wants to role-play a buyer–seller dialogue with Alex about these potential closing approaches so he will have a chance to practice them *before* making the actual sales call on Tracy.

Alex's Role

Work with Rhonda to develop a list of specific closing methods likely to be relevant in the Happy Teeth call on Tracy. Develop a specific dialogue for the role play in which Tracy (role-played by Rhonda) responds differently to the different closing approaches—sometimes accepting, sometimes expressing concerns/objections, and sometimes neutral or nonresponsive. Develop dialogue that allows Alex to respond properly to each reaction expressed by Tracy. Refer to the sample buyer/seller dialogues in the section on closing methods for ideas on developing the list and the role-play dialogue.

Rhonda's Role

Work with Alex on the above.

Assignment

Present a 7–10 minute role play in which Alex plays himself in a mock sales call on Tracy (Rhonda gets to role-play Tracy). Focus only on the *closing* part of the sales dialogue. Use as many of the closing methods in the chapter as you find appropriate to the situation. Vary Rhonda's responses so that Alex can use different approaches to moving the sale forward after each. In some cases Rhonda should come up with concerns/objections after the trial close so that Alex can demonstrate proper negotiation techniques to overcome the concern and then try to close again. At the end of the mock sales call, Rhonda should take no more than 5 minutes to provide constructive feedback/coaching to Alex on how well he used the closing methods.

DISCUSSION QUESTIONS

1. What images of "closers" did you have before reading this chapter? List as many negative stereotypes of closing as you can. How has the chapter's point that "closing should become a natural part of the communication process" between buyers and sellers changed our opinion of closing?

2. Why is attitude so important to successful closing? What are some aspects of a positive attitude that you believe contribute to success in closing (and in selling in general)?

3. Once a salesperson sees one or more buying signals from a prospect, he or she should trial close. What happens if the prospect doesn't close at that point? Why is this outcome actually favorable for continuing the dialogue with the buyer and moving toward closing?

4. Why is it important to be able to use different closing methods in different situations?

5. A sage of selling once said, "Your job as a salesperson is to do 80 percent listening and 20 percent talking." Do you agree? Why or why not?

6. Review the list of common closing mistakes in the chapter. Give specific examples of how each might affect your success in a sales call.

7. What is it about postsale follow-up that makes it one of the most important ways to enhance long-term customer relationships? What specific things can you do in follow-up to accomplish this?

8. Consider the statement "Customer complaints are customer opportunities—but only if we know about them." Do you agree or disagree? Why?

9. How do CRM and the use of databases in selling enhance closing and follow-up?

MINI-CASE 9 ST. PAUL COPY MACHINES

Paula Phillips arrived back at her office at St. Paul Copy Machines around 4:00 on Tuesday afternoon. As she sat behind her desk looking dejected, her sales manager, Jeff Baker, showed up to ask how that afternoon's sales call had gone.

Paula had been scheduled to meet at 2:00 p.m. with a few representatives from Direct Mailers Inc. to finalize their purchase of a high-speed, multifunction copy machine. Direct Mailers uses these high-end machines to copy direct-mail pieces it sends out for a wide array of clients. The pieces are typically coupons that companies pay to have sent to local residents in an effort to entice customers to visit their businesses and begin to buy their products or services. Because Direct Mailers' clients require high-quality reproductions of their coupons, Paula has already made several sales calls on buying center members at Direct Mailers to get to know their operations and their specific requirements for a copy machine.

At today's meeting, Paula had planned to present to the Direct Mailers' representatives the copy machine that would fulfill all of their needs, resulting in an order for a new machine. However, once Jeff saw the look on her face, he knew that things had not gone as planned.

JEFF: Hi, Paula. How did it go at Direct Mailers today?

PAULA: You don't want to know. I'm not sure we'll be able to salvage this sale.

JEFF: Why don't you tell me what happened and we'll see if there's anything that can be done to give us another shot at the sale.

PAULA: Well, it started when I first walked in there. You know how things have been sort of rough with me lately. I haven't made a sale all month, so I probably didn't have the best attitude going in. Nevertheless, I made my presentation and it seemed to be going great.

JEFF: What kind of questions did they ask?

PAULA: The standard questions about warranty, when the copier could be delivered and installed, purchase price, annual operating cost, and how much more productive they can be with this new machine versus what they currently own. I handled all of these questions and they still were reluctant to make a decision today.

JEFF: What closing technique did you use?

PAULA: The one I always use—the balance sheet method. This method has worked for me in the past and I've used it on dozens of buyers. Not all of them buy from me, of course, but hey, you can't have success all of the time, can you? Plus, I get enough buyers that I make my quota most years. I mean, what else can I do?

JEFF: How many items did you end up with on both sides of the balance sheet?

PAULA: On the "reasons for buying" side I had six items and on the "remaining questions" side I had three items. I know that sounds like quite a few remaining questions, but at least the reasons for buying were greater. They were going along with the proposal pretty well at this point in the presentation. In fact, I'm pretty sure that they had decided to purchase the copier. It had gotten to the point where we were standing around chitchatting about various things.

JEFF: What kinds of things?

PAULA: You know, things like how much their business could improve with a new copier and how much more efficient they could be from an operational standpoint. You know the feeling and the look of how people relax when they have made a decision. We had reached that point and I thought it was done. I waited about 15 more minutes to pull out the contract for them to sign because they seemed to be having a good time talking about these issues among themselves.

JEFF: What do you suppose made them change their mind?

PAULA: In the conversation, someone mentioned all of the money they had just spent on supplies to operate their current machine—copy toner and stuff like that. Before I knew it, they had decided that too much money had been sunk into those supplies and they couldn't justify a new copier. Having spent money on supplies for the current machine wasn't even on the balance sheet list of "remaining questions." It just came out of the blue and then I was stuck.

JEFF: It's obvious that you're tired. Why don't you use the rest of today to finish your paperwork and make sure you have everything you need to see your clients tomorrow. We'll talk about this some more when you get into the office tomorrow afternoon.

As Paula finished her paperwork and checked her schedule for Wednesday, Jeff pondered what their conversation would include the next day.

Questions

1. What mistake(s) common closing mistakes did Paula make in her sales call with the representatives from Direct Mailers Inc.?

2. Why do you think Paula's closing method did not work? What could she have done differently to give it a better chance to work? What *other* closing methods might have worked better in her attempt to get this sale? Write a brief script for what Paula could have said using one of the closing methods you just identified.

3. What do you recommend Paula do now? Are there any key follow-up activities she should undertake to get another opportunity to make this sale with Direct Mailers?

Appendix: Checklist for Using Effective Closing Skills

For some strange reason, many salespeople who can present a flawless case for their products or services and calmly overcome the toughest of objections suddenly flounder at the point of asking for the order. Yet asking for the order is the logical conclusion of everything that has preceded it, from qualifying the prospect to giving the presentation. Since few prospects volunteer their order, salespeople seldom ring up a sale without asking for it.

This extensive set of questions will help you determine where you stand in using closing skills effectively. The idea is to get you to think about where you might need some coaching and practice in the important area of closing the sale.

1. Do you ask for the order several times during the course of your presentation?
2. Do you try for a close on the first call?
3. Do you regularly ask prospects which alternative (models, payment plans, delivery schedules, etc.) they prefer rather than whether they are interested?
4. Is your presentation enthusiastic and positive, suggesting that you fully expect to get the order?
5. If necessary, can you usually give compelling, plausible reasons for buying immediately?
6. Do you avoid giving the impression of high pressure in your requests for the order?
7. If the prospect hesitates, do you tactfully try to determine the reasons for his or her reservations, then answer them fully and persuasively?
8. Failing to get an explicit yes, do you proceed to try to get your prospect to do something (get figures, call in an assistant for backup information, show you where the display would be placed) that may be interpreted as approval of your proposition?
9. Do you unobtrusively introduce your order form early in your presentation?
10. Are you usually prepared to meet the standard objections to your product or service?
11. Have you the tools for an order at hand, ready to use (catalog, spec sheets, order form, etc.)?
12. Do you ever arrive armed with the order form already filled out (based on an intelligent estimate of the prospect's needs) and requiring only a signature?
13. If you've dealt with the customer before, are you familiar with his or her buying patterns, idiosyncrasies, pet peeves, and complaints?
14. Do you usually have a fairly accurate idea of the prospect's creditworthiness and ability to pay?
15. Before calling on the person with authority to buy, do you ever visit other departments or buying center members to determine the firm's needs and otherwise gather "selling ammunition"?
16. Can you describe three good ways any prospect is losing out by not buying your product immediately?

17. Are there any tax advantages to your proposition that might make it more appealing to your prospects?

18. How do you handle the buyer who seems impressed by your offer but hesitates, explaining, "I'll have to discuss it with my partner (boss, committee, spouse, etc.)"?

19. Are you ever guilty of behaving in a manner that tells your prospect, "I don't really expect an order now"?

20. Conversely, are you ever so obviously elated by the possibility of getting the order that the customer backs away?

21. Are your presentations benefit-oriented so the prospect is continually aware of what he or she will gain by buying?

22. Do you always maintain control of your sales calls—or does the prospect frequently control the agenda?

23. Have you ever been so afraid of being turned down that you did not ask for the order?

24. Do you keep some reserve ammunition for the end of your presentation—some benefit or advantage tucked away in your back pocket that you can use in a final attempt to get the prospect to buy?

25. Do you always know in advance your product is right for the prospect?

26. When you fail to close, do you get out of the prospect's place of business quickly but not abruptly?

27. When you do close, do you get out of the prospect's place of business quickly but not abruptly?

28. Suppose you feel your price is the one thing standing in the way of a sale. How can you make it more palatable to the prospect (delayed billing, financing help, trade-ins, leasing plans, etc.)?

29. How can you convince a prospect who says "I want to think it over" that any delay in the purchase of your product is unwise?

30. Do you demonstrate your product to prospects?

31. Do you usually manage to get the prospect to participate in the demonstration in some way, by handling something, examining, reading, operating, or testing it?

32. Do you tend to assume a prospect will never buy from you if he or she says no on your first call?

33. How often do you call on a prospect before giving up?

34. Do you keep up to date on personnel changes in the firms you already deal with on the assumption that the next buyer is, for all practical purposes, a brand-new prospect?

35. Do you keep in touch with prospects who have turned you down to find out if circumstances have changed in your favor?

36. In a typical presentation, how many times do you ask for the order?

37. A prospect turns you down, claiming satisfaction with the present supplier. How, in terms of personal service, can you break through this loyalty barrier?

38. Describe three ways you can ask for the order without literally asking for it (e.g., "Shall we bill you this month or next?").

39. How is your product unique? That is, how is it genuinely different from all the competition?

40. Can you name the person with the authority to buy in three of your largest prospects' offices?

41. When was the last time you simply gave up on a sale, convinced that pursuing it any further was a waste of time? Think. Has anything (business conditions, your product line, your price, the prospect's needs, etc.) changed since then that may provide a reason for trying again?

42. You ask for the order from an out-of-town prospect who tells you he or she prefers to buy locally. Your answer?

43. The prospect puts you off with "I have a reciprocal arrangement with your competition." What's your answer to that one?

44. When you run into an objection that you cannot answer, do you make it your business to find a convincing answer that you can use the next time you encounter it?

45. You sense the prospect isn't saying yes because of doubts about his or her own judgment. How do you go about changing his or her mind?

46. The prospect tells you that she needs a little more time to decide and suggests that you call back in a few days. When you do make that phone call, how do you ask for the order this time?

47. When was the last time you reassessed your customer's needs (by talking to him or her or an associate, taking stock of what he or she has on hand, projecting future growth, etc.)?
48. In your presentations, are you fully aware of your prospect's biggest problem and prepared to show how buying from you will solve it or alleviate it?
49. How will your product help your prospect become more competitive?
50. With three specific prospects in mind, what are the best times of the year in each case to ask for the order? Why?
51. Similarly, what are the least promising times of year to ask for the order in each case. Why?
52. If you can somehow help a prospect use or sell more of your product profitably, it follows that he or she will buy more. How can you help your two toughest prospects get more profit out of your product?
53. What information (sales, product, research, news items, etc.) is currently of help in closing sales?
54. Are you using that information with all of your prospects to the best possible advantage?
55. If your product is part of a full line, do you regularly try for tie-in sales?
56. Do you check back on former customers who, for one reason or another, have stopped buying from you?
57. What percentage of your sales calls do you turn into actual sales?
58. On which call are most of your initial sales made (first, second, third, fourth)?
59. Which of your prospects do you think are ripe for a close this week?
60. When, specifically, are you going to ask them for their orders?

Closing is a natural and expected part of a client relationship. As a challenging and rewarding part of a salesperson's professional activities, it deserves your best efforts.

Adapted from: Ted Pollock, "How Good a Closer Are You?" *American Salesman* (June 2003), pp. 18–23.

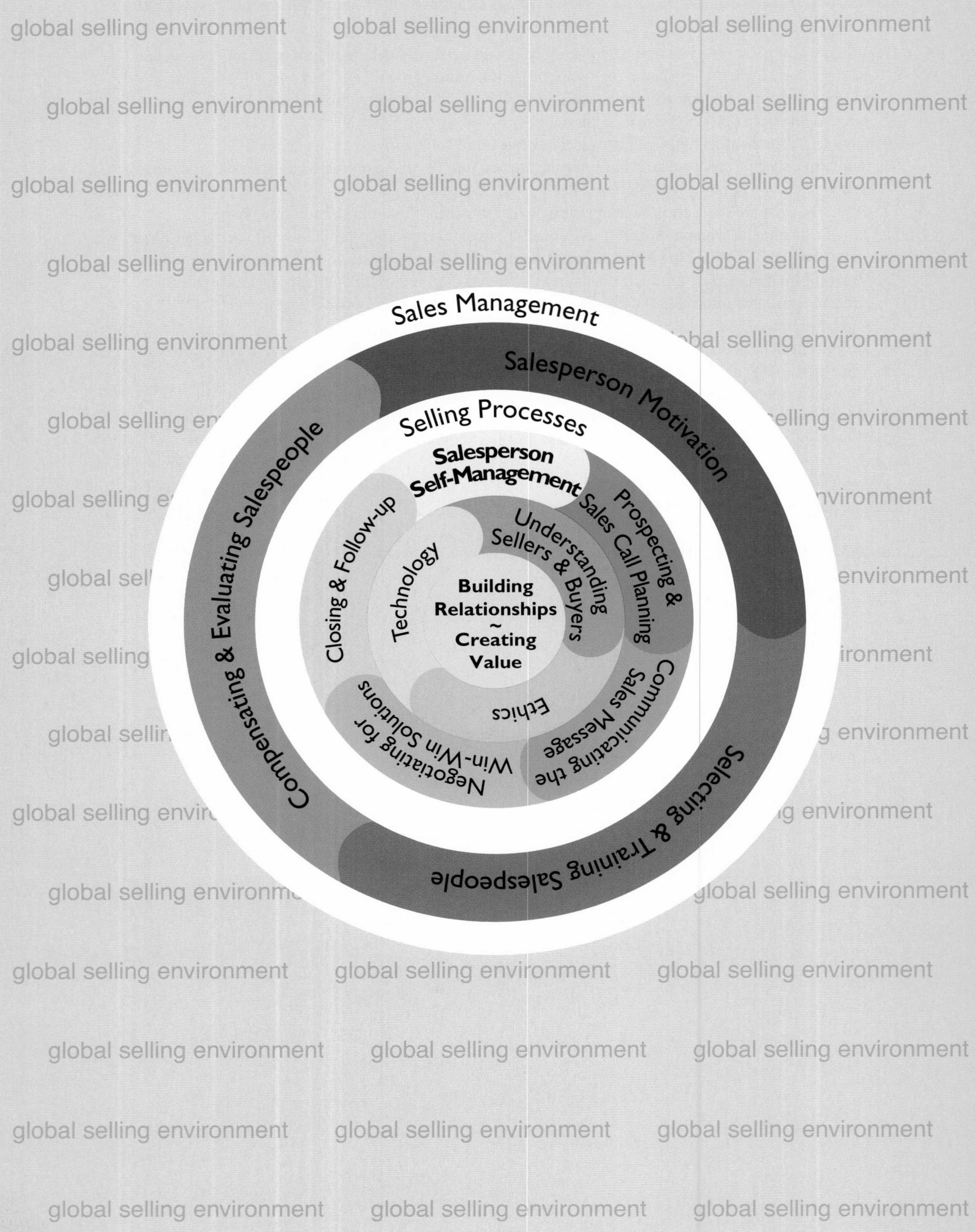
global selling environment
Sales Management
Salesperson Motivation
Selecting & Training Salespeople
Compensating & Evaluating Salespeople
Selling Processes
Salesperson Self-Management
Prospecting & Sales Call Planning
Understanding Sellers & Buyers
Communicating the Sales Message
Negotiating for Win-Win Solutions
Closing & Follow-up
Technology
Ethics
Building Relationships ~ Creating Value

Salesperson Self-Management

LEARNING OBJECTIVES

To salespeople, time is literally money, and managing their territory and time well is critical to long-term success in relationship selling.

After reading this chapter, you should be able to:

- Understand salespeople's role in time and territory management.
- Explain efficient time management tools for salespeople.
- Discuss territory management techniques.
- Describe the sales manager's role in time and territory management.
- Determine how salespeople should allocate their time.
- Design an effective sales territory.
- Measure sales territory performance.

EXPERT ADVICE

EXPERT: Tom Kadien
President of Epedx (the distribution arm of International Paper)

TOPIC: Time management and the importance of experience

SUMMARY: Mr. Kadien discusses the importance of planning the sales call and spending time with the customer. He notes how experienced salespeople tend to have the greatest efficiency and, consequently, spend the most time in front of the customer solving their problems. One of the keys is the experienced salesperson's ability to learn how to do important tasks, such as manage client orders inside the company more efficiently, which gives them more time to focus on the customer relationship. Mr. Kadien estimates the experienced salespeople spend as much as 50 percent of their time with the customer while inexperienced salespeople may only spend half that much time.

NEXT STEPS: Go to the website for *Contemporary Selling* (www.routledge.com/cw/Johnston), watch the chapter 10 video and then read the chapter. You will find an Expert Advice follow-up at the end of the chapter with questions that connect elements of the video to your learning.

THE IMPORTANCE OF SALESPERSON SELF-MANAGEMENT

In Part Two of this book, we have been discussing the relationship-selling process. Part Three will focus on the issues and activities of the sales manager. However, this chapter is about an activity in which salespeople and their managers both play critical roles: time and territory management. Salespeople are in the field and responsible for managing their time and territory effectively, but without careful management design and monitoring, they cannot tap the full potential of the territory. The Contemporary Selling model at the beginning of the chapter highlights the salesperson self-management area.

How important is time management in selling? Go to Google at www.google.com and type in "time management and sales." You will find dozens of companies offering courses and seminars in time and territory management for salespeople.[1] For further proof, visit Amazon at www.amazon.com or Barnes & Noble at www.barnesandnoble.com and type in "time management." The search engine will identify dozens of books dedicated to helping salespeople manage their time more effectively.

A simple calculation will help demonstrate the importance of time management. Suppose a salesperson works 47 weeks a year (subtracting vacation and other miscellaneous time off) for 8 hours a day. That gives a total work time of 1,880 hours in a year. However, a salesperson has many responsibilities, including traveling, completing reports, researching and dealing with customer concerns, and a host of other activities designed to build successful customer relationships. These activities total, on average, 67 percent of the salesperson's time. In our example that totals 1,260 hours for the year, which leaves only 620 hours—14 hours a week—of face-to-face selling time with customers. If a salesperson produces $500,000 in sales per year, that means for every hour in front of the customer he or she must generate $806.45. Time is precious, and the ability to manage time and territory is essential to success for both the salesperson and sales manager.

Specific reasons why salespeople and managers care about time and territory management are detailed in Exhibit 10.1.

EXHIBIT 10.1 WHY TIME AND TERRITORY MANAGEMENT IS IMPORTANT

Reasons for Salespeople	Reasons for Sales Managers
1. Increase productivity.	1. Ensure territory and customer coverage.
2. Improve customer relationships.	2. Minimize sales expenses.
3. Enhance personal confidence.	3. Assess sales performance.
	4. Align company policies with customer expectations.

Reasons for Salespeople

Salespeople's ability to manage their time and territory is essential for three reasons. Salespeople who are efficient time and effective territory managers (1) increase productivity, (2) improve customer relationships, and (3) enhance personal confidence. Let's examine each result more closely.

Increase Productivity. The more effective and efficient salespeople are in managing their territory and time, the more productive they are in the job. Management designs territories so that salespeople must exert maximum effort to reach the territory's full sales potential. If a salesperson is not efficient in managing time and effective in managing the customers in the territory, he or she will not hit the sales targets set by the company.

At the same time, salespeople have many duties to accomplish in relatively little face-to-face time with customers. Time management makes sure that every minute with customers is productive. This is especially true in territories that require a lot of travel, where salespeople must manage time and territory so they can focus on relationship building.

Improve Customer Relationships. One of the most constructive tools salespeople use to build customer relationships is effectively managing customer time. Wasting the customer's time never leads to a better relationship. When the salesperson is on time, deals with customer concerns, and makes maximum use of the customer's time, the customer relationship often improves. Remember, customers don't see the entire organization. They see the salesperson. When the salesperson is efficient and effective, it raises the customers' opinion of the entire organization. Building successful customer relationships means the salesperson knows when to see customers and what to say (and not say) while with them. Time and territory management are critical to that process.

Enhance Personal Confidence. What makes people confident? The answer is certainly complex and varies by individual. However, research suggests that capable time and territory management skills go a long way toward improving salespeople's confidence that they can get the job done. Having the time to prepare properly for each customer enhances the salesperson's comfort level and confidence and reduces stress.

Reasons for Sales Managers

Good sales managers know that skillful time and territory management is essential to (1) ensure territory and customer coverage, (2) minimize sales expenses, (3) assess sales performance, and (4) align company policies with customer expectations. Creating relationships that both satisfy customers and motivate salespeople depends in large part on helping salespeople manage their time and territory.

Ensure Territory and Customer Coverage. The single most effective way to make sure the company has the right relationships with its customers is to create territories that define where and how customers will interact with the company. Clearly, not all customers will be treated the same; however, defining the customer relationship and creating territories (which we will discuss later in this chapter) is vital to ensure that all customers have a salesperson (or sales team) to build the relationship.

In today's selling environment, territory and customer coverage is much more difficult and demanding. Unique customer relationships may require salespeople to move between established territories. Some argue that this makes territories less important, but in fact the opposite is true. Not all customers warrant special treatment. Territory management ensures the company aligns the sales force appropriately with various customers.

Minimize Sales Expenses. Running a sales force is expensive, and a territory structure helps manage sales expenses. Creating territories eliminates duplication and maximizes salespeople's face-to-face customer time while minimizing nonselling time. Few management activities have greater potential to reduce sales expenses than designing, creating, and monitoring the performance of sales territories.

Assess Sales Performance. How well is a product selling in Kansas? Why hasn't our best customer, Gracie Incorporated, been buying as much from us in the last six months? Why are sales so high in our upstate New York territory? Sales managers ask questions like these every day, and territory management is critical to getting answers. By investing in a territory management system, managers can evaluate individual territories, districts, regions, or even countries to identify problems before they get too big and positive trends in time to capitalize on them.

ETHICAL DILEMMA

YOUTH OR EXPERIENCE

Frank Lay, vice president of sales for Red Dot Graphics, faces a difficult decision. The company specializes in high-quality, difficult graphic printing and has a number of national clients.

Business is very good in the Nashville district and Red Dot management decided a new territory was needed to maximize the area's sales potential. After meeting with the local district sales manager, Larry Van Dyke, Frank selected the area that would be carved out for a new territory. It would include several high-volume existing clients and a number of large prospective customers (in other words, it would be a territory with high potential). Frank knew the area well since he had been the district sales manager in Nashville just prior to being promoted to vice president of sales. Company policy dictates that local district managers select which salespeople fill a particular territory.

Frank thinks Jim Henderson should be assigned that territory. Jim has been with the company for many years. While his performance has diminished in recent years, Frank feels this opportunity will reenergize Henderson. After all, it's not Henderson's fault that several large clients in his territory moved to different locations. Finally, Frank and Jim have been friends for many years. They both started at Red Dot about the same time. Last night Jim called to tell Frank he really wanted the opportunity to show what he could do in this new territory.

Van Dyke, on the other hand, believes Sylvia Beckett is the best candidate. She has been with the company only one year but has demonstrated an ability to increase business with her clients and exceeded her sales goals. Despite her short tenure, her performance justifies a promotion to a new, more challenging territory. Van Dyke thinks this opportunity would give her the chance to be a real star with the company.

As Frank sits at his desk, he is trying to decide whether to violate company policy and overrule Larry Van Dyke's decision to put Beckett in the new territory. Frank believes that Henderson deserves this chance to prove he can still perform at a high level, but he knows this move could have a negative effect on both Van Dyke and Sylvia Beckett.

Questions to Consider

1. What would you do with a salesperson who had been a high performer in the past but was currently not performing well?
2. Should Frank Lay give the new territory to Jim Henderson?
3. If you were Larry Van Dyke, what would be your reaction to Frank Lay's decision to put Jim Henderson in the new territory?

Align Company Policies with Customer Expectations. As we discussed in chapter 5, the ability to collect data by product, customer, and territory, analyze it, and make decisions based on it helps managers make better decisions about recruiting, training, compensation, and a host of other key management activities. In addition, specific customer feedback provides a consistent, organized mechanism for managers to hear the customers' needs and align company strategy with those needs. For example, salespeople can be hired with explicit qualifications (experience, background) to fit into specific territories or certain salespeople can receive training based on territory analysis and need identification.

SALESPEOPLE'S ROLE IN SALESPERSON SELF-MANAGEMENT

We began the chapter talking about the roles played by the salesperson and sales manager in time and territory management. Managers analyze customers and design territories to put together the most efficient and effective territory structure (as we shall see in the next section). However, once management identifies the basic territory requirements (customers, call frequency, call duration, nonselling time), salespeople have the flexibility—indeed, the responsibility—to manage their time and territory effectively. Two key questions drive salespeople in time and territory management:

- What is the most efficient use of my time?
- What is the most effective way to manage my territory?

Note that, although we are focusing on salespeople assigned to territories, all salespeople need to be good time and territory managers. In some industries, such as insurance, companies do not assign specific territories; they allow salespeople to prospect for customers in a large geographic area. For example, if you go to the State Farm Insurance website (www.statefarm.com), click on "Insurance," then click on "Find an Agent," you will see methods for identifying the nearest agent. Type in your zip code and you will see a number of agents who are close to you. Even salespeople in these situations need to be good time managers.

Efficient Time Management

Time—everyone seems to need more of it, but unfortunately there is only so much to go around. Given the demands on their time, salespeople must become efficient time managers if they wish to be successful. For years people have examined the backgrounds and characteristics of successful salespeople, and good time management is one strength they list consistently. To manage their time efficiently, salespeople must (1) identify their personal and professional priorities, and (2) develop a time management plan.

Identify Personal and Professional Priorities. What's important to you? That is a critical question in salesperson self-management. People spend time doing what they want to do or they spend time on things they don't want to do, which eventually makes them less productive, frustrated, and even unhappy. Does this mean that you will enjoy every minute of being a salesperson (or whatever career you choose)? Of course not. However, it does mean that successful salespeople are successful in part because selling is consistent with their life and career goals. The process becomes even more complex when you consider aligning personal, professional and team priorities.[2] Exhibit 10.2 shows the relationship between your personal and professional (sales) priorities.

Choosing priorities falls into two broad categories: personal and professional. Salespeople must identify their goals for each of these priorities. First, they must make choices about their personal priorities in life and career. Life priorities deal with basic choices in life. For example, is your family important to you? Most people would say yes, but just how important has a big effect on the choices you make in a career. Salespeople travel a lot, and those with children may not want to be away from their family. Complicating the decision is that people often begin with one set of priorities but, as life changes (they get married or have a baby or get divorced), their priorities change. Life priorities need to be reevaluated every so often to make sure that career and professional priorities are consistent (refer to Exhibit 10.3 for a discussion on the importance of priorities).

Career priorities deal with what kind of sales career you want to have over time. Historically, there are two basic choices: (1) a sales career, leading to a position as a senior account or key account executive or (2) sales management. But there are other concerns too. For example, do you want to work for the same company (which usually means moving to new locations over time)? Or is your home more important (which means you may change companies over time)?

EXHIBIT 10.2 PRIORITY CHECKLIST

Personal	Life	Family	How important is my family?
		Life goals	Do I live to work or work to live?
		Personal wealth	How important is personal wealth?
	Career	Goals	What are my career goals?
		Ambition	Would I do anything to succeed?
		Trade-offs	What trade-offs am I prepared to make to be successful? (Example: Would I take a job if it meant moving my children to a new location?)
Professional	Account	Sales volume	Is the customer buying more now than last year?
		Satisfaction	Is the customer satisfied with my company/me?
		Sales potential	What is the potential for new business with this customer?
	Activity	New sales calls	How many new sales calls have I made this year?
		New customers	Am I finding new customers or relying on existing customers?
		Sales/expense ratio	What is my ratio of sales to expenses compared to last year?

EXHIBIT 10.3 TAKE CONTROL OF YOUR LIFE

One result of today's "connected world" is that time has become a very valuable commodity. This is particularly true for salespeople who must manage a variety of relationships including customers, company, and family. People often focus on being more efficient, getting more "stuff" done. As a result, time management is more about efficiency—doing more things faster—than effectiveness—doing the right things better. However, efficiency is not always the answer and misses the point. Consider that doing the incorrect things more efficiently does not make that person a good time manager. It is possible the individual feels good because more activities are getting done but, at the end of day, he or she may not have accomplished the things needed to make their life better.

Put simply, salespeople, indeed all of us, would benefit from better priortization. Identify what is really important and focus on those activities. So many people jump from one crisis to another with a focus on efficiency (how many fires can be put out) versus effectiveness (am I putting out the most important fires). To this, time management experts speak about (1) setting goals, (2) developing focus, (3) talking to the right people at the right time, (4) managing expectations (yours and those around you), (5) controlling technology (before it controls you), (6) organizing your life, and (6) putting both your mind and emotions to work.

Adapted from Michael Guld, "Effectively Manage Your Multi-Tasking Day," *American Salesman* 53 (Issue 7, July 2008), pp. 25–29.

Professional priorities concern the sales task at hand and fall into two areas. Account priorities relate to goals and objectives for individual customers, such as increased sales or greater customer satisfaction year over year. Often these are the primary measures of individual sales performance (which we talk about in chapter 13). Activity priorities include goals such as number of new accounts, number of sales calls per week or month, and sales-to-expense ratio. These objectives are often identified by management or by management working with the salesperson to set specific performance goals for a given period of time.

Develop a Time Management Plan. Once you have identified personal and professional priorities, the next step is to develop a time management plan. The basic steps in a time management plan are not difficult to understand. The problem for most people is implementing the steps and sticking with the plan over time. The real benefits of a time management plan come when you incorporate behavioral changes into your everyday thinking.[3] A good time management plan has three basic elements:

1. Daily event schedule. What are you going to do today?
2. Weekly/monthly planning calendar. What are you going to do this week? This month?
3. Organization of critical information. How do you control the information you need to be a good time manager?

DAILY EVENT SCHEDULE. Creating a daily to-do list is a time management tool almost everyone has tried at least once. The process involves sitting down in the morning or the previous evening, thinking about the specific tasks you want to accomplish, and prioritizing them. There are variations on this process, but all time management counselors, such as Franklin Covey, advise taking control of events and prioritizing what you need to accomplish every day. It is important to write them down either on a piece of paper or in a cell phone because writing down the tasks affirms their importance. A schedule you keep in your head is too easily changed because often things that come up during the day seem to be more important at the time.

WEEKLY/MONTHLY PLANNING CALENDAR. Daily event schedules are important, but everyone (especially salespeople) must plan for longer periods of time. The list of demands on their time is endless and changes every day. Salespeople have to plan everything from customer meetings to sales training seminars. An event one year out has a different level of commitment from an event scheduled for tomorrow, and certainly salespeople need to be flexible enough to change their schedule as needed. However, a calendar of events and tasks is essential for medium- and long-term planning.

ORGANIZATION OF CRITICAL INFORMATION. Salespeople are required to keep a lot of information close at hand and accessible. In addition to their own schedules, they need customer contact information, key facts about their company's products/services, customer order and transaction data, and current memos, emails, or other correspondence. The ability to organize and create a system for easy access is important to time management.

Even just 10 years ago the primary system for tracking, storing, and accessing information was a filing system with drawers full of folders. Now, of course, the primary way to access information is through computers. For salespeople, that usually means laptops. Cell phones have become so powerful and interface with laptops so easily they have become an extension of the computer. One caveat, however: The laptop or cell phone is only as good as the information in it. Salespeople must regularly update their systems to keep the information as current as possible.[4]

Effective Territory Management

Although management is responsible for designing effective territories, it is most often the salesperson's task to map out a specific routing pattern and call schedule. For example, management may tell a salesperson that a certain group of customers need to be called on once a week, another group twice a month, and a third group once a month. It is the salesperson's job to define a plan that will accomplish those customer call frequencies. In addition, salespeople are constantly communicating to management changes in the customer relationship that can affect the company's perception of the customer and ultimately the call frequency.

Effective territory management involves two steps: (1) develop a territory management plan and (2) provide territory feedback to management.

Develop a Territory Management Plan. The most basic component of a territory management plan is the routing schedule, the plan for reaching all customers in a given time period and territory. It is developed with management input, but ultimately it is the salesperson's responsibility to maintain and adjust the schedule. There are three basic goals in developing an effective routing schedule:

1. Maximize face-to-face selling time with customers.
2. Minimize nonselling time.
3. Provide adequate territory coverage across all customers.

Historically, managers would sit down with salespeople and a map to determine the most effective routes. Now sophisticated programs do the work. Companies like TerrAlign provide comprehensive software packages that design territories and map out individual sales call patterns. (Check out its ads in Exhibit 10.4.) Many of these packages interface with CRM programs and individual personal management packages like Microsoft Outlook.[5]

The second component of a territory management plan is communication. Salespeople know that successful territory management involves using technology to maximize their effectiveness. Customers want answers to questions now and often will not wait until the next scheduled visit, so salespeople use email and wireless technologies to deal with customer and company issues quickly. But immediate communication does not preclude face-to-face customer time. Customer questions can be answered in an email or phone call, but sales presentations and relationship building require one-on-one time with the customer.

Provide Territory Feedback to Management. Managing a sales territory is not a static procedure. Managers develop territories based on the best available information at the time, but conditions change literally overnight. Customers, competitors, and the general environment are changing all the time. Salespeople bring in new customers, existing customers move to different suppliers, and many other events can change the dynamics of a territory.

It is imperative that salespeople provide feedback to management on what is happening in the sales territory. Management does receive a great deal of information in the sales analysis (coming up in the next section), but salespeople are working in the territory and often develop an understanding that extends beyond the numbers. Analyses of customer, product, or territory sales cannot convey nuances in the customer relationship. For example, management changes at a customer can signal potential changes in purchasing patterns. This information would be known to the salesperson but not necessarily show up in current sales numbers.

This kind of feedback is important for two reasons. First, management needs to know this information so it can be aware of any potential problems or opportunities before it is too late. Second, salespeople can benefit from a shared information community. Once a feedback system is created, salespeople in one territory can hear about insights (or problems) from other salespeople around the country. Such information sharing can be extremely helpful for salespeople in the field.

SALES MANAGERS' ROLE IN TIME AND TERRITORY MANAGEMENT

While salespeople bear ultimate responsibility for how they use their time, sales managers play a critical role in designing and creating territories that enable salespeople to be effective and efficient. Essentially

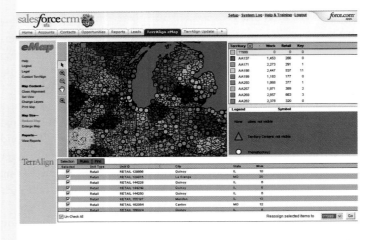
Source: The TerrAlign Group, Inc. 800-437-9601. Used by permission.

there are two activities sales managers must do well to maximize the efficiency of salespeople's time and the potential of sales territories:

- Design the most effective sales territories.
- Measure the sales performance of the company's products, customers, and territories.

Design the Most Effective Sales Territories

Sales managers strive to make all sales territories roughly equal with respect to the amount of sales potential they contain and the amount of work it takes a salesperson to cover them effectively. When the sales potential is basically the same across all territories, it is easier to evaluate each salesperson's performance and to compare salespeople.

Equal workloads also tend to improve sales force morale and diminish disputes between management and the sales force. Sales managers should also consider the impact of particular territory structures and call frequencies. It is difficult (if not impossible) to achieve a perfect balance with respect to all these factors.

Sales managers should do their best to ensure fairness and equity in territory design. Salespeople do not perform well when their managers fail to consider the long-term effects of poor territory design. While managers should design territories based on rules and company priorities, and not for specific salespeople, they should consider personal issues. As we discussed, people's priorities change over time, affecting their relationship with customers and their territory. The five steps in territory design are illustrated in Exhibit 10.5.

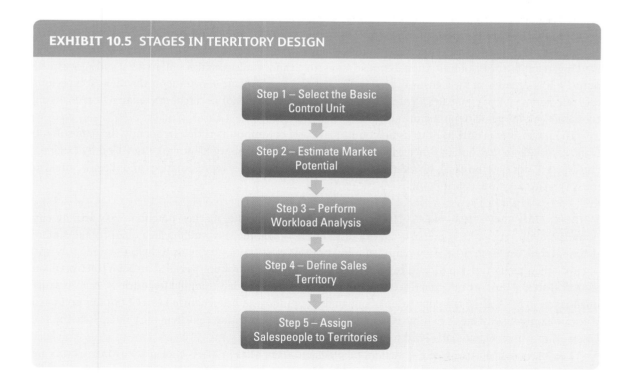

EXHIBIT 10.5 STAGES IN TERRITORY DESIGN

Step 1 – Select the Basic Control Unit

Step 2 – Estimate Market Potential

Step 3 – Perform Workload Analysis

Step 4 – Define Sales Territory

Step 5 – Assign Salespeople to Territories

Step 1: Select the Basic Control Unit. The first step is for the manager to identify what is called the basic control unit. This is the fundamental geographic area used to form sales territories (county or city, for example). As a general rule, small geographic control units are preferable to large ones because low-potential accounts may be hidden by their inclusion in areas with high potential. This makes it difficult to pinpoint the true market potential, which is a primary reason for forming geographically defined sales territories in the first place. Also, small control units make it easier to adjust sales territories when conditions warrant. It is much easier to reassign the accounts in a particular county from one salesperson to another, for example, than it is to reassign all the accounts in a state.

The size of the basic control unit depends on many factors. Small, growing companies with a national distribution can manage the entire country with a relatively small number of salespeople. Business-to-business companies generally have fewer customers who are often concentrated in a limited number of areas (the automobile industry around Detroit, technology companies in Silicon Valley and the northeastern United States), which makes delineating basic control units easier. Business-to-consumer companies face a more difficult challenge, as they need a large sales force to cover a very large market area like the United States.

Getting the size and configuration of the territory correct is difficult and requires constant monitoring. Too small and the company will not maximize the full potential of the sales force (and increase sales expenses). Too large (the more common dilemma) and the organization can create problems in customer coverage and salesperson performance. As salespeople are asked to spread themselves over more customers (or geography) they may not be able to satisfy the requirements of each customer. In addition, they may not be able to discern important from less critical customers because of territory call demands. Performance can suffer and customers become dissatisfied.

While there are a number of basic control units, such as states and trading areas, we will focus on those most commonly used, which include counties, cities or metropolitan statistical areas (MSAs), and zip code areas.

COUNTIES. Counties are probably the most widely used basic geographic control unit. They permit a more fine-tuned analysis of the market than do states, given that there are over 3,000 counties and only 50 states in the United States. One dramatic advantage of using counties as control units is the wealth of statistical data available by county. The *County and City Data Book,* published biennially by the Bureau of the Census, is a great source of information on such things as population, education, employment, income, housing, banking, manufacturing output, capital expenditures, retail and wholesale sales, and mineral and agricultural output.[6] It is available at the Census Bureau website. Another advantage of counties is that their size permits easy reassignment from one sales territory to another. Thus, sales territories can be altered to reflect changing economic conditions without major upheaval in basic service.

The most serious drawback to using counties as basic control units is that frequently they are still too large, especially in metropolitan areas. Los Angeles County, Cook County (Chicago), Dade County (Miami), and Harris County (Houston), for example, may require several sales representatives and must be divided into even smaller basic control units.

METROPOLITAN STATISTICAL AREAS. Historically, when most of the market potential was within city boundaries, the city was a good basic control unit. But now that the surrounding area often contains more potential than the central city, companies employ broader classification systems to help them identify and organize their territories. Developed by the Census Bureau, the control unit is called an MSA (metropolitan statistical area). MSAs are integrated economic and social units with a large population nucleus. Any area that qualifies as an MSA and has a population of one million or more can be recognized as a CMSA (consolidated metropolitan statistical area). Exhibit 10.6 ranks the 10 largest population centers in the United States by size based on the most recent data (2010 Census).

The heavy concentration of population, income, and retail sales in MSAs explains why many firms are content to concentrate their field selling efforts in those areas. Such a strategy minimizes travel time and expense.

ZIP CODE AND OTHER AREAS. In really large metropolitan areas when the city or MSA boundaries are too large, companies use zip code areas as basic control units. The U.S. Postal Service has defined more than 36,000 five-digit zip code areas. An advantage of zip code areas is that they are likely to be relatively similar in age,

EXHIBIT 10.6 THE 10 LARGEST CMSAS IN DECREASING ORDER OF SIZE

Rank	Area	2010 Population (in thousands)
1	New York–northern New Jersey–Long Island, NY–NJ–PA	18,897,109
2	Los Angeles–Long Beach–Santa Ana, CA	12,828,837
3	Chicago–Naperville–Joliet, IL–IN–WI	9,461,105
4	Dallas–Fort Worth–Arlington, TX	6,371,773
5	Houston—Sugar Land—Baytown TX	6,086,538
6	Philadelphia–Camden–Wilmington, PA–NJ–DE–MD	5,965,343
7	Washington–Arlington–Alexandria, DC–VA–MD–WV	5,582,170
8	Miami–Fort Lauderdale–Pompano Beach, FL	5,564,635
9	Atlanta–Sandy Springs–Marietta, GA	5,268,860
10	Boston–Cambridge–Quincy, MA–NH	4,552,402

Adapted from "Estimated Ten Largest CMSA/MSAs in Decreasing Order of Size," U.S. Bureau of the Census website www.census.gov.

income, education, and other socioeconomic data and to even display similar consumption patterns (unlike residents within an MSA).

Although the Census Bureau does not publish a lot of data by zip code area, an industry has developed to tabulate such data by arbitrary geographic boundaries. The *geodemographers,* as they are typically called, combine census data with their own survey data or data they gather from such administrative records as motor vehicle registrations or credit transactions to produce customized products for their clients.

Typically geodemographers analyze census data to identify homogeneous groups that describe the American population. Claritas, a subsidiary of the Nielsen company and one of the leaders in the industry, uses over 500 demographic variables in its PRIZM system when classifying residential neighborhoods.[7] This system breaks the population of the United States into 15 groups and over 60 specific market segments based on consumer behavior and lifestyle. Each type has a name that endeavors to describe the people living there: Urban Gold Coast, Shotguns and Pickups, Pools and Patios, and so on.

Claritas and its competitors will do a customized analysis for whatever geographic boundaries a client specifies. Or a client can send a list of the zip code addresses from its customer database, and the geodemographer will attach the cluster codes. For more information about PRIZM, visit the Claritas website at www.claritas.com. These analyses are expensive, but they give companies, especially B2C organizations, tremendous insight into specific market segments.

Step 2: Estimate Market Potential. Step 2 in territory design involves estimating market potential by considering the likely demand from each customer and prospect in a basic control unit. This works much better for B2B products than for B2C goods because B2B customers are typically fewer in number and more easily identified. Furthermore, each typically buys much more product than a B2C buyer. This makes it worthwhile to identify at least the larger prospects by name, estimate the likely demand from each, and add up these estimates to produce an estimate for the territory as a whole.

In B2C markets, historical data and market research results are combined with feedback from salespeople to estimate market potential in a given territory. Companies seek precise figures, but market potential is just an estimate and subject to change for a variety of reasons.

Step 3: Perform Workload Analysis. The next step is to determine how much work is required to cover each territory. Ideally, managers like to form sales territories that are equal in both potential and workload.

Although step 2 should produce territories roughly equal in potential, they will probably require a decidedly unequal amount of work to cover adequately. In this step, managers estimate the amount of work involved in covering each territory and try to match the sales potential with the workload of each salesperson.

ACCOUNT ANALYSIS. Typically, the workload analysis considers each customer in the territory, emphasizing the larger ones. The analysis is often conducted in two stages. First, the manager does an account analysis to estimate the sales potential (the share of total market potential a company expects to achieve) for each customer and prospect in the territory. Then the sales potential estimate is used to decide how often each account should be called on and for how long. The manager determines total effort required to cover the territory by considering the:

- Number of accounts.
- Number of calls to be made on each account.
- Duration of each call.
- Estimated amount of nonselling and travel time.

CRITERIA FOR CLASSIFYING ACCOUNTS. Sales potential is only one of several criteria for determining an account's attractiveness to the firm. In addition, the factors that affect the productivity of an individual sales call are likely to change from firm to firm. Factors likely to affect the productivity of the sales call include:

- Competitive pressures. How many competitors are actively targeting the account?
- Prestige. Is the account a market leader, or does it influence other companies in the industry?
- Size. How big is the account?
- Number and level of buying influences. How many individuals are responsible for buying decisions inside the account?[8]

Determining account call rates. Once the specific factors affecting the productivity of a sales call have been isolated, they can be treated in various ways. Customer accounts can be divided along two dimensions that reflect (1) the customer's sales potential and (2) the company's ability to capitalize on that potential (competitive advantage or disadvantage). Each account is then placed in the account planning guide matrix in Exhibit 10.7. The guide uses account potential and the firm's competitive account advantage (disadvantage) to classify accounts into four cells that require different call frequencies. The heaviest account call rates in the sample matrix depicted in Exhibit 10.7 would be on accounts in cells 1, 2, and possibly 3, depending on the firm's ability to overcome its competitive disadvantages. The lowest planned call rates would be on accounts in cell 4.

DETERMINING CALL FREQUENCIES ACCOUNT BY ACCOUNT. Accounts do not have to be divided into classes and call frequencies set at the same level for all accounts in the class. Instead, the firm might want to determine the workload in each tentative territory on an individual account basis. One popular approach is to estimate the likely sales to be realized from each account as a function of the number of calls on that account. There are many methods for doing this. In one common approach, someone in the sales organization (typically the salesperson serving the account but sometimes the sales manager) estimates the sales-per-sales-call function to determine the optimal number of calls to make on each account. Much of this work is now done by sophisticated programs that optimize call frequencies and even design sales territories (refer to our earlier discussion on TerrAlign). CRM systems like those from Oracle provide a wealth of opportunity for data collection toward estimating future sales based on calls on particular customers.

Determine total workload. When the account analysis is complete, a workload analysis can be performed for each territory. To determine the total amount of face-to-face contact (direct selling time), multiply the

EXHIBIT 10.7 ACCOUNT PLANNING GUIDE

	Strong	**Weak**

High
 	
Account potential
 	
Low
	Opportunity
	  Account offers good opportunity. It has high potential and sales organization has a differential advantage in serving it.
	
	Strategy
	  Commit high levels of sales resources to take advantage of the opportunity.
	
	1
		Opportunity
		  Account may represent a good opportunity. Sales organization must overcome its competitive disadvantage and strengthen its position to capitalize on the opportunity.
		
		Strategy
		  Either direct a high level of sales resources to improve position and take advantage of the opportunity or shift resources to other accounts.
		
		2

	Opportunity
	  Account offers stable opportunity since sales organization has differential advantage in serving it.
	
	Strategy
	  Allocate moderate sales resources to maintain current advantage.
	
	3
		Opportunity
		  Account offers little opportunity. Its potential is small and the sales organization is at a competitive disadvantage in serving it.
		
		Strategy
		  Devote minimal resources to the account or consider abandoning it altogether.
		
		4

Competitive strength

Source: Mark W. Johnston and Greg W. Marshall, *Sales Force Management*, 11th ed. (London: Routledge, 2013).

call frequency of each type of account by the number of such accounts. Combine the amount of direct selling time with estimates of the nonselling and travel time required to determine the total amount of work involved in covering that territory.

Step 4: Define Sales Territories. Step 4 in territory planning defines the boundaries of the sales territories. While attempting to balance potentials and workloads across territories, the analyst must keep in mind that the sales volume potential per account changes over time. It is also likely to vary with the number of calls made. Computer call allocation models such as TerrAlign consider this. However, many sales managers rely on personal intuition or historical data, which do not take workload changes into account.

Clearly there is a relationship between account attractiveness and account effort. Account attractiveness affects how hard the account should be worked. At the same time, the number and length of calls affect the sales likely to be realized from the account. Yet these relationships are not directly recognized in many managerial decisions used to determine territory workloads. The firm needs a mechanism for balancing potentials and workloads when adjusting the initial territories if it is not using a computer model. Critical customer relationships will certainly affect account attractiveness and may necessitate adjustments to the overall territory configuration.

Step 5: Assign Salespeople to Territories. After territory boundaries are established, the analyst determines which salesperson to assign to which territory. In the past, these assignments ignored differences in abilities among salespeople and in the effectiveness of different salespeople with different customers. At this stage in territory planning, the analyst should consider such differences and attempt to assign each salesperson to the territory where he or she can contribute the most to the company's success.

Unfortunately, the ideal match cannot always be accomplished. Changing territory assignments can upset salespeople. It would be too disruptive to an established sales force with established sales territories to change practically all account coverage. If the firm is operating without assigned sales territories, then the realignment might be closer to the ideal. However, a firm with established territories typically must be content to change assignments incrementally and on a more limited basis.

The assignment of salespeople to sales territories also incorporates personal considerations. The firm may not want to change call assignments for particular accounts because of the potential for lost business. It may not want to reduce sales force size even if the analysis suggests it should because of morale problems associated with downsizing. Even increasing sales force size can be disruptive. More salespeople means more sales territories, which means redrawing existing boundaries, changing quotas, and disrupting potential for incentive pay. In sum, sales managers want to consider the people involved when they redraw territory boundaries and minimize disruptions to existing personal relationships between salespeople and customers.

Measure Sales Territory Performance

Once the territories have been developed and the salespeople assigned to them, it is important for the manager to monitor how well sales are doing. This is different from evaluating a salesperson's individual performance (which we will examine in chapter 13). Here we are looking at how well the product, customer, or territory itself is doing relative to its potential. The process may be a relatively simple one of comparing company sales in two time periods or it may involve detailed comparisons of all sales (or sales-related) data among themselves, with external data, and with like figures for earlier time periods.

The major advantage of even the most elementary sales analysis is the ability to identify those products, customers, or territories in which the firm's sales are concentrated. A heavy concentration is very common. Often 80 percent of the customers or products account for only 20 percent of total sales. Conversely, and more significantly, the remaining 20 percent of the customers or products account for 80 percent of the total sales volume. This is often called the 80:20 rule, or the concentration ratio.[9]

The same phenomenon applies to territories. A few of the company's territories often account for most of its sales. The 80:20 rule describes the general situation (although, of course, the exact concentration ratio varies).

Managers who wish to undertake a sales analysis must decide the (1) sources of information and (2) types of information they wish to focus on in the analysis. Exhibit 10.8 provides an overview of the nature of these decisions.

Sources of Information for Sales Analysis. A key decision for sales managers is what sources of information to use in the analysis. The firm first must determine the types of comparisons that it wants to make to determine how well customers, products, and territories are doing. A comparison with sales in other territories will require less analysis than a comparison against market potential or quota or against the average sales in the territory for the last five years.

EXHIBIT 10.8 KEY DECISIONS IN SALES ANALYSIS

Sources of Information	Types of Aggregation
Sales invoice	Geographic region
Salesperson call reports	Salesperson territory
Salesperson expense reports	Customer
Warranty cards	Customer size
Store scanner data	Customer location
CRM system	Product size and category
ERP system	Size of order
Customer industry classification	

The firm also needs to decide the extent to which preparing the sales report should be integrated with preparing other types of reports. These may include inventory or production reports or sales reports for other company units such as other divisions.

The document with the most information is usually the sales invoice. From this, the following information can usually be extracted:

- Customer name and location.
- Product(s) or service(s) sold.
- Volume and dollar amount of the transaction.
- Salesperson (or agent) responsible for the sale.
- End use of product sold.
- Location of customer facility where product is to be shipped and/or used.
- Customer's industry, class of trade, and/or distribution channel.
- Terms of sale and applicable discount.
- Freight paid and/or to be collected.
- Shipment point for the order.
- Transportation used in shipment.[10]

Other documents provide more specialized output. Some of the more important of these are listed in Exhibit 10.9. As you have learned, CRM systems facilitate the capturing of customer information, which can be analyzed and applied to particular sales analysis questions.

Software that links processes such as bid estimation, order entry, shipping, billing systems, and other work processes is called an enterprise resources planning (ERP) system. Boeing uses an ERP system to price out airplanes.[11] Each airline and private customer fits out each jet differently, so the salesperson's proposal has to account for each different item in order to derive a price. Also, commission has to be paid on the sale, parts have to be ordered for manufacturing, delivery has to be scheduled. The ERP helps manage all of these functions. As with CRM, the information generated through enterprise software is an invaluable resource in sales analysis. Firms like Oracle and IBM market ERP systems that are integrated throughout the companies and cost millions of dollars to install and maintain.

Types of Information Aggregation for Sales Analysis. The second major decision managers must make when designing a sales analysis is what they want to study (products, customers, territories). The most common and instructive procedure is to assemble and tabulate sales by some appropriate groupings, such as these:

EXHIBIT 10.9 SOURCES OF INFORMATION FOR SALES ANALYSIS

Cash register receipts
Type (cash or credit) and dollar amount of transaction by department
   by salesperson

Salespeople's call reports
Customers and prospects called on (company and individual seen;
   planned or unplanned calls)
Products discussed
Orders obtained
Customers' product needs and usage
Other significant information about customers
Distribution of salespeople's time among customer calls, travel, and
   office work
Sales-related activities: meetings, conventions, etc.

Salespeople's expense accounts
Expenses by day by item (hotel, meals, travel, etc.)

Individual customer (and prospect) records
Name and location and customer number
Number of calls by company salesperson (agent)
Sales by company (in dollars and/or units by product or service by
   location of customer facility)
Customer's industry, class of trade, and/or trade channel
Estimated total annual usage of each product or service sold by
   the company
Estimated annual purchases from the company of each such product
   or service
Location (in terms of company sales territory)

Financial records
Sales revenue (by products, geographic markets, customers, class
   of trade, unit of sales organization, etc.)
Direct sales expenses (similarly classified)
Overhead sales costs (similarly classified)
Profits (similarly classified)

Credit memos
Returns and allowances

Warranty cards
Indirect measures of dealer sales
Customer service

Source: Mark W. Johnston and Greg W. Marshall, *Sales Force Management*, 11th ed. (London: Routledge, 2013).

- Salesperson territories divided by state, county, MSA, or zip code.
- Customer or customer size.
- Product or package size.
- Size of order.

The kind of information a company uses depends on things like its size, diversity of product line, geographic extent of sales area, number of markets, and customers it serves. Different people in the organization may want different analyses. Product managers will focus on territory-by-territory sales of their products. On the other hand, sales managers will likely be much more interested in territory by salesperson or customer analyses and only secondarily interested in the territory sales broken out by product. Global Connection summarizes sales analysis reports for a major B2C food products company.

GLOBAL CONNECTION

SALES REPORTS IN A CONSUMER FOOD PRODUCTS COMPANY

Report Name	Purpose	Report Access[*]
Region	To provide sales information in units and dollars for each sales office or center in the region as well as a regional total	Appropriate regional manager
Sales office or center	To provide sales information in units and dollars for each district manager assigned to a sales office	Appropriate sales office or center manager
District	To provide sales information in units and dollars for each account supervisor and retail salesperson reporting to the district manager	Appropriate district manager
Salesperson summary	To provide sales information in units and dollars for each customer on whom the salesperson calls	Appropriate salesperson
Salesperson customer/product	To provide sales information in units and dollars for each customer on whom the salesperson calls	Appropriate salesperson
Salesperson/product	To provide sales information in units and dollars for each product that the salesperson sells	Appropriate salesperson
Region/product	To provide sales information in units and dollars for each product sold within the region. Similar reports would be available by sales office and by district	Appropriate regional manager
Region/customer class	To provide sales information in units and dollars for each class of customer located in the region. Similar reports would be available by sales office and by district	Appropriate regional manager

[*]Salespeople were assigned accounts in sales districts. Salespeople were assigned one or, at most, a couple of large accounts and were responsible for all the grocery stores, regardless of geography, affiliated with these large accounts, or they were assigned a geographic territory and were responsible for all the stores within that territory. All sales districts were assigned to sales offices or sales centers. The centers were, in turn, organized into regions.

Source: Mark W. Johnston and Greg W. Marshall, *Sales Force Management*, 11th ed. (London: Routledge, 2013).

EXPERT ADVICE: FOLLOW-UP    Chally Group
WORLDWIDE

After watching the video of Mr. Kadien and reading the chapter, consider the following questions:

1. What do you think contributes to the "experience curve" that longtime salespeople use to be more efficient in managing all the tasks associated with building a customer relationship? Are there things companies could do to shorten that curve for less experienced salespeople?
2. How much time should salespeople spend in front of the customer?

SUMMARY

One of the most important activities for both salespeople and sales managers is the efficient and effective management of time and territory. Salespeople who are good time and territory managers can increase productivity, improve customer relationships, and enhance their confidence. Sales managers also benefit by ensuring territory and customer coverage, minimizing sales expenses, assessing the sales performance of customers and products, and aligning company policies with customer expectations.

Salespeople have two fundamental questions to answer in time and territory management. What is the most efficient use of my time? What is the most effective way to manage my territory? Salespeople should identify their personal and professional priorities and develop a time management plan. They should also develop a territory management plan and provide territory feedback to management.

Sales managers have two fundamental tasks to complete in time and territory management. First, they must design the most effective sales territories. The overall success of a salesperson in any territory is based in part on how well management designs the territory. The second major task is measuring the sales performance of the company's products, customers, and territories. Territories are the fundamental unit of measure for evaluating various critical aspects of the company's business, such as the success of various products, how well customers are doing compared to other customers, or historical purchasing patterns.

KEY TERMS

personal priorities	daily event schedule	routing schedule	account analysis
life priorities	weekly/monthly planning calendar	sales territory	sales potential
career priorities		basic control unit	account call rates
professional priorities	organization of critical information	metropolitan statistical area (MSA)	account attractiveness
account priorities			80:20 rule
activity priorities	call frequency	market potential	enterprise resources planning (ERP)
time management plan	territory management plan	workload analysis	

ROLE PLAY

BEFORE YOU BEGIN

Before getting started, please go to the Appendix of chapter 1 to review the profiles of the characters involved in this role play, as well as the tips on preparing a role play.

Characters Involved

Rhonda Reed
Any one of the five account managers you would like to include in the role play.

Setting the Stage

Upland has asked all district managers to assist each of their account managers in developing a personal plan for continuous improvement in time and territory management. Rhonda has decided that the best way to approach this task is to ask each of her people to develop a page of bullet points for discussion and then meet individually to debrief the plan and provide input and ideas. To prepare these notes, each salesperson will follow the guidelines from the chapter sections on efficient time management and effective territory management.

Rhonda Reed's Role

Rhonda will meet with whichever account manager the other role-play partner chooses to be. Rhonda will listen as the account manager goes over the key bullet points for improving his or her time and territory management. Ultimately, Rhonda will provide advice and suggestions on the plan and (with the account manager) come to an agreement on what steps to implement.

Account Manager's Role

Choose one of the five account managers to prepare the plan and meet with Rhonda. Pick a manager you think will be the most interesting character for this role play. Then develop the list of time and territory management improvement items. You may use leeway in fleshing out specific personal and job issues for discussion points in the meeting. Just be sure to thoroughly cover the key points from the chapter sections on efficient time management and effective territory management.

Assignment

Work together to develop and execute the role-play discussion on improving time and territory management between Rhonda and one of her account managers. Limit the meeting to 12–15 minutes. Be sure to agree on a plan for the account manager to put into practice.

DISCUSSION QUESTIONS

1. Suppose you are a salesperson working 50 weeks per year, five days a week, eight hours a day. You want to make $50,000 per year, which is based on a 10 percent commission of gross sales. How many hours of face time with customers can you expect in any given year? How much will you have to generate in sales per hour to make $50,000?

2. As sales manager, you realize your salespeople need to be more efficient and effective in managing their time and territory. As you deliver the opening comments at an all-day seminar on time and territory management, your best salesperson stands and asks why this is so important. How do you respond?

3. You are vice president of sales for your company and are speaking with your sales managers from around the country. You have been asked by the CEO to prepare a 5-minute presentation on why time and territory management is so important to the company. What do you say?

4. Complete the priority checklist in Exhibit 10.2. What do your responses to the checklist tell you about your career choices?

5. You are sales manager for an office supply distributor in a large metropolitan area. What do you use as your basic control unit in creating territories? Why?

6. What are the criteria used for estimating the total effort required by a salesperson to cover a territory?

7. You are sales director for a company with 1,125 customers generating $30 million in sales. Calculate the number of customers and sales generated using the 80:20 rule.

8. What is the most useful source of information on customers generated by any company? Identify all the possible data available on that source.

9. What are the primary ways data is aggregated in sales analysis?

10. Identify five types of sales reports a consumer products company might generate. Specify the purpose of such a report and who should have access.

MINI-CASE 10 DIAGNOSTIC SERVICES INC.

Diagnostic Services Inc. (DSI) is a new company. It has been in business for only one year, offering diagnostic services to physicians in the Tampa/St. Petersburg, Miami, and Orlando markets. DSI carries the latest technology, including magnetic resonance imaging (MRI) machines, computerized tomography (CT) scanners, and electron beam tomography (EBT) scanners. The EBT scanners are the state of the art in medical diagnostic equipment, and DSI is one of only three companies in each market to have them. DSI executives are particularly excited about having the EBT scanners in all three locations, because these machines detect potential health problems much earlier than previous medical tests could. The EBT scanners are very flexible. They can perform individual organ scans (for example, a heart scan, a lung scan, or a spleen scan) or they can perform a full-body scan. DSI plans to use the machines to expand its market base and brand awareness in the markets in which it operates.

DSI has operated for the past 12 months with six sales representatives, two for each metropolitan area. Until recently, the company has not had a sales manager. Company executives, all of whom are medical doctors, thought the motivation of each sales representative would be enough to make the company successful. However, after disappointing results in the first year of operation, the management team decided to hire a sales manager to bring some order and direction to the sales force's efforts.

DSI recently hired Lydell Washington as the sales manager. Lydell has 15 years of sales and sales manager experience with a pharmaceutical company. For the last two years his district finished second in sales productivity for the entire company. DSI management told Lydell his mission is to increase the sales force's productivity and name recognition throughout the three-market area by using the new EBT technology.

In his first month with the company, Lydell spent a day with each sales rep making sales calls. By the time Lydell met with the sixth rep, Cindy Minnis, he already knew how to increase the sales force's productivity. He had noticed consistency across the sales force to his questions about their workdays. Cindy's responses were no different from the others. When Lydell asked which doctors she called on, she replied: "I call on all types of doctors. Wherever I find an office I'll stop in and talk to them. I don't care if they are pediatricians, obstetricians, or cardiologists. I'll talk to anyone who will see me."

After Lydell suggested that the physicians most likely to use the company's diagnostic equipment were cardiologists, oncologists, neurologists, and internists, Cindy said, "Really? No one ever told me that."

Next Lydell asked Cindy how many doctors she called on per day. "Only about five, sometimes six. My territory is so large I can't seem to get around to very many offices in a day. Sometimes I run into Mike, the other DSI rep in this area, at an office. There should be something we can do to prevent us from showing up at the same office on the same day." Lydell knew 10 calls per day is the industry standard and many times reps can do more.

Finally, Lydell asked Cindy what kind of information she provided back to the home office about her activity in the field. She answered, "Not much really. I keep some notes on who I've talked to and what we discussed, but until now I haven't had anyone to send them to. I guess that will change now that you're onboard."

After his visit with Cindy, Lydell returned to his office and began to design a plan to increase the company's sales productivity.

Questions

1. What are some of the problems that DSI's salespeople have experienced as a result of not having had the direction of a sales manager for the first 12 months?

2. Describe the process Lydell should follow to design territories for the six sales reps currently employed by DSI. What sources of information are available for Lydell as he designs these territories?

3. What types of information should Lydell use to conduct a sales analysis of his reps' territories? Why?

MANAGING THE CONTEMPORARY SELLING PROCESS

CHAPTER 11
Salesperson Performance:
Behavior, Motivation, and Role
Perceptions

CHAPTER 12
Recruiting, Selecting, and Training
Salespeople

CHAPTER 14
Global Sales Perspectives on
Contemporary Selling

CHAPTER 13
Compensating and Evaluating
Salespeople

PART THREE
To this point we have focused on the roles of salesperson and customer in the contemporary selling process. As we have observed, building a successful buyer–seller relationship is a complex process involving a lot of hard work by the salesperson. However, there are other critical issues in the contemporary-selling process. In this section we will explore the difficult task of managing the sales force as well as global selling.

Chapter 11 examines salesperson performance from both the salesperson's and sales manager's perspective. It discusses role perceptions and motivation, which are both key elements in the model. Sales force recruitment, selection, and training are investigated in Chapter 12. Chapter 13 focuses on the critical management function — evaluation and how it is applied to develop effective sales compensation and incentive programs. Finally, Chapter 14 explores the unique challenges of global selling.

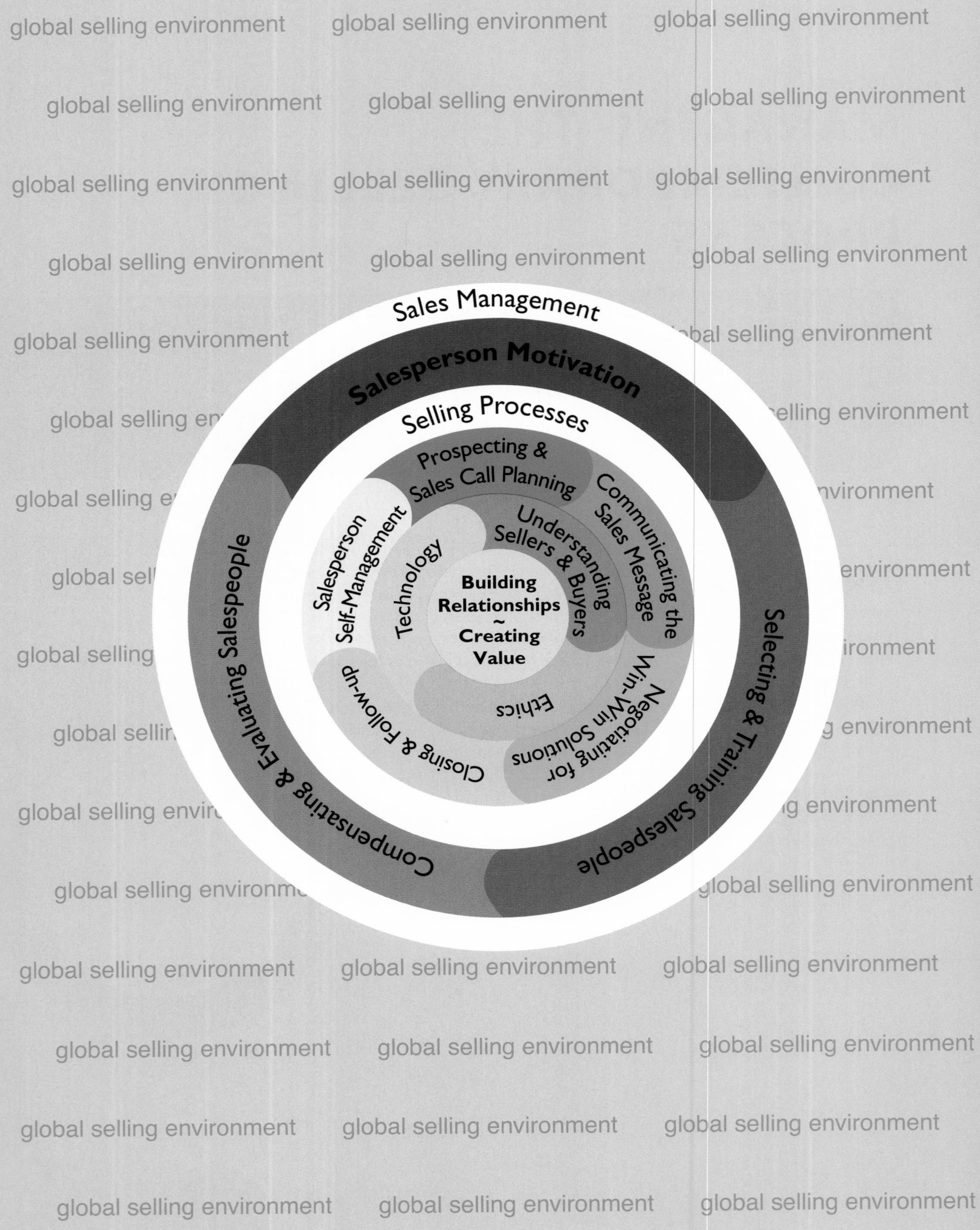

Salesperson Performance: Behavior, Motivation, and Role Perceptions

LEARNING OBJECTIVES

How a salesperson performs is the result of a complex interaction among many factors, including the individual's personal characteristics, motivation, and perceptions of the job. Sales managers must have a clear understanding of salesperson performance to maximize the performance potential of their people. This chapter will present a model of salesperson performance and lay the groundwork for chapters 12 through 14. It also focuses on a key element in the model: the salesperson's role perceptions.

Sales managers must motivate and direct the behavior of sales reps toward the company's goals, so they must understand why sales reps behave the way they do. This chapter offers a model for understanding salesperson performance.

After reading this chapter, you should be able to:

- Understand the model of salesperson performance.
- Identify the various components that make up the model.
- Discuss the role perception process.
- Understand why salespeople are susceptible to role issues.

EXPERT ADVICE

EXPERT: Mr. David B. Edmonds
Senior Vice President, Worldwide Services, FedEx Corporation

TOPIC: Salesperson motivation, performance and sales careers.

SUMMARY: Mr. Edmonds discusses the low turnover rate of salespeople at FedEx and atributes much of their success to hiring the right people, training them well, and finding successful tools to motivate them. He also charts the typical career path for a salesperson, starting in the inside sales department, then moving to outside sales (smaller to larger customers). He reinforces that the biggest challenge in creating a great sales force is a focus on continuous improvement and education. He also discusses the new professionalism of sales and how it has changed dramatically from some of the old stereotypes.

NEXT STEPS: Go to the website for *Contemporary Selling* (www.routledge.com/cw/Johnston), watch the video for Chapter 11 and then read the chapter. You will find an Expert Advice follow-up at the end of the chapter with questions that connect elements of the video to your learning.

WHY IS IT IMPORTANT FOR MANAGEMENT TO UNDERSTAND SALESPERSON PERFORMANCE?

Understanding the model of salesperson performance is extremely important to the sales manager, because almost everything the sales manager does influences sales performance. For example, the way the sales manager organizes and deploys the sales force can affect salespeople's perceptions of the job. How the manager selects salespeople and the kind of training they receive can affect their aptitude and skill. The compensation program and the way it is administered can influence motivation and overall sales performance.

As our focus changes to managing the sales force, refer back to the model for Contemporary Selling at the beginning of the chapter and note the shift from relationship selling to sales management. This chapter will concentrate on salesperson performance (motivation).

SALESPERSON PERFORMANCE

A salesperson's performance is a function of five factors: (1) role perceptions, (2) aptitude, (3) skill level, (4) motivation, and (5) personal, organizational, and environmental variables.[1] These factors are shown in Exhibit 11.1. The success of any salesperson is a complex combination of these forces, which can influence his or her performance positively or negatively.

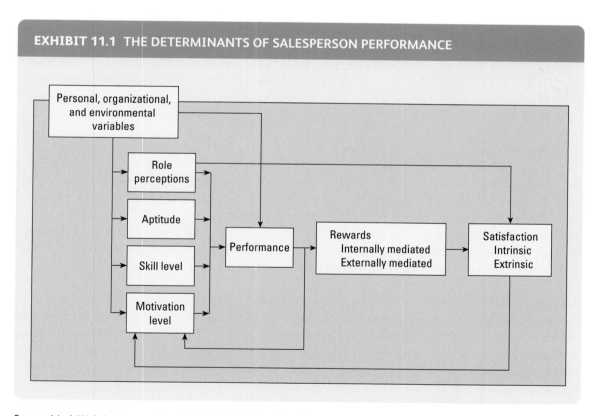

EXHIBIT 11.1 THE DETERMINANTS OF SALESPERSON PERFORMANCE

Source: Mark W. Johnston and Greg W. Marshall, *Sales Force Management*, 11ed. (London: Routledge, 2013).

Although not pictured in the model, the determinants interact with each other. For example, if the salesperson has native ability and the motivation to perform but lacks understanding of how the job should be done, he or she will likely perform at a low level. Similarly, a salesperson who has the ability and accurately perceives how the job should be performed but lacks motivation will likely perform poorly. As you can see already, understanding and improving salesperson performance is challenging. Take the short quiz in Exhibit 11.2 and see how well you would do as a sales manager.

EXHIBIT 11.2 TEST YOUR MANAGEMENT SKILLS

Let's assess your sales management skills. Answer the questions below; all are True/False. Check your answers at the end of the Discussion Questions.

1. If you monitor expenses regularly and your salespeople know that you are checking their expense reports, it is still necessary to have a written expense policy and procedures document.
2. Sales incentive programs should always focus on financial compensation.
3. Require salespeople to get permission for job-related travel.
4. When performance does not meet company expectations the sales manager should confront the salesperson directly.
5. Salespeople should not allow family responsibilities to conflict with work during regular business hours.
6. Promotion is not the long-term goal of a salesperson.
7. Sales training should focus on delivering critical product updates and company information.
8. Good salespeople are born with the inherent abilities to be good.
9. There should be one set of rewards applied across the entire sales organization.
10. Sales managers are responsible for making sure the salesperson understands company performance expectations.

Role Perceptions

The *role* of a salesperson is the set of activities or behaviors to be performed by any person occupying that position. This role is defined largely through the expectations, demands, and pressures communicated to the salesperson by his or her role partners. These partners include people both outside and within the firm who have a vested interest in how the salesperson performs the job—top management, the salesperson's sales manager, customers, and family members. Salespeople's perceptions of these expectations strongly influence their definition of their role in the company and behavior on the job.

Defining Role Perceptions. The role perceptions component of the model for salesperson performance has three dimensions: perceived role conflict, perceived role ambiguity, and role inaccuracy. **Perceived role conflict** arises when a salesperson believes the role demands by two or more of his or her role partners are incompatible. Thus, he or she cannot possibly satisfy them all at the same time. A salesperson suffers from perceptions of conflict, for example, when a customer demands a delivery schedule or credit terms the salesperson believes will be unacceptable to company superiors.

Perceived role ambiguity occurs when a salesperson believes he or she does not have the information necessary to perform the job adequately. The salesperson may be uncertain about what some role partners expect in certain situations, how he or she should satisfy those expectations, or how his or her performance will be evaluated and rewarded.

Role inaccuracy is the degree to which the salesperson's perceptions of demands from his or her role partners—particularly company superiors—are not accurate and is different from role ambiguity in that the salesperson feels certain about what should be done. However, the salesperson's belief is wrong. It differs from role conflict in that the salesperson does not see any inconsistencies because the rep does not realize his or her perceptions are inaccurate.

Why Are Role Perceptions Important? How salespeople perceive their roles will have significant consequences for them. Role perceptions can produce dissatisfaction with the job. They can also affect a salesperson's motivation.[2] These effects can increase sales force turnover and hurt performance. However, role stress (role conflict and ambiguity) does not necessarily imply a negative job outcome (quitting). Believe it or not, a certain degree of role conflict and ambiguity enables salespeople to make creative decisions that can be beneficial to the customer and the organization.

Because they spend so much time out of the office and with customers, B2B salespeople are particularly vulnerable to role inaccuracy, conflict, and ambiguity. Several personal factors (such as traveling, work demands) and organizational factors (such as infrequent meetings with their supervisor) can affect people's role perceptions. Fortunately, many of these factors can be controlled or influenced by sales management policies and methods, so sales managers can help their salespeople perform better.[3]

Sales Aptitude: Are Good Salespeople Born or Made?

Stable, self-sufficient, self-confident, goal-directed, decisive, intellectually curious, accurate—these are personal traits one major personnel testing company says a successful salesperson should have. Sales ability has sometimes been thought to be a function of (1) physical factors such as age and physical attractiveness, (2) aptitude factors such as verbal intelligence and sales expertise, and (3) personality characteristics such as empathy and sociability. However, there is no proof that these types of broad aptitude measures, by themselves, affect sales performance. It's an open question whether the presence or absence of such traits is determined by a person's genetic makeup and early life experiences or whether they can be developed through training, supervision, and experience after the person is hired for a sales position. In other words, the question is: Are good salespeople born or made?

Many sales executives seem unsure about what it takes to become a successful salesperson. When forced to choose, a majority of managers say they believe good salespeople are made rather than born. By a margin of seven to one, the respondents in a survey of sales and marketing executives said training and supervision are more critical determinants of selling success than the rep's inherent personal characteristics.[4] But many of those respondents also described someone they knew as "a born salesperson," and a minority argued that personal traits are critical determinants of good sales performance.

Thus, while most managers believe the things a firm does to train and develop its salespeople are the most critical determinants of their success, many also believe that certain basic personal traits—such as a strong ego, self-confidence, decisiveness, and a drive to achieve—are requirements. Most likely both sets of factors play crucial roles in shaping a salesperson's performance. Exhibit 11.3 highlights five traits considered critical for sales success.

Sales Skill Levels

Role perceptions determine whether the salesperson knows what to do in performing a job, and aptitude determines whether the individual has the necessary native abilities. Skill levels are the individual's learned proficiency at performing the necessary tasks.[5] They include such learned abilities as interpersonal skills, leadership, technical knowledge, and presentation skills. The relative importance of each of these skills, and the need for other skills, depends on the selling situation. Different kinds of skills are needed for different types of selling tasks.

Aptitude and skill levels are thus related constructs. Aptitude consists of relatively enduring personal abilities, while skills are proficiencies that can improve rapidly with learning and experience. A salesperson

---

EXHIBIT 11.3 PERSONAL TRAITS THAT LEAD TO SALES SUCCESS

Are good salespeople born or made? As we have seen, this question is difficult to answer. However, leading sales managers agree all good salespeople possess at least a few basic personality traits. Recently, managers and sales experts identified the following five traits of successful salespeople:

Optimistic. Have you ever noticed how the best reps tend to look on the bright side? Optimism may also determine how resilient a salesperson will be.

Flexible. Being able to adjust to difficult situations is key to success in sales. "A salesperson needs to be able to accept 15 nos before you get a yes."

Self-motivated. Most experts and managers believe motivation cannot be taught. Whether it's being driven by money or recognition or simply pride, the best salespeople tend to have an inherent competitive drive.

People person. Simply put, you can't sell if your customers don't like you. Being friendly and sociable is a hallmark of salespeople who network and maintain long-term customer relationships.

Empathetic. This intuitive, perceptive ability underlies virtually all other emotional intelligence skills because it involves truly understanding the customer. Empathetic salespeople tend to have good listening and communication skills.

---

for Cisco Systems selling multimillion-dollar network switching equipment needs different skill sets from someone selling BMWs to consumers.

The salesperson's past selling experience and the extensiveness and content of the firm's sales training programs influence skill level. While American companies spend large amounts of money on sales training, very little is known concerning the effects of these training programs on salespeople's skills, behavior, and performance. We will discuss training the sales force in much greater detail in chapter 12.

Motivation

Motivation is how much the salesperson wants to expend effort on each activity or task associated with the job. These activities include calling on existing and potential new accounts, developing and delivering sales presentations, and filling out orders and reports.

Defining Motivation. The salesperson's motivation to expend effort on any task seems to be a function of the person's (1) expectancies and (2) valences for performance. **Expectancies** are the salesperson's estimates that expending effort on a specific task will lead to improved performance on some specific dimension. For example, will increasing the number of calls made on potential new accounts lead to increased sales? **Valences for performance** are the salesperson's perceptions of the desirability of attaining improved performance on some dimension(s). For example, does the salesperson find increased sales important?

A salesperson's valence for performance on a specific dimension, in turn, seems to be a function of the salesperson's (1) instrumentalities and (2) valences for rewards. **Instrumentalities** are the salesperson's estimates that improved performance on that dimension will lead to increased attainment of particular rewards. For example, will increased sales lead to increased compensation? **Valences for rewards** are the salesperson's perceptions of the desirability of receiving increased rewards as a result of improved performance. Does the salesperson find increased compensation attractive enough to put in the time calling on more prospects?

Why Is Motivation Important? Sales managers constantly try to find the right mix of motivation elements to direct salespeople to do certain activities, but rewards that motivate one salesperson may not motivate another. The manager of a leading consulting company in Chicago gave his top performer a new mink coat.

The only problem was that the individual was opposed to wearing fur. Rewarding the salesperson was a great idea, but the form of the reward led to problems for the sales manager.

A salesperson's motivation is not directly under the sales manager's control, but it can be influenced by things the sales manager does, such as how he or she supervises or rewards the individual. In addition it is influenced by a a number of personal variables such as the individual's career stage.[6] Since motivation strongly influences performance, the sales manager must be sensitive to the way various factors affect each rep. Exhibit 11.4 explores ways to motivate and retain your star salespeople.

EXHIBIT 11.4 MOTIVATE YOUR STAR SALESPEOPLE FOR FREE

Most sales managers believe that it costs a lot of money to motivate and retain your best salespeople. They think that financial rewards are the only way to keep those stars from leaving the company. However, consider five ways to motivate your star salespeople for practically nothing.

1. *Understand personal difference.* What motivates one rep may leave another cold. Get to know your salespeople and their likes and dislikes.
2. *Encourage balance.* Successful people need to juggle work along with family and friends. Respect their personal lives.
3. *Praise good work.* Find salespeople doing something worthwhile, like sharing leads, and notice it.
4. *Get out.* Be supportive, visible, and available. Don't hide in your office.
5. *Don't play favorites.* Even a hint of favoritism can undermine a sales team.

Organizational, Environmental, and Personal Factors

It is difficult to separate organizational, environmental, and personal variables. The sales performance model in Exhibit 11.1 suggests that they influence sales performance in two ways: (1) by directly facilitating or constraining performance and (2) by influencing and interacting with the other performance determinants, such as role perceptions and motivation. Many questions remain unanswered concerning the effects of these factors on sales performance.

Organizational and Environmental Variables. Organizational factors include the company marketing budget, current market share for products, and the degree of sales force supervision. There is an indirect and direct relationship between performance and environmental factors like territory potential, the salesperson's workload, and the intensity of competition.

When you look at sales territory design (remember the discussion from chapter 10), a salesperson's performance increases as he or she becomes more satisfied with the territory's design and structure. Including salespeople in the territory design process may seem intuitive, but managers sometimes find it difficult to balance the needs of the organization with the input of the salespeople. Sales managers have learned, however, that including them in the decision-making process on key issues such as territory design and technology decisions may increase their performance over time.[7] As we discussed in chapter 10, computer territory mapping software helps sales managers and salespeople work together to create the most profitable and efficient territory configurations.[8] In the long term this can lead to less role ambiguity and more job satisfaction, as well as better performance.

Personal Variables. Personal and organizational variables (such as job experience, the manager's interaction style, and performance feedback) affect the amount of role conflict and ambiguity salespeople perceive. In addition, their desire for job-related rewards (such as higher pay or promotion) differs with demographic characteristics such as age, education, family size, career stage, and organizational climate and other characteristics such as coping strategies that can impact a wide range of salesperson attitudes and behaviors.[9]

As the role of salespeople has evolved into building and maintaining customer relationships, they have been asked to engage in a whole range of activities that can be described as being good corporate citizens. These behaviors are called **organizational citizenship behaviors** and encompass four basic types of activity: (1) sportsmanship, (2) civic virtue, (3) conscientiousness, and (4) altruism. Sportsmanship is a willingness on the salesperson's part to endure less than optimum conditions (like slow reimbursement of expenses or reduced administrative support) without complaining to superiors or other salespeople. Civic virtue is a proactive behavior that includes making recommendations to management that will improve the overall performance of the organization (e.g., providing feedback from customers even when it is not complimentary). Conscientiousness is the willingness to work beyond the normal expectations of the job (late at night or on weekends). Altruism refers to helping others in the organization (for example, mentoring younger salespeople).

There is a growing understanding that salespeople who engage in these activities perform better on both outcome-based measures (sales volume) and behavior-based measures (customer satisfaction). Measuring and evaluating salesperson performance will be discussed in chapter 13. Engaging in activities that enhance the overall organization becomes even more important as the focus shifts to relationship selling.

Rewards

Exhibit 11.1 indicates that performance affects the salesperson's rewards. However, the relationship between performance and rewards is very complex. For one thing, a firm may choose to evaluate and reward different dimensions of sales performance. A company might evaluate its salespeople on total sales volume, quota attainment, customer satisfaction, profitability of sales, new accounts generated, services provided to customers, or some combination of these. Different firms use different dimensions. Even firms that use the same performance criteria are likely to have different emphases.

A company can also bestow a variety of rewards for any given level of performance. There are two types of rewards—extrinsic and intrinsic. Extrinsic rewards are those controlled and bestowed by people other than the salesperson, such as managers or customers. They include such things as pay, financial incentives, security, recognition, and promotion. Intrinsic rewards are those that salespeople primarily attain for themselves. They include such things as feelings of accomplishment, personal growth, and self-worth.

Satisfaction

The **job satisfaction** of salespeople refers to all the characteristics of the job that salespeople find rewarding, fulfilling, and satisfying—or frustrating and unsatisfying. Satisfaction is a complex job attitude, and salespeople can be satisfied or dissatisfied with many different aspects of the job. There are seven dimensions to sales job satisfaction: (1) the job itself, (2) pay, (3) company policies and support, (4) supervision, (5) co-workers, (6) promotion and advancement opportunities, and (7) customers. See Exhibit 11.5 for a summary. Salespeople's total satisfaction with their jobs is a reflection of their satisfaction with each element. For example, recent research suggests that salespeople's satisfaction goes down if they perceive that new technologies like Internet sales cannibalize their own sales efforts.[10]

Like rewards, the seven dimensions of satisfaction can be grouped, into intrinsic and extrinsic components. *Extrinsic satisfaction* is based on the extrinsic rewards bestowed on the salesperson, such as pay, company policies and support, supervision, fellow workers, chances for promotion, and customers. *Intrinsic satisfaction* is based on the intrinsic rewards the salesperson obtains from the job, such as satisfaction with the work itself.

EXHIBIT 11.5 JOB SATISFACTION DIMENSIONS

Job satisfaction consists of the following dimensions:

1. The job itself.
2. Pay (all forms of financial rewards, including salary and commission).
3. Company policies and support (procedures such as expense policies, reports, paperwork).
4. Supervision (immediate sales manager, senior sales management in the company).
5. Co-workers (other salespeople, people on the sales team, staff).
6. Promotion and advancement (opportunities to move up in the company).
7. Customers (friendliness, ease of working with people).

Salespeople's satisfaction is also influenced by their role perceptions.[11] Salespeople who perceive a great deal of conflict in job demands tend to be less satisfied than those who do not. So do those who experience great uncertainty in what is expected from them on the job.

Finally, a salesperson's job satisfaction is likely to affect his or her motivation to perform, as suggested by the feedback loop in Exhibit 11.1. The relationship between satisfaction and motivation is complex and varies by individual.

HOW SALESPEOPLE INFLUENCE PERFORMANCE

Clearly, the salesperson has the most significant effect on his or her own performance. Two areas that influence performance in relationship selling are the salesperson's role perceptions and the many factors that influence those perceptions. As we have seen, the salesperson's role is complex and has conflicting demands.

The Salesperson's Role Perceptions

Role perceptions have important implications for sales managers and affect salesperson performance in many ways. For example, feelings of ambiguity, conflict, and inaccurate role perceptions can cause anxiety and stress, which can lead to lower performance. Fortunately, the sales manager can minimize the negative consequences of role perceptions by the kind of salespeople that are hired, training methods, the incentives used to motivate them, criteria used to evaluate them, and the way they are supervised.

What makes understanding and managing role perceptions even more complicated is that not all the consequences of role ambiguity, role conflict, and role accuracy are negative. Eliminating all ambiguity and conflict would reduce the challenge for a salesperson and can actually limit long-term performance. The sales manager's job is to create an environment that will stimulate and motivate salespeople while reducing the negative effects of role stress that are a natural part of selling. The salesperson's role is defined through a three-step process:[12] role partners communicate expectations, salespeople develop perceptions, and salespeople convert these perceptions into behaviors.

Stage 1: Role Partners Communicate Expectations. First, expectations and demands concerning how the salesperson should behave, together with pressures to conform, are communicated to the salesperson by people with a vested interest in how he or she performs the job. These people include the rep's immediate superior, other executives in the firm, customers and members of customers' organizations, and the salesperson's family. They all try to influence the person's behavior, either formally through organizational

GLOBAL CONNECTION

WHEN JOB AND FAMILY COLLIDE IN THE 21ST CENTURY

Companies demand much from their salespeople and managers. Travel and entertaining are part of the sales environment. The challenge of balancing home and work demands has never been greater. It is not surprising that, as the demands of the job increase, the conflict between work and family grows as well. In addition, the trend toward working longer hours shows no signs of slowing down. American workers tend to work longer hours than their counterparts in Europe, even when they would rather spend more time with their family.

Employers are increasingly worried about productivity problems among workers with conflicting job and family responsibilities. But the Families and Work Institute, a nonprofit research and planning group, says the family also bears a heavy burden. In a recent study, over half of the respondents said they had felt overworked in the last three months. The study suggested overworked employees:

1. Experience more conflict between the demands of the job and home.
2. Feel less successful in their personal relationship with spouses and children.
3. Get less sleep.
4. Experience more stress.

Technology that lets employees be in almost constant contact with the office and customers has also led to increases in work-related stress and conflict between job and home. Nearly 40 percent of the employees who said they are heavy users of technology reported being overworked. Half of employees who believe they are unnecessarily accessible feel they are overworked and experience higher levels of job-related stress.

Over 40 percent of employees who feel overworked reported being angry with their employers often or very often. Nearly half said they were going to look for employment elsewhere in the next year. These two outcomes can have serious negative consequences for the company, since the salesperson is the primary connection to customers.

Families are paying an even higher price. More than a quarter of respondents said they are often or very often not in as good a mood as they would like when they get home at night. And 28 percent often or very often do not have enough energy to do things with their families.

The findings, which echo those of similar studies by the Institute, have major implications. One key finding is summarized as follows. "Of particular concern are the negative spillover effects that demanding and hectic jobs can have on the quality of workers' personal lives and well-being. This spillover is reflected in high stress, poor coping, bad moods, and insufficient time and energy for people who are personally important, creating 'problems' that, in turn, spill over into work and impair job performance." Despite the sobering reality of job–family conflict, people are finding ways to get balance. Occasionally, that means a new career; more often it means making family a more significant priority.

Indeed, this work–life balance is an issue around the world as even European workers, who have traditionally worked fewer hours than workers in Asia or the United States, are reporting highers levels of work-related stress. It is clear that it is difficult for employees around the world to find the right balance between work and life.

Adapted from Fernanado Jaramillo, Jay Prakash Mulki, and James S. Boles, "Workplace Stressors Job Attitude, and Job Behaviors: Is Interpersonal Conflict the Missing Link," *Journal of Personal Selling & Sales Management* 31 (Issue 3, Summer 2011), pp. 339–56; Mahmoud Darrat, Douglas Amyx, and Rebecca Bennett, "An Investigation into the Effects of Work-Family Conflict and Job Satisfaction on Saleperson Deviance," *Journal of Personal Selling & Sales Management* 30 (Issue 3, Summer 2010), pp. 43–60; James T. Bond, Ellen Galinsky, and Michele Conlin, "Work-Life Balance: How to Get a Life and Do Your Job," *BusinessWeek* (August 14, 2008), www.businessweek.com/magazine/content/08_34/64097036727134.htm.

policies, operating procedures, and training programs or informally through social pressures, rewards, and sanctions.

The salesperson's family members can have a significant effect on job perceptions. Their demands are much more likely to differ from one salesperson to the next than the expectations of customers or management. So no matter what the company expects in hours of work, customer relationships, travel, and the like, a substantial number of salespeople are likely to be in conflict with their families' expectations. That is becoming an increasingly serious problem for today's workers, as Global Connection indicates.

Stage 2: Salespeople Develop Perceptions. The second part of the role definition process involves salespeople's perception of the expectations and demands of those around them (sales manager, customers, loved ones). Salespeople perform according to what they think these individuals expect, even when their perceptions of those expectations are not accurate. To really understand why salespeople perform the way they do, it is necessary to understand what they think the members of the role set expect.

At this stage of the role definition process, three factors can wreak havoc with a salesperson's job performance and mental well-being. As Exhibit 11.6 shows, the salesperson may suffer from role ambiguity, role conflict, or role inaccuracy.

Stage 3: Salespeople Convert Perceptions to Behaviors. The final step in the role definition process involves the salesperson's conversion of role perceptions into actual behavior. Both job behavior and attitudes can be affected if there is role ambiguity or conflict, or if these perceptions are inaccurate. High levels of perceived ambiguity and conflict are directly related to high stress and tension and low job satisfaction. Also, feelings of uncertainty or conflict and the actions taken to resolve them can have a strong impact on job performance.[13] At a minimum, the salesperson's performance is less likely to meet management's

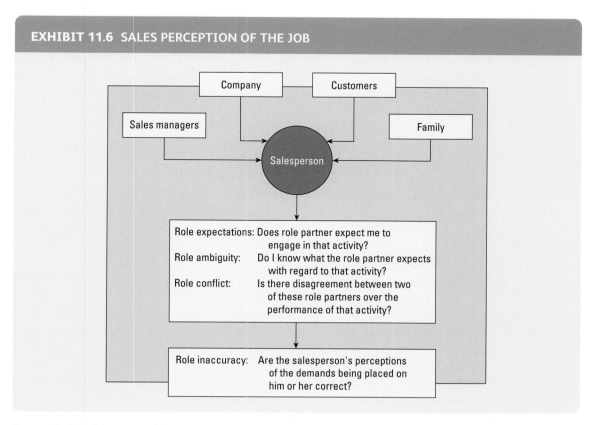

EXHIBIT 11.6 SALES PERCEPTION OF THE JOB

Source: Mark W. Johnston and Greg W. Marshall, *Sales Force Management,* 11th ed. (London: Routledge, 2013).

expectations when the rep is uncertain about what those expectations are or feels conflicting expectations from customers or family.

The Salesperson's Role Is Affected by Many Factors

Several characteristics of the salesperson's role make it susceptible to role conflict, role ambiguity, and the development of inaccurate role perceptions. Salespeople operate at the boundary of the firm, interact with many people, and are often considered innovators inside the organization.

Boundary Position. Salespeople are likely to experience more role conflict than other individuals in a company because they work at the boundary of their firms. Key members affecting the salesperson's role—customers—are external to the organization, so salespeople receive demands from organizations that have diverse goals, policies, and problems. Since both the customer and the salesperson's own organization want a salesperson's behavior to be consistent with their different goals, the demands on the salesperson are often incompatible.

For example, a customer may question the salesperson on the company's long-term commitment to meet his or her needs. You will remember the problems associated with Research in Motion's first versions of their tablet computer. Even now Research in Motion salespeople get asked about the long-term viability of the company in light of the product's problems. Management told them to be honest and explain to customers what the company was doing to fix product issues. They had to balance confidentiality with customers' legitimate concerns about the future ability of the company to meet existing product and customer service pledges. Salespeople get caught in the middle. To satisfy the demands of one partner, they must deal with the concerns and demands of the other.

Another problem that arises from the salesperson's boundary position is that the individuals in one organization (for example, the salesperson's company) often don't appreciate the expectations and demands made by others (customers or loved ones). A customer may not know company policies or the constraints under which the salesperson must operate. Or the sales rep's superiors may formulate company policies without understanding the needs of certain customers. Even someone who is aware of the other's demands may not understand the reasoning behind them and may consider them arbitrary or illegitimate.

The nature of selling also increases the likelihood salespeople will experience role ambiguity. Contact with customers, though regular, is probably infrequent and often brief. Under such conditions, it is easy for a salesperson to feel uncertain or to misjudge what the customers really expect in delivery, service, or how they really feel about the rep's service.

The "Remote" Sales Force. Increasingly, salespeople operate from remote offices (often their home) and spend very little time in their company's offices. This can increase role stress and lead to lower performance over time. Benefits of a remote sales force include lower costs and stronger relationships as salespeople get closer to their customers. But being separated from the organization may lead to alienation and isolation, which can lower satisfaction and performance.

Managers help salespeople feel less isolated by remaining in regular contact and assuring the reps that they are still a vital part of the organization. Salespeople also need feedback on their performance from managers and learn how to improve their selling skills (training). Many companies, including Johnson & Johnson and Hewlett-Packard, have salespeople who work remotely from their homes with great results.

Interaction with Many People. Salespeople interact with many diverse individuals. One salesperson may sell to hundreds of customers, and each expects his or her own particular needs and requirements to be satisfied. People within the firm rely on the salesperson to execute company policies with customers and increase the firm's revenue. The specific design of a product and the delivery and credit terms quoted by the salesperson directly affects people in the engineering, production, and credit departments, for example. All these people may hold definite beliefs about how the salesperson should perform the job and may pressure the individual to conform to their expectations.

The large number of people from diverse departments and organizations who depend on the salesperson increases the probability that at least some demands will be incompatible. It also means the salesperson's perceptions of some demands will be inaccurate and he or she will be uncertain about others.

Selling in a Team. The complex nature of the relationship between company and customer has created a need for salespeople to work in teams that include specialists from many parts of the company (technical, manufacturing, logistics, and others). As we have discussed, the role of salesperson has evolved from selling to customers to managing the relationship between the company and customers. Companies as diverse as Sun Microsystems, 3M, Siemens, and Sony have created sales teams managed by salespeople. Inside salespeople and customer service reps create additional contact with the customer that often requires greater coordination with the field representatives. This may create role conflict as salespeople deal with the expectations and demands of many individuals in the sales team and the organization as a whole.

Innovative Role. Salespeople are frequently called on to produce new, innovative solutions to nonroutine problems. This is particularly true when they are selling highly technical products or engineered systems designed to customer's specifications. Even salespeople who sell standardized products must display some creativity in matching the company's offerings to each customer's particular needs. With potential new accounts, this is an extremely difficult but critical task.

As a result of their innovative roles, salespeople tend to experience more conflict than other employees because they must have flexibility to perform at a high level. They must also have the authority to develop and carry out innovative solutions. This need for flexibility often brings the salesperson into conflict with standard operating procedures of the firm and the expectations of co-workers who want to maintain the status quo. The production manager, for example, may frown on orders for nonstandard products because of the adverse effects on production costs and schedules—although marketing (especially the salespeople) desires flexible production schedules and the ability to sell custom-designed products.

Workers with innovative roles also tend to experience more role ambiguity and inaccurate role perceptions because they face unusual situations where they have no standard procedures or past experience to guide them. Consequently, they are often uncertain about how their role partners expect them to proceed. Their perceptions are more likely to be inaccurate because of the nonroutine nature of the task. The flexibility needed to fulfill an innovative role can have unforeseen negative consequences.

HOW MANAGERS INFLUENCE PERFORMANCE

While salespeople are most responsible for their own performance, sales managers also play a critical role. Managers affect all elements in the model of sales performance, though in this section we focus on two: role perceptions and motivation. (Chapters 12 and 13 will look at how managers influence other factors in the model.)

Role Perceptions

Given that role conflict and ambiguity produce mostly negative consequences for salespeople, the question is: Can sales management do anything to reduce conflicts and ambiguities or help salespeople deal with them when they occur? Yes. There are many things management can do to manage salesperson conflict and ambiguity.

Role Conflict. Experienced salespeople perceive less conflict than less experienced representatives. Perhaps salespeople who experience a great deal of conflict become dissatisfied and quit, whereas those who stay on the job do not perceive as much conflict.

Also, successful sales representatives also learn with experience how to deal with conflict. They learn that demands that initially appear to conflict can turn out to be compatible or perhaps they find out how to resolve conflicts so they are no longer stressful. They build up psychological defense mechanisms to screen out conflicts and ease tension. Sales training programs can prepare salespeople to deal with job-related conflicts and teach them to do their job better.

When their sales managers structure and define their jobs, salespeople seem to experience more conflict. Perhaps too close supervision decreases a salesperson's flexibility in dealing with the diverse role expectations with which salespeople must contend (customers, management, and family). Peter Sowden, vice president of business development for Polytex Fibers, puts it this way: "Most salespeople love autonomy and flexibility. I find the greatest compliment is to be left alone to run my territory as if it were my own business."[14] Another way to reduce role conflict, then, is to give salespeople a greater voice in what they do and how they do it.

Role Ambiguity. There are also things management can do to reduce role ambiguity. Since it too depends on experience, training should help salespeople cope with it. More importantly, it also depends on the manager's supervisory style. Close supervision may actually reduce ambiguity, though salespeople should have some influence over the standards used to control and evaluate their performance. Closely supervised salespeople are more aware of their supervisors' expectations and demands, and inconsistent behaviors can be brought to their attention more quickly.

ETHICAL DILEMMA

THE COST OF POOR ETHICAL DECISIONS

Due to increasing reports of unethical behavior on the part of its sales force, top management of PrimeTech industries recently held a meeting to denounce the alleged practices. Ron Yeaple, CEO and founder of the company, said these activities are never tolerated and anyone found violating company policies was subject to immediate dismissal.

Frank Harris has been a salesperson with PrimeTech for 10 years. In the past he has performed at or above the average and received sales awards from time to time. However, his recent performance has been less than what both he and the company had hoped. Recently, Frank learned his future with the company was being reevaluated by management. He knew his performance over the next few months was critical.

Two months ago Frank began calling on a large potential new customer, First Line Manufacturing. The potential with this company was very big and it seemed receptive to Frank's company and products. Frank believed obtaining a large contract with this company would secure his job, so he provided gifts (a DVD player, an expensive bottle of wine), charging them against his expense account disguised as other expenses. However, after hearing Mr. Yeaple's remarks, he realizes that his actions have violated company policy.

Questions to Consider

1. What should Frank Harris do?
2. Can you be ethical and still violate company policy on ethical practices?
3. If you were Ron Yeaple, would you fire Frank Harris?

Similarly, salespeople who have input in determining the standards by which they are evaluated are more familiar with these standards, which tends to reduce role ambiguity. Another way to reduce ambiguity is by reducing the number of people who report directly to the sales manager. An increase in the number of people who report to a manager also increases a salesperson's perceived role ambiguity. Reducing it allows closer supervision, and tends to make job-related issues clearer to salespeople.[15]

As you can see, close supervision can be a two-edged sword. While it can reduce ambiguity, it can increase role conflict and job dissatisfaction when salespeople feel they don't have enough latitude to deal effectively with customers or enough creative input to service their accounts. The problem is particularly acute when sales managers use coercion and threats to direct their salespeople.[16] Sales managers must walk a very fine line in how closely and by what means they supervise their sales force.

Motivation

Through company policies, the sales manager can directly facilitate or hinder a salesperson's motivation. They may also influence salespeople's performance indirectly, however, by affecting their interest in company rewards and the size and accuracy of their expectancies and instrumentalities. How do sales executives motivate their sales forces? Check out Exhibit 11.7.

EXHIBIT 11.7 SECRETS OF MOTIVATION

Sales managers must overcome a number of challenges to successfully motivate their sales force. Often the challenges are easy to identify, although they may be difficult to address, such as compensation. However, some problems are less easy to recognize, although their impact on sales force motivation can be dramatic. Let's look at two of those issues.

A persistent perception held by many sales managers is that salespeople can learn how to become successful on their own. In other words salespeople have an innate ability to identify what they need to know, learn it, and then be able to apply to their own situation. For the top 5 percent of sales performers, that is true, but what about the other 95 percent? The reality is that the vast majority of salespeople don't know what they don't know. Most salespeople invest very little in their own sales education and most sales managers fail in providing useful skills. Success-oriented sales managers value a "best practices" approach to selling, searching for skills and information that benefit their salespeople, then creating an environment for salespeople to learn and practice those skills. The result is a more confident, motivated salesperson. Incorporating "best practices" throughout the sales force raises the performance and motivation for everyone, not just the top 5 percent.

Another widely held perception is that sales performance mediocrity must be tolerated. The theory often used in those situations is, "It's better to have somebody in that territory than no one." The "solution" may be to reassign the individual to a less desirable territory (usually in an attempt to force the individual to leave the company) or engage the individual in discussion to identify and address the problem.

While those ideas may work for that individual, most sales managers, unfortunately, fail to consider the effect mediocre performance has on the rest of the sales force. The belief that performance issues are person-specific can inflict serious damage on the motivation of the entire sales force. Sales managers need to address performance issues directly, seeking regular, meaningful input on what is working (and not working), what motivates each individual, and what can be done to improve their performance. In a very real sense sales managers need to consistently focus on improving performance individually and across the entire sales force.

Adapted from Dave Kahle, "Are there Best Practices for Salespeople," *American Salesman* 53 (Issue 2, February 2008), pp. 11–15; and Paul Cherry, "How to Motivate Your Sales Team to Achieve Next Level Selling," *American Salesman* 52 (Issue 11, November 2007), pp. 8–12.

Motivation and Managerial Leadership. One well-regarded theory of leadership suggests that managers can attain good performance by increasing salespeople's personal rewards and making the path to those rewards easier to follow—by providing instructions and training, reducing roadblocks and pitfalls, and increasing the opportunities for personal satisfaction.[17]

Effective leaders match their style and approach to the needs of their sales force and the kinds of tasks they must perform. When the salesperson's task is well defined, routine, and repetitive, the leader should seek ways to increase the intrinsic rewards, perhaps by assigning a broader range of activities or giving the rep more flexibility to perform tasks. When the salesperson's job is complex and ambiguous—as is the case in most selling situations—he or she is likely to be happier and more productive when the leader provides more guidance and structure. One of the challenges is critically examining the manager–salesperson relationship. In general salespeople respond well to managers who display a genuine concern for their salespeople (servant leadership).[18]

The more accurate salespeople's role perceptions are, the more motivated they're likely to be. Salespeople work at the boundary of their companies, dealing with customers and other people who may make conflicting demands. Salespeople frequently face new, nonroutine problems. However, closely supervised salespeople can learn more quickly what is expected of them and how they should perform their job. On the other hand close supervision can increase role conflict, since it can reduce flexibility in accommodating and adapting to customers' demands.

Another factor is how often salespeople communicate with their managers. The more frequent the communication, the less role ambiguity salespeople are likely to experience and the more accurate their expectancies and instrumentalities are. Again, too frequent contact with superiors may increase a representative's feelings of role conflict.

Incentive and Compensation Policies

Management policies and programs concerning rewards, such as recognition and promotion, can influence the desirability of such rewards in the salesperson's mind. If, for example, a large proportion of the sales force receives some formal recognition each year, salespeople may think such recognition is too common, too easy to obtain, and not worth much. If very few representatives receive formal recognition, however, recognition may not motivate simply because the odds of attaining it are so low. The same kind of relationship is likely to exist between the proportion of salespeople promoted into management each year (the **opportunity rate**) and the importance salespeople place on promotion. In addition, a critical issue is the question of fairness and how rewards are dispensed across the organization, if rewards are not perceived to be fair it can impact a wide range of employees attitudes and motivation.[19]

Another issue is preferential treatment for stars. The goal of recognition and other forms of incentives is to motivate people to do better, but what happens when one star demands and receives much more than the average or even much more than the company's other top performers? A few years ago, baseball player Alex Rodriguez (A-Rod) was on the market to the highest bidder. One of the teams considering recruiting Rodriguez was the New York Mets. However, the Mets withdrew from consideration when they realized that, while they could afford Rodriguez, the effect on team morale would be negative. General manager of the Mets at the time, Steve Phillips said, "It's not about an individual. It's about 25 players that join together as a team. When that is compromised, it becomes difficult to win." The same is true for a sales force. A company's policies on the kinds and amounts of financial compensation paid to "star" salespeople are also likely to affect their motivation. When an individual is basically satisfied with his or her pay, money become less important and the value of that reward to that person is reduced.

Finally, the reward mix offered by the firm is a factor. **Reward mix** is the relative emphasis placed on salary versus commissions or other incentive pay and nonfinancial rewards. It is likely to influence a salesperson's value estimates of certain rewards and help determine into which job activities and types of performance he or she will put the greatest effort. The question from a manager's viewpoint is how to design an effective reward mix for directing the sales force's efforts toward the activities most important to the overall success of the firm's sales program. This leads to a discussion of the relative advantages and drawbacks of alternative compensation and incentive programs—the topic of chapter 13.

EXPERT ADVICE: FOLLOW-UP   Chally Group
WORLDWIDE

After watching the video of Mr. Edmonds and reading the chapter, consider the following questions:

1. How does the long-term focus on customers at companies like FedEx impact a salesperson's motivation and performance?
2. How would a salesperson's motivation and performance change based on their work in the inside sales department versus moving to an outside sales position?

SUMMARY

This chapter presents a model (Exhibit 11.1) for understanding the performance of salespeople. It examines the first component of the model, the salesperson's role perceptions.

A salesperson's performance is a function of five basic factors: (1) role perceptions, (2) aptitude, (3) skill level, (4) motivation, and (5) organizational, environmental, and personal variables. There is substantial interaction among the components. A salesperson who is deficient in any one may perform poorly.

Salespeople's role perceptions are defined largely through the expectations, demands, and pressures communicated by role partners (people both within and outside the company who are affected by the way they perform the job). The role of salesperson is defined through a three-step process: (1) role partners communicate expectations and demands concerning how the salesperson should behave in various situations, together with pressures to conform; (2) the salesperson perceives these expectations and demands; and (3) the salesperson converts these perceptions into actual behavior.

The three major variables in role perception are role accuracy, ambiguity, and conflict. Role accuracy is the degree to which the salesperson's perceptions of his or her role partners' demands are accurate. Role ambiguity occurs when the salesperson does not believe he or she has the information to perform the job adequately. Role conflict arises when a salesperson believes the demands of two or more of his or her role partners are incompatible.

Salespeople's performance affects the rewards they receive. There are two basic types of rewards: extrinsic rewards, which are controlled and bestowed by people other than the salesperson, and intrinsic rewards, which are those that people primarily attain for themselves.

The rewards received have a major impact on a salesperson's satisfaction with the job and the total work environment. Satisfaction is also of two types. Intrinsic satisfaction comes from the intrinsic rewards the salesperson obtains from the job, such as satisfaction with the work and the opportunities it provides for personal growth and a sense of accomplishment. Extrinsic satisfaction comes from the extrinsic rewards bestowed on the salesperson, such as pay, promotion, and supervisory and company policies.

The salesperson's role is affected by many factors. They work on the boundary of the organization between the company and customer. Much of the time they are working away from the office and interact with many diverse individuals. Finally, the role of salesperson is one of the most innovative in the company.

The manager plays an important part by having a profound influence on role perceptions (conflict, ambiguity). In addition managers affect a salesperson's motivation through reward and compensation plans and other company policies.

KEY TERMS

perceived role conflict

perceived role ambiguity

role inaccuracy

expectancies

valences for performance

instrumentalities

valences for rewards

organizational citizenship behaviors

job satisfaction

opportunity rate

reward mix

ROLE PLAY

BEFORE YOU BEGIN

Before getting started, please go to the Appendix of chapter 1 to review the profiles of the characters involved in this role play, as well as the tips on preparing a role play.

Characters Involved

Alex Lewis

Abe Rollins

Setting the Stage

Over the past couple of years, Alex Lewis's children (a 12-year-old boy and 14-year-old girl) have become more and more involved in sports and other extracurricular activities that require frequent travel to other cities for competition, sometimes road trips 100 miles or more away from home. A parent must accompany the child on each trip. Alex's wife, Sonya, holds a professional position that involves overnight travel three or four nights per month. Alex's sales territory involves only minimal overnight travel (an occasional night here and there, generally not more than two or three nights per quarter). Thus, he often plays Mr. Mom at home when his wife is on the road. Sometimes both he and Sonya have to be out of town at the same time. Sonya's parents live in the area and can watch the children when that happens.

Although Alex's job performance has consistently been quite good, the stress of the family–work conflict is beginning to take its toll. Unless something changes, he expects the stress to increase in the next few years until his children get their drivers' licenses.

Alex knows that Abe Rollins went through a similar situation back when his four children were teenagers and somehow Abe survived with both marriage and career intact. Like Sonya, Abe's wife is employed in a professional position, but unlike Sonya, Kate does not travel for work. Alex wants to visit with Abe to get some ideas on how to balance the various roles required to be successful at Upland and at home. He calls Abe and sets an appointment to meet over lunch.

Alex Lewis's Role

Alex is to meet with Abe and lay out his concerns about the role requirements of his job and the role requirements of his family. He needs to listen more than talk, as Abe has a lot of insight on how to strike a successful role balance and how to prioritize roles successfully.

Abe Rollins's Role

Abe will play the role of the trusted, experienced senior account manager. He needs to come to the lunch meeting prepared to discuss all aspects of role conflict, role ambiguity, role stress, job satisfaction, and especially family–work conflict. Basically Abe needs to help Alex develop a game plan to put balance back into his work and family life, and especially to ensure that Alex continues to be motivated to do a good job. The elements needed to prepare for this discussion are all in the chapter.

Abe should ask relevant questions and provide appropriate advice. Abe will do most of the talking in the role play, with Alex sharing information and listening. Alex should end up with a game plan to follow to continue his record of good performance and at the same time maintain a healthy family life.

Assignment

Work together to develop and execute the role-play dialogue surrounding the issues described. Limit the lunch meeting to 12–15 minutes. Be sure to end up with an agreed-upon, specific plan for change that will reduce Alex's role stress. In addition to changes Alex can make, some of the changes may involve recommendations to make to Rhonda later regarding Alex's territory. Assume that both Rhonda and Upland want their account managers to have high motivation and satisfaction and low role stress.

DISCUSSION QUESTIONS

1. A salesperson's past and present performances affect his or her expectations for future performance. After experiencing several failures, many new salespeople quit their sales job within a few months because they assume that selling is not for them. What role can a sales manager play in such situations?

2. The president of Part-I-Tyme, manufacturer of salty snack foods, is dismayed over the dismal sales results for the past six months. A new product, a deluxe cookie, had been taste-tested and consumers' responses were very positive. Part-I-Tyme's sales force consists of over 5,000 truck-driver distributors who have excellent reputations with their customers. Part-I-Tyme's president is convinced that the sales force enthusiastically supports the new product line, but it's obvious that something is wrong. How would you determine the nature of the problem? Can you use the model of salesperson performance in this situation?

3. Although many aptitude tests exist, their ability to predict sales performance has been weak. How do you account for this?

4. Frequently, sales managers use contests and recognition rewards to motivate the sales force. If sales managers understand salesperson performance, why is it necessary to employ these additional techniques?

5. "I want sales representatives who can stand on their own. Once they have been through training and show how to apply their knowledge, it shouldn't be necessary for me to constantly tell them how they are doing. The stars always shine; it's the other reps who need my attention." Comment on this statement. Do you agree or disagree?

6. A sales representative for Lead-In Technologies is faced with a demand from an important customer that is in direct conflict with company policies. The customer wants several product modifications with no change in price. What can the sales rep do to handle this conflict?

7. Salespeople for the Ansul Company, a manufacturer of fire prevention systems for B2B applications, have been told they will now have to sell small fire extinguishers to the retail market. The salespeople have never sold in the retail market before and have no background in this area. What role problems are likely to occur?

8. Maria Gomez-Simpson, a customer service rep with Mar-Jon Associates, spends considerable time traveling to various customer offices. As a result, she often arrives home late. Maria asked her manager if she could rearrange her Thursday work schedule to attend an evening class at a local college. Which of the following statements best reflects how to manage the conflict created by Maria's request?

  a. "Since we're talking about only one night, go ahead, sign up for the course, and we'll work out the details."
  b. "We need to discuss this first to see if you can be back most Thursdays in time for your course and still get the job done."
  c. "We know that you get home late on certain days, but it's part of the job. Maybe you can take the course some other time."

ANSWER KEY FOR QUIZ IN EXHIBIT 11.2

1. True
2. False
3. True
4. False
5. False
6. True
7. False
8. False
9. False
10. True

MINI-CASE 11 ACE CHEMICALS

Dave Parrett, sales manager for Ace Chemicals, is wrestling with the issue of how to get Kay Powers back on track. Kay has been with the company 20 years. Historically, she had been one of the company's top salespeople, but her performance has fallen off during the past three or four years.

That concerns Dave, because Kay calls on some of Ace's largest accounts. She earned each of those assignments. When she joined Ace Chemicals, Kay turned heads with her performance. She secured business in companies the firm had never previously served. Customers were extremely pleased with the service she provided. Ace received more unsolicited compliments on how she serviced her accounts than on any other salesperson. Her call reports indicated she made more calls in a week than almost any other salesperson with the company, and her sales showed it. She regularly exceeded the quotas she was assigned.

All this has changed in the last few years. Kay has developed very few new accounts. Complaints from customers, while not the highest in the sales force, have shown a marked increase. Kay seems to start later and quit earlier than she used to. She makes fewer calls most weeks than most of the other salespeople. She has barely met her quota in three of the last five years and fell short of it once. Yet she is still a good enough salesperson that her annual income (salary and commissions) exceeds six figures.

Senior management is pushing to increase productivity. Several younger salespeople are eager to move into larger, more demanding accounts. Dave contemplated the future and considered his next move.

Questions

1. Attempt to discern why Kay's performance has deteriorated and offer training and assistance to help improve her performance.

2. If you were Dave Parrett, what would you do in this situation?

3. What do you with a salesperson who is no longer great?

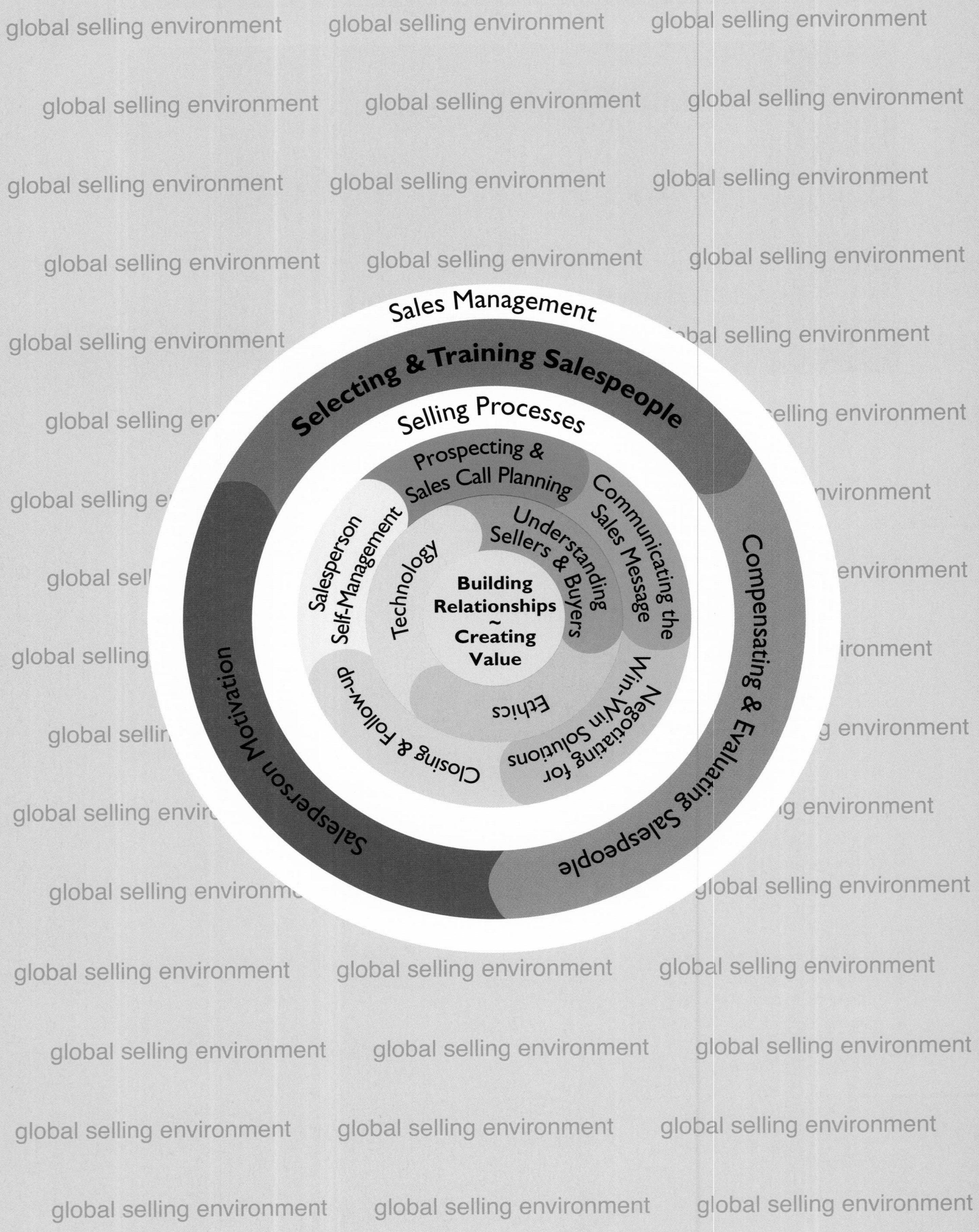

Recruiting, Selecting, and Training Salespeople

LEARNING OBJECTIVES

Perhaps more than any other function of the sales manager, successfully recruiting new salespeople, then training them well.

is critical to the long-term success of the organization. As markets expand both domestically and internationally, companies seek qualified new candidates to fill sales positions while talented people inside the company are being recruited by competitors. Competition for talented candidates is fierce and the direct and indirect costs of poor recruiting are high. At the same time salespeople operate in a highly dynamic environment and must be able to assimilate a great deal of information to make them effective with customers. A key element in enhancing the success of current salespeople and preparing new salespeople is training. For all these reasons, recruiting, selecting, and training salespeople has become a very important part of the sales manager's job. This chapter describes the process of recruiting new salespeople into the organization, then training the entire sales force.

After reading this chapter, you should be able to:

- Understand the key issues that drive the recruitment and selection of salespeople.
- Understand a job analysis and how selection criteria are determined.
- Define the sources for new sales recruits.
- Explain the selection procedures.
- Identify the key issues and objectives in sales training.
- Discuss how to develop sales training programs.
- Define the topics covered in a sales training program.
- Understand the various methods for conducting sales training.
- Explain how to measure the costs and benefits of sales training.

EXPERT ADVICE

EXPERT: Mr. Bill Scannell
Vice President, EMC

TOPIC: Recruiting, selecting, and training salespeople.

SUMMARY: Mr. Scannell looks at the critical process of recruiting and hiring the right salespeople. He discusses the growing understanding that professional selling requires professional skills and highlights the positive impact collegiate sales programs have on the recruiting at EMC. Mr. Scannell also outlines the company's approach to training with a focus on getting salespeople in front of the cusomter as soon as possible, even if that means telesales or customer service. Finally, he speaks to the "lifelong" learning approach of the company, providing learning throughout the salesperson's career.

NEXT STEPS: Go to the website for *Contemporary Selling* (www.routledge.com/cw/Johnston), watch the video for chapter 12 and then read the chapter. You will find an Expert Advice follow-up at the end of the chapter, with questions that connect elements of the video to your learning.

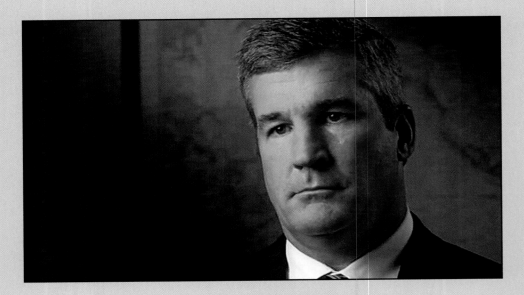

RECRUITMENT AND SELECTION ISSUES

Sales managers must resolve a number of important issues when recruiting and selecting new salespeople for relationship selling. Refer to the Contemporary Selling model to see where we are. To better understand the recruiting and selection process for salespeople, refer to Exhibit 12.1. The decision process has four stages: establishing policy, analyzing the job, attracting applicants, and evaluating applicants. The recruiting process is complex and involves many criteria. Test your skills at hiring in Exhibit 12.2 and see what kind of candidate you would choose for a sales position. Let's examine this process in greater detail.

EXHIBIT 12.1 THE DECISION PROCESS FOR RECRUITING AND SELECTING SALESPEOPLE

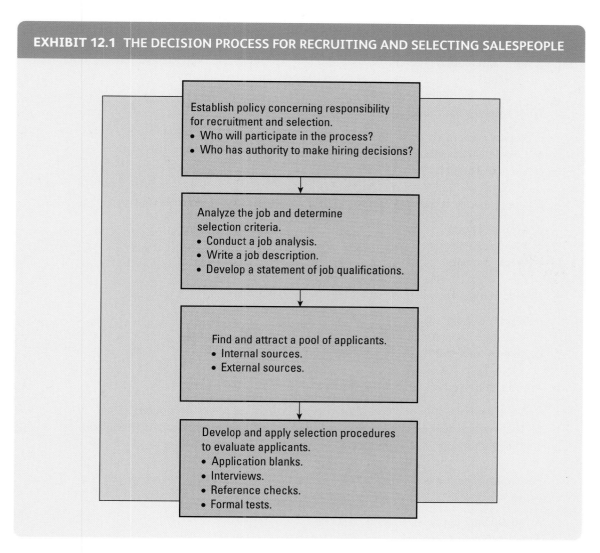

Source: Mark W. Johnston and Greg W. Marshall, *Sales Force Management*, 11th ed. (London: Routledge, 2013).

EXHIBIT 12.2   THE HIRING QUIZ

Managers are always searching for tools that will help them make better hiring decisions. Here is a quiz that helps the sales manager identify the right candidate. By completing the survey they get insights on the primary and secondary characterisitics of the "right" salesperson and also whether candidates should be recruited from college, inside the firm, or a competitive hire.

1. Are you in an industry with

   a. Relatively few well-known competitors and few changes in relation to new products and service (1 point)
   b. New competition entering the market and rapid changes to products and services introduced (2 points)

2. What category fits your product?

   a. Capital equipment (1 point)
   b. Consumer (2 points)
   c. Service (3 points)

3. If your product is technical in nature, what is your level of technical sales support?

   a. Strong (1 point)
   b. Average (2 points)
   c. Weak (3 points)

4. How do you market your product?

   a. Heavily (1 point)
   b. Very little (2 points)
   c. Rely on sales staff to do it (3 points)

5. Are you interested in

   a. The development of additional business within existing accounts (1 point)
   b. The management of an existing line of business within mature accounts (2 points)
   c. The promotion of a new product to prospective customers (3 points)

6. How much time can you afford to hire and train new sales staff before receiving a return on your investment?

   a. 30–90 days (1 point)
   b. 91–180 days (2 points)
   c. 181 days or more (3 points)

7. Will your sales staff work in an office where

   a. Direct supervisor is present (1 point)
   b. No direct supervisor is present (3 points)

8. Will your sales staff

   a. Rely on other sales personnel to prospect and qualify potential customers (2 points)
   b. Qualify prospects themselves (0 points)

9. How much time will you spend training your new hire?

   a. More than 80 hours (1 point)
   b. 41–80 hours (2 points)
   c. 0–40 hours (3 points)

10. How much time will you spend coaching and counseling your new sales staff?

   a. More than 20 hours per week (1 point)
   b. 12–20 hours per week (2 points)
   c. 0–10 hours per week (3 points)

How to Score

1. Add your total points from questions 1–10.
2. Match your point total to the corresponding point totals following.
3. Your ideal candidate will possess the characteristics indicated for the point total.

Primary Characteristic of Salesperson

13 points or less	Tenacity, rapport building, work standards, oral communication, ability to learn
14–18 points	Leadership, planning and organization, job motivation, presence
19–28 points	Persuasiveness, negotiation, analysis, initiative, written communication

Secondary Characteristic of Salesperson

13 points or less	Planning and organization, listening, job motivation, initiative, written communication
14–18 points	Analysis, tenacity, oral communication, written communication, rapport building
19–28 points	Independence, listening, oral communication, presence, planning

Source of Sales Recruits

13 points or less	New college graduate or hire from within
14–18 points	Hire from within or competitive hire
19–28 points	Competitive hire

Adapted from Walt Shedd, "Ten Stops to Top Sale Professionals," www.sellingpower.com

Establish Responsibility

An MBA student at the authors' school was recently recruited for a sales job with a major software company. She was interviewed extensively, not only by the sales manager (her prospective supervisor) but also by higher-level executives in the firm, including a regional vice president of marketing. All this attention from top-level managers surprised the candidate. She asked, "Is it common for so many executives to be involved in recruiting new salespeople?"

The student's question raises the issue of who should have the primary responsibility for recruiting and selecting new salespeople. The way a company answers this question typically depends on the size of the sales force and the kind of selling involved. In firms with small sales forces, the recruitment and selection of new people is a primary responsibility of the top-level sales manager. In larger, multilevel sales forces, however, attracting and choosing new recruits is usually too extensive and time consuming for a single executive. Authority for recruitment and selection is commonly delegated to lower-level sales managers or staff specialists.

In some firms, members of the human resources department (or outside HR specialists) instead of the sales management staff assist and advise sales managers in hiring new salespeople. This approach helps reduce duplication of effort and avoids friction between the sales and HR departments. One disadvantage is that HR specialists may not be as knowledgeable about the job to be filled and the qualifications necessary as a sales manager. Even when the HR department or outside specialist helps attract and evaluate applicants, the sales manager typically has the final say in whom to hire.

Finally, when the firm sees its sales force as a training ground for sales and marketing managers, either HR executives or other top-level managers may participate in recruiting to make sure the new hires have management potential. This was the situation in the firm that interviewed our MBA student. Although it offered her "just a sales job," company executives saw that job as a stepping stone to management responsibilities.

Analyze the Job and Determine Selection Criteria

Research relating salespeople's personal characteristics to sales aptitude and job performance suggests there is no single set of traits and abilities sales managers can use to help them decide which recruits to hire. Different sales jobs require different activities, and people with different personality traits and abilities should be hired to fill them. The first activities in the recruitment and selection process thus should be the following:

1. Conduct a **job analysis** to determine what activities, tasks, responsibilities, and environmental influences are involved in the job to be filled.
2. Write a job description that details the findings of the job analysis.
3. Develop a statement of **job qualifications** that describe the personal traits and abilities a person should have to perform the job.

Most companies, particularly larger ones, have written job descriptions for sales positions. Unfortunately, those job descriptions are often out of date and do not accurately reflect the current scope and content of the positions. The responsibilities of a given sales job change as the customers, the firm's account management policies, the competition, and other environmental factors change. When this happens, companies need to conduct new analyses and update descriptions to reflect those changes. When firms create new sales positions new tasks also need to be identified.

Consequently, a critical first step in the hiring process is for management to make sure the job to be filled has been analyzed recently and the findings have been written out in great detail. Without a detailed, up-to-date description, the sales manager will have difficulty deciding what kind of person is needed and prospective recruits will not really know what is expected of them. Consider Ethical Dilemma #1 and the challenges companies face in identifying the right kind of candidates.

ETHICAL DILEMMA #1

THE YOUTZ OR EXPERIENCE CHALLENGE

Craig McMillan faced a difficult choice. His company, Cutting Edge Logistics, had experienced significant growth in the last five years, and as vice president of sales he had been one of the key people in watching the company grow from just under $100 million to over $500 million in sales. Based in Chicago, the company had hired experienced salespeople from competitors to help grow quickly and had used generous financial packages to keep them motivated and loyal.

However, as McMillan reviewed the sales for the last four quarters, he noticed a disturbing trend. Many of these salespeople were older and performance had begun to drop off. He knew he needed to hire new salespeople, but he was unsure if he should use the old model (experienced salespeople from competitors) or a new model of hiring less experienced salespeople fresh out of college who could communicate with younger buyers and decision makers at the client companies. The old model had been hugely successful and he was afraid that a new one would alienate salespeople who had been with the company for years. McMillan was afraid that changing the hiring model could destroy morale, yet he knew the sales force needed greater diversity.

Question to Consider

1. Craig McMillan has called you for advice. What would you tell him?

Job Analysis and Determination of Selection Criteria. Information about each selling job's content should come from two sources: (1) the current occupant of the job and (2) the sales manager who supervises that person.

Current job occupants should be observed and/or interviewed to determine what they actually do. Sales managers at various levels should be asked what they think the job occupant should be doing in view of the firm's strategic sales program and account management policies. It is not uncommon for the person who analyzes a job to discover the salespeople are doing extra work that management is not aware of and slacking off on some activities management believes are important. Such misunderstandings and inaccurate role perceptions illustrate the need for accurate, detailed job descriptions.[1]

Job Descriptions. Job descriptions written to reflect a consensus between salespeople and their managers can serve several useful functions. In addition to guiding the firm's recruiting efforts, they can guide the design of a sales training program that will provide new salespeople with the skills to do their job effectively and improve their understanding of how the job should be done. They can also serve as standards for evaluating each salesperson's job performance, as discussed in chapter 11.

In many companies there are a variety of sales positions. Some may not even include the word "sales" in the job title. Go to Monster.com and type in "sales" and you will find hundreds of job listings. Note that each description spells out many of the items identified below and require a variety of different skills and experience. Detailed job descriptions, such as those you see on Monster.com, tell both the company and the potential salesperson exactly what the expectations are before employment, which vastly increases the rep's chances of success.

Good job descriptions of sales jobs typically identify the following dimensions and requirements:

1. The nature of product(s) or service(s) to be sold.
2. The types of customers to be called on, including policies concerning how often calls are to be made and the personnel within customer organizations who should be contacted (e.g., buyers, purchasing agents, plant supervisors).

3. The specific tasks and responsibilities to be carried out, including planning tasks, research and information collection activities, specific selling tasks, other promotional duties, customer servicing activities, and clerical and reporting duties.

4. The relationships between the job occupant and other positions within the organization. To whom does the job occupant report? What are the salesperson's responsibilities to the immediate superior? How and under what circumstances does the salesperson interact with members of other departments, such as production or engineering?

5. The mental and physical demands of the job, including the amount of technical knowledge the salesperson should have concerning the company's products, other necessary skills, and the amount of travel involved.

6. The environmental pressures and constraints that might influence job performance, such as market trends, the strengths and weaknesses of the competition, the company's reputation among customers, and resource and supply problems.

Determining Job Qualifications and Selection Criteria. Determining the qualifications of a prospective employee is the most difficult part of the recruitment and selection process. The problem is that nearly all these characteristics play at least some role in choosing new salespeople. No firm, for instance, would actively seek sales recruits who are unintelligent or lacking in self-confidence. At the same time, not many job candidates will possess high levels of *all* desirable characteristics. The task, then, is to decide which traits and abilities are most important for which job and which are less critical. Also, some thought should be given to trade-offs among the qualification criteria. Will a person with a deficiency in one important attribute still be considered acceptable if he or she has outstanding qualities in other areas? For example, will the firm want someone with only average verbal ability and persuasiveness if that person has a great deal of ambition and persistence?

Deciding on Selection Criteria. Simply examining the job description can assist decision makers looking for key qualifications in new salespeople. If the job requires extensive travel, for instance, management might prefer applicants who are younger, have few family responsibilities, and want to travel. Similarly, statements in the job description concerning technical knowledge and skill can help management determine what educational background and previous job experience to look for when selecting from a pool of candidates.

Larger firms go one step further and evaluate the personal histories of their existing salespeople to determine what traits differentiate between good and poor performers. This analysis seldom produces consistent results across different jobs and different companies. It can produce useful insight, however, when applied to a single type of sales job within a single firm. The assumption is that there may be a cause-and-effect relationship between such attributes and job performance. If new employees have attributes similar to those of people who are currently performing the job successfully, they may also be successful.[2] Another compelling reason to analyze personal history is to validate the selection criteria the firm is using, as required by government equal employment opportunity regulations.

Find and Attract Applicants

This is one area where some firms do not spend enough time and money. They attempt to hold down recruiting costs in hopes that a good training program can convert marginal recruits into solid sales performers. Unfortunately, several determinants of sales success are difficult or impossible to change through training or experience. Therefore, spending the money and effort to find well-qualified candidates can be a profitable investment. In certain industries finding enough qualified individuals can be a challenge. For example, the life insurance industry reports that it must interview 60 to 120 people to find one good hire.[3]

In view of the difficulties in attracting qualified people to fill sales positions, a well-planned and well-implemented recruiting effort is usually a crucial part of the firm's hiring program. The primary objective of the recruiting process should not be to maximize the total number of job applicants. Too many recruits can overload the selection process, forcing managers to use less thorough screening and evaluation procedures. Intel, for example, receives thousands of applications every day. Besides, numbers do not ensure quality. The focus should be on finding a few good recruits.

Self-selection by prospective employees is the most efficient means of selection, so the recruiting effort should discourage unqualified people from applying. For example, many companies recruit via the Internet. Companies like Cisco Systems and IBM have a screening procedure by which candidates can provide certain key pieces of data about themselves and the company will search its job openings to look for a match.

Recruiting communications should point out both the attractive and unattractive aspects of the job to be filled, spell out the required qualifications, and state the likely compensation. This will encourage only qualified and interested people to apply for the job. Also, recruiting efforts should focus only on sources where fully qualified applicants are likely to be found.

Internal Sources. Sales managers go to a number of places to find recruits or leads on potential recruits. Internal sources are people already employed by the firm, while external sources include people in other firms (who are often identified and referred by current members of the sales force), advertisements, recruiting agencies, educational institutions, and the Internet.

When the job involves technical selling that requires substantial product knowledge and industry experience, firms focus more heavily on employees in other departments within the company and on personal referrals of people working for other firms in the industry.[4] Surveys suggest that more than half of U.S. manufacturers hire at least some of their salespeople from other internal departments.

Recruiting current company employees for the sales force has distinct advantages:

1. Company employees have established performance records, and they are more of a known quantity than outsiders.
2. Recruits from inside the firm should require less orientation and training because they are already familiar with the company's products, policies, and operations.
3. Recruiting from within can bolster company morale, as employees become aware that opportunities for advancement are available outside of their own department or division.

External Sources. Although it is a good idea to start with internal sources when recruiting new salespeople, most of the time there will not be enough qualified internal candidates to meet the needs of a firm's sales force. As a result, the vast majority of companies must expand the search to include external sources like people from other firms, ads, professional recruiting agencies, educational institutions, and the Internet.

All of the recruiting issues faced by sales managers are magnified as companies expand globally and seek to hire salespeople in new international markets. Cultural differences, language barriers, and legal restrictions create additional concerns about hiring the right people for the sales position. The key is for a company to do its homework and research each new market before deciding to enter it. For example, in many European countries it is much more difficult to terminate the contract of an employee than in the United States, so it's even more crucial to hire the right people. It is important for a company to understand the legal requirements of hiring new salespeople.

REFERRAL OF PEOPLE FROM OTHER FIRMS. In addition to being potential sales employees themselves, company personnel can provide management with leads to potential recruits from outside the firm. Current salespeople are in a good position to provide leads to new recruits. They know the requirements of the job, they often have contacts with other salespeople who may be willing to change jobs, and they can do much to help "sell" an available job to potential recruits. Consequently, many sales managers make sure their salespeople

GLOBAL CONNECTION

PROS AND CONS OF HIRING SALESPEOPLE FROM COMPETITORS

Competitors are often used as a source for new salespeople. In considering competitor salespeople for a new position, it is important to understand the pros and cons. Let's take a closer look at the advantages and disadvantages.

Pros

Reduce the learning curve. Competitor salespeople take less time to get up to speed and selling for the company. For example, they already know the industry and are frequently familiar with the company's products having sold against them in the past.

External motivator. There is nothing like an external competitor to get your existing salespeople motivated. Quite often hiring salespeople from competitors motivates your current salespeople to demonstrate they are better than the new hire.

Knowledge base. Someone who knows the customers, products, and market environment has a distinct advantage over an "outsider." The more experienced a competitor's salesperson, the less they need to learn and the more value they can add to the company immediately. In addition, much of the knowledge experienced salespeople bring to the table is not easily trained; rather, it is the result of spending time in the field.

Cons

Square Peg in Round Hole. The single biggest concern in hiring salespeople from competitors is assimilating those individuals into the company culture and getting them to learn the policies and procedures. It can be difficult for a salesperson trained in one sales culture to "unlearn" what they currently know and successfully adapt to a new culture. The real problem occurs when those salespeople interact with customers; the resulting culture clash can spill over into the customer relationship.

Customer Trust. It is unsettling for a customer who has seen a salesperson marketing one company's products suddenly switch companies and argue that these new products do a better job of meeting the customer's needs. If it is not handled properly customers question the honesty of the salesperson. By extension they also may question the honesty of the company. Again, these types of circumstances can do significant harm to the customer relationship.

Short-Term Versus Long-Term Strategy. Hiring competitor salespeople does offer some short-term benefits (lower training costs, reduced learning curve) but at a price. There is evidence to suggest these salespeople are less loyal and have the potential to create greater cultural conflict that younger, less experienced salespeople trained in the company culture, policies, and procedures. The question becomes, "does the company want to take a long- or short-term approach to building the sales force?" Younger, less experienced salespeople will take longer to become profitable in the field but may be a better investment long term.

are aware of the company's recruiting needs. Some companies offer bonuses as incentives for their salespeople to recruit new prospects. Referrals from current employees must be handled tactfully to avoid hard feelings if the applicant is rejected later. The question of whether a firm should recruit salespeople from its competitors is controversial. Such people are knowledgeable about the industry from their experience; however, there are some disadvantages. Global Connection highlights the pros and cons of hiring salespeople from the competition.

ADVERTISEMENTS. A less selective way to attract job applicants is to advertise the position. When a technically qualified or experienced person is needed, an ad might be placed in an industry trade or technical journal. More commonly, ads are placed in the personnel or marketplace sections of local newspapers to attract applicants for less demanding sales jobs that don't require special qualifications. A well-written ad can be very effective for attracting applicants—though that is not necessarily a good thing. When a firm's ads attract large numbers of applicants who are unqualified or only marginally interested, the firm must engage in costly screening to separate the wheat from the chaff.[5]

PROFESSIONAL RECRUITING AGENCIES. While **employment agencies** are sometimes used to find recruits, often for more routine sales jobs like retail sales, relationship selling usually requires more sophisticated outside professionals. These agencies specialize in finding applicants for more demanding sales jobs. When the company clearly understands the demands of the job and knows the kind of candidates it is looking for, these organizations can be helpful.

EDUCATIONAL INSTITUTIONS. College and university placement offices are a common source of recruits for firms that require salespeople with high intelligence or technical backgrounds. Most educational institutions allocate resources to "career management" departments that help graduates develop their careers. Educational institutions are an effective source when the sales job is viewed as a first step toward a career in management. Good grades are at least some evidence the person can think logically, budget time efficiently, and communicate reasonably well.

But college graduates generally have less selling experience and are likely to require extensive orientation and training in the basics of salesmanship. Also, college-educated sales recruits tend to "job hop" unless their jobs are challenging and promotions are rapid. One insurance company stopped recruiting college graduates when it found that they did not stick around very long. Such early turnover is sometimes more the fault of the company than of the recruits. When recruiters paint an unrealistic picture of the demands and rewards of the job, or when they recruit people who are overqualified, high turnover is often the result.[6]

Junior colleges and vocational schools are another source of sales recruits that has expanded rapidly in recent years. Many such schools have programs explicitly designed to prepare people for selling careers. Firms that recruit from such programs do not have to contend with the negative attitudes toward selling they sometimes encounter in four-year college graduates.

THE INTERNET. Increasingly companies are seeking applications over the Internet. Younger candidates are as comfortable submitting applications over the Internet as they are filling them out on paper. In high-tech industries, the Internet application process demonstrates a comfort level with technology. Finally, by targeting the Internet application to specific job postings, the company can direct the information to the right people very efficiently. For example, Internet applications to Dell include a unique job reference and number so that the information can be sent to the right people at a specific geographic location.

While the use of the Internet to recruit salespeople is clearly increasing, the unique aspects of the sales position coupled with the need to meet and interview individuals in person make it a difficult tool for recruiting purposes. However, it makes a good screening device since a large number of applications can be processed easily. Companies like IBM receive thousands of applications every day for positions throughout the company. The Internet can process these applications to the right people efficiently and effectively.

Develop and Apply Selection Procedures

After the job qualifications have been determined and some applicants have been recruited, the final task is to determine which applicants best meet the qualifications and have the greatest aptitude for the job. To gain the information needed to evaluate each prospective employee, firms typically use some combination of the following **selection procedures**:[7]

1. Application
2. Personal interviews
3. Reference checks
4. Psychological tests:
    a. Intelligence
    b. Personality
    c. Aptitude/skills

Research into these selection tools has found that composites of psychological test scores are the best predictors of a potential salesperson's future job performance. Evaluations based on personal interviews are the worst.[8] Surprisingly, the way firms actually use the various selection tools is not consistent with their demonstrated validity. Almost all companies use personal interviews, while psychological tests are the least used selection tool—although their use is increasing again. Large firms are somewhat more thorough in the use of psychological tests—and the development of detailed job descriptions—than smaller firms.

Some of the practical advantages and limitations of the various tools are discussed next.

Applications. Although professional salespeople often have résumés to submit to prospective employers, many human resources experts believe a standard company application form makes it easier to assess applicants. A well-designed application blank obtains the same information in the same form from all candidates. The primary purpose of the application form is to collect information about the recruit's physical characteristics and personal history. Forms typically ask for facts about the candidate's physical condition, family status, education, business experience, military service, participation in social organizations, and outside interests/activities. They can also screen for basic qualifications such as educational experience. A second function of the application form is to help managers prepare for personal interviews with job candidates. A study at one pharmaceutical firm found that common application information—such as candidates' tenure in their previous jobs and their amount of sales experience—was able to distinguish salespeople likely to stay with the hiring company from those who were more likely to quit.[9]

Personal Interviews. In addition to probing the applicant's history, **personal interviews** reveal insights into the applicant's mental abilities and personality. A manager can assess a candidate's communication skills, intelligence, sociability, aggressiveness, empathy, ambition, and other traits the job demands. Different managers use many different interviewing approaches to accomplish these objectives. The primary methods for conducting personal interviews can all be classified as either structured or unstructured. In *structured interviews,* each applicant is asked the same predetermined questions. This approach is particularly good when the interviewer is inexperienced at evaluating candidates. At the other end of the spectrum of interviewing techniques is the *unstructured interview,* which seeks to get the applicant talking freely on a variety of subjects. The interviewer asks only a few questions to direct the conversation to topics of interest, such as the applicant's work experience, career objectives, and outside activities. The rationale for this approach is that allowing the applicant to talk freely yields significant insight into his or her character and motivations. The interviewer is free to spend more time on topics where the applicant's responses are interesting or unusual.

Regardless of what interviewing techniques are used, more managers rely on interviews than any other selection tool to evaluate sales candidates. Yet there is evidence that evaluations based on personal interviews are among the least valid predictors of job performance. Does this mean many firms are doing a less than optimal job of evaluating and selecting new salespeople? Are there ways to improve the accuracy of impressions gained from interviews? These questions are explored in Exhibit 12.3.

EXHIBIT 12.3 PERSONAL INTERVIEWS: AN IMPORTANT TEST FOR SELECTING SALESPEOPLE

Personal interviews are both the most commonly used method of selecting salespeople and the one sales managers consider most helpful. But assessments of evaluations based on personal interviews across a variety of occupations suggest they are disappointing predictors of future job performance. One analysis found that evaluations based on interviews have a low correlation with candidates' subsequent performance. Other research offers a more favorable view of the personal interviewing process and suggests that interviews are more useful when several different people interview the candidate.

Sales managers often take a more pragmatic view.

- Presentation—Is the candidate prepared? Do they bring visual aids?
- Personality—If appropriate, is the candiadate a risk taker? How do they handle questions?
- Experience—Does the candidate's cultural orientation match the company's own culture?

It is clear the sales manager should play an active role in interviewing prospective salespeople. The interview should seek to draw out a candidate's basic skills, such as product knowledge, as well as presentation and oral communication skills. It is also important to note that, while interviews are important, they work best when used with other assessment tools that provide additional insights into the individual. One metaphor of the job candidate is that he or she is like an iceberg, with only 10 percent of the individual visible during a standard interview. Things like education and skill sets are easier to evaluate; however, critical skills like problem solving and decision making represent the 90 percent that is hidden, making them more difficult to assess but more important to consider.

As part of the interview process, companies may employ a *realistic job preview,* a process of having the recruit work with a salesperson in order to learn more about the job. Often this involves an assessment of the candidate after the job preview. In addition, the realistic job preview gives the candidate the opportunity to see what the job is really like before they accept the position

REQUIREMENTS FOR INTERVIEWS AND APPLICATIONS. Because it is illegal to discriminate in hiring on the basis of race, sex, religion, age, or national origin, a firm should not ask for such information on its job application forms or during personal interviews. It is wise to avoid all questions in any way related to such factors. Then there will be no question in the applicant's mind about whether the hiring decision was biased or unfair. This is easier said than done, however, because some innocent questions can be viewed as attempts to gain information that might be used to discriminate against a candidate. Exhibit 12.4 offers guidelines concerning the kinds of illegal or sensitive questions managers should avoid when conducting employment interviews and designing application forms.

References. If an applicant passes the face-to-face interview, a reference check is often the next step. Some sales managers question the value of references because "they always say nice things." However, with a little resourcefulness, reference checks can be a valuable selection tool.

Checking references can ensure the accuracy of factual data about the applicant. It is naive to assume that everything a candidate writes on a résumé or application form is true. Facts about previous job

EXHIBIT 12.4   ILLEGAL OR SENSITIVE QUESTIONS TO ELIMINATE FROM EMPLOYMENT APPLICATIONS AND INTERVIEWS

Nationality and Race

Comments or questions relating to the race, color, national origin, or descent of the applicant—or his or her spouse—must be avoided. Applicants should not be asked to supply a photo of themselves when applying for a job. If proficiency in another language is an important part of the job, the applicant can be asked to demonstrate that proficiency but cannot be asked whether it is his or her native language. Applicants may be asked if they are U.S. citizens but not whether they—or their parents or spouse—are naturalized or native-born Americans. Applicants who are not citizens may be asked whether they have the legal right to remain and work in the United States.

Religion

Applicants should not be asked about their religious beliefs or whether the company's workweek or the job schedule would interfere with their religious convictions.

Sex and Marital Status

Except for jobs where sex is clearly related to job performance—as in a TV commercial role—the applicant's sex should not enter the hiring discussion. Applicants should not be asked about their marital status, whether or not their spouse works, or even whom the prospective employer should notify in an emergency. A woman should not be asked whether she would like to be addressed as Mrs., Miss, or Ms. Applicants should not be asked any questions about their children, babysitting arrangements, contraceptive practices, or planned family size.

Age

Applicants may be asked whether they are minors or age 70 or over, because special laws govern the employment of such people. With those exceptions, however, applicants should not be asked their age or date of birth.

Physical Characteristics, Disabilities, Handicaps, and Health Problems

In view of the Americans with Disabilities Act, all such questions are best avoided. However, once an employer has described the job, applicants can be asked whether they have any physical or mental condition that would limit their ability to perform the job.

Height and Weight

While not illegal, such questions are sensitive, since they may provide a basis for discrimination against females or Americans of Asian or Spanish descent.

Bankruptcy or Garnishments

The bankruptcy code prohibits discrimination against individuals who have filed bankruptcy.

Arrests and Convictions

Questions about past arrests are barred. Applicants can be asked about past convictions, but the employer should include a statement that the nature and circumstances of the conviction will be considered.

Adapted from C. David Shepherd and James C. Heartfield, "Discrimination Issues in the Selection of Salespeople: A Review and Managerial Suggestions," *Journal of Personal Selling & Sales Management* (Fall 1991, p. 71).

experience and college degrees should be checked. The discovery of false data on a candidate's application raises a question about basic honesty as well as about what the candidate is trying to hide. References can supply additional information and opinions about a prospect's aptitude and past job performance. Calling a number of references and probing them in depth can be time consuming and costly, but it can also produce worthwhile information and protect against expensive hiring mistakes.[10]

Psychological Tests. A final set of selection tools used by many firms consists of tests aimed at measuring an applicant's mental abilities and personality traits. The most common tests are intelligence, aptitude, and personality tests. Within each category, there are a variety of different tests used by different companies.

INTELLIGENCE TESTS. Intelligence tests are useful for determining whether an applicant has sufficient mental ability to perform a job successfully. Sales managers tend to believe these are the most useful tests for selecting salespeople. General intelligence tests are designed to measure overall mental abilities by examining how well the applicant comprehends, reasons, and learns.

APTITUDE TESTS. Aptitude tests are designed to determine whether an applicant has an interest in, or the ability to perform, certain tasks and activities. This can determine whether applicants' interests are similar to those of people who are successful in a variety of different occupations, including selling. Other tests measure abilities, such as mechanical or mathematical aptitude, that might be related to success in particular selling jobs.

One problem with at least some aptitude tests is that, instead of measuring a person's native abilities, they measure his or her current skill level at certain tasks. At least some skills needed for successful selling can be taught, or improved, through a well-designed training program. Rejecting applicants because they currently do not have the necessary skills can mean losing people who could be trained to be successful salespeople.

PERSONALITY TESTS. Many general personality tests evaluate an individual on numerous traits. The Myers Briggs Personality Type, for instance, measures 16 traits such as extroversion, sensing, thinking, and judging. Such tests, however, contain many questions, require substantial time to complete, and gather information about some traits that may be irrelevant for evaluating future salespeople.

More limited personality tests have been developed in recent years that concentrate on only a few traits thought to be directly relevant to a person's future success in sales.[11] The Multiple Personal Inventory, for example, uses a small number of "forced-choice" questions to measure the strength of two personality traits: empathy with other people and ego drive.

CONCERNS ABOUT THE USE OF TESTS. During the 1950s and early 1960s, tests—particularly general intelligence and sales aptitude tests—were widely used as selection tools for evaluating potential salespeople. However, due to legal concerns and restrictions posed by civil rights legislation and equal opportunity hiring practices, use of these tests was cut back until recently. Current evidence suggesting that properly designed and administered tests are a valid selection tool has spurred an increase in their popularity.[12] Despite the empirical evidence, however, managers continue to be wary of tests, and many firms do not use them. There are a number of reasons for these negative attitudes. For one thing, despite the evidence that tests are relatively accurate, some managers continue to doubt their validity for predicting the success of salespeople in their specific firm. No mental abilities or personality traits have been found to relate to performance across a variety of selling jobs in different firms. Thus, specific tests that measure such abilities and traits may be valid for selecting salespeople for some jobs but invalid for others.

Also, tests for measuring specific abilities and characteristics do not always produce consistent scores. Some commercial tests have not been developed using the most scientific measurement procedures, so their reliability and validity are questionable. Even when a firm believes a particular trait, such as empathy or sociability, is related to job performance, there is still a question about which test should be used to measure that trait.

Another concern about testing involves the reactions of the subjects. A reasonably intelligent, test-wise person can fudge the results of many tests by giving answers he or she thinks management wants rather than answers that reflect the applicant's feelings or behavior. Also, many prospective employees view extensive testing as a burden and perhaps an invasion of privacy. Therefore, some managers fear that requiring a large battery of tests may turn off candidates and reduce their likelihood of accepting a job with the firm.

Finally, any test that discriminates between people of different races or sexes is illegal. Some firms have abandoned the use of tests rather than risk getting into trouble with the government. Exhibit 12.5 outlines some guidelines for the appropriate use of tests.

As you can see, the process of recruiting and selecting the right salesperson is complex and requires a great deal of analysis and insight. Keep in mind that sales managers must balance the time needed to recruit and select salespeople with their other job demands. While the process is time consuming, sales managers understand the importance of selecting the best individual for the job.

EXHIBIT 12.5 GUIDELINES FOR USING TESTS

1. *Test scores should be a single input in the selection decision.* Managers should not rely on them to do the work of other parts of the selection process, such as interviewing and checking references. Candidates should not be eliminated solely on the basis of test scores.

2. *Applicants should be tested only on those abilities and traits that management, on the basis of a thorough job analysis, has determined to be relevant for the specific job.* Broad tests that evaluate a large number of traits not relevant to a specific job are probably inappropriate.

3. *When possible, tests with built-in "internal consistency checks" should be used.* Then the person who analyzes the test results can determine whether the applicant responded honestly or was faking some answers. Many tests ask similar questions with slightly different wording several times throughout the test. If respondents are answering honestly, they should always give the same response to similar questions.

4. *A firm should conduct empirical studies to ensure the tests are valid for predicting an applicant's future performance in the job.* Hard evidence of test validity is particularly important in view of the government's equal employment opportunity requirements.

ISSUES IN SALES TRAINING

Once the individual is recuited, he or she needs additional instruction (training) to make them an effective salesperson. Even experienced salespeople need to understand the company's policies and procedures as well specific knowledge of the company's products and services. People new to selling will require even more training. This is why sales training is a critical task for sales managers in the contemporary selling process. Training salespeople is a huge industry. According to the latest data, American companies spent more than $171 billion on training in 2012. It is not surprising, then, that the subject of sales training produces considerable interest among managers at all levels of a company.

Sales managers have a variety of objectives for training. A national account manager wants sales training to provide specific details about certain industries and to teach salespeople how to develop close relationships with customers—a critical issue, especially with large national accounts. A regional market manager will be interested in teaching salespeople to deal with the complex problems of local customers. Product managers, of course, hope salespeople have expertise in product knowledge, specifications, and applications. Even managers outside the marketing function, such as human resource managers, will have a stake in the sales training process. They know that highly regarded sales training programs enhance the firm's ability to recruit and retain salespeople. A few firms have developed such strong sales training programs that graduates say completing them is like earning a second degree or an MBA.

When determining sales training needs, three issues must be considered:[13]

- *Who should be trained?* (new and/or experienced salespeople?)
- *What should be the primary emphasis in the training program?* (relationship building, product knowledge, company knowledge, customer knowledge, and/or generic selling skills such as time management or presentation skills?)
- *How should the training process be structured?* (on-the-job training and experience versus a formal and more consistent centralized program, field initiatives and participation versus headquarters programs, in-house training versus outside expertise?)

Sales training is an ongoing process. Sales training for new recruits tries to instill in a relatively short time a vast amount of knowledge that has taken skilled sales reps years and years to acquire. Sales training for experienced salespeople may be needed due to new product offerings, changes in market structure, new technologies, competitive activities, and so on, plus a desire to reinforce and upgrade critical selling skills. Although some sales managers think sales training has only one objective—for example, to increase motivation—others identify a variety of objectives.

OBJECTIVES OF SALES TRAINING

Although the specific objectives of sales training may vary from firm to firm, there is some agreement on the broad objectives. Sales training is undertaken to improve relationships with customers, increase productivity, improve morale, lower turnover, and improve selling skills (like better management of time and territory). Exhibit 12.6 summarizes the objectives of sales training programs.

EXHIBIT 12.6 OBJECTIVES OF SALES TRAINING

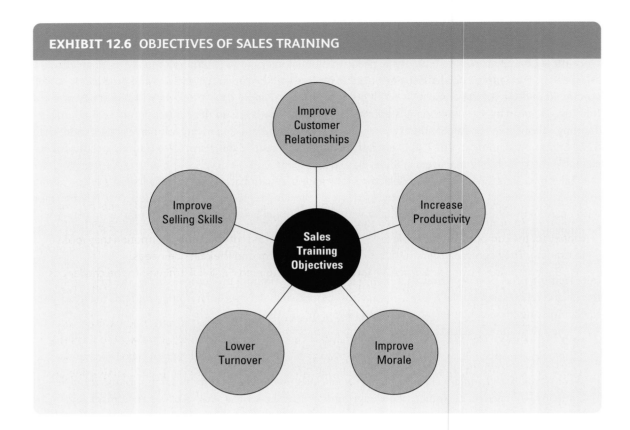

Improve Customer Relationships

As we have discussed, building successful sales relationships is difficult and requires a significant commitment from salespeople and their company. One benefit of effective sales training is continuity in customer relationships. Having the same salesperson call on a given customer for an extended period of time can enhance the relationship between the company and the customer, especially when the salesperson can handle customer questions, objections, and complaints (the topics covered in many sales training programs). Inadequately trained salespeople usually cannot provide these benefits, and customer relations suffer.

Increase Productivity

An important objective of sales training is giving salespeople the skills they need to improve their performance and make a positive contribution to the firm. In a relatively short time, sales training attempts to teach the skills of successful sales force members. The time it takes for a new salesperson to achieve satisfactory productivity is thus shortened considerably. The productivity of sales training receives strong support from companies like Cisco Systems, which credits much of its success to having the best-trained sales force in the industry. That success has been dramatic: Cisco's revenue rose from $18.9 billion in 2003 to $43.2 billion in 2012.[14]

Improve Morale

How does sales training lead to better morale? One objective of sales training is to prepare trainees to perform tasks so their productivity increases as quickly as possible. When sales trainees know what is expected of them, they are less likely to experience frustration that arises from trying to perform a job without adequate preparation. Without training, the salesperson may not be able to answer customers' questions, leading to frustration and lower morale.

Creating the right format for sales training is a very challenging task. Exhibit 12.7 describes how to create an effective training experience, which is not based on motivational hype but rather on delivering specific skills and techniques to enhance the salesperson's ability to be successful in the field.[15]

EXHIBIT 12.7 CREATING A POWER SALES TRAINING EXPERIENCE

Many training professionals will tell you salespeople are the toughest audience. Motivational pep talks and PowerPoint presentations that do not provide real tools *now* will anger salespeople and waste money for the company. Salespeople tend to be independent and critical of the information they receive in training. They demand training that is geared toward them and their unique needs.

Experts suggest two key elements in successful sales training. First, link training to the challenges reps face right now. Second, provide specific tools for them to use. Incorporate forms that enable them to organize information.

Above all, sales training cannot be boring. Inordinate amounts of reading and theory will not work with salespeople. They will turn off the trainer, and the training experience will be wasted from the company's perspective. Keep the agenda open so that issues raised by salespeople can be dealt with at the training session. Telling salespeople you will get back with them will not work. They want the information now.

Lower Turnover

If sales training can lead to improved morale, lower **turnover** should result. Young, inexperienced salespeople are more likely to get discouraged and quit than their experienced counterparts. Turnover can lead to customer problems, since many customers prefer continuity with a particular salesperson. When a salesperson suddenly quits, the customer may transfer business to other suppliers rather than wait for a new representative. Sales training can help mitigate such problems.

The pharmaceutical industry has focused a lot of effort on improving its sales training programs. Industry experts estimate that turnover can cost twice as much as a salesperson's compensation package and cite training as the most significant factor in improving the retention rate of high-performing salespeople.[16]

Improve Selling Skills

Many companies believe that improving basic selling skills can lead to improved performance in the field. As we discussed in chapter 10, time and territory management is a subject of many sales training programs. How much time should be devoted to calls on existing accounts and how much to calls on potential new accounts? How often should each class of account be called on? What is the most effective way of covering the territory to reduce miles driven and time spent? Many sales training programs provide answers to these questions.[17]

DEVELOPING SUCCESSFUL SALES TRAINING PROGRAMS

There is no doubt that sales training is an important function. However, implementing it creates a number of challenges. For example, top management may not be dedicated to sales training or the training program may not be adequately funded. Some salespeople resent the intrusion on their time and resist making the changes suggested by training programs.[18]

This pessimistic view of sales training stems from two problems. First, management too often expects training will be a panacea for all of the company's sales problems. If those problems are not resolved, budget cutting often starts with the sales training program. Sales training is viewed as a cost of doing business rather than an investment that pays future dividends.

The second problem is that too many sales training programs are conducted without any thought of measuring the benefits. Evaluation is difficult, but considering the millions of dollars devoted to sales training, it is essential for management to take the time to develop a cost-effective training program that delivers on specific, measurable objectives.

Analyze Needs

The starting point in creating an effective sales training program is to analyze the needs of the sales force (see Exhibit 12.8). An important first step is to travel with salespeople, observing them and asking what they need to know that will help them perform more effectively. Local sales managers are a useful source of information because they are closest to the salespeople. Other sources include company records on turnover data, performance evaluations, and sales/cost analyses. Attitudinal studies of the sales force are also helpful. On the other hand, sending questionnaires to customers is less useful because they either don't have time to fill them out or are not particularly interested in providing good feedback. The **sales training analysis** should answer three basic questions:

- Where in the organization is training needed?
- What should be the content of the training program?
- Who needs the training?

Determine Objectives

Specific, realistic, and measurable objectives are essential to a sales training program. They may include learning about new products, sales techniques, or procedures. It pays to keep the objectives simple. Management may want a 10 percent sales increase, which then becomes the broad objective of the training program. The specific objective might be to teach sales reps how to call on new accounts, which will help achieve the broad objective.

Develop and Implement the Program

At this point, management must decide whether to develop the training program in-house or hire an outside organization. Small companies often use outside training professionals. Large companies develop most of their own programs, though they may employ outside agencies like our experts at the beginning of each chapter to handle specific training topics.

Outside suppliers should be screened carefully. One sales manager was embarrassed when a company he hired put on an "entertaining song and dance routine" that cost $45,000 but failed to have any lasting effect. Outside sources can be cost effective if they meet the company's objectives.

EXHIBIT 12.8 ANALYZING THE TRAINING NEEDS OF THE SALES FORCE

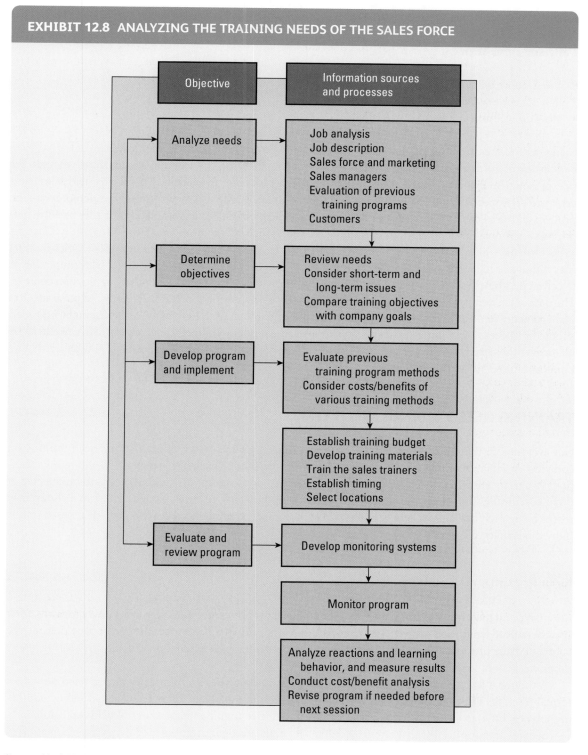

Source: Mark W. Johnston and Greg W. Marshall, *Sales Force Management*, 11th ed. (London: Routledge, 2013).

Evaluate and Review the Program

Designing a measurement system is the next step.

- What do we want to measure?
- When do we want to measure?
- How do we measure the training?

Using tests to measure learning is not difficult, but measuring application in the field is. Whether a salesperson learns to demonstrate a product can be evaluated during the training session. But whether the salesperson demonstrates effectively in front of a customer is harder to evaluate. This is why field sales managers are an important link: They provide follow-up and feedback on how well sales reps demonstrate the product and also coach the reps on how to demonstrate the product. Finally, evaluations of sales performance provide additional proof of the value of training, although such information must be used carefully. Changes in performance, like sales increases, may be due to other factors. To claim they are due solely to sales training may ultimately reflect negatively on the training effort. Since measurement is crucial, the sales trainer needs to collect data before training starts. The needs analysis provides relevant information about program content. The data collection process should provide sales trainers with information that will justify the program. Top management wants to know if the benefits exceed or equal the costs. Keeping top management informed about the success of training programs contributes to overall credibility. Determining what needs to be included in a sales training program often presents some interesting challenges; consider the sales training implications in Ethical Dilemma #2.

TRAINING NEEDS CHANGE WITH TIME

Not everyone in the sales force needs the same training. Certainly newly hired recruits need training on company products and policies. Then, when procedures or products change, everyone should receive additional training. However, if certain sales reps are having a sales slump, the training needs to be directed at them specifically. To include the entire force may create problems. Salespeople who aren't in a slump may resent being included and let others know it. As you can see, training needs vary a great deal based on the individuals involved.

New Recruits

Most large and medium-size companies have programs for training new sales recruits. These programs differ considerably in length and content, however. The differences often reflect variations in company policies, the nature of the selling job, and types of products and services sold. Even within the same industry, sales training programs vary in length, content, and technique.

Although a few companies have no preset time for training sales recruits, most have a fixed period for formal training. The time varies from just a couple of days in the office, followed by actual selling and on-the-job coaching, to as long as two or three years of intensive training in a number of fields and skills.

Second, training needs vary because of differences in the needs and aptitudes of the recruits. Experienced recruits have less need for training than inexperienced recruits, although most large firms require every new hire to go through some formal training. One industrial firm requires a one-week program for experienced recruits and a two- to three-year program for inexperienced recruits.

A final reason the length of training programs varies is company philosophy. Some sales managers believe training for new recruits should be concentrated at the beginning of their career; others think it should be spread over a longer time and include a large dose of learning by doing. Indeed, many companies promote

ETHICAL DILEMMA #2

IS IT FAIR TO MEASURE PERFORMANCE WITHOUT THE PROPER TOOLS?

Beverly Hart is wondering how to solve the problem that confronts her as she looks out the corner office window at Bottom Line Consulting. As head of worldwide marketing for the company, she is responsible for a sales force of 1,000 consultants around the world. Earlier today she received a phone call from the CEO, Sarah Klein, who was upset about a conversation she had yesterday with the president of World Mart, a company with huge potential for new business. Bottom Line had obtained only a small contract for a customer analysis study, but both Klein and Hart had targeted World Mart for future growth. Unfortunately, the president told Klein the research conducted by Bottom Line was unacceptable and it was unlikely the company would be receiving any new business from World Mart. After investigating the situation, Klein found that Bottom Line had made some mistakes in the study and the results were not valid.

Klein told Hart the lead account representative for World Mart, Jeff Blake, should be fired for losing the account due to mistakes on the study. After Klein hung up, Hart gave Blake a call. She asked him what happened and how he had made such blunders. Jeff said that, while he took responsibility for the errors, he felt he had been poorly prepared for the task. He reminded Beverly his instructions were to get new business, any new business, from World Mart. It was understood that Bottom Line needed to get its foot in the door to build new business opportunities with the company.

He went on to say he had received no training in conducting this kind of research. Contributing to the problem was the fact that World Mart had given him a short window to complete the study and told Blake if Bottom Line was unable to do the job, they would find someone who could. Hart knew he was right. The company had been pressuring him to get new business from World Mart but not really given him the tools to get the job done. Indeed, four customers had asked for similar studies in the last two months, but Bottom Line still did not offer training on marketing research methods. On the other hand, Blake had gone ahead and done the study, making mistakes that invalidated the results.

Hart ponders the fact that both Klein and Blake are right. Mistakes were made in the study; however, Blake was never given the training to get the job done. She realizes that Klein will be unhappy with her if she learns that Blake was not given the training he needed.

Questions to Consider

1. What critical management issue does Beverly Hart face as she deals with the current crisis?
2. Did the CEO overreact in telling Hart to fire Jeff Blake?
3. Should Beverly Hart fire Jeff Blake? Why or why not?

lifelong learning. General Electric's many companies deliver training throughout a salesperson's career because GE believes the need to learn never ends.

Experienced Salespeople

After new salespeople are assigned to field positions, they quickly become involved in customer relationships, competitive developments, and other related matters. Over time, their knowledge of competitors and market conditions becomes dated. Even their personal selling styles may become less effective. Sales reps also require refresher or advanced training programs because of changes in company policies and product lines. Few companies halt training after the trainee has completed the basics. As discussed previously, most managers agree that the need to learn is a never-ending process and even the most successful sales rep can benefit from refresher training.

Additional training often occurs when a sales representative is being considered for promotion. In many companies, a promotion means more than moving from sales to district sales manager. It can mean being assigned better customers, transferring to a better territory, moving to a staff position, or being promoted to sales management. Whenever salespeople are assigned new customers or new territories, additional sales training helps them assimilate their new responsibilities.

SALES TRAINING TOPICS

For new trainees, the content of sales training tends to remain constant. Most programs cover product or service knowledge, market/industry orientation, company orientation, and selling skills like time and territory management. Beyond these standard topics is a vast array of subjects. They range from the logical (such as training sales reps how to use the company's new computerized procedures, instructing the sales force how to build relationships, and educating the sales reps in team selling procedures) to some questionable topics, such as training sales reps to modify their presentation based on whether the customer is left-brained or right-brained. Exhibit 12.9 identifies the primary topics covered in sales training programs.

EXHIBIT 12.9 TOPICS IN SALES TRAINING

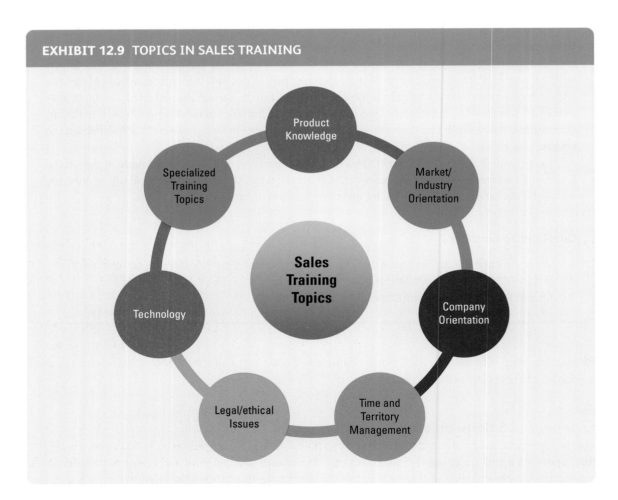

Product Knowledge

Although product knowledge is one of the most important topics, knowing when and how to discuss the subject in a sales call is probably even more important. More time is typically spent on product knowledge than any other subject (although the time spent varies with the product sold).

Companies that produce technical products, such as computer and other technology-related companies, spend more time on product knowledge than do manufacturers of nontechnical products. Hewlett-Packard, Intel, and others spend a great deal of time educating salespeople on their products and services because it is critical that the right product or service be applied to each customer's unique application.

Product knowledge involves knowing not only how the product is made but also how it is used—and, in some cases, how it should not be used. One producer of machine tools gives newly hired sales engineers extensive in-plant exposure to technical and engineering matters. Before field assignment, they spend time in a customer's plant, where they are taught machine setup and operations under realistic conditions.

Product knowledge is not limited to those products the salesperson will eventually sell. Customers often want to know how competitive products compare with each other on price, construction, performance, and compatibility. They expect salespeople to show them how the seller's products can be coordinated with competitive products, as in a computer installation that involves products made by different manufacturers. One manufacturer that supplies paper towels to industrial firms exposes sales trainees to competitive towel dispensers so they will know which dispensers handle their paper towels.

A major objective in training product knowledge is to enable a salesperson to give potential customers the information they need for rational decision making. As we discussed in chapter 7, many benefits accrue to salespeople as they acquire product knowledge:

1. Pride and confidence in product quality.
2. Self-assurance emanating from technical knowledge of product makeup.
3. Communication with customers through the use of the operational vocabulary peculiar to the industry.
4. Understanding of product functioning that allows effective diagnosis of customer problems.[19]

All these benefits improve the customer–salesperson relationship.

Market/Industry Orientation

Sales training in market/industry orientation covers both broad and specific factors. From a broad viewpoint, salespeople need to know how their particular industry fits into the overall economy. Economic fluctuations affect buying behavior, which affects selling techniques. Information about inflationary pressure, for example, may be used to persuade prospective buyers to move their decision dates up. If the sales force is involved in forecasting sales and setting quotas, knowledge of the industry and the economy is essential. From a narrower viewpoint, salespeople must have detailed knowledge about present customers. They need to know their buying policies, patterns, and preferences and the products or services these customers produce. In some cases, salespeople need to be knowledgeable about their customers' customers.

Company Orientation

New salespeople must be aware of company policies that affect their selling activities. Like all new employees, they need to learn the company's policies on such items as salary structure and company benefits. New salespeople learn about company policies and procedures by working in various departments, such as credit, order processing, advertising, sales promotion, and shipping. In addition, salespeople work inside sales for a time before being assigned to a field sales position. They process customer orders, maintain contact with customers (email, phone), and sometimes serve as the company contact for a group of customers.

Time and Territory Management

As we discussed in chapter 10, new and even experienced salespeople can benefit from training in how to manage their time and territories. Management also considers time management a critical issue. Blue Cross Blue Shield instituted Internet-based learning so salespeople could spend more time with their customers. Dan Goettsch, sales training manager, states, "One of the big issues here is the notion that selling time is a very precious commodity. Any time [out of the field] is costly for sales folks."[20]

Legal/Ethical Issues

You learned in chapter 4 that statements (or misstatements) made by salespeople have legal and ethical implications. Lapses in ethical conduct have been known to lead to legal problems. Exhibit 12.10 describes

EXHIBIT 12.10   TRAINING ETHICS IN THE SALES FORCE

The insurance industry has been plagued by deceptive sales practices for years. Indeed, the industry has suffered from a bad reputation, as many salespeople followed unethical (and even illegal) sales techniques. One company, the Liberty Mutual Insurance, has created a number of policies and procedures to help ensure that its sales force behaves in an ethical manner.

One of the policies requires all agents and support staff to take an ethics course taught by agency managers. The sales professionals are given study materials on ethics and take an exam.

As stated in the company's policy statement on ethics, Liberty Mutual wants their salespeople to adhere to the highest ethical standards.

Liberty Mutual's reputation for integrity is tested every day by the way you treat clients. Honesty, fairness and keeping commitments must be hallmarks of the way you do business.

- Sell products and services on their merits. Describe them truthfully and without exaggeration.
- Explain contracts, products, services, and investment opportunities clearly and accurately.
- Ensure that commitments are honored and that all your clients receive the highest quality service.
- Scrupulously follow compliance procedures applicable to your company. When in doubt consult the compliance department of your company or its legal counsel.

Liberty Mutual has also joined the Insurance Marketplace Standards Association, an association of companies that promotes high ethical standards in the sale and service of life insurance, annuities, and long-term care products. As of 2012, only a small percentage of more than 1,000 life insurance companies in the United States had been awarded membership in IMSA, yet they represent the vast majority of all life insurance business. To belong, a company must follow the IMSA code of ethical business conduct. A key component of the IMSA code is training salespeople in the products and services of their company and in techniques for presenting that information in an ethical way. Ethics training and the commitment of the company and industry are essential to making it work successfully.

Source: Adapted from websites for Liberty Mutual (www.libertymutual.com) and Insurance Marketplace Standards Association (www.imsaethics.org), March 2013.

one industry's response to ethical problems. When major insurance companies allowed sales reps to engage in unethical practices (such as selling whole-life insurance policies as annuities), the legal settlements ran into millions of dollars. National organizations like the Insurance Marketplace Standards Association support ongoing mandatory ethics training for salespeople.

Technology

Laptop computers are standard issue for salespeople today. Many companies (for example, Procter & Gamble and IBM) are also creating home offices for their sales forces that eliminate the need to go out to an office at all. With a high-speed network connection, laptop or desktop computer, printer, and cell phone, a salesperson is almost totally self-sufficient. Salespeople use laptops or other mobile devices to plan their call activities, submit orders, send reports, check on inventory, receive both customer and company messages, and present product and service demonstrations. In some cases, the sales rep can access the company's decision support system (DSS) to learn what products have been selling in an area or for a specific customer.

Effective use of technology allows salespeople more face-to-face customer contact time. It also lets them respond much faster to customers. With cell phones, they can be in contact with customers almost all the time. Add to these the direct network connections that companies such as General Motors and Ford have with their suppliers, and it's no wonder that many customers report much better communication with the salespeople who call on them.

Specialized Training Topics

Sales training topics may be very specific. Price objections are common in sales transactions, and sales managers are not pleased if reps offer discounts too quickly. Johnson Controls Inc., a manufacturer of automated control systems based in Atlanta, instituted a training program on price negotiations. The company found that many salespeople were more comfortable reducing market price than building value. One solution was to provide salespeople with detailed financial information to help customers see the added value of Johnson's pricing policies.[21]

SALES TRAINING METHODS

The most common methods of sales training are **on-the-job training** (OJT), individual (one-on-one) instruction, in-house classes, and external seminars. Recognizing that different subjects require different methods, companies use a variety of techniques. Overlap exists within a given method. On-the-job training includes individual instruction (coaching) and in-house classes held at district sales offices. District sales personnel attend external seminars as well.

The design, development, and sale of training materials is big business these days. However, the use of outside sources is not without controversy. Companies question whether they should spend money on external sales training sources. Verizon, like many other companies, has established outsourcing partnerships that provide training programs for all types and levels of employees. It hired an outside training company, Acclivus, to improve the problem-solving skills of its sales and customer service staff. However, the outsourcing partnership did not eliminate the training function at Verizon. The net effect was to enhance the company's training capabilities.[22]

On-the-Job Training

The mere mention of on-the-job training sometimes scares new sales recruits. The thought of learning by doing is psychologically troubling for many people, often due to incorrect perceptions of OJT. On-the-job training is not a "sink or swim" approach in which the trainee is handed an order book and a sales manual and told, "Go out and sell."

On-the-job training is a very effective way of learning for salespeople. Indeed, it is said that three-fourths of all learning at work takes place informally. The Education Development Center identifies five keys for effective on-the-job informal training:

1. *Teaming.* Bringing together people with different skills to address issues.
2. *Meetings.* Setting aside times when employees at different levels and positions can get together and share thoughts on various topics.
3. *Customer interaction.* Including customer feedback as part of the learning process.
4. *Mentoring.* Providing an informal mechanism for new salespeople to interact and learn from more experienced ones.
5. *Peer-to-peer communication.* Creating opportunities for salespeople to interact for mutual learning.[23]

When on-the-job training and coaching occur together, it is called one-on-one training. Observation is an integral part of the process. For managers, helping salespeople reach their full potential means spending time with them one on one. One consultant specializing in sales performance states, "Managers play an essential role in cultivating talent. They need to take on a coaching role." Providing individual feedback can lead to greater salesperson satisfaction. One salesperson sums up the benefits of one-on-one feedback this way: "For my entire sales career, my manager went on calls with me at least two days every month. The [sales] classes never would have had an impact without coaching."[24]

OJT often involves job rotation—assigning new salespeople to different departments where they learn about such things as manufacturing, marketing, shipping, credits and collections, and servicing procedures. After on-the-job training, many sales trainees proceed to formal classroom training.

Internet (Online)

The Internet has revolutionized the delivery of training not just in sales but across the entire organization. Indeed, it's now possible for companies to deliver quality learning experiences to their customers online. Companies find the Internet very effective and very efficient in delivering information. Online training is growing at a very rapid rate and companies are literally spending billions on online training methods. Exhibit 12.11 highlights one way the Internet is being used in sales training.

IBM invests a great deal of time and resources in the delivery of online training to its sales force of over 300,000 worldwide. Its Internet-based training strategy involves delivering small incremental packets of information on products and customers in time to complete specific projects currently on the salesperson's activity list. Online chat groups help salespeople gather even more information and provide feedback on current activities.

Do online training programs work? Can they train salespeople to interact with customers effectively? The answers have not been well documented. As with all methods, salespeople need a great deal of information to do their jobs well. Online training can be very effective in delivering certain kinds of information but will not likely eliminate the need for one-on-one training for salespeople. Even as technology improves and interactive online training effectively simulates the sales environment, the ability for trainers and managers to provide real time, specific feedback to a salesperson highlights the need for companies to implement a wide range of training tools.

EXHIBIT 12.11 INTERNET SALES SIMULATION

Real estate companies are experimenting with a variety of Internet-based sales training tools to improve agent performance. One area receiving a lot of attention is sales simulation programs. Align Mark has created a sales simulation that tests salespeople on various real estate sales tasks.

Using actors and interactive video, the Sales Simulator assesses the agent's ability to deal with customer objections or handle a difficult customer. After watching a video clip, the agent is asked to respond to a menu of possible options. Which option provided the best choice in the situation? Which option was the worst choice? A score is given for each response and the agent performance is evaluated.

Each agent taking the simulation receives a report that gives his or her score as well as an overall assessment of strengths and weaknesses. The report gives the agent feedback in four critical areas:

- Analyzing the customer's needs.
- Active listening.
- Managing the sales process.
- Influencing and closing.

Perhaps most importantly, agents are also given specific tools to improve their performance. Sophisticated, interactive simulations like these are not cheap. Align Mark's Real Estate Sales Simulator starts at $300 per salesperson.

Source: Adapted from AlignMark website (www.alignmark.com).

Classroom Training

For most companies, formal classroom training is an indispensable part of sales training—although very few rely on it exclusively. The Internet now allows much of the information delivered in a classroom to be sent directly to salespeople in the field, yet classroom training still has one major advantage—the opportunity for interaction among sales trainees. Reinforcement and ideas for improvement can come from other sales trainees. Interaction is so important that many companies divide sales trainees into teams for case presentations, which forces them to become actively involved.

Classroom training also has its disadvantages. It is expensive and time consuming. It requires recruits to be brought together and facilities, meals, transportation, recreation, and lodging to be provided for them. In an attempt to cut costs, sales managers sometimes cover too much material in too short a time. This results in less retention of information. Sales managers must avoid the tendency to add more and more material because the additional exposure is often gained at the expense of retention and opportunity for interaction.

Role Playing

As you already know, role playing is an important part of the learning experience. The sales trainee acts out a part, most often a salesperson, in a simulated buying session. The buyer may be either a sales instructor or another trainee. Role playing is widely used to develop selling skills, but it can also test whether the trainee can apply knowledge taught via other methods of instruction. The trainee, the trainer, and other trainees critique the trainee's performance immediately after the role-playing session.

Role-playing critiques can be harsh sometimes if the critique is conducted only in the presence of the sales trainee and only by the instructor. When role playing is handled well, most trainees identify their own strengths and weaknesses without input from other trainees.

MEASURING THE COSTS AND BENEFITS OF SALES TRAINING

Sales training is a time-consuming and very costly activity. Is all this effort worth the cost? Does sales training produce enough benefits to justify its existence? If done properly, sales training can be one of the best ways to increase the satisfaction and performance of salespeople. However, as Exhibit 12.12 discusses, there are many obstacles in the way of a successful training strategy.

EXHIBIT 12.12 SALES TRAINING ROADBLOCKS

Companies spend billions on training, yet they find it difficult to determine the real value of it. Unfortunately, there are many problems associated with the development of effective training programs. Here are nine common problems that inhibit training success in many sales organizations?

1. *Training can't solve the problem.* The real cause of many problems inside the sales force is often something that won't be solved by more training. A training specialist in the Northwest got a call from the head of a manufacturing company asking for training on its new products. Upon investigation the trainer found out the sales force was unhappy because the commission had been cut to 10 percent (it had been 20 percent). The issue was not training but compensation.
2. *Your busy, jaded salespeople are not open to learning new skills.* Salespeople never have enough time. When they are away from their customers, sales performance takes the hit. They want to see results immediately.
3. *Managers don't support the training program.* Not surprisingly, salespeople are reluctant to participate actively in training if management does not support it.
4. *Conflicting methods and philosophies are taught at different sessions.* Everyone should be familiar with previous training so that conflicting information is not presented to the sales force.
5. *The training isn't relevant to the company's pressing needs.* It is crucial to have frontline managers provide at least some input into the content of training programs.
6. *The training format doesn't fit the need.* Many companies fail to match the need with the format. For example, a half-day seminar might work to change salesperson attitudes, but will almost never be successful in providing detailed information about a new product. A common problem is a failure to build in practice time when salespeople can try out what they've learned in the training. If you give them a half-day seminar on new selling skills and then let them go, those skills will probably not work.
7. *E-learning is overused or used in the wrong situations.* While e-learning can be successful, many companies fail to consider whether it is the right way to deliver the training.
8. *There's no follow-up after training.* Companies spend millions on training but don't follow up. The result is that salespeople don't feel compelled to use it.
9. *The trainer can't relate to the sales team.* It is a fact of human nature that if a person is not interesting, people lose interest. A trainer must be able to connect with his or her audience.

Is the measurement process that difficult? After all, if sales training is supposed to lead to better productivity, improved morale, and lower turnover, why not measure the changes in these variables after training has occurred? Some sales managers have done just that. They instituted sales training and shortly afterwards sales increased, so they assumed, sales training was the reason. Right? Wrong!

Unless the research is designed properly, it is hard to say what caused the sales increase. The reason may have been improved economic conditions, competitive activity, environmental changes, and/or seasonal trends, among others. Research must isolate these contaminating effects to identify the benefits directly attributable to training.

Measurement Criteria

If it is important to measure training, what characteristics of sales training should be assessed? Exhibit 12.13 is an evaluation options matrix. A company could single out one method to measure effectiveness, but using several criteria will yield more accurate results. Measuring what participants learned, for example, is not enough because the obtained knowledge may not produce desired behavior changes. Yet the program might be considered a failure if nothing was learned or if what was learned was not helpful. The solution is to specify the objectives and content of the sales training program, the criteria used to evaluate the program, and the design of the research so benefits can be unambiguously determined.

EXHIBIT 12.13 EVALUATION OPTIONS MATRIX

Evaluation level: What is the question?	Information required: What information to collect?	Method: How to collect?
Reaction Did participants respond favorably to the program?	**Attitudinal** Understanding of concepts, ability to use skills	**Evaluation:** 1. Surveys 2. Interviews with participants
Learning Did participants learn concepts or skills?		Before and after tests
Behavior Did participants change their on-the-job behavior?	On-the-job behavior	1. Behavior ratings 2. Before and after critical incident review
Results What personal or organizational results occurred?	Changes in sales, productivity	Cost/benefit analysis

Source: Mark W. Johnston and Greg W. Marshall, *Sales Force Management*, 11th ed. (London: Routledge, 2013).

Measuring Broad Benefits

Broad benefits of sales training include improved morale and lower turnover. Morale can be partially measured by studies of job satisfaction. This approach is feasible with experienced sales personnel. Suppose, for instance, a company measured job satisfaction as part of a needs analysis and found evidence of problems. A follow-up job satisfaction study after the corrective sales training program would determine if morale changed noticeably.

Measuring reactions and learning in sales training is important for both new and experienced personnel. Most companies measure reactions by asking participants to complete an evaluation form either immediately after the session or several weeks later. Enthusiasm may be high right after a session, but sales training effectiveness is much more than a warm feeling.

Measuring what sales trainees learned requires tests. To what extent did they learn the facts, concepts, and techniques covered in the training session? Objective examinations are needed.

Measuring Specific Benefits

Enjoying the program and learning something are not enough. Specific measures are needed to examine behavior and results. The effectiveness of sales training aimed at securing more new customers, for example, is assessed, in part, by examining call reports to see whether more new customers are being called on. Results can also be measured by tracking new-account sales to see whether they have increased. If the specific objective of sales training is to increase the sales of more profitable items, the checking on overall sales profitability is a valid measure of training effectiveness. If reducing customer complaints is the objective, then it is appropriate to consider whether customer complaints do in fact decrease.

The measurement of both specific and broad benefits presumes the sales training program is designed to achieve certain goals. The goals should be established before training begins. When specific objectives have been determined, the best training program can be developed to achieve these objectives. Most training programs have several objectives, so multiple measurements of their effectiveness are a necessary part of evaluating their benefits.

Many sales training evaluation measures are simple, consisting primarily of reactions to the program. Meaningful evaluation measures, such as learning, behavior, and results, are not used often enough, while the weakest or easiest-to-collect measures—staff comments and feedback from supervisors and trainees—are used the most.[25]

EXPERT ADVICE: FOLLOW-UP

After watching the video of Mr. Scannell and reading the chapter, consider the follow questions:

1. What do you think is the most important quality/characteristic to look for in hiring a professional salesperson?
2. Why is turnover a problem in the recruit and selection process?

SUMMARY

This chapter reviewed the recruitment and selection of new salespeople. The issues discussed ranged from who is responsible for these tasks to the impact on selection procedures of federal legislation barring job discrimination. Two factors are primary in determining who is responsible for recruiting and selecting salespeople: (1) the size of the sales force and (2) the kind of selling involved.

After responsibility is allocated, recruitment and selection is a three-step process: (1) job analysis and description, (2) recruitment of a pool of applicants, and (3) selection of the best applicants from the available pool.

The job analysis and description phase includes a detailed examination of the job to determine what activities, tasks, responsibilities, and environmental influences are involved. This analysis may be conducted by someone in the sales management ranks or by a job analysis specialist. That person must prepare a job description that details the findings of the job analysis. The job description is used to develop a statement of job qualifications, which describes the personal traits and abilities an employee should have to perform the tasks involved.

The pool of recruits can come from a number of sources, including (1) people within the company, (2) people in other firms, (3) advertisements, (4) recruiting agencies, (5) educational institutions, and (6) the

Internet. Each source has its own advantages and disadvantages. Some, such as ads, typically produce a large pool. The key question for the sales manager is which source or combination of sources is likely to produce the largest pool of good, qualified recruits.

Once the qualifications necessary to fill a job have been determined and applicants have been recruited, the final task is to determine which applicant best meets the qualifications and has the greatest aptitude for the job. To make this determination, most firms use some or all of the following tools and procedures: (1) applications, (2) face-to-face interviews, (3) reference checks, and (4) intelligence, aptitude, and personality tests. Although most employers find the interview and then the application most helpful, each device seems to perform some functions better than the others do. This may explain why most firms use a combination of selection tools.

Sales training is a varied and ongoing activity that is time consuming and expensive. Most companies engage in some type of sales training. In fact, most sales managers require it for everybody, regardless of their experience. Some common objectives of sales training are to improve customer relations, increase productivity, improve morale, lower turnover, and teach selling skills (like time and territory management).

Sales training programs vary greatly in length. Industry differences account for variations not only in length but also in program content. Company policies, the nature of the selling job, and the types of products and services offered also contribute to differences in time spent and topics covered.

Sales training is very expensive. It's generally considered beneficial, but accurate measurement of the benefits is difficult. It is hard to isolate the effects produced solely by sales training from those that might have been produced by other factors, such as changes in the economy or the nature of competition. Evaluation methods should be designed carefully, and both broad and specific benefits should be measured.

KEY TERMS

job analysis	internal sources	selection procedures	sales training analysis
job qualifications	external sources	personal interviews	on-the-job training (OJT)
job description	employment agencies	turnover	role playing

ROLE PLAY #1

BEFORE YOU BEGIN

Before getting started, please go to the Appendix of chapter 1 to review the profiles of the characters involved in this role play, as well as the tips on preparing a role play. This particular role play requires that you be familiar with the chapter 2 role play.

Characters Involved

Rhonda Reed
Another student in the class, who will role-play himself or herself as a job candidate for the vacant Territory 106 in Rhonda's district at Upland Company.

Setting the Stage

Back in the role play in chapter 2, new hire Bonnie Cairns met with district manager Rhonda Reed to prepare for doing some campus recruiting at Stellar College, which is Bonnie's alma mater. This was necessary because Territory 106 is currently vacant. Rocky Lane, who was the account manager in Territory 106 for 15 months, left a few weeks ago because he came to the conclusion that sales was not the right career track for him. Since then, Rhonda has corresponded with Rocky's most important customers to determine what needs to be done while the territory is vacant. Despite Rocky's decision to leave sales, the customers have told Rhonda that they were mostly happy with Rocky and Upland's service. Rhonda is relieved that the new person hired for Territory 106 will not be inheriting a mess.

The campus interviews Rhonda and Bonnie conducted at Stellar College went very well, and Rhonda has a shortlist of seven candidates she wants to visit within a more formal setting. Below is the general process Upland follows when recruiting from colleges and universities:

1. The district manager (possibly accompanied by an account manager) gets on the list to conduct brief informational interviews (15–20 minutes) with students on campus.
2. Top candidates from the campus visit are called back and invited to interview with the district manager in a more formal setting.
3. Remaining finalists are assigned to spend a "typical day" working with an Upland Company account manager. At the end of the day, the district manager and account manager take the candidate to dinner to debrief the experience and determine if the candidate still holds a strong interest in pursuing a position with Upland.
4. A final interview is then conducted. Each remaining candidate is asked to participate in an impromptu role-play sales call on a client.
5. A hiring decision is made, references are checked, and an offer is made contingent on the candidate passing a physical examination.

With regard to the Territory 106 position, Rhonda is at stage 2 of the process and needs to conduct the first in-depth interview with each of the seven candidates who emerged from the campus visit. An appointment has been set for one candidate.

Rhonda Reed's Role

Before the interview, Rhonda must analyze the job and determine the selection criteria. To do this, follow the process outlined in the chapter. You may exercise some leeway in developing the content for this assignment, but be sure the various criteria seem to be a good fit for sales positions such as those at Upland. Prepare a one- or two-page typed summary of this information. Rhonda will need to review the candidate's résumé again prior to the interview and develop some questions for a structured job interview. She will want to ask good questions to determine whether or not to keep this candidate in the finalist pool. Remember to use good active listening skills and let the candidate do much of the talking.

Job Candidate's Role

The other student involved in this role play will play himself or herself as the actual job candidate. Develop a one- or two-page résumé for yourself targeted toward an account manager job at Upland Company. If your actual résumé does not qualify you for the position, you can fictionalize your qualifications for purposes of this role play. Also, assume you are about to graduate and could start the job in the next month or so. Rhonda can share with you in advance the job description and other relevant information that a candidate would likely have before arriving at an interview. Prepare for the interview by coming up with some good questions to ask that will help you decide whether you want to pursue the position further. Use good active listening skills during the interview.

Assignment

Work together to develop and execute the role play of the job interview. Although interviews of this type are usually 45–60 minutes, here do a shortened version of about 15 minutes. At the end of the interview, leave it that the candidate remains interested and Rhonda will call him or her after completing the other first-round interviews (probably within the next week).

ROLE PLAY #2

BEFORE YOU BEGIN

Before getting started, please go to the Appendix of chapter 1 to review the profiles of the characters involved in this role play, as well as the tips on preparing a role play. In addition, you will need to review the following exhibits and accompanying discussion from chapter 2: Exhibit 2.3 (Success Factors for Salespeople) and Exhibit 2.4 (Sales Job Factors and Selected Associated Activities).

Characters Involved

Bonnie Cairns
Justin Taylor

Setting the Stage

Bonnie has been with the company only a few weeks. During that time, she spent the first full week at the Upland Company's initial sales training program at the home office. This program is a comprehensive introduction to the company, its products, and the knowledge, skill, and other factors necessary for successful relationship selling at Upland.

After returning home from that first week of intensive training, new Upland account managers spend the second week riding with their district manager, calling on customers together. This allows the district manager to reinforce in the field what the new account manager learned in the training class. During the third and fourth weeks with the company, a new Upland account manager is turned over to a mentor within the district, who is another more experienced account manager. In Bonnie's case, her mentor is Justin Taylor. Rhonda assigned Justin to this role because he is interested in eventually moving into management with Upland, and she believes this experience will be good training for him (as well as for Bonnie!).

During the two weeks of mentorship, the trainer doesn't work with the new account manager every day. Justin and Bonnie will make calls together four days during the two weeks, which represents on-the-job training. This is to allow Bonnie to use the other days to begin to get her feet wet calling on a few customers by herself. In addition to the on-the-job training component of these two weeks, Upland also requires the mentor to work with the new account manager during this time period to identify specific success factors that can be practiced and reinforced through role play between the mentor and the trainee. These may be selling activities, knowledge or skill factors, or other factors important to the job. After identifying these factors, the mentor and trainee work together to develop and execute several role plays over the course of the two weeks to allow the new account manager to build confidence with these key success factors.

Bonnie Cairns's Role

Bonnie needs to work with Justin, with Justin taking the lead, to identify two or three specific factors that she can benefit from practicing through role play. From chapter 2, Exhibits 2.3 and 2.4, and the accompanying discussion provide you with some possible factors and activities that can be the focus of this role-play training. Bonnie and Justin will decide on two or three relevant factors or activities, develop a role-play script to demonstrate effective use of these factors or activities, and then execute the role-play training session. In the role play, Bonnie will play herself.

Justin Taylor's Role

As mentioned earlier, in his role as Bonnie's mentor Justin can both contribute to her training and also contribute to his experience as a trainer in preparation for achieving his goal of being promoted to district manager. He wants to do a very good job of putting together this role play, and will work with her to identify two or three specific factors that Bonnie can benefit from practicing through role play. Once the factors are jointly identified and the script jointly developed, Justin will role-play a part that is appropriate to each situation (her buyer, her district manager, or some other appropriate character—these parts can stay the same or change as different success factors are built into the role play). Afterward, Justin should assume his mentor role and provide constructive feedback on how well Bonnie demonstrated the knowledge, skills, or other factors represented by the role play.

Assignment

Work together to develop and execute the role-play dialogue surrounding the issues described above. Limit the overall role play to 12–15 minutes.

DISCUSSION QUESTIONS

1. The sales manager for one of the nation's largest producers of consumer goods has identified eight factors that appear to be related to effective performance. The manager of human resources, who is concerned about high turnover rates among the sales force, would like to use this information to improve the company's recruiting and hiring process. The key factors are:

    Setting priorities
    Initiative and follow-through
    Working effectively with others
    Creativity and innovation
    Thinking and problem solving
    Leadership
    Communication
    Technical mastery

How could these factors become part of the company's recruiting and hiring process? How would you define these factors and determine if applicants for sales positions possess them?

2. What are the advantages of using the Internet to conduct preliminary job interviews?

What problems is a company that uses computer-aided interviewing likely to encounter?

3. College recruiters were discussing some of the students they had interviewed one day. One interviewer described an applicant with excellent credentials as follows: "She looked too feminine, like she would need someone to take care of her, and she was not all that serious about a sales job with us." When asked to explain her comments, the interviewer said, "Under her jacket she wore a flowery blouse with little flowing sleeves and a lace collar." The other recruiter countered, "What do a flowery blouse, flowing sleeves, and a lace collar have to do with performance?" Comment.

4. One expert contends that sales training is not at all complicated. He predicts that, regardless of advances in communication, resources, technology, and training tools, the basic selling skills that trainers teach salespeople will change very little from those that have been successful during the past 50 years. What will change, according to the expert, is how salespeople are trained to use these skills effectively. Do you agree with this prediction?

5. The CEO of the company asks you to justify the 10 percent increase in sales training expenditures for next year. How would you satisfy this request by the CEO?

6. As sales manager for a nationwide electrical products distributor, you are about to roll out a new line of electrical products. What method would you use to train the 500 salespeople in your national sales force on the new products?

MINI-CASE 12.1 RIGHT TIMES UNIFORM

Steven Zhang, regional director of sales for Right Times Uniform Company, is reviewing the résumés and applications and his own notes on three job candidates he interviewed for a vacant sales position in the Salt Lake City area. In a few minutes, Steven will meet with Peggy Phillips, regional sales trainer, and Tony Brooks, district sales manager, to choose whom to hire for the vacancy in Tony's district.

Right Times Uniform provides uniforms to a variety of businesses throughout the country. The professional-looking uniforms allow the businesses' employees to present a consistent, professional appearance to their customers. Like other companies in this industry, Right Times Uniform provides its customers' employees enough uniforms to use for an entire week. At the end of the week, a Right Times Uniform customer service driver picks up the dirty uniforms and leaves clean ones for all employees for the next week.

The sales process for Right Times involves a salesperson visiting a prospect, determining if the prospect is a candidate for Right Times' services, and selling that prospect on the advantages of using Right Times Uniforms. Whether or not a company is a prospect for Right Times depends on the number of employees it has and the importance of their presenting a professional image to the public. The range of customers Right Times Uniforms serves is vast, from Joe's Mechanic Shop with five employees all the way to some of the nicest downtown hotels with over 200 employees.

STEVEN: Let's talk about our final three candidates for this position. I have an application, résumé, and my interview notes for David, Kathy, and Tim. Do we have any more information on these three people?

TONY: No, we don't. We all have the same information. One thing you and Peggy may not know is how these people became aware of this job opening. David is the cousin of Richard, one of the reps in my district working down in Provo. Kathy saw our ad in the local newspaper and Tim found out about the opening from our website. The local newspaper and our company website are the only places where we published the job opening.

STEVEN: I'm worried about Tim as a potential employee. He comes from New Orleans, where a high percentage of the population is Catholic. If he's Catholic, how will he fit into our community here in Salt Lake?

PEGGY: I asked him his religion. He looked sort of uncomfortable about the question but said he has lived in several places around the country and he didn't see any special problems with fitting in here.

TONY: Tim is not the one I'm concerned about. David is the one who indicated on his application that he was convicted of a felony. I asked him and he said there was a DUI on his record from 10 years ago, when he was 20 years old. Richard never said anything about this when he recommended David. Evidently David learned his lesson because he finished college and has several years of good sales experience with an office supplies company. However, do we want a felon on our payroll?

STEVEN: I think David's record and his lack of a repeat incidence in the last 10 years speak for themselves. What about Kathy?

PEGGY: Did you notice that engagement ring on Kathy's finger? She's obviously in the middle of a very big life change and likely will be distracted by that for some time. I asked her when the wedding is and she said in six months. Her fiancé is a software engineer who may or may not be staying in Utah for the long term. His family is in Seattle and we all know there are plenty of job opportunities for people in his line of work there. Plus, Kathy's likely to want to have children soon. I asked her about those plans. She hesitated but finally said that while they want to have children, they haven't set a deadline for that yet. However, she's 33 years old and the clock is ticking. I'm guessing she'll be out on maternity leave sooner rather than later.

STEVEN: We have a lot to consider. What do you say we look at their sales experience and see if we can come to some conclusion?

With that comment, the conversation steered toward the sales experience of the three candidates and their potential to perform the job at hand. After a discussion of about 30 minutes, a decision on whom to offer the job to was made and the meeting ended. One last decision made by the group was that if the person getting the offer didn't take the job, they would try to get another pool of candidates.

Questions

1. Analyze the recruitment and selection process used by Right Times Uniform Company. What was the source of this pool of candidates? What changes, if any, do you recommend to the process?

2. What tests do you recommend the company use to help select its salespeople? Discuss the advantages and disadvantages of such tests.

3. What do you think of some of the questions that were asked of these job candidates? Did the company expose itself to any potential problems by asking them? If so, how?

MINI-CASE 12.2 HOUSE HANDY PRODUCTS

House Handy Products manufactures plastic products and utensils for use in a number of situations. The company produces and sells a vast range of products that can be used in the home (plastic cooking utensils, food storage containers, dish drainers, laundry baskets, etc.), in the garage (garbage cans, workbench and garden tool organizers), and recreationally (coolers, plastic cups, plates and eating utensils, fishing tackle boxes, etc.). The company is extremely innovative and introduces many new products every year. In fact, House Handy's CEO has set the goal to have products introduced in the previous five years account for 65 percent of current-year sales. This goal puts tremendous pressure on the research and development department to design, test, and develop potential new products. It also requires the sales force stay knowledgeable about the new products and work hard to have them stocked by retail partners.

House Handy's products are sold in full-line discount stores, national grocery store chains, and home and garden stores located throughout the United States, Canada, and Puerto Rico. Each representative is responsible for up to 25 retail outlets in his or her territory. Sales reps call on specific department managers (housewares, sporting goods, grocery) in the stores and seek to develop relationships that lead to mutually beneficial results for both the department and House Handy. The relationship-building process includes:

1. Managing the inventory of their products in the store and placing orders when inventory needs replenishing.
2. Troubleshooting any problems (for example, shipping or billing errors) that may occur.
3. Working with the department manager to secure shelf space for the many new products that House Handy introduces every year.
4. Building end-of-aisle and point-of-purchase displays to give the company's products more visibility and enhance the profit potential of House Handy's products for the department.
5. Expediting orders when necessary.
6. Working with store managers when they want to run a promotion that takes their product out of the departments in which it is usually located. For example, at the beginning of spring, during the week before Memorial Day, and around the Fourth of July, coolers are moved to a point-of-purchase display near the entrance of each store.

House Handy's sales force consists of both new recruits and more experienced representatives. About 35 percent of the sales force have two years of experience or less with the company. The company recruits most of its new salespeople from universities around the country. It divides the United States into four regions and identifies 12 universities in each region as target universities. They are chosen based on the strength of their academic programs, the student body's work ethic, and the willingness of graduates to relocate to other areas of the region. The Canadian and Puerto Rican locations follow similar strategies adapted for their specific situations.

New recruits are assigned to a sales territory where they will work for a district manager. District managers typically are responsible for 15 to 20 sales representatives. The company assigns a mentor to each recruit to answer any questions he or she has. Initial training comes in the form of product manuals. Recruits are told, "Walk around the stores and see for yourself what goes on." Training for each new product is also done through product manuals.

Questions

1. What type of training do you recommend that House Handy provide new members of its sales force? How should this training differ from that provided to the company's more experienced sales reps?

2. Discuss the various methods House Handy could use to provide its sales force with ongoing training. What method or methods of training would make the most sense for House Handy's sales force? Justify your response.

3. Suppose House Handy implements a comprehensive training program for not just new recruits but also experienced reps. How can House Handy's VP of sales determine if she is getting any return on the money she invests in training the sales force? What specific items would you recommend she measure to make that determination?

global selling environment

Sales Management

Compensating & Evaluating Salespeople

Selling Processes

Prospecting & Sales Call Planning

Communicating the Sales Message

Salesperson Self-Management

Technology

Understanding Sellers & Buyers

Building Relationships ~ Creating Value

Selecting & Training Salespeople

Salesperson Motivation

Closing & Follow-up

Ethics

Negotiating for Win-Win Solutions

Compensating and Evaluating Salespeople

LEARNING OBJECTIVES

This chapter provides an overview of key issues related to compensating salespeople, including the types of compensation and especially incentive forms of compensation available and when to offer each. It also provides insight into effective salesperson performance evaluation, which should be a process that provides a forum for constructive dialogue between a salesperson and the sales manager, focused on future professional development and performance success. To successfully execute a performance review, sales managers must have a strong working knowledge of different measures of performance that are appropriate to a particular selling situation. Then they must conduct the appraisal in a positive and constructive manner that allows the salesperson to build on current strengths and proficiencies and make performance improvements where warranted.

After reading this chapter, you should be able to:

- Discuss the advantages and limitations of straight salary, straight commission, and combination compensation plans.
- Explain how and why a bonus component to compensation might be used as an incentive.
- Understand the effective use of sales contests, as well as the potential pitfalls of their use.
- Identify key nonfinancial rewards and how and why they might be important.
- Discuss making decisions on the mix and level of compensation.
- Explain the difference between performance and effectiveness.
- Identify objective measures of salesperson performance, both output and input.
- Use ratio analysis as an objective approach to salesperson performance measurement.
- Discuss key issues related to subjective measurement of salesperson performance and the forms that might be used to administer such an evaluation.
- Understand how a sales manager can make the performance review process more productive and valuable for the salesperson.
- Explain the benefits of 360-degree feedback.

EXPERT ADVICE

EXPERT: Anjai ("A.J.") Gandi
              Managing Director of the Sales Practice of the Corporate Executive Board

TOPIC: Rewards.

SUMMARY: Mr. Gandi builds a strong case for the value of salesperson compensation that he calls "pay at risk." By this, he means receiving a significant portion of total compensation that is "at risk" purely based on the salesperson's own performance. Salespeople can't afford to just rest on their laurels — they've got to go out and prove themselves every compensation period. And there aren't really too many jobs with that direct a link between pay and performance, so the financial attractiveness of the sales role is exceptional. He also believes that the career satisfaction aspect of the job is terrific as well because today's sales person is doing far more problem solving and consultative selling than they are doing transactional selling.

NEXT STEPS: Go to the website for *Contemporary Selling* (www.routledge.com/cw/Johnston), watch the chapter 13 video, and then read the chapter. You will find an Expert Advice follow-up at the end of the chapter with questions that connect elements of your learning.

OVERVIEW OF SALESPERSON COMPENSATION AND INCENTIVES

Chapter 11 introduced the concept of rewards. The way the reward structure is implemented in a sales organization is through the compensation plan. Three basic questions drive successful compensation plans:

1. Which compensation method is most appropriate for motivating specific kinds of selling activities in specific selling situations?
2. How much of a salesperson's total compensation should be earned through incentives?
3. What is the best mix of financial and nonfinancial compensation and incentives for motivating the sales force?

In most firms, the total financial compensation paid to salespeople has several components, each of which may be designed to achieve different objectives. The core of sales compensation plans consists of a salary and incentive payments. A salary is a fixed sum of money paid at regular intervals. The amount of salary paid to a given salesperson is usually a function of that salesperson's experience, competence, and time on the job, as well as the sales manager's judgments about the quality of the individual's performance. Salary adjustments are useful to reward salespeople for performing customer relationship-building activities that may not directly result in sales in the short term, such as prospecting for new customers or providing postsale service. They can also help adjust for differences in sales potential across territories.

Many firms that pay their salespeople a salary also offer additional incentive pay to encourage good performance. Incentives may take the form of commissions tied to sales volume or profitability, or bonuses for meeting or exceeding specific performance targets (e.g., meeting quotas for particular products or particular types of customers). Such incentives direct salespeople's efforts toward specific strategic objectives during the year, as well as provide additional rewards for top performers. A commission is a payment based on short-term results, usually a salesperson's dollar or unit sales volume. Since a direct link exists between sales volume and the amount of commission received, commission payments are useful for increasing reps' selling efforts.

A bonus is a payment made at management's discretion for achieving or surpassing some set level of performance. Commissions are typically paid for each sale; in contrast, a bonus is typically not paid until the salesperson surpasses some level of total sales or other aspect of performance. The size of the bonus might be determined by the degree to which the salesperson exceeds the minimum level of performance required to earn it. Thus, bonuses are usually *additional incentives* to motivate salespeople to reach high levels of performance, rather than part of the basic compensation plan. Bonuses are almost never the sole form of compensation. Rather, they are combined with other compensation elements.

Attaining a quota is often the minimum requirement for a salesperson to earn a bonus. Quotas can be based on goals for sales volume, profitability of sales, or various account-servicing activities. To be effective, quotas (like goals) should be specific, measurable, and realistically attainable. Therefore, bonuses can be a reward for attaining or surpassing a predetermined level of performance on any dimensions for which quotas are set.

In addition to these incentives, many firms conduct sales contests to encourage extra effort aimed at specific short-term objectives. For example, a contest might offer additional rewards for salespeople who obtain a specified volume of orders from new customers or who exceed their quotas for a new product during a three-month period. Contest winners might be given additional cash, merchandise, or travel awards.

Finally, a foundation of most compensation plans is a package of employee benefits designed to satisfy the salesperson's basic needs for security. Benefits typically include medical and disability insurance, life insurance, and a retirement plan, among others. The types and amount of benefits in a compensation plan are usually a matter of company policy and apply to all employees. The benefit package a firm offers its salespeople should be comparable to competitors' plans to avoid being at a disadvantage when recruiting new sales talent.

The key forms of financial compensation of salespeople are summarized in Exhibit 13.1.

EXHIBIT 13.1 COMPONENTS AND OBJECTIVES OF FINANCIAL COMPENSATION PLANS

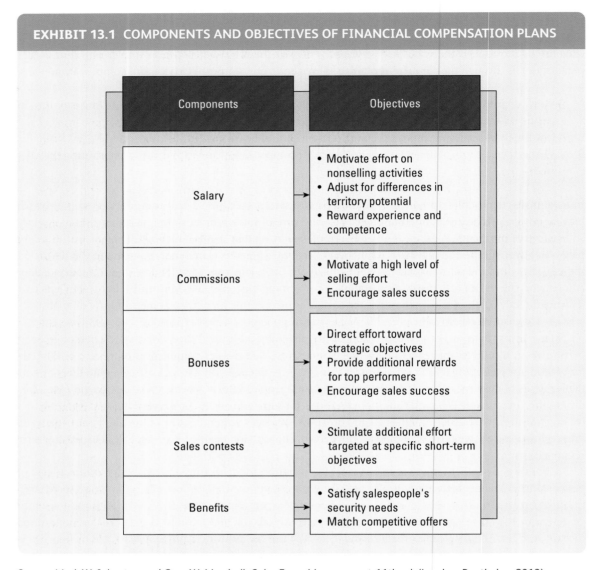

Source: Mark W. Johnston and Greg W. Marshall, *Sales Force Management*, 11th ed. (London: Routledge, 2013).

It is important to know that, beyond financial compensation, a variety of nonfinancial incentives exist. These might take the form of opportunities for promotion or various types of recognition for performance, such as special awards and mention in company newsletters. Nonfinancial incentives will be discussed in more detail later in the chapter.

When it comes to rewards in general, a critical axiom in management is to reward what is expected. Although this may sound intuitively obvious and one might assume it would occur logically as a result of clear goals connected to a well-designed and executed compensation plan, nonetheless it is not uncommon for a disconnect to occur. Sales managers who find that their salespeople's behaviors do not seem to match their organization's goals might ask if their reward systems pay off salespeople for behaviors other than those sought by the firm. This issue, which is exacerbated because of the global scope of contemporary selling, is discussed further in Global Connection.

GLOBAL CONNECTION

THE PERILS OF REWARDING A WHILE HOPING FOR B

Steven Kerr coined the phrase "rewarding A while hoping for B" way back in 1975 in a now classic article in the *Academy of Management Review.* His premise was this: "Very frequently, organizations establish reward systems that pay off one behavior even though the rewarder hopes dearly for some other behavior." This concept has strong application in sales force compensation plans, especially in today's complex global selling environment.

Sales managers who step back, ponder the vastness of their global sales force, and wonder why their salespeople's behaviors do not seem to match their organization's goals might ask if their reward systems pay off salespeople for behaviors other than those sought by the firm. In the past, rewarding salespeople was easier. The focus was on individual salespeople approaching customers on a transaction-to-transaction basis. The focus today is on not just the salesperson but the whole organization working together toward developing long-term customer relationships. Do straight commission plans make sense in this environment? Not likely, since they motivate individual sales efforts, not teamwork.

Take hypothetical salesperson Chris, who is the senior representative on a sales team responsible for his firm's business in the Asia-Pacific Rim. To achieve goals that yield desired results, Chris often has to rely in part on the performance of teammates back at the home country operation in the U.K. who represent other functional areas of the firm. With this arrangement, unlike many salespeople of the past, she cannot personally and directly control much of the customer relationship and selling process. Chris can marshal internal organizational resources and apply them to the relationship-building process in her region and can certainly serve as a "point person" for managing those relationships, but she *cannot* directly control the actions of the whole global team. Clearly, in such a situation standard compensation and incentive systems are inadequate.

Firms cannot expect salespeople to focus on operating effectively within a global team or on securing, building, and maintaining long-term relationships with profitable customers across the vast diversity of global customers if the reward system doesn't recognize the inherent differences and challenges and compensate them for the necessary adaptive behaviors. That is, in the context of Steven Kerr's original premise, today "hoping for B" should be matched by "rewarding B." In the global selling environment, incentives must be rethought and performance appraisal instruments refashioned to reflect the goals and behavior required for success today.

Steven Kerr had it right in 1975: "For an organization to act upon its members, the formal reward system should positively reinforce desired behaviors, not constitute an obstacle to be overcome."

Questions to Consider

1. What are the most important things a sales manager can do to consistently avoid subjecting salespeople to "rewarding A while hoping for B"?
2. Put yourself into the shoes of a salesperson for whom rewards do not match expectations. In what ways do you believe this disconnect would impact how you perform in your job? That is, what problems would it create for you?

Kerr's original article was updated and republished as follows: Steven Kerr, "On the Folly of Rewarding A, While Hoping for B," *Academy of Management Executive* 9 (Issue 1, 1995), pp. 7–14.

STRAIGHT SALARY, STRAIGHT COMMISSION, AND COMBINATION PLANS

Three primary methods of compensating salespeople are (1) straight salary, (2) straight commission, and (3) a combination of base salary plus incentive pay in the form of commissions, bonuses, or both. In recent years, the steady trend has been away from both straight salary and straight commission plans toward combination plans. Today, combination plans are by far the most common form of compensation.

In essence, managers seek to create a "pay for performance" plan that uses both salary and incentive programs to maximize salespeople's performance. Unfortunately, creating such programs is very complex, and companies often choose a program based on convenience or cost effectiveness rather than actual benefits to the company.[1] There is much variety in preferences for rewards among salespeople. And each approach has clear positives and negatives. Exhibit 13.2 highlights the three main compensation approaches, along with advantages and disadvantages of each.

EXHIBIT 13.2 COMPENSATION METHODS FOR SALESPEOPLE

Compensation Method	Especially Useful	Advantages	Disadvantages
Straight Salary	When compensating new sales reps; when firm moves into new sales territories that require developmental work; when sale reps must perform many nonselling activities	Provides sales rep with maximum security; gives sales manager more control over sales reps; is easy to administer; yields more predictable selling expenses	Provides no incentive; necessitates closer supervision of sale reps' activities; during sales declines, selling expenses remain at same level
Straight Commission	When highly aggressive selling is required; when nonselling tasks are minimized; when company cannot closely control sales force activities	Provides maximum incentive; by increasing commission rate, sales managers can encourage reps to sell certain items; selling expenses relate directly to selling resources	Sales reps have little financial security; sales manager has minimum control over sales force; may cause reps to provide inadequate service to smaller accounts; selling costs are less predictable
Combination	When sales territories have relatively similar sales potential; when firm wishes to provide incentive but still control sales force activities	Provides certain level of financial security; provides some incentive; selling expenses fluctuate with sales revenue; sales manager has some control over reps' nonselling activities	Selling expenses are less predictable; may be difficult to administer

Source: Mark W. Johnston and Greg W. Marshall, *Sales Force Management*, 11th ed. (London: Routledge, 2013).

Whether base salary is combined with commission payments or bonuses, managers must answer several questions when designing effective combination compensation plans. (1) What is the appropriate size of the incentive relative to the base salary? (2) Should a ceiling be imposed on incentive earnings? (3) When should the salesperson be credited with a sale? (4) Should team incentives be used? If so, how should they be allocated among members of a sales team? (5) How often should the salesperson receive incentive payments? Each of these issues will now be considered in detail.

Proportion of Incentive Pay to Total Compensation. What proportion of total compensation should be incentive pay? The sales manager's decision should be based in large measure on the degree of relationship selling involved in the job. When the firm's primary selling approaches relate directly to short-term sales (such as increasing dollar or unit sales volume, or profitability), a large incentive component should be offered. When customer service and other nonsales objectives are deemed more important, the major emphasis should be on the base salary component of the plan. This gives management more control over rewarding the sales force's relationship-selling activities.

When the salesperson's selling skill is the key to sales success, the incentive portion should be relatively large. However, when the product has been presold through advertising and the salesperson is largely an order taker, or when the sales job involves a large proportion of missionary or customer service work, the incentive component should be relatively small.

If a particular combination plan is not very effective at motivating salespeople, the incentive portion is probably too small to generate much interest. Companies are always challenged to hire and retain the best salespeople. One approach is to open up the incentive component to negotiation on an individual basis. Salespeople who seek greater security can focus on more fixed compensation (salary); risk takers can opt for the potential to earn even higher total compensation by placing more of their compensation in incentive-based rewards.[2] Such individualized approaches must allow a salesperson to change his or her compensation allocation periodically, perhaps annually.

Incentive Ceilings. Should there be a ceiling or cap on incentive earnings to ensure top salespeople do not earn substantially more money than other employees? This issue is dealt with in very different ways across companies and industries. Strong arguments can be made on both sides. Part of the difference in how different firms handle this issue seems to reflect variation in average compensation levels. Firms in relatively low-paying industries are more likely to impose caps than those in higher-paying fields.

One argument in favor of ceilings is that they ensure top salespeople will not earn so much that other employees in the firm (sometimes even managers) suffer resentment and low morale. Ceilings also protect against windfalls—such as increased sales due to the introduction of successful new products—where a salesperson's earnings might become very large without corresponding effort. Finally, ceilings make a firm's maximum potential sales compensation expense more predictable and controllable.

A strong counterargument can be made, however, that ceilings ultimately reduce motivation and dampen the sales force's enthusiasm. Also, some salespeople may reach the earnings maximum early and be inclined to take it easy for the rest of the year.

The issue of incentive ceilings has become a growing problem in contemporary selling, especially in a team-selling environment. As team selling brings individuals from around the company to help with a customer, the question becomes how much the sales rep should make in a sale resulting from the efforts of many individuals. This problem gets worse as the size of each sale grows larger and is especially relevant with key accounts.

Another problem with incentive ceilings occurs when the customer is a global firm. How much should the sales rep who is servicing the customer's headquarters in his or her territory be compensated for a sale in another part of the world? The solution that many companies have chosen is capping incentive compensation.[3]

Some desired effects of ceilings can be accomplished without arbitrary limits on the sales force's motivation if management pretests any new or revised compensation plan before implementing it. Sales managers can do this by analyzing the sales performance records of selected reps to see how they would have come out under the proposed compensation system. Particular attention should be given to the compensation that the best and poorest performers would have earned to ensure that the plan is both fair and reasonable.

When Is a Sale a Sale? When incentives are based on sales volume or other sales-related aspects of performance, the precise meaning of a *sale* should be defined to avoid confusion and irritation. Most incentive plans credit a salesperson with a sale when the order is accepted by the company, less any returns and allowances. Occasionally, though, it makes good sense to credit the salesperson with a sale only after the goods have been shipped or payment has been received from the customer. This is particularly true when the time between receipt of an order and shipment of the goods is long and the company wants its salespeople to maintain close contact with customers to prevent cancellations and other problems. As a compromise, some plans credit salespeople with half a sale when the order is received and the other half when payment is made.

Team versus Individual Incentives. The increasing use of cross-functional teams to win new customers and service major accounts raises some important questions about the kinds of incentives to include in a combination compensation plan. Should incentives be tied to the overall performance of the entire team, should separate incentives be keyed to the individual performance of each team member, or both? If both group and individual incentives are used, which should be given greater weight? Sales managers must address these questions when designing team-based incentives.

When Should a Salesperson Receive Incentive Payments? One survey of over 500 compensation plans found that 21 percent paid salespeople incentive earnings on an annual basis, 3 percent paid semiannually, 24 percent paid quarterly, and 52 percent made monthly payments. In general, plans offering salary plus commission were more likely to involve monthly incentive payments, while salary plus bonus plans more often made incentive payments on a quarterly or annual schedule.

Shorter intervals between performance and the receipt of rewards increase the motivating power of the plan. However, short intervals add to the computation required, increase administrative expenses, and may make the absolute amount of money received appear so small salespeople are not very impressed with their rewards. Quarterly incentive payments often are an effective compromise.

OTHER TYPES OF COMPENSATION

Sales Contests

Sales contests are short-term incentive programs designed to motivate sales reps to accomplish specific sales objectives. Although contests should not be considered part of a firm's ongoing compensation plan, they offer salespeople both financial and nonfinancial rewards. Contest winners often receive prizes in cash, merchandise, or travel. They also receive recognition and a sense of accomplishment.

Successful contests require the following:

- Clearly defined, specific objectives.
- An exciting theme.
- Reasonable probability of rewards for all salespeople.
- Attractive rewards.
- Promotion of the event by the company and effective follow-through.[4]

Although many sales managers believe contests motivate special efforts from salespeople, contests can cause a few problems—particularly if they are poorly designed or implemented.

Some critics argue that contests designed to stimulate sales volume may produce fleeting results with no lasting improvement in market share. Salespeople may "borrow" sales from before and/or after the contest to increase their volume during the contest. That is, they may hold back orders before the contest and rush orders that would normally not be placed until after it. As a result, customers may be overstocked, causing sales volume to fall off for some time after the contest ends.

Contests may also hurt the cohesiveness and morale of the sales force, especially when they make individual reps compete against each other for rewards and when the number of rewards is limited.

Finally, some firms use sales contests to cover up faulty compensation plans. Salespeople should not have to be compensated a second time for what they are already being paid to do. Contests should be used only on a short-term basis to motivate special efforts beyond the normal performance expected of the sales force. If a firm has to conduct frequent contests to maintain acceptable sales performance, it should reexamine its entire compensation and incentive program.

Expense Accounts

Expense items incurred by sales reps in the field—travel, lodging, meals, and entertaining customers—can be substantial. Although field selling expenses vary across industries and types of sales jobs, nearly $16,000 per year is the average for a salesperson, and the amount may be much higher.[5] The growing trend of creating home offices for salespeople has increased expenses related to technology (laptops, tablets, smartphones, teleconferencing) but reduced some travel expenses. Expense reimbursement plans, or **expense accounts**, range from unlimited reimbursement for all "reasonable and allowable" expenses to plans where salespeople must pay all expenses out of their total compensation. Obviously, an expense account enhances a salesperson's overall compensation.

When deciding which form of expense reimbursement to use, sales managers must make trade-offs between tight control aimed at holding down total expenses and the financial well-being—and subsequent motivation level—of salespeople. Some expense items (such as entertainment expenses, club dues, and the costs of personal services while the salesperson is away from home) can be considered either legitimate business expenses that should be reimbursed by the company or personal expenses that the rep should pay. Company policies and reimbursement plans that treat such costs as business expenses increase the salesperson's total financial compensation but also increase the firm's total selling costs.

Nonfinancial Rewards

Two types of rewards that are nonfinancial in nature are opportunities for advancement and recognition programs.

Opportunities for Advancement. It is a mistake to think that a firm's sales force compensation plan is the only way to improve sales performance. In fact, most sales managers consider opportunities for promotion and advancement second only to financial incentives as effective sales force motivators. This is particularly true for young, well-educated salespeople, who tend to view their jobs as stepping stones to top management. One common career path is from salesperson to district sales manager to top sales management. A rep that has been with a firm for several years without making it into sales management may start to believe such a promotion will never happen. He or she may begin to concentrate solely on financial rewards or lose motivation and not work as hard at the job.

To overcome this problem, some firms have instituted two career paths for salespeople. One leads to management, the other to more advanced positions within the sales force. The latter usually involves responsibility for dealing with key accounts or leading sales teams. Even if a salesperson doesn't move into management, he or she can still work toward a more prestigious and lucrative position within the sales force. To make advanced sales positions more attractive as promotions, many firms provide extra perquisites (perks) including higher compensation, a better car, and perhaps a nicer office.

Recognition Programs. Like contests, effective recognition programs should offer everyone in the sales force a reasonable chance of winning. But if everyone achieves recognition, the program is likely to lose some of its appeal because the winners feel no special sense of accomplishment. Consequently, effective programs often recognize the best performers across several dimensions. For example, winners might include reps with the highest sales volume for the year, the biggest percentage increase in sales, the biggest dollar increase, the highest number of new customers, the largest sales per account, and the best customer retention record.

Recognition is an attractive reward because it makes a salesperson's peers and superiors aware of the outstanding performance. Communicating the winner's achievements through recognition at a sales meeting, publicity in the local press, company website postings announcements in the company newsletter, and other ways is an essential part of a good recognition program. Firms typically give special awards that have low monetary but high symbolic value, such as trophies, plaques, or rings. Finally, as Exhibit 13.3 points out, objectivity and good taste are important ingredients of recognition programs (as they are for contests and other incentives).

EXHIBIT 13.3 GUIDELINES FOR EFFECTIVE FORMAL RECOGNITION PROGRAMS

Regardless of its size or cost, any recognition program should incorporate the following features:

- The program must be strictly performance-based, with no room for subjective judgments. If people suspect that it is in any way a personality contest, the program will not work. The winners should be clear to anyone looking at the data.
- It should be balanced. The program should not be so difficult that only a few can hope to win or so easy that just about everyone does. In the first case, people will not try; in the second, the program will be meaningless.
- A ceremony should be involved. If rings are casually passed out or plaques sent through the mail, a lot of the glamor of the program will be lost.
- The program must be in good taste. If not, it will be subject to ridicule and, rather than motivate people, it will leave them uninspired. No one wants to be part of a recognition program that is condescending or tacky. The program should make people feel good about being part of the company.
- There must be adequate publicity. In some cases, sales managers do such a poor job of explaining a program or promoting it to their own salespeople that no one seems to understand or care about it. Prominent mention of the program on the company website and in company publications is the first step to overcoming this handicap.

Source: Mark W. Johnston and Greg W. Marshall, *Sales Force Management*, 11th ed. (London: Routledge, 2013).

DECIDING ON THE MIX AND LEVEL OF COMPENSATION

Not all salespeople find the same kinds of rewards equally attractive. Needs and preferences vary depending on personalities, demographic characteristics, and lifestyles. No single reward—including money—is likely to motivate all of a firm's salespeople. Similarly, a mix of rewards that motivates a sales force at one time may lose its appeal as the members' personal circumstances and needs change and as new salespeople are hired. In view of this, a wise first step in designing a sales compensation and incentive package is to determine the reps' current preferences for various rewards.[6]

The decision about how much total compensation (base pay plus any incentives) a salesperson may earn is crucial in designing an effective motivation program. The starting point for this decision is to determine the gross amount of compensation necessary to attract, retain, and motivate salespeople who can manage the firm's customer relationships. This also depends on the specific type of sales job in question, the size of the firm and the sales force, and the resources available to the firm.

Chapter 2 introduced several types of sales jobs, and it is important to note that average total compensation varies substantially across them. In general, more complex and demanding sales jobs, which require salespeople with special qualifications, offer higher compensation than more routine sales jobs. To compete for the best talent, a firm should determine how much total compensation other firms in its industry or related ones provide people in similar jobs. Then the firm can decide whether to compensate its salespeople an average or above average amount relative to these other firms. Few companies consciously pay below average (although some do so without realizing it) because below-average compensation generally cannot attract selling talent.

The decision about whether to offer average or premium total compensation depends in part on the size of the firm and its sales force. Large firms with good reputations in their industries and large sales forces generally offer only average total compensation. Firms like Intel and Cisco can attract sales talent because of their reputation in the marketplace and because they are big enough to offer advancement into management. Such firms can hire younger people (often just out of school) as sales trainees and put them through an extensive training program. This allows them to provide relatively low total compensation because they do not have to pay a market premium to attract older, more experienced salespeople.

In contrast, smaller firms often cannot afford extensive training programs. They may have to offer above-average compensation to attract experienced sales reps from other firms.

Dangers of Paying Salespeople Too Much

Some firms, regardless of their size or position in their industries, offer their salespeople opportunities to make very large amounts of money. The rationale for such high compensation is that it will attract the best talent and motivate sales reps to continue working for higher and higher sales volumes. This leads some sales managers to think there's no such thing as paying salespeople too much, since in their view compensation relates directly to volume of sales.

Unfortunately, overpaying salespeople relative to what other firms pay for similar jobs and relative to what other employees in the same firm are paid for nonsales jobs can cause major problems. For one thing, compensation is usually the largest element of a firm's selling costs, so overpaying salespeople increases selling costs and reduces profits. Also, it can cause resentment and low morale among the firm's other employees and executives when salespeople earn more money than even top management. It becomes virtually impossible to promote good salespeople into managerial positions because of the financial sacrifice they would have to make.

Finally, it is not clear that offering unlimited opportunities to earn higher pay is always an effective way to motivate salespeople to continually increase the selling effort. At some compensation level, the next dollar earned would likely show diminishing returns in terms of motivation.

Dangers of Paying Salespeople Too Little

Overpaying salespeople can cause problems, but it is critically important not to underpay them. Holding down sales compensation may appear to be a convenient way to hold down selling costs and enhance profits, but this is usually not true in the *long run*. When buying talent in the labor market, a company tends to get what it pays for. If poor salespeople are hired at low pay, poor performance will almost surely result. If good salespeople are hired at low pay, the firm is likely to have high turnover, with the resulting higher costs for recruiting and training replacements and lost sales.

In the high-flying days of the initial e-commerce boom of the late 1990s, many technology companies offered low salaries but stock options that promised salespeople (and everyone else in the firm) great wealth when the options were cashed in later. However, as the technology sector fell on more difficult economic times, the value of stock options diminished to the point where many technology companies have gone back to financial compensation as the primary motivator.[7]

This raises a question of cause and effect. Are firms more successful when they create the opportunity for a big payday that does not always happen or when they pay people what they are worth plus an incentive for outstanding performance? Paying what it takes to attract and keep a competent sales force seems a more likely path to high performance in contemporary selling than being overly creative with the latest financial gimmicks designed to recruit but not necessarily retain the best people.

The overall importance of management having a stake in ensuring that the overall compensation system is fair and equitable is illustrated in a poignant way in Ethical Dilemma #1.

EVALUATING SALESPERSON PERFORMANCE

Performance versus Effectiveness

The process of evaluating the performance of salespeople is very important. A key issue in this process is the distinction among the concepts of behavior, performance, and effectiveness.[8] Although role perceptions, aptitude, skill level, and motivation level are directly linked to performance (as discussed in chapter 11), they are directly linked to behavior as well.

Behavior refers to what salespeople do—the tasks on which they expend effort while working. These tasks might include calling on customers, writing orders, preparing sales presentations, sending follow-up communications, and the like. These are the sales activities discussed in chapter 2.

Think of **performance** as behavior evaluated in terms of its contribution to the goals of the organization. In other words, performance reflects whether a salesperson's behavior is good or bad, appropriate or inappropriate, in light of the organization's goals and objectives. Note that behavior and performance are both influenced by relevant sales activities, which depend on the types of sales jobs in question.

Before we discuss salesperson evaluation further, let's also distinguish between performance and effectiveness. By definition, **effectiveness** refers to some summary index of organizational outcomes for which an individual is at least partly responsible. Examples include sales volume, market share, profitability of sales, and customer retention rate. The crucial distinction between performance and effectiveness is that the latter does not refer to behavior directly. Rather, it is a function of additional factors not under the individual salesperson's control, including, for example, top management policies, sales potential or difficulty of a territory, and actions of competitors.

It is generally agreed that salespeople should be evaluated solely on those phases of sales performance over which they exercise control and should not be held responsible for factors beyond their control. If a company's method of measuring salesperson performance is to result in valid comparisons, yardsticks for objective or subjective evaluation must distinguish between factors within a salesperson's control versus those outside his or her control.

Quotas, which you learned about earlier in the chapter, are a critical benchmark on which salesperson performance evaluations are based. For example, percentage of quota attained should be an acceptable measure of performance because quotas supposedly consider variations in environmental factors across territories. True, a comparison of salespeople's percentage of quota attained is a better measure of their performance than a comparison that simply looks at each rep's level of absolute sales or market share— assuming the quotas were done well. However, that is a big assumption. Sometimes quotas are arbitrary and not based on an objective assessment of all the factors that facilitate or constrain a salesperson's ability to make a sale. This is especially true if quota development relies too heavily on historical trends and not enough on emerging trends in a given sales territory.

ETHICAL DILEMMA #1

WHAT'S FAIR IS FAIR

Jack Trimble (vice president of sales for New World Technologies) is hesitating. He knows he has to make the call, but he's unsure what to tell Lupe Gonzalez, a veteran salesperson at New World. Lupe has just had the most successful year of her career. Indeed, she got the largest order of anyone in the history of the company. For two years she had been calling on Lockwood Jones Industries, one of the largest military contractors in the world, with very limited success. Although the company had placed small orders for a few products, Lupe had been unable to get a large order.

Recently, however, Lockwood Jones was awarded a huge contract from the Pentagon for a new jet fighter. The company's vice president for purchasing told Lupe it was going to make New World the primary supplier of several key components. He also mentioned that New World was chosen because it has the extra capacity to handle the contract—the biggest single contract ever received by New World. Lupe believes her hard work in cultivating the relationship with Lockwood Jones has paid off big for New World, and she's expecting a substantial incentive reward.

Although Jack is thrilled with Lupe's success and knows she will very likely win "salesperson of the year," he is also faced with a difficult problem. While the sales force is paid a salary (which averages nearly $100,000 per person across the entire sales force), every year a bonus is awarded based on hitting sales targets. The bonus uses a pool of money set aside at the beginning of the year by upper management. This process was created to help management budget for expenses in any given year. The size of the bonus pool is announced at the beginning of each year and all the reps know they are working toward a piece of it.

In the 20 years of the company's existence, this process has worked well. New World has experienced steady growth and everyone in the company looks forward to the bonus at the end of the year. However, Lupe's success in landing the big order from Lockwood Jones has thrown the bonus system into chaos! Based on the existing formula for calculating bonuses, Lupe's share would equal 90 percent of the total bonus pool, or $450,000. No one anticipated the size of the order from Lockwood Jones, and Jack is faced with an incentive system that does not take into account the implications of such success.

The company has 10 salespeople, including Lupe. All of them managed to hit their sales target for the year. While Jack intended to raise the bonus pool by 10 percent to accommodate everyone's success, he knows it is impossible to adjust the pool enough to award Lupe the full amount she expects. In addition, although Lupe has worked hard, there is a sense that she was simply in the right place at the right time. Finally, Jack believes the rest of the sales force would react very negatively to Lupe receiving such a large bonus.

On the one hand, Lupe has won the largest single contract in the history of the company and on paper earned a huge bonus based on the existing bonus pool formula. On the other hand, the bonus pool system will not accommodate such a large payout to one person. In addition, is it fair to give Lupe the full amount when she has benefited in large part because the company simply had excess capacity?

Questions to Consider

1. What should Jack do to resolve this situation? How should he explain it to Lupe, the rest of the sales force, and his superiors?
2. If you were Lupe, how would you react if you did not receive the full expected amount?

Even when quotas are done well, the measure "percentage of quota attained" still omits much about a salesperson's performance. For one thing, it ignores the profitability of sales. Sales reps can be compared with respect to profitability, or the return they produce on the assets under their control. It is difficult to establish quotas that accurately consider the many factors affecting the sales a rep should be able to produce in a territory, but determining the appropriate standards of profitability for each territory is even more difficult.

Even if good sales and profit standards could be developed, the problem of evaluating salespeople would not be solved because neither measure incorporates activities that may have no short-term payout but still have substantial consequences to the firm in the long run. These include the time devoted to laying the groundwork for a long-term client relationship, particularly when developing a potentially large account. Other activities that often go unmeasured are building long-term goodwill for the company and developing a detailed understanding of the capabilities of the products being sold. Thus, other measures beyond sales and profits are needed to evaluate salesperson performance more directly.

These other performance measures fall into two broad categories: (1) objective measures and (2) subjective measures.[9] **Objective measures** reflect statistics the sales manager can gather from the firm's internal data. These measures are best used when they reflect elements of the sales process. **Subjective measures** typically rely on personal evaluations by someone inside the organization, usually the salesperson's immediate supervisor, of how he or she is doing. Subjective measures are generally gathered via direct observation of the salesperson by the manager but may involve input from customers or other sources.

OBJECTIVE MEASURES OF PERFORMANCE

Objective measures fall into three major categories: (1) output measures, (2) input measures, and (3) ratios of output and/or input measures. Exhibit 13.4 lists some of the more common output and input measures.

The use of outputs, inputs, and ratios to measure salesperson performance is a recognition of the nature of the overall selling process. As you have learned, some sales processes, especially those that contribute to securing, building, and maintaining long-term relationships with profitable customers, can take months or years. Within the selling process, salespeople engage in activities with (or in pursuit of) the prospect or buyer. The manager can measure those activities and compare them with results for each stage. By examining this performance evidence, the manager can pinpoint areas for improvement by each salesperson or identify changes needed in the sales strategy to align it with how buyers want to buy.

Output measures show the results of the efforts expended by the salesperson. They include a variety of information about orders and various account measures. Many objective measures of performance evaluation focus on the efforts sales reps expend rather than the results of those efforts. Evaluating these efforts requires **input measures** of performance. Input measures include various aspects of calls, time and time utilization, expenses, and nonselling activities.

Input measures are important for two key reasons. First, efforts or desirable behaviors are much more directly controllable than results in the short term. If a rep's sales fall short of quota, the problem may lie with the person, the quota, or a change in the environment. On the other hand, if the number of calls a salesperson makes falls short of the target, it is clear that a majority of the problem lies with the individual.[10]

Second, in selling there is often a time lag between inputs and outputs. A particularly large sale may be the result of several years of effort. Thus, focusing on the efforts (behaviors) themselves lets the sales manager evaluate and coach the salesperson during the selling process into making changes that can improve the output (results).

EXHIBIT 13.4 COMMON OUTPUT AND INPUT MEASURES USED TO EVALUATE SALESPEOPLE

Output Measures	Input Measures
Orders • Number of orders • Average size of orders • Number of canceled orders **Accounts** • Number of active accounts • Number of new accounts • Number of lost accounts • Number of overdue accounts • Number of prospective accounts	**Calls** • Total number of calls • Number of planned calls • Number of unplanned calls **Time and time utilization** • Days worked • Calls per day (call rate) • Selling time versus nonselling time **Expenses** • Total • By type • As a percentage of sales • As a percentage of quota **Nonselling activities** • Letters to prospects • Phone calls to prospects • Number of formal proposals developed • Advertising displays set up • Number of meetings held with distributors/dealers • Number of training sessions held with distributor/dealer personnel • Number of calls on distributor/dealer customers • Number of service calls made • Number of overdue accounts collected

Source: Mark W. Johnston and Greg W. Marshall, *Sales Force Management*, 11th ed. (London: Routledge, 2013).

Ratio Measures

Just as a focus on outputs other than straight sales volume and profit can provide useful information on how salespeople are performing, so can analysis of input factors. Combining the various outputs and/or inputs in selected ways, typically in various **ratio measures**, can yield further insights.[11] Exhibit 13.5 lists some of the ratios commonly used to evaluate salespeople. They are grouped under expense ratios, account development and servicing ratios, and call activity and/or productivity ratios.

SUBJECTIVE MEASURES OF PERFORMANCE

A useful distinction exists between the quantitative nature of objective measures of performance just discussed and the qualitative nature of the subjective performance measures discussed in this section. Quantitative measures focus on the outputs and inputs of what salespeople do; qualitative measures reflect behavioral or process aspects of what they do and how well they do it. This difference in what is being measured leads to marked differences in how objective and subjective measurements are taken and how they are used.

EXHIBIT 13.5 COMMON RATIOS USED TO EVAULATE SALESPEOPLE

Expense Ratios

- Sales expense ratio = $\dfrac{\text{Expense}}{\text{Sales}}$

- Cost per call ratio = $\dfrac{\text{Total costs}}{\text{Number of calls}}$

Account Development and Servicing Ratios

- Account penetration ratio = $\dfrac{\text{Accounts sold}}{\text{Total accounts available}}$

- New-account conversion ratio = $\dfrac{\text{Number of new accounts}}{\text{Total number of accounts}}$

- Lost account ratio = $\dfrac{\text{Prior accounts not sold}}{\text{Total number of accounts}}$

- Sales per account ratio = $\dfrac{\text{Sales dollar volume}}{\text{Total number of accounts}}$

- Average order size ratio = $\dfrac{\text{Sales dollar volume}}{\text{Total number of orders}}$

- Order cancellation ratio = $\dfrac{\text{Number of canceled orders}}{\text{Total number of orders}}$

- Account share = $\dfrac{\text{Salesperson's business from account}}{\text{Account's total business}}$

Call Activity and/or Productivity

- Calls per day ratio = $\dfrac{\text{Number of calls}}{\text{Number of days worked}}$

- Calls per account ratio = $\dfrac{\text{Number of calls}}{\text{Number of accounts}}$

- Planned call ratio = $\dfrac{\text{Number of planned calls}}{\text{Total number of calls}}$

- Orders per call (hit) ratio = $\dfrac{\text{Number of orders}}{\text{Total number of calls}}$

Source: Mark W. Johnston and Greg W. Marshall, *Sales Force Management*, 11th ed. (London: Routledge, 2013).

In many ways, it is more difficult to assess salespeople qualitatively versus quantitavely. Quantitative measures can require a detailed analysis of a salesperson's call report, an extensive time utilization analysis, or an analysis of the type and number of nonselling activities employed. However, once the measurement procedure is set up, it typically can be conducted fairly and consistently.

When assessing qualitative performance factors, even a well-designed measurement process that is firmly in place leaves much room for bias in the evaluation. **Bias** in a performance evaluation represents a difference from objective reality, usually based on errors by the evaluator (the sales manager). Even well-designed systems rely on the personal judgment of the individuals charged with evaluation. Typically, the manager rates the salesperson on a performance appraisal form on a number of attributes, such as the following:

1. *Sales results.* Volume of sales, sales to new accounts, and selling of the full product line.
2. *Job knowledge.* Knowledge of company policies, prices, and products.
3. *Management of territory.* Planning activities and calls, controlling expenses, and handling reports and records.
4. *Customer and company relations.* The salesperson's standing with customers, associates, and company.
5. *Personal characteristics.* Initiative, personal appearance, personality, resourcefulness, and so on.

Note the mix of objective and subjective performance measures. Most formal performance evaluations of salespeople involve a combination of these two types of criteria.

Problems with Subjective Performance Measurement

Common problems with performance appraisal systems that rely on subjective rating forms, particularly those using the simple checklist type, include the following:[12]

1. *Lack of an outcome focus.* The most useful type of performance appraisal highlights areas for improvement and the actions the employee must take to implement such improvements. For this to occur, the key behaviors in accomplishing the tasks assigned must be identified. Unfortunately, many companies have not taken this step. They have simply identified attributes thought to be related to performance without systematically assessing whether the attributes actually are critical. One type of performance appraisal, called BARS (behavioral anchored rating scale), helps overcome this weakness by identifying behaviors that are more versus less effective with respect to the goals established for the person. BARS will be discussed in detail shortly.
2. *Ill-defined personality traits.* Many performance evaluation forms use personality factors as attributes. For salespeople, these attributes might include such things as initiative and resourcefulness. Although these attributes are intuitively appealing, their actual relationship to performance is open to question.[13]
3. *Halo effect.* A halo effect is a common phenomenon with any performance evaluation form. Halo means the rating assigned to one characteristic may significantly influence the ratings assigned to all other characteristics, as well as the overall rating. The halo effect holds that a sales manager's overall evaluations can be predicted quite well from his or her rating of the salesperson on the single performance dimension the manager believes is most important. For example, a salesperson tends to be very prompt in getting assignments in prior to deadlines, therefore the manager harbors a halo effect that he or she is excellent on other performance dimensions. Different branch or regional managers may have different beliefs about what is most important, compounding the problem.
4. *Leniency or harshness.* Some sales managers rate at the extremes. Some are very lenient and rate every salesperson as good or outstanding on every attribute; others do just the opposite. This behavior is often a function of their own personalities and their perceptions of what comprises outstanding performance, rather than of any fundamental differences in how the salespeople are actually performing. Different managers' use of different definitions of performance can undermine the whole performance appraisal system.

5. *Central tendency.* Some managers err in the opposite direction. They never or rarely rate people at the ends of the scale. They stick to middle of the road, play-it-safe ratings. Such ratings reveal very little about true differences in performance. This can be particularly troublesome when a company attempts to use a history of poor performance as the basis of a termination decision. Some companies have instituted forced ranking systems partly to circumvent managers' leniency, harshness, or central tendency in their evaluations—but ranking systems have their own problems.

6. *Interpersonal bias.* Our perceptions of other people and the social acceptability of their behaviors are influenced by how much we like or dislike them personally. Many sales managers' evaluations of sales reps are similarly affected. Furthermore, research suggests a salesperson can use personal influence or impression management strategies on the manager to bias evaluations upward.

7. *Organizational uses influence.* Performance ratings are often affected by the use to which they will be put within the organization. If promotions and monetary payments hinge on the ratings, a manager who values the friendship and support of subordinates may be lenient. It is not difficult to imagine the dilemma of a district sales manager if other district sales teams receive consistently higher compensation increments and more promotions than his or her group. On the other hand, when appraisals are used primarily for the development of subordinates, managers tend to pinpoint weaknesses more freely and focus on what is wrong and how it can be improved.[14]

By now, it should be clear that performance evaluation is fraught with opportunities for biases and inaccuracies to creep into the process. An **outcome bias** occurs when a sales manager allows the outcome of a rep's decision or series of decisions to overly influence his or her performance ratings.

Avoiding Errors in Subjective Performance Evaluation

To guard against distortions in the performance appraisal system, many firms provide extensive training to sales managers on how to complete the forms and conduct the appraisal process. Common instructions issued with such forms include the following:

1. Read the definition of each attribute thoroughly and carefully before rating.
2. Guard against the common tendency to overrate.
3. Do not let personal likes or dislikes influence your ratings. Be as objective as possible in your subjective ratings.
4. Do not permit your evaluation of one factor to influence your evaluation of another.
5. Base your rating on the observed performance of the salesperson, not on potential abilities.
6. Never rate an employee on a few instances of good or poor work, but rather on general success or failure over the whole period.
7. Have sound reasons for your ratings.[15]

These admonitions can help, particularly when the evaluator must supply reasons for ratings. However, they do not resolve problems with the form's design (the selection of attributes for evaluation and how they are presented). A trend in performance appraisal directed at resolving this issue is the BARS.

BARS Systems

A **BARS (behaviorally anchored rating scale)** system concentrates on the behaviors and other performance criteria the individual can control. The system focuses on the fact that a number of factors affect any employee's performance. However, some of these factors are more critical to job success than others, and in evaluation it is important to focus on the key success factors for contemporary selling as identified and discussed in chapter 2. Implementing a BARS system for evaluating salespeople requires identifying the specific behaviors relevant to their performance. The evaluation must rate these behaviors using the appropriate descriptions.[16]

To develop a BARS system, management identifies the key behaviors with respect to performance using critical incidents. Critical incidents are occurrences that are vital (critical) to performance. Managers and sales reps could be asked to identify some outstanding examples of good or bad performance and to detail why they were good or bad.[17] The performances are then reduced to a smaller number of performance dimensions.

Next, the group of critical incidents is presented to a select group of sales personnel (perhaps top salespeople and sales managers), who assign each critical incident to an appropriate performance dimension. An incident is typically kept in if 60 percent or more of the group assigns it to the same dimension as did the instrument development group. The sales personnel group is also asked to rate the behavior described in the critical incident on a 7- or 10-point scale with respect to how effectively or ineffectively it represents performance on the dimension.

Incidents that generate good agreement in ratings, typically indicated by a low standard deviation, are considered for the final scale. The particular incidents chosen are determined by their location along the scale, as measured by the mean scores. Typically, the final scale has six to eight anchors. Exhibit 13.6 shows a BARS scale that resulted from such a process for the attribute "promptness in meeting deadlines."

EXHIBIT 13.6 A BARS SCALE WITH BEHAVIORAL ANCHORS FOR THE ATTRIBUTE "PROMPTNESS IN MEETING DEADLINES"

Very high
This indicates the more-often-than-not practice of submitting accurate and needed sales reports.

10.0 — Could be expected to promptly submit all necessary field reports even in

9.0 — the most difficult of situations.

8.0 — Could be expected to promptly meet deadlines comfortably in most report completion situations.

7.0 —

6.0 — Is usually on time and can be expected to submit most routine field sales reports in proper format.

Moderate
This indicates regularity in promptly submitting accurate and needed field sales reports.

5.0 —

4.0 — Could be expected to regularly be tardy in submitting required field sales reports.

3.0 — Could be expected to be tardy and submit inaccurate field sales reports.

2.0 —

1.0 — Could be expected to completely disregard due dates for filing almost all reports.

Very low
This indicates irregular and unacceptable promptness and accuracy of field sales reports.

0.0 — Could be expected to never file field sales reports on time and resist any managerial guidance to improve this tendency.

Source: Mark W. Johnston and Greg W. Marshall, *Sales Force Management*, 11th ed. (London: Routledge, 2013).

A key advantage of a BARS system is that it requires sales managers to consider in detail a wide range of components of a salesperson's job performance. It must also include clearly defined anchors for those performance criteria in specific behavioral terms, leading to thoughtful consideration by managers of just what comprises performance. Of course, by nature a BARS emphasizes behavior and performance rather than effectiveness. When used in tandem with appropriate objective measures (sales and profit analyses and output, input, and ratio measures), BARS can handle subjective evaluation criteria, providing as complete a picture as possible of a salesperson's overall performance and effectiveness.

BARS systems are not without their limitations, though. For one thing, the job-specific nature of their scales suggests they are most effective in evaluating salespeople performing very similar functions. They might be good for comparing one national account rep to another national account rep or two territory reps against each other, but they could suffer major shortcomings if used to compare a national account rep against a territory rep because of differences in responsibilities in these positions. BARS systems can also be relatively costly to develop since they require a good deal of up-front time from many people.[18]

360-DEGREE PERFORMANCE FEEDBACK

As you learned in chapter 5, one important attraction of CRM systems is their inherent ability to provide feedback from a wide range of constituents and stakeholders. Although much of this information is used for product development and formulation of the overall marketing message, CRM systems typically also facilitate the gathering, analysis, and dissemination of a great deal of information directly relevant to the performance of the sales force.

To take full advantage of the information generated by enterprise software such as CRM, the firm as a whole must embrace the philosophy that the customer is a customer of the *company,* not just of the individual salesperson. You have seen that the complex and often lengthy process of developing and managing customer relationships almost always involves more than just a salesperson and a purchasing agent. An effective CRM system should be gathering data at all the touchpoints where members of a selling organization interact with members of a buying organization and where members of a selling organization interact internally to build a business relationship with a customer.

Such a comprehensive information management process allows us to rethink the nature of input data for use in salesperson performance evaluation. Rather than relying on purely objective measures or on subjective measures generated by one person (the sales manager), evaluators can receive information from multiple sources. This concept, called 360-degree performance feedback, opens the door to a new era in using the performance appraisal process as an effective tool for salesperson development and improvement.

Among the sources of feedback useful to salespeople are external customers, internal customers (people within your firm who may not have external customer contact but who nonetheless add value that will ultimately benefit external customers), other members of the selling team, anyone who reports directly to the sales manager (such as sales assistants), and of course the sales manager.[19] Integrating feedback from these and other relevant sources of performance information into the formal evaluation process (and thus onto the evaluation form) can provide the impetus for a more productive dialogue between the sales manager and salesperson at performance review time. Ethical Dilemma #2 provides a fascinating example of how customer feedback could be impacted by a rejected client request for unethical behavior by their salesperson.

Related to 360-degree feedback is self-evaluation. Sales organizations should encourage salespeople to prepare an honest assessment of their own performance against the established objective and subjective performance criteria. This should be prepared *before* the formal performance review session with the sales manager.[20] The best sales organizations use this process to begin setting sales unit goals for the next period and especially to establish a professional development program to help move salespeople toward the fulfillment of their personal goals on the job.

In Chapter 11 you learned that intrinsic rewards are those that salespeople primarily attain for themselves. They include such things as feelings of accomplishment, personal growth, and self-worth and

ETHICAL DILEMMA #2

THE SPECIAL ARRANGEMENT

Terri Jensen is reviewing the semiannual customer satisfaction scores for the sales force at Planet Plastics. As eastern region vice president of sales, she had played an important part in getting senior management to support using customer satisfaction surveys as part of the compensation package for each salesperson. These surveys were initially criticized by the sales force, but over the last two years they have come to see the scores as a successful part of the salesperson evaluation process. Customers appreciate the opportunity to provide feedback, and salespeople realize the benefits of keeping their customers satisfied—*and* 25 percent of their incentive compensation is tied to these customer satisfaction reports.

However, as Terri looks at the reports she notices a disturbing problem. Jason Zaderhorn, a young salesperson in Nashville, received very low scores from his largest customer, Mercury Manufacturing. These numbers mean that Jason will not be eligible for any of the compensation tied to customer satisfaction this year. Terri knows why Jason's scores are so low. Jason emailed her a month ago and later called about a serious problem at Mercury. The director of purchasing in Mercury's Nashville plant had called Jason into his office and said that if Planet Plastics wanted to continue as the lead plastics supplier for Mercury, there would need to be a "special arrangement." Jason knew at once the purchasing director meant some form of bribe.

Planet Plastics has always held to the highest ethical standards. While Jason said he would check with his boss, he knew that Planet would not participate in bribes just to keep the business. Terri affirmed Jason's perspective in a phone call. Jason told the purchasing director that Planet felt it deserved the business based on performance and would not be involved with any "special arrangements." (He was careful not to use the inflammatory word "bribe" with the purchasing director.)

Mercury is Planet's second largest customer worldwide. Jason is responsible for several of its facilities in the Nashville area, but Mercury has business around the world and Planet has been its supplier for 10 years. This is a difficult situation. Terri knows why Jason's customer satisfaction scores are low, but if she explains why to senior management at Planet, it will get back to Mercury's facilities around the world. This could put the entire account at risk.

On the other hand, Jason has done well on other accounts, and it is not fair to withhold his bonus based on the feedback from this one customer. If Terri does give Jason the bonus, how will she explain it to the executive vice president of sales—who just happens to be coming into her office later today?

Questions to Consider

1. What should Terri Jensen tell the executive vice president of sales?
2. Should Jason get a bonus? If so, how might it be calculated?
3. How should Jason, Terri, and Planet Plastics respond to Mercury?

can be very powerful motivators. Allowing salespeople to have direct input by establishing personal growth goals on the job, and then institutionalizing the achievement of those goals via the formal performance evaluation process, goes a long way toward providing a workplace atmosphere where they can realize their intrinsic rewards.

It is important to involve salespeople directly in all phases of the performance appraisal process. When appraisals provide clear criteria whose development included input by salespeople, and the appraisals are perceived as fair and are used in determining rewards, salesperson job satisfaction increases. Thus, the critical determinants of appraisal effectiveness are not purely criteria-driven. Instead, they are largely determined by appraisal process factors that managers can influence, such as buy-in by those being appraised and fairness of the appraisal process.[21]

An old adage in human resource management holds that if an employee is surprised by anything he or she is told during a formal performance review, the manager is not doing a very good job. Performance evaluation should not be a cathartic event that happens once or twice a year. Such an approach can cause great trepidation by both employees and managers and often leads managers to procrastinate in conducting the review and minimize the time spent with the employee during the review.

Great sales organizations use the performance evaluation process to facilitate *ongoing* dialogue between salespeople and their managers. A key goal should be to facilitate professional and personal development by providing salespeople the feedback and tools they need to achieve their goals in the job. To make this happen, sales managers must carry on the dialogue beyond just the periodic formal appraisal event into day-to-day communication with salespeople. Importantly, this developmental perspective on performance evaluation requires sales managers to not just give feedback but also listen and respond to feedback and questions from the salespeople.

Ultimately, sales organizations need to work toward developing a **performance management system**, which requires a commitment to integrating all the elements of feedback on the process of serving customers. The result is performance information that is timely, accurate, and relevant to the firm's overall customer management initiative.[22] The pieces of the performance puzzle are integrated in such a way that the salesperson does not have to wait on the manager for a formal validation of performance. Instead, under a performance management system approach, salespeople take the lead in goal setting, performance measurement, and adjustment of their own performance.[23] The concept of performance management is analogous to Total Quality Management (TQM) approaches that advocate the empowerment of employees to take ownership of their own jobs and conduct their own analyses of performance against goals, creating a culture of self-management. To successfully implement a performance management system, sales managers must shift their leadership style to that of a partner in a mutually shared process.

EXPERT ADVICE: FOLLOW-UP   Chally Group WORLDWIDE

After watching the video of Mr. Gandi and reading the chapter, consider the following questions:

1. Consider his central point about salesperson compensation being "pay at risk." What is your personal opinion about that aspect of a sales job? Do you agree with him that it is a huge advantage to making sales jobs attractive? Why or why not?
2. What are some specific examples of types of sales jobs that might be the best fit to his favored compensation approach—that is, heavy incentive and lighter base salary?

SUMMARY

To manage the contemporary selling process effectively, sales managers must address the firm's compensation system. Which rewards do salespeople value? How much of each is optimum? How should the rewards be integrated into a total compensation system? This chapter provides insights to these issues.

In determining the most effective form of financial compensation, the firm must decide whether to use (1) straight salary, (2) straight commission, or (3) a combination of base salary and incentive pay such as commissions, bonuses, or both. Most companies today use a combination approach. The base salary gives salespeople a stable income while allowing the company to reward them for performing tasks not directly related to short-term sales. The incentive portion of a combination plan provides direct rewards to motivate salespeople to expend effort to improve their sales volume or other aspect of their quota. To be effective, the incentive has to be large enough to generate interest among salespeople.

Sales contests are often part of incentive compensation. In addition, nonfinancial incentives such as opportunity for advancement and recognition programs can play an important role in a firm's compensation system. Often, salespeople qualify for the use of expense accounts, which of course also add to total compensation. Overall, the sales manager must determine an appropriate mix and level of compensation for salespeople that maximizes the compensation plan's motivational value, is fair, and is consistent with the firm's resources.

In terms of salesperson evaluation, the concepts of performance and effectiveness are different. Performance is a salesperson's behavior evaluated in terms of its contribution to the goals of the organization. Effectiveness is an organizational outcome for which a salesperson is at least partly responsible, usually examined across a variety of indexes.

Salespeople may be evaluated based on objective and subjective criteria. Objective measures reflect statistics a sales manager can gather from a firm's internal data and other means. They may be categorized as output measures (the results of the efforts expended by salespeople) and input measures (the efforts they expend achieving the results). Objective measures also may take the form of ratios that combine various outputs and/or inputs. On the other hand, subjective measures typically rely on personal evaluations, usually by the sales manager, of how the salesperson is doing. Managers should pay attention to both objective and subjective measures in evaluating salespeople.

A variety of potential pitfalls exist in performance measurement, especially regarding subjective measures. These problems often take the form of various errors or biases in the evaluation, which result in an inaccurate performance appraisal that the salesperson rightly perceives as unfair. Sales organizations and their managers must take great care to conduct the performance evaluation process as fairly and accurately as possible. BARS systems aid in this process.

In addition, 360-degree feedback in the performance review, including a strong component of self-evaluation by the salesperson, can greatly improve the usefulness of the performance evaluation process.

KEY TERMS

compensation plan	employee benefits	objective measures	BARS (behaviorally anchored rating scale)
salary	nonfinancial incentives	subjective measures	
incentive pay	expense accounts	output measures	360-degree performance feedback
commission	perquisites (perks)	input measures	
bonus	behavior	ratio measures	self-evaluation
quota	performance	bias	performance management system
sales contests	effectiveness	outcome bias	

ROLE PLAY #1

BEFORE YOU BEGIN

Before getting started, please go to the Appendix of chapter 1 to review the profiles of the characters involved in this role play, as well as the tips on preparing a role play.

Characters Involved

Rhonda Reed
Justin Taylor

Setting the Stage

Upland Company uses a limited reimbursement plan for salesperson expenses. Basically, salespeople submit receipts monthly to Rhonda for all allowable and reasonable expenses. Rhonda reviews these and forwards them to the home office for processing and payment. Annually, Rhonda provides each salesperson a budget for expenses based on mutually agreed on needs. Salespeople receive a small bonus for finishing the year within their budget. It's not unusual for a salesperson's expenses to exceed budget for a given month—though several months of exceeding budgeted expenses would be problematic.

Over the past four months, Rhonda has noticed a marked upward trend in Justin Taylor's expenses. Not only are his average monthly expenses running 23 percent higher than those of anyone else in District 10, but also his expenses for last month are 32 percent higher than his average monthly expenses just six months ago. This has put the whole district's expense budget in the red year-to-date, and the home office has noticed. Rhonda has set up a meeting with Justin to discuss this and develop a plan to reduce his expenses so they are more in line with the budget and with the other reps in the district.

Note: Rhonda sent Justin an email about this problem two months ago. He replied that he would watch expenses more closely. Last month she talked to him about it in person while riding with him to call on an account, but he did not seem concerned and continually shifted the conversation to how well his sales were going for the year.

Rhonda Reed's Role

Rhonda wants to ask questions to find out exactly why Justin's expenses are so high. She does not want to squelch his motivation, as he is an outstanding performer and in fact is leading the district in sales increase year-to-date at 22 percent. However, she needs to counsel him and help him develop a set of objectives and action plans to get his expenses back in line. She knows Justin wants to move into management with Upland and sees this meeting as a coaching opportunity to help him learn more about expense control—a critical sales management function.

Justin Taylor's Role

Although Justin has done a great job selling to his customers this year, he has lost control of his expenses. This has not been intentional. He is not cheating or doing anything unethical. He simply is not keeping good tabs on his expenditures versus his budget. He comes into the meeting ready to focus on what a great year he is having in sales, and when Rhonda focuses the conversation on his expense problem, he claims his big sales increase should offset any expense overruns. He will not veer from that position until Rhonda does a good job of coaching him. At the end of the encounter, he and Rhonda must have set specific objectives and action plans to correct the problem.

Assignment

Work with another student to develop a 7–10 minute coaching session between Rhonda and Justin on these issues. Be sure to play the parts in accordance with the guidance above. This should not be a "you are in trouble" session, but instead a "here's a learning and professional growth opportunity" session.

ROLE PLAY #2

BEFORE YOU BEGIN

Before getting started, please go to the Appendix of chapter 1 to review the profiles of the characters involved in this role play, as well as the tips on preparing a role play.

Characters Involved

Rhonda Reed

Zane Cleary, regional sales manager for Upland Company. Zane is Rhonda's direct supervisor and reports to the vice president of sales, Leslie Skipper. Upland has four regions in the United States, each containing 15 to 20 districts.

Setting the Stage

Leslie Skipper recently announced that Upland will be undertaking a full review of its salesperson performance evaluation process. A committee has been named to lead this initiative, including all four regional sales managers and four select district managers (one from each region). Because Rhonda is very highly regarded within the organization, she has been named to the committee.

Leslie has charged the group with designing the best possible performance evaluation system for salespeople at Upland without regard to "how it has been done in the past." In two weeks, the committee will hold its first formal meeting at the home office to kick off the discussions. Zane Cleary has scheduled a trip to Rhonda's city this week so they can develop some ideas and notes before the big meeting.

Rhonda Reed's Role

Rhonda needs to come to the meeting with Zane prepared to discuss what might comprise an ideal performance evaluation system for Upland. She reviews material on objective and subjective performance measures as well as the concept of 360-degree feedback. It will be important for her to discuss various measurement options with Zane, consider the pros and cons of each as well as their applicability to Upland's particular situation, and come up with some clear goals that Upland would like to accomplish through its salesperson performance evaluation process.

Zane Cleary's Role

Zane wants to go into the big committee meeting at the home office prepared to share and support the ideas that he and Rhonda develop now. He will remind Rhonda that they can start with a clean slate to develop and recommend a great salesperson performance evaluation process for Upland without regard to how it has been done in the past.

Like Rhonda, Zane needs to come to the meeting prepared to discuss what might comprise an ideal performance evaluation system for Upland. He too reviews material on objective and subjective performance measures as well as 360-degree feedback. It will be important for him to discuss various measurement options with Rhonda, consider the pros and cons of each as well as their applicability to Upland's situation, and come up with some clear goals that Upland would like to accomplish through its salesperson performance evaluation process.

Assignment

Work with another student to prepare a 15–20 minute role-play dialogue for the meeting between Rhonda and Zane. Be sure to cover the issues outlined and reach a conclusion that includes the necessary deliverables for the big meeting at the home office. To do this successfully, you will need to review carefully the material in chapter 13.

DISCUSSION QUESTIONS

1. We know that the use of selling teams is common practice today. These teams sometimes include both salespeople and other employees. As with individual salespeople, the success of these teams depends in part on the reward systems used to motivate and recognize performance. How would you develop a compensation plan that motivates members of a selling team? How can you ensure the plan is fair for everybody involved?

2. When OfficeSolutions, a software producer, went into business, it needed to establish market share quickly. To accomplish this, it decided to pay the sales force a straight commission. After two years, the company had a large base of business, but customers began to complain that salespeople were not spending enough time with them on postsale service and problem solving. The salespeople said they did not make any money on problem solving and would rather spend their time finding new customers. What's more, salespeople spent little or no time selling the new products on which OfficeSolutions was staking its future. They said they could sell the old products more easily and earn more money for both themselves and the company. How might the company rework its compensation plan to begin to resolve this issue?

3. A sales manager says, "You can never hold enough sales contests for your salespeople. The more, the merrier. They are guaranteed to increase your business." Evaluate this statement.

4. Assume you are taking a selling job right out of college. What would be your own ideal compensation mix? Why?

5. What are the pros and cons of placing ceilings on salesperson incentives? If you were a sales manager, would you ever advocate incentive ceilings? If so, in what situation(s) and why?

6. Given the following information from evaluations of the performance of different sales representatives, what can you conclude about why the reps are not achieving quota? (Assume each is not making quota.)

    a. *Rep 1:* Achieved goals for sales calls, phone calls, and new accounts; customer relations are good; no noticeable deficiencies in any areas.
    b. *Rep 2:* Completed substantially fewer sales calls than goal. Many phone calls, but primarily with one firm. Time management analysis shows the sales rep spends a disproportionately large amount of time with one firm. New accounts are low; all other areas good to outstanding.
    c. *Rep 3:* Number of sales calls low, below goal. Telephone calls, email correspondence, proposals all very low and below goal. Evaluation shows poor time utilization. Very high amount of service-related activities in rep's log; customer relations extremely positive; recently has received a great deal of feedback from customers on product function.

7. Is sales just a numbers game, as one sales manager claims? She believes that all you have to do is make the right number of calls of the right type, and the odds will work in your favor. Make 10 calls, get one sale. So to get two sales, make 20 calls. Is this the right approach? Why or why not?

8. Jackie Hitchcock, recently promoted to district sales manager, faced a new problem she wasn't sure how to resolve. The district's top sales rep is also the district's number one problem. Brad Coombs traditionally leads the company in sales but also in problems. He has broken every rule, bent every policy, deviated from guidelines, and been less than truthful. Jackie knew Brad had never done anything illegal, but she was worried that something serious could happen. Brad also does not prepare call reports on time, fails to show up at trade shows, and doesn't attend sales training programs.

How should Jackie handle this problem? How does a sales manager manage a maverick sales rep? Specifically, how can the performance evaluation process help Jackie deal with Brad?

MINI-CASE 13.1 MEDTECH PHARMACEUTICALS

DOUG: Now that it looks like we are going to get approval on these two new cancer drugs, we need to get a sales force out there selling them for us and we need to do it quickly.

HAROLD: I agree. We've put so much time and effort over the last three years into developing the drugs, conducting the clinical trials, and getting them through the FDA approval process that we forgot to consider what would happen when that approval came through. We have to make sure the sales force has the right incentive to see a lot of doctors and generate sales. Our window of opportunity for these drugs is only seven years, so we have to maximize our return during that time.

BECKY: Based on my experience with other sales organizations, paying our sales force based solely on commission should generate the sales we're looking for. Salespeople love to make money, and if they know that the more they sell the more they'll make, we'll be in good shape.

DOUG: Good idea, Becky. Harold, put together a sales organization and start assembling your sales force. With FDA approval expected within the next six weeks, we'll need to move quickly.

With that conversation as the backdrop, MedTech Pharmaceuticals was in business. MedTech began when Doug Reynolds left his position as a university research fellow to start a new company. Doug's work as a molecular biologist gave him an idea for a new cancer treatment compound that could be used to treat the deadliest form of skin cancer, melanoma. This new drug can treat melanoma without surgery (which is the typical treatment for this type of cancer). Doug also speculated that a different variation of the drug compound would treat a more common but less deadly type of skin cancer called basal-cell carcinoma. Doug thought that these new drugs would be in great demand in the future because, as baby boomers age, many will be afflicted with skin cancer.

Based on the promise shown by this new drug, Doug was able to secure venture capital financing to develop the compound and submit it for approval by the Food and Drug Administration. To facilitate the development and approval process, Becky Smith was hired from another pharmaceutical company because of her expertise in conducting clinical trials and responding to FDA inquiries about the effects of the drug on patients. Harold Moran was hired to be the business manager. When the conversation above took place, Harold was the only person in the company with the expertise to develop a sales force that could successfully introduce the products.

Four Years Later

In the four years since MedTech received FDA approval, it has employed a sales force of 150 representatives organized geographically across the United States, calling on oncologists and dermatologists whose primary specialty is treating skin cancer. Each sales rep reports to one of 10 sales managers. The sales managers all report to Harold. Sales of the new drugs have been good but have not met the company's expectations. Several of the sales managers have mentioned to Harold that a regular program of sales contests would create more excitement among the sales force and provide greater motivation to increases sales. Harold's response is always, "The salespeople are getting paid 100 percent commission. That should be enough incentive for them to generate more sales."

The sales managers also have mentioned that reimbursing sales reps for entertainment expenses would allow them to compete on a level playing field, since most pharmaceutical companies reimburse physician entertainment expenses. However, the U.S. Internal Revenue Service has clamped down on certain types of client entertaining, and the American Medical Association as well as the leading associations of pharmaceutical manufacturers have taken a strong stand against pharmaceutical reps exerting undue influence over physician purchases through entertainment and free gifts. MedTech currently provides a $250 per month car allowance and another $50 per month for incidental expenses. This reimbursement plan was implemented four years ago when the sales force began, and neither the dollar amounts nor the types of expenses reimbursed have changed since.

In light of the disappointing sales numbers and the impending expiration (in three years) of the company's patent on the two drugs, recently Harold has been listening to his sales managers more closely. He's concerned that a number of the salespeople may leave the company to pursue other opportunities. Consequently, he is considering changes to the overall compensation program at MedTech Pharmaceuticals.

Questions

1. Discuss the advantages and disadvantages of MedTech Pharmaceuticals paying employees on a straight commission basis. What specific changes would you recommend Harold make to the compensation program? Why?

2. What do you think of Harold's opinion about sales contests? Are contests an appropriate incentive in this situation? Why or why not?

3. Assume that the decision is made to proceed with a sales contest. Use your knowledge from this chapter to design a sales contest that MedTech can implement to generate enthusiasm among the sales force and increase sales for the company. Describe the contest's objective, its theme, how many of the reps should be winners, and what types of rewards the contest should provide.

4. What do you think about MedTech's expense reimbursement plan? What do you believe should be changed, and why?

MINI-CASE 13.2 AMERICAN FOOD PROCESSORS

Jamie Walker, regional vice president of sales for American Food Processors (AFP), is looking at the performance numbers of his sales force for the past year. He is starting to get that sinking feeling he gets every year at this time. Once again he has to evaluate the performance of his sales force, and he is not looking forward to the exercise. The problem is that Jamie really likes all of his sales reps as people. Because of that, he would like to use more subjective criteria in evaluating them. He thinks they all do a good job, and many of them have extenuating circumstances that just don't show up in the objective performance data the company requires him to use.

Jamie knows from having been a sales rep himself for eight years before getting into sales management that various things come up each year that can drastically affect a salesperson's territory. A large customer may go out of business, a competitor may place renewed emphasis on gaining accounts in a certain territory, or the economy may simply be poor for some customers. Any one of these events or many others can significantly impair a salesperson's performance, and the rep has little to no influence on these events. Nonetheless, AFP's evaluation process for the time being is numbers-driven. Jamie will have to get to work calculating the required ratios and rank ordering his sales reps before holding his annual performance review meetings with each rep next week.

In looking at the performance data, Jamie immediately sees an example of why objective performance information by itself is not the best way to evaluate a sales force. The standard number of days any representative could work in his or her territory for the year was 240 (52 weeks/year 5 days/week – 10 holidays – 10 travel and meeting days). Since Steve Rogers has been with the company for just over a year, he gets only one week of vacation. However, Marti Edwards combined her two weeks of vacation with six weeks of maternity leave when her baby was born. Such discrepancies in the number of days worked affects the evaluation process, but going strictly by the numbers doesn't allow for any consideration of those extenuating circumstances. Jamie also notices that Rick Randall, who was originally on his way to having a breakout year, barely exceeded quota. One of Rick's largest customers went bankrupt nine months into the year, and he had a hard time recovering from that setback.

Table 1 Current Year Sales Performance Data

Sales Rep	Previous Year's Sales	Current Year's Sales	Current Sales Quota	Total Number of Accounts
Steve Rogers	$480,000	$481,000	$575,000	1,100
Adam Murphy	750,000	883,000	835,000	1,600
Vicki Doyle	576,000	613,000	657,000	1,150
Rick Randall	745,000	852,000	850,000	1,350
Brenda Palmer	765,000	860,000	850,000	1,300
David Chen	735,000	835,000	825,000	1,400
Marti Edwards	665,000	670,000	720,000	1,600
Kim McConnell	775,000	925,000	875,000	1,700

Sales Rep	Number of Orders	Annual Sales Expenses	Number of Calls	Number of Days Worked
Steve Rogers	780	$9,300	1,300	235
Adam Murphy	1,970	12,300	1,800	223
Vicki Doyle	1,020	7,500	1,650	228
Rick Randall	1,650	11,000	1,700	230
Brenda Palmer	1,730	11,300	1,750	232
David Chen	1,790	11,500	1,750	220
Marti Edwards	960	10,800	1,550	200
Kim McConnell	1,910	12,800	1,850	225

As Jamie continues to ponder the task before him, he knows that the other three regional sales VPs are working on the same assignment. He also begins to realize (as he does every year) that there are as many extenuating circumstances as there are salespeople and that considering them all when evaluating performance would be an impossible task. Maybe looking at only the numbers and ratios is the fairest method after all.

Questions

1. Using the information provided in Table 1, rank Jamie's sales representatives from best to worst by calculating and considering the following ratios: sales growth, sales to quota, sales per account, average order size, sales expense, calls per day, and orders per call (hits).

2. Suppose you are Jamie Walker and you're holding the annual review meeting with each of these sales reps. What recommendations will you give to the four lowest-ranking reps to improve their sales?

3. What are some of the limitations of using only ratios to evaluate members of AFP's sales force? How could Jamie improve the performance evaluation process so that other information is considered? If Jamie could convince AFP to consider other performance information, what other information do you recommend he use?

Sales Management

Salesperson Motivation

Selling Processes

Compensating & Evaluating Salespeople

Selecting & Training Salespeople

Prospecting & Sales Call Planning

Communicating the Sales Message

Salesperson Self-Management

Technology

Understanding Sellers & Buyers

Building Relationships ~ Creating Value

Closing & Follow-up

Ethics

Negotiating for Win-Win Solutions

global selling environment

Global Perspectives on Contemporary Selling

LEARNING OBJECTIVES

While the basic concepts and practices of contemporary selling—identify, communicate, and deliver value to the customer—are universal, it is also true that the global business environment creates unique challenges for both the salesperson and sales manager. This chapter will define these challenges and present current business practices for success. In that regard it extends contemporary selling to the global marketplace, something that every company is struggling to do in this hyper-competitive environment.

Salespeople must be able to understand and work successfully in a global business environment, and the size or location of the company, size of their customers, or nature of their competition doesn't matter. Sales managers need to know how to manage the sales force in any complex and dynamic market environment.

After reading this chapter you should be able to:

- Understand the importance of global sales in contemporary selling
- Identify the key challenges facing salespeople in a global sales environment
- Understand the impact of a global sales challenges on managing the sales force.

EXPERT ADVICE

EXPERT: Mr. Tom Kadien
President, Epedx (distribution arm of International Paper)

TOPIC: Importance of salespeople who understand global markets and solutions.

SUMMARY: Mr. Kadien speaks of the value of a global sales force that is able to understand customers and their needs, then bring the company's resources together in order to create a solution. This can be a challenge when working with large global customers whose supply chain stretches all over the world. Salespeople need to understand the complexity of a global supply chain as well as the local logistics of distribution in countries as diverse as Vietnam, China, Germany, and Brazil. In a very real sense they are consultants for their customers, creating solutions to the customer's problems.

NEXT STEPS: Go the website for *Contemporary Selling* (www.routledge.com/cw/Johnston), watch the video for chapter 14, and then read the chapter. You will find an Expert Advice follow-up at the end of the chapter with questions that connect elements of the video to your learning.

SELLING IS GLOBAL

We have talked throughout the book about the fundamentals of selling—identify the customers' needs, develop and communicate a solution to meet those needs, and work with the customer to enhance their business—and they are true all over the world. At the same time, it is important to recognize that there are distinct and profound differences in the sales process itself, as well as managing salespeople from country to country and region to region globally. The global sales environment exists outside the company's home but influences the company, its operations, and customers. In this chapter we bring together all that we have talked about, from the Contemporary Selling process to managing the contemporary sales force, and consider the impact of the global sales environment.

We first examine the importance of considering a global perspective. Some sales managers may argue that they are too small or their customers have no global operations or any one of dozens of reasons why it is not important to study the global sales environment. Unfortunately, people who take this approach fail to realize that the global sales environment impacts every salesperson and we will see how. Next we delineate the various global challenges in the sales process. From culture to ethics, the global sales environment impacts the sales process and is a differentiator between sales success and failure. The final section of the chapter will focus on managing the contemporary sales process and how global issues impact everything from sales structure to salesperson evaluation. Let's start by considering how a global marketplace impacts the contemporary selling process.

The Global Marketplace and Contemporary Selling

Consider how business has changed since 2000. Classic American companies like IBM now generate more than half their revenue outside the United States, the largest car company in the world is now Japanese (Toyota), China has become a world economic power, much of Europe now operates with a single currency (the Euro), and everyone from consumers to businesses are doing business on the Internet. With all these changes and many, many more, it is not surprising then that the nature of contemporary selling has adapted as well. From globalization to technology, economic forces to political/legal changes contemporary selling has been impacted by the global marketplace.[1] Exhibit 14.1 highlights several well-known U.S.-based companies and the percentage of their revenue generated outside of America.

EXHIBIT 14.1	U.S.-BASED COMPANIES AND THE PERCENTAGE OF REVENUE GENERATED OUTSIDE AMERICA
Company	**Percentage of Revenue Outside of U.S. (%)**
Qualcomm	95
Avon	79
Coca-Cola	69
3M	65
Nike	64
Apple	62
Chevron	58
Heinz	56

In his classic book on the influence of globalization on society and business, *The World is Flat*, Thomas L. Friedman offered two important Rules for business in the 21st Century. One of his rules addressed small firms, "And the small shall act big . . . One way small companies flourish in the flat world is by learning to act really big. And the key to being small and acting big is being quick to take advantage of all the new tools for collaboration to reach farther, faster wider and deeper." He goes on to elaborate how important it is for small companies to learn the customer's business and move faster than the competition, essentially reinforcing the principles of contemporary selling.

A second rule that Friedman suggests for big companies is, "And the big shall act small . . . One way that big companies learn to flourish in the flat world is by learning how to act really small and enabling their customers to act really big."[2] Again, Friedman argues against the tendency of big companies to lose focus on their customers; in essence they become more important than their customers. In a global sales environment there are always competitors willing to respond to the customer, and "big" doesn't always win.

Globalization is the "development of an increasingly integrated global economy marked by free trade, free flow of capital and the tapping of cheaper foreign labor markets."[3] The definition speaks to the integrated nature of markets around the world and need for companies (and salespeople) to move around the world to meet the needs of those markets. Increasingly companies consider the world not as individual markets but as the sum of its parts, designing a product in one country, engineering it in another, manufacturing it in a third, and distributing it throughout the world. Airbus, the world's largest commercial jet aircraft manufacturer, designs their aircraft in Europe but outsources the component manufacturing to over 3,000 suppliers all over the world, then assembles all those parts at a single location in France. Finally, the company must deliver its products to customers all over the world. It may be easier to think about global decisions if you build jet aircraft, but consider Swedish apparel retailer H&M (Hennes and Mauritz) which has seen dramatic growth in the last 10 years, with over 1,600 stores in 30 countries. One of the keys to the company's success has been its global business model. With in-house designers (located in Stockholm, Sweden) the company designs its own clothes and then uses 700 independent suppliers in Europe and Asia to coordinate a complex manufacturing and distribution process. The end result is high fashion at reasonable prices for younger women.

For many there is an understanding that selling to large global customers like Airbus or H&M requires global knowledge of the contemporary selling process. However, regional or even local companies must also know how to manage the effects of globalization. For example, construction companies throughout the world have learned the hard way about China's sustained economic growth because of the shortages in key construction components such as concrete. Consider one local construction company in central Florida. In recent years they have had to work with new materials and manage customer expectations due to the shortage of critical components, in essence learning to work in a global marketing environment despite being a local (central Florida) company. In one case, the company was forced to work with a customer to develop cost-effective alternatives when shortages in concrete pushed out the project time line. Gaining that level of understanding has been important to the company but also its customers.

GLOBAL CHALLENGES IN THE SALES PROCESS

The contemporary sales process has been dramatically affected by changes in the global sales environment. These changes impact the way the customer approaches and interacts with the customer, conducts the sales presentation, and, ultimately, the salesperson's decisions about the customer relationship. In this section we explore the three most critical global challenges to the contemporary sales process: the impact of culture on the salesperson and the customer, the impact of the global sales environment on business practices, and the effect of technology on the sales process globally.

Culture

Culture has a considerable influence on everyone's perception of the world. Every culture creates its own set of norms, accepted behaviors, and beliefs that manifest themselves as cultural differences. Culture is a system of values, beliefs, and morals shared by a particular group of people that permeates over time.[4] Consider the use of entertainment as a business tool. Many American companies severely restrict this aspect of the buyer–seller relationship, yet in Asian cultures, salespeople are expected to spend time with customers in social situations before the purchase. These culture clashes can create personal ethical dilemmas for salespeople and by extension for management. Another area where there are significant cultural differences is gift giving: in Asia and Latin America, gifts are an integral part of the relationship-building experience. However, many Western-based companies do not allow the giving of gifts, particularly expensive gifts, to customers.

The "one-size-fits-all" approach does not work when you are selling to customers in the United States, Germany, and China. Companies have adjusted their selling policies to different countries.[5] But these policies can become so inconsistent they affect customer relationships. For example, many Middle Eastern cultures do not let women take a leadership role in business. Many Middle Eastern customers will not readily accept even the most talented saleswoman. The company must decide whether to send the best person, potentially a woman, or one who fits the cultural norms of the customer. Companies like General Electric encourage their salespeople to be receptive to local business customs in dealing with customers and try to match salespeople with customers' cultural sensitivities. Let's examine three key cultural elements and see how they impact the contemporary sales process.

Language is one of the essential building blocks and the primary communication tool in a society. At the most basic level it is important to understand the language, making sure that words are being properly understood. At the same time, language does much more; it is important in conveying the society's value. Salespeople need to understand the language of their customers to express themselves clearly and be understood correctly. In addition, most industries have a "language" of their own where terms are defined and widely recognized among customers and companies. The words used by the salesperson speak not only to the specific meaning of the word but also to the cultural values of the word. In native English-speaking countries (England, Australia, United States) the word "contract' has a specific meaning defined by cultural custom and legal precedent. However, in some Asian countries, such as Japan, the cultural meaning of "contract" is different and implies a relationship between two parties that extends beyond the formal boundaries of the legal definition.

In a salesperson's home country, language is less of an issue, as the cultural context of the conversation is the same for both the customer and salesperson. If a word is misunderstood the customer or salesperson will quickly understand the problem and define a mutually understood context for the meaning of the word. However, when salesperson and customer do not share a common culture and language, those subtle meanings can get lost. In Asia it is common for customers to show approval for a sales presentation even if they have questions or concerns. Their culture is one of respect and there is a conscious effort to minimize conflict. While the salesperson believes the customer's lack of objections signals approval, the customer may actually be thinking that this product does not meet their needs at all. It is important for the salesperson to know the language and the cultural context for the conversation.

Cultural values are a society's ideals expressed as beliefs and they can play an important role in shaping the salesperson–customer relationship. In many Latin countries (Argentina, Colombia, and others), the family plays a significant role in an individual's life and there is a cultural value of maintaining a balance between work and family. The focus on the family helps shape people's choices about work schedules and stands in contrast to the American value of hard work and commitment to "get the job done." Are American salespeople and customers concerned about spending time with their families? Of course they are, but American culture values hard work and sacrifice, while Latin culture values family. It is important to understand these cultural values differences when working with customers—for example, their schedules may be less open to meetings on Monday or Friday.

These differences can also be reflected in other values. For example, American culture places a high value on individualism, while many Asian cultures value more group consensus. Even countries next door to one another can have different cultural systems. The German and French cultures, while very close geographically, have evolved very differently. Global Connection highlights the differences in negotiating between Chinese and American cultures.

GLOBAL CONNECTION

DIFFERENCES IN NEGOTIATING BETWEEN CHINESE AND AMERICAN CULTURES

	American	Chinese
Their Basic Cultural Values and Ways of Thinking		
	Individualist	Collectivist
	Egalitarian	Hierarchical
	Information oriented	Relationship oriented
	Reductionist	Holistic
	Sequential	Circular
	Seeks the truth	Seeks the way
	The argument culture	The haggling culture
How They Approach the Negotiation Process		
Nontask sounding	Quick meetings	Long courting process
	Informal	Formal
	Make cold calls	Draw on intermediaries
Information exchange	Full authority	Limited authority
	Direct	Indirect
	Proposals first	Explanations first
Means of persuasion	Aggressive	Questioning
	Impatient	Enduring
Terms of agreement	Forging a "good deal"	Forging a long-term relationship

Questions to Consider

1. You are a key account salesperson with Hewlett-Packard, negotiating a contract for a significant order of network servers with a large Chinese bank. Describe how you would go about making the sale and how the process would differ from the sale to a large American bank?
2. Do you think it is easier for a Chinese businessperson to come to the United States and learn how to do business or for an American businessperson go to China and do business?
3. Do you think it is important for American businesspeople to learn Chinese? Why or why not?

Notice the major differences in the critical selling step in the Contemporary Selling process. Salespeople must understand these differences in order to avoid breaching local business custom.

One of the most challenging cultural values for salespeople to understand is the time. Western European and American cultures, for example, place a high value on using time efficiently. They tend to carve the day into minutes and hours, trying to be as efficient and effective as possible in any given period of time. Outlook (Microsoft's calendar and email software application) and other calendar applications break a day into smaller increments of time, even as small as 15 minutes, and it is possible to set up the applications to notify or even block someone from "double-booking" a calendar event. This focus on maximizing the effectiveness of any given period of time is not a cultural value of Asian and Latin American cultures, which look at time very differently. These cultures view time as much more flexible and less distinct. For salespeople this is an important difference. When a salesperson from a Latin American or Asian company calls on an American customer, the customer will consider the time of the sales call to be firmly fixed, but for an American or Western European salesperson calling on a Latin American or Asian customer they may be frustrated to find out their meeting time is more flexible.

A third cultural value that is important in the global sales environment is the focus on the salesperson–customer relationship. Asian and Latin American cultures extend the business relationship beyond "work" and seek to develop a more personal relationship with their vendors. It is not uncommon for Asian customers to want initial sales meetings focused on personal relationship-building activities (dinner, sporting events like golf) rather than a formal sales presentation or negotiations. As you can imagine, this can be exasperating for someone outside the culture, particularly someone coming from a "time-sensitive" culture.

Differences in cultural values also play a role in defining an individual's ethics. It's a challenge for managers to balance corporate ethics rules with the business practices of cultures around the world. American companies face a particularly tough challenge because ethics rules in the United States tend to be much tougher than in many parts of the world. The Foreign Corrupt Practices Act (1977) forbids U.S. companies to bribe foreign officials. In 1998 the law was amended to allow for small payments that are consistent with cultural norms.[6] When corporate policies conflict with local cultural practices, salespeople are in a difficult position. If they follow corporate policy, they may lose the business, but if they follow local business customs, they may violate company ethics policies. As you can see, it is critical for members of management to be aware of their salespeople's customer experiences and to impart company policies clearly to avoid ethical problems. Even highly ethical salespeople and managers find themselves faced with very difficult choices. Given the challenges of selling across cultures, it is essential that managers understand how these differences impact their sales efforts, and recent research suggests that salespeople are much more comfortable making tough ethical decisions when their companies have a defined and consistently applied code of conduct, reinforce ethical principles in their training, and enforce corporate ethical policies.[7]

In chapter 4 we discussed the ethical and legal issues in Contemporary Selling, but it is important to note the role of culture in shaping and defining an individual's ethics. Consider the issues of bribery and various cultural differences that exist around the world. In Germany and France, bribes have been actually tax deductible as a business expense until recently and, in many Latin American countries, despite laws to the contrary, it is a common business practice.[8] American companies are not allowed to engage in bribery under the Foreign Corrupt Practices Act.

The final cultural element that salespeople need to consider is nonverbal communication. In chapter 7 we discussed the importance of nonverbal communication in the context of individual differences (everyone conveys and responds to nonverbal communication differently); here we will at look at nonverbal communication in the context of cultural differences. Simple gestures that are taken for granted in someone's home culture could have very different meanings in another culture. Consider the classic "thumbs-up," which in American and European cultures means things are going well or according to plan; however, in many Islamic and Asian cultures that gesture is considered rude and offensive. Consider the impression a salesperson would leave with an Asian or Islamic customer by giving that gesture as a positive sign during a sales presentation. Another example is the widely used gesture for "OK," which is generally recognized around the world to mean that things are going well. However, doing that in France or Latin America has very negative connotations, while in Australia it means zero. As with the earlier example, it is important for the salesperson to have a very good understanding of local gestures before presuming to use his or her own.

Business Practices

As you will recall from previous marketing courses, marketers have a set of tools they use to develop the company's value proposition, then deliver and communicate that value to the customer. This "toolkit" is known as the marketing mix and consists of four elements (product, price, distribution, and promotion).[9] These elements are profoundly affected by a company's decision to move into global markets and, in turn, impact the contemporary sales process. Salespeople must be able to work with their customers wherever they are in the world, and to deliver the same level of service and product quality (at least, that is the expectation). At the same time, the complex nature of global supply chains puts pressure on the salesperson's internal operations. Finally, all organizations must adjust to a rapidly changing global economic backdrop. In this section we will examine five critical business practices that are affected by the global sales environment.

One of the first challenges in the global sales environment is the question of **equivalent products**, which refers to the degree to which products are comparable around the world. On the one hand, salespeople argue that products be customized to fit the needs of individual customers. On the other hand, operations/production management generally argue for more standardization because of logistical challenges in getting various components and production challenges in making the product. Even in large trading zones like the European Union, where the member countries have sought to create more unified products, there remain hundreds of differences in many products, such as cars. For a company whose customers include automobile manufacturers, this presents some unique problems in selling the right product for the right market.

At the same time, smaller companies face similar tough choices. Many smaller companies throughout the EU have traditionally made products for their home markets; now, with the expansion and opening of new markets in Europe, these small companies must decide whether or not to continue focusing on their home market or expand to new markets with different product specifications. It becomes more difficult if smaller companies count global companies among their customers, since local providers are frequently held to consistent standards across markets. In addition, smaller companies often find it difficult to get important market information in the first place.[10]

One of the other challenges facing companies today, no matter their size, is the need to introduce products quickly to many markets at the same time. With today's distribution and communication systems, customers in China may wait weeks, but won't wait months, for a new product. This creates the challenge of **complex logistics networks** to manage the distribution of products to markets around the world. Salespeople must coordinate their customer presentations and manage expectations so that product changes, upgrades, and new product introductions occur with minimal disruption for the customer or their own company's operations.

Pricing for global markets is a complex and difficult issue for salespeople. As a fundamental component of the value proposition, it is essential that the customer clearly understand the price and its relationship to the overall value of the product. For many years, companies would charge a competitive price in their home market, higher prices in foreign markets where strong competition was present, and still higher prices in developing markets where market conditions were less competitive. This was usually justified by telling the customer that higher manufacturing or service delivery costs or increased shipping costs were the reason for the price difference. Today, of course, almost every market is competitive and customers (no matter their size) have access to a great deal more information about the costs of the products they purchase. Information about products and their pricing structure is universally available and customers need that information to leverage better prices and terms from their suppliers. Exhibit 14.2 demonstrates the complexity of global pricing by comparing prices for an Apple iPad across six countries.

ETHICAL DILEMMA

INFORMATION AND ETHICAL DECISIONS

Susan Benson was sitting at her desk wondering about her next move and thinking back to a conversation with her largest client—Acton Pharmacies, the largest pharmacy chain in Australia. Susan was the key account manager in Australia for G&G Products, a worldwide manufacturer of consumer healthcare products, responsible for the Acton Pharmacy account. Her primary contact at Acton was Bo Wellington, vice president of purchasing. Ms. Wellington recently became aware of a new line of baby products that G&G was getting to introduce around the world. While the products had been announced, and several countries (including the United States and China) were slated to get the products in the next 30 days, a timetable for delivery to other markets had not been announced. The products had already passed all necessary product-testing protocols and were approved for sale in Australia.

Ms. Wellington called Susan in to let her know that, as G&G's largest customer in Australia, she expected preferential treatment in terms of getting the product for Acton and wanted Susan to work with her on a timeline for introducing the product through Acton Pharmacies. Susan's boss and the country manager for G&G products in Australia was Grace Jensen, who had notified everyone just last week about the company's plans for introducing the product in Australia. At the meeting she made it clear that all information about the new products was to be kept confidential for the next 60 days while senior management worked out the plans for introducing the products. Susan knew that Ms. Wellington was looking to leverage Acton's position in the market to gain a competitive advantage over their competitors by introducing this new product first.

A few minutes ago, Ms. Wellington had called Susan to ask about G&G's specific plans for the new products and let her know again that Acton expected to receive preferential treatment. Susan decided to tell her some of the company's plans for the product rollout and that she would work with her to give Acton exclusive distribution for the product rollout. Now, as she contemplates what she should do, she turns to see Grace Jensen standing in the door, asking Susan how things are going with Acton Pharmacies.

Questions to Consider

1. Given the importance of Acton Pharmacies to G&G in Australia, was Susan wrong in giving Ms. Wellington information about the introduction of the new products?
2. Should she tell Grace Jensen about her conversation with Ms. Wellington and her commitment to secure exclusive rights for Acton on the product rollout?
3. What should Susan do now?

Customers appreciate that transportation costs, currency exchange rates, and tariffs are different around the world but they also expect, and increasingly demand, their suppliers provide consistent pricing for all purchases, no matter where that product is purchased. Global, even local, customers are confident that if one company cannot match pricing for a particular product, someone else will. They believe that the location of manufacturing and the costs of shipping products are a constant; in other words, there is no difference in cost because of where the product is produced.

This challenge makes global pricing strategies very problematic. There is a tendency in many companies to charge their largest customers competitive prices while asking smaller customers to pay a premium. However, as mentioned previously, that strategy is quickly becoming obsolete as even very small, local customers have access to information about shipping and manufacturing costs. This is coupled with the

EXHIBIT 14.2　PRICE COMPARISON FOR APPLE IPAD ACROSS SIX COUNTRIES

Country	Apple iPad, 16GB, Wi-Fi Only Price
United States	$499
Great Britain	$637 (399 British pounds)
France	$652 (489 Euros)
Germany	$639 (479 Euros)
China	$474 (2988 Chinese yuan)
Australia	$564 (539 Australian dollars)

fact that sophisticated transportation and communication systems take away the "local" advantage that many companies have relied on for years, essentially arguing that we are your "hometown" provider and will provide better service. Even small customers almost anywhere in the world can purchase a product and have it within a few days and receive customer support via the Internet or telephone. For the salesperson, it means having a clear understanding of the value proposition as an essential part of the contemporary sales process, as we have discussed throughout this book. If the salesperson cannot accurately define the value of their products to the customer, no matter where that customer is in the world, the customer will base their purchase decision on who has the lowest price—essentially turning the product into a commodity.

As a critical component of a company's promotion program, sales needs to be particularly sensitive to adjustments in the **global marketing communications**. As we noted earlier, at the most basic level it is important that local customers receive communications in their own language. However, the challenge of global marketing communications is much more complex, involving coordination and consistency of messaging as well as accuracy and timing of customer communication.

When a company updates its website it must also have available all other marketing collateral (information sheets, product brochures, pricing sheets). This can be a challenge if the company has many markets spread around the world. At the same time, if the information needs to be translated, all translations should convey the same information—not surprisingly, this includes salespeople, who need to be trained and updated on any changes to the company's product portfolios and pricing structure. If the customer can see it on the company's website, they expect the salesperson to be knowledgeable. This can create an internal conflict for the company: they don't want to release information too early because it can give competitors an advantage; however, and this is particularly true of salespeople, it is important that salespeople clearly understand and be able to deliver an effective sales message to the customer. As a result, they need to receive relevant information and be trained when necessary. All of this takes time.

Often companies will alert the sales force that changes are going to occur (product enhancement, new product introduction or changes in the pricing) and let them know that additional training will be forthcoming. The key is to be able to address customer questions and concerns. With customers having access to a great deal more information, they are often asking salespeople about the "latest product buzz" and it is essential salespeople be informed about their own products (and hopefully their competitors). Hearing about these kinds of changes from the customer is frustrating and embarrassing for the salesperson and appears unprofessional to the customer.

Technology

Technology has fundamentally changed the contemporary sales process. In many respects it has improved the customer–salesperson relationship but technology also creates new challenges for the salesperson. Let's consider these changes from the perspective of both the customer and the salesperson.

The "old" customer–salesperson relationship model was based on the assumption that a company's best customers demanded the most "face" time. Salespeople would call on them more frequently and seek to build a personal relationship with their key decision makers. While it is still true that a company's largest customers require the unique benefits that personal selling brings to the customer–salesperson relationship, it is also true that customers are redefining what a successful relationship means. The Internet now allows customers to have an immediate, personalized, and comprehensive relationship with their suppliers without a salesperson. They can order, check on order status, review product information, and receive customer service. All of these activities used to fall under the job description of the salesperson. When the Internet was becoming a dominant business tool in the late 1990s, many salespeople became concerned that this would eliminate or greatly reduce the need for the personal selling function, but just the opposite has happened. The Internet has increased the need for professional salespeople who can identify the customer's needs and deliver effective solutions. This is especially true in global sales. Indeed, most companies realize that a well-trained sales force is a huge competitive advantage in the global sales environment. In developing countries like Vietnam, companies often find that salespeople can use their product knowledge to gain the trust of their customers and win business.[11]

Technology has also impacted the global salesperson. Customers demand instant access to their salesperson and today's technology enables that to happen. This has created a lot of pressure for global account managers as they struggle to accommodate the challenges of instant access, 24/7. Consider that many companies (IBM, Disney, Coca-Cola) have large operations in the United Kingdom that service customers as far away as the Middle East and even Asia. Salespeople based in London must be able to reach customers by phone or email even though they may be several time zones away. In addition, salespeople must be able to work with colleagues around the world to service their global customers.[12]

In addition, communication is now mobile and salespeople must be able to access and effectively use this new technology. For example, tablet computers are an essential business tool for salespeople and customers expect more effective sales presentations, faster and more accurate information, and better customer service overall from their salespeople. This means salespeople need to understand and be able to use these new technologies. Finally, technology enables "virtual sales teams" composed of individuals from around the world to effectively communicate with customers no matter where they are located. This is especially helpful with technical products where a limited number of people with sufficient skills (product knowledge and application, customer knowledge) are available.

Another challenge for many companies in a rapidly changing mobile technology environment is choosing the technology platform, developing the content for the platform, then giving salespeople the tools to use it effectively. In addition, salespeople must work within the constraints of local market conditions. In cities like São Paolo and Rio de Janeiro, both in Brazil, there is good access to Wi-Fi and cellular data networks, but in smaller cities coverage is not as good and a salesperson can find that his or her tablet (or laptop) is not as effective.

The use of technology in global markets becomes a very difficult problem for smaller companies, who need to balance the cost of the technology against the benefits. Increasingly local customers demand high customer service and large customers demand exceptional customer service, which means that salespeople need to know how to use technology and have access to customer information. When a customer contacts a company about a product inquiry, or a customer service question, they expect the salesperson to know, and this is true if that customer is local or a large global company.

GLOBAL CHALLENGES IN MANAGING THE SALES PROCESS

As we have seen, the impact of global business on the contemporary sales process is profound. However, the influence is perhaps even more profound in managing the sales process. Almost every aspect of sales management is affected.

Sales Organizational Structure

When a company makes a decision to move into markets outside of its home country, one of the first decisions it has to make is how to structure its international operations and an essential component of that structure is the sales force. Companies historically have created sales organizational structures built around one or more of three criteria: products, customers, or geography. While there are advantages and disadvantages to each one, there has been a trend in recent years for companies to move toward a sales structure focused on the customer, often combined with a second criterion such as product. For example, IBM creates sales teams focused on their customers, then brings in product specialists to help support these teams with product specific information. The salesperson knows the customer well and looks for solutions to the customers' needs based on IBM's product and service competencies.

Most sales organizations start with generalists, people who know as much as possible about all the companies' products; however, as companies evolve customers demand salespeople with more expertise in more specialized areas around their own needs. As we have discussed throughout the book, one of the keys to building a successful customer relationship is a thorough understanding of the customer's business and how the company's products and services can meet their needs. Once a company develops a set of major customers (accounts) in its home country, it generally creates a new sales position most frequently called "key account manager," whose job is to manage large, important customers.

Many companies adopt a similar approach when they move to global markets and create **global account managers** (GAM), who are responsible for managing customers across country boundaries. Ultimately, these individuals are both the internal champion for the customer inside the firm and a salesperson for the company when dealing with the customer. They must have excellent selling skills but also good managerial abilities as they are frequently called to manage how the company's personnel interface with the customer. With large customers and companies this may run into hundreds, even thousands, of people.

Generally, global accounts are managed in one of three ways. First, a company may have traditional sales organizations in each country (or use strategic partners) and the global account manager acts as an internal consultant working with local salespeople to manage the customer in each country. In this structure the GAM has no formal authority and the "local" national sales managers in each country manage the accounts. The second approach is a matrix configuration where the GAM reports to a global accounts sales executive at the company's headquarters while also working directly with local sales managers to manage the account in country. In this arrangement authority for the account is shared between the GAM and local sales manager. While these two approaches represent a majority of sales structures, this is changing, as companies move to a third structure. This structure is customer focused and pulls responsibility for global accounts away from local managers and gives it to the GAM. The global account manager is responsible for managing and setting the strategic goals for each account. They are also the primary point of contact for the customer with the company around the world. Local salespeople are used to facilitate local implementation issues with the account, working with the global account manager.[13]

Hire the Right People in a Global Sales Environment

You will recall that we discussed the importance of hiring the right people in chapter 12. In that discussion we mentioned that the future of the organization rests on hiring people that are able to effectively communicate the company's value proposition to the customers and manage the customer–company relationship. When a company moves to global markets three additional factors are added to the process.

First, the company must decide on the qualifications for the job. Keep in mind that a global sales position, whether it is called global account manager or something else, is different from a sales position in a company's home country. Many companies have found that using a sales job description from their home country does not translate well to a global position in other countries. Take educational experience, for example; many professional sales positions require a college education. But countries around the world have different educational systems and degrees, which can make it difficult to equate educational experience across cultures.[14] For example, in some countries such as Germany people getting a master's degree are allowed to use the title "Doctor." However, in the United States, that title is used to reference individuals who have earned a Ph.D.

Second, legal protections for employees vary widely around the world and companies must be careful to follow the law as they move into new markets. In countries like Germany, once an employee passes a probationary period it becomes very difficult for that individual to be let go. While this does provide employees a level of confidence about their job security, it also means companies are more careful about their hiring practices.

Finally, the company needs to consider the type of individual for the position. As companies expand into global markets their employment options increase—more specifically, a company can choose to hire local nationals in each country, expatriates (generally this involves bringing in employees from the company's home country), or nationals from a third country. For many years, companies around the world sent a significant number of expatriates to run their global operations. At the time there were reasons why this was a good option. The expatriates know the company and its products and are frequently familiar with the customers. Today, however, those advantages have diminished, as qualified individuals are now available around the world. While it is certainly true that companies still send expatriates around the world for specific assignments, the vast majority of global salespeople are hired from the ranks of qualified local applicants.[15] Hiring local people does have some risks. In China, for example, there is a shortage of qualified salespeople in many fields (technical areas in particular), which can make it difficult to fill a position. In addition, because of the shortage of qualified applicants in some areas the cost of hiring the right person is high. Nationals from a third country are also an option, and in large companies you will see people from all over the world being moved from country to country. This may be due to customer considerations; perhaps the individual has particular skills that would be useful in this market. Often it is because companies are looking to develop potential managers by giving them broad international experience. Companies like Sony seek to diversify their workforce and broaden the talent pool inside the company. See Exhibit 14.3 for a breakdown of employee diversity according to region around the world.

Training for Effective Global Selling

The challenge in global sales training is to understand that training needs vary a great deal around the world. While everyone agrees that salespeople need to be trained on new products and/or changes to company policies, the most important training needs are quite different across global markets. For example, in China the hierarchical management structure can create barriers for salespeople who need to be able to speak to decision makers in a higher position. (This tends to be less of a concern for British or French salespeople.) The result is that Chinese salespeople often need training on how to address and sell to people in supervisory positions. Cultural differences need to be a considered in creating a sales training program, particularly for topics such as effective communication, customer relationship building and account management.

In addition to the changes in training content based on cultural differences, trainers must be aware of technological issues in putting together sales training. As we discussed earlier, the technology infrastructure differs widely around the world, which makes relying on a web-based training program difficult in countries like Thailand or many African nations. At the same time, developers of web-based training need to consider

EXHIBIT 14.3 EMPLOYEE DIVERSITY BY REGION FOR SONY CORPORATION

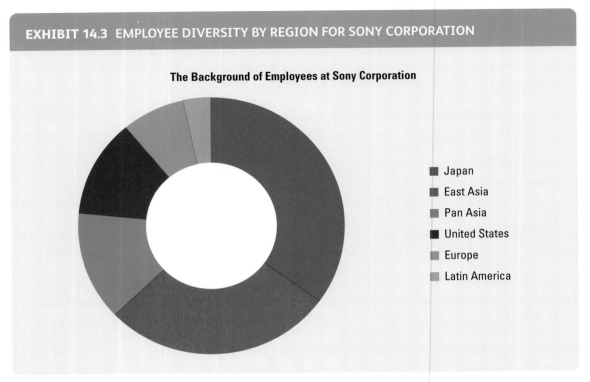

The Background of Employees at Sony Corporation

- Japan
- East Asia
- Pan Asia
- United States
- Europe
- Latin America

Note: East Asia = Mainland China, Hong Kong, Taiwan, South Korea; Pan Asia = Southeast Asia, Middle East, Africa, Oceania.

Adapted from Sony website, March 2012, http://www.sony.net/SonyInfo/csr_report/employees/info/index.html

those cultural differences when designing the training programs. The concern is that the training becomes country-specific and lacks broad applicability across different global markets.

A third challenge is that salespeople in a company's home country generally have a better understanding of the company's culture, since they frequently get to visit headquarters and benefit from knowing the culture of the home country. For salespeople working in markets outside the company's home market this becomes more challenging. The issue becomes even more important when one considers that the salesperson is responsible for the customer relationship. As a result, many companies make an extra effort to train salespeople in global markets to understand not only the products and policies but also the corporate culture.

Motivation of the Global Salesperson

As discussed in chapter 11, motivating any individual is challenging and sales managers must use a variety of tools to motivate their sales force. The key difference between motivating the sales force in a sales manager's home country and salespeople in global markets is the impact of the individual's cultural needs, goals, and behaviors. As we discussed earlier, cultural values vary widely around the world and it probably comes as no surprise that what motivates someone in the United Kingdom will not work with someone from Brazil, Japan, or Australia. Researchers have identified six bipolar dimensions that define cultural differences around the world[16] and also serve to define individual's work-related needs and motivation (see Exhibit 14.4).

Understanding broad cultural differences is an important first step in motivating the global salesperson but the sales manager must link individual cultural differences with company programs and goals. The nature of most global sales positions requires people to be independent, which runs counter to some cultures such as Japan, where group consensus is a core cultural value. Sales managers must constantly assess whether

EXHIBIT 14.4 SIX DIMENSIONS OF CROSS-CULTURAL DIFFERENCES

Universalism (Rules, codes, laws and generalizations)	*Particularism* (Exceptions, special circumstances, unique relations)
Individualism (Personal freedom, human rights, competitiveness)	*Communitarianism* (Social responsibility, harmonious relationships, cooperation)
Specificity (Atomistic, reductive analytic, objective)	*Diffusion* (Holistic, elaborative, synthetic, relational)
Achieved Status (What you have done, your track record, your accomplishments)	*Ascribed Status* (Who you are, your potential, your connections)
Inner Direction (Conscience and convictions are located inside the individual)	*Outer Direction* (Examples and influences are located outside the individual)
Sequential Time (Time is a race along a course)	*Synchronous Time* (Time is a dance of fine coordination)

Source: Charles M. Hampden-Turner and Fons Trompenaars, *Building Cross-Cultural Competence: How to Create Wealth from Conflicting Values* (New Haven, CN: Yale University Press, 2000).

the individual is a good fit with the company's culture, which is likely based on the company's home country. An individual's motivation may be a great fit with a corporate culture from his home country but not a good fit with another corporate culture. Some Americans find working in German-based companies challenging because of the traditional hierarchical managerial structure. Americans are used to making decisions and following an action plan, while German companies generally take more time planning and vetting decisions through more levels of management.

Compensation of the Global Salesperson

Compensating salespeople is complex and it is difficult to create an effective plan that rewards and motivates the salesperson while helping the company reach its goals. We examined this issue in chapter 13 but, as you might guess, there are unique challenges facing the management team when they expand the compensation program to a global sales force. Initially sales managers must strike the proper balance between company goals and the specific characteristics of a global market. Consider sales executives in Germany and France. Both of the European countries are characterized by high income tax rates, so many companies adjust their compensation programs to pay less compensation in Euros but cover the cost of housing and other perks such as cars and even vacations. These kind of local adjustments are needed to motivate and retain good executives across the organization, not just in sales.

Moreover, sales managers must consider balancing overall company goals against specific country objectives. In emerging markets, for example, salespeople generally spend a lot more time developing new business and less time servicing existing customers, while established markets often require a higher level of customer service. While overall corporate goals may be seeking to improve customer service and compensation programs adjusted to reward people who hit customer service metrics, the local sales manager in a developing market may want the sales force focused on new business goals. In situations like this, local sales managers will often seek permission from senior management to adjust reward programs to reflect the needs of the specific market while maintaining some element of the compensation plan on the overall corporate objectives.

Another challenge is balancing compensation programs around the world. Currency fluctuations, local costs of living, and base-compensation packages can all create anomalies in compensation systems over time. The goal is that salespeople in the same position performing at the same level of success should be compensated more or less equally all over the world. If anomalies in the compensation do appear and are not adjusted, the results can be lower morale and performance inside the sales force. At the same time it is difficult to for sales managers to fine-tune compensation systems and any changes in one country will be known by other salespeople in the company.

Evaluation of the Global Sales Force

Evaluation is a critical part of managing the contemporary sales process. This process comes to be even more important for the global sales force when we bear in mind that salespeople reside all over the world, making it difficult for many senior sales executives to see an individual's performance firsthand. Evaluating the local sales manager becomes particularly important and speaks to the importance of a well-understood performance evaluation system.

At the same time, it is critical to realize that an effective performance evaluation system adjusts for differences across global markets. Consider our earlier discussion on cultural differences and the dimension of Individualism versus Communitarianism. For a salesperson from Japan, who values working in teams, evaluating the sales force on individual performance may actually work against the prevailing culture inside that group of salespeople.[17] It is important to define evaluation, not only in terms of corporate metrics but also metrics that fit the culture.

EXPERT ADVICE: FOLLOW-UP   <Chally Group> WORLDWIDE

After watching the video of Mr. Kadien and reading the chapter, consider the following questions:

1. What challenges do you think a salesperson from Epedx faces in working with global customers?
2. Is a global representative with Epedx a salesperson or consultant? If salesperson, what is the primary focus? If consultant, what is his or her primary focus?

SUMMARY

The fundamentals of contemporary selling are true all over the world. However, it is important to appreciate that there are clear and profound differences in the sales process as well as managing salespeople from country to country and region to region globally. The global sales environment exists outside the company's home but influences the company, its operations, and its customers. This chapter considered the impact of the global sales environment on the contemporary selling process and managing the contemporary sales force.

We first examined the importance of considering a global perspective. Some sales managers may argue that they are too small or their customers have no global operations or give any one of dozens of reasons why it is not important to study the global sales environment. Unfortunately, people who take this approach fail to realize that the global sales environment impacts every salesperson. Next we delineated the various global challenges in the sales process. From culture to ethics, the global sales environment impacts the sales process and can be a differentiator between sales success and failure. The final section in the chapter focused on managing the contemporary sales process and how global issues impact everything from sales structure to salesperson evaluation (organizational structure, marketing mix, hiring, training, compensation, and evaluation).

KEY TERMS

globalization

culture

cultural differences

language

cultural values

equivalent products

complex logistics networks

pricing for global markets

global marketing communications

global account manager

DISCUSSION QUESTIONS

1. In Thomas Friedman's book *The World is Flat*, he states the big companies should "learn how to act small and enable their customers to act really big." What do you think that means? How might that statement impact a global sales force and the way they interact with their customers?

2. You are a small manufacturer of specialty medical devices located in Chicago, Illinois, and the market for your product is cardiologists in the United States. Does globalization affect your business? If so, why and how?

3. You are the global sales manager for a consumer food products company that is getting ready to roll out a new product. As part of the introduction your global sales force is being asked to do a number of in-store demonstrations in grocery stores around their market. This means working weekends for three months. One of the largest global regions for your products is Latin America. How will your decision to work weekends be received among your Latin American sales force? What would you do to ensure the sales force accepts this short-term policy?

4. You are the global sales manager for Samsung responsible for sales of their tablet computers. The company has just announced a new model that will be available in five countries starting next month (Japan, Korea, United States, United Kingdom, and France). The product is expected to be very popular and you have been asked to develop a strategy for rollout for the rest of the world. Due to limited production the rollout must occur over six months, so some countries will have to wait that long before receiving the new tablet. What would you suggest salespeople in other countries tell their customers (large electronics retailers)?

5. As sales manager for a global technology company, you have been tasked with opening up a new market in Asia. One of your responsibilities is to create a sales force consisting of 20 new salespeople. The job description describes someone with good technical skills and selling ability in the B2B technology market. Would you focus on hiring local nationals, expatriates, or third-country nationals? Why?

MINI-CASE 14 GEN TECH CORPORATION

Barry Randolph is a global marketing manger for Gen Tech Corporation, a leading manufacturer of computer accessories. The company has market-leading products in several categories, including keyboards and cases for laptops and tablet computers. One of Barry's responsibilities is working with the Gen Tech global sales force as well as overall marketing communications for the company's line of laptop and tablet computer cases.

Recently he became aware of a problem in their Asian markets. While many of the company's products were manufactured in Asia, particularly China, local Asian markets paid a premium for Gen Tech's products relative to the price of their products in the United States or Western Europe. This was due to the perceived quality of the product in Asia and the power of Gen Tech's brand in these markets. The problem was that several large retailers wanted Gen Tech to lower their prices to match the pricing structure of Gen Tech's products in the United States. Senior management had told Barry to "hold the line" on the pricing structure, but he was finding this to be difficult. Salespeople were asking Barry to drop the price, or some of these retailers would like to reduce the amount of Gen Tech products in their stores.

At Gen Tech the local sales force in each global market was under the supervision of the country manager and Barry had no direct control over their activities. While this had worked well for many years, it was now creating problems for Gen Tech, as salespeople (and their country managers) were putting a lot of pressure on Barry and Gen Tech management to lower prices in an effort to retain these important retailers.

Questions

1. What are the challenges for a company like Gen Tech when they maintain different pricing structures for their products around the world?

2. How should Barry Randolph and Gen Tech resolve the issue of variable price structures for their products?

3. What management structure would you recommend Gen Tech follow in managing their global sales operations?

Glossary

A

Account analysis estimating the sales potential for each customer and prospect in the territory.

Account attractiveness the degree to which a customer is desirable to the company, such as generating new business.

Account call rates a calculation of the number of times a particular account is called on in a given time (week, month, or year).

Account priorities goals and objectives for individual customers.

Active listening carefully monitoring the dialogue with the customer, watching for buying signals (verbal and nonverbal).

Activity priorities goals and objectives for specific sales related activities (i.e., number of new accounts).

Adaptive selling the altering of sales behaviors during a customer interaction or from one situation to another based on information the sales rep gathers about the nature of the selling situation.

Advantage a particular product/service characteristic that helps meet the customer's needs.

Alternative choice close gives the prospect options (neither of which is not to buy at all). It focuses on making the choice between viable options—options the prospect is most likely to accept.

Approach the first part of the sales presentation. It is a transition point from the greeting to the main body of your presentation, where the primary sales message will be delivered to the customer.

Assessment approach a sales strategy in which you ask the customer to complete a set of questions, collect the data, analyze the information, and make a presentation based on your analysis.

Assumptive close a closing technique in which a salesperson assumes the buyer accepts the sales presentation and the sale will be successfully completed.

Attitude a state of mind or feeling with regard to a person or thing (or product or service).

Autonomy the degree of independence the salesperson can exercise in making his or her own decisions in the day-to-day operation of the job.

Average cost of a sales call has been estimated to be as much as $242, depending on the industry. This cost is increasing by about 5 percent per year.

B

Balance sheet close also known as **t-account close**, gets the salesperson directly involved in helping the prospect see the pros and cons of placing the order by creating a list of "Reasons for Buying" and "Remaining Questions" on paper.

BARS (behaviorally anchored rating scale) an approach to performance appraisal directed at resolving problems related to the selection of attributes for evaluation and how they are presented on the form.

Basic control unit the fundamental geographic area used to form sales territories—county or city, for example.

Behavior refers to what salespeople do—that is, the tasks on which they expend effort while working.

Benefit is the favorable outcome to the buyer from the advantage found in the product feature.

Bias refers to the degree to which performance evaluations differ from objective reality, usually based on errors by the evaluator (in our case, the sales manager).

Bird dogs, or spotters are people who come into contact with an unusually large number of people in the course of their daily routine. Salespeople use bird dogs as their eyes and ears in the marketplace.

Blended technology sales call a sales call on a buyer that includes some in-person salespeople and some via electronic means.

Blogs online journals and forums that are generally publicly accessible.

Bonus a payment made at the discretion of management for achieving or surpassing some set level of performance.

Bounce-back occurs when a salesperson turns a customer concern into a reason for action. The bounce-back is effective in many different situations (appointment setting, negotiating, and closing).

Brand equity the value inherent in a brand name in and of itself.

Bribe a financial present given to a buyer to manipulate his or her purchase decision.

Business climate a set of unwritten norms and rules that influence the behavior of individuals. Every organization has a business climate. See also *corporate culture.*

Business ethics moral principles and standards that guide behavior in the world of business. The purpose of such principles and standards is to define right and wrong behavior for salespeople. See also *ethics.*

Business-to-business (B2B) market (previously called *industrial selling*)—the sale of goods and services to buyers who are not the end users. Relationship selling is much more predominant in the B2B market than the B2C market.

Business-to-consumer (B2C) market the sale of goods and services to end-user consumers (retail selling).

Buying center all the people who participate in purchasing or influencing the purchase of a particular product. Buying center members include initiators, users, influencers, gatekeepers, buyers, deciders, and controllers.

Buying signals verbal and nonverbal cues that the customer is ready to make a commitment to purchase.

Buy-now close also sometimes referred to as the **impending event** close or standing-room-only close, creates a sense of urgency with the buyer that, if he or she doesn't act today, something valuable will be lost.

C

Call frequency the number of times the salesperson calls on certain customers or classes of customers (for example, retail stores with less than a certain amount of sales in a given period). It is expressed as so many times per week, month, and year.

Call reluctance occurs when salespeople resist prospecting because (of all the activities required in successful relationship selling) it is the one that involves making cold calls. Salespeople must overcome call reluctance.

Career priorities priorities that deal with what kind of sales career one wants to have over time.

Caveat emptor ("Let the buyer beware") adage that defined the 20th Century sales model. It was generally considered the buyer's responsibility to uncover any untruths in the seller's statements.

Centers of influence people who are in a position to persuade a salesperson's potential customers.

Closing the sale obtaining a commitment from the prospect or customer to make a purchase. It is one of the most important sales call goals.

Code of ethics formulated through learning a sense of right and wrong. Employees make ethical decisions using two ethical frameworks—their own personal code of ethics and the company's ethical code.

Cold calls, also referred to as **canvassing**—telephoning or going to see potential prospects in person without invitation.

Collusion occurs when competing companies get together and fix prices, divide up customers or territories, or act in a way to harm a third party (often another competitor or a customer).

Commission a payment based on short-term results, usually a salesperson's dollar or unit sales volume.

Compensate for deficiencies moving the customer from focusing on a feature in which your product performs poorly to one in which it excels.

Compensation all monetary rewards professional salespeople receive.

Compensation plan is the method used to implement the reward structure in an organization.

Competitor defamation harming a competitor by making unfair or untrue statements about the company, its products, or the people that work for it.

Competitor obstruction the practice of impeding competitor access to a customer.

Complex logistics networks intricate supply-chain management systems designed to manage the distribution of products to markets around the world.

Conferences events held by the sales organization to provide a forum for prospecting. Conferences typically combine information sessions with social outings and are usually held in attractive locations.

Confidentiality the sharing of sensitive information between salespeople and customers—an important aspect of relationship selling.

Consultative selling the set of skills, strategies, and processes that works most effectively with buyers who demand, and are willing to pay for, a sales effort that creates new value and provides additional benefits beyond the product.

Corporate culture developed through establishment of a well-defined mission together with a successful corporate history and top management's values and beliefs. Corporate cultures shape employee attitudes and actions and help determine the plans, policies, and procedures salespeople and their managers can implement.

Cultural differences the unique manifestations of a specific set of norms, accepted behaviors, and beliefs created by every culture.

Cultural values the set of ideals expressed as beliefs adopted by a particular culture.

Culture a system of values, beliefs, and morals shared by a specific group of people that lasts over time.

Customer advocacy a customer is satisfied, loyal, and willing to spread the word that he or she is pleased with you.

Customer benefit approach a sales technique that involves starting the presentation with a solution to at least one of the customer's problems, creating an instant win–win situation.

Customer-centric firms that put the customer at the center of everything that happens both inside and outside the organization.

Customer complaints concerns raised by the customer about some aspect of the relationship. They may involve service problems, the salesperson's performance, pricing concerns, product quality, or any other issue that creates a problem for the customer.

Customer delight exceeding customer expectations to a surprising degree; is a powerful way to gain customer loyalty.

Customer loyalty when salespeople give customers many reasons not to switch to competitors. Your value proposition must be strong enough to move customers past mere satisfaction and into a commitment to you and your products for the long run.

Customer mindset the salesperson's belief that understanding and satisfying customers, whether internal or external to the organization, is central to doing his or her job well. It is through this customer mindset that a customer orientation comes alive within a sales force.

Customer orientation the importance that a firm places on customers. Customer-oriented organizations instill an organizationwide focus on understanding customer requirements, generate an understanding of the marketplace, disseminate that knowledge to everyone in the firm, and align system capabilities internally so that the organization responds effectively with innovative, competitively differentiated, satisfaction-generating products and services.

Customer relationship management (CRM) a comprehensive business model for increasing revenues and profits by focusing on customers. CRM uses advanced technology to maximize the firm's ability to add value to customers and develop long-term customer relationships.

Customer satisfaction the degree to which customers like the product, service, and relationship.

Customer value when the customer weighs the costs (monetary and otherwise) of a relationship with a seller, and the benefits realized from that relationship outweigh the costs.

D

Daily event schedule one of the basic elements in a good time management plan. It involves a daily to-do list with specific tasks.

Data mining sorting the information warehoused in a database to learn more about current and potential customers.

Data warehouse a comprehensive, customer-centric approach to handling customer data and transforming it into useful information for developing customer-focused strategies and programs.

Deception occurs when a manager and/or salesperson are not being totally honest with each other.

Defer is postponing the customer concern until salespeople have had the chance to explain other material.

Demarketing a process that a company may engage in during periods of shortage that may involve a part, or all, of its product line. The process seeks to reduce demand in the short run.

Derived demand demand for goods and services derived from the customers' demand for the goods or services it produces or markets.

Development a long-term road map or career track for a salesperson so he or she can realize professional goals.

Direct close the most straightforward closing approach, in which the salesperson simply asks for the order.

Direct denial an immediate and unequivocal rejection of a customer statement.

Directories published books of contacts (available from a variety of sources) that can serve as lead generators.

Dishonesty providing false or deliberately inaccurate information to customers.

E

Effectiveness refers to some measure of organizational outcomes for which a salesperson is at least partly responsible.

Effort the core of motivation. That is, motivation may be thought of as the amount of effort a salesperson chooses to expend on each activity or task associated with the job.

80:20 rule 80 percent of a company's business comes from 20 percent of its customers.

Empathy a salesperson's identification with and understanding of the buyer's situation, feelings, and motives.

Employee benefits part of a compensation package designed to satisfy the salesperson's basic needs for security. They typically include medical and disability insurance, life insurance, and a retirement plan.

Employment agencies companies that specialize in the placement of individuals in jobs. Some companies focus on certain types of jobs, like sales, and others are general employment agencies.

Endless chain referral occurs when the salesperson asks an open-ended question during each customer contact in an effort to gather the names of potential prospects, who in turn will provide more leads.

Enterprise resource planning (ERP) software that links bid estimation, order entry, shipping, billing systems, and other work processes.

Enterprise selling the set of skills, strategies, and processes that work most effectively with strategically important customers who demand an extraordinary level of value creation from a key supplier. The primary function of enterprise selling is to leverage the sales organization's corporate assets to contribute to the customer's strategic success.

Equivalent products the degree to which products are comparable around the world. Products that are very similar around the world are considered equivalent (for example, many technology products are very similar around the world).

Ethics moral principles and standards that guide behavior. Importantly, social values set the standards for ethical behavior. A particular action may be legal but not ethical.

Expectancy the salesperson's estimate of the probability that expending effort on a task will lead to improved performance on some dimension.

Expectancy theory of motivation provides the framework for motivating salespeople.

Expense account a formal reimbursement plan for travel, lodging, meals, entertainment, and other expenses incurred by sales reps in the field.

External environment, or **macroenvironment** the issues that arise outside the control of the selling organization. Examples include the Federal Reserve raising interest rates or the government regulating a product. See also *internal environment*.

External sources for recruits include people in other firms (who are often identified and referred by current members of the sales force), educational institutions, ads, and employment agencies.

Extrinsic rewards the rewards bestowed on the salesperson by people or organizations outside the individual, most notably the company. See also *intrinsic rewards*.

F

FAB an acronym that stands for "features, advantages, and benefits." By applying the FAB approach, salespeople can make the company's products and services relevant for the customer.

Feature is any material characteristic or specification of the company's products and services.

Firing a customer a rather harsh way to express the idea that a customer does not generate enough profit, and thus needs to find alternative sources or channels for products needed.

Follow-up one of the most important ways to add value through excellent service after the sale. Effective follow-up is one way that salespeople and their firms can improve customer perceptions of service quality, customer satisfaction, and customer loyalty and retention rates.

Formalization the structure, processes and tools, and managerial knowledge and commitment that are formally established in support of a firm's culture.

Formula presentation a prepared outline that directs the overall structure of the presentation but enables the salesperson to gain customer feedback and adjust the presentation. A formula presentation is highly structured but increases customer interaction by soliciting more information.

4 Ps of marketing product, place or distribution, price, and promotion. They are also known as the marketing mix.

G

Gamification approaching other tasks and turning them into a videogame-like platform.

Gift a nonfinancial present.

Global account manager the individual in an organization responsible for managing large global customer accounts, whose responsibilities include managing and setting strategic goals for the account and facilitating local implementation issues as they come up around the world.

Global marketing communications the coordination of complex messaging that is consistent around the world, as well as the accuracy and timing of customer communication.

Globalization the process of creating an increasingly integrated global economy generally represented by free trade, free flow of capital, and the searching out of low-cost foreign labor markets.

I

Inbound telemarketing gives prospects a way to receive more information from the sales organization via the telephone.

Incentive pay is the compensation paid by commission or bonus that direct salespeople's efforts toward specific strategic objectives during a given time period.

Incentives financial as well as nonfinancial rewards. Nonfinancial incentives include recognition programs, promotions to better territories or to management positions, or opportunities for personal development.

Indirect denial is less threatening than a direct denial and involves agreeing with the customer and validating their objection before explaining why it is untrue or misdirected.

Industrial selling an old term for business-to-business (B2B) selling. See *business-to-business market*.

Input measures objective measures of performance that focus on the efforts sales representatives expend rather than the results of those efforts.

Inside salespeople salespeople who do not call on clients face-to-face. Telemarketers are inside salespeople.

Instrumentalities are the salesperson's estimates that improved performance will lead to attaining particular rewards.

Integrated marketing communications (IMC) ensures that all the messages about a company and its products are consistent.

Internal customers people within a firm who may not have direct external customer contact but who nonetheless add value that will ultimately benefit the people and companies that buy the firm's products and services.

Internal environment, or **organizational environment** issues that arise inside the company and are controllable by the firm. Examples include hiring more support staff or improving quality control. See also *external environment*.

Internal marketing marketing inside a firm to provide a consistency of messages among employees and to show that management is uniform in supporting key strategic themes.

Internal sources for recruits, consist of people already employed in other departments within the firm.

Intimate space the space within 2 feet of a person. This space is reserved for family and close friends. Salespeople who violate this space are considered rude and even offensive.

Intrinsic rewards the rewards inherent to satisfaction derived from elements of the job or role itself. The salesperson bestows intrinsic rewards on himself or herself. See also *extrinsic rewards*.

J

Job analysis determines what activities, tasks, responsibilities, and environmental influences are involved in the job.

Job description used to develop a statement of job qualifications, which lists and describes the personal traits and abilities a person should have to perform the tasks and meet the responsibilities involved.

Job enlargement the fact that the sales role today is broader and contains substantially more activities than it once did.

Job qualifications are the personal traits and abilities a person should have to perform the job.

Job satisfaction refers to all the characteristics of the job that sales reps find rewarding, fulfilling, and satisfying. Job dissatisfaction refers to aspects they find frustrating and unsatisfying.

Junk mail unsolicited mass direct mail that many customers throw away.

K

Key account one of a firm's largest customers (especially one with a buying center) whose potential business over time represents enough dollars and entails enough cross-functional interaction among various areas of both firms to justify the high costs of the team approach. Key accounts generally have a senior salesperson as the key account manager (KAM).

Key success factors the various skills and knowledge components required to perform the sales role successfully. Identifying these key success factors in contemporary selling is the first step in recruiting and selecting good salespeople.

L

Language an essential building block of culture and the primary communication tool in a society.

Lead the name of someone who might have the potential to buy from the sales company. See also *prospects*.

Libel defamation in which unfair or untrue *written* statements materially harm the reputation of a competitor or the personal reputation of anyone working for it.

Life priorities personal priorities that deal with basic choices in life.

Lifetime value of a customer an estimate of the present value of the stream of future profits expected over a customer's lifetime of purchases.

M

Margin refers to profit made by the firm.

Market orientation the operationalization or implementation of the marketing concept. Actions taken by a firm that is market oriented are focused on aligning all the various organizational processes and functions toward maximizing the firm's success in the competitive marketplace.

Market potential combines historical data and market research results with feedback from salespeople to estimate the potential sales for all similar products in a given area.

Marketing concept an overarching business philosophy where companies turn to customers for input in making strategic decisions about what products to market, where to market them, how to get them to market, at what price, and how to communicate with customers about the products.

Marketing mix the 4 Ps of marketing, which is the toolkit marketers use to develop marketing strategy (product, place or distribution, price, and promotion).

Matrix organization an organization of direct reports and supporting internal consultants who bring their collective expertise to bear for a client.

Memorized presentation a very structured presentation that focuses on the product and is based on the memorization of specific canned statements and questions. Companies and salespeople who adopt a memorized presentation strategy believe they can make a compelling argument for the product without spending time learning more about the customer's problems and needs.

Mentors managers in sales organizations who work with their salespeople to enhance their effectiveness during sales presentations and help them improve their skill sets.

Metropolitan statistical area (MSA) an integrated economic and social unit with a large population nucleus.

Minor point close occurs when the salesperson focuses the buyer on a small element of the decision. The idea is that agreeing on something small reflects commitment to the purchase and lets the salesperson move forward with the deal.

Modified rebuy where a customer wants to modify the product specs, prices, or other terms it has been receiving from existing suppliers and will consider dealing with new suppliers to make changes.

Motivation refers to an individual's choice to initiate action on a certain task, expend a certain amount of effort on that task, and persist in expending effort over a period of time.

N

Need analysis occurs when a firm determines the best solution to the customer's requirements by combining knowledge of the company's products and services with the recognition of customer needs. The salesperson must make the analysis quickly, often during the presentation.

Need identification involves questioning customers to discover their needs.

Need satisfaction occurs when the salesperson presents the company's solution (products and services) to a customer's needs.

Need satisfaction presentation a sales presentation in which the focus is on customers and satisfying their needs. As much as 50–60 percent of the first half of the presentation is spent asking questions, listening, and determining the customer's real needs.

Negotiation a process in which a sales organization works with customers to develop a win–win solution to their problems. It is at the heart of the relationship selling process.

Networking using contacts—personal, professional, everyone a sales rep meets—to develop leads.

New-task purchase occurs when a customer is buying a relatively complex and expensive product or service for the first time.

Nonfinancial incentives incentives in addition to financial compensation such as opportunities for promotion or various types of recognition for performance like special awards and citations.

Nonverbal communication communication that does not involve words, such as someone's facial expressions, posture, eye contact, gestures, and even dress.

O

Objections concerns that some part of a product offering (solution) does not fully meet the buyer's need. The objection may be over price, delivery, terms of agreement, timing, or myriad other potential elements of a deal.

Objective measures of salesperson performance reflect statistics the sales manager can gather from the firm's internal data. These measures are best used when they reflect elements of the sales process. See also *subjective measures of salesperson performance*.

On-the-job (OJT) training individual instruction (coaching) and in-house classes held close to where the salesperson is working, such as district sales offices.

Opportunity rate the proportion of salespeople promoted into management in a year.

Organization of critical information ability to organize and create a system for easy access to information critical to effective time management.

Organizational citizenship behaviors encompass four basic types of activities: (1) sportsmanship, (2) civic virtue, (3) conscientiousness, and (4) altruism.

Outbound telemarketing involves making unsolicited phone calls to leads in an attempt to qualify them as prospects.

Outcome bias occurs when a sales manager allows the outcome (rather than the process) of a decision or a series of decisions made by a salesperson to overly influence his or her performance ratings.

Output measures objective measures of performance that represent the results of efforts expended by a salesperson.

Outside salespeople salespeople that call on clients in person.

Outsourced sales force entails hiring sales agents—who usually work for a broker organization—who specialize in selling particular types of product lines within the hiring firm's channel of distribution.

Outsupplier a potential supplier that is not on a buyer's approved vendor list. An outsupplier's objective is to move the customer away from the automatic reordering procedures of a straight rebuy toward the more extensive evaluation processes of a modified rebuy.

P

Perceived risk in a buying center, is based on the complexity of the product and situation, the relative importance of the purchase, time pressure to make a decision, and the degree of uncertainty about the product's efficacy.

Perceived role ambiguity occurs when a salesperson lacks sufficient information about the job and its requirements.

Perceived role conflict arises when a salesperson believes that the demands of two or more of his or her role partners are incompatible.

Perceived value whether or not something has value is in the eye of the beholder—the customer.

Performance behavior evaluated in terms of its contribution to the goals of the organization. Performance has a normative element reflecting whether a salesperson's behavior is good or bad, appropriate or inappropriate, in light of the organization's goals and objectives.

Performance gap the difference between what a salesperson promised and what he or she delivers to a buyer. Performance gaps result in customer complaints.

Performance management system integrates all the elements of feedback on the process of serving customers so that performance information is timely, accurate, and relevant to the customer management aspects of the firm.

Perquisites (perks) might include higher compensation, a better automobile, better office facilities, and the like to provide incentives for top salespeople to move into more advanced sales positions.

Personal interviews structured and unstructured, the most common method of selecting salespeople and the one sales managers consider most helpful.

Personal priorities what's really important to a given individual. See also *professional priorities*.

Personal space the space of 2–3 feet around a person. It should not be violated except for a handshake.

Persuasive communication hoping to convince someone to do something or win someone over to a particular course of action.

Preapproach planning the sales call before actually making the initial approach to set the appointment.

Price discrimination the practice of giving different prices or discounts to different customers who purchase the same quality and quantity of products and services.

Pricing for global markets the process of creating a pricing strategy around the world that maximizes revenue and profit while remaining competitive in individual markets.

Problem-solving presentation approach considered the most complex and difficult sales presentation strategy. It is based on a simple premise that the customer has problems and the salesperson is there to solve them by creating win–win solutions.

Product demonstration a sales presentation for a product (like a car) for which demonstrating the product is a critical part of the presentation.

Professional priorities an individual's goals and objectives for his or her work life and career. See also *personal priorities*.

Promotion mix, or **marketing communications mix**, includes personal selling, advertising, sales promotion, public relations and publicity, and direct marketing.

Prospecting pursuing leads that you hope will develop into customers as a way to fill your pipeline of future business.

Prospects leads who meet certain criteria to qualify as potential customers. Prospects are considered to be a set of *very likely* potential customers.

Public space the space greater than 12 feet around a person. It is the most accessible space around the customer.

Q

Qualifying the prospect the process of analyzing a lead to see if the person meets the criteria to be a prospect.

Question method asking customers questions in the approach to involve them right from the start and get customer feedback to position you for success in the presentation.

Quota the minimum requirement a salesperson must reach to earn a bonus. Quotas can be based on goals for sales volume, profitability of sales, or various account servicing activities.

R

Ratio measures Combining various outputs and/or inputs measures of performance in selected ways.

Reciprocity the practice of suppliers buying from one another.

Referral occurs when an existing customer sends business to his or her salesperson.

Rejection not the way a salesperson should take the failure to get an order or close a deal. Such outcomes are not personal rejections.

Relationship selling has the central goal of securing, building, and maintaining long-term relationships with profitable customers. Relationship selling works to add value through all possible means.

Repeat purchase, or **straight rebuy** occurs when a customer buys the same product under the same circumstances again and again. It tends to be much more routine than new-task purchase or modified rebuy.

Restraint of trade forcing a dealer or other channel member to stop carrying its competitors' products as part of its arrangement with the dealer.

Retail selling involves selling goods and services to end-user consumers for their own personal use.

Retention rate how long a salesperson or company keeps customers.

Return on customer investment how much time, money, and other resources are invested in a customer divided by how much the company earns from that customer's purchases.

Reward mix relative emphasis placed on salary versus commission or other incentive pay and nonfinancial rewards.

Role inaccuracy the degree to which the salesperson's perceptions of his or her role partners' demands are accurate.

Role playing a popular technique in which the sales trainee acts out a part, most often a salesperson, in a simulated buying session.

Routing schedule the plan for reaching all customers in a given time period and territory.

S

Salary a fixed sum of money paid at regular intervals.

Sales contests get reps to compete for prizes like vacations and clothes. They encourage extra effort aimed at specific short-term objectives.

Sales management the way the various aspects of relationship selling are managed within the salesperson's firm.

Sales potential the share of total market potential a company expects to achieve.

Sales presentation the delivery of information relevant to solving the customer's needs. It often involves a product demonstration.

Sales pressure the pressure exerted on the salespeople. It is one of the ethical issues in the relationship between managers and salespeople. Management should define clear sales goals without threatening undue pressure.

Sales territory an area defined by the company that includes customers or potential customers for the salesperson to call on. It is often designated geographically.

Sales training analysis investigates the training needs of a sales force and results in a plan for management to conduct a training program designed to benefit a particular salesperson or, more likely, an entire sales force.

Selection procedure a process that results in hiring the best sales rep from the available pool of applicants.

Self-evaluation means salespeople prepare an assessment of their own performance against the established objective and subjective performance criteria. This is part of 360-degree performance feedback and should be done before the formal performance review session with the manager.

Selling center brings together individuals from around the organization (marketing, customer service, sales, engineering, and others) to help salespeople do their jobs more effectively.

Service recovery a well-handled follow-up to customer problems that solidifies long-term customer relationships.

Silence a closing tool in which a salesperson sits back, stays quiet, and lets the customer talk.

Single-source supplier only one vendor used by a firm for a particular good or service to minimize the variation in quality of production inputs.

Slander defamation in which unfair or untrue *oral* statements materially harm the reputation of a competitor or the personal reputation of anyone working for it.

Slotting allowances fees retailers charge sales organizations for guaranteed shelf space. They cover the cost of setting up a new item in their IT system, programming it into inventory, and ultimately distributing it to stores.

Social media Internet-based platforms that allow users to create their own content and share it with others that access the site. These platforms all aim to build community and communication-sharing among users.

Social responsibility the responsibility a company has toward its stakeholders: customers, employees, shareholders, suppliers, the government, creditors, and a host of other entities, who expect the company to act in an ethical manner.

Social space the space from 4 to 12 feet, often the space between customer and salesperson in a personal sales presentation.

Solution selling a relationship selling approach in which the salesperson's primary role is to move the buyer toward visualization of a solution to his or her problem (need).

Spam junk email. Many email users (especially business users) filter spam out of their inboxes before they even view the messages.

SPIN strategy a comprehensive selling approach based on a series of four questions about the situation, problem, implication, and need payoff.

Stall occurs when customers ask for more time because they wish to delay the final decision for several reasons.

Straight rebuy occurs when a customer reorders an item he or she has purchased many times. See also *repeat purchase*.

Strategic partnerships formal relationships where companies' assets are shared for mutual advantage.

Subjective measures of salesperson performance typically relies on personal evaluations by someone inside the organization, usually the salesperson's immediate supervisor. They are generally gathered via direct observation but may involve input from customers or other sources. See also *objective measures of salesperson performance*.

Summary-of-benefits close a relatively formal way to close by going back over some or all of the benefits accepted, reminding the buyer why those benefits are important, and then asking a direct closing question (or perhaps ending with a choice or some other method).

Supply-chain management the way firms manage every element in the channel of distribution. Firms that have excellent supply-chain management add a great deal of value for customers.

Sustainability a movement succinctly defined as firms doing well by doing good across the multifaceted aspects of their operations, which significantly impacts relationships with client firms as well as with the public at large.

T

Team selling these structures commonly make the salesperson responsible for working with the entire selling team in order to manage the customer relationship.

Technology the making, usage, and knowledge of tools, techniques, crafts, systems, or methods of organization in order to solve a problem or serve some purpose.

Technology acceptance model (TAM) a model has been well tested and consistently predicts that salesperson attitude and behavioral intentions to use a technology are positively impacted by the perceived usefulness and perceived ease of use of the technology by the salesperson.

Telecommuting working from a remote or virtual office, often at home, and seldom traveling to company offices.

Telemarketing selling by telephone. It is a support provided to salespeople by many firms and may be outbound, inbound, or both. Recent legislation limits outbound telemarketing.

Tenacity sticking with a task, even through difficulty and adversity.

Territory management plan defines where and how customers will interact with the company, in order to maintain the right relationship with its customers. It involves designing and monitoring the territory and tapping its full potential.

360-degree performance feedback solicits information for performance evaluation simultaneously from multiple sources, such as external customers, internal customers, selling team members, sales assistants, the sales manager, and the salesperson himself or herself.

Time management plan a schedule of goals based on identification of personal and professional priorities.

Touchpoints various points at which a firm has contact with its prospects and customers for the purpose of acquiring, retaining, or cross-selling customers. Examples include a call center, salesperson, distributor, store, branch office, website, or email.

Trade shows major industry events in which companies doing business in a particular industry gather together to display their new products and services.

Training generally focuses on building specific skill and knowledge sets needed to succeed in a job.

Transactional selling the approach of conducting business as a series of discrete transactions. Transactional selling creates its value by stripping costs and making acquisition easy.

Trial close at any time during the sales process, the salesperson tries to close upon detecting one or more buying signals. The buyer may or may not actually be ready to commit. If commitment is achieved, it is considered *the* close. If commitment is not achieved, the trial close can uncover buyer objections that must be overcome. A trial close can involve any of the closing methods discussed in the book.

Trial offer an offer that allows the customer to use a product (perhaps in a small quantity) without a commitment to purchase.

Trust a belief by one party that the other party will fulfill its obligations in a relationship.

Turnover the number of people who leave the organization in a given time period (usually one year). Turnover is often expressed as a percentage (those who leave versus the total sales force).

U

Uniform Commercial Code (UCC) a group of regulations that defines the legal implications of selling. Consisting of nine articles, and modified by each state, the UCC sets out the rules and procedures for almost all business practices in the United States.

Utility the want-satisfying power of a good or service.

V

Valence for performance the salesperson's perception of the desirability of improving performance on a given dimension.

Valence for rewards the salesperson's perceptions of the desirability of receiving increased rewards as a result of improved performance.

Value the net bundle of benefits derived by the customer from the product you are selling.

Value-added selling works to add value through all possible means. Examples include better customer service, enhanced product quality, or improved buyer–seller communication. A value-added selling approach changes much of the sales process to a relationship approach.

Value chain envisioned by Michael Porter of Harvard to identify ways for a selling firm to add customer value.

Value proposition the communication of value, which is the net bundle of benefits that the customer derives from the product you are selling.

Virtual office a location outside the company's offices where a salesperson works from (often his or her home).

W

Warm calls a prospecting approach in which the salesperson makes a personal visit or phone call based on some pre-work in leads qualifying via one of the other sources of prospects.

Weekly/monthly planning calendar one of the basic elements in a good time management plan. Salespeople use it to create lists with specific tasks they want to accomplish in longer periods of time.

Word of mouth a powerful source of leads that have a strong chance of resulting in qualified prospects.

Work/family conflict a lack of balance between work and family life, usually involving work encroaching on family.

Workload analysis a determination of how much work is required to cover each sales territory.

Endnotes

CHAPTER 1

1 Benson P. Shapiro, Adrian J. Slywotsky, and Stephen X. Doyle, *Strategic Sales Management: A Boardroom Issue,* Case #9 (Cambridge, MA: Harvard Business School, 1994), pp. 1–23.
2 Karen Norman Kennedy, Felicia G. Lassk, and Jerry R. Goolsby, "Customer Mind-Set of Employees Throughout the Organization," *Journal of the Academy of Marketing Science* 30 (Spring 2002), pp. 159–71.
3 Neil Rackham and John DeVincentis, *Rethinking the Sales Force: Redefining Selling to Create and Capture Customer Value* (New York: McGraw-Hill, 1999).
4 Tom Reilly, "Relationship Selling at Its Best, *Industrial Distribution* 95 (September 2006), p. 29; Tom Reilly, *Value-Added Selling: How to Sell More Profitably, Confidently, and Professionally by Competing on VALUE, Not Price* (New York: McGraw-Hill, 2003).
5 Sean Valentine and Tim Barnett, "Ethics Code Awareness, Perceived Ethical Values, and Organizational Commitment, *Journal of Personal Selling & Sales Management* 23 (Fall 2003), p. 359; Jennifer Gilbert, "A Matter of Trust," *Sales & Marketing Management* (March 2003), pp. 31–35.
6 Michael T. Bosworth, *Solution Selling: Creating Buyers in Difficult Selling Markets* (New York: McGraw-Hill, 1995).
7 Kenneth B. Yap and Jillian C. Sweeney, "Zone-of-Tolerance Moderates the Service Quality-Outcome Relationship," *Journal of Services Marketing* 21 (Issue 2, 2007), pp. 137–48; Valarie Zeithaml, A. Parasuraman, and Leonard L. Berry, *Delivering Quality Service: Balancing Customer Perceptions and Expectations* (New York: The Free Press, 1990).
8 Mark P. Leach, Annie H. Liu, and Wesley J. Johnston, "The Role of Self-Regulation Training in Developing the Motivation Management Capabilities of Salespeople," *Journal of Personal Selling & Sales Management* 25 (Summer 2005), pp. 269–81; Mrugank V. Thakor and Ashwin W. Joshi, "Motivating Salesperson Customer Orientation: Insights from the Job Characteristics Model," *Journal of Business Research* 58 (May 2005), pp. 584–92; John P. Campbell and Robert D. Pritchard, "Motivation Theory in Industrial and Organizational Psychology," in *Handbook of Industrial and Organizational Psychology,* ed. Marvin D. Dunnette (Chicago: Rand McNally, 1976), p. 65.
9 Greg W. Marshall, Daniel J. Goebel, and William C. Moncrief, "Hiring for Success at the Buyer-Seller Interface," *Journal of Business Research* 56 (March 2003), pp. 247–55.
10 William L. Cron, Alan J. Dubinsky, and Ronald E. Michaels, "The Influence of Career Stages on Components of Salesperson Motivation," *Journal of Marketing* 52 (January 1988), pp. 78–92; William L. Cron, "Industrial Salesperson Development: A Career Stage Perspective," *Journal of Marketing* (Fall 1984), pp. 41–52.
11 Jerome A. Colletti and Mary S. Fiss, *Compensating New Sales Roles: How to Design Rewards That Work in Today's Selling Environment,* 2nd ed. (New York: AMACOM, 2001).
12 HR Chally Group, *The Chally World Class Excellence Research Report: The Route to the Summit* (Dayton, OH: HR Chally Group, 2007). Leonard L. Berry, *On Great Service: A Framework for Action* (New York: The Free Press, 1995).

CHAPTER 2

1 Nancy E. Waldeck, Ellen Bolman Pullins, and Melissa Houlette, "Media as Factor in Student Perceptions for Sales Jobs: A Framework for Research," *Journal of Personal Selling & Sales Management* 30 (Fall 2010), pp. 343–54.

2 This classic line of research on job satisfaction of salespeople was initiated by Gilbert A. Churchill, Jr., Neil M. Ford, and Orville C. Walker, Jr., in the article "Organizational Climate and Job Satisfaction of the Sales Force," *Journal of Marketing Research* (November 1976), pp. 323–32. Measurement approaches and study results within this domain have remained relatively stable for nearly 30 years.

3 Nic Sale, "The Way We Will All Work," *Global Telecoms Business* (July/August 2007), p. 1.

4 Julia Chang, "Desperately Seeking Sales Stars," *Sales & Marketing Management* 158 (October 2006), pp. 45–47.

5 Greg W. Marshall, Daniel J. Goebel, and William C. Moncrief, "Hiring for Success at the Buyer–Seller Interface," *Journal of Business Research* 56 (April 2003), pp. 247–55.

6 Dawn R. Deeter-Schmelz, Daniel J. Goebel, and Karen Norman Kennedy, "What Are the Characteristics of an Effective Sales Manager? An Exploratory Study Comparing Salesperson and Sales Manager Perspectives," *Journal of Personal Selling & Sales Management* 28 (Winter 2008), p. 7; Stephen B. Castelberry and C. David Shepherd, "Effective Interpersonal Listening and Personal Selling," *Journal of Personal Selling & Sales Management* (Winter 1993), pp. 35–49.

7 Bulent Menguc and Seigyoung Auh, "Creating a Firm-Level Dynamic Capability through Capitalizing on Market Orientation and Innovativeness," *Journal of the Academy of Marketing Science* 34 (Winter 2006), pp. 63–73; Rosemary P. Ramsey and Ravi S. Sohi, "Listening to Your Customers: The Impact of Perceived Salesperson Listening Behavior on Relationship Outcomes," *Journal of the Academy of Marketing Science* 25 (Spring 1997), pp. 127–37.

8 George R. Franke and Jeong-Eun Park, "Salesperson Adaptive Selling Behavior and Customer Orientation: A Meta-Analysis," *Journal of Marketing Research* 43 (November 2006), p. 34; Barton A. Weitz, Harish Sujan, and Mita Sujan, "Knowledge, Motivation, and Adaptive Behavior: A Framework for Improving Selling Effectiveness," *Journal of Marketing* 50 (October 1986), pp. 174–91.

9 William C. Moncrief III, "Selling Activity and Sales Position Taxonomies for Industrial Sales Forces," *Journal of Marketing Research* 23 (August 1986), pp. 261–70.

10 Greg W. Marshall, William C. Moncrief, and Felicia G. Lassk, "The Current State of Sales Force Activities," *Industrial Marketing Management* 28 (January 1999), pp. 87–98.

11 William A. O'Connell and William Keenan, Jr., "The Shape of Things to Come," *Sales & Marketing Management* (January 1990), pp. 36–41.

12 Michelle Marchetti, "The Cost of Doing Business," *Sales & Marketing Management* (September 1999), p. 56.

13 O'Connell and Keenan, p. 38.

14 Derek A. Newton, *Sales Force Performance and Turnover* (Cambridge, MA: Marketing Science Institute, 1973), p. 3.

15 Adam Rapp, "Outsourcing the Sales Process: Hiring a Mercenary Sales Force," *Industrial Marketing Management* 38 (May 2009), pp. 411-18.

16 Donald W. Jackson, Jr., Janet E. Keith, and Richard K. Burdick, "Purchasing Agents' Perceptions of Industrial Buying Center Influence: A Situational Approach," *Journal of Marketing* (Fall 1984), pp. 75–83.

17 P. Fraser Johnson and Michiel R. Leenders, "Building a Corporate Supply Chain Function," *Journal of Supply Chain Management* 44 (July 2008), pp. 39–52; Richard G. Jennings and Richard E. Plank, "When the Purchasing Agent Is a Committee: Implications for Industrial Marketing," *Industrial Marketing Management* 24 (November 1995), pp. 411–19.

18 Frank Jacob and Michael Ehret, "Self-Protection versus Opportunity Seeking in Business Buying Behavior: An Experimental Study," *Journal of Business & Industrial Marketing* 21 (Issue 2, 2006), p. 106; V. W. Mitchell, "Buy-Phase and Buy-Class Effects on Organizational Risk Perceptions and Reductions in Purchasing Professional Services," *Journal of Business & Industrial Marketing* 13 (Issue 6, 1998), pp. 461–78.

19 Jennings and Plank.

20 Mark A. Moon and Susan Forquer Gupta, "Examining the Formation of Selling Centers: A Conceptual Framework," *Journal of Personal Selling & Sales Management* (Spring 1997), pp. 31–42.

21 Geoffrey Brewer, "Lou Gerstner Has His Hands Full," *Sales & Marketing Management* (May 1998), pp. 36–41.

22 Louis V. Gerstner, Jr., *Who Says the Elephant Can't Dance? Inside IBM's Historic Turnaround* (New York: Harper-Business, 2002).

23 Rodrigo Guesalagaa and Wesley Johnston, "What's Next in Key Account Management Research? Building the Bridge between the Academic Literature and the Practitioners' Priorities," *Industrial Marketing Management* 39 (October 2010), pp. 1063–68.

24 Paolo Guenzi, Laurent Georges, and Catherine Pardoc, "The Impact of Strategic Account Managers' Behaviors on Relational Outcomes: An Empirical Study," *Industrial Marketing Management* 38 (April 2009), pp. 300–11.

25 Keith A. Richards and Eli Jones, "Key Account Management: Adding Elements of Account Fit to an Integrative Theoretical Framework," *Journal of Personal Selling & Sales Management* 29 (Fall 2009), pp. 305–20.

26 Donald W. Barclay and Michele D. Bunn, "Process Heuristics in Organizational Buying: Starting to Fill a Gap," *Journal of Business Research* 59 (February 2006), p. 186; Wesley J. Johnston and Jeffrey E. Lewin, "Organizational Buying Behavior: Toward an Integrative Framework," *Journal of Business Research* 35 (January 1996), pp. 1–15.

CHAPTER 3

1 Bill Brooks, "Ten Ways to Add Value and Defeat Price Objections," *American Salesman* 50 (November 2005), pp. 3–4.
2 Lewis Hershey, "The Role of Sales Presentations in Developing Customer Relationships," *Services Marketing Quarterly* 26 (Issue 3, 2005), p. 41.
3 Roger D. Blackwell, *From Mind to Market* (New York: HarperBusiness, 1997), pp. 182–83. 5. Hershey, p. 41.
4 Avinash Malshe and Ravipreet S. Sohi, "Sales Buy-In of Marketing Strategies: Exploration of its Nuances, Antecedents, and Contextual Conditions," *Journal of Personal Selling & Sales Management* 29 (Summer 2009), pp. 207-26; Kenneth Le Meunier-FitzHugh and Nigel F. Piercy, "Exploring the Relationship between Market Orientation and Sales and Marketing Collaboration," *Journal of Personal Selling & Sales Management* 31 (Summer 2011), pp. 287–96.
5 Philip Kotler, Neil Rackham, and Suj Krishnaswamy, "Ending the War between Sales and Marketing," *Harvard Business Review* Hershey, p. 41. (July–August 2006), pp. 68–78.
6 Michael E. Porter, *Competitive Advantage* (New York: Simon & Schuster, 1985).
7 Frederick F. Reichheld, *Loyalty Rules! How Leaders Build Lasting Relationships in the Digital Age* (Cambridge, MA: Harvard Business School Press, 2001).
8 David A. Garvin, "Competing on the Eight Dimensions of Quality," *Harvard Business Review* (November/December 1987), pp. 101–09.
9 Rosemary P. Ramsey and Ravipreet S. Sohi, "Listening to Your Customers: The Impact of Perceived Salesperson Listening Behavior on Relationship Outcomes," *Journal of the Academy of Marketing Science* 25 (Spring 1997), pp. 127–37; John Swan and Johannah Nolan, "Gaining Customer Trust: A Conceptual Guide for the Salesperson," *Journal of Personal Selling & Sales Management* (November 1985), pp. 39–48.
10 Valarie A. Zeithaml, Mary Jo Bitner, and Dwayne D. Gremler, *Services Marketing: Integrating Customer Focus across the Firm*, 4th ed. (Chicago: McGraw-Hill/Irwin, 2005).
11 David A. Aaker and Erich Joachimsthaler, *Brand Leadership: Building Assets in the Information Society* (New York: The Free Press, 2000).

CHAPTER 4

1 Mahmoud Darrat, Douglas Amyx, and Rebecca Bennett, "An Investigation into the Effects of Work-Family Conflict and Job Satisfaction on Salesperson Deviance," *Journal of Personal Selling & Sales Management* 30 (Issue, 3, Summer 2010), pp. 239–52; William T. Ross and Diana C. Robertson, "A Typology of Situational Factors: Impact on Salesperson Decision Making about Ethical Issues," *Journal of Business Ethics* (September 2003), pp. 213–25; Willem Verbeke, Cok Ouwerkerk, and Ed Peelen, "Exploring the Contextual and Individual Factors on Ethics Decision Making of Salespeople," *Journal of Business Ethics* 15 (1996), pp. 1175–87.
2 O. C. Ferrell, John Fraedrich, and Linda Ferrell, *Business Ethics: Ethical Decision Making and Cases*, 7th ed. (Boston: Houghton-Mifflin, 2008), p. 7.
3 Sean Valentine, "Ethics Training, Ethical Context, and Sales and Marketing Professional's Satisfaction with Supervisors and Coworkers," *Journal of Personal Selling & Sales Management* 29 (Issue 3, Summer 2009), pp. 227–42; Jennifer Gilbert, "A Matter of Trust," *Sales & Marketing Management* (March 2003), p. 32.
4 John D. Hansen and Robert J. Riggle, "Ethical Salesperson Behavior in Sales Relationships," *Journal of Personal Selling & Sales Management* 29 (Issue 3, Spring 2009), pp. 151–66; Thomas N. Ingram, Raymond W. LaForge, and Charles H. Schwepker, Jr., "Salesperson Ethical Decision Making: The Impact of Sales Leadership and Sales Management Control Strategy," *Journal of Personal Selling & Sales Management* (Fall 2007), p. 301; Frank Sonnennberg, "Trust Me . . . Trust Me Not," *Journal of Business Strategy* (February 1994), pp. 14–16; and Fredrick Trawick, John Swan, Gail McGee and David Rink, "Influence of Buyer Ethics and Salesperson Behavior on Intention to Choose a Supplier," *Journal of the Academy of Marketing Science* (Winter 1991), pp. 17–23.
5 Michael Bendixen and Russell Abratt, "Corporate Identity, Ethics and Reputation in Supplier-Buyer Relationship," *Journal of Business Ethics* (November 2007), pp. 69–75; Fredrick Trawick, Fred Morgan, and Jeffery Stoltman, "Influence of Buyer Ethics and Salesperson Behavior on Intention to Choose a Supplier," *Journal of the Academy of Marketing Science* (Winter 1991), pp. 17–24.

6 Dawn Myers, "You Get What You Give So Make it Good," *Promotional Products Business* (June 1998), pp. 105–11.

7 Erin Strout, "Are Your Salespeople Ripping You Off?" *Sales & Marketing Management* (February 2001), pp. 56–62.

8 Betsy Cummings, "An Affair to Remember," *Sales & Marketing Management* (August 2001), pp. 50–57.

9 Charles H. Schwepker and David J. Good, "Transformational Leadership and its Impact on Sales Force Moral Judgment," *Journal of Personal Selling & Sales Management* 30 (Issue 4, Fall 2010), pp. 299–318; James B. DeConinck and Julie T. Johnson, "The Effects of Perceived Supervisor Support, Perceived Organizational Support, and Organizational Justice on Turnover Among Salespeople, *Journal of Personal Selling & Sales Management* 20 (Issue 4, Fall 2009), pp. 333–51; Rowena Crosbie, "Who Defines Ethics in Your Organization," *Industrial and Commercial Training* (2008), pp. 181–98; Charles Schwepker, O. C. Ferrell, and Thomas Ingram, "The Influences of Ethical Climate and Ethical Conflict on Role Stress in the Sales Force," *Journal of the Academy of Marketing Science* 25 (Spring 1997), pp. 106–16.

10 Christophe Fournier, John F. Tanner, Lawrence B. Chonko, and Chris Manolis, "The Moderating Role of Ethical Climate on Salesperson Propensity to Leave," *Journal of Personal Selling & Sales Management* 30 (Issue 4, Winter 2010), pp. 7-22; Scott John Vitell and Anusorn Singhapakdi, "The Role of Ethics Institutionalization in Influencing Organizational Commitment, Job Satisfaction, and Esprit de Corps," *Journal of Business Ethics* (August 2008), pp. 343–55; Charles Schwepker, "Ethical Climate's Relationship to Job Satisfaction, Organizational Commitment and Turnover Intention in the Sales Force," *Journal of Business Research* 54 (2001), pp. 39–52.

11 John F. Veiga, Timothy D. Golden, and Kathleen Dechant, "Why Managers Bend the Company Rules," *Academy of Management Executive* (May 2004), pp. 84–97; Debbie LeClair, O. C. Ferrell, and Linda Ferrell, "Federal Sentencing Guidelines for Organizations: Policy Issues for International Marketing," *Journal of Public Policy and Marketing* 16 (Spring 1997), pp. 27–37.

12 Douglas B. Grisaffe and Fernando Jaramillo, "Toward Higher Levels of Ethics: Preliminary Evidence of Positive Outcomes," *Journal of Personal Selling & Sales Management* (Fall 2007), pp. 355–68; Thomas G. Brashear, James S. Boles, Danny N. Bellenger, and Charles M. Brooks, "An Empirical Test of Trust-Building Processes and Outcomes in Sales Manager-Salesperson Relationships," *Journal of the Academy of Marketing Science* 31 (Issue 2, Spring 2003), pp. 189–200; and Willem Verbeke, Cok Ouwerkerk, and Ed Peelen, "Exploring the Contextual and Individual Factors on Ethical Decision Making of Salespeople," *Journal of Business Ethics* 15 (Fall 1996), pp. 1175–87.

CHAPTER 5

1 Ajay K. Kohli and Bernard J. Jaworski, "Market Orientation: The Construct, Research Propositions, and Managerial Implications," *Journal of Marketing* 54 (April 1990), pp. 1–18; John C. Narver and Stanley F. Slater, "The Effect of a Market Orientation on Business Profitability," *Journal of Marketing* (October 1990), pp. 20–35.

2 Chally Group Worldwide, *The World Class Excellence Report: The Route to the Summit* (Dayton, OH: Chally Group Worldwide, 2007).

3 The Data Warehouse Institute, Industry Study 2000 Survey, p. 1.

4 www.PricewaterhouseCoopers.com.

5 Don Peppers and Martha Rogers, *One to One B2B: Customer Development Strategies for the Business-to-Business World* (New York: Doubleday, 2001).

6 Ronald S. Swift, *Accelerating Customer Relationships: Using CRM and Relationship Technologies* (Upper Saddle River, NJ: Prentice Hall PTR, 2000), p. 42.

7 Stanley A. Brown, ed., *Customer Relationship Management: A Strategic Imperative in the World of E-Business* (Toronto: John Wiley & Sons Canada, 2000), pp. 8–9.

8 Sharad Borle, Siddharth S. Singh, and Dipak C. Jain, "Customer Lifetime Value Measurement," *Management Science* 54 (January 2008), pp. 100–14.

9 Swift, *Accelerating Customer Relationships*, pp. 39–42.

10 Ray McKenzie, *The Relationship-Based Enterprise: Powering Business Success through Customer Relationship Management* (New York: McGraw-Hill, 2001), pp. 7–8.

11 Ibid., p. 8.

12 Howard P. Stevens and Geoffrey James, *Selling in the Internet Age: How the Web is Transforming the Buyer/Seller Relationship* (Dayton, OH: Chally Group Worldwide, 2012).

13 National Science Foundation, "Industry, Technology, and the Global Marketplace: International Patenting Trends in Two New Technology Areas," *Science and Engineering Indicators 2002,* http://www.nsf.gov/statistics/seind02/c6/c6s5.htm, retrieved July 1, 2011.

14 Paul Christ and Rolph Anderson, "The Impact of Technology on Evolving Roles of Salespeople," *Journal of Historical Research in Marketing* 3 (February 2011), pp. 173–93.

15 Leroy Robinson, Jr., Greg W. Marshall, and Miriam B. Stamps, "An Empirical Investigation of Technology Acceptance in a Field Sales Force Setting," *Industrial Marketing Management* 34 (May 2005), pp. 407–15.

16 Greg W. Marshall, William C. Moncrief, John M. Rudd, and Nick Lee, "Revolution in Sales: The Impact of Social Media and Related Technology on the Selling Environment," *Journal of Personal Selling & Sales Management* 32 (Summer 2012), pp. 251–65.

CHAPTER 6

1 John Boe, "Six Powerful Prospecting Tips," *American Salesman* 52 (October 2007), pp. 23–25.

2 John J. Bowen, Jr., "Relationship Marketing," *Advisor's Edge* 8 (June 2005), p. 37.

3 Ralph Kisiel, "Dealers Discover Social Networking Sites: MySpace, YouTube, Others Help Reach Sales Prospects," *Automotive News* (February 4, 2008); Jon Swartz, "Social Networking Sites Work to Turn Users into Profits," *USA Today* (May 12, 2008).

4 Frank Belschak, Willem Verbeke, and Richard P. Bagozzi, "Coping with Sales Call Anxiety: The Role of Sales Perseverence and Task Concentration Strategies," *Journal of the Academy of Marketing Science* 34 (Summer 2006), pp. 403–18; Willem Verbeke and Richard P. Bagozzi, "Sales Call Anxiety: Exploring What It Means When Fear Rules a Sales Encounter," *Journal of Marketing* 63 (July 2000), pp. 88–101.

5 Robert McGarvey, "Ice Cubes to Eskimos," *Entrepreneur* (August 2000), pp. 68–76.

CHAPTER 7

1 Christian Homburg, Michael Müller, and Martin Klarmann, "When Should the Customer Really Be King? On the Optimum Level of Salesperson Customer Orientation in Sales Encounters," *Journal of Marketing* 75 (Issue 2, March 2011), pp. 55–74; Subhra Chakrabarty, Gene Brown, and Robert E. Widing, "Closed Influence Tactics: Do Smugglers Win in the Long Run? *Journal of Personal Selling & Sales Management* 30 (Issue 1, Winter 2010), pp. 23–32; Pradeep Bhardwaj, Yuxin Chen, and David Godes, "Buyer-Initiated vs. Seller-Initiated Information Revelation," *Management Science* (June 2008), pp. 1104–15; Marvin A. Jolson, "Broadening the Scope of Relationship Selling," *Journal of Personal Selling & Sales Management* (Fall 1997), pp. 75–88.

2 Tim Oliver Brexendorf, Silke Muhlmeier, Torsten Tomczak, and Martin Eisend, "The Impact of Sales Encounters on Brand Loyalty," *Journal of Business Research* 63 (Issue 10, November 2010), pp. 1148–55. Jennifer Wiggins Johnson and Adam Rapp, "Avatars as Salespeople: Communication Style, Trust, and Intentions," *Journal of Business Research* 63 (Issue 8, August 2010), pp. 793–800.

3 Lillian H. Chaney and Catherine G. Green, "Effective Presentations," *American Salesman* (June 2004), pp. 22–28; Tony L. Henthorne, Michael S. Latour, and Alvin Williams, "Initial Impressions in the Organizational Buyer-Seller Dyad: Sales Management Implications," *Journal of Personal Selling & Sales Management* (Summer 1992), pp. 57–65.

4 Julie Hill, "Nail Your First Three Minutes to Avoid Going Down in Flames," *Presentations* (February 1999), p. 28.

5 Dan Hill, "Emotionomics, Winning Hearts and Minds," *American Salesman* (March 2008), pp. 12–14; Erika Rasmusson, "The 10 Traits of Successful Salespeople," *Sales & Marketing Management* (February 1999), p. 34.

6 Author interview with financial consultant, June 2003.

7 Edward C. Bursk, "Low Pressure Selling," *Harvard Business Review* (July/August 2006), pp. 150–65; Dorothy Leeds, "The Art of Asking Questions," *Training and Development* (January 1993), p. 58.

8 Neil Rackham, *SPIN Selling* (New York: McGraw-Hill, 1988); and Huthwaite, Inc. website (www.huthwaite.com), June 2003.

9 Tanya Drollinger, Lucette B. Comer, and Patricia T. Warrington, "Development and Validation of Active Empathetic Listening Scale," *Psychology & Marketing*, February 2006, pp. 161–79; John Stewart, *Bridges Not Walls: A Book about Interpersonal Communication,* 8th ed. (New York: McGraw-Hill, 2001).

10 Stephen J. Newell, Joseph J. Belonanx, Jr. Michael W. McCardle, and Richard E. Plank, "The Effect of Personal Relationships and Consultative Task Behaviors on Buyer Perceptions of Salesperson Trust, Expertise, and Loyalty," *Journal of Marketing Theory and Practice* 19 (Issue 3, Summer 2011), pp. 307–16; Keving D. Bradfor, J. Michael Crant, and Joan M. Phillips, "How Suppliers Affect Trust with Their Customers: The Role of Salesperson Job Satisfaction and Perceived Customer Importance," *Journal of Marketing Theory and Practice* 17 (Issue 4, Spring 2009), pp. 383–94.

11 Bill Brooks, "How to Present Your Product with No Resistance," *American Salesman* (November 2006), pp. 27–31; Sarah Lorge, "Selling a Product That's Ahead of Its Time," *Sales & Marketing Management* (July 1999), p. 15.

12 Othman Boujena, Wesley J. Johnston, and Dwight R. Merunka, "The Benefits of Sales Force Automation: A Customer's Perspective" *Journal of Personal Selling & Sales Management* 29 (Issue 2, Spring 2009), pp. 137–50.

CHAPTER 8

1　Subhra Chakrabarty, Gene Brown, and Robert E. Widing, "Closed Influence Tactics: Do Smugglers Win in the Long Run?" *Journal of Personal Selling & Sales Management* 30 (Issue 1, Winter 2010), pp. 23–32; Tom Batchelder, "A More Human Approach to Sales," *American Salesman* (June 2008), pp. 7–13; Tom Riley, "Step up Your Negotiating Success," *Personal Selling Power* (April 1990), p. 40.

2　Micheal Soon Lee, "10 Common Negotiating Mistakes That Cost You Thousands," *American Salesman* (September 2007), pp. 25–29; Joe F. Alexander, Patrick L. Schul, and Denny E. McCorkle, "An Assessment of Selected Relationships in a Model of the Industrial Marketing Negotiation Process," *Journal of Personal Selling & Sales Management* 14 (Summer 1994), pp. 25–39.

3　*Webster's Online Dictionary* (www.m-w.com), January 2009.

4　Marvin Jolson, "Broadening the Scope of Relationship Selling," *Journal of Personal Selling & Sales Management* 17 (Fall 1997), pp. 75–88.

5　www.wired.com, January 2009.

6　Kim Sydow Campbell, Lenita Davis, and Lauren Skinner, "Rapport Management during the Exploration Phase of the Salesperson-Customer Relationship," *Journal of Personal Selling & Sales Management* (Fall 2006), pp. 359–73; Judy A. Wagner, Noreen M. Klein, and Janet E. Keith, "Selling Strategies: The Effects of Suggesting a Decision Structure to Novice and Expert Buyers," *Journal of the Academy of Marketing Science* 29 (Summer 2001), pp. 289–306.

7　Joanne Lynch and Leslie de Chernatony, "Winning Hearts and Minds: Business-to-Business Branding and the Role of the Salesperson," *Journal of Marketing Management* (February 2007), pp. 123–37; Kenneth Evans, Robert E. Kleine, Timothy D. Landry, and Lawrence A. Crosby, "How First Impressions of a Customer Impact Effectiveness in an Initial Sales Encounter," *Journal of the Academy of Marketing Science* 28 (Fall 2000), pp. 512–26.

8　Krongjit Laochumnanvanit and David H. B. Bednall, "Consumers' Evaluation of Free Service Trial Offers," *Academy of Marketing Science Review* (January 2005), pp. 1–17; Julie Johnson, Hiram C. Barksdale, and James S. Boles, "The Strategic Role of the Salesperson in Reducing Customer Defection in Business Relationships," *Journal of Personal Selling & Sales Management* 21 (Spring 2001), pp. 123–34.

9　Jeffrey E. Lewin, "Business Customer's Satisfaction: What Happens When Suppliers Downsize?" *Industrial Marketing Management* 38 (Issue 3, April 2009), pp. 283–99.

CHAPTER 9

1　Roger Fisher, William Ury, and Bruce Patton, *Getting to Yes: Negotiating Agreement without Giving In*, 3rd ed. (New York: Penguin Books USA, 2011).

2　Sean Dwyer, John Hill, and Warren Martin, "An Empirical Investigation of Critical Success Factors in the Personal Selling Process for Homogeneous Goods," *Journal of Personal Selling & Sales Management* 20 (Summer 2000), pp. 151–59.

3　James W. Pickens, *The Art of Closing Any Deal: How to Be a Master Closer in Anything You Do* (New York: Warner Books, 2003).

4　Tom Reilly, "Salespeople: Develop the Means to Handle Rejection," *Personal Selling Power* (July/August 1987), p. 15.

5　Pickens, pp. 263–95; Stephan Schiffman, *Getting to "Closed"* (Chicago: Dearborn Trade Publishing, 2002).

6　Greg W. Marshall, Daniel J. Goebel, and William C. Moncrief, "Hiring for Success at the Buyer-Seller Interface," *Journal of Business Research* 56 (April 2003), pp. 247–55.

7　Valarie A. Zeithaml, Mary Jo Bitner, and Dwayne D. Gremler, *Services Marketing: Integrating Customer Focus across the Firm*, 4th ed. (Chicago: McGraw-Hill/Irwin, 2005).

8　Joël Le Bon and Douglas E. Hughes, "The Dilemma of Outsourced Customer Service and Care: Research Propositions from a Transaction Cost Perspective," *Industrial Marketing Management* 38 (May 2009), pp. 404–10.

9　Douglas Amyx and Shahid Bhuian, "Salesperf: The Salesperson Service Performance Scale," *Journal of Personal Selling & Sales Management* 29 (Fall 2009), pp. 367–76.

10　Gabriel R. Gonzalez, K. Douglas Hoffman, Thomas N. Ingram, and Raymond W. LaForge, "Sales Organization Recovery Management and Relationship Selling: A Conceptual Model and Empirical Test," *Journal of Personal Selling & Sales Management* 30 (Summer 2010), pp. 223–38.

11　Frederich F. Reichheld, "Loyalty and the Renaissance of Marketing," *Marketing Management* 2 (1994), pp. 10–21.

CHAPTER 10

1 Google website (www.google.com), January 2013.
2 C. Jay Lambe, Kevin L. Webb, and Chiharu Ishida, "Self-Managing Selling Teams and Team Performance: The Complementary Roles of Empowerment and Control," *Industrial Marketing Management*, 38 (Issue 1, January 2009), pp. 5–16.
3 Dave Kahle, "Salespeople: Position Yourselves with Power," *American Salesman*, November 2007, pp. 14–21; William Kendy, "Time Management," *Selling Power,* July 2000, pp. 34–36.
4 Jim Morgan, "Customer Information Management (CIM): The Key to Successful CRM in Financial Services," *Journal of Performance Management* (May 2007), pp. 47–66; Daniel Tynan, "Leveraging Your Needs," *Sales & Marketing Management* (December 2003), p. 23.
5 TerrAlign website (www.terralign.com), January 2013.
6 *County and City Data Book* (www.census.gov), January 2013.
7 PRIZM website (www.claritas.com), January 2013.
8 Judy A. Siguaw, Sheryl E. Kimes, and Jule B. Gassenheimer, "B2B Sales Force Productivity: Applications of Revenue Management Strategies to Sales Management," *Industrial Marketing Management*, October 2003, pp. 539–51; Andris A. Zoltners and Sally E. Lorimer, "Sales Territory Alignment: An Overlooked Productivity Tool," *Journal of Personal Selling & Sales Management* 20 (Issue 3, Summer 2000), pp. 139–50.
9 Mark W. Johnston and Greg W. Marshall, *Sales Force Management,* 11th ed. (London: Routledge, 2013), p. 163.
10 Ibid., p. 166.
11 Ibid.

CHAPTER 11

1 Mark W. Johnston, and Greg W. Marshall, *Sales Force Management,* 11th ed. (London: Routledge, 2013), p. 201.
2 C. Fred Miao and Kenneth R. Evans, "The Impact of Salesperson Motivation on Role Perceptions and Job Performance—A Cognitive and Affective Perspective, *Journal of Personal Selling & Sales Management* (Winter 2007), pp. 89–106; Jeffrey K. Sager, Junsub Yi, and Charles M. Futrell, "A Model Depicting Salespeople's Perceptions," *Journal of Personal Selling & Sales Management* 18 (Issue 3, Summer 1998), pp. 1–22.
3 Paolo Guenzi, Luigi M. De Luca, and Gabrielle Troilo, "Organizational Drivers of Salespeople's Customer Orientation and Selling Orientation,*" Journal of Personal Selling & Sales Management* 31 (Issue 3, Summer 2011), pp. 369–86; Jeffrey E. Lewin and Jeffrey K. Sager, "An Investigation of the Influence of Coping Resources in Salesperson's Emotional Exhaustion," *Industrial Marketing Management* 38 (Issue 7, October 2009), pp. 798–805; Thomas E. DeCarlo, R. Kenneth Teas, and James C. McElroy, "Salesperson Performance Attributions Process and the Formulation of Expectancy Estimates," *Journal of Personal Selling & Sales Management* 17 (Issue, 3, 1997), pp. 1–17.
4 Bill Brooks, "Self-Management and Character, *American Salesman* (February 2006), pp. 19–22; Rene Y. Darmon, "Where Do the Best Sales Force Profit Producers Come From?" *Journal of Personal Selling & Sales Management* 13 (Issue 3, 1993), pp. 17–29.
5 Peter A. Redaya, Roger Marshall, and A. Parasuraman, "An Interdisciplinary Approach to Assessing the Characteristics and Sales Potential of Modern Salespeople," *Industrial Marketing Management* 38 (Issue 7, October 2009), pp. 838–44; Joseph O. Rentz, C. David Shepherd, Armen Tashchian, Pratibha A. Dabholkar, and Robert T. Ladd, "A Measure of Selling Skill: Scale Development and Validation," *Journal of Personal Selling & Sales Management* (Winter 2002), pp. 13–22; Siew Meng Leong, Paul S. Busch, and Deborah Roedder John, "Knowledge Bases and Salesperson Effectiveness: A Script Theoretic Analysis," *Journal of Marketing Research* 26 (May 1990), pp. 164–78.
6 C. Fred Miao, Donald J. Jund, and Kenneth R. Evans, "Re-examining the Influence of Career Stages on Salesperson Motivation: A Cognitive and Affective Perspective," *Journal of Personal Selling & Sales* Management 29 (Issue 3, Spring 2009), pp. 243–56; Francie Dalton, "Motivating the Unmotivated," *American Salesman* (June 2007), pp. 6–10; Audrey Bottjen, "Incentives Gone Awry," *Sales & Marketing Management* (May 2001), p. 72.
7 Vincent Onyemah, Scott D. Swain, Richard Hanna, "A Social Learning Perspective on Sales Technology Usage: Preliminary Evidence from an Emerging Economy," *Journal of Personal Selling & Sales Management* 30 (Issue 2, Spring 2010), pp. 131–42; Michael W. Pass, Kenneth R. Evans, and John L. Schlacter, "Sales Force Involvement in CRM Information Systems: Participation, Support, and Focus," *Journal of Personal Selling & Sales Management* (Summer 2004), pp. 229–42; Nicholas G. Paparoidamis, "Learning Orientation and Leadership Quality: Their Impact on Salespersons' Performance," *Management Decision* (July 2005), pp. 1054–64; Arthur Baldauf, David W. Cravens, and Nigel F. Piercy, "Examining Business Strategy, Sales Management, and Salesperson Antecedents of Sales Organization Effectiveness," *Journal of Personal Selling & Sales Management* 21 (Issue 2, Spring 2001), pp. 109–22; Ken Grant, David W. Cravens, George S. Low, and William C. Moncrief, "The Role of Satisfaction and Territory

Design on Motivation, Attitudes, and Work Outcomes of Salespeople," *Journal of the Academy of Marketing Science* (Spring 2001), pp. 165–78.

8 TerrAlign website (www.terralign.com), December 2012.

9 Denny Bristow, Douglas Amyx, Stephen B. Castleberry, and James J. Cochran, "A Cross Generational Comparison of Motivational Factors in a Sales Career Among Gen-X and Gen-Y College Students," *Journal of Personal Selling & Sales Management* 31 (Issue 1, Winter 2011), pp. 77-86; Brian Rutherford, JungKun Park, and Sang-Lin Han, "Increasing Job Performance and Decreasing Salesperson Propensity to Leave: An Examination of an Asian Sales Force," *Journal of Personal Selling & Sales Management* 31 (Issue 2, Summer 2011), pp. 171–84; William A. Weeks and Christophe Fournier, "The Impact of Time Congruity on Salesperson's Role Stress: A Person-Job Fit Approach," *Journal of Personal Selling & Sales Management* 30 (Issue 1, Winter 2010), pp. 73–90; Adam Rapp, Raj Agnihotri and Thomas L. Baker, "Concepetualizing Salesperson Competitive Intelligence: An Individual Level Perspective," *Journal of Personal Selling & Sales Management* 31 (Issue 2, Spring 2011), pp. 141–56; Jeffrey E. Lewin and Jeffrey K. Sager, "The Influence of Personal Characteristics and Coping Strategies on Salesperson's Turnover Intentions," *Journal of Personal Selling & Sales Management* 30 (Issue 4, Fall 2010), pp. 355–70; Michael Segalla, Dominique Rouzies, Madeleine Besson, and Barton A. Weitz, "A Cross-National Investigation of Incentive Sales Compensation," *International Journal of Research in Marketing*, December 2006, pp. 419–30; William A. Weeks, Terry W. Loe, Lawrence B. Chonko, Carlos Ruy Martinez, and Kirk Wakefield, "Cognitive Moral Development and the Impact of Perceived Organizational Ethical Climate on the Search for Sales Force Excellence: A Cross-Cultural Study," *Journal of Personal Selling & Sales Management* 26 (Issue 2, Spring 2006), pp. 205–21; Donald W. Jackson, Stephen S. Tax and John W. Barnes, "Examining the Salesforce Culture: Managerial Applications and Research Propositions," *Journal of Personal Selling and Sales Management* 14 (Issue 4, Fall 1994), pp. 1–14.

10 Dheeraj Sharma, Jule B. Gassenheimer and Bruce L. Alford, "Internet Channel and Cannibalization: An Empirical Assessment of Sales Agents' Perspective," *Journal of Personal Selling & Sales Management* 30 (Issue 3, Summer 2010), pp. 209–22; James S. Boles, John Any Wood, and Julie Johnson, "Interrelationships of Role Conflict, Role Ambiguity, and Work-Family Conflict with Different Facets of Job Satisfaction and the Moderating Effects of Gender," *Journal of Personal Selling & Sales Management* 23 (Issue 2, Spring 2003), pp. 99–113.

11 Ibid.

12 Jeffrey K. Sager, Junsub Yi, and Charles M. Futrell, "A Model Depicting Salespeople's Perceptions," *Journal of Personal Selling & Sales Management* 18 (Issue 3, Summer 1998), pp. 1–22.

13 Dee K. Knight, Hae-Jung Kim, and Christy Crutsinger, "Examining the Effects of Role Stress on Customer Orientation and Job Performance of Retail Salespeople," *International Journal of Retail & Distribution Management* (2007), pp. 381–99; Theresa B. Flaherty, Robert Dahlstrom, and Steven J. Skinner, "Organizational Values and Role Stress as Determinants of Customer-Oriented Selling Performance," *Journal of Personal Selling & Sales Management* 19 (Issue 2, Spring 1999), pp. 1–18.

14 Peter Sowden, "What Motivates Me," *Sales & Marketing Management* (May 2003), p. 22.

15 Subhra Chakrabarty, Diana T. Oubre, and Gene Brown, "The Impact of Supervisory Adaptive Selling and Supervisory Feedback on Salesperson Performance," *Industrial Marketing Management* (June 2008), pp. 447–60; Farrand J. Hartenian, J. Hadaway, and Gordon J. Badovick, "Antecedents and Consequences or Role Perceptions: A Path Analytic Approach," *Journal of Applied Business Research* 10 (Spring 1994), pp. 40–50.

16 Fernando Jaramillo, Jay Prakash Mulki, and Paul Solomon, "The Role of Ethical Climate on Salesperson's Role Stress, Job Attitudes, Turnover Intention, and Job Performance," *Journal of Personal Selling & Sales Management*, Summer 2006, pp. 271–90; Eli Jones, Donna Massey Kantak, Charles M. Futrell, and Mark W. Johnston, "Leader Behavior, Work-Attitudes, and Turnover of Salespeople: An Integrative Study," *Journal of Personal Selling & Sales Management* 16 (Issue 2, Spring 1996), pp. 13–23.

17 James B. DeConinck and Julie T. Johnson, "The Effects of Perceived Supervisor Support, Perceived Organizational Support and Organizational Justice on Turnover Among Salespeople," *Journal of Personal Selling & Sales Managemenet* 29 (Issue 4, Fall 2009), pp. 333–51; Nigel F. Piercy, David W. Cravens, and Nikala Leanea, "Sales Management Control Level and Competencies: Antecedents and Consequences," *Industrial Marketing Management* 38 (Issue 38, May 2009), pp. 459–67; Mark P. Leach, Annie H. Liu, and Wesley J. Johnston, "The Role of Self-Regulation Training in Developing the Motivation Management Capabilities of Salespeople," *Journal of Personal Selling & Sales Management* (Summer 2005), pp. 269–81; Susan M. Keaveney and James E. Nelson, "Coping with Organizational Role Stress: Intrinsic Motivational Orientation, Perceived Role Benefits, and Psychological Withdrawal," *Journal of the Academy of Marketing Science* 21 (Spring 1993), pp. 113–24.

18 Fernando Jaramillo, Douglas B. Grisaffe, Lawrence B. Chonko, and James A. Roberts, "Examining the Impact of Servant Leadership on Sales Force Performance," *Journal of Personal Selling & Sales Management* 29 (Issue 3, Summer 2009), pp. 257–76; James B. DeConinick, "The Effects of Leader-Member Exchange and Organizational Identification on Performance and Turnover Among Salespeople," *Journal of Personal Selling & Sales Management* 21 (Issue 1, Winter 2011), pp. 21–34.

19 Todd J. Arnold, Timothy D. Landry, Lisa K. Scheer, and Simona Stan, "The Role of Equity and Work Environment

in the Formation of Salesperson Distributive Fairness Judgements," *Journal of Personal Selling & Sales Management* 29 (Issue 1, Winter 2008–09), pp. 61–80; Tara Burnthorne Lopez, Chistopher D. Hopkins, and Mary Anne Raymond, "Reward Preferences of Salespeople: How Do Commissions Rate?" *Journal of Personal Selling & Sales Management* (Fall 2006), pp. 381–99; Susan K. DelVecchio, "The Quality of Salesperson–Manager Relationship: The Effect of Lattitude, Loyalty and Competence," *Journal of Personal Selling & Sales Management* 18 (Issue 1, Winter 1998), pp. 31–48; Vincent Alonzo, "Perks for Jerks," *Sales & Marketing Management* (February 2001), pp. 38–40.

CHAPTER 12

1 William Weeks and Christophe Fournier, "The Impact of Time Congruity on Salesperson's Role Stress: A Person-Job Fit Approach," *Journal of Personal Selling & Sales Management* 20 (Issue 1, Winter 2010), pp. 73–90; Kenneth R. Evans, John L. Schlacter, Roberta J. Schultz, and Dwayne D. Gremler, "Salesperson and Sales Manager Perceptions of Salesperson Job Characteristics and Job Outcomes: A Perceptual Congruence Approach," *Journal of Marketing Theory and Practice* (Fall 2002), pp. 30–45; Thomas Rollins, "How to Tell Competent Salespeople from the Other Kind," *Sales & Marketing Management* (September 1990), pp. 116–18, 145–46.

2 Peter R. Dickson, Walfried M. Lassar, Gary Hunter, and Samit Chakrovort, "The Pursuit of Excellence in Process Thinking and Customer Relationship Management," *Journal of Personal Selling & Sales Management* 29 (Issue 2, Spring 2009, pp. 111–24; Diane Coutu, "HBR Case Study: We Googled You," *Harvard Business Review* (June 2007), pp. 37–45; Thomas Rollins, "How to Tell Competent Salespeople from the Other Kind," *Sales & Marketing Management* (September 1990), pp. 116–18, 145–46; see also Timothy J. Trow, "The Secret of a Good Hire: Profiling," *Sales & Marketing Management* (May 1990), pp. 44–55.

3 Carole Ann King, "Frustration Mounts as Recruiting Gets Harder," *National Underwriter* (March 19), 2001, pp. 6–7.

4 David Ice, "Looking to Hire New Reps?" *Agency Sales* (January 2008), p. 7; Jim Pratt, "Recruiting Talented Sales Associates," *Transaction World Magazine* (May 2001) (www.transactionworld.com).

5 Brian P. Matthews and Tom Redman, "Recruiting the Wrong Salespeople: Are the Job Ads to Blame?" *Industrial Marketing Management* (October 2001), pp. 541–59; Marianne Matthews, "If Your Ads Aren't Pulling Top Sales Talent . . .," *Sales & Marketing Management* (February 1990), pp. 73–79.

6 Dawn R. Deeter-Schmelz and Karen Norman Kennedy, "A Global Perspective on the Current State of Sales Education in the College Curriculum, *Journal of Personal Selling & Sales Management* 31 (Issue 1, Winter 2011), pp. 55–76. Michael A. Wiles and Rosann L. Spiro, "Attracting Graduates to Sales Positions and the Role of the Recruiter Knowledge: A Re-Examination," *Journal of Personal Selling & Sales Management* (2004), pp. 39–52; Audrey Bottjen, "The Benefits of College Recruiting," *Sales and Marketing Management* (April 2001), p. 20.

7 Alan J. Dubinsky, Rolph E. Anderson, and Rajiv Mehta, "Selection, Training, and Performance Evaluation of Sales Managers: An Empirical Investigation," *Journal of Business-to-Business Marketing* (1999), pp. 37–51; E. James Randall and Cindy H. Randall, "Review of Salesperson Selection Techniques and Criteria: A Managerial Approach," *International Journal of Research in Marketing* 7 (1990), pp. 81–95.

8 Donald M. Truxillo, Talya N. Bauer, Michael A. Campion, and Matthew E. Paronto, "A Field Study of the Role of Big Five Personality in Applicant Perceptions of Selection, Fairness, Self, and the Hiring Organization," *International Journal of Selection and Assessment* (September 2006), pp. 269–81; Neil M. Ford, Orville C. Walker Jr., and Gilbert A. Churchill Jr., "Selecting Successful Salespeople: A Meta-Analysis of Biographical and Psychological Selection Criteria," *Review of Marketing*, ed. Michael J. Houston (Chicago: American Marketing Association, 1988), pp. 90–131.

9 Myron Gable, Charles Hollon, and Frank Dangello, "Increasing the Utility of the Application Blank: Relationship between Job Application Information and Subsequent Performance and Turnover of Salespeople," *Journal of Personal Selling and Sales Management* (Summer 1992), pp. 39–55.

10 Joe Mullich and Shari Caudron, "Cracking the Ex-Files," *Workforce Management* (September 2003), pp. 51–54; Arthur Bragg, "Checking References," *Sales & Marketing Management* (November 1990), pp. 68–71.

11 Margaret Jenkins and Richard Griffith, "Using Personality Constructs to Predict Performance: Narrow or Broad Bandwidth," *Journal of Business and Psychology* (December 2004), pp. 255–70; Seymour Adler, "Personality Tests for Salesforce Selection: Worth a Fresh Look," *Review of Business* (Summer 1994), pp. 27–31.

12 Robert P. Tett and Neil D. Christiansen, "Personality Tests at the Crossroads: A Response to Morgeson, Campion, Dipboyes, Hollenbeck, Murphy, and Schmitt," *Personnel Psychology* (Winter 2007), pp. 967–94; Marvin A. Jolson and Lucette B. Comer, "The Use of Instrumental and Expressive Personality Traits as Indicators of a Salesperson's Behavior," *Journal of Personal Selling & Sales Management* 17 (Issue 1, Winter 1997), pp. 29–43.

13 Frank Cespedes, *Organizing and Implementing the Marketing Effort: Text and Cases* (Reading, MA: Addison-Wesley, 1991), pp. 87–88.

14 Annual Report for Cisco Systems, 2012, online at www.Ciscosystems.com.

15 Shikhar Sarin, Trina Sego, Ajay K. Kohli, and Goutam Challagalla, "Characteristics that Enhance Training

Effectiveness in Implementing Technological Change in Sales Strategy: A Field-Based Exploratory Study," *Journal of Personal Selling & Sales Management* 30 (Issue 2, Spring 2010), pp. 143–56; Rebecca Aronauer, "The Classroom vs. E-Learning," *Sales and Marketing Management* (October 2006), p. 21; Mark McMaster, "A Tough Sell: Training the Salesperson," *Sales & Marketing Management,* January 2001, p. 42.

16　Jean C. Mowrey and Scott Hull, "Beyond Training," *Pharmaceutical Executive* (April 2001), pp. 108–22.

17　Alfred Pelham, "Sales Force Involvement in Product Design: The Influence on the Relationships Between Consulting-Oriented Sales Management Programs and Performance," *Journal of Marketing Theory and Practice* (Winter 2006), pp. 37–56; Judy A. Wagner, Noreen M. Klein, and Janet E. Keith, "Selling Strategies: The Effects of Suggesting a Decision Structure to Novice and Expert Buyers," *Journal of the Academy of Marketing Science* 29 (Issue 3, Summer 2001), pp. 289–306.

18　Thomas L. Powers, Thomas E. DeCarlo, and Gouri Gupte, "An Update on the Status of Sales Management Training, *Journal of Personal Selling & Sales Management* 30 (Issue 4, Fall 2010), pp. 319–26; Andrew B. Artis and Eric G. Harris, "Self-Directed Learning and Sales Force Performance: An Integrated Framework," *Journal of Personal Selling & Sales Management* (Winter 2007), pp. 9–21; "What's the Problem with Sales Training?" *Training Today* (March 1990), p. 167; Kathleen McLaughlin, "Training's Top 50 Edward Jones," *Training Magazine* (March 2001), p. 20.

19　Adel I. EI-Ansary, "Sales Force Effectiveness Research Reveals New Insights and Reward-Penalty Patterns in Sales Force Training," *Journal of Personal Selling & Sales Management* 13 (Issue 2, Spring 1993), pp. 83–90.

20　Erika Rasmusson, "Training Goes Virtual," *Sales & Marketing Management* (September 2000), p. 48.

21　Johnson Controls website (www.jci.com), January 2013.

22　Verizon website (www.verizon .com), January 2013.

23　Education Development Center (www.edc.org), November 2008; and Kevin Dobbs, "When Learning Really Happens," *Sales & Marketing Management* (November 2000), p. 98.

24　Elana Harris, "Stars in the Making," *Sales & Marketing Management* (March 2001), p. 61.

25　Ashraf M. Attia, Earl D. Honeycutt Jr., and M. Asri Jantan, "Global Sales Training: In Search of Antecedent, Mediating, and Consequence Variables," *Industrial Marketing Management* (April 2008), pp. 181–201; Robert C. Erffmeyer, K. Randall Russ, and Joseph F. Hair, Jr., "Needs Assessment and Evaluation in Sales-Training Programs," *Journal of Personal Selling & Sales Management* 11 (Winter 1991), pp. 17–31.

CHAPTER 13

1　Bruce Talgan, "Real Pay for Performance," *Journal of Business Strategy* (May/June 2001), pp. 19–22.

2　C. Bram Cadsby, Fei Song, and Francis Tapon, "Sorting and Incentive Effects of Pay for Performance: An Experimental Investigation," *Academy of Management Journal* 50 (April 2007), p. 387; James W. Walker, "Perspectives on Compensation," *Human Resource Planning* 24 (June 2001), pp. 6–8.

3　Arun Sharma, "Customer Satisfaction-Based Incentive Systems: Some Managerial and Salesperson Considerations," *Journal of Personal Selling & Sales Management* (Spring 1997), pp. 61–70.

4　Joel Silver, "Building an Effective Sales Incentive Program," www.saleslobby.com, January 2002.

5　Cengiz Yilmaz and Shelby D. Hunt, "Salesperson Cooperation: The Influence of Relational, Task, Organizational, and Personal Factors," *Journal of the Academy of Marketing Science* (Fall 2001), pp. 335–57.

6　S. Scott Sands, "Ineffective Quotas: The Hidden Threat to Sales Compensation Plans," *Compensation and Benefits Review* 32 (March–April 2000), pp. 35–42.

7　Kemba J. Dunham, "Back to Reality: To Lure Workers, Dot-Coms Are Having to Focus on Something Besides Options, Such as Salaries," *The Wall Street Journal* (April 12, 2001), p. R5.

8　V. Kumar, Rajkumar Venkatesan, and Werner Reinartz, "Implications of Adopting a Customer-Focused Sales Campaign," *Journal of Marketing* 72 (September 2008), p. 50; Charles E. Pettijohn, Linda S. Pettijohn, and A.J. Taylor, "Does Salesperson Perception of the Importance of Sales Skills Improve Sales Performance, Customer Orientation, Job Satisfaction, and Organizational Commitment, and Reduce Turnover?" *Journal of Personal Selling & Sales Management* 27 (Winter 2007), p. 75; Ramon A. Avila, Edward F. Fern, and O. Karl Mann, "Unraveling Criteria for Assessing the Performance of Salespeople: A Causal Analysis," *Journal of Personal Selling & Sales Management* 8 (May 1988), pp. 45–54; and Richard E. Plank and David A. Reid, "The Mediating Role of Sales Behaviors: An Alternative Perspective of Sales Performance and Effectiveness," *Journal of Personal Selling & Sales Management* 14 (Summer 1994), pp. 43–56.

9　Sven A. Haugland, Igunn Myrtveit, and Arne Nygaard, "Market Orientation and Performance in the Service Industry: A Data Envelopment Analysis," *Journal of Business Research* 60 (November 2007), p. 1191; Bernard Jaworksi, Vlasis Stathakopoulos, and Shanker Krishan, "Control Combinations in Marketing: Conceptual Framework and Empirical Evidence," *Journal of Marketing* 57 (January 1993), pp. 57–69.

10　David W. Cravens, Thomas N. Ingram, Raymond W. LaForge, and Clifford E. Young, "Behavior-Based and Outcome-Based Salesforce Control Systems," *Journal of Marketing* 57 (October 1993), pp. 47–59.

11 Lee Froschheiser, "Unlock the Power and Potential of Your Team," *American Salesman* 53 (May 2008), p. 5; Alan Test, "Selling Is Still a Numbers Game," *American Salesman* 38 (June 1993), pp. 10–14; and Pete Frye, *The Complete Selling System* (Dover, NH: Upstart Publishing Co., 1992).

12 Benton Cocanougher and John M. Ivancevich, "BARS Performance Rating for Sales Personnel," *Journal of Marketing* 42 (July 1978), pp. 87–95.

13 Arun Sharma, Michael Levy, and Heiner Evanschitzky, "The Variance in Sales Performance Explained by the Knowledge Structures of Salespeople," *Journal of Personal Selling & Sales Management* 27 (Spring 2007), p. 169; Lyndon E. Dawson, Jr., Barlow Soper, and Charles E. Pettijohn, "The Effects of Empathy on Salesperson Effectiveness," *Psychology and Marketing* 9 (July/August 1992), pp. 297–310; and Neil M. Ford, Orville C. Walker, Jr., Gilbert A. Churchill, Jr., and Steven W. Hartley, "Selecting Successful Salespeople: A Meta-Analysis of Biographical and Psychological Selection Criteria," in *Annual Review of Marketing,* ed. Michael J. Houston (Chicago: American Marketing Association, 1987), pp. 90–131.

14 Cocanougher and Ivancevich, "BARS Performance Rating," p. 89.

15 Greg W. Marshall, John C. Mowen, and Keith J. Fabes, "The Impact of Territory Difficulty and Self versus Other Ratings on Managerial Evaluations of Sales Personnel," *Journal of Personal Selling & Sales Management* 12 (Fall 1992), pp. 35–47.

16 Cocanougher and Ivancevich, "BARS Performance Rating," pp. 90–99.

17 Mary Jo Bitner, Bernard H. Booms, and Mary Stanfield Tetreault, "The Service Encounter: Diagnosing Favorable and Unfavorable Incidents," *Journal of Marketing* 54 (January 1990), pp. 71–84.

18 Roger J. Placky, "Appraisal Scales That Measure Performance Outcomes and Job Results," *Personnel* 60 (May/June 1983), pp. 57–65.

19 Scott Wimer and Kenneth M. Nowack, "13 Common Mistakes Using 360-Degree Feedback," *Training & Development* 52 (May 1998), pp. 69–78.

20 "Give Yourself a Job Review," *American Salesman* (May 2001), pp. 26–27.

21 Charles E. Pettijohn, Linda S. Pettijohn, and Michael d'Amico, "Characteristics of Performance Appraisals and Their Impact on Sales Force Satisfaction," *Human Resource Development Quarterly* 12 (Summer 2001), pp. 127–39.

22 William Fitzgerald, "Forget the Form in Performance Appraisals," *HR Magazine* 40 (December 1995), p. 134.

23 Helen Rheem, "Performance Management: A Progress Report," *Harvard Business Review* (March/ April 1995), p. 11.

CHAPTER 14

1 Nikolaos G. Panagopoulos, Nick Lee, Ellen Bolman Pullins, George J. Avlonitis, Pascal Brassier, Paolo Guenzi, Anna Humenberger, Piotr Kwiatek, Terry W. Loe, Elina Oksanen-Ylikoski, Robert M. Peterson, Beth Rogers, and Dan C. Weilbaker, "Internationalizing Sales Research: Current Status, Opportunities, and Challenges, *Journal of Personal Selling and Sales Management* 31 (Issue 3, 2011), pp. 219–42.

2 Thomas Friedman, *The World is Flat*, (New York: Farrar, Straus, and Giroux, 2005), pp. 345–52.

3 Merriam-Webster online dictionary, 2012, http://www.merriam-webster.com/dictionary/globalization.

4 Greg W. Marshall and Mark W. Johnston, *Marketing Management*, 1st ed. (New York: McGraw-Hill, 2009), p. 186.

5 John D. Hansen, Tanuja Singh, Dan C. Weilbaker, and Rodrigo Guesalaga, "Cultural Intelligence in Cross Cultural Selling: Propositions and Directions for Future Research," *Journal of Personal Selling and Sales Management* 31 (Issue 3, 2011), pp. 243–54.

6 Carole Hotchkiss, "The Sleeping Dog Stirs: New Signs of Life in Efforts to End Corruption in International Business," *Journal of Public Policy and Marketing* 54 (2001), pp. 39–52.

7 Joel E. Urbany, Thomas J. Reynolds, and Joan M. Phillips, 2008, "How to Make Values Count in Everyday Decisions," *MIT Sloan Management Review* (Summer 2008), pp. 75–87; O. C. Ferrell, Thomas N. Ingram, and Raymond W. LaForge, "Initiating Structure for Legal and Ethical Decisions in a Global Sales Organization," *Industrial Marketing Management* 29 (Issue 6, 2000), pp. 555–64.

8 Martine Milliet-Erbinder, March 2012, "Writing off Tax Deductibility," *OECD Observer*, http://www.oecdobserver. org/news/fullstory.php/aid/245/Writing_off_tax_deductibility_.html.

9 Marshall and Johnston, *Marketing Management*, p. 13.

10 Rajshekhar G. Javalgi, Elad Granot, and Thomas G. Brashear, "Qualitative Methods in International Sales Research: Cross Cultural Considerations," *Journal of Personal Selling and Sales Management* 31 (Issue 2, 2011), pp. 151–70.

11 Mayer-Brown, "Guide to Doing Business in Vietnam," March 2012, http://www.mayerbrown.com/publications/A-Guide-to-Doing-Business—-Vietnam-10-10-2011/.

12 Vishag Badrinarinarayanan, Sreedhar Madhavaram, and Elad Granot, "Global Virtual Sales Teams (GVST): A Conceptual Framework of the Influence of Intellectual and Social Capital on Effectiveness, *Journal of Personal Selling and Sales Management,* V. 31 (Issue 3, 2011), pp. 7–20.

13 Julian Birkinshaw, Omar Toulan, and David Arnold, 2001, "Global Account Management in Multinational Corporations: Theory and Evidence," *Journal of International Business Studies,* (Issue 2, 2011) 32, pp. 231–248.

14 Dawn R. Deeter-Schmelz and Karen Norman Kennedy, "A Global Perspective on the Current State of Sales Education in the College Curriculum, *Journal of Personal Selling and Sales Management* 31 (Issue 1, 2011), pp. 55–76.

15 Darin W. White, R. Keith Absher, and Kyle A. Huggins, "The Effects of Hardiness and Cultural Distance on Sociocultural Adaptation in an Expatriate Sales Manager Position," *Journal of Personal Selling and Sales Management* 31 (Issue 3, 2011), pp. 325–38.

16 Charles Hampden-Turner and Fons Trompenaars, *Building Cross-Cultural Competence: How to Create Wealth from Conflicting Values* (New Haven, CN: Yale University Press, 2000).

17 Bruce R. Money and John L. Graham, "Sales Performance, Pay and Job Satisfaction: Tests of a Model Using Data Collected in the U.S. and Japan," *Journal of International Business Studies* 30 (Issue 1, 1999), pp. 149–72.

Index

Accenture plc. 87
accountability 87, 100
account analysis 248, 375
account attractiveness 249–50, 375
account call rates 248, 375
account classification 248
account planning guide 249
account priorities 242, 375
Acer 119
acquisition of new customers 74, 113
acting big/small 360
active listening 172–3, 200, 214, 375
activities of selling process 38–40
activity priorities 242, 375
adaptive selling 37, 375
Adelphia 99
advancement opportunities 333–4
advantage 173, 375
advertising 57; for recruits 293; word-of-mouth 138, 389
AIDA strategy 162
Airbus 360
AlignMark 311
alternative choice close 215, 375
Altria Group Inc. 87
altruism 268
always-accessible conflicts 270, 367
Amazon 17, 237
ambition 34
AMD 174
American Airlines 42–3, 45
Amway 19
Amyx, Douglas 270
analysis and refinement 114
Anderson, Rolph 117
Anheuser-Busch 41
anticipation of objections 178, 199, 206–7
Apple 19, 67–8, 118–19, 122, 194, 359, 364, 366
application forms 294
approach 148, 166–8, 375
aptitude 265

aptitude tests 297
arm and hand gestures 179
Asia 361, 363, 367
assessment approach 167, 375
assigning territories 250
assumptive close 214–15, 375
assurance 220
attitude 217–19, 375
authority 134, 204–5; ethical dilemmas 220–1
autonomy 13, 32–3, 375
average cost of a sales call 40, 376
Avon 19, 41, 359

B2B/B2C sales 4, 21, 41–2, 48, 121–2, 247, 253, 376
Badrinarayanan, Vishag 44
balance sheet close 216, 376
Bank of America 170
Barnes & Noble 237
BARS systems 341–4, 376
basic control unit 245–7, 376
Bates, Suzanne 68
Baxter International 16
Bayham, Alan G. 136
Beechcraft 49
behavior 48, 97, 221–2, 268, 271–2, 313, 329, 336, 376
    see also BARS systems; ethical issues/dilemmas
benefit 199, 376
benefits 173–4, 376
benefits-cost ratio 59–60, 67
Bennett, Rebecca 270
best practices approach 275
Bezos, Jeff 17
bias 341–2, 376
bids/proposals 47; preparation 148, 153–4
billing problems 222
bird dogs 139, 376
Birst 124
blended technology sales calls 121, 376
blogs 122, 141, 376
Blue Cross Blue Shield 308
BMS 14–15, 87

body language/movements 179–80
Boeing 41–2, 197
Boles, James S. 270
Bond, James T. 270
bonuses 327, 376; ethical dilemmas 337
bounce-back 203, 376
boundary positions 272
brand equity 67, 376
Brazil 367
bribes 88–9, 363, 376
Brooks, Bill 165
Budweiser 42
business climates 102, 376
business ethics 85, 376
business users, sales to 41
buyers 10, 43; behavioural types 134–6;
    objections 12–13, 38, 178, 193–204, 206–7,
    379, 384
buyer-seller relationships 36, 153, 238; ethics 84–6,
    88–9; global perspectives 363; initiation of 164–8;
    negotiating win-win solutions 193; quality of 65;
    and training 300; trust 85
buy-in 167
buying centers 42–5, 376
buying signals 213, 218–19, 376
buy-now close 216, 377

call frequencies 243, 248, 377
call rates 248
call reluctance 145, 148, 377
Campbell Soup Company 87
canvassing 143
career development 14, 31–5; advancement
    opportunities 333–4; success factors 35–8;
    types of jobs 40–2
career priorities 240, 377
Caterpillar 18–19
caveat emptor 88, 377
Celebrex 42
Census Bureau 246–7
centers of influence 139, 377
central tendency 342
CEO positions 34–5, 61
Cessna 49
Chally Group 56, 115, 118, 123–5
change conflict 169, 175, 194–5
channel deliverables 64
Charles Schwab 16
cheating 90
Cherry, Paul 275
Chevron 359
China 19, 30, 360, 364, 369
Christ, Paul 117
Cisco Systems 16, 88, 266, 290, 300
civic and professional groups 139
civic virtue 268
Claritas 247
clarity of communication 199
classroom training 311
Clayton Act 96
close supervision 274–5
closing 13, 213–14, 377; checklist 231–3; common
    mistakes 219–20; dealing with rejection 216–18;
    discussion questions 228; expert advice 212, 226;
    fear of 220; identifying buying signals 218–19;

methods 214–16; mini-case 229–30; role plays
    227–8; skills 38
Cloud9 124
cloud-based sites 121
CNL Investments 93
Coca-Cola 67, 87, 359, 367
codes of ethics/conduct 98–100, 377; Dell 85–6, 99
cold calls 143, 377
collusion 97, 377
combination plans 330–1
commission 327, 330–1, 377
commodity markets 68
communicating value categories 63
communication barriers 133–4
communication of sales message 12, 159; and buyer
    types 134–6; expert advice 158, 183
communication skills 176
communication tools 121
Company Online Applications 123
company orientation 307–8
company policies, ethical issues 92–5
company websites 140, 366
compensation 14–15, 276–7, 377; global perspectives
    371–2; methods 330; mix and level 334–6
compensation for product deficiencies 202, 377
compensation management 124
compensation plans 327–8, 377
competition 18–19
competitor defamation 97–8, 377
competitor obstruction 97, 377
complaint behaviour 221–3
complex logistics networks 364, 377
concentration ratio 250
conferences 143, 377
confidence 165, 238
confidentiality 90, 377
confrontational stances 201–2
Conlin, Michele 270
conscientiousness 268
consistency of message 58, 64, 161–2
consultative selling 7–10, 377
contemplative buyers 135
control of presentations 162
controllers 43
Core Values statements 93
corporate citizenship 86–7
corporate code of ethics 98–9
corporate cultures 15–16, 378; unethical 93–4
corporate image 67
Corporate Social Responsibility 86–7
costs: of sales 40, 90, 238, 376; of training 312–14
counties as basic control units 246
County and City Data Book 246
coverage 238
Covey, Franklin 242
Cravens, David W. 58
credibility 175
credit and billing problems 222
critical information, organization of 242–3
critical questions in sales calls 153
CRM (customer relationship managememt) 5, 12,
    18, 35, 39, 62, 73, 111–16; key terms 126;
    process cycle 114; and prospecting 136, 145;
    software 44
CRM process cycle: ethical dilemmas 115–16

CRM systems 145, 243, 248; follow-up 225–6; and performance evaluation 344; and prospecting 136, 144
CROA (Corporate Responsibility Officers Association) 87
cross-functional selling teams 42
CSO Insights 125
cultural change 9
cultural differences 85, 179, 361, 369–71, 378
cultural environments 19–20
cultural values 361–3, 378
customer acquisition 113
customer advocacy 138, 378
customer agreement 162, 170–1, 174–5
customer benefit approach 59–60, 166, 378
customer-centric firms 5, 15, 111–12, 114, 378
customer-centricity 59, 378
customer delight 13, 69
customer expectations management 69, 221–3, 225, 239
customer interaction 114, 162 see also buyer-seller relationships
customer involvement in demonstrations 177
customer loyalty 5, 60, 113, 138, 225; to other companies 195
customer mindset 5–6
customer objections 12–13, 38, 178, 193–204, 206–7, 379, 384
customer orientation 5, 111
customer profitability 113
customer retention 113, 225
customer satisfaction 60, 174, 225
customers, ethical issues 88–90
customer training problems 222
customer value 113, 378
customization 364

daily event schedule 242, 378
Darrat, Mahmoud 270
data collection questions 169–70
data mining 114, 379
data warehouse 114, 379
Death of a Salesman (Miller) 31
deception 92, 379
decision making 43, 115; DSS support systems 309; stages 45–8; stalling 197
deferred objections 204, 379
defining of sales territories 249–50
delivery problems 222
Dell 41, 60, 85–6, 99, 119, 178
demarketing 20, 379
demographics 19
demonstration tools 177–8
denial of objections 201–2
derived demand 45, 379
determinants of salesperson performance 263–4
developing countries 367
development 14, 34–5, 379
DeVincentis, John 8
Dillard's Department Store 45
direct buyers 135
direct close 215, 379
direct denial 201, 379
direct marketing 57
directories 140, 379
direct sellers 19, 41
discounts 98

discussion questions 23–4; closing 228; CRM and technology 127; ethical issues 104–5; global perspectives 373; negotiating win-win solutions 207; performance, motivation, role perceptions 279–80; pricing 207; prospecting and sales call planning 151; recruitment 318–19; rewards and evaluation 350–1; sales careers 51–2; sales presentations 186–7; selection 318–19; time and territory management 255–6; training 318–19; value-added selling 71
dishonesty 88, 379
Disney 367
distribution 18, 121, 364
diversity of interactions 272–3
Do Not Call Registry 142
Dow Jones 124
DSS support systems 309
Dun & Bradstreet Reference Book 139

Eades, Keith 9
e-commerce 17
economic environments 18–19, 67
Edmonds, David B. 4, 20, 84, 102, 158, 183, 262, 277
educational experience 369
educational institutions: recruitment from 293
effectiveness 336, 379
effort expended 13–14, 379
80:20 rule 250, 379
email 140–1
email etiquette: global connections 223–5
EMC 284
emotional elements 199–200, 203, 222
empathy 214, 220–2, 266, 379
employee benefits 327, 379
employee diversity 369–70
employers, ethical issues 90–1
employment agencies 293, 379
endless chain referrals 138–9, 379
energy resources 20
Enron 85–6, 94
enterprise resource planning 251, 379
enterprise selling 8, 379
entertainment 88–9
environmental factors 20, 266
Epedx 358, 372
equal workloads 245
equivalent products 364, 379
ERP systems 251, 379
ethical checklist 101
ethical companies 93–4
ethical dilemmas: authority concerns 220–1; autonomy 33; bonuses 337; bribes/retirement funds 89; CRM process cycle 115–16; declining accounts 66; global perspectives 364–5; performance evaluation 345; performance issues 274; pricing and false invoices 195–6; recruitment and selection 289; technology and sales presentations 181, 183; telemarketing 142; time and territory management 239; training 304–5
ethical issues 10–11, 380; with company policies 92–5; with customers 88–90; with employers 90–1; global perspectives 363; for management 91–5; renewed emphasis 85–6; for salespeople 85–95; with salespeople 92; and training 308–9
European Union 364–5

evaluation of performance 336–8; objective measures 338–9; and rewards 332; subjective measures 339–44
evaluation of training programs 304, 313
Excel 178
expectancy 271, 380
expectancy theory 14, 380
expense accounts 333, 380; role play 347–8
expenses 90–1, 94
experience, importance of 236
expert advice: closing 212, 226; communication of sales message 158, 183; global B2B sales 4, 21, 49; global perspectives 358, 372; motivation, performance, sales careers 262, 277; peddlers and drummers 132, 149; pricing and negotiation 192, 205; recruiting, selecting, training 284, 314; rewards 326, 346; sales role/job characteristics 30, 49; service as value-added 56, 69; technology as a change driver 110, 126; time management 236, 254; trust in customer relationships 84, 100
external environments 15, 17–20, 380
external sources of recruits 291, 380
extrinsic rewards 33–4, 268, 380

FAB approach 153, 160, 173–4, 194, 202, 380
Facebook 119, 122, 141
face-to-face interaction 367
facial expressions 179
features 173, 380
FedEx 4, 58, 64, 84, 158, 262, 277
feedback 48, 114, 162, 243
feel-felt-found technique 202–3
filter gatekeepers 43
financial resources 17
firing customers 62, 113, 380
firm infrastructure 61
first impressions 164–6
Fisher, Roger 213
flexibility 160, 162, 266, 273
follow-up 13, 17, 48, 144, 220–6, 380; skills 37
Ford 309
Ford, Henry 193, 195
Foreign Corrupt Practices Act 363
formalization 111, 380
formula presentation 162, 380
Fortune 100 firms 14
4 Ps of marketing 57, 59, 380
Four Square 141
France 363, 371
Friedman, Thomas L. 360
Friedman, Walter 132, 149
friends and relatives 139
frontier opportunities 123
FTC (Federal Trade Commission) 141

Galinsky, Ellen 270
gamification 123, 380
gaming technology 125–6
Gandhi, A. J. 30, 49, 326, 346
Gap Inc. 87
gatekeepers 43
General Electric 35, 41–2, 305, 361
General Mills 16
General Motors 309
generational difference 125–6, 134, 141–3

generic value chain 61
geodemographers 247
Germany 363, 369, 371
Gerstner, Lou 45, 64
gifts 88–9, 361, 380
Gillette 16
Glengarry Glen Ross (Mamet) 31
global accounts managers 368, 380
global business practices 364–6; expert advice 4, 21, 49
global challenges: sales management 368–72; sales process 360–8
global connections 9–10, 15; categories of prospects 134–6; email etiquette 223–5; first impressions 164–5; negotiating price 197; negotiations (Chinese and American) 362; personal brand 67–8; recruitment 292–3; rewards 329; sales reports 253; technology 118–19; virtual sales teams 44; work-family conflicts 270
globalization 16, 360, 381
global markets 291, 359–60; communications 366, 381
global perspectives: expert advice 358, 372; mini-case 374
global selling environment 15–20
GM 44
goals 15, 92, 144–6; presentation 163–4
Goebel, Daniel J. 36
Goettsch, Dan 308
Goldstein, Leonard 49
Google 140, 237
Google Maps 121, 164
Goolsby, Jerry R. 6
GPS technology 121
Granot, Elad 44
greeting customers 165–6
grooming and attire 147–8, 165
growth 137
Gschwandtner, Gerhard 110, 126, 212, 226
Guld, Michael 241

halo effect 341
Hampden-Turner, Charles M. 371
Hanes 41
hard-sell 31
Harrison, Craig 176
Heartfield, James C. 297
Heinz 359
Hennes & Mauritz 360
Hewlett-Packard 89, 119, 272
hierarchical structures 49
hiring quiz 286–7
Home Depot 89
Hoovers 124
HRM (human resource management) 16, 61, 288, 346
100 Best Corporate Citizens Methodology 87
Huthwaite Inc. 170
Hyundai 46

IBM 34, 42, 45, 64, 67, 87, 251, 290, 293, 309–10, 359, 367–8
image 147–8
IMC (integrated marketing communications) 57–9, 64
Immelt, Jeff 34–5
implication questions 170–1
inappropriate environments 181
inappropriate relationships 91

inbound logistics 60
inbound telemarketing 141–2, 381
incentive ceilings 331–2
incentive pay 327, 331–2, 381
incentives 14–15, 276–7, 381
India 19
indirect denial 202, 381
individual codes of ethics 99–100
industry orientation 307
influencers 43, 49
information delivery 162
information sources 250–3
initiating relationships 164–8
initiators 42, 49
innovation 273
input measures 338–9, 381
inside salespeople 141, 381
InsideView 124
installation problems 222
institutions, sales to 41
instrumentalities 266, 381
insuppliers 49
integrated marketing communications 57–8, 63–4, 381
Intel Corp. 87, 174
intelligence tests 297
interactive presentations 163
internal customers 58, 344, 381
internal environments 15–17, 381
internal marketing 58, 381
internal sources of recruits 291, 381
Internet 359, 367; and prospecting 140–1, 146; and recruitment 293–4; and training 310–11
interpersonal buyers 135
interruptions, dealing with 180–1
interviews 294–5
intimate space 180, 381
intrinsic rewards 33, 268, 381

James, Geoffrey 125
Japan 370–2
Jaramillo, Fernanado 270
Jigsaw 124
job analysis 288–9, 381
job characteristics: expert advice 30; and technology 115–18
job descriptions 289–90, 382
job enlargement 39, 382
job qualifications 288, 290, 382
job rotation 310
job satisfaction 32, 268–9, 382
job security 369
job types 40–2
Johnson Controls Inc. 87, 309
Johnson & Johnson 64, 272
Johnston, Mark W. 249, 252–3, 263, 271, 285, 303, 313, 328, 330, 334, 339–40, 343
junk mail 143, 382

Kadien, Tom 192, 205, 236, 254, 358, 372
Kahle, Dave 275
Kamen Wiping Materials Co. Inc. 49
Kennedy, Karen Norman 6
Kerr, Steven 329
key accounts 45, 368, 382
key success factors 14, 35–8, 382

Kiwanis 139
knowledge: of company 174; of competitors 194; of products 307, 366–7; in sales presentations 173–4
knowledge discovery 114
knowledge transmission 160
Komatsu 18

Lafley, A. G. 34
language issues 361, 382
Lassk, Felicia G. 6
Latin America 361, 363, 367
leadership 276
leads 133, 382; generation of 124; ranking of 134
Lear Corporation 46–7
Lectors 121
legal issues 95–8; definitions 95–6; environments 19; recruitment 295–7; training 308–9
leniency/harshness 341
Lenovo 119, 173–4, 178
libel 98, 382
Liberty Mutual 308
life priorities 240, 382
lifetime value of customers 7, 61–3, 74, 113, 382
LinkedIn 122, 124, 137, 139, 141
listening skills 36, 171–3, 200, 214, 222
losing customers 137

macroenvironments 15, 17–20, 380
MADDEN test 133–4
Madhavaram, Sreedhar 44
Makana 124
Mamet, David 31
management skills 264
managerial leadership 276
managerial positions 35
mapping software 121
MapQuest 121, 164
margin 61, 382
marketing 57–8; and technology 113
marketing concept 57, 111, 382
marketing mix 57–60, 111, 114, 364, 383
marketing mix programs 57, 59, 65
market orientation 111, 307, 382
market planning 114
market potential 247, 382
Marriott 44
Marshall, Greg W. 36, 249, 252–3, 263, 271, 285, 303, 313, 328, 330, 334, 339–40, 343
Mary Kay 19, 41
mass marketing 112–13
matrix organizations 44, 383
McDonald's 67
measurement: input 338–9, 381; output 338–9, 384; of performance (objective) 338–9; of performance (subjective) 339–44; ratio 339–40, 386; territory performance 250–3; of training 313
memorable presentations 160–1
memorized presentations 161–2, 383
mentoring 145, 148, 383
Merck 67
metropolitan statistical areas 246–7, 383
Microsoft 42, 87, 122, 178, 243
Middle East 361, 367
Miller, Arthur 31

mini-cases: Ace Chemicals 280–1; American Food Processors 352–4; BestValue Computers 71–2; Bright Colors Paints 187–8; Creekside Outdoor Gear 23–4; Diagnostic Services Inc. 256–7; Gen Tech Corporation 374; Health Sense Pharmaceuticals 106–7; House Handy Products 321–2; MedTech Pharmaceuticals 351–2; Mid-Town Office Products 208; National Agri-Products 52–3; New World Manufacturing 127–8; Right Times Uniform 319–20; St Paul Copy Machines 229–30; Strong Point Financial Services 151–2
minor point close 215, 383
missionary seller 41
misuse of company resources 90–1
Mitsubishi 178
mobile technologies 118–19, 194, 367
modified rebuys 49, 383
Moncrief, William C. 36, 39
Monster.com 123, 289
Moody's Industrial Manual 139
Moore's Law 119
morale 276, 300–1, 313
motivation 13–14, 266–7, 275–6, 383; global perspectives 370–1
Mulcahy, Anne 35
Mulki, Jay Prakash 270
multi-level personal interactions 37, 49
multiple prospecting approaches 144

natural disasters 20
natural environments 20
need 45–6, 133; analysis 163, 194, 383; identification 163, 168–71, 383; satisfaction 162–3, 174–5, 383
need payoff questions 171
negativity 195, 199–200
negotiation 12–13, 383; basic points 198–200; customer objections 193–8; expert advice 192, 205; strategies 200–4
networking 34, 139–40, 383
new-business sellers 42, 74
new-task purchases 49, 383
Nielsen 247
Nike 67–8, 87, 359
9/11 attacks 20
Nissan 46
no-excuses approach 222
nonfinancial incentives 328, 333–4, 383
nonlinear process 213–14
nonselling activities 40
nonverbal communication 179–80, 363–4, 383
Northwestern Mutual Life Insurance 139

objections 12–13, 200, 203, 384; anticipation of 178, 199, 206–7; deferred 204, 379; denial of 201–2; negotiation 193–8; overcoming 38; role play 206–7
objective measures of performance 338–9, 384
objectives 15, 163–4, 177; training 299–301
Office Suite 178
oil prices 20
one-to-one marketing 112–13
ongoing dialogue 121
online training 310–11
on-the-job training 309–10, 384
open-ended questions 169
operations 60

opportunities for advancement 333–4
opportunity rates 276, 384
optimism 266
Oracle 44, 160, 248, 251
order routines 48
organizational buying process: decision stages 45–8; participants 42–5; types of situations 49
organizational citizenship behaviours 268, 384
organizational factors 15–17, 266, 368, 381
organizational uses influence 342
organized approach 37, 242–3, 384
outbound logistics 60
outbound telemarketing 141, 384
outcome bias 341–2, 384
output measures 338–9, 384
outside salespeople 141, 384
outsourced sales forces 42, 384
outsuppliers 49, 384
overpayment 335

Palm 194
Palmisano, Sam 34
participants, organizational buying 42–5
Patton, Bruce 213
PDA functions 194
Pekel, Jon 101
Peppers, Don 113
perceived benefits 198
perceived risk 43, 384
perceived role conflict/ambiguity 264, 384
perceived value 57, 60, 63, 384
perceptions, salespeople 271–2
performance 274–6, 385; ethical dilemmas 274; managers' influence 273–7; mini-case 280–1; salespeople's influence 269–73
performance evaluation 15, 48, 238, 336–8; ethical dilemmas 345; global perspectives 372; mini-cases 352–4; objective measures 338–9; role play 349–50; subjective measures 339–44; by territories 250–3
performance gaps 221–2, 385
performance management systems 346
personal code of ethics 99–100
personal connection 165–6, 175–6, 195–6, 363
personal factors 250, 266–8
personal interviews 294–5, 385
personality tests 297
personality traits 265–6, 341
personal planning skills 38
personal priorities 240, 385
personal selling 57
personal space 180, 385
persquisites 334, 385
persuasive communication 12, 385
Pfizer 42, 67, 123
Phillips, Steve 276
Pickens, James W. 216
Piercy, Nigel F. 58
Pinterest 141
plain-speaking 199
planning 164–5, 199; account 249; calendar 242, 389; enterprise resource 251, 379; market 114; prospecting 144–5; sales call 12, 44, 145–8; skills 38
plug-in packages 121
political environments 19
Pollock, Ted 233

Polytex Fibers 274
pop-ups 140
Porter, Michael E. 61
PowerPoint 121, 164, 178
preapproach 145–8, 219, 385
preferential treatment 276–7
preparation *see* planning
presentations 168–75, 386; control of 162; distractions 180–1; ethical dilemmas 181–2; first impressions 164–6; formula 162, 380; goals 163–4; interactive 163; knowledge 173–4; memorable 160–1; memorized 161–2, 383; preparation for 159–63; problem-solving 163, 167, 385; relationship-building 168–75; role play 184–6; sales manager's role 181, 183; strategies 161–3; success factors 159–61, 175–81; technology 181–2; tools 121; types 147
press coverage 64
pressures 92, 386
price/pricing 67–9, 197–8; concessions 198, 309; discrimination 98, 385; ethical dilemmas 195–6; expert advice 192, 205; global perspectives 364–6, 385
PricewaterhouseCoopers 111
priorities: checklist 241; personal and professional 240, 242
privacy concerns 140
PRIZM system 247
proactive follow-up 223
problem anticipation/recognition 45
problem questions 170–1
problem-solving presentation 163, 167, 385
Procter & Gamble 17, 34, 41, 45, 65, 162, 309
procurement 61
product capabilities 17
product deficiences compensation 202
product demonstration 168, 175–8, 385
product development 19
product focus 98, 161
productivity increase 237–8; training 300
product knowledge 307, 366–7
product performance problems 222
product quality 63–4
professionalism 67
professional priorities 242, 385
profitability 61
profit margin spreadsheet 73–7
promotional vehicles 57
promotion mix 57, 111, 114, 385
proposals/bids 47; preparation 148, 153–4
prospecting 12, 133–7, 385; importance of 136–7; by non-salespeople 144; systematic planning 144–5; types of buyers 134–6
prospects 12, 385; researching 146–7; sources of 137–44
psychological tests 297–8
public relations and publicity 57
public space 180, 385
punctuality 165

Qualcomm 359
qualifications 288, 290
qualifying the prospect 133–4, 385
quantifiable justifications 73–81
question strategy 167, 201, 385

question types 169–71
quotas 327, 336–8, 385

Rackham, Neil 8, 170–1
ratio measures 339–40, 386
raw materials 20
real estate laws 96
realistic job previews 295
real-time access/communications 121
reciprocity 97, 386
recognition programs 334
record-keeping 144, 222
recruiting agencies 293
recruiting sites 122–3
recruitment 14, 35–6, 285–98; ethical dilemmas 289; global connections 292–3; global perspectives 368–9; legal issues 295–7; mini-case 319–20
recruits, training 304–5
references 296–7
referrals 138–9, 166, 386; of recruits 291–2
regulations 141
rehearsal 177, 180
Reichheld, Frederick 63, 113
rejection 216–18, 386
relationship selling 5–8, 13–14, 57, 61, 69, 73–81, 115, 137, 145, 153, 159, 168, 178, 193, 331, 338, 386; quantifiable justifications 73–81; relationship-building 57–8, 367; sales presentations 168–75
reliability 220
remote sales forces 272
repeat purchases 49, 386
reputation 67
research 145–6, 164
research and development (R&D) 17
Research in Motion 272
resellers, sales to 41
responsibilities 34; recruiting 288; social 86, 387
responsiveness 220
restraint of trade 97, 386
restricted questions 169
results focus 144
retail selling 41, 386
retention 62, 74, 113, 386
retirement funds, ethical dilemmas 89
return on customer investment 6–7, 114, 386
return on investment spreadsheet (ROI) 73–4, 77–81
reward mix 276, 386
rewards 32–5, 268; expert advice 326, 346; global connections 329; mini-cases 351–2
rights abuse 92
risk 194–5, 200
Robinson-Patman Act 96
Rodriguez, Alex 276
Rogers, Martha 113
role ambiguity/conflict 271, 273–5
role inaccuracy 264–5, 271, 386
role partners 269–70
role perceptions: managers 273–5; salespeople 264–5, 269–72
role plays 21, 25–7, 145, 311, 386; anticipation of customer objections 206–7; closing 227–8; ethical issues 103–4; expense accounts 347–8; external environment factors 22; performance evaluation 349–50; preapproach 150; recruitment drive 50–1; sales presentations 184–6; selection process 315–17;

time and territory management 255; training 317–18; value proposition development 70; work-life balance 278–9
Rotary International 139
routing schedules 243, 386

safety/status quo buyers 135
salaries 327, 330–1, 386
sales analysis information sources 250–3
sales calls: blended technology 121, 376; cost of 40, 376; critical questions in 153; manager's role 148–9; planning 12, 145–8
sales contests 327, 332–3, 347, 386
sales cycle acceleration 124
sales force technology 123–5
SalesGenie 124
sales invoices as sources of information 251
sales management 5, 13–15, 35, 125, 386; expert advice 262; global challenges 368–72; performance evaluation (find all) 341; policies to encourage legal behaviour 97
sales manager's role 148–9; closing and follow-up 226; ethics 10–11, 86; influence on performance 273–7; negotiating win-win solutions 204–5; prospecting and sales call planning 148–9; sales presentations 181, 183; time and territory management 238–9, 243–53
sales-marketing communications 59
sales-marketing integration 124
Sales & Marketing Management magazine 10, 16
sales message communication 12
salespeople: assigning to territories 250; ethical issues with 92; expectancies 266; expert advice 132, 149; influence on performance 269–73; inside/outside 141; performance 263–9; role in time and territory management 240–3; role perceptions 264–5, 269–72; time and territory management 237–8; types 132, 149
sales planning 44
sales potential 248, 386
Sales Practice of the Corporate Executive Board 30
sales presentations see presentations
sales process, global challenges 360–8
sales promotions 57
Sales Proposal Handbook 153
sales proposal preparation 148, 153–4
sales reports, global connections 253
sales role: expert advice 30; and technology 115–18
sales territory 386; design 245–50
sales training analysis 302–3, 387
Samsonite 45
Samsung 119
Scannell, Bill 284, 314
screen gatekeepers 43
search for suppliers 47
seating in presentations 166
Second Life 123
selection 285–98, 387; criteria 288, 290; ethical dilemmas 289; global perspectives 368–9; mini-case 319–20; of order routines 48; procedures 294–8; role play 315–17; of salespeople 14; of suppliers 47
self-esteem 217
self-evaluation 344, 387
self-management 13, 346
self-motivation 266

seller profiles 153
selling centers 44–5, 387
selling costs 40
Selling Power magazine 110, 212
selling process 12–13; activities 38–40
service capabilities 17, 60
service quality 65–6, 220
service recovery 222, 387
services, unique properties 65–6
set questions 162
sexual harassment 91
Sharp, Dan 172
Shedd, Walt 287
Shepherd, C. David 297
Sherman Antitrust Act 96
shortages 20
Siebel Systems 44
silence 214, 387
single-source suppliers 47, 387
situation questions 170–1
skills 14, 41, 118; closing 38; communication 176; follow-up 37; levels of 265–6, 301; listening 36, 171–3, 200, 214, 222; management 264; planning 38; time management 38, 139; and training 301; verbal 37
Skype 121
slander 98, 387
slotting allowances 48, 387
Smartphone Apps 122
SMEI Sales and Marketing Creed 99–100
Snap 121
sociability 266
social environments 19–20
social media 121–2, 141, 387
social responsibility 86, 387
social space 180, 387
software acceptance and usage problems 116
solution selling 9, 12, 387
Sony 369–70
sources of sales analysis information 250–3
sourcing prospects 137–44
Southwest Airlines 68
Sowden, Peter 274
spam 140, 387
spatial elements 180
special treatment 89
Spectra Energy Corp. 87
SPIN selling 153, 170, 387
sportsmanship 268
spotters 139
stalling decision making 197, 387
standardization 364
Standard & Poor's Corporation Record Service 139
State Farm Insurance 139, 240
stereotypes 30–2, 159, 217
Stevens, Howard 56, 69, 123, 125
straight rebuys 49, 387
strategic partnerships 67, 387
subjective measures of performance 339–44, 387
success factors 14, 35–8; sales presentations 159–61
summary-of-benefits close 215–16, 388
supply-chain capabilities 17, 64
supply-chain management 64, 388
sustainability 20, 388
Sweden 360

Swift, Ronald, S. 112–14
synergy, sales-marketing 64–5, 174

talk/listen ratio 161–2, 171, 220
tangibles 220
Target 89
targeting 113
Teal, Thomas 63
team selling 14–15, 44–5, 174, 273, 388; incentives 332
technical environments 19
technically complex products 47
technical sellers 42
technological capabilities 17, 38, 44, 61
technology 11, 67, 181, 388; ethical dilemmas 181–2; expert advice 110; global perspectives 367; historical perspective 118–20; informational decade 120–5; key terms 126; and marketing evolution 112; post-1980 120; and presentations 181; of selling 115–18; and training 309; value-adding 67
technology acceptance model 125–6, 388
telecommunication 34
telecommuting 34, 388
telemarketing 141, 388
tenacity 37, 217–18, 388
TerrAlign 243–4, 248
territory management 243; discussion questions 255–6; ethical dilemmas 239; importance of 237–9; mini-case 256–7; role play 254–5; salepeople's role 240–3; sales manager's role 243–53; training 308
territory management plans 243, 388
territory performance measurement 250–3
The Office TV show 31
third-party endorsements 203
Thomas Registry of American Manufacturers 139
3M 19, 359
360-degree performance feedback 344–6, 388
timeframes 197, 203
time investment 8, 40
time management 240–3; discussion questions 256; ethical dilemmas 239; expert advice 236, 254; global perspectives 363; importance of 237–9; mini-case 256–7; role play 254–5; salepeople's role 240–3; sales manager's role 243–53; skills 38, 139; tools 122; training 308
time management plans 242, 388
timezone differences 44
Toshiba 119
Total Quality Management 346
touchpoints 111, 114, 388
Toyota 63, 359
trade servicer 41
trade shows 143, 388
training 14, 134, 145, 183, 265–6, 299–314, 388; changing/updating 304–6; costs and benefits 312–14; developing programs 302–4; ethical dilemmas 304–5; global perspectives 369–70; issues 299; legal issues 308–9; methods 309–11; mini-case 321–2; new recruits/experienced salespeople 304–6; objectives 299–301; roadblocks 312; role plays 317–18; topics 306–9
transactional selling 7, 35, 69, 388
transparency 87
trial close 219, 388
trial offers 204, 389
Trompenaars, Fons 371

trust 65, 175, 195, 199, 389; expert advice 84
turnover 301, 389; and training 301
Twitter 119, 122, 137, 141

underpayment 335–6
underpromise and overdeliver approach 13, 69, 175
unfair corporate policies 94–5
unfair treatment 89
Uniform Commercial Code 95–6, 103, 389
Unilever 20
United Kingdom 367
unlawful business activities 96–8
unrestricted questions 169
UPS 170
Ury, William 213
users 42–3, 48
utility 59–60, 389

valences for performance/rewards 266, 389
validation of objections 200
validation questions 170
value 5, 389; in the sales message 62–9
value-added selling 57–9, 63, 73, 133, 198, 225, 389; global connection 9–10; time investment 8
value analysis in financial terms 153
value chain 60–1, 389
value concepts 59–62
value creation 47
value propositions 5, 59–60, 62, 153, 178, 197–8, 200, 389; explaining 160; quantifiable justifications 73–81, 153
variety 32, 40
verbal skills 37
Verizon 309
virtual offices 34, 367, 389
virtual worlds 123
Voice Thread 121
volatile markets 45

Wallace, Doug 101
Walmart 17, 45, 49, 61, 198
warm calls 143, 389
web-based training 369–70
WebEx 121
weekly/monthly planning calendar 242, 389
Welch, Jack 35
whole-business understanding 34
win-win solutions 12, 163, 193, 198–205, 213–14
WKRP in Cincinnati TV show 31
Word 178
word-of-mouth advertising 138, 389
work-family conflicts 361, 389; global connections 270
working conditions 34
work-life balance 34, 270; role play 278–9
workload analysis 247–9, 389
work-withs 148
written correspondence 142–3

Xactly 124
Xerox 35, 41, 134
XpedX 192

YouTube 122

Zimmerman, Eilene 34
zip code areas as basic control units 246–7